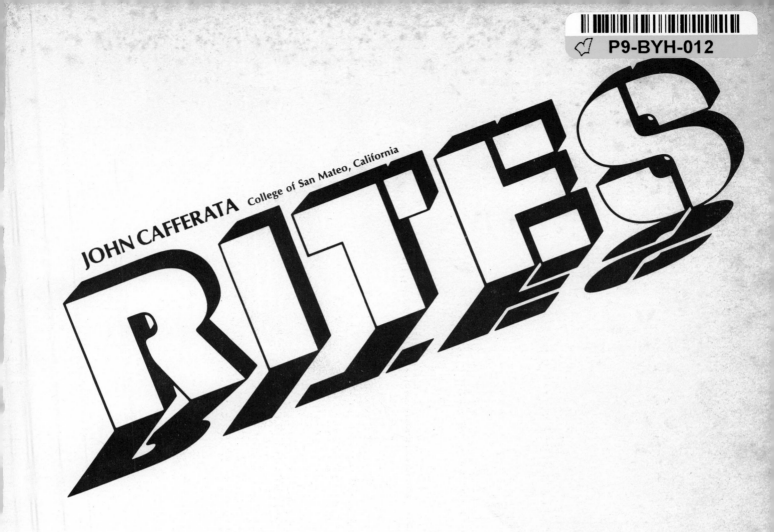

JOHN CAFFERATA College of San Mateo, California

RITES

**McGraw-Hill
Book Company**

New York
St. Louis
San Francisco
Auckland
Düsseldorf
Johannesburg
Kuala Lumpur
London
Mexico
Montreal
New Delhi
Panama
Paris
São Paulo
Singapore
Sydney
Tokyo
Toronto

Library of Congress Cataloging in Publication Data

Cafferata, John, comp.
  Rites.

  1. Anthologies.   I. Title.
PN6014.C24   808.8'035   73-19686
ISBN 0-07-009561-2

This book was set in Optima and Palatino
by Monotype Composition Company, Inc.
The editors were Lyle Linder and James R. Belser;
the designer was J. E. O'Connor;
the production supervisor was Joe Campanella.
Cover photograph by John Briggs.
George Banta Company, Inc., was printer and binder.

ACKNOWLEDGMENTS

James Agee, "A Mother's Tale," from *The Collected Prose of James Agee*. Copyright © 1968, 1969 by The James Agee Trust. Reprinted by permission of Houghton Mifflin.

Simone de Beauvoir, from *The Coming of Age*. Copyright 1970 by Éditions Gallimard. English translation © 1972 by Andre Deutsch, Weidenfeld and Nicolson and G. P. Putnam's Sons. Reprinted by permission of G. P. Putnam's Sons.

Bruno Bettelheim, from *Symbolic Wounds*. Copyright 1954 by The Free Press, a Corporation. Reprinted by permission of Macmillan Publishing Company, Inc.

Joseph Campbell, from *The Hero with a Thousand Faces*. Bollingen Series XVII. Copyright © 1949 by Bollingen Foundation. Reprinted by permission of Princeton University Press.

Albert Camus, "The Myth of Sisyphus," from *The Myth of Sisyphus and Other Essays*, translated by Justin O'Brien. Copyright © 1955 by Alfred A. Knopf, Inc. Reprinted by permission.

Padraic Colum from Orpheus: Myths of the World. Macmillan Publishing Co., Inc.

Mircea Eliade, from *Rites and Symbols of Initiation*. Copyright © 1958 by Mircea Eliade. Reprinted by permission of Harper & Row, Publishers, Inc.

T. S. Eliot, "The Love Song of J. Alfred Prufrock," from *Collected Poems, 1909–1962*. Copyright 1936 by Harcourt Brace Jovanovich, Inc., copyright 1963, 1964 by T. S. Eliot. Reprinted by permission of Harcourt Brace Jovanovich, Inc., and Faber and Faber, Ltd.

Albert Ellis, from *The American Sexual Tragedy*. Reprinted by permission of Lyle Stuart, Inc.

F. Scott Fitzgerald, "Babylon Revisited," from *Taps at Reveille* by F. Scott Fitzgerald. Copyright 1931 by The Curtis Publishing Company, renewed copyright © 1959 by Frances S. F. Lanahan. Reprinted by permission of Charles Scribner's Sons.

Sigmund Freud, from *Civilization and Its Discontents*, translated from the German and edited by James Strachey. Copyright © 1961 by James Strachey. Reprinted by permission of W. W. Norton & Company, Inc., Sigmund Freud Copyrights Ltd., The Institute of Psycho-Analysis, and The Hogarth Press Ltd.

Erich Fromm, from *The Forgotten Language*. Copyright 1951 by Erich Fromm. Reprinted by permission of Holt, Rinehart and Winston, Inc.

Eugene David Glynn, "Television and the American Character," from *Television's Impact on American Culture*, edited by William Y. Eliott. Copyright © 1956. Reprinted by permission of Michigan State University Press.

M. Esther Harding, from *Woman's Mysteries*, by M. Esther Harding. Copyright © 1971 by the C. G. Jung Foundation for Analytical Psychology. Reprinted by permission of G. P. Putnam's Sons.

Ernest Hemingway, "The Three-Day Blow," from *In Our Time*. Copyright 1925 by Charles Scribner's Sons; renewal copyright 1953 by Ernest Hemingway. Reprinted by permission of Charles Scribner's Sons.

Karen Horney, M.D., *Feminine Psychology*, edited and with an introduction by Harold Kelman, M.D. Copyright © 1967 by W. W. Norton Company, Inc. Reprinted by permission.

C. G. Jung, from *The Collected Work of C. G. Jung*, ed. by G. Adler, M. Fordham, and H. Read, translated by R. F. C. Hull, Bollingen Series XX, Vol. 17, *The Development of Personality*. Copyright © 1954 by Bollingen Foundation; Bollingen Series XX, Vol. 9i, *The Archetypes and the Collective Unconscious*. Copyright © 1959 and 1969 by Bollingen Foundation; Vol. 9ii, AION. Copyright © 1959 by Bollingen Foundation. Reprinted by permission of Princeton University Press.

Franz Kafka, "The Metamorphosis," from *The Penal*

Colony by Franz Kafka, translated by Willa and Edwin Muir. Copyright © 1948 by Schocken Books Inc. Reprinted by permission.

Lao Tzu, "The Breath of Life," "Read Words Are Not in Vain," "The Universe Is Deathless," from *The Way of Life according to Lao Tzu*, translated by Witter Bynner. Reprinted by permission of The John Day Company, Inc.

D. H. Lawrence, "Give Her a Pattern," from *Phoenix II: Uncollected, Unpublished and Other Prose Works by D. H. Lawrence*, edited by Warren Roberts and Harry T. Moore. "The Prussian Officer" from *The Complete Short Stories of D. H. Lawrence, Vol. I*. All rights reserved. Reprinted by permission of The Viking Press, Inc.

Archibald MacLeish, "The End of the World," from *Collected Poems of Archibald MacLeish 1917–1952*. Copyright © 1962 by Archibald MacLeish. Reprinted by permission of Houghton Mifflin Company.

Norman Mailer, "Superman Comes to the Supermarket," from *The Presidential Papers* by Norman Mailer. Copyright © 1960, 1961, 1962, 1963 by Norman Mailer. Reprinted by permission of G. P. Putnam's Sons.

Herbert Marcuse, "The Images of Orpheus and Narcissus," from *Eros and Civilization* by Herbert Marcuse. Copyright 1955, 1956 by the Beacon Press. Reprinted by permission.

Margaret Mead, "To Both Their Own," from *Male and Female* by Margaret Mead. Copyright © 1935, 1950, 1963 by Margaret Mead. Reprinted by permission of William Morrow & Company, Inc.

Kate Millet, "Theory of Sexual Politics," from *Sexual Politics* by Kate Millet. Copyright © 1969, 1970 by Kate Millet. Reprinted by permission of Doubleday & Company, Inc.

Marianne Moore, "Poetry," from *Collected Poems* by Marianne Moore. Copyright 1935 by Marianne Moore, renewed 1963 by Marianne Moore and T. S. Eliot. Reprinted by permission of Macmillan Publishing Company, Inc.

Edwin Muir, "The Bridge of Dread," "The Heroes," from *Collected Poems* by Edwin Muir. Copyright © 1960 by Willa Muir. Reprinted by permission of Oxford University Press, Inc.

Erich Neumann, from *The Origins and History of Consciousness*, translated by R. F. C. Hull, Bollingen Series XLII. Copyright © 1954 by Bollingen Foundation. Reprinted by permission of Princeton University Press.

Julia Randall, "A Scarlet Letter about Mary Magdalene." Reprinted by permission of the University of North Carolina Press.

Arthur Rimbaud, "By Way of Preface," from *Illuminations*, translated by Louise Varèse. Copyright © 1946, 1957 by New Directions Publishing Corporation. Reprinted by permission.

Richard Rive, "The Beach," from *An African Treasury* edited by Langston Hughes. © 1960 by Langston Hughes. Reprinted by permission of Crown Publishers, Inc.

Theodore Roethke, "Dolour," "In a Dark Time," from *Collected Poems of Theodore Roethke*. "Dolour" copyright 1943 by Modern Poetry Association, Inc.; "In a Dark Time" copyright © 1960 by Beatrice Roethke, Administratrix of the Estate of Theodore Roethke. Reprinted by permission of Doubleday & Company, Inc.

Isaac Bashevis Singer, "Yanda," *The Seance and Other Stories* by Isaac Bashevis Singer. Copyright © 1968 by Isaac Bashevis Singer. Reprinted by permission of Farrar, Straus & Giroux, Inc.

Barbara Stanford with Gene Stanford, "In the Beginning There Was Nothing," "In the Beginning Were Ice and Fire," "In the Beginning Was Chaos," "In the Beginning and Forever Was the One," "In the Beginning—Was There a Beginning?," "In the Beginning Was a Black World of Fire," "Out of the Earth," "Changing Woman," "Sati and Siva," "Adam and Eve," "Pandora," "Woman Must Be Obedient," "Deirdre of the Sorrows," "Secrets of Manhood," "Three Foolish Men," "Rama," "Dionysus," "Revenge in Zen," "Truth and Falsehood," "Cheyenne Council of 44," "The Phoenix and the Sparrow," "The House of Atreus," "Arjuna's Duty," "The Five Nations," "Persephone," "Osiris" from *Myth and Modern Man*. Copyright © 1972 by Barbara Dodds Stanford and Gene Stanford. Reprinted by permission of Simon & Schuster, Washington Square Press Division.

M. Stein, A. Vidich, and B. White (editors), from *Identity and Anxiety*. Copyright 1960 by The Free Press. Reprinted by permission of Macmillan Publishing Company.

Wallace Stevens, "Of Modern Poetry," from *The Collected Poems of Wallace Stevens*. Copyright 1942 by Wallace Stevens, renewed 1970 by Holly Stevens. Reprinted by permission of Alfred A. Knopf, Inc.

John M. Synge, from "Riders to the Sea," from *The Complete Plays of John M. Synge*. Copyright 1935 by The Modern Library, Inc. Reprinted by permission of Random House, Inc.

Dylan Thomas, "In My Craft of Sullen Art," "Fern Hill," from *The Poems of Dylan Thomas*. Copyright 1946 by New Directions Publishing Corporation. Reprinted by permission of New Directions Publishing Corporation, J. M. Dent & Sons, Ltd., and the Trustees for the Copyrights of the late Dylan Thomas.

Lionel Tiger, from *Men in Groups*. Copyright © 1969 by Lionel Tiger. Reprinted by permission of Random House, Inc.

Lionel Trilling, "Of This Time, of That Place." Copyright 1943, © 1971 by Lionel Trilling. Reprinted by permission of the Viking Press, Inc.

Parker Tyler, "The Awful Fate of the Sex Goddess," from *Sex, Psyche, Etcetera in the Film* by Parker

PHOTO CREDITS

Chapter I

Richard Gonzalez. *2, 6, 25–26, 34–35, 54* (top and bottom), *55* (top left, lower left, top right), *57*

Courtesy Lyle Stuart. *9*

William Blake, *Body of Abel*. Courtesy The Tate Gallery, London. *40*

Transmutations woodcut, Felicity of San Francisco. *65*

Courtesy Philip Morris. *62*

Gauguin, Eugene Henri Paul. *Ia Orana Maria*. Oil on canvas. H 44¾, W 34½ inches. Signed and dated (at lower right): P. Gauguin. Inscribed (at lower left) *Ia Orana Maria*. The Metropolitan Museum of Art. Bequest of Samuel A. Lewisohn, 1951. *87* (top)

Ajanta, India. *Mara*, Musee Guinet, Paris. *87* (second from top)

Murillo, Bartolome Esteban. Spanish 1618–1692. *The Virgin and Child*. Oil on canvas 64¼ × 43 inches. The Metropolitan Museum of Art. Rogers Fund, 1943. *87* (third from top)

Greek coin, *Head of Athena*. Silver, diameter one inch. The Metropolitan Museum of Art. Gift of Edmund Kerper, 1952. *87* (bottom)

Courtesy National General Pictures Corporation. *88* (top)

R. Capa, Magnum Photos. *88* (second from top)

Burt Glinn, Magnum Photos. *88* (third from top)

Bruce Davidson, Magnum Photos. *88* (bottom)

Chapter II

Albrecht Durer, German, 1471–1528. *Adam and Eve*. Engraving. Centennial Gift of Landon Clay. Courtesy Museum of Fine Arts, Boston. *126*

Courtesy Lyle Stuart. *128*

Richard Gonzalez. *130–131, 134, 144, 196*

William Blake, *God Judging Adam*. The Tate Gallery, London. *145*

Courtesy Hiram Walker, Incorporated. *185* (top)

Courtesy R. J. Reynolds Tobacco Company. *185* (lower)

Reproduced by special permission of *Playboy* Magazine; copyright © 1969 by Playboy. *197*

Chapter III

Goya, *Los Fusilamientos dels tres de Mayo*. The Prado, Madrid. *226*

Sandro Botticelli, *The Birth of Venus*, Uffizi Gallery, Florence. *227*

Courtesy Lyle Stuart. *231*

Statue of a Youth, Roman copy of a Greek work of the V Century (450–425 B.C.) Marble. The Metropolitan Museum of Art, Fletcher Fund, 1926. *238* (top)

Gilgamesh, The British Museum. *238* (center)

Peter Paul Rubens, Gefangennahme Simsons. Alte Pinakothek München. *238* (bottom)

Axel Poignant. *253*

Richard Gonzalez. *282, 293*
David Hurn, Magnum Photos. *286*
C. Allori, *Judith*, Galleria Pitti, Florence. *299*
Egyptian Sculpture, Ptolemaic. *Seated Isis with Horus on Her Lap.* Bronze statuette. The Metropolitan Museum of Art. Gift of Darius Ogden Mills, 1904. *301*
D. Stock, Magnum Photos. *309*
Michelangelo, *Leda and the Swan.* Royal Academy of Arts, London. *344*

Chapter IV

C. Capa, Magnum Photos. *348*
Michelangelo, *Pieta*, The Vatican, Rome. *350*
Courtesy Lyle Stuart. *352*
From *Man and His Symbols* edited by Carl G. Jung and M. L. von Franz, © 1964 Aldus Books Limited, London. *353*
Rougier, Time, Inc. *382*
Wayman, Time, Inc. *386*
E. Erwitt, Magnum Photos. *414*
Constantine Manos, Magnum Photos. *415* (top)
Cornell Capa, Magnum Photos. *415* (bottom)
Leonardo da Vinci, *The Cartoon for St. Anne.* Reproduced by the courtesy of the Trustees, The National Gallery, London. *419*
Richard Gonzalez. *426, 486*
Michelangelo, *The Last Judgement,* detail of Christ and the Virgin. The Vatican, Rome. *440*

Courtesy Lyle Stuart. *442*
Philippe Luzy. *446*
Dennis Stock, Magnum Photos. *448*
El Greco (Domenico Theotocopuli). (1541–1614). *The Adoration of the Shepherds.* Oil on canvas. The Metropolitan Museum of Art, The Rogers Fund, 1905. *451* (upper left)
Paul Gauguin, *The Yellow Christ.* Albright-Knox Art Gallery, Buffalo, New York. *451* (lower left)
El Greco, *Ascension of Christ,* The Prado, Madrid. *451* (right)
Kuan Yin: Goddess of the South Sea, Porcelain, Tehua ware. The Cleveland Museum of Art, Gift of Mrs. R. Henry Norweb. *463*
S. Dali, *Metamorphosis of Narcissus,* The Edward James Foundation. *479*
Courtesy Lyle Stuart. *481*
Wide World Photos. *482*

Chapter V

Richard Gonzalez. *502, 504, 505, 519*
Warriors Arming, detail from reverse of a calyz krater signed by Euphronios and Euxitheos. Attic, ca. 515 B.C. Terracotta. The Metropolitan Museum of Art. Purchase, Gift of Darius Ogden Mills, Gift of J. Pierpont Morgan and Bequest of Joseph H. Durkee, by exchange. *518*
Ronald Guilmette. *521*

CONTENTS

Preface   x

Introduction   xi

1 RITES OF PASSAGE   1

Ecclesiastics—A TIME FOR EVERYTHING	4	Sigmund Freud THE ORIGINS OF CULTURE	36
Hindu Scriptures RIG-VEDA—A TIME		William Blake THE ECCHOING GREEN	39
FOR CREATION	5	Emily Dickinson	39
Zuni Myth	12	Nathaniel Hawthorne MY KINSMAN,	
Tewa Indians SONG OF THE SKY LOOM	12	MAJOR MOLINEUX	42
Maori Myth	13	Lao Tzu THE BREATH OF LIFE	58
Genesis	15	Lao Tzu THE UNIVERSE IS DEATHLESS	58
Hindu Myth	17	Theodore Roethke IN A DARK TIME	59
Aztec Myth	19	Plato THE ALLEGORY OF THE CAVE	60
Norse Myth	19	Lionel Trilling OF THIS TIME,	
Greek Myth	20	OF THAT PLACE	66
Navajo Myth	22	C. G. Jung THE PRINCIPAL ARCHETYPES	89
Mircea Eliade MODERN MAN'S NEED		Franz Kafka THE METAMORPHOSIS	95
TO UNDERSTAND THE RITES OF PASSAGE	27	Dylan Thomas FERN HILL	122

2 RITES OF SEPARATION   124

ADAM AND EVE	136	Nathaniel Hawthorne THE BIRTHMARK	154
Hindu Myth SATI AND SIVA	137	Albert Ellis PATTERNS OF ROMANTIC LOVE	163
Swahili Myth	139	Margaret Mead MALE AND FEMALE	
The Rose of Sharon from "SONG OF		IN AMERICA	177
SOLOMON"	140	Navajo Myth	187
Ibibian Myth	141	Kate Millett From "THEORY OF	
Greek Myth PANDORA	142	SEXUAL POLITICS"	188
William Blake LONDON	146	D. H. Lawrence GIVE HER A PATTERN	193
William Blake THE GARDEN OF LOVE	146	D. H. Lawrence THE PRUSSIAN OFFICER	198
Erich Neumann THE SEPARATION		F. Scott Fitzgerald BABYLON REVISITED	212
OF THE WORLD PARENTS	147		

3 RITES OF INITIATION: A SECOND BIRTH 224

Edwin Muir   BRIDGE OF DREAD   229
Julia Randall   A SCARLET LETTER ABOUT MARY MAGDALENE   230
African Myth   THE SECRETS OF MANHOOD   233
The Marines   AN INITIATION INTO MANHOOD   234
GILGAMESH   239
Homer   THE DEATH OF HECTOR   244
RAMA . . . A HOLY NAME   248
Bruno Bettelheim   SYMBOLIC WOUNDS   254
Ernest Hemingway   THE THREE-DAY BLOW   273
Richard Rive   THE BENCH   278
Alfred, Lord Tennyson   ULYSSES   284
Joseph Campbell   THE HERO TODAY   287
Eugene Glynn   TELEVISION AND THE AMERICAN CHARACTER   295
Irish Myth   DEIDRE OF THE SORROWS   300

Egyptian Myth   ISIS, THE GODDESS OF FERTILITY   302
Giovanni Verga   THE SHE-WOLF   306
Parker Tyler   THE AWFUL FATE   311
M. Esther Harding   THE MYSTERIES OF WOMAN   316
Genesis   JUDAH AND TAMAR   326
Herodotus   THE CULT OF MYLITTA   328
Kshemendra   THE RISE AND FALL OF A HARLOT   330
Hrotswitha   THAIS AND THE MONK   333
Richard Head   A VISIT TO MOTHER CRESSWELL   337
Stephen Crane   MAGGIE GOES ON THE TURF   340
William Butler Yeats   LEDA AND THE SWAN   345

4 RITES OF WORD MAGIC 346

Padhraic Pearse   THE MOTHER   351
Suzanne K. Langer   ON THE ORIGIN OF LANGUAGE   354
Erich Fromm   THE NATURE OF SYMBOLIC LANGUAGE   355
Senegalese Myth   THE FALSEHOOD OF TRUTH   360
Chinese Myth   THE PHOENIX   361
Japanese Myth   THE ZEN MASTER   361
Genesis   CAIN AND ABEL   363
Abraham Lincoln   THE GETTYSBURG ADDRESS   364
Greek Myth   THE CURSE OF BLOOD   365
PSALM 137   366
Hindu Myth   ARJUNA'S DUTY   367
Iroquois Myth   THE PIPE OF PEACE   368
Paul   ROMANS 12, A LETTER   369
Matthew   THE SERMON ON THE MOUNT   371
John F. Kennedy   INAUGURAL ADDRESS   374
Herbert Marcuse   THE IMAGES OF ORPHEUS AND NARCISSUS   377
Shakespeare   MARK ANTONY'S SPEECH   383

Norman Mailer   SUPERMAN COMES TO THE SUPERMARKET   387
Arthur Rimbaud   BY WAY OF A PREFACE   407
Marianne Moore   POETRY   408
Lao Tzu   READ WORDS ARE NOT VAIN   408
John Keats   THE POET   408
Alexander Pope   RIDDLE OF THE WORLD   409
Walt Whitman   I SIT AND LOOK OUT   409
Emily Dickinson   I DIED FOR BEAUTY   409
Ralph Waldo Emerson   THE TEST (MUSA LOQUITUR)   409
Sir John Davies   MAN   410
Shakespeare   WHY IS MY VERSE SO BARREN OF NEW PRIDE   410
Wallace Stevens   OF MODERN POETRY   410
Dylan Thomas   IN MY CRAFT OR SULLEN ART   411
THE BOOK OF RUTH   416
Eric R. Wolf   THE VIRGIN OF GUADALUPE   420
John Millington Synge   RIDERS TO THE SEA   428
Karen Horney   MISTRUST BETWEEN THE SEXES   436

5 RITES OF RENEWAL; FROM DEATH TO IMMORTALITY 438

John Donne DEATH 443
THE TWENTY-THIRD PSALM 444
THE NINETIETH PSALM 444
Greek Myth DIONYSUS 449
James Agee A MOTHER'S TALE 452
ISHTAR'S DESCENT INTO THE WORLD
BELOW 466
Sophocles ELECTRA'S SPEECH 469
Sophocles ANTIGONE'S SPEECH 469
Shakespeare CLEOPATRA'S SPEECH 470
George Bernard Shaw JOAN'S SPEECH 471
Isaac Bashevis Singer YANDA 473
W. B. Yeats THE SECOND COMING 477
Greek Myth NARCISSUS 480
Jeremiah THE END OF THE WORLD 483
Archibald MacLeish THE END OF THE
WORLD 483
Henry David Thoreau WHERE I LIVED
AND WHAT I LIVED FOR 488
Walt Whitman TO A LOCOMOTIVE
IN WINTER 490

Samuel Butler THE BOOK OF THE
MACHINES 491
Thomas Wolfe ONLY THE DEAD
KNOW BROOKLYN 496
Theodore Roethke DOLOUR 498
William Blake THE TYGER 503
Simone de Beauvoir FRANK TALK ABOUT
A FORBIDDEN SUBJECT 506
T. S. Eliot THE LOVE SONG
OF J. ALFRED PRUFROCK 512
William Faulkner ACCEPTANCE OF THE
NOBEL PRIZE 517
Edwin Muir THE HEROES 518
John Donne NO MAN IS AN ISLAND 520
Albert Camus THE MYTH OF SISYPHUS 521
Shakespeare KING LEAR 523
William Blake JERUSALEM 523
Jean Pumphrey THERE, OUT OF THE SOUND
OF THE SEA 525

PREFACE

> But in order to speak about all to all, one has to speak of what all know and the reality common to all. The sea, the rain, necessity, desire, and the struggle against death—these are things that unite us all.
>
> **Albert Camus**
> *Resistance, Rebellion, and Death*

These words by Albert Camus capture the spirit and purpose of this book. We all begin in patterns of silence until language transforms us, making it possible for us to enter the realm of the human community. We use the medium of language to create images of a self, to interpret our world, and to share these definitions and interpretations with one another. Yet, there are limits to expression when it is confined by a specific place and time. There are ambiguities that arise from the diversity of our specific worlds that can mar our full understanding of the human condition. To transcend these limitations, the collected materials in this book provide access to the myths from our collective past which offer us the various ways that cultures have attempted to explain what it means to be a human being. Joseph Campbell believes that myths not only reveal our past, but they are also "symbols which evoke and direct our psychological energies." If we allow ourselves to see Campbell's point of view, to see the symbols as they cut across time and place, then perhaps we might begin to see contemporary problems from a perspective beyond the moment, beyond the limitations of the self.

Those who are familiar with literature know that artists have always been concerned with the expression of the contradictions inherent in the human condition. Macbeth laments that life is a "tale told by an idiot, full of sound and fury signifying nothing." Cordelia bemoans her fate when she discovers how others have wronged her father during her absence when she says, "We are not the first who wishing the best have incurred the worst." Exposed to these images, we suddenly face a universe that is too vast and incomprehensible for our finite imaginations. We often withdraw because of our fear to express fear of the unknown. To create form out of this moment-to-moment chaos, many cultures created "rites of passage" to help life flow more evenly as we move from birth to death. These rites serve as the title and metaphor for this attempt to articulate the paradoxes present in any attempt to explain human destiny. The human vision is rich and varied, and the more we understand human choices the greater our chance for a meaningful life. We need to understand the inner patterns that mold the core of our literature and give us insight into ourselves. Alexander Pope said: "Nothing human is alien to me," and language is the key which opens us to experience the possibilities inherent in Pope's statement. From Ecclesiasties to Albert Camus, this selection of literature unfolds a vision of life which reveals the human effort to express our intellectual and emotional perceptions of the world. This is a book for those of us who are overwhelmed by the vast amount of knowledge available to us through language. If we begin to understand how others, and we too, make assumptions about the world, then, hopefully, we will understand that which "unites us all."

Acknowledgment

With deep appreciation to Richard Gonzalez for his photography and the ideas he contributed for the making of this book.

John Cafferata

INTRODUCTION

The central paradox of life: Man/Woman lives inside of a world and a world lives inside of man/woman.

Human beings are born, and they die. In between these two significant events, we struggle to live in a complex state of emotional and intellectual moments which characterize our interaction within a world. To emerge from this chaotic experience, we create forms to bring a sense of order to bridge the difficulties which coexist within our mind and the "external" world in which we reside. To explain and give meaning to the process of existence, mythical tales are narrated to explore the conflicts between our instinctual drives* and the repressed wishes, fears, and conflicts which they motivate. At the center of these myths, we see enacted: (1) the process of birth, (2) the ordeals and trials which establish and maintain the process of life on earth, (3) the unanswerable and undeniable realization that all who live must die, and (4) an attempt to extend the meaning of life into a world beyond the scope of life. At this stage, the "sacred" philosophies of cultures embody the reasons for the entire process. To ease the pain for individuals as they move through these time-space categories, cultures establish rituals which introduce the individuals into the community and afford them an explanation of the community's concept of the world. In the study of primitive life, anthropologists would tend to agree with the findings of Claude Levi-Strauss that there is an amazing similarity between widely divergent groups of people as they create myths to explain the flood, the slaying of monsters, incest, and sibling rivalry.

The purpose and force implicit in these

* Behavior that is governed by, or the result of, reactions below the conscious level.

myths become the underlying symbols of identification embodied in those rituals which function as a means to intergrate the individual into a culture's explanation of the mysterious encounter with the cycle of life. Unfortunately, we live at a point in time when neither our myths nor our rituals seem to serve as a means for individuals to achieve a balance between the "inner" and "outer" worlds. Because of this: we have lost our awareness of the past; we are uncertain of the future; and, consequently, we lack confidence in the present. Modern life needs to create new myths to remind us that we have not lost our potential, but that we have merely misplaced our ability to effectively direct our energies as we encounter crisis situations. In other times, cultures created certain "rites of passage" to serve as connecting links for individuals as they moved from one phase of life to another. For example, a hunter would be forced to undergo ordeals of suffering before he would be permitted to become a full member of the tribe. If he successfully withstood those ordeals which were placed in his way, he was accepted as a man. This meant that he would be allowed knowledge of tribal myths which explain and give meaning to (1) tribal customs and (2) rituals which enable members to enter a world beyond the measure of time. These "rites" seem no longer visible to us, but they continue to remain in the imprint of our collective psyche. They often emerge when we feel uncertain about our place in the scheme of nature. In America, we were able to glimpse these rites following the murder of President John F. Kennedy on November 22, 1963. As a nation, we were shocked out of our isolated concerns for individual security. The funeral allowed us to experience catharsis, as a result of the untimely death of the slain hero, and fear, because his death revealed that we too were vulnerable. The media responded by exposing us to a riderless horse which symbolized our inability to transcend the limitations of mortality. And when Mrs. Kennedy extended her hand to signal the eternal flame to begin, we hoped that the knowledge of one man's journey might serve as an illumination for all to find meaning in the human condition. In this instant, we seemed to be linked together. We participated in a ritualistic enactment which linked the leader with his people and the people with one another. Perhaps if modern consciousness could find connecting links within the accumulated knowledge of our past, we might once again feel a sense of awe about the inherent possibilities of the future.

For this reason, the theme "rites of passage" is the organic principle which generates the structure and meaning of this book. The term was originally used by Arnold Van Gennep to interpret how individuals made the transition from one stage in life to the next.

The word "rites" refers to those ceremonies which enable individuals to make the passage from one point in life to another. For example, marriage is a rite which recognizes the movement from individual to sexual union. These rituals closely resemble the rhythmic patterns revealed in nature. Spring marks the celebration of fertility. Today, we still have symbols which convey these meanings. Both the rabbit and the egg are symbolic elements which signal the process of procreation and fertility. We celebrate Christmas as a symbolic rite which signals the possibility of hope in the midst of winter. The bringing in of the tree is reminiscent of the pagan festival of lights which served as a reminder of the sun's power. And the birth of the Christ child signals the possibility of salvation during the dead of winter. The songs of every age reveal the human need for an understanding of the passage of individuals from one point in life to the next.

In tribal ceremonies of birth, initiation, marriage, and burial, we see rites which brought the individual into relationship with the collective. The rites transformed the individual into a member of the tribe which made it possible not only for one to see the world unfold but to know one's essence as well. The new identity brought the individual into contact with others in order to share the whole meaning of the universe. This concept of a second birth as an adult provided human beings with the needed symbols in times of catastrophe. These rites balanced the contradiction between the persistence and maintenance of forms and the desire to move forward in harmony with the changing patterns of life. These rituals function as models for members of the group to imitate, and concurrently they express the needs of the group. The chaos of "life-crisis" situations was suddenly transformed into an orderly and meaningful form which provided the development and movement which characterizes the growth of human awareness.

One of the most universal rituals was the initiation ceremony which marked the end of childhood and the acceptance of adult status within the group. Writing about these rites, Mircea Eliade states:

Initiation represents one of the most significant spiritual phenomena in the history of humanity. It is an act that involves not only the religious life of the individual, in the modern meaning of the word "religion"; it involves his *entire* life. It is through initiation that, in primitive and archaic societies, man becomes what he is and what he should be—a being open to the life of the spirit, hence one who participates in the culture into which he was born. For as we shall soon see, *the puberty initiation represents above all the revelation of the sacred—and, for the primitive world, the sacred means not only everything that we now understand by religion, but also the whole body of the tribe's mythological and cultural traditions.* In a great many cases puberty rites, in one way or another, imply the revelation of sexuality—but, for the entire premodern world, sexuality too participates in the sacred. In short, through initiation, the candidate passes beyond the natural mode—the mode of the child—and gains access to the cultural mode; that is, he is introduced to spiritual values. From a certain point of view it could almost be said that, for the primitive world, it is through initiation that men attain the status of human beings; before initiation, they do not yet fully share in the human condition precisely because they do not yet have access to the religious life. This is why initiation represents a decisive experence for any individual who is a member of a premodern society; it is a fundamental existential experience because through it a man becomes able to assume his mode of being in its entirety.[1]

[1] Mircea Eliade, *Rites and Symbols of Initiation*, p. 3.

According to Erich Neumann, "The goal of all initiation ceremonies is transformation." These rites complete the separation of the individual from his or her family, mark the passing of life into middle and finally old age, or signal the transition which takes place between the process of life and death. According to Van Gennep, an examination of the content and form of these rites reveals a universal pattern. He claims that the three stages found everywhere are separation, initiation, and return, and that in the past this pattern reveals how human beings have attempted to come to terms with the various stages of transition. For example, funeral rites have marked the separation of life to death to afterlife. Initiation rites have made possible the transformation of boy and girl into sexually mature man and woman. The return from any of these experiences marks the insights and knowledge gained by those who crossed the boundaries which express the crucial problems found during the life experience.

The focus of this book on the rites of passage theme has revealed how primitive man created ceremonies to ease the anxiety accompanying changes as individuals move through the various stages of life. These rites served as models for others to imitate. They also created patterns for living which assured individuals of the continuity of life. This led to a belief in the individual's ability to survive in an "external" world. This discussion now shifts to an exploration of the second half of the central paradox of life: the world that lives inside us. This realm raises certain important and significant questions: What images govern the "inner" worlds of human beings? What forces shape and mold human behavior from within? What universal questions has man attempted to find answers for? What does it mean to be a human being? And how do we ascertain what is the purpose of life? These questions are of course unanswerable, but they reveal how human beings have created images and symbols to transcend the limitations of a subjective point of view.

We need to find a perspective which will help us to understand our part in the total picture of life. One of the most perceptive and influential thinkers on this subject is the Swiss psychologist Carl Gustav Jung. He explored in his patients what evidence there was that the past continued to haunt the present. Jung states:

Our life is indeed the same as it ever was. At all events, in our sense of the word it is not transitory; for the same physiological and psychological processes that have been man's for hundreds of thousands of years still endure, instilling into our inmost hearts this profound intuition of the "eternal" continuity of the living. But the self, as an inclusive term that embraces our whole living organism, not only contains the deposit and totality of all past life, but is also a point of departure, the fertile soil from which all future life will spring. This premonition of futurity is as clearly impressed upon our innermost feelings as is the historical aspect. The idea of immortality follows legitimately from these psychological premises.[2]

To explain the workings of our "inner" patterns, Jung focuses our attention on the need to develop an expanded concept of self. To add significance to our life spans, we need to investigate what universal problems have plagued us. According to Jung, this will bring us in contact with "the totality of all past life." This image of life helps us develop a new consciousness which makes possible the apprehension of an unfolding, moving and changing world. Jung states:

The person who lives without myth lives without roots, without links to the collective self which is finally what we are all about. He is literally isolated from reality. The person who lives with a myth gains "a sense of wider meaning" to his existence and is raised "beyond mere getting and spending."[3]

The study of myth opens us to experience new dimensions of awareness which give us "a wider sense of meaning." Unfortunately to allow this energy to flow from without to within and back out again, we must face the pain of knowing the limitations of our perceptions of the world. We must deal with our illusions of the world and the world as it is. We need to recognize that our planet is not the center of the universe, and that we are not gods ruling over all creation and life. This causes fear and anxiety. The study of myth brings us to see all the possibilities inherent in the stream of life. For both Campbell and Jung, the study of myth

[2] *Two Essays*, p. 190. Modern biology has attempted to explain it on the basis of the "eternal life" of the original cell.
[3] Carl Gustav Jung, M.-L. von Franz, et al., *Man and His Symbols*, pp. 76–78.

becomes the exploration of the human imagination since time immemorial.

Jung began his search into the past while he was associated with the founder of modern psychology, Sigmund Freud. Freud taught Jung of the personal unconscious—that vast area within human beings where all personal experiences become registered, but oftentimes are unaccessible. This led Freud to the theory of repression in which he contended that individuals inhibit certain content from becoming conscious because of an "inner" fear. For example, the child's awareness of separation from the mother forms the basis, according to Freud, of all anxiety associated with being abandoned. This may appear in one's life in certain forms of behavior which Freud characterized as neurotic. An example would be the individual who refuses to leave his or her house because of a fear of being left alone. Freud traced this fear to an early experience, and he found this located in the individual's unconscious. Freud also discovered what he called "archaic remnants" of our link with the past. He did not pursue this element, but one of his students did. That student was Carl Jung. He accepted Freud's theory of the personal unconscious, but he expanded on the archaic remnants theme as a metaphor to explain our link with the past. Jung states:

> A more or less superficial layer of the unconscious is undoubtedly personal. I call it the *personal unconscious*. But this personal unconscious rests upon a deeper layer, which does not derive from personal experience and is not a personal acquisition but is inborn. This deeper layer I call *collective unconscious*. I have chosen the term "collective" because this part of the unconscious is not individual but universal; in contrast to the personal psyche, it has contents and modes of behavior that are more or less the same everywhere and in all individuals. It is, in other words, identical in all men and thus constitutes a common substrate of a suprapersonal nature which is present in every one of us.[4]

Jung labeled those elements found within the personal unconscious as complexes, and those found in the collective unconscious, he called archetypes. These archetypes became the center of his study as a means to explain the human psyche. Jung also believed that these archetypes were part of the inherited structure of the human mind. He states:

> Like every animal, he [man] possesses a preformed psyche which breeds true to his species and which, on closer examination, reveals distinct features traceable to family antecedents. We have not the slightest reason to suppose that there are certain human activities or functions that could be exempted from this rule.[5]

To understand this complex term, we need to explore how the archetypes emerge from the unconscious and in what ways they become visible to our conscious perceptions. We might first begin by defining the meanings contained within the word: (1) "arche" refers to the original source of energy which projects images from the unconscious into the conscious. This becomes the source of the psyche's strength. (2) "Type" refers to a particular mold which casts certain patterns which carries with it a particular form of meaning. An example of this mold would be the role set for males and females to follow in order to know what it means to be a member of one sex or the other. These patterns become visible to us through an investigation of the myriad ways the human psyche translates and describes an "external" world. These translations are flashed to a magnetic field which is highly charged with energy, and this energy is released as the image is combined with symbol to express the archetype. This expression makes possible the concept of consciousness. Jung found the archetypes in the dreams, fantasies, visions, and myths recorded from ancient to modern times. For Jung,

> An archetypal content expresses itself, first and foremost, in metaphors. If such a content should speak of the sun and identify it with the lion, the king, the hoard of gold guarded by the dragon, or the power that makes for the life and health of man, it is neither the one thing nor the other, but the unknown third thing that finds more or less adequate expression in all these similes, yet —to the perpetual vexation of the intellect— remains unknown and not to be fitted into a formula.[6]

Archetypal images become those universal patterns which appear everywhere as an expression of those forms which convey and exhibit

[4] Jung, *The Archetypes and the Collective Unconscious*, in *The Collected Works*, 1959, Vol. 9, Part 1, p. 3.

[5] *Ibid.*, p. 78.
[6] Carl Jung, *The Psychology of the Child Archetype*, p. 137.

certain patterns of behavior as metaphors to express our need to understand the unknown.

According to Jung, the archetypes become visible to us only through the forms which are projected in human behavioral patterns. They form the basis for the "self-portrait of the instincts." Biologists have long acknowledged these patterns of behavior in lower animals. For instance, the nesting of birds, the ritual dance of the bee, the spinning of the web by the spider, and the migratory habits of all animals are manifestations of an instinctive drive to act out behavior which comes from the remotest beginnings of the species. Human beings also show evidence of evolutionary instinctual patterns of behavior. For Jung, these elements become the contents of the archetypes which are the "innate forms of the mind." Jung says:

> ... The unconscious, as the totality of all archetypes, is the deposit of all human experience right back to its remotest beginnings. Not, indeed, a dead deposit, a sort of abandoned rubbish heap, but a living system of reactions and aptitudes that determine the individual's life in invisible ways—all the more effective because invisible. It is not just a gigantic historical prejudice, so to speak, an a priori historical condition; but it is also the source of the instincts, for the archetypes are simply the forms which the instincts assume.[7]

> ... archetypes are not disseminated only by tradition, language, and migration, but ... can rearise spontaneously, at any time, at any place, and without any outside influence. ... This statement ... means that there are present in every psyche forms which are unconscious but nonetheless active—living dispositions, ideas in the Platonic sense, that preform and continually influence our thoughts and feelings and actions.[8]

We are not conscious of the influence of the archetypes in determining how we respond to various situations and symbols. Although they arise spontaneously, Jung says:

> The archetypes are not whimsical inventions, but autonomous elements of the unconscious psyche which were there before any invention was thought of. They represent the unalterable structure of a psychic world whose "reality" is attested by the determining effects it has upon the conscious mind.[9]

> Archetypes may be considered the fundamental elements of the conscious mind, hidden in the depths of the psyche. ... They are systems of readiness for action, and at the same time *images and emotions*. They are inherited with the brain structure—indeed they are its psychic aspect.[10]

The archetypes are absorbed into the instinctual sphere, but only through the images which both evoke and signify how they represent the structure of the human psyche.

The symbolic expression of archetypes reveals how the human psyche is fascinated by and attracted to certain images which we strive to interpret. The symbol becomes the energy transformer which also becomes the "molder of our consciousness." For an example, let us discuss the archetype of the way which underlies the rites of passage theme. As far as we can deduce, this archetype first appeared among the prehistoric people of the ice age. In a ritual which was for the most part unconscious, the way led these early individuals into mountain caves. These caves were often hidden and inaccessible, but there the first "temples" became visible. They adorned the walls of these caves with the representations of animals, upon whose killing existence depended.

The magical and sacred significance of these paintings, as well as of the caves in which they are found, is almost unquestionable today, but it is evident that these early places were difficult to reach. The path which led to them formed a part of the ritual which was responsible for creating these mountain temples. At a later stage of conscious development, the archetype of the way is represented in temples from Egypt to Java. At this stage of development, the worshiper is compelled to follow a ritual way from the periphery to the center of the shrine. Christ's movement up Calvary is another example of a more highly developed use of the way. In modern times, the movement between our "inner" and "outer" worlds is a manifestation of the archetype of the way. We often take for granted such expressions as the "inner path" or the companion symbols of orientation and disorientation. These expressions are part of the archetype of the way. The

---

[7] "The Structure of the Psyche," par. 339.

[8] "Psychological Aspects of the Mother Archetype," pars. 153f.

[9] "The Phenomenology of the Spirit in Fairytales" (C. W. 9, i), par. 451.

[10] "Mind and Earth," in *Contributions*, p. 118 (modified). [C. W. 10.]

original use of this symbol began long ago in the unconscious behavior of those early people who carved a path toward finding a sacred place. We who follow in their footsteps seek the wisdom accompanying the archetypal pattern of the way.

There are myriad uses of the archetype of the way as a means to attain knowledge about temporal and sacred existence. Followers of Christ believe that he is the Way to attain eternal peace and harmony. Theories which explain the workings of the universe are often conceived in terms of a pattern of steps. The path toward understanding is reached only as one completes the way. Dante's version of hell is conceived in terms of movement down through the stages of sin up to purgatory and finally into heaven. Dante has guides to help him through this difficult passage. The world of literature abounds with tales of those who trod the path toward enlightenment. As a means to understand how one might view the total picture of life, Northrop Frye, the literary critic, focuses on the history of literature from preliterate to modern times. Frye uses the categories of ritual, myth, and folk tale as examples of primitive people's literary history. Frye states:

> The myth is the central informing power that gives archetypal significance to the ritual and archetypal narrative to the oracle. Hence the myth *is* the archetype, though it might be convenient to say myth only when referring to narrative, and archetype when speaking of significance. In the solar cycle of the day, the seasonal cycle of the year, and the organic cycle of human life, there is a single pattern of significance, out of which myth constructs a central narrative around a figure who is partly the sun, partly vegetative fertility and partly a god or archetypal human being. The crucial importance of this myth has been forced on literary critics by Jung and Frazer in particular. . . .[11]

He recognizes the movement of ideas which develops a more universal picture of the human situation. His study carves a path which leads to a comprehension of the total body of literature "as an order of words." Frye develops the following pattern as a means to comprehend the various stages of literary development as a symbolic expression of the movement from human ignorance to knowledge. Frye's way is as follows:

1 The dawn, spring and birth phase. Myths of the birth of the hero, of revival and resurrection, of creation and (because the four phases are a cycle) of the defeat of the powers of darkness, winter and death. Subordinate characters: the father and the mother. The archetype of romance and of most dithyrambic and rhapsodic poetry.

2 The zenith, summer, and marriage or triumph phase. Myths of apotheosis, of the sacred marriage, and of entering into Paradise. Subordinate characters: the companion and the bride. The archetype of comedy, pastoral and idyll.

3. The sunset, autumn and death phase. Myths of fall, of the dying god, of violent death and sacrifice and of the isolation of the hero. Subordinate characters: the traitor and the siren. The archetype of tragedy and elegy.

4. The darkness, winter and dissolution phase. Myths of the triumph of these powers; myths of floods and the return of chaos, of the defeat of the hero, and Götterdämmerung myths. Subordinate characters: the ogre and the witch. The archetype of satire (see, for instance, the conclusion of *The Dunciad*).[12]

Frye's theory of literary history resembles Carl Jung's theory of archetypes and Joseph Campbell's study of myth.

Symbols which are associated with the archetype of the way bring us to view the multiple levels of meaning associated with the archetype. Only the symbol can provide us with the means to combine diverse elements and create a unified impression. These symbolic forms become the rulers of our "inner" world. They also provide us with a metaphor which creates for us a particular world view. For example, Alan Watts describes Christ's descent into hell as a symbolic expression of the human attempt to attain consciousness. Watts contends that this symbol transforms the idea into an image and allows us to understand "the necessity of knowing one's very depths." Watts states:

> . . . the descent into the depths is almost invariably one of the great tasks of "the hero with a thousand faces," of the Christ in his many forms. Hades or Hell may here be understood as the Valley of the Shadow, the experience of impotence and despair in which "I" die and Christ comes to life. The descent is likewise a figure of the descent of consciousness into the unconscious, of the necessity of knowing one's very depths. For so long as the unconscious remains unexplored it is possible to retain the naïve feeling of the insularity and separateness of the con-

[11] Northrop Frye, *Fables of Identity*, p. 15.

[12] Ibid., p. 16.

scious ego. Its actions are still taken to be free and spontaneous movements of the "will," and it can congratulate itself upon having motivations which are purely "good," unaware of the "dark" and hidden forces of conditioning which actually guide them.[13]

To become aware of the "dark" forces which guide us, we must investigate the symbolic content behind the acts of expression. The symbols provide us with the material which is invisible in the unconscious until made conscious by the symbol. We need to look at the contradictions of opposites in order to understand the structure of the archetype of the way. Eric Neumann states:

> The symbolism of the archetype is its manifestation in specific psychic images, which are perceived by consciousness and which are different for each archetype. The different aspects of an archetype are also manifested in different images. Thus, for example, the terrible aspect and the life-giving, "kindly" aspect of an archetype appear in diverging images.[14]

In the archetype of the way, we see the positive and negative elements contained together. Let us use Watt's description of Christ's descent into hell. The negative aspect is the association of Christ with death and the kingdom of the eternal dead. The positive aspect is revealed when Christ returns to inform us that death is only a transitional stage before experiencing the way toward eternal life. In order for one to know the way, one must come to terms with the diverse images and symbols associated with the archetype.

The focus of this discussion has been on the central paradox of life: Man/Women lives inside a world and a world lives inside man/women. This focus illustrates the principle which generates this book. The use of "rites of passage" provides the reader with a metaphor to depict what individuals have done in order to get through life-crisis situations. The emphasis on the archetype of the way provides the reader with a metaphor to depict how individuals have attempted to come to terms with "inner" contradictions between the world as they see it and as they would like it to be. To explore the ramifications of these two metaphors, this book is divided into the following chapters. Chapter 1 focuses on the human concept of time as a means to impose order on chaos. Time becomes the symbol which makes it possible for individuals to express the creation of life as an ongoing process. Chapter 2 focuses on the transition from boy to man and from girl to woman. The myths and literature deal with the crisis of love between the sexes. Chapter 3 brings together the hero and the temptress as opposite archetypal symbols who undergo trials in order to be born a second time as a man and a woman. Chapter 4 uses language as word magic to explore how the political leader seeks to use symbols as a means to bring together his people. His archetypal counterpart is the madonna who serves as both life giver and life taker. Chapter 5 begins with a depiction of those gods and goddesses who descend into the underworld in order to return to provide us the knowledge to go beyond this world of time and space. The second part of the chapter focuses on existentialism as the modern world's philosophy to explain this time of transition. Since much of what went before us is now in a state of change, we might say that everyone is undergoing a rite of passage.

[13] Alan Watts, *Myth and Ritual in Christianity*, p. 168.
[14] Erich Neumann, *The Great Mother*, p. 3.

RITES OF

Life is transition. So are the youth and wealth of a man. Wives, children, friends and relatives are the passing shadows in life. Only virtue and good deeds endure. . . . The rest is the changeful life, the wave of the ocean.

Gesuis Purana

In this picture, the distance between the sky and the earth reflects the dimensions possible in the explanation of human existence. For primitive man, sacred time became the measurement of the movement between birth, death, and rebirth. The gods often existed somewhere in the heavens, and were often identified with the sun. Life was closely associated with the rhythmic motions of nature. For modern man, profane time becomes the measure of the way we move between life and death. Science is the means by which men and women travel beyond the limits of earthly existence. Nature no longer seems to have mysterious elements because understanding is attained through the illusion of explanation.

Touching the Flow of Time

A TIME FOR EVERYTHING
ECCLESIASTICS

To every *thing there is* a season, and a time to every purpose under the heaven: a time to be born, and a time to die; a time to plant, and a time to pluck up *that which is* planted; a time to kill, and a time to heal; a time to break down, and a time to build up; a time to weep, and a time to laugh; a time to mourn, and a time to dance; a time to cast away stones, and a time to gather stones together; a time to embrace, and a time to refrain from embracing; a time to get, and a time to lose; a time to keep, and a time to cast away; a time to rend, and a time to sew; a time to keep silence, and a time to speak; a time to love, and a time to hate; a time of war, and a time of peace. What profit hath he that worketh in that wherein he laboreth?

I have seen the travail, which God hath given to the sons of men to be exercised in it. He hath made every *thing* beautiful in his time: also he hath set the world in their heart, so that no man can find out the work that God maketh from the beginning to the end. I know that *there is* no good in them, but for a *man* to rejoice, and to do good in his life. And also that every man should eat and drink, and enjoy the good of all his labor, it *is* the gift of God. I know that, whatsoever God doeth, it shall be for ever: nothing can be put to it, nor any thing taken from it: and God doeth *it,* that *men* should fear before him. That which hath been is now; and that which is to be hath already been; and God requireth that which is past.

To Create from Nothing...

A TIME FOR CREATION
FROM THE *RIG VEDA:* HINDU SCRIPTURES

Then was not non-existent nor existent: there was
no realm of air, no sky beyond it.
What covered in, and where? and what gave shelter?
Was water there, unfathomed depth of water?
Death was not then, nor was there aught immortal:
no sign was there, the day's and night's divider.
That One Thing, breathless, breathed by its own
nature: apart from it was nothing whatsoever.
Darkness there was: at first concealed in darkness
this All was undiscriminated chaos.
All that existed then was void and formless: by the
great power of warmth was born that unit.
Who verily knows and who can here declare it,
whence it was born and whence comes this
creation?
The gods are later than this world's production.
Who knows then whence it first came into being?
He, the first origin of this creation, whether he
formed it all or did not form it,
Whose eye controls this world in highest heaven, he
verily knows it, or perhaps he knows not.

...Everything

To see a world in a grain of sand
And a heaven as a wild flower,
Hold infinity in the palm of your hand
And eternity in an hour.

William Blake

Men must endure
Their coming hither even as their going hence,
Ripeness is all.

King Lear, **William Shakespeare**

The Journey of Life begins with the Child's Need

A new World has just been born, a fresh, pure, rich world with all its potentialities intact and unworn by time ... the World as it was on the first day of Creation. This idea, which is ... very widespread, reveals the religious man's desire to deliver himself from the weight of his past, to escape the work of Time, and to begin his life again *ab ovo.*
Mircea Eliade

Where did I come from?
How did I get get here?
How do men and women differ?
What will I become?
Is death the end?

Encountering the Wheel of Time

WHEEL of FORTUNE.

Time is a symbol used by human beings to impose order and meaning on the life experience. Nature becomes the symbolic representation of the time-life cycle. Spring signals the beginning of the life process, and winter brings us to an end of this cycle. Each season becomes an integral link in the chain of events which help make the next season possible. Thus in the midst of winter, the celebration of the new year imitates this movement. The previous year is represented by an old man posing as father time. The new year is represented by a young child. The old man must die in order to make it possible for the child to grow and become the next year. In the dead of winter, this child signifies the hope of life which will appear in the coming spring. In past societies, "rites of passage" were created to help individuals make the transition from one stage of life to the next. These rites brought nature and the human community together to celebrate their interdependence. Time is the symbolic concept which helps make it possible for an individual to become a part of the collective.

THE BEGINNING

I was born a thousand years ago, born in the culture of bows and arrows ... born in an age when people loved the things of nature, and spoke to it as though it had a soul.

Chief Dan George

The Purposes and Functions of Myth Are:

To give human beings a perspective
To give meaning and direction to the life experience
To understand what forces influence and direct our actions
To hold the mirror up to nature and see what images are reflected
To view the evolution of the human mind
To name and express the unexpressible
To help human beings go beyond their illusions
To understand how "inner" experiences have been interpreted
To balance the contradictions between life and death
To bring experience from the realm of possibility into the world of actuality
To provide us with a means to express our common joys and woes

Primitive man often looked to the sunrise as a symbolic representation of how the world began. The sun became the symbol of the light of knowledge. Heroes were created to undergo certain ordeals to overcome the forces of darkness which threatened to destroy the light of consciousness. In antiquity, Greeks believed that Apollo was the god of light who had triumphed over the god of darkness, Dionysus. These myths become the narration of humanity's struggle to move from birth to death to rebirth in order to demonstrate the movement from ignorance to knowledge.

THE CENTER OF THE WORLD:
The Moment When Night Meets Day

ZUNI MYTH

Mother Earth and Father Sky lay together and conceived all beings, but they were not ready for creation yet. So they assumed human forms and talked together. They prepared the land for the coming of the creatures by bringing rain and corn to earth and planting corn in the sky to serve as guiding stars.

At last, in the innermost womb of Mother Earth, life began to appear. The first forms of life were wormlike crawling creatures. Only one of these creatures was able to find his way out of the deep darkness of the fourth womb. He went through the inner paths and finally came to the light of the sun. There he prayed to the Sun Father for all of the other things that were still inside the inner womb.

The Sun Father created twins who were to finish his work of creation. The twins crawled back into the womb on spiderweb threads and began to teach the newly created beings so they would be prepared for a world of light. When they were ready, the twins made a ladder of vines and trees and made the creatures climb it. The second womb in which they arrived was much larger, but still dark. Here the people increased rapidly and soon were ready to climb the ladder to the third world. As they climbed this time, the twins separated them into different groups: yellow, brown-gray, red, white, black, and all colors mixed.

Finally they arrived in the birth channel of the earth. Here they were warned about the coming light of the sun, but were still not prepared for its brilliance. They came up at night and were certain that the star Sirius was the sun. When morning came they were terrified at the great light. But gradually they learned to love the light and to grow into wise and thankful people under the warm rays of the sun.

SONG OF THE SKY LOOM
TEWA INDIANS

O our Mother the Earth, O our Father the Sky,
Your children are we, and with tired backs
We bring you the gifts you love.
Then weave for us a garment of brightness;
May the warp be the white light of morning,
May the weft be the red light of evening,
May the fringes be the falling rain,
May the border be the standing rainbow.
Thus weave for us a garment of brightness,
That we may walk fittingly where birds sing,
That we may walk fittingly where grass is green,
O our Mother the Earth, O our Father the Sky.

FROM NOTHING CAME . . .

MAORI: NEW ZEALAND NATIVES

MAORI

And from nothing came darkness, and then light, and finally the sky and the earth. And Rangi, the sky, and Papa, the earth, came together in love and had many children.

But Rangi and Papa were joined inseparably, so that their children had no place to live but were squeezed into the tight darkness between them. At last their offspring crept together to confer about their fate. Tu, the god of man and war, said, "Let's kill Rangi and Papa so we'll be freed."

But Tane, the god of the forest, said, "No, let's try to separate them. If we try hard enough, we can push the sky away and keep Mother Earth to nurse us."

So first Rongo, god of cultivated food, tried to force the heaven and earth apart. But he failed. Then Tangaroa, god of all the animals that live in the sea, tried, but he, too, had no luck. Then Haumia, father of wild plants, also tried and failed. Warlike Tu then took his knife and hacked away the sinews that bound earth and heaven, but he still could not separate them.

At last, Tane, god of the trees, placed his shoulders against the earth and his feet against the sky and pressed with all of his might. He thrust the sky above him and held him there.

Now at last all of the children of Rangi and Papa could stand up and see the light.

Since there was room upon the earth, Tane decided to make some people. He went to the spot where Rangi's blood had fallen when Tu chopped on him and picked up some of the clay. Tane was a god, but he had a man's interest, so he made a woman. Soon she had a beautiful daughter whom he named Hine Titama.

When Hine Titama grew up she was very beautiful, so Tane also married her and she bore him several children. But she did not know that Tane was her father.

One day she asked Tane, "Who is my father?"

For a long time Tane did not answer. At last he told her the truth.

Hine Titama cried out in horror, "How could you make me commit such a dreadful crime! I can't bear to live with this shame!"

So Hine Titama ran sorrowfully to her grandmother Papa in the deep, dark center of the earth. There she was comforted. And since that time all of mankind has followed her on the trail of death.

AND GOD CREATED MAN IN HIS IMAGE....

GENESIS

Chapter 1

In the beginning God created the heaven and the earth.

2 And the earth was without form, and void; and darkness was upon the face of the deep. And the Spirit of God moved upon the face of the waters.

3 And God said, let there be light: and there was light.

4 And God saw the light, that it was good: and God divided the light from the darkness.

5 And God called the light Day, and the darkness he called Night. And the evening and the morning were the first day.

6 ¶ And God said, Let there be a firmament in the midst of the waters, and let it divide the waters from the waters.

7 And God made the firmament, and divided the waters which were under the firmament from the waters which were above the firmament: and it was so.

8 And God called the firmament Heaven. And the evening and the morning were the second day.

9 ¶ And God said, Let the waters under the heaven be gathered together unto one place, and let the dry land appear: and it was so.

10 And God called the dry land Earth; and the gathering together of the waters called he Seas: and God saw that it was good.

11 And God said, Let the earth bring forth grass, the herb yielding seed, and the fruit tree yielding fruit after his kind, whose seed is in itself, upon the earth: and it was so.

12 And the earth brought forth grass, and herb yielding seed after his kind, and the tree yielding fruit, whose seed was in itself, after his kind: and God saw that it was good.

13 And the evening and the morning were the third day.

14 ¶ And God said, Let there be lights in the firmament of the heaven to divide the day from the night; and let them be for signs, and for seasons, and for days, and years:

15 And let them be for lights in the firmament of the heaven to give light upon the earth: and it was so.

16 And God made two great lights; the greater light to rule the day, and the lesser light to rule the night: he made the stars also.

17 And God set them in the firmament of the heaven to give light upon the earth.

18 And to rule over the day and over the night, and to divide the light from the darkness: and God saw that it was good.

19 And the evening and the morning were the fourth day.

20 And God said, Let the waters bring forth abundantly the moving creature that hath life, and fowl that may fly above the earth in the open firmament of heaven.

21 And God created great whales, and every living creature that moveth, which the waters brought forth abundantly, after their kind, and every winged fowl after his kind: and God saw that it was good.

22 And God blessed them, saying, Be fruitful, and multiply, and fill the waters in the seas, and let fowl multiply in the earth.

23 And the evening and the morning were the fifth day.

24 ¶ And God said, Let the earth bring forth the living creature after his kind, cattle, and creeping thing, and beast of the earth after his kind: and it was so.

25 And God made the beast of the earth after his kind, and cattle after their kind, and every thing that creepeth upon the earth after his kind: and God saw that it was good.

26 ¶ And God said, Let us make man in our image, after our likeness: and let them have dominion over the fish of the sea, and over the fowl of the air, and over the cattle, and over all the earth, and over every creeping thing that creepeth upon the earth.

27 So God created man in his own image, in the image of God created he him; male and female created he them.

28 And God blessed them, and God said unto

them, Be fruitful, and multiply, and replenish the earth, and subdue it: and have dominion over the fish of the sea, and over the fowl of the air, and over every living thing that moveth upon the earth.

29 ¶ And God said, Behold, I have given you every herb bearing seed, which is upon the face of all the earth, and every tree, in the which is the fruit of a tree yielding seed; to you it shall be for meat.

30 And to every beast of the earth, and to every fowl of the air, and to every thing that creepeth upon the earth, wherein there is life, I have given every green herb for meat; and it was so.

31 And God saw every thing that he had made, and, behold, it was very good. And the evening and the morning were the sixth day.

Chapter 2

Thus the heavens and the earth were finished, and all the host of them.

2 And on the seventh day God ended his work which he had made; and he rested on the seventh day from all his work which he had made.

3 And God blessed the seventh day, and sanctified it: because that in it he had rested from all his work which God created and made.

4 ¶ These are the generations of the heavens and of the earth when they were created, in the day that the LORD God made the earth and the heavens.

5 And every plant of the field before it was in the earth, and every herb of the field before it grew: for the LORD God had not caused it to rain upon the earth, and there was not a man to till the ground.

6 But there went up a mist from the earth, and watered the whole face of the ground.

7 And the LORD God formed man of the dust of the ground, and breathed into his nostrils the breath of life; and man became a living soul.

8 ¶ And the LORD God planted a garden eastward in Eden; and there he put the man whom he had formed.

9 And out of the ground made the LORD God to grow every tree that is pleasant to the sight, and good for food; the tree of life also in the midst of the garden, and the tree of knowledge of good and evil.

10 And a river went out of Eden to water the garden; and from thence it was parted, and became into four heads.

11 The name of the first is Pison: that is it which compasseth the whole land of Havilah, where there is gold;

12 And the gold of that land is good: there is bdellium and the onyx stone.

13 And the name of the second river is Gihon: the same is it that compasseth the whole land of Ethiopia.

14 And the name of the third river is Hiddekel: that is it which goeth toward the east of Assyria. And the fourth river is Euphrates.

15 And the LORD God took the man, and put him into the garden of Eden to dress it and to keep it.

16 And the LORD God commanded the man, saying, Of every tree of the garden thou mayest freely eat:

17 But of the tree of the knowledge of good and evil, thou shalt not eat of it: for in the day that thou eatest thereof thou shalt surely die.

18 ¶ And the LORD God said, It is not good that the man should be alone; I will make him an help meet for him.

19 And out of the ground the LORD God formed every beast of the field, and every fowl of the air; and brought them unto Adam to see what he would call them: and whatsoever Adam called every living creature, that was the name thereof.

20 And Adam gave names to all cattle, and to the fowl of the air, and to every beast of the field; but for Adam there was not found an help meet for him.

21 And the LORD God caused a deep sleep to fall upon Adam, and he slept: and he took one of his ribs, and closed up the flesh instead thereof;

22 And the rib, which the LORD God had taken from man, made he a woman, and brought her unto the man.

FROM ONE SPIRIT WORLDS BEGIN TO SPIN OFF:

HINDU MYTH

The whole world, everything that exists, comes from the One, the Absolute, the Universal Spirit, or Iswara. The Universal Spirit is manifested in three forms: Brahma, the creator, Vishnu, the preserver, and Siva, the destroyer. The world itself exists and disappears as Brahma sleeps and wakes up. Each time Brahma awakens, the world of physical beings appears. When he goes to sleep, the world is absorbed into the Universal Spirit. A day in Brahma's life is equal to 43,200,000 years on earth. Eventually, after 100 years of Brahma's life, the entire universe, including Brahma himself, will be absorbed into Iswara and remain for 100 years.

The world between cycles of creation is sometimes pictured as Vishnu lying motionless on a thousand-headed cobra called Ananta, or eternity, floating on an infinite and unmoving ocean of milk. Then from Vishnu's navel a lotus emerges with Brahma seated on it. Before beginning the work of creation, Brahma submits to a number of austerities to build up his spiritual power. Then he begins by creating opposites—gods and demons.

Another way of visualizing the beginning of creation in the Hindu tradition is as a golden, cosmic egg floating on the waters. At the beginning of the cycle of creation, the egg breaks open to reveal Purusha, a manifestation of the Ultimate Being with a thousand thighs, a thousand eyes, a thousand faces, and a thousand heads. Purusha offers himself as a sacrifice for the creation of the universe, and from each of his limbs an object of creation appears. From his mouth issue the Brahmans and the gods. From his abdomen come demons. From his thighs come the merchant caste and cattle. Manual workers and horses come from his feet. In this picturesque way, the myth emphasizes that all of creation has come from the One and will return to it.

Vishnu is most closely involved in human affairs, for frequently his work requires that he come to earth in human form to save the world from premature destruction. Usually his task is to kill a demon who has gained tremendous spiritual powers through meditation and threatens to overpower the gods.

At times Vishnu appears as an animal. One appearance was as a fish when the great flood came. He appeared to the great sage Manu as a fish, warned Manu to build a boat, and floated near him so that Manu could anchor his boat to him.

In another story of the flood, the earth was held under the waters by a demon. Vishnu took the form of a boar and dived deep into the depths, where he killed the demon and raised the earth back to its proper place.

Other appearances were as a lion, as a dwarf who had the power to grow to gigantic size, and as two important heroes, Rama and Krishna.

The final appearance of Vishnu is yet to come. He will appear riding on a white horse and will bring in the end of the age—and the work of Siva.

Siva, the third of the trinity, is the god of destruction—the destruction of the old, worn-out world. He prepares the way for all to be reabsorbed into the Eternal One and for the re-creation of the world. Siva is also associated with asceticism—the destruction of evil in the human being so that the individual soul may be reabsorbed into the One and be freed from the world of illusion.

Sacrifice of Human Life to Ensure the Continuation of the World...

Creation in many mythologies appears to be a bloody, painful process. Self-mutilation is a common form of sacrifice in these rituals. The Norse god Odin sacrifices one of his eyes to attain knowledge, and in Australia, Africa, and the Middle East, young men undergo circumcision to attain their manhood. Other peoples believed that human life must be offered to appease the gods; the Aztecs believed that they must kill people every day in order to feed the sun and keep it in the sky. Greeks sacrificed bulls; Africans, cocks; Hebrews, lambs; and Incas, llamas as a means to secure a treaty, or alliance, with their gods.

THE BLOOD OF LIFE

AZTEC

AZTEC MYTH

No one knows. Man only knows that this earth has been created and destroyed many, many times. And it will be destroyed again.

The last time the world was destroyed and re-created, there were no men on it. Quetzalcoatl, the plumed serpent god, saw that the earth was empty. So he went to the world of the dead and collected the bones of the dead people of the past. He gathered the bones together, but they did not live because they had no blood. So Quetzalcoatl cut himself and gave mankind his own blood so that they might live.

Since the god's blood was shed for man, man must continue to shed his blood so the gods can continue to live. Human beings must be sacrificed regularly or the sun and the earth will die.

A Daily Prayer
O Gods! All your names (and forms) are to be revered, saluted, and adored; all of you who have sprung from heaven, and earth, listen here to my invocation.
—from the *Rig Veda*

NORSE MYTH

And the two came together and formed a mist. And from these mists, Ymir, the frost giant, was formed. Next, the mist formed a great cow who fed Ymir. The cow gained her nourishment by eating the ice and frost, but one day as she was eating, a hair appeared. As she continued eating, she uncovered the whole head of some new being. At last she kicked free the whole body of the god Bori.

Ymir, in the meantime, continued to grow from the cow's milk and had a number of children from the mist. One of his daughters married Bori, and they had sons and grandsons. His grandsons Odin, Vili, and Ve decided that Ymir, the frost giant, was evil and that they should kill him.

From the dead frost giant's body the new gods made the earth. From his blood they made the seas. They built the mountains out of his bones and the trees out of his hair.

From the body of Ymir grew a mighty ash tree, Yggdrasil, which supports the whole universe. This tree has three immense roots: the first goes to Midgard, the land of man; the second goes to Jotunheim, the land of the giants; and the third to Niflheim, the region of death. The root to Midgard is carefully guarded by the Norns, or fates.

The gods built themselves a home called Asgard which can be reached only by crossing the rainbow, Bilfrost. There Odin lives with his wife, Frigga, and sons Thor, Vithar, Bragi, Balder, and Hoder.

NORSE

THE KILLING OF THE FATHERS
GREEK

Greek theology was not formulated by priests nor even by prophets, but by artists, poets, and philosophers. The great civilizations of the East were dominated by a sacerdotal caste, and the temple became for them the center of intellectual, no less than of religious life. In Greece nothing of this sort ever happened. There was no priestly class guarding from innovating influence a sacred tradition enshrined in a sacred book. There were no divines who could successfully claim to dictate the terms of belief from an inexpugnable fortress of authority. One consequence was that the conception of deity could be dissociated from cult, and enlarged to include beings and things which no one ever dreamed of connecting with the obligation of worship.

—from *Greek Religious Thought from Homer to Alexander*
F. M. Comford

Night, mist, and ether whirled in confusion until at last they formed themselves into an egg. Gathering speed, the whirling chaos suddenly split in two, forming Father Heaven (Uranus) and Mother Earth (Gaea). And between them floated Eros, or Love.

As Love touched him, Uranus showered a fertile rain on Gaea and from her womb sprang mountains, woods, and meadows. Then came living creatures: hundred-handed monsters, one-eyed Cyclops, and gigantic Titans. Uranus was horrified at the sight of the hundred-handed monsters and banished them to a deep pit called Tartarus.

Gaea was insulted by this treatment that her children were given, for she loved them all even if they were ugly, so she plotted with her youngest son, Cronus, to kill Uranus. That night the son waited for his father with a sickle and when Uranus came by, Cronus leaped out and slashed the old god to bits. The blood of the great sky god fell upon the sea and was washed up on the shore of Cythera in ocean foam. And from this blood sprang the beautiful goddess of love and beauty, Aphrodite.

But Cronus was an even worse ruler than his father, Uranus. To begin with, he did not free his hundred-handed monster brothers, whose imprisonment was supposedly the reason he had killed his father. Gaea was so angry at Cronus that

she vowed that one of his own children would dethrone him, just as he had dethroned his father.

Cronus thought he was too smart for her. He went ahead and married his sister Rhea and waited for the children to come along. As soon as they were born, he swallowed them so they would not be able to dethrone him. Five children—Hestia, Demeter, Hera, Poseidon, and Hades—were born and immediately swallowed by their father. But Rhea did not like this treatment of her children any better than Gaea had appreciated the imprisonment of her monsters.

So when she became pregnant with her sixth child, Rhea decided that she would trick her husband. When it was time for the baby to be born, she slipped off to a cave in Crete and left the infant there in charge of a gentle nymph. Then she returned to Cronus with a large stone wrapped in swaddling clothes. Cronus did not bother to unwrap the bundle, but swallowed it whole, not noticing that the taste and texture were somewhat different from his first five children.

So, Zeus, the youngest child of Cronus, lived and grew to manhood. His grandmother, Gaea, who had prompted Cronus to kill Uranus, was now more than eager to have Cronus overthrown, so she gave the young god an herb which would make Cronus vomit. Zeus managed to slip it into his food, and Cronus went into a vomiting fit. First the stone came up, and then the five brothers and sisters, who were—amazingly—still alive. The six children placed the stone at Delphi, where it stands today, and fled away to begin plotting their father's downfall.

Thus began the great battle of the gods. Cronus and all his Titan brothers, with their gigantic strength, were arrayed against the young gods. But Gaea was still trying to rescue her monster children from Tartarus and offered their services to Zeus if he would let them loose. So Zeus flew to Tartarus and let loose the Cyclops and the hundred-handed monsters, and with their help he conquered the Titans. The Cyclops were so grateful at being freed that they made the thunderbolt and lightning. They gave Poseidon a magic trident which could cause the earth to shake, and they gave Hades a magic helmet which made him invisible.

Zeus and his two brothers divided the control of the world, with Zeus receiving the heavens and earth, Poseidon the sea, and Hades the underworld. Zeus and his family made their homes on Mount Olympus, where they feasted on ambrosia and watched the affairs of men.

Zeus married his sister Hera, who was also known as Juno, but he was never very faithful. In fact, most of the heroes of Greece could trace their ancestry to Zeus and one of his human lovers, whom he usually visited in the form of an animal such as a swan or a bull. Hera was very jealous of Zeus and did her best to bring his human lovers and children to a sad end.

Zeus also had affairs with other goddesses, particularly the goddess Leto. Hera fiercely attacked Leto and drove her from land to land. Pregnant with twins, Leto fled from country to country until she came to a desolate floating island called Delos and there at last delivered her daughter, Artemis. A rather precocious child, Artemis assisted at the birth of her twin brother, Apollo, a few hours later.

Apollo was the god of light, music, and masculine beauty. He made known the will of the gods, gave judgments, and offered purification from sin through his oracle at Delphi, where he inspired the priestess to speak his message.

His sister Artemis was a virgin huntress, protectress of wild things, and goddess of the moon. As Greek culture spread, she took on the names and characteristics of other goddesses of the moon, so she is variously known as Cynthia, Selena, Hecate, and Diana, and her character varied from the chaste, shy goddess of the wood who killed a man who saw her naked, to the multi-breasted fertility goddess of Ephesus.

Hermes, or Mercury, was another of Zeus' rather precocious offspring. On the day of his birth he invented the lyre and stole Apollo's cattle. However, the clever trickster made friends with his brother by giving him the lyre, and Apollo was so enraptured with the beautiful music of this instrument that he forgot all about punishing Hermes for stealing his cattle. Hermes became the chief messenger of the gods and the conductor of dead souls to Hades, the land of the dead.

Athena's birth was the most unusual of all the Olympian gods; for she sprang fully grown and in complete armor from Zeus' head. Always one of Zeus' favorites, she was allowed to carry his breastplate. Athena represented wisdom, justice, and law, and was associated with the city of Athens, which she won in a contest with Poseidon. She greatly admired courage and frequently assisted heroes in their exploits.

Strangely, the children of Zeus' legitimate wife, Hera, were among the less attractive of the gods. Hephaestus, or Vulcan, was born lame, and Hera was so upset that she threw the child from Mount Olympus. Only when he became powerful by learning to shape iron and bronze did the gods invite him back.

Their other child, Ares or Mars, was the god of war. Unlike the other gods, who were willing to fight only when they needed to, Ares simply enjoyed the blood and gore—at least as long as it was from others. When he joined in the Trojan War, he was quickly wounded and came scampering back whimpering to his disgusted father.

So the Greek universe was peopled with gods and goddesses representing many different aspects of the world but behaving in very human fashion. Two dynasties of gods have been overthrown since the world emerged from chaos, and Zeus himself may someday be overthrown, perhaps by man.

NAVAJO

THE BRINGING OF FIRE . . . .

Our ancestry is firmly rooted in the animal world, and to its subtle, antique ways our hearts are yet pledged. Children of all animal kind, we inherited many a social nicety as well as the predator's way. But most significant of all our gifts, as things turned out, was the legacy bequeathed us by those killer apes, our immediate forebears. Even in the long days of our beginnings we held in our hand the weapon, an instrument somewhat older than ourselves.

Robert Ardrey

Prometheus, a Titan who had helped Zeus against Cronus, was given the job of creating man and the animals for earth. Epimetheus, his brother, was to help.

Epimetheus began on the lower animals and became so excited with them that he gave away all of the good gifts of courage, wisdom, swiftness, warm coats, powerful claws, and wings.

Prometheus came to find what Epimetheus was doing and was very disturbed that there was nothing left for man. Since man must be better than the animals, there was nothing to do but make him like the gods.

So Prometheus took some earth and water and shaped man to look like the gods. He made him to stand upright so that he could look up at the stars instead of the earth. But he could not give man the powers of the gods, and the new creature was still too weak to rule over the world as he was supposed to.

At last, in desperation, Prometheus went to heaven and lit a torch at the chariot of the sun and brought to man the gift of fire. With the fire he brought men civilization and the ability to warm their homes and make weapons.

Zeus was furious at Prometheus, for he felt that man was now too

powerful and might threaten the gods. So he created woman, Pandora, to weaken man and cause him trouble.

As for Prometheus, Zeus bound him to a rock on Mount Caucasus. There he was tormented for ages by a vulture who preyed on his liver, which was continually replenished, so that the torture would continue forever.

At last, however, Prometheus was freed. Some stories say that Hercules decided that freeing Prometheus would be the greatest deed man could do and with his mighty strength killed the vulture and broke the chains. Another myth says that the centaur Chron, after being wounded and in great pain, offered to die in Prometheus' place and so free the hero.

NAVAJO:

The first world was inhabited by insects and insectlike people. It was such an unpleasant place that all of the insects made themselves wings and flew to the sky to look for a new home. Finally they found a crack in the sky and emerged into the second world.

The second world was a blue world of birds who strongly resented the invasion of the insect people. There was constant fighting, and at last the insect people followed the voice of the blue wind to the third world.

The third world, or yellow world, began to look more like the world we now know, and people and animals began to look more like they do now. There were four mountains in this land, one in each direction, and the mountain people began to teach First Man and First Woman how to plant corn and how to build homes. They also warned everyone not to bother the water monster.

But the coyote did not heed the warnings. He went to the home of the water monster and kidnapped his two children.

Suddenly the oceans rose and the land began to flood. All of the people and animals gathered on top of the highest mountain. The people planted a giant reed on top of the mountain and climbed up inside it. Finally after four days of climbing the giant reed, they reached the fourth world.

This fourth world was even more beautiful than those before, and here were other people and other kinds of animals. Here First Man and First Woman learned more about growing corn and the proper roles for the sexes.

But the coyote still had the children of the water monster, and First People were horrified to find the waters of their new world suddenly rising. Again they planted a reed and began to climb, but this time they could not reach all the way. Nor could they find a hole. So the yellow hawk tried to scratch a hole in the dome. The heron and the buzzard also helped, but the locust was the one who finally succeeded in getting through. Then the spider spun a rope so that everyone could climb up through the hole.

The new world was only a small island, so the ants went first, carrying the soil of the fourth world. The other people followed, carrying seeds of corn and other treasures from the fourth world.

The people had not even gotten settled in the fifth world when the waters there started rising. This time First Man and First Woman decided that someone must have offended the water monster. They searched everyone, and of course, found his children with the coyote. They took them to the lake and put them in a small boat. The waters went down immediately and floods have never again destroyed man's world.

Man is at bottom a wild terrific animal. We know him only in connection with the taming and training which is called civilization.

Arthur Schopenhauer

Straight is the gate and narrow the way which leadeth to Life, And few there be to find it.

Matthew 7:14

?

In each of the preceding myths, we see examples of the way a culture attempts to explain the process of creation. The following questions direct your focus of attention on how these myths contain both truths and illusions about man's conception of the way a world began:

1 How do these myths attempt to transcend the barriers of time and space?

2 What cultural attitudes toward nature emerge as we compare and contrast the ways these myths present us with a conception of a world?

3 What image of the human species emerges as we examine the powers attached to the founding spirit, i.e., a god, in each of these myths?

4 How do each of these myths create patterns of behavior for the (a) father; (b) mother; and (c) children? What does this suggest about the family as a social institution?

5 In which of these myths do men give birth to life? What does this suggest about the powers of the male in that society?

6 How do these myths both create and justify the need for human sacrifice? What does this express about their conception of death?

7 Though these myths vary in detail, to what degree do they express similar patterns of thought and behavior?

8 Each of the creation myths expresses a rite of passage.
   a How do they explain a world before creation?
   b How do they give us clues to acquire the means to survive during the life process?
   c How do they explain the contradiction between life and death, or creation and destruction?
   d How do they explain a life after death?

THE UNIVERSAL SELF
(A Hindu account of the creation)

In the beginning this universe was Self alone, in the shape of a person. He, looking round, saw nothing but his Self. He first said, "This is I"; therefore he became by name. Therefore to this day, if a man is asked, he first says, "This is I," and then says the other name which he may have. . . . In the beginning this was Self alone, one only. He desired, "Let there be a wife for me that I may have offspring, and let there be wealth so that I may offer sacrifices." Truly this is the whole desire, and, even if one wishes, one cannot get more than this.

—from the *Upanishads*

> We cannot duplicate God's work, but we come very close.
>
> *Newsweek,* **1967**

Will wonders never cease: The Golden Gateway

In this picture, the skyscraper symbolizes modern man's struggle to imprison himself in a world of concrete to create the illusion that the transformation of nature is nearly accomplished. These "external" forms create the image that modern life is not subject to the destruction of time. In "Modern Man's Need to Understand the Rites of Passage," Mircea Eliade discusses how the loss of initiation rites in the twentieth century has created this vacuum.

CULTURE ORGANIZES THE TRANSITION INTO RITUAL

Despite all our technology,
We still ask:
WHAT IS MAN?
The Bible Statement is:

WHEN I CONSIDER THE HEAVENS,
THE WORK OF THY FINGERS
THE MOON AND THE STARS,
WHICH THOU HAST ORDAINED.

WHAT IS MAN THAT THOU ART MINDFUL
    OF HIM?
FOR THOU HAST MADE HIM A LITTLE
    LOWER THAN THE ANGELS.
AND HAST CROWNED HIM WITH GLORY
    AND HONOR.
THOU MAKEST HIM TO HAVE DOMINION
    OVER
THE WORKS OF THY HANDS:
THOU HAST PUT ALL THINGS UNDER HIS
    FEET.

PSALMS 8:3–6

MODERN MAN'S NEED TO UNDER-STAND THE RITES OF PASSAGE

MIRCEA ELIADE

It has often been said that one of the character-istics of the modern world is the disappearance of any meaningful rites of initiation. Of primary importance in traditional societies, in the modern Western world significant initiation is practically nonexistent. To be sure, the several Christian communions preserve, in varying degrees, ves-tiges of a mystery that is initiatory in structure. Baptism is essentially an initiatory rite; ordina-tion to the priesthood comprises an initiation. But it must not be forgotten that Christianity triumphed in the world and became a universal religion only because it detached itself from the climate of the Greco-Oriental mysteries and proclaimed itself a religion of salvation acces-sible to all.

Then, too, we may well ask whether the mod-ern world as a whole can still justifiably be called Christian. If a "modern man" does indeed exist, it is in so far as he refuses to recognize himself in terms familiar to the Christian view of man or, as European scholars express it, in terms of Christian "anthropology." Modern man's originality, his newness in comparison with traditional societies, lies precisely in his determination to regard himself as a purely his-torical being, in his wish to live in a basically desacralized cosmos. To what extent modern man has succeeded in realizing his ideal is an-other problem, into which we shall not enter here. But the fact remains that his ideal no longer has anything in common with the Chris-tian message, and that it is equally foreign to the image of himself conceived by the man of the traditional societies.

It is through the initiation rite that the man of the traditional societies comes to know and to assume this image. Obviously there are num-erous types and countless variants of initiation, corresponding to different social structures and cultural horizons. But the important fact is that all premodern societies (that is, those that lasted in Western Europe to the end of the Middle Ages, and in the rest of the world to the first World War) accord primary importance to the ideology and techniques of initiation.

The term initiation in the most general sense denotes a body of rites and oral teachings whose purpose is to produce a decisive alteration in the religious and social status of the person to be initiated. In philosophical terms, initiation is equivalent to a basic change in existential con-dition; the novice emerges from his ordeal en-dowed with a totally different being from that which he possessed before his initiation; he has become *another*. Among the various categories of initiation, the puberty initiation is particu-larly important for an understanding of premod-ern man. These "transition rites" are obligatory for all the youth of the tribe. To gain the right to be admitted among adults, the adolescent has to pass through a series of initiatory ordeals: it is by virtue of these rites, and of the revelations that they entail, that he will be recognized as a responsible member of the society. Initiation introduces the candidate into the human com-munity and into the world of spiritual and cul-tural values. He learns not only the behavior patterns, the techniques, and the institutions of adults but also the sacred myths and traditions of the tribe, the names of the gods and the his-tory of their works; above all, he learns the mystical relations between the tribe and the Supernatural Beings as those relations were es-tablished at the beginning of Time.

Every primitive society possesses a consistent body of mythical traditions, a "conception of the world"; and it is this conception that is gradu-ally revealed to the novice in the course of his initiation. What is involved is not simply in-struction in the modern sense of the word. In order to become worthy of the sacred teaching, the novice must first be prepared spiritually. For what he learns concerning the world and human life does not constitute knowledge in the mod-ern sense of the term, objective and compartmentalized information, subject to indefinite correction and addition. The world is the work of Supernatural Beings—a divine work and hence sacred in its very structure. Man lives in a universe that is not only supernatural in origin, but is no less sacred in its form, sometimes even in its substance. The world has a "history": first, its creation by Supernatural Beings; then, everything that took place after that—the coming of the civilizing Hero or the mythical Ancestor, their cultural activities, their demiurgic adventures, and at last their disappearance.

This "sacred history"—mythology—is exemplary, paradigmatic: not only does it relate how things came to be; it also lays the foundations for all human behavior and all social and cultural institutions. From the fact that man was created and civilized by Supernatural Beings, it follows that the sum of his behavior and activities belongs to sacred history; and this history must be carefully preserved and transmitted intact to succeeding generations. Basically, man is what he is because, at the dawn of Time, certain things happened to him, the things narrated by the myths. Just as modern man proclaims himself a historical being, constituted by the whole history of humanity, so the man of archaic societies considers himself the end product of a mythical history, that is, of a series of events that took place *in illo tempore*, at the beginning of Time. But whereas modern man sees in the history that precedes him a purely human work and, more especially, believes that he has the power to continue and perfect it indefinitely, for the man of traditional societies everything significant—that is, everything creative and powerful—that has ever happened took place *in the beginning*, in the Time of the myths.

In one sense it could almost be said that for the man of archaic societies history is "closed"; that it exhausted itself in the few stupendous events of the beginning. By revealing the different modes of deep-sea fishing to the Polynesians at the beginning of Time, the mythical Hero exhausted all the possible forms of that activity at a single stroke; since then, whenever they go fishing, the Polynesians repeat the exemplary gesture of the mythical Hero, that is, they imitate a transhuman model.

But, properly considered, this history preserved in the myths is closed only in appearance. If the man of primitive societies had contented himself with forever imitating the few exemplary gestures revealed by the myths, there would be no explaining the countless innova-

tions that he has accepted during the course of Time. No such thing as an absolutely closed primitive society exists. We know of none that has not borrowed some cultural elements from outside; none that, as the result of these borrowings, has not changed at least some aspects of its institutions; none that, in short, has had no history. But, in contrast to modern society, primitive societies have accepted all innovations as so many "revelations," hence as having a superhuman origin. The objects or weapons that were borrowed, the behavior patterns and institutions that were imitated, the myths or beliefs that were assimilated, were believed to be charged with magico-religious power; indeed, it was for this reason that they had been noticed and the effort made to acquire them. Nor is this all. These elements were adopted because it was believed that the Ancestors had received the first cultural revelations from Supernatural Beings. And since traditional societies have no historical memory in the strict sense, it took only a few generations, sometimes even less, for a recent innovation to be invested with all the prestige of the primordial revelations.

In the last analysis we could say that, though they are "open" to history, traditional societies tend to project every new acquisition into the primordial Time, to telescope all events in the same atemporal horizon of the mythical beginnings. Primitive societies too are changed by their history, although sometimes only to a very small degree; but what radically differentiates them from modern society is the absence of historical consciousness in them. Indeed, its absence is inevitable, in view of the conception of Time and the anthropology that are characteristic of all pre-Judaic humanity.

It is to this traditional knowledge that the novices gain access. They receive protracted instruction from their teachers, witness secret ceremonies, undergo a series of ordeals. And it is primarily these ordeals that constitute the religious experience of initiation—the encounter with the sacred. The majority of initiatory ordeals more or less clearly imply a ritual death followed by resurrection or a new birth. The central moment of every initiation is represented by the ceremony symbolizing the death of the novice and his return to the fellowship of the living. But he returns to life a new man, assuming another mode of being. Initiatory death signifies the end at once of childhood, of ignorance, and of the profane condition.

For archaic thought, nothing better expresses

the idea of an end, of the final completion of anything, than death, just as nothing better expresses the idea of creation, of making, building, constructing, than the cosmogony. The cosmogonic myth serves as the paradigm, the exemplary model, for every kind of making. Nothing better ensures the success of any creation (a village, a house, a child) than the fact of copying it after the greatest of all creations, the cosmogony. Nor is this all. Since in the eyes of the primitives the cosmogony primarily represents the manifestation of the creative power of the gods, and therefore a prodigious irruption of the sacred, it is periodically reiterated in order to regenerate the world and human society. For symbolic repetition of the creation implies a reactualization of the primordial event, hence the presence of the Gods and their creative energies. The return to beginnings finds expression in a reactivation of the sacred forces that had then been manifested for the first time. If the world was restored to the state in which it had been at the moment when it came to birth, if the gestures that the Gods had made *for the first time* in the beginning were reproduced, society and the entire cosmos became what they had been then—pure, powerful, effectual, with all their possibilities intact.

Every ritual repetition of the cosmogony is preceded by a symbolic retrogression to Chaos. In order to be created anew, the old world must first be annihilated. The various rites performed in connection with the New Year can be put in two chief categories: (1) those that signify the return to Chaos (e.g., extinguishing fires, expelling "evil" and sins, reversal of habitual behavior, orgies, return of the dead); (2) those that symbolize the cosmogony (e.g., lighting new fires, departure of the dead, repetition of the acts by which the Gods created the world, solemn prediction of the weather for the ensuing year). In the scenario of initiatory rites, "death" corresponds to the temporary return to Chaos; hence it is the paradigmatic expression of the *end of a mode of being*—the mode of ignorance and of the child's irresponsibility. Initiatory death provides the clean slate on which will be written the successive revelations whose end is the formation of a new man. We shall later describe the different modalities of birth to a new, spiritual life. But now we must note that this new life is conceived as the true human existence, for it is open to the values of spirit. What is understood by the generic term "culture," comprising all the values of spirit, is accessible only to those who have been initiated. Hence participation in spiritual life is made possible by virtue of the religious experiences released during initiation.

All the rites of rebirth or resurrection, and the symbols that they imply, indicate that the novice has attained to another mode of existence, inaccessible to those who have not undergone the initiatory ordeals, who have not tasted death. We must note this characteristic of the archaic mentality: the belief that a state cannot be changed without first being *annihilated*—in the present instance, without the child's dying to childhood. It is impossible to exaggerate the importance of this obsession with beginnings, which, in sum, is the obsession with the absolute beginning, the cosmogony. For a thing to be well done, it must be done as it was done *the first time*. But the first time, the thing—this class of objects, this animal, this particular behavior —did not exist: when, in the beginning, this object, this animal, this institution, came into existence, it was as if, through the power of the Gods, being arose from nonbeing.

Initiatory death is indispensable for the beginning of spiritual life. Its function must be understood in relation to what it prepares: birth to a higher mode of being. As we shall see farther on, initiatory death is often symbolized, for example, by darkness, by cosmic night, by the telluric womb, the hut, the belly of a monster. All these images express regression to a preformal state, to a latent mode of being (complementary to the precosmogonic Chaos), rather than total annihilation (in the sense in which, for example, a member of the modern societies conceives death). These images and symbols of ritual death are inextricably connected with germination, with embryology; they already indicate a new life in course of preparation. Obviously, as we shall show later, there are other valuations of initiatory death—for example, joining the company of the dead and the Ancestors. But here again we can discern the same symbolism of the beginning: the beginning of spiritual life, made possible in this case by a meeting with spirits.

For archaic thought, then, man is *made*—he does not make himself all by himself. It is the old initiates, the spiritual masters, who make him. But these masters apply what was revealed to them at the beginning of Time by the Supernatural Beings. They are only the representatives of those Beings; indeed, in many cases they incarnate them. This is as much as to say that in order to become a man, it is necessary to resemble a mythical model. Man recognizes himself as such (that is, as man) to the extent to which he is no longer a "natural man," to which he is made a second time, in obedience to a paradigmatic and transhuman canon. The initiatory new birth is not natural, though it is sometimes expressed in obstetric symbols. This birth requires rites instituted by the Supernatural Beings; hence it is a divine work, created by the power and will of those Beings; it belongs, not to nature (in the modern, secularized sense of the term), but to sacred history. The second, initiatory birth does not repeat the first, biological birth. To attain the initiate's mode of being demands knowing realities that are not a part of nature but of the biography of the Supernatural Beings, hence of the sacred history preserved in the myths.

Even when they appear to be dealing only with natural phenomena—with the course of the sun, for example—the myths refer to a reality that is no longer the reality of Nature as modern man knows it today. For the primitive, nature is not simply natural; it is at the same time supernature, that is, manifestation of sacred forces and figure of transcendental realities. To know the myths is not (as was thought in the past century) to become aware of the regularity of certain cosmic phenomena (the course of the sun, the lunar cycle, the rhythm of vegetation, and the like); it is, first of all, to know what has happened in the world, has *really* happened, what the Gods and the civilizing Heroes *did*— their works, adventures, dramas. Thus it is to know a divine history—which nonetheless remains a "history," that is, a series of events that are unforeseeable, though consistent and significant.

In modern terms we could say that initiation puts an end to the natural man and introduces the novice to culture. But for archaic societies, culture is not a human product, its origin is supernatural. Nor is this all. It is through culture that man re-establishes contact with the world of the Gods and other Supernatural Beings and participates in their creative energies. The world of Supernatural Beings is the world in which things took place for the first time—the world in which the first tree and the first animal came into existence; in which an act, thenceforth religiously repeated, was performed for the first time (to walk in a particular posture, to dig a particular edible root, to go hunting during a particular phase of the moon); in which the

Gods or the Heroes, for example, had such and such an encounter, suffered such and such a misadventure, uttered particular words, proclaimed particular norms. The myths lead us into a world that cannot be described but only "narrated," for it consists in the history of acts freely undertaken, of unforeseeable decisions, of fabulous transformations, and the like. It is, in short, the history of everything significant that has happened since the Creation of the world, of all the events that contributed to making man as he is today. The novice whom initiation introduces to the mythological traditions of the tribe is introduced to the sacred history of the world and humanity.

It is for this reason that initiation is of such importance for a knowledge of premodern man. It reveals the almost awesome seriousness with which the man of archaic societies assumed the responsibility of receiving and transmitting spiritual values.

. . . [M]odern man no longer has any initiation of the traditional type. Certain initiatory themes survive in Christianity; but the various Christian denominations no longer regard them as possessing the values of initiation. The rituals, imagery, and terminology borrowed from the mysteries of late antiquity have lost their initiatory aura; for fifteen centuries they have formed an integral part of the symbolism and ceremonial of the Church.

This is not to say that there have not existed, and do not still exist, small groups seeking to revive the "esoteric" meaning of the institutions of the Catholic Church. The attempt of the writer J. K. Huysmans is the best known, but his is not the only one. These efforts have met with almost no response outside of the restricted circles of writers and amateur occultists. It is true that for the past thirty years or so Catholic authorities have shown much interest in images, symbols, and myths. But this is due primarily to the revival of the liturgical movement, to the renewed interest in Greek patrology, and to the increasing importance accorded to mystical experience. None of these trends was initiated by an esoteric group. On the contrary, the Roman Church quite visibly has the same desire to live in history and to prepare its adherents to face the problems of contemporary history as the Protestant churches have. If many Catholic priests are far more interested in the study of symbols today than Catholic priests in general were thirty years ago, it is not in the sense in which Huysmans and his friends were interested, but in order the better to understand the difficulties and crises of their parishioners. It is for the same reason that psychoanalysis is increasingly studied, and applied, by the clergy of various Christian denominations.

To be sure, we find today a considerable number of occult sects, secret societies, pseudo-initiatory groups, hermetistic or neospiritualistic movements, and the like. The Theosophical Society, Anthroposophy, Neo-Vedantism, Neo-Buddhism are merely the best-known expressions of a cultural phenomenon found almost everywhere in the Western world. It is no new phenomenon. Interest in occultism, accompanied by a tendency to form more or less secret societies or groups, already appears in Europe in the sixteenth century and reaches its height in the eighteenth. The only secret movement that exhibits a certain ideological consistency, that already has a history, and that enjoys social and political prestige is Freemasonry. The other self-styled initiatory organizations are for the most part recent and hybrid improvisations. Their interest is chiefly sociological and psychological; they illustrate the disorientation of a part of the modern world, the desire to find a substitute for religious faith. They also illustrate the indomitable inclination toward the mysteries, the occult, the beyond—an inclination that is an integral part of the human being and that is found in all ages on all levels of culture, especially in periods of crisis.

Not all the secret and esoteric organizations of the modern world include entrance rites or initiation ceremonies. Initiation is usually reduced to instruction obtained from a book. (The number of initiatory books and periodicals published throughout the world is amazing.) As for occult groups requiring a formal initiation, what little is known about them shows that their "rites" are either sheer inventions or are inspired by certain books supposed to contain precious revelations concerning the initiations of antiquity. These so-called initiation rites frequently betoken a deplorable spiritual poverty. The fact that those who practice them can regard them as infallible means of attaining to supreme gnosis shows to what a degree modern man has lost all sense of traditional initiation. But the success of these enterprises likewise proves man's profound need for initiation, that is, for regeneration, for participation in the life of spirit. From one point of view, the pseudo-initiatory sects and groups perform a positive function, since they help modern man to find a spiritual meaning for his drastically desacralized existence. A psychologist would even say that the extreme spuriousness of these pretended initiation rites is of little significance, the important fact being that the deep psyche of the participant regains a certain equilibrium through them.

The majority of the pseudo-occult groups are hopelessly sterile. No important cultural creation whatever can be credited to them. On the contrary, the few modern works in which initiatory themes are discernible—James Joyce's *Ulysses*, T. S. Eliot's *The Waste Land*—were created by writers and artists who make no claim to have been initiated and who belong to no occult circle.

And so we come back to the problem on which we touched earlier—that initiatory themes remain alive chiefly in modern man's unconscious. This is confirmed not only by the initiatory symbolism of certain artistic creations—poems, novels, works of plastic art, films—but also by their public reception. Such a massive and spontaneous acceptance proves, it seems to us, that in the depth of his being modern man is still capable of being affected by initiatory scenarios or messages. Initiatory motifs are even to be found in the terminology used to interpret these works. For example, such and such a book or film will be said to rediscover the myths and ordeals of the Hero in quest of immortality, to touch upon the mystery of the redemption of the world, to reveal the secrets of regeneration through woman or love, and so on.

It is not surprising that critics are increasingly attracted by the religious implications, and especially by the initiatory symbolism, of modern literary works. Literature plays an important part in contemporary civilization. Reading itself, as a distraction and escape from the historical present, constitutes one of the characteristic traits of modern man. Hence it is only natural that modern man should seek to satisfy his suppressed or inadequately satisfied religious needs by reading certain books that, though apparently "secular," in fact contain mythological figures camouflaged as contemporary characters and offer initiatory scenarios in the guise of everyday happenings.

The genuineness of this half-conscious or unconscious desire to share in the ordeals that regenerate and finally save a Hero is proved, among other things, by the presence of initiatory themes in the dreams and imaginative activity of modern man. C. G. Jung has stressed the fact that the process that he terms individuation, and that, in his view, constitutes the ultimate goal of human life, is accomplished through a series of ordeals of initiatory type.

As we said before, initiation lies at the core of any genuine human life. And this is true for two reasons. The first is that any genuine human life implies profound crises, ordeals, suffering, loss and reconquest of self, "death and resurrection." The second is that, whatever degree of fulfillment it may have brought him, at a certain moment every man sees his life as a failure. This vision does not arise from a moral judgment made on his past, but from an obscure feeling that he has missed his vocation; that he has betrayed the best that was in him. In such moments of total crisis, only one hope seems to offer any issue—the hope of beginning life over again. This means, in short, that the man undergoing such a crisis dreams of new, regenerated life, fully realized and significant. This is something other and far more than the obscure desire of every human soul to renew itself periodically, as the cosmos is renewed. The hope and dream of these moments of total crisis are to obtain a definitive and total *renovatio*, a renewal capable of transmuting life. Such a renewal is the result of every genuine religious conversion.

But genuine and definitive conversions are comparatively rare in modern societies. To us, this makes it all the more significant that even nonreligious men sometimes, in the depths of their being, feel the desire for this kind of spiritual transformation, which, in other cultures, constitutes the very goal of initiation. It does not fall to us to determine to what extent traditional initiations fulfilled their promises. The important fact is that they proclaimed their intention, and professed to possess the means, of transmuting human life. The nostalgia for an initiatory renewal which sporadically arises from the inmost depths of modern nonreligious man hence seems to us highly significant. It would appear to represent the modern formulation of man's eternal longing to find a positive meaning in death, to accept death as a transition rite to a higher mode of being. If we can say that initiation constitutes a specific dimension of human existence, this is true above all because it is only in initiation that death is given a positive value. Death prepares the new, purely spiritual birth, access to a mode of being not subject to the destroying action of Time.

1 Define and explain Eliade's discussion of initiation rites.
2 Discuss Eliade's emphasis on primitive man's need to express a conception of the world from the following perspectives:
   a What is the function of "sacred history" in the initiation rites?
   b How does time represent primitive man's attempt to explore the dimensions of experience?
   c How were their myths charged with magico-religious power?
   d What is the symbolic purpose of myth?
   e Why is "the return to the beginning" so important?
   f What is the symbolic significance of death?
   g Explain what is meant by this line: "For archaic thought, then, man is made—he does not make himself all by himself."
   h What is the value of a "second birth"?
   i How did primitive man use nature as a metaphor to explain his spiritual values?
3 Discuss Eliade's concern with modern man's need to understand initiation rites from the following perspectives:
   a In what ways does the initiation theme appear in the modern world?
   b What evidence is there to see modern man's desire to find substitutes for religious beliefs?
   c What is the purpose of the contemporary interest in the occult?
   d What is the relation between literature and the initiation motif?
   e Why is initiation an important aspect in understanding the basis of human life?
   f Why do we need to find a positive meaning in death?
   g How does the concern for an understanding of the unconscious express our need to be a part of experience?
   h Explain what is meant by this line: "to accept death as a transition . . . to a higher mode of being."
   i In what ways do you see the initiation theme in your beliefs about the world in which you live?

The Past Experienced as the Present

In the twentieth century, the past is represented in the present through those replicas which characterize a particular age. The photograph above of the Acropolis is an example of such a representation of a time past. Modern visitors to Greece seek to become part of that time in the ruins which remain. This link makes it possible for the modern individual to touch the collective past of Western civilization thereby connecting profane time, a manifestation of mortality, to sacred time, a manifestation of immortality, and blending the modern period with the classical.

UP AGAI
THE
WAL
SDS

Who is up against the wall?

Civilization progresses at the expense of individual happiness.

Sigmund Freud

Now that you have achieved total perfection enlightment

You may expect to be just as miserable as ever

THE ORIGINS OF CULTURE

SIGMUND FREUD

The development of civilization appears to us as a peculiar process which mankind undergoes, and in which several things strike us as familiar. We may characterize this process with reference to the changes which it brings about in the familiar instinctual dispositions of human beings, to satisfy which is, after all, the economic task of our lives. A few of these instincts are used up in such a manner that something appears in their place which, in an individual, we describe as a character-trait. The most remarkable example of such a process is found in the anal erotism of young human beings. Their original interest in the excretory function, its organs and products, is changed in the course of their growth into a group of traits which are familiar to us as parsimony, a sense of order and cleanliness—qualities which, though valuable and welcome in themselves, may be intensified till they become markedly dominant and produce what is called the anal character. How this happens we do not know, but there is no doubt about the correctness of the finding. Now we have seen that order and cleanliness are important requirements of civilization, although their vital necessity is not very apparent, any more than their suitability as sources of enjoyment. At this point we cannot fail to be struck by the similarity between the process of civilization and the libidinal development of the individual. Other instincts [besides anal erotism] are induced to displace the conditions for their satisfaction, to lead them into other paths. In most cases this process coincides with that of the *sublimation* (of instinctual aims) with which we are familiar, but in some it can be differentiated from it. Sublimation of instinct is an especially conspicuous feature of cultural development; it is what makes it possible for higher psychical activities, scientific, artistic or ideological, to play such an important part in civilized life. If one were to yield to a first impression, one would say that sublimation is a vicissitude which has been forced upon the instincts entirely by civilization. But it would be wiser to reflect upon this a little longer. . . . It is impossible to overlook the extent to which civilization is built up upon a renunciation of instinct, how much it presupposes precisely the non-satisfaction (by suppression, repression or some other means?) of powerful instincts. This "cultural frustration" dominates the large field of social relationships between human beings. As we already know, it is the cause of the hostility against which all civilizations have to struggle.

our scientific work, and we shall have much to explain here. It is not easy to understand how it can become possible to deprive an instinct of satisfaction. Nor is doing so without danger. If the loss is not compensated for economically, one can be certain that serious disorders will ensue.

But if we want to know what value can be attributed to our view that the development of civilization is a special process, comparable to the normal maturation of the individual, we must clearly attack another problem. We must ask ourselves to what influences the development of civilization owes its origin, how it arose, and by what its course has been determined.

The task seems an immense one, and it is natural to feel diffidence in the face of it. But here are such conjectures as I have been able to make.

After primal man had discovered that it lay in his own hands, literally, to improve his lot on earth by working, it cannot have been a matter of indifference to him whether another man worked with or against him. The other man acquired the value for him of a fellow-worker, with whom it was useful to live together. Even earlier, in his ape-like prehistory, man had adopted the habit of forming families, and the members of his family were probably his first helpers. One may suppose that the founding of families was connected with the fact that a moment came when the need for genital satisfaction no longer made its appearance like a guest who drops in suddenly, and, after his departure, is heard of no more for a long time, but instead took up its quarters as a permanent lodger. When this happened, the male acquired a motive for keeping the female or, speaking more generally, his sexual objects, near him; while the female, who did not want to be separated from her helpless young, was obliged, in their interests, to remain with the stronger male. In this primitive family one essential feature of civilization is still lacking. The arbitrary will of its head, the father, was unrestricted. In *Totem and Taboo* [1912–13] I have tried to show how the way led from this family to the succeeding stage of communal life in the form of bands of brothers. In overpowering their father, the sons had made the discovery that a combination can be stronger than a single individual. The totemic culture is based on the restrictions which the sons had to impose on one another in order to keep this new state of affairs in being. The taboo-observances were the first "right" or

"law." The communal life of human beings had, therefore, a two-fold foundation: the compulsion to work, which was created by external necessity, and the power of love, which made the man unwilling to be deprived of his sexual object—the woman—and made the woman unwilling to be deprived of the part of herself which had been separated off from her—her child. Eros and Ananke [Love and Necessity] have become the parents of human civilization too. The first result of civilization was that even a fairly large number of people were now able to live together in a community. And since these two great powers were co-operating in this, one might expect that the further development of civilization would proceed smoothly towards an even better control over the external world and toward a further extension of the number of people included in the community. Nor is it easy to understand how this civilization could act upon its participants otherwise than to make them happy.

Before we go on to enquire from what quarter an interference might arise, this recognition of love as one of the foundations of civilization may serve as an excuse for a digression which will enable us to fill a gap which we left in an earlier discussion. We said there that man's discovery that sexual (genital) love afforded him the strongest experiences of satisfaction, and in fact provided him with the prototype of all happiness, must have suggested to him that he should continue to seek the satisfaction of happiness in his life along the path of sexual relations and that he should make genital erotism the central point of his life. We went on to say that in doing so he made himself dependent in a most dangerous way on a portion of the external world, namely, his chosen love-object, and exposed himself to extreme suffering if he should be rejected by that object or should lose it through unfaithfulness or death. For that reason the wise men of every age have warned us most emphatically against this way of life; but in spite of this it has not lost its attraction for a great number of people.

A small minority are enabled by their constitution to find happiness, in spite of everything, along the path of love. But far-reaching mental changes in the function of love are necessary before this can happen. These people make themselves independent of their object's acquiescence by displacing what they mainly value from being loved on to loving; they protect themselves against the loss of the object by directing their love, not to single objects but to all men alike; and they avoid the uncertainties and disappointments of genital love by turning away from its sexual aims and transforming the instinct into an impulse with an *inhibited aim*. What they bring about in themselves in this way is a state of evenly suspended, steadfast, affectionate feeling, which has little external resemblance any more to the stormy agitations of genital love, from which it is nevertheless derived. Perhaps St. Francis of Assisi went furthest in thus exploiting love for the benefit of an inner feeling of happiness. Moreover, what we have recognized as one of the techniques for fulfilling the pleasure principle has often been brought into connection with religion; this connection may lie in the remote regions where the distinction between the ego and objects or between objects themselves is neglected. According to one ethical view, whose deeper motivation will become clear to us presently, this readiness for a universal love of mankind and the world represents the highest standpoint which man can reach. Even at this early stage of the discussion I should like to bring forward my two main objections to this view. A love that does not discriminate seems to me to forfeit a part of its own value, by doing an injustice to its object; and secondly, not all men are worthy of love.

The love which founded the family continues to operate in civilization both in its original form, in which it does not renounce direct sexual satisfaction, and in its modified form as aim-inhibited affection. In each, it continues to carry on its function of binding together considerable numbers of people, and it does so in a more intensive fashion than can be effected through the interest of work in common. The careless way in which language uses the word 'love' has its genetic justification. People give the name 'love' to the relation between a man and a woman whose genital needs have led them to found a family; but they also give the name 'love' to the positive feelings between parents and children, and between the brothers and sisters of a family, although *we* are obliged to describe this as 'aim-inhibited love' or 'affection'. Love with an inhibited aim was in fact originally fully sensual love, and it is so still in man's unconscious. Both—fully sensual love and aim-inhibited love—extend outside the family and create new bonds with people who before were strangers. Genital love leads to the formation of new families, and aim-inhibited love to "friendships' which become valuable from a cul-

tural standpoint because they escape some of the limitations of genital love, as, for instance, its exclusiveness. But in the course of development the relation of love to civilization loses its unambiguity. On the one hand love comes into opposition to the interests of civilization; on the other, civilization threatens love with substantial restrictions. . . .

?

Freud contends that "culture is based on restrictions" and that "love (Eros) and necessity (Ananki) are the parents of human civilization." This description of the origins of culture would not be possible without the medium of language, and the development of culture closely parallels the development of a language. Without symbolic expression, it would not have been possible to create a magic circle in order to draw together the members of the tribe. Language provides the human imagination with the means to transcend the categories of time and space. At the same instant, language brings us to view the restrictions placed on individuals born into a particular culture. To clarify the confusion surrounding individual desire versus cultural taboos, the poet creates a vision which enables us to perceive how we perceive the world in motion. The poet uses time as a metaphor to weave together: the spiritual voices of our past; the necessity of our involvement in the present; and the possibility of our sharing a future together.

THE ECCHOING GREEN[1]
WILLIAM BLAKE

The Sun does arise,
And make happy the skies.
The merry bells ring
To welcome the Spring.
The skylark and thrush,
The birds of the bush,
Sing louder around
To the bells' cheerful sound;
While our sports shall be seen
On the Ecchoing Green.

Old John, with white hair,
Does laugh away care,
Sitting under the oak,
Among the old folk.
They laugh at our play,
And soon they all say:
Such, such were the joys,
When we all, girls and boys,
In our youth time were seen,
On the Ecchoing Green.

Till the little ones, weary,
No more can be merry;
The sun does descend,
And our sports have an end:
Round the laps of their mothers
Many sisters and brothers,

Like birds in their nest,
Are ready for rest;
And sport no more seen,
On the darkening Green.

[1] The spelling of "Ecchoing" is Blake's.

EMILY DICKINSON

I started Early—Took my Dog—
And visited the Sea—
The Mermaids in the Basement
Came out to look at me—

And Frigates—in the Upper Floor
Extended Hempen Hands—
Presuming Me to be a Mouse—
Aground—upon the Sands—

But no Man moved Me—till the Tide
Went past my simple Shoe—
And past my Apron—and my Belt
And past my Boddice—too—

And made as He would eat me up—
As wholly as a Dew
Upon a Dandelion's Sleeve—
And then—I started—too—

And He—He followed—close behind—
I felt His Silver Heel
Upon my Ankle—Then my Shoes
Would overflow with Pearl—

Until We met the Solid Town—
No One He seemed to know—
And bowing—with a Mighty look—
At me—The Sea withdrew—

Law as Order: The Guilty Condem the Innocent through the Ritual of Murder:

Blake depicts the act of murder with a human face. Cain executes his brother Abel to punish him for receiving all the love. When emotions become frustrated, violence expresses what language cannot.

Could I have used my tongue,
I would not have struck him.
Billy Budd, **Herman Melville**

The act of murder reveals a human face in Blake's vision of Cain's execution of Abel. This primal act reveals the underlying aggression which exists between brothers. Cain was motivated to act because the Lord favored Abel. The punishment for his crime was banishment from the group. He became a scapegoat who had to be removed because he acted out the collective desire to remove, by violence, the favored son. Abel, on the other hand, became the sacrifical victim who sheds his blood. The symbolic function of blood in ritual ceremonies was used as a gesture to the divine spirit to end any kind of misfortune which had befallen the group. Abel's blood is spilled to fertilize the ground as a ritual enactment of the tribe's desire to ensure its survival. The victim and executioner were symbolically linked through the blood of brothers to depict the way the innocent and guilty are necessary to explain the causes of evil and why men die. The individual is bound to the group to protect the social order which is established through the culture's taboos. In *The Golden Bough,* Sir James Frazer discusses the ritual murder of the scapegoat king as a necessary function of primitive society. This ceremony served a double function: (1) The expulsion of evil from the group; and (2) the sacrifical death of the divine ruler whose potency is renewed by a young successor. The bonds of kinship link the fathers and sons, and the scapegoat becomes the symbol to express the tensions which exist as the sons overthrow parental authority. Nathaniel Hawthorne in "My Kinsman, Major Molineux" demonstrates this ritual process. The story involves a young man's initiation into society. The search for the kinsman becomes a quest for recognition of adult male status. The rejection of Major Molineux is carried out in a ritual ceremony reminiscent of the scapegoat-king murder. As Molineux is tarred and feathered, the young man joins the group to ridicule authority. This act "frees" the individual from dependence on either a benevolent or malignant paternal order. This pattern is synonymous with the American experience in the Revolutionary War. Independence was gained as colonial power was overthrown. Hawthorne weds the individual to the group to express the underlying taboo of the son's removal of a father figure and the need to remove the chief evil that possessed the consciousness of his culture. Molineux is the scapegoat who makes possible the transfer of power. On another level, the story revolves around the human desire to be fairly treated by some "external" force. The young man is the second son of a clergyman, and because of his position within the family, he will not inherit his father's farm. Has this happened because of divine intervention, or is this a quirk of fate? If the Lord loves man, then why must the innocent be punished with the guilty? The scapegoat symbolizes the contradictions between these divergent points of view. The mask of innocence enables Robin to project onto Molineux the evil which reflects "a fiend of fire and a fiend of darkness." This reveals what exists within Robin, and this knowledge unites Robin with the scapegoat. This symbolic union mirrors the son's desire to rid himself of any paternal authority. We are left to ponder that whether one is innocent or guilty, death is the price all must pay for life.

My Kinsman, Major Molineux

Nathaniel Hawthorne

After the kings of Great Britain had assumed the right of appointing the colonial governors, the measures of the latter seldom met with the ready and generous approbation which had been paid to those of their predecessors, under the original charters. The people looked with most jealous scrutiny to the exercise of power which did not emanate from themselves, and they usually rewarded their rulers with slender gratitude for the compliances by which, in softening their instructions from beyond the sea, they had incurred the reprehension of those who gave them. The annals of Massachusetts Bay will inform us, that of six governors in the space of about forty years from the surrender of the old charter, under James II, two were imprisoned by a popular insurrection; a third, as Hutchinson[1] inclines to believe, was driven from the province by the whizzing of a musket-ball; a fourth, in the opinion of the same historian, was hastened to his grave by continual bickerings with the House of Representatives; and the remaining two, as well as their successors, till the Revolution, were favored with few and brief intervals of peaceful sway. The inferior members of the court party, in times of high political excitement, led scarcely a more desirable life. These remarks may serve as a preface to the following adventures, which chanced upon a summer night, not far from a hundred years ago.[2] The reader, in order to avoid a long and dry detail of colonial affairs, is requested to dispense with an account of the train of circumstances that had caused much temporary inflammation of the popular mind.

It was near nine o'clock of a moonlight evening, when a boat crossed the ferry with a single passenger, who had obtained his conveyance at that unusual hour by the promise of an extra fare. While he stood on the landing-place, searching in either pocket for the means of fulfilling his agreement, the ferryman lifted a lantern, by the aid of which, and the newly risen moon, he took a very accurate survey of the stranger's figure. He was a youth of barely eighteen years, evidently country-bred, and now, as it should seem, upon his first visit to town. He was clad in a coarse gray coat, well worn, but in excellent repair; his under garments[3] were durably constructed of leather, and fitted tight to a pair of serviceable and well-shaped limbs; his stockings of blue yarn were the incontrovertible work of a mother or a sister; and on his head was a three-cornered hat, which in its better days had perhaps sheltered the graver brow of the lad's father. Under his left arm was a heavy cudgel formed of an oak sapling, and retaining a part of the hardened root; and his equipment was completed by a wallet, not so abundantly stocked as to incommode the vigorous shoulders on which it hung. Brown, curly hair, well-shaped features, and bright, cheerful eyes were nature's gifts, and worth all that art could have done for his adornment.

The youth, one of whose names was Robin, finally drew from his pocket the half of a little province bill of five shillings, which, in the depreciation in that sort of currency, did but satisfy the ferryman's demand, with the surplus of

---

[1] Thomas Hutchinson, *The History of the Colony and Province of Massachusetss Bay,* Boston, 1764.
[2] The story was written in 1828 or 1829.

[3] Knee breeches.

a sexangular piece of parchment, valued at three pence. He then walked forward into the town, with as light a step as if his day's journey had not already exceeded thirty miles, and with as eager an eye as if he were entering London city, instead of the little metropolis of a New England colony. Before Robin had proceeded far, however, it occurred to him that he knew not whither to direct his steps; so he paused, and looked up and down the narrow street, scrutinizing the small and mean wooden buildings that were scattered on either side.

"This low hovel cannot be my kinsman's dwelling," thought he, "nor yonder old house, where the moonlight enters at the broken casement; and truly I see none hereabouts that might be worthy of him. It would have been wise to inquire my way of the ferryman, and doubtless he would have gone with me, and earned a shilling from the Major for his pains. But the next man I meet will do as well."

He resumed his walk, and was glad to perceive that the street now became wider, and the houses more respectable in their appearance. He soon discerned a figure moving on moderately in advance, and hastened his steps to overtake it. As Robin drew nigh, he saw that the passenger was a man in years, with a full periwig of gray hair, a wide-skirted coat of dark cloth, and silk stockings rolled above his knees. He carried a long and polished cane, which he struck down perpendicularly before him at every step; and at regular intervals he uttered two successive hems, of a peculiarly solemn and sepulchral intonation. Having made these observations, Robin laid hold of the skirt of the old man's coat, just when the light from the open door and windows of a barber's shop fell upon both their figures.

"Good evening to you, honored sir," said he, making a low bow, and still retaining his hold of the skirt. "I pray you tell me whereabouts is the dwelling of my kinsman, Major Molineux."

The youth's question was uttered very loudly; and one of the barbers, whose razor was descending on a well-soaped chin, and another who was dressing a Ramillies wig,[4] left their occupations, and came to the door. The citizen, in the mean time, turned a long-favored countenance upon Robin, and answered him in a tone of excessive anger and annoyance.

His two sepulchral hems, however, broke into the very centre of his rebuke, with most singular effect, like a thought of the cold grave obtruding among wrathful passions.

"Let go my garment, fellow! I tell you, I know not the man you speak of. What! I have authority, I have—hem, hem—authority; and if this be the respect you show for your betters, your feet shall be brought acquainted with the stocks by daylight, tomorrow morning!"

Robin released the old man's skirt, and hastened away, pursued by an ill-mannered roar of laughter from the barber's shop. He was at first considerably surprised by the result of his question, but, being a shrewd youth, soon thought himself able to account for the mystery.

"This is some country representative," was his conclusion, "who has never seen the inside of my kinsman's door, and lacks the breeding to answer a stranger civilly. The man is old, or verily—I might be tempted to turn back and smite him on the nose. Ah, Robin, Robin! even the barber's boys laugh at you for choosing such a guide! You will be wiser in time, friend Robin."

He now became entangled in a succession of crooked and narrow streets, which crossed each other, and meandered at no great distance from the water-side. The smell of tar was obvious to his nostrils, the masts of vessels pierced the moonlight above the tops of the buildings, and the numerous signs, which Robin paused to read, informed him that he was near the centre of business. But the streets were empty, the shops were closed, and lights were visible only in the second stories of a few dwelling-houses. At length, on the corner of a narrow lane, through which he was passing, he beheld the broad countenance of a British hero swinging before the door of an inn,[5] whence proceeded the voices of many guests. The casement of one of the lower windows was thrown back, and a very thin curtain permitted Robin to distinguish a party at supper, round a well-furnished table. The fragrance of the good cheer steamed forth into the outer air, and the youth could not fail to recollect that the last remnant of his travelling stock of provision had yielded to his morning appetite, and that noon had found and left him dinnerless.

[4] A wig having a long plait behind tied with a bow at the top and the bottom.

[5] An inn would often be named after a famous personage, whose picture would appear on a sign projecting from above the main entry.

"Oh, that a parchment three-penny might give me a right to sit down at yonder table!" said Robin, with a sigh. "But the Major will make me welcome to the best of his victuals; so I will even step boldly in, and inquire my way to his dwelling."

He entered the tavern, and was guided by the murmur of voices and the fumes of tobacco to the public-room. It was a long and low apartment, with oaken walls, grown dark in the continual smoke, and a floor which was thickly sanded, but of no immaculate purity. A number of persons—the larger part of whom appeared to be mariners, or in some way connected with the sea—occupied the wooden benches, or leather-bottomed chairs, conversing on various matters, and occasionally lending their attention to some topic of general interest. Three or four little groups were draining as many bowls of punch, which the West India trade had long since made a familiar drink in the colony. Others, who had the appearance of men who lived by regular and laborious handicraft, preferred the insulated bliss of an unshared potation, and became more taciturn under its influence. Nearly all, in short, evinced a predilection for the Good Creature[6] in some of its various shapes, for this is a vice to which, as Fast Day sermons of a hundred years ago will testify, we have a long hereditary claim. The only guests to whom Robin's sympathies inclined him were two or three sheepish countrymen, who were using the inn somewhat after the fashion of a Turkish caravansary;[7] they had gotten themselves into the darkest corner of the room, and heedless of the Nicotian[8] atmosphere, were supping on the bread of their own ovens, and the bacon cured in their own chimney-smoke. But though Robin felt a sort of brotherhood with these strangers, his eyes were attracted from them to a person who stood near the door, holding whispered conversation with a group of ill-dressed associates. His features were separately striking almost to grotesqueness, and the whole face left a deep impression on the memory. The forehead bulged out into a double prominence, with a vale between; the nose came boldly forth in an irregular curve, and its bridge was of more than a finger's breadth; the eyebrows were deep and shaggy, and the eyes glowed beneath them like fire in a cave.

While Robin deliberated of whom to inquire respecting his kinsman's dwelling, he was accosted by the innkeeper, a little man in a stained white apron, who had come to pay his professional welcome to the stranger. Being in the second generation from a French Protestant, he seemed to have inherited the courtesy of his parent nation; but no variety of circumstances was ever known to change his voice from the one shrill note in which he now addressed Robin.

"From the country, I presume, sir?" said he, with a profound bow. "Beg leave to congratulate you on your arrival, and trust you intend a long stay with us. Fine town here, sir, beautiful buildings, and much that may interest a stranger. May I hope for the honor of your commands in respect to supper?"

"The man sees a family likeness! the rogue has guessed that I am related to the Major!" thought Robin, who had hitherto experienced little superfluous civility.

All eyes were now turned on the country lad, standing at the door, in his worn three-cornered hat, gray coat, leather breeches, and blue yarn stockings, leaning on an oaken cudgel, and bearing a wallet on his back.

Robin replied to the courteous innkeeper, with such an assumption of confidence as befitted the Major's relative. "My honest friend," he said, "I shall make it a point to patronize your house on some occasion, when"—here he could not help lowering his voice—"when I may have more than a parchment three-pence in my pocket. My present business," continued he, speaking with lofty confidence, "is merely to inquire my way to the dwelling of my kinsman, Major Molineux."

There was a sudden and general movement in the room, which Robin interpreted as expressing the eagerness of each individual to become his guide. But the innkeeper turned his eyes to a written paper on the wall, which he read, or seemed to read, with occasional recurrences to the young man's figure.

"What have we here?" said he, breaking his speech into little dry fragments. " 'Left the house of the subscriber, bounden servant,[9] Hezekiah Mudge,—had on, when he went away, gray coat, leather breeches, master's

---

[6] Applied humorously to intoxicating liquor, but originally signifying that part of God's creation which ministers to the material comfort of man. See I Timothy 4:4, "Every creature of God is good."

[7] A public building in which travelers prepare and eat the food they have brought with them.

[8] Filled with tobacco smoke (from the name of Jacques Nicot, who introduced tobacco into France in 1560).

[9] An indentured servant, bound by contract to serve for a certain time before obtaining his freedom.

third-best hat. One pound currency reward to whosoever shall lodge him in any jail of the providence.' Better trudge, boy; better trudge!"

Robin had begun to draw his hand towards the lighter end of the oak cudgel, but a strange hostility in every countenance induced him to relinquish his purpose of breaking the courteous innkeeper's head. As he turned to leave the room, he encountered a sneering glance from the bold-featured personage whom he had before noticed; and no sooner was he beyond the door, than he heard a general laugh, in which the innkeeper's voice might be distinguished, like the dropping of small stones into a kettle.

"Now, is it not strange," thought Robin, with his usual shrewdness,—"is it not strange that the confession of an empty pocket should outweigh the name of my kinsman, Major Molineux? Oh, if I had one of those grinning rascals in the woods, where I and my oak sapling grew up together, I would teach him that my arm is heavy though my purse be light!"

On turning the corner of the narrow lane, Robin found himself in a spacious street, with an unbroken line of lofty houses on each side, and a steepled building at the upper end, whence the ringing of a bell announced the hour of nine. The light of the moon, and the lamps from the numerous shop-windows, discovered people promenading on the pavement, and amongst them Robin had hoped to recognize his hitherto inscrutable relative. The result of his former inquiries made him unwilling to hazard another, in a scene of such publicity, and he determined to walk slowly and silently up the street, thrusting his face close to that of every elderly gentleman, in search of the Major's lineaments. In his progress, Robin encountered many gay and gallant figures. Embroidered garments of showy colors, enormous periwigs, gold-laced hats, and silver-hilted swords glided past him and dazzled his optics. Travelled youths, imitators of the European fine gentlemen of the period, trod jauntily along, half dancing to the fashionable tunes which they hummed, and making poor Robin ashamed of his quiet and natural gait. At length, after many pauses to examine the gorgeous display of goods in the shop-windows, and after suffering some rebukes for the impertinence of his scrutiny into people's faces, the Major's kinsman found himself near the steepled building, still unsuccessful in his search. As yet, however, he had seen only one side of the thronged street; so Robin crossed,

and continued the same sort of inquisition down the opposite pavement, with stronger hopes than the philosopher seeking an honest man, but with no better fortune. He had arrived about midway towards the lower end, from which his course began, when he overheard the approach of some one who struck down a cane on the flag-stones at every step, uttering at regular intervals, two sepulchral hems.

"Mercy on us!" quoth Robin, recognizing the sound.

Turning a corner, which chanced to be close at his right hand, he hastened to pursue his researches in some other part of the town. His patience now was wearing low, and he seemed to feel more fatigue from his rambles since he crossed the ferry, than from his journey of several days on the other side. Hunger also pleaded loudly within him, and Robin began to balance the propriety of demanding, violently, and with lifted cudgel, the necessary guidance from the first solitary passenger whom he should meet. While a resolution to this effect was gaining strength, he entered a street of mean appearance, on either side of which a row of ill-built houses was straggling towards the harbor. The moonlight fell upon no passenger along the whole extent, but in the third domicile which Robin passed there was a half-opened door, and his keen glance detected a woman's garment within.

"My luck may be better here," said he to himself.

Accordingly, he approached the door, and beheld it shut closer as he did so; yet an open space remained, sufficing for the fair occupant to observe the stranger, without a corresponding display on her part. All that Robin could discern was a strip of scarlet petticoat, and the occasional sparkle of an eye, as if the moonbeams were trembling on some bright thing.

"Pretty mistress," for I may call her so with a good conscience, thought the shrewd youth, since I know nothing to the contrary,—"my sweet pretty mistress, will you be kind enough to tell me whereabouts I must seek the dwelling of my kinsman, Major Molineux?"

Robin's voice was plaintive and winning, and the female, seeing nothing to be shunned in the handsome country youth, thrust open the door, and came forth into the moonlight. She was a dainty little figure, with a white neck, round arms, and a slender waist, at the extremity of which her scarlet petticoat jutted out over a hoop, as if she were standing in a balloon. Moreover, her face was oval and pretty, her hair dark beneath the little cap, and her bright eyes possesed a sly freedom, which triumphed over those of Robin.

"Major Molineux dwells here," said this fair woman.

Now, her voice was the sweetest Robin had heard that night, yet he could not help doubting whether that sweet voice spoke Gospel truth. He looked up and down the mean street, and then surveyed the house before which they stood. It was a small, dark edifice of two stories, the second of which projected over the lower floor, and the front apartment had the aspect of a shop for petty commodities.

"Now, truly, I am in luck," replied Robin, cunningly, "and so indeed is my kinsman, the Major, in having so pretty a housekeeper. But I prithee trouble him to step to the door; I will deliver him a message from his friends in the country, and then go back to my lodgings at the inn."

"Nay, the Major has been abed this hour or more," said the lady of the scarlet petticoat; "and it would be to little purpose to disturb him to-night, seeing his evening draught was of the strongest. But he is a kind-hearted man, and it would be as much as my life's worth to let a kinsman of his turn away from the door. You are the good old gentleman's very picture, and I could swear that was his rainy-weather hat. Also he has garments very much resembling those leather small-clothes. But come in, I pray, for I bid you hearty welcome in his name."

So saying, the fair and hospitable dame took our hero by the hand; and the touch was light, and the force was gentleness, and though Robin read in her eyes what he did not hear in her words, yet the slender-waisted woman in the scarlet petticoat proved stronger than the athletic country youth. She had drawn his half-willing footsteps nearly to the threshold, when the opening of a door in the neighborhood startled the Major's housekeeper, and, leaving the Major's kinsman, she vanished speedily into her own domicile. A heavy yawn preceded the appearance of a man, who, like the Moonshine of Pyramus and Thisbe,[10] carried a lan-

tern, needlessly aiding his sister luminary in the heavens. As he walked sleepily up the street, he turned his broad, dull face on Robin, and displayed a long staff, spiked at the end.

"Home, vagabond, home!" said the watchman, in accents that seemed to fall asleep as soon as they were uttered. "Home, or we'll set you in the stocks by peep of day!"

"This is the second hint of the kind," thought Robin. "I wish they would end my difficulties, by setting me there to-night."

Nevertheless, the youth felt an instinctive antipathy towards the guardian of midnight order, which at first prevented him from asking his usual question. But just when the man was about to vanish behind the corner, Robin resolved not to lose the opportunity, and shouted lustily after him,—

"I say, friend! will you guide me to the house of my kinsman, Major Molineux?"

The watchman made no reply, but turned the corner and was gone; yet Robin seemed to hear the sound of drowsy laughter stealing along the solitary street. At that moment, also, a pleasant titter saluted him from the open window above his head; he looked up, and caught the sparkle of a saucy eye; a round arm beckoned to him, and next he heard light footsteps descending the staircase within. But Robin, being of the household of a New England clergyman, was a good youth, as well as a shrewd one; so he resisted temptation, and fled away.

He now roamed desperately, and at random, through the town, almost ready to believe that a spell was on him, like that by which a wizard of his country had once kept three pursuers wandering, a whole winter night, within twenty paces of the cottage which they sought. The streets lay before him, strange and desolate, and the lights were extinguished in almost every house. Twice, however, little parties of men, among whom Robin distinguished individuals in outlandish attire, came hurrying along; but, though on both occasions, they paused to address him, such intercourse did not at all enlighten his perplexity. They did but utter a few words in some language of which Robin knew nothing, and perceiving his inability to answer, bestowed a curse upon him in plain English and hastened away. Finally, the lad determined to knock at the door of every mansion that might appear worthy to be occupied by his kinsman, trusting that perseverance would overcome the fatality that had hitherto

[10] In Shakespeare's *A Midsummer-Night's Dream*, Act V, Scene 1, a man with a lantern represents the moon in a comically inept performance of the tragic love story of Pyramus and Thisbe.

thwarted him. Firm in this resolve, he was passing beneath the walls of a church, which formed the corner of two streets, when as he turned into the shade of its steeple, he encountered a bulky stranger, muffled in a cloak. The man was proceeding with the speed of earnest business, but Robin planted himself full before him, holding the oak cudgel with both hands across his body as a bar to further passage.

"Halt, honest man, and answer me a question," said he, very resolutely. "Tell me, this instant, whereabouts is the dwelling of my kinsman, Major Molineux!"

"Keep your tongue between your teeth, fool, and let me pass!" said a deep, gruff voice, which Robin partly remembered. "Let me pass, or I'll strike you to the earth!"

"No, no, neighbor!" cried Robin, flourishing his cudgel, and then thrusting its larger end close to the man's muffled face. "No, no, I'm not the fool you take me for, nor do you pass till I have an answer to my question. Whereabouts is the dwelling of my kinsman, Major Molineux?"

The stranger, instead of attempting to force his passage, stepped back into the moonlight, unmuffled his face, and stared full into that of Robin.

"Watch here an hour, and Major Molineux will pass by," said he.

Robin gazed with dismay and astonishment on the unprecedented physiognomy of the speaker. The forehead with its double prominence, the broad hooked nose, the shaggy eyebrows, and fiery eyes were those which he had noticed at the inn, but the man's complexion had undergone a singular, or, more properly, a twofold change. One side of the face blazed an intense red, while the other was black as midnight, the division line being in the broad bridge of the nose; and a mouth which seemed to extend from ear to ear was black or red, in contrast to the color of the cheek. The effect was as if two individual devils, a fiend of fire and a fiend of darkness, had united themselves to form this infernal visage. The stranger grinned in Robin's face, muffled his party-colored features, and was out of sight in a moment.

"Strange things we travellers see!" ejaculated Robin.

He seated himself, however, upon the steps of the church-door, resolving to wait the appointed time for his kinsman. A few moments were consumed in philosophical speculations upon the species of man who had just left him; but having settled this point shrewdly, rationally, and satisfactorily, he was compelled to look elsewhere for his amusement. And first he threw his eyes along the street. It was of more respectable appearance than most of those into which he had wandered; and the moon, creating, like the imaginative power, a beautiful strangeness in familiar objects, gave something of romance to a scene that might not have possessed it in the light of day. The irregular and often quaint architecture of the houses, some of whose roofs were broken into numerous little peaks, while others ascended, steep and narrow, into a single point, and others again were square; the pure snow-white of some of their complexions, the aged darkness of others, and the thousand sparklings, reflected from bright substances in the walls of many; these matters engaged Robin's attention for a while, and then began to grow wearisome. Next he endeavored to define the forms of distant objects, starting away, with almost ghostly indistinctness, just as his eye appeared to grasp them; and finally he took a minute survey of an edifice which stood on the opposite side of the street, directly in front of the church-door, where he was stationed. It was a large, square mansion, distinguished from its neighbors by a balcony, which rested on tall pillars, and by an elaborate Gothic window, communicating therewith.

"Perhaps this is the very house I have been seeking," thought Robin.

Then he strove to speed away the time, by listening to a murmur which swept continually along the street, yet was scarcely audible, except to an unaccustomed ear like his; it was a low, dull, dreamy sound, compounded of many noises, each of which was at too great a distance to be separately heard. Robin marvelled at this snore of a sleeping town, and marvelled more whenever its continuity was broken by now and then a distant shout, apparently loud where it originated. But altogether it was a sleep-inspiring sound, and, to shake off its drowsy influence, Robin arose, and climbed a window-frame, that he might view the interior of the church. There the moonbeams came trembling in, and fell down upon the deserted pews, and extended along the quiet aisles. A fainter yet more awful radiance was hovering around the pulpit, and one solitary ray had dared to rest upon the open page of the great Bible. Had nature, in that deep hour, become a worshipper in the house which man had builded? Or was that heavenly light the visible sanctity of the place,—visible because no earthly and impure feet were within the walls? The scene made Robin's heart shiver with a sensation of loneliness stronger than he had ever felt in the remotest depths of his native woods; so he turned away and sat down again before the door. There were graves around the church, and now an uneasy thought obtruded into Robin's breast. What if the object of his search, which had been so often and so strangely thwarted, were all the time mouldering in his shroud? What if his kinsman should glide through yonder gate, and nod and smile to him in dimly passing by?

"Oh that any breathing thing were here with me!" said Robin.

Recalling his thoughts from this uncomfortable track, he sent them over forest, hill, and stream, and attempted to imagine how that evening of ambiguity and weariness had been spent by his father's household. He pictured them assembled at the door, beneath the tree, the great old tree, which had been spared for its huge twisted trunk and venerable shade, when a thousand leafy brethren fell. There, at the going down of the summer sun, it was his father's custom to perform domestic worship, that the neighbors might come and join with him like brothers of the family, and that the wayfaring man might pause to drink at that fountain, and keep his heart pure by freshening the memory of home. Robin distinguished the seat of every individual of the little audience; he saw the good man in the midst, holding the Scriptures in the golden light that fell from the western clouds; he beheld him close the book and all rise up to pray. He heard the old thanksgivings for daily mercies; the old supplications for their continuance, to which he had so often listened in weariness, but which were now among his dear remembrances. He perceived the slight inequality of his father's voice when he came to speak of the absent one; he noted how his mother turned her face to the broad and knotted trunk; how his elder brother scorned, because the beard was rough upon his upper lip, to permit his features to be moved; how the younger sister drew down a low hanging branch before her eyes; and how the little one of all, whose sports had hitherto broken the decorum of the scene, understood the prayer for his playmate, and burst into clamorous

grief. Then he saw them go in at the door; and when Robin would have entered also, the latch tinkled into its place, and he was excluded from his home.

"Am I here, or there?" cried Robin, starting; for all at once, when his thoughts had become visible and audible in a dream, the long, wide, solitary street shone out before him.

He aroused himself, and endeavored to fix his attention steadily upon the large edifice which he had surveyed before. But still his mind kept vibrating between fancy and reality; by turns, the pillars of the balcony lengthened into the tall, bare stems of pines, dwindled down to human figures, settled again into their true shape and size, and then commenced a new succession of changes. For a single moment, when he deemed himself awake, he could have sworn that a visage—one which he seemed to remember, yet could not absolutely name as his kinsman's—was looking towards him from the Gothic window. A deeper sleep wrestled with and nearly overcame him, but fled at the sound of footsteps along the opposite pavement. Robin rubbed his eyes, discerned a man passing at the foot of the balcony, and addressed him in a loud, peevish, and lamentable cry.

"Hallo, friend! must I wait here all night for my kinsman, Major Molineux?"

The sleeping echoes awoke, and answered the voice; and the passenger, barely able to discern a figure sitting in the oblique shade of the steeple, traversed the street to obtain a nearer view. He was himself a gentleman in his prime, of open, intelligent, cheerful, and altogether prepossessing countenance. Perceiving a country youth, apparently homeless and without friends, he accosted him in a tone of real kindness, which had become strange to Robin's ears.

"Well, my good lad, why are you sitting here?" inquired he. "Can I be of service to you in any way?"

"I am afraid not, sir," replied Robin, despondingly; "yet I shall take it kindly, if you'll answer me a single question. I've been searching, half the night, for one Major Molineux; now, sir, is there really such a person in these parts, or am I dreaming?"

"Major Molineux! The name is not altogether strange to me," said the gentleman, smiling. "Have you any objection to telling me the nature of your business with him?"

Then Robin briefly related that his father

was a clergyman, settled on a small salary, at a long distance back in the country, and that he and Major Molineux were brothers' children. The Major, having inherited riches, and acquired civil and military rank, had visited his cousin, in great pomp, a year or two before; had manifested much interest in Robin and an elder brother, and, being childless himself, had thrown out hints respecting the future establishment of one of them in life. The elder brother was destined to succeed to the farm which his father cultivated in the interval of sacred duties; it was therefore determined that Robin should profit by his kinsman's generous intentions, especially as he seemed to be rather the favorite, and was thought to possess other necessary endowments.

"For I have the name of being a shrewd youth," observed Robin, in this part of his story.

"I doubt not you deserve it," replied his new friend, good-naturedly; "but pray proceed."

"Well, sir, being nearly eighteen years old, and well grown, as you see," continued Robin, drawing himself up to his full height, "I thought it high time to begin in the world. So my mother and sister put me in handsome trim, and my father gave me half the remnant of his last year's salary, and five days ago I started for this place, to pay the Major a visit. But, would you believe it, sir! I crossed the ferry a little after dark, and have yet found nobody that would show me the way to his dwelling; only, an hour or two since, I was told to wait here, and Major Molineux would pass by."

"Can you describe the man who told you this?" inquired the gentleman.

"Oh, he was a very ill-favored fellow, sir," replied Robin, "with two great bumps on his forehead, a hook nose, fiery eyes; and, what struck me as the strangest, his face was of two different colors. Do you happen to know such a man, sir?"

"Not intimately," answered the stranger, "but I chanced to meet him a little time previous to your stopping me. I believe you may trust his word, and that the Major will very shortly pass through this street. In the mean time, as I have a singular curiosity to witness your meeting, I will sit down here upon the steps and bear you company."

He seated himself accordingly, and soon engaged his companion in animated discourse. It was but of brief continuance, however, for a noise of shouting, which had long been remotely audible, drew so much nearer that Robin inquired its cause.

"What may be the meaning of this uproar?" asked he. "Truly, if your town be always as noisy, I shall find little sleep while I am an inhabitant."

"Why, indeed, friend Robin, there do appear to be three or four riotous fellows abroad to-night," replied the gentleman. "You must not expect all the stillness of your native woods here in our streets. But the watch will shortly be at the heels of these lads and"—

"Ay, and set them in the stocks by peep of day," interrupted Robin, recollecting his own encounter with the drowsy lantern-bearer. "But, dear sir, if I may trust my ears, an army of watchmen would never make head against such a multitude of rioters. There were at least a thousand voices went up to make that one shout."

"May not a man have several voices, Robin, as well as two complexions?" said his friend.

"Perhaps a man may; but Heaven forbid that a woman should!" responded the shrewd youth, thinking of the seductive tones of the Major's housekeeper.

The sounds of a trumpet in some neighboring street now became so evident and continual, that Robin's curiosity was strongly excited. In addition to the shouts, he heard frequent bursts from many instruments of discord, and a wild and confused laughter filled up the intervals. Robin rose from the steps, and looked wistfully towards a point whither people seemed to be hastening.

"Surely some prodigious merry-making is going on," exclaimed he. "I have laughed very little since I left home, sir, and should be sorry to lose an opportunity. Shall we step round the corner by that darkish house, and take our share of the fun?"

"Sit down again, sit down, good Robin," replied the gentleman, laying his hand on the skirt of the gray coat. "You forget that we must wait here for your kinsman; and there is reason to believe that he will pass by, in the course of a very few moments."

The near approach of the uproar had now disturbed the neighborhood; windows flew open on all sides; and many heads, in the attire of the pillow, and confused by sleep suddenly broken, were protruded to the gaze of whoever had leisure to observe them. Eager voices hailed each other from house to house, all demanding the explanation, which not a soul could give. Half-dressed men hurried towards the unknown commotion, stumbling as they went over the stone steps that thrust themselves into the narrow foot-walk. The shouts, the laughter, and the tuneless bray, the antipodes of music, came onwards with increasing din, till scattered individuals, and then denser bodies, began to appear round a corner at the distance of a hundred yards.

"Will you recognize your kinsman, if he passes in this crowd?" inquired the gentleman.

"Indeed, I can't warrant it, sir; but I'll take my stand here, and keep a bright lookout," answered Robin, descending to the outer edge of the pavement.

A mighty stream of people now emptied into the street, and came rolling slowly towards the church. A single horseman wheeled the corner in the midst of them, and close behind him came a band of fearful wind-instruments, sending forth a fresher discord now that no intervening buildings kept it from the ear. Then a redder light disturbed the moonbeams, and a dense multitude of torches shone along the street, concealing, by their glare, whatever object they illuminated. The single horseman, clad in a military dress, and bearing a drawn sword, rode onward as the leader, and, by his fierce and variegated countenance, appeared like war personified; the red of one cheek was an emblem of fire and sword; the blackness of the other betokened the mourning that attends them. In his train were wild figures in the Indian dress, and many fantastic shapes without a model, giving the whole march a visionary air, as if a dream had broken forth from some feverish brain, and were sweeping visibly through the midnight streets. A mass of people, inactive, except as applauding spectators, hemmed the procession in; and several women ran along the sidewalk, piercing the confusion of heavier sounds with their shrill voices of mirth or terror.

"The double-faced fellow has his eye upon me," muttered Robin, with an indefinite but an uncomfortable idea that he was himself to bear a part in the pageantry.

The leader turned himself in the saddle, and fixed his glance full upon the country youth, as the steed went slowly by. When Robin had freed his eyes from those fiery ones, the musicians were passing before him, and the torches were close at hand; but the unsteady brightness of the latter formed a veil which he could not penetrate. The rattling of wheels over the stones sometimes found its way to his ear, and confused traces of a human form appeared at intervals, and then melted into the vivid light. A moment more, and the leader thundered a command to halt: the trumpets vomited a horrid breath, and then held their peace; the shouts and laughter of the people died away, and there remained only a universal hum, allied to silence. Right before Robin's eyes was an uncovered cart. There the torches blazed the brightest, there the moon shone out like day, and there, in tar-and-feathery dignity, sat his kinsman, Major Molineux!

He was an elderly man, of large and majestic person, and strong, square features, betokening a steady soul; but steady as it was, his enemies had found means to shake it. His face was pale as death, and far more ghastly; the broad forehead was contracted in his agony, so that his eyebrows formed one grizzled line; his eyes were red and wild, and the foam hung white upon his quivering lip. His whole frame was agitated by a quick and continual tremor, which his pride strove to quell, even in those circumstances of overwhelming humiliation. But perhaps the bitterest pang of all was when his eyes met those of Robin; for he evidently knew him on the instant, as the youth stood witnessing the foul disgrace of a head grown gray in honor. They stared at each other in silence, and Robin's knees shook, and his hair bristled, with a mixture of pity and terror. Soon, however, a bewildering excitement began to seize upon his mind; the preceding adventures of the night, the unexpected appearance of the crowd, the torches, the confused din and the hush that followed, the spectre of his kinsman reviled by that great multitude,—all this, and, more than all, a perception of tremendous ridicule in the whole scene, affected him with a sort of mental inebriety. At that moment a voice of sluggish merriment saluted Robin's ears; he turned instinctively, and just behind the corner of the church stood the lantern-bearer, rubbing his eyes, and drowsily enjoying the lad's amazement. Then he heard a peal of laughter like the ringing of silvery bells; a woman twitched his arm, a saucy eye met his, and he saw the lady of the scarlet petticoat. A sharp, dry cachinnation appealed to his memory, and, standing on tiptoe in the crowd, with his white apron over his head, he beheld the courteous little innkeeper. And lastly, there sailed over the heads of the multitude a great, broad laugh, broken in the midst by two sepulchral hems; thus, "Haw, haw, haw,—hem, hem,—haw, haw, haw, haw!"

The sound proceeded from the balcony of the opposite edifice, and thither Robin turned his eyes. In front of the Gothic window stood the old citizen, wrapped in a wide gown, his gray periwig exchanged for a nightcap, which was thrust back from his forehead, and his silk stockings hanging about his legs. He supported himself on his polished cane in a fit of convulsive merriment, which manifested itself on his solemn old features like a funny inscription on a tombstone. Then Robin seemed to hear the voices of the barbers, of the guests of the inn, and of all who had made sport of him that night. The contagion was spreading among the multitude, when all at once, it seized upon Robin, and he sent forth a shout of laughter that echoed through the street,—every man shook his sides, every man emptied his lungs, but Robin's shout was the loudest there. The cloud-spirits peeped from their silvery islands, as the congregated mirth went roaring up the sky? The Man in the Moon heard the far bellow. "Oho," quoth he, "the old earth is frolicsome to-night!"

When there was a momentary calm in that tempestuous sea of sound, the leader gave the sign, the procession resumed its march. On they went, like fiends that throng in mockery around some dead potentate, mighty no more, but majestic still in his agony. On they went, in counterfeited pomp, in senseless uproar, in frenzied merriment, trampling all on an old man's heart. On swept the tumult, and left a silent street behind.

"Well, Robin, are you dreaming?" inquired the gentleman, laying his hand on the youth's shoulder.

Robin started, and withdrew his arm from the stone post to which he had instinctively clung, as the living stream rolled by him. His cheek was somewhat pale, and his eye not quite as lively as in the earlier part of the evening.

"Will you be kind enough to show me the way to the ferry?" said he, after a moment's pause.

"You have, then, adopted a new subject of inquiry?" observed his companion, with a smile.

"Why, yes, sir," replied Robin, rather dryly. "Thanks to you, and to my other friends, I have at last met my kinsman, and he will scarce desire to see my face again. I begin to grow weary of a town life, sir. Will you show me the way to the ferry?"

"No, my good friend Robin,—not to-night, at least," said the gentleman. "Some few days hence, if you wish it, I will speed you on your journey. Or, if you prefer to remain with us, perhaps, as you are a shrewd youth, you may rise in the world without the help of your kinsman, Major Molineux."

?

The pattern of Hawthorne's story resembles the pattern of a young man's rite of passage from adolescence to adulthood. Robin's journey begins in darkness and separation. He crosses the river to be initiated into the life of the townspeople. The quest for his kinsman provides Hawthorne with the material to test Robin. The ceremony marking the end of his journey is the procession which introduces the old military leader. Robin moves from "pity and terror," Aristotle's definition of the two major elements which produce a catharsis in the audience because of their identification with the tragic hero's fate, to the individual whose "shout . . . was the loudest there." At this moment, Robin renounces his past and accepts the group's norms as his own. His "second birth" as a man is now complete. The expulsion of Major Molineux ends Robin's search. The Major becomes the scapegoat leader who must be removed in order to unite the individual to the group. The search for independence is made possible by the son's replacement of the father. The anxiety and guilt which result from this is the source of energy which propels Hawthorne's character to give up his nostalgia for a past. The following questions focus on the theme of initiation into the American way of life as expressed in Hawthorne's story:

1 Discuss Robin's movement from youth to adulthood from the following perspectives:
   a What does Robin represent before the initiation ceremony which introduces Major Molineux?
   b What tests is Robin presented with? How do these tests contradict Robin's assertion that he is a "shrewd youth"?

What is revealed about Robin in the incident with the girl in the red petticoat? What cultural taboo is presented to Robin in this incident?
   c What is revealed to Robin in his dream? What does the dream reveal about his "inner" conflicts? What does the dream suggest about what is taboo in Robin's culture? What parts of himself must Robin repress in order to survive in this culture?
   d What attitudes toward authority symbols emerge from Hawthorne's contrasting images of father figures? How do these images provide Robin with models to imitate? Do you think the American attitude toward authority symbols has changed since Hawthorne's time? Explain!
   e What does Robin learn from his initiation? What does the story suggest about the individual's relation to group pressure? Discuss what Robin confronts in Major Molineux. What does this suggest about social taboos?

2 Use Eliade's essay to interpret how this story combines both the primitive and modern concern for initiation rites.

3 According to Freud, how might the concept of guilt be used as a device to inhibit Robin from acting out his desires? In what ways does the story validate or invalidate Freud's concept of the Oedipus complex?

4 What evidence is there that we still need scapegoats in contemporary America? What do these scapegoat's reveal about the individual's and the group's desire to act out a social taboo?

Everything lives, everything acts, everything corresponds. . . . It is a transparent network that covers
the world, and its fine threads communicate from
one to the other to the planets and the stars.
Gerard De Nerval

Understanding the Transparent Network: To Interpret the Picture is to Name and Know the Cultural Belief!

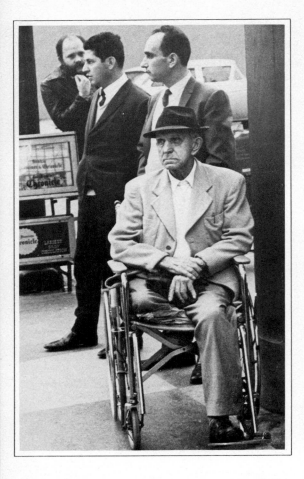

Answer the following questions:

1 Select one or more of these pictures and write a brief character sketch in which you describe the kind of individual you feel each person represents.

2 How does each of these pictures express the transition from individual to member of society? What cultural attitudes are expressed by the people in these pictures?

3 Explain whether or not you believe any of these individuals is "up against a wall." How would you use Freud's essay to interpret what civilization has created in the people depicted here?

4 Which of these people might be thought of as a scapegoat? Discuss what characteristics enable you to make a choice. Which of the individuals resembles a character in Hawthorne's "Major Molineaux"? What reasons would you cite to explain your choice?

Socrates said, "Know thyself," in order to seek answers to this ancient question, we must pass into the world of dreams to unlock the door to our unconscious.

Wordsworth Describes The Human Mind As:

An active power to fasten images
Upon his brain; and on their picture lines
Intensely brooded, even till they acquire
The liveliness of dreams.

How do I know the way of all things at the
Beginning?
By that which is within me.

Tao Te Ching

The Breath of Life

LAO TZU

The breath of life moves through a deathless **valley**
Of mysterious motherhood
Which conceives and bears the universal seed,
The seeming of a world never to end,
Breath for men to draw from as they will:
And the more they take of it, the more remains.

The Universe is Deathless

LAO TZU

The universe is deathless,
Is deathless because, having no finite self,
It stays infinite.
A sound man by not advancing himself
Stays the further ahead of himself,
By not confining himself to himself
Sustains himself outside himself:
By never being an end in himself
He endlessly becomes himself.

The artist must prophesy, not in the sense that he foretells things to come, but that he tells his audience, at the risk of their distress, the secrets of their own heart. His business as an artist is to speak out, to make a clean breast. But what he has to utter is, not as the individualistic theory of art would have us think, his own secrets. As a spokesman of his community the secrets he must utter are theirs. The reason why they need him is that no community altogether knows its own heart, and by failing in this knowledge a community deceives itself on the one subject concerning which ignorance means death. Art is the community's medicine for the worst disease of the mind, the corruption of consciousness.
The Principles of Art, R. G. Collingwood

In a Dark Time

THEODORE ROETHKE

In a dark time, the eye begins to see,
I meet my shadow in the deepening shade;
I hear my echo in the echoing wood—
A lord of nature weeping to a tree.
I lived between the heron and the wren.
Beasts of the hill and serpents of the den.

What's madness but nobility of soul
At odds with circumstance? The day's on fire!
I know the purity of pure despair,
My shadow pinned against a sweating wall.
That place among the rocks—is it a cave,
Or winding path? The edge is what I have.

A steady storm of correspondences!
A night flowing with birds, a ragged moon,
And in broad day the midnight come again!
A man goes far to find out what he is—
Death of the self in a long, tearless night,
All natural shapes blazing unnatural light.

Dark, dark my light, and darker my desire.
My soul, like some heat-maddened summer fly,
Keeps buzzing at the sill. Which I is I?
A fallen man. I climb out of my fear.
The mind enters itself, and God the mind,
And one is One, free in the tearing wind.

Was nature kind? The heart's core tractable?
All waters waver, and all fires fail.
Leaves, leaves, lean forth and tell me what I am;
The single tree turns into purest flame.
I am a man, a man at intervals
Pacing a room, a room with dead-white walls;
I feel the autumn fail—all that slow fire
Denied in me, who has denied desire.

Both Lao Tzu and Theodore Roethke are concerned with the self encounter and the experience of time. Each poet presents us with an image of the divided self struggling to be a part of the whole. The following questions direct our awareness of the mazes in life and the experience of death.

Compare and contrast Lao Tzu and Theodore Roethke from the following perspectives:

1 How does each poet define the concept of self?
2 How does each poet bridge the "inner" experience with the "outer" world? What does this suggest about the conscious and unconscious?
3 What is the purpose of death in both works of art?
4 What is the function of the spiritual in both poems?
5 How does the self undergo a second birth as a human being?
6 What is the concept of union in both poems?
7 How does one learn to go beyond a "finite" world?
8 How does each poet reveal a way for individuals to transcend the here and now?

Initiation: From Darkness to Light Understanding the Shadows Behind the Images

PLATO

Next, said I, here is a parable to illustrate the degrees in which our nature may be enlightened or unenlightened. Imagine the condition of men living in a sort of cavernous chamber underground, with an entrance open to the light and a long passage all down the cave.[1] Here they have been from childhood, chained by the leg and also by the neck, so that they cannot move and can see only what is in front of them, because the chains will not let them turn their heads. At some distance higher up is the light of a fire burning behind them; and between the prisoners and the fire is a track[2] with a parapet built along it, like the screen at a puppet-show, which hides the performers while they show their puppets over the top.

I see, said he.

Now behind this parapet imagine persons carrying along various artificial objects, including figures of men and animals in wood or stone or other materials, which project above the parapet. Naturally, some of these persons will be talking, others silent.[3]

It is a strange picture, he said, and a strange sort of prisoners.

Like ourselves, I replied; for in the first place prisoners so confined would have seen nothing of themselves or of one another, except the shadows thrown by the fire-light on the wall of the Cave facing them, would they?

Not if all their lives they had been prevented from moving their heads.

And they would have seen as little of the objects carried past.

Of course.

Now, if they could talk to one another, would they not suppose that their words referred only to those passing shadows which they saw?[4]

Necessarily.

And suppose their prison had an echo from the wall facing them? When one of the people crossing behind them spoke, they could only suppose that the sound came from the shadow passing before their eyes.

No doubt.

In every way, then, such prisoners would recognize as reality nothing but the shadows of those artificial

---

[1] The *length* of the "way in" (*eisodos*) to the chamber where the prisoners sit is an essential feature, explaining why no daylight reaches them.

[2] The track crosses the passage into the cave at right angles, and is *above* the parapet built along it.

[3] A modern Plato would compare his Cave to an underground cinema, where the audience watch the play of shadows thrown by the film passing before a light at their backs. The film itself is only an image of "real" things and events in the world outside the cinema. For the film Plato

has to substitute the clumsier apparatus of a procession of artificial objects carried on their heads by persons who are merely part of the machinery, providing for the movement of the objects and the sounds whose echo the prisoners hear. The parapet prevents these persons' shadows from being cast on the wall of the Cave.

[4] Adam's text and interpretation. The prisoners, having seen nothing but shadows, cannot think their words refer to the objects carried past behind their backs. For them shadows (images) are the only realities.

objects.[5]

Inevitably.

Now consider what would happen if their release from the chains and the healing of their unwisdom should come about in this way. Suppose one of them set free and forced suddenly to stand up, turn his head, and walk with eyes lifted to the light; all these movements would be painful, and he would be too dazzled to make out the objects whose shadows he had been used to see. What do you think he would say, if someone told him that what he had formerly seen was meaningless illusion, but now, being somewhat nearer to reality and turned towards more real objects, he was getting a truer view? Suppose further that he were shown the various objects being carried by and were made to say, in reply to questions, what each of them was. Would he not be perplexed and believe the objects now shown him to be not so real as what he formerly saw?

Yes, not nearly so real.

And if he were forced to look at the fire-light itself, would not his eyes ache, so that he would try to escape and turn back to the things which he could see distinctly, convinced that they really were clearer than these other objects now being shown to him?

Yes.

And suppose someone were to drag him away forcibly up the steep and rugged ascent and not let him go until he had hauled him out into the sunlight, would he not suffer pain and vexation at such treatment, and, when he had come out into the light, find his eyes so full of its radiance that he could not see a single one of the things that he was now told were real?

Certainly he would not see them all at once.

He would need, then, to grow accustomed before he could see things in that upper world. At first it would be easiest to make out shadows, and

then the images of men and things reflected in water, and later on the things themselves. After that, it would be easier to watch the heavenly bodies and the sky itself by night, looking at the light of the moon and stars rather than the Sun and the Sun's light in the day-time.

Yes, surely.

Last of all, he would be able to look at the Sun and contemplate its nature, not as it appears when reflected in water or any alien medium, but as it is in itself in its own domain.

No doubt.

And now he would begin to draw the conclusion that it is the Sun that produces the seasons and the course of the year and controls everything in the visible world, and moreover is in a way the cause of all that he and his companions used to see.

Clearly he would come at last to that conclusion.

Then if he called to mind his fellow prisoners and what passed for wisdom in his former dwelling-place, he would surely think himself happy in the change and be sorry for them. They may have had a practice of honouring and commending one another, with prizes for the man who had the keenest eye for the passing shadows and the best memory for the order in which they followed or accompanied one another, so that he could make a good guess as to which was going to come next.[6] Would our released prisoner be likely to covet those prizes or to envy the men exalted to honour and power in the Cave? Would he not feel like Homer's Achilles, that he would far sooner "be on earth as a hired servant in the house of a landless man"[7] or endure anything rather than go back to his

old beliefs and live in the old way?

Yes, he would prefer any fate to such a life.

Now imagine what would happen if he went down again to take his former seat in the Cave. Coming suddenly out of the sunlight, his eyes would be filled with darkness. He might be required once more to deliver his opinion on those shadows, in competition with the prisoners who had never been released, while his eyesight was still dim and unsteady; and it might take some time to become used to the darkness. They would laugh at him and say that he had gone up only to come back with his sight ruined; it was worth no one's while even to attempt the ascent. If they could lay hands on the man who was trying to set them free and lead them up, they would kill him.[8]

Yes, they would.

Every feature in this parable, my dear Glaucon, is meant to fit our earlier analysis. The prison dwelling corresponds to the region revealed to us through the sense of sight, and the fire-light within it to the power of the Sun. The ascent to see the things in the upper world you may take as standing for the upward journey of the soul into the region of the intelligible; then you will be in possession of what I surmise, since that is what you wish to be told. Heaven knows whether it is true; but this, at any rate, is how it appears to me. In the world of knowledge, the last thing to be perceived and only with great difficulty is the essential Form of Goodness. Once it is perceived, the conclusion must follow that, for all things, this is the cause of whatever is right and good; in the visible world it gives birth to light and to the lord of light, while it is itself sovereign in the intelligible world and the parent of intelligence and truth. Without having had a vision of this Form no one can act with wisdom, either in his own life or in matters of state.

[5] The state of mind called *eikasia* in the previous chapter.

[6] The empirical politician, with no philosophic insight, but only a "knack of remembering what usually happens" (*Gorg.* 501 A). He has *eikasia* = conjecture as to what is likely (*eikos*).

[7] This verse, being spoken by the ghost of Achilles, suggests that the Cave is comparable with Hades.

[8] An allusion to the fate of Socrates.

Look at the images from our Modern Cave Walls:

BELIEVE ... ;

ENDORSE ... ;

Obey

ALLEGORY OF THE CAVE

"The Allegory of the Cave" presents the individual with the means to move from darkness to light, or from ignorance to knowledge. This movement is similar to the individual's transformation during a rite of passage. The time in the cave is a time for understanding one's illusions of the world, and the world of sunlight is a time for the contemplation of wisdom.

1   What does the image of the cave symbolize?

2   What do "the shadows thrown by firelight" suggest about the nature of subjective experience?

3   Why are the people in the cave prisoners?

4   Explain why anyone would prefer the image of a world to the experience in a world. Does fantasy seem more exciting than our experiences?

5   What forms are made visible by the sunlight?

6   How does Plato suggest that one might come to know the nature of the soul?

7   Does Plato believe that any idea is irrelevant?

8   What is the significance of Plato's definitions of universal "truths"?

9   How does one learn to see multilevels of "reality," rather than stare at reflections on the cave's wall?

10   How would one relate Plato's essay to the poems by Lao Tzu and Theodore Roethke?

Interpreting the Message within the Message

1   Have the people toward whom this advertisement is directed emerged from watching the images which appear on the wall of Plato's cave?

2   How does this advertisement use the woman to express rites of passage?

3   What cultural attitude toward time does this advertisement express?

4   What fears do you see expressed in this advertisement?

An initiation ceremony which presents the individual with the means to attain self-discovery or self-deception!

As the child grows and develops, he or she is transformed from individual into social being through the ritual of education. Within the framework of this process, one learns the goals and values which either bring acceptance or rejection according to our social standards. This creates a dilemma for those individuals who attempt to understand the contradictions between private feelings and public behavior. In the lithograph, "Transmutations" by Felicity, we see a depiction of what lies beneath the social mask one wears. The face is opened for us to descend into the "inner" world of the human psyche. A light casts a shadow on a ladder which will enable us to descend on a journey which could bring about self-discovery or self-deception. This forces a confrontation between what I am—the social masks one wears to convey the role one chooses to play, and who I am—the "inner" images which reflect a thinking, feeling, acting being in relation to an "external" world. The underlying implications inherent in the question of what I am involve an exploration of those assumptions each of us makes about the world in which we live and how we choose to act in response to them. The underlying implications of who I am involve an exploration of how each of us attempts to reconcile the differences between social approval and individual preference. For many the pressure to conform to a social role far outweighs the necessity of understanding what lies behind the mask. In "Of This Time, of That Place," Lionel Trilling creates a situation which reveals how an individual chooses social acceptance over individual integrity.

The story takes place in an Eastern college where Joseph Howe, a young instructor, struggles to understand the differences between who and what he is. Howe's social mask reflects the image of a man who has learned what symbols are necessary in order for one to succeed in his culture. These social labels inform us of what Howe is, but they do not reveal any insight into who he is. To dramatize this conflict, Trilling confronts Howe with two students who symbolically represent the opposing forces with which he is struggling. The man with a respect for the intellect is depicted by Tertan, a young genius who appears insane to both Howe and the others in the story. The man of success is depicted by Blackburn, a young man who as student-body vice president and manager of the debating team would do anything to get ahead.

Joseph Howe joins forces with those who become members of the "thrice woven circle" which establishes them as members of a social machine which produces educated men and women who become passive, timid individuals seeking to ascend the ladder of success. The camera is an apt symbol to frame the picture of those who choose to adapt to this institution which will shape and mold their destinies. Trilling's vision of Howe enables us to focus on what happens to those who fail to choose self-discovery over self-deception. Howe's path has lead him to accept his social mask at the expense of expressing what he feels. Nowhere in the story do we see examples of the expression of passion or even of anger. Howe is also unable to express compassion for the suffering of Tertan, and for that matter he is unable to express concern for those who join with him in the ceremony of graduation. This initiation into the ritual of education transforms the individual to seek the rewards of success, but it does not make it possible for one to identify or participate with other human beings. The voice of the collective rules over the lives of those men and women who live in this place at this time.

In *Transmutations,* we see the landscape of the mind's eye. The "inner" world appears in darkness. The ladder points the way out. This theme of understanding what lies beneath appearances makes it possible for an individual to transcend the experience of a self caught in time.

OF THIS TIME OF THAT PLACE

LIONEL TRILLING

It was a fine September day. By noon it would be summer again, but now it was true autumn with a touch of chill in the air. As Joseph Howe stood on the porch of the house in which he lodged, ready to leave for his first class of the year, he thought with pleasure of the long indoor days that were coming. It was a moment when he could feel glad of his profession.

On the lawn the peach tree was still in fruit and young Hilda Aiken was taking a picture of it. She held the camera tight against her chest. She wanted the sun behind her, but she did not want her own long morning shadow in the foreground. She raised the camera, but that did not help, and she lowered it, but that made things worse. She twisted her body to the left, then to the right. In the end she had to step out of the direct line of the sun. At last she snapped the shutter and wound the film with intense care.

Howe, watching her from the porch, waited for her to finish and called good morning. She turned, startled, and almost sullenly lowered her glance. In the year Howe had lived at the Aikens', Hilda had accepted him as one of her family, but since his absence of the summer she had grown shy. Then suddenly she lifted her head and smiled at him, and the humorous smile confirmed his pleasure in the day. She picked up her bookbag and set off for school.

The handsome houses on the streets to the college were not yet fully awake, but they looked very friendly. Howe went by the Bradby house where he would be a guest this evening at the first dinner party of the year. When he had gone the length of the picket fence, the whitest in town, he turned back. Along the path there was a fine row of asters and he went through the gate and picked one for his buttonhole. The Bradbys would be pleased if they happened to see him invading their lawn and the knowledge of this made him even more comfortable.

He reached the campus as the hour was striking. The students were hurrying to their classes. He himself was in no hurry. He stopped at his dim cubicle of an office and lit a cigarette. The prospect of facing his class had suddenly presented itself to him and his hands were cold; the lawful seizure of power he was about to make seemed momentous. Waiting did not help. He put out his cigarette, picked up a pad of theme paper, and went to his classroom.

As he entered, the rattle of voices ceased, and the twenty-odd freshmen settled themselves and looked at him appraisingly. Their faces seemed gross, his heart sank at their massed impassivity, but he spoke briskly.

"My name is Howe," he said, and turned and wrote it on the blackboard. The carelessness of the scrawl confirmed his authority. He went on, "My office is 412 Slemp Hall, and my office-hours are Monday, Wednesday and Friday from eleven-thirty to twelve-thirty."

He wrote, "M., W., F., 11:30–12:30." He said, "I'll be very glad to see any of you at that time. Or if you can't come then, you can arrange with me for some other time."

He turned again to the blackboard and spoke over his shoulder. "The text for the course is Jarman's *Modern Plays,* revised edition. The Co-op has it in stock." He wrote the name, underlined "revised edition" and waited for it to be taken down in the new notebooks.

When the bent heads were raised again he began his speech of prospectus. "It is hard to explain—" he said, and paused as they composed themselves. "It is hard to explain what a course like this is intended to do. We are going to try to learn something about modern literature and something about prose composition."

As he spoke, his hands warmed and he was able to look directly at the class. Last year on the first day the faces had seemed just as cloddish, but as the term wore on they became gradually alive and quite likable. It did not seem possible that the same thing could happen again.

"I shall not lecture in this course," he continued. "Our work will be carried on by discussion and we will try to learn by an exchange of opinion. But you will soon recognize that my opinion is worth more than anyone else's here."

He remained grave as he said it, but two boys understood and laughed. The rest took permission from them and laughed too. All Howe's private ironies protested the vulgarity of the joke, but the laughter made him feel benign and powerful.

When the little speech was finished, Howe picked up the pad of paper he had brought. He announced that they would write an extemporaneous theme. Its subject was traditional, "Who I am and why I came to Dwight College." By now the class was more at ease and it gave a ritualistic groan of protest. Then there was a stir as fountain pens were brought out and the writing-arms of the chairs were cleared, and the paper was passed about. At last, all the heads bent to work, and the room became still.

Howe sat idly at his desk. The sun shone through the tall clumsy windows. The cool of the morning was already passing. There was a scent of autumn and of varnish and the stillness of the room was deep and oddly touching. Now and then a student's head was raised and scratched in the old, elaborate students' pantomime that calls the teacher to witness honest intellectual effort.

Suddenly a tall boy stood within the frame of the open door. "Is this," he said, and thrust a large nose into a college catalogue, "is this the meeting place of English 1A? The section instructed by Dr. Joseph Howe?"

He stood on the very sill of the door, as if refusing to enter until he was perfectly sure of all his rights. The class looked up from work, found him absurd and gave a low mocking cheer.

The teacher and the new student, with equal pointedness, ignored the disturbance. Howe nodded to the boy, who pushed his head forward and then jerked it back in a wide elaborate arc to clear his brow of a heavy lock of hair. He advanced into the room and halted before Howe, almost at attention. In a loud, clear voice he announced, "I am Tertan, Ferdinand R., reporting at the direction of Head of Department Vincent."

The heraldic formality of this statement brought forth another cheer. Howe looked at the class with a sternness he could not really feel, for there was indeed something ridiculous about this boy. Under his displeased regard the rows of heads dropped to work again. Then he touched Tertan's elbow, led him up to the desk and stood so as to shield their conversation from the class.

"We are writing an extemporaneous theme," he said. "The subject is, 'Who I am and why I came to Dwight College.' "

He stripped a few sheets from the pad and offered them to the boy. Tertan hesitated and then took the paper, but he held it only tentatively. As if with the effort of making something clear, he gulped, and a slow smile fixed itself on his face. It was at once knowing and shy.

"Professor," he said, "to be perfectly fair to my classmates"—he made a large gesture over the room—"and to you"—he inclined his head to Howe—"this would not be for me an extemporaneous subject."

Howe tried to understand. "You mean you've already thought about it—you've heard we always give the same subject? That doesn't matter."

Again the boy ducked his head and gulped. It was the gesture of one who wishes to make a difficult explanation with perfect candor. "Sir," he said, and made the distinction with great care, "the topic I did not expect, but I have given much ratiocination to the subject."

Howe smiled and said, "I don't think that's an unfair advantage. Just go ahead and write."

Tertan narrowed his eyes and glanced sidewise at Howe. His strange mouth smiled. Then in quizzical acceptance, he ducked his head, threw back the heavy, dank lock, dropped into a seat with a great loose noise and began to write rapidly.

The room fell silent again and Howe resumed his idleness. When the bell rang, the students who had groaned when the task had been set now groaned again because they had not finished. Howe took up the papers, and held the class while he made the first assignment. When he dismissed it, Tertan bore down on him, his slack mouth held ready for speech.

"Some professors," he said, "are pedants. They are Dryasdusts.[1] However, some professors are free souls and creative spirits. Kant, Hegel and Nietzsche were all professors." With this pronouncement he paused. "It is my opinion," he continued, "that you occupy the second category."

Howe looked at the boy in surprise and said with good-natured irony, "With Kant, Hegel and Nietzsche?"

Not only Tertan's hand and head but his whole awkward body waved away the stupidity. "It is the kind and not the quantity of the kind," he said sternly.

Rebuked, Howe said as simply and seriously as he could, "It would be nice to think so." He added, "Of course I am not a professor."

This was clearly a disappointment but Tertan met it. "In the French sense," he said with composure. "Generically, a teacher."

Suddenly he bowed. It was such a bow, Howe fancied, as a stage-director might teach an actor playing a medieval student who takes leave of Abelard[2]—stiff, solemn, with elbows close to the body and feet together. Then, quite as suddenly, he turned and left.

A queer fish, and as soon as Howe reached his office, he sifted through the batch of themes and drew out Tertan's. The boy had filled many sheets with his unformed headlong scrawl. "Who am I?" he had begun. "Here, in a mundane, not to say commercialized academe, is asked the question which from time long immemorially out of mind has accreted doubts and thoughts in the psyche of man to pester him as a nuisance. Whether in St. Augustine (or Austin as sometimes called) or Miss Bashkirtsieff or Frederic Amiel or Empedocles,[3] or in less lights of the intellect than these, this posed question has been ineluctable."

Howe took out his pencil. He circled "academe" and wrote "vocab." in the margin. He underlined "time long immemorially out of mind" and wrote "Diction!" But this seemed inadequate for what was wrong. He put down his pencil and read ahead to discover the principle of error in the theme. "Today as ever, in spite of gloomy prophets of the dismal science (economics) the question is uninvalidated. Out of the starry depths of heaven hurtles this spear of query demanding to be caught on the shield of the mind ere it pierces the skull and the limbs be unstrung."

Baffled but quite caught, Howe read on. "Materialism, by which is meant the philosophic concept and not the moral idea, provides no aegis against the question which lies beyond the tangible (metaphysics). Existence without alloy is the question presented. Environment and heredity relegated aside, the rags and old clothes of practical life discarded, the name and the instrumentality of livelihood do not, as the prophets of the dismal science insist on in this connection, give solution to the interrogation which not from the professor merely but veritably from the cosmos is given. I think, therefore I am (cogito etc.)[4] but who

[1] Generic name used by Thomas Carlyle (1795–1881) in *Sartor Resartus* for a pedantic scholar; derived from the fictitious writer of prefaces to several of Scott's novels.

[2] French scholastic philosopher and theologian (1079–1142) who was extremely popular as a teacher.

[3] St. Augustine (354–430), church father, author of *Confessions, City of God*, etc.; Maria Constantinowna Bashkirtsieff (1860–1884), Russian artist whose diaries were published in 1887; Henri Frédéric Amiel (1821–1881), Swiss scholar, poet, and philosopher; Empedocles (ca. 490–430 B.C.), Greek philosopher, poet, and statesman.

[4] *Cogito, ergo sum* (Latin, I think, therefore I am), a famous phrase of the philosopher René Descartes (1596–1650).

am I? Tertan I am, but what is Tertan? Of this time, of that place, of some parentage, what does it matter?"

Existence without alloy: the phrase established itself. Howe put aside Tertan's paper and at random picked up another. "I am Arthur J. Casebeer, Jr.," he read. "My father is Arthur J. Casebeer and my grandfather was Arthur J. Casebeer before him. My mother is Nina Wimble Casebeer. Both of them are college graduates and my father is in insurance. I was born in St. Louis eighteen years ago and we still make our residence there."

Arthur J. Casebeer, who knew who he was, was less interesting than Tertan, but more coherent. Howe picked up Tertan's paper again. It was clear that none of the routine marginal comments, no "sent. str." or "punct." or "vocab." could cope with this torrential rhetoric. He read ahead, contenting himself with underscoring the errors against the time when he should have the necessary "conference" with Tertan.

It was a busy and official day of cards and sheets, arrangements and small decisions, and it gave Howe pleasure. Even when it was time to attend the first of the weekly Convocations he felt the charm of the beginning of things when intention is still innocent and uncorrupted by effort. He sat among the young instructors on the platform, and joined in their humorous complaints at having to assist at the ceremony, but actually he got a clear satisfaction from the ritual of prayer, and prosy speech, and even from wearing his academic gown. And when the Convocation was over the pleasure continued as he crossed the campus, exchanging greetings with men he had not seen since the spring. They were people who did not yet, and perhaps never would, mean much to him, but in a year they had grown amiably to be part of his life. They were his fellow-townsmen.

The day had cooled again at sunset, and there was a bright chill in the September twilight. Howe carried his voluminous gown over his arm, he swung his doctoral hood by its purple neckpiece, and on his head he wore his mortarboard with its heavy gold tassel bobbing just over his eye. These were the weighty and absurd symbols of his new profession and they pleased him. At twenty-six Joseph Howe had discovered that he was neither so well off nor so bohemian as he had once thought. A small income, adequate when supplemented by a sizable cash legacy, was genteel poverty when the cash was all spent. And the literary life—the room at the Lafayette,[5] or the small apartment without a lease, the long summers on the Cape,[6] the long afternoons and the social evenings—began to weary him. His writing filled his mornings, and should perhaps have filled his life, yet it did not. To the amusement of his friends, and with a certain sense that he was betraying his own freedom, he had used the last of his legacy for a year at Harvard. The small but respectable reputation of his two volumes of verse had proved useful—he continued at Harvard on a fellowship and when he emerged as Doctor Howe he received an excellent appointment, with prospects, at Dwight.

He had his moments of fear when all that had ever been said of the dangers of the academic life had occurred to him. But after a year in which he had tested every possibility of corruption and seduction he was ready to rest easy. His third volume of verse, most of it written in his first years of teaching, was not only ampler but, he thought, better than its predecessors.

There was a clear hour before the Bradby dinner party, and Howe looked forward to it. But he was not to enjoy it, for lying with his mail on the hall table was a copy of this quarter's issue of *Life and Letters,* to which his landlord subscribed. Its severe cover announced that its editor, Frederic Woolley, had this month contributed an essay called "Two Poets," and Howe, picking it up, curious to see who the two poets might be, felt his own name start out at him with cabalistic power—Joseph Howe. As he continued to turn the pages his hand trembled.

Standing in the dark hall, holding the neat little magazine, Howe knew that his literary contempt for Frederic Woolley meant nothing, for he suddenly understood how he respected Woolley in the way of the world. He knew this by the trembling of his hand. And of the little world as well as the great, for although the literary groups of New York might dismiss Woolley, his name carried high authority in the academic world. At Dwight it was even a revered name, for it had been here at the college that Frederic Woolley had made the distin-

---

[5] Hotel that was well-known as a gathering place for intellectuals and bohemians in New York's Greenwich Village.
[6] Cape Cod.

guished scholarly career from which he had gone on to literary journalism. In middle life he had been induced to take the editorship of *Life and Letters,* a literary monthly not widely read but heavily endowed, and in its pages he had carried on the defense of what he sometimes called the older values. He was not without wit, he had great knowledge and considerable taste, and even in the full movement of the "new" literature he had won a certain respect for his refusal to accept it. In France, even in England, he would have been connected with a more robust tradition of conservatism, but America gave him an audience not much better than genteel. It was known in the college that to the subsidy of *Life and Letters* the Bradbys contributed a great part.

As Howe read, he saw that he was involved in nothing less than an event. When the Fifth Series of *Studies in Order and Value* came to be collected, this latest of Frederic Woolley's essays would not be merely another step in the old direction. Clearly and unmistakably, it was a turning point. All his literary life Woolley had been concerned with the relation of literature to morality, religion, and the private and delicate pieties, and he had been unalterably opposed to all that he had called "inhuman humanitarianism." But here, suddenly, dramatically late, he had made an about face, turning to the public life and to the humanitarian politics he had so long despised. This was the kind of incident the histories of literature make much of. Frederic Woolley was opening for himself a new career and winning a kind of new youth. He contrasted the two poets, Thomas Wormser, who was admirable, Joseph Howe, who was almost dangerous. He spoke of the "precious subjectivism of Howe's verse. "In times like ours," he wrote, "with millions facing penury and want, one feels that the qualities of the *tour d'ivoire* are well-nigh inhuman, nearly insulting. The *tour d'ivoire* becomes the *tour d'ivresse,*[7] and it is not self-intoxicated poets that our people need." The essay said more: "The problem is one of meaning. I am not ignorant that the creed of the esoteric poets declares that a poem does not and should not *mean* anything, that it *is* something. But poetry is what the poet makes it, and if he is a true poet he makes what his society needs. And what is needed now is the tradition in which Mr. Wormser writes, the true tradition

[7] The ivory tower becomes the tower of intoxication, or madness.

of poetry. The Howes do no harm, but they do no good when positive good is demanded of all responsible men. Or do the Howes indeed do no harm? Perhaps Plato would have said they do, that in some ways theirs is the Phrygian music that turns men's minds from the struggle. Certainly it is true that Thomas Wormser writes in the lucid Dorian mode[8] which sends men into battle with evil."

It was easy to understand why Woolley had chosen to praise Thomas Wormser. The long, lilting lines of *Corn Under Willows* hymned, as Woolley put it, the struggle for wheat in the Iowa fields, and expressed the real lives of real people. But why out of the dozen more notable examples he had chosen Howe's little volume as the example of "precious subjectivism" was hard to guess. In a way it was funny, this multiplication of himself into "the Howes." And yet this becoming the multiform political symbol by whose creation Frederic Woolley gave the sign of a sudden new life, this use of him as a sacrifice whose blood was necessary for the rites of rejuvenation, made him feel oddly unclean.

Nor could Howe get rid of a certain practical resentment. As a poet he had a special and respectable place in the college life. But it might be another thing to be marked as the poet of a willful and selfish obscurity.

As he walked to the Bradbys', Howe was a little tense and defensive. It seemed to him that all the world knew of the "attack" and agreed with it. And, indeed, the Bradbys had read the essay but Professor Bradby, a kind and pretentious man, said, "I see my old friend knocked you about a bit, my boy," and his wife Eugenia looked at Howe with her childlike blue eyes and said, "I shall *scold* Frederic for the untrue things he wrote about you. You aren't the least obscure." They beamed at him. In their genial snobbery they seemed to feel that he had distinguished himself. He was the leader of Howeism. He enjoyed the dinner party as much as he had thought he would.

And in the following days, as he was more preoccupied with his duties, the incident was forgotten. His classes had ceased to be mere groups. Student after student detached himself from the mass and required or claimed a place in Howe's awareness. Of them all it was Tertan who first and most violently signaled his sepa-

[8] The Phrygian and Dorian modes were scales used in Greek and ecclesiastical music; the Phrygian was brisk and spirited and the Dorian, bold and grave.

rate existence. A week after classes had begun Howe saw his silhouette on the frosted glass of his office door. It was motionless for a long time, perhaps stopped by the problem of whether or not to knock before entering. Howe called, "Come in!" and Tertan entered with his shambling stride.

He stood beside the desk, silent and at attention. When Howe asked him to sit down, he responded with a gesture of head and hand, as if to say that such amenities were beside the point. Nevertheless, he did take the chair. He put his ragged, crammed briefcase between his legs. His face, which Howe now observed fully for the first time, was confusing, for it was made up of florid curves, the nose arched in the bone and voluted in the nostril, the mouth loose and soft and rather moist. Yet the face was so thin and narrow as to seem the very type of asceticism. Lashes of unusual length veiled the eyes and, indeed, it seemed as if there were a veil over the whole countenance. Before the words actually came, the face screwed itself into an attitude of preparation for them.

"You can confer with me now?" Tertan said.

"Yes, I'd be glad to. There are several things in your two themes I want to talk to you about." Howe reached for the packet of themes on his desk and sought for Tertan's. But the boy was waving them away.

"These are done perforce," he said. "Under the pressure of your requirement. They are not significant; mere duties." Again his great hand flapped vaguely to dismiss his themes. He leaned forward and gazed at his teacher.

"You are," he said, "a man of letters? You are a poet?" It was more declaration than question.

"I should like to think so," Howe said.

At first Tertan accepted the answer with a show of appreciation, as though the understatement made a secret between himself and Howe. Then he chose to misunderstand. With his shrewd and disconcerting control of expression, he presented to Howe a puzzled grimace. "What does that mean?" he said.

Howe retracted the irony. "Yes. I am a poet." It sounded strange to say.

"That," Tertan said, "is a wonder." He corrected himself with his ducking head. "I mean that is wonderful."

Suddenly, he dived at the miserable briefcase between his legs, put it on his knees, and began to fumble with the catch, all intent on the difficulty it presented. Howe noted that his suit was worn thin, his shirt almost unclean. He became aware, even, of a vague and musty odor of garments worn too long in unaired rooms. Tertan conquered the lock and began to concentrate upon a search into the interior. At last he held in his hand what he was after, a torn and crumpled copy of *Life and Letters*.

"I learned it from here," he said, holding it out.

Howe looked at him sharply, his hackles a little up. But the boy's face was not only perfectly innocent, it even shone with a conscious admiration. Apparently nothing of the import of the essay had touched him except the wonderful fact that his teacher was a "man of letters." Yet this seemed too stupid, and Howe, to test it, said, "The man who wrote that doesn't think it's wonderful."

Tertan made a moist hissing sound as he cleared his mouth of saliva. His head, oddly loose on his neck, wove a pattern of contempt in the air. "A critic," he said, "who admits *prima facie* that he does not understand." Then he said grandly, "It is the inevitable fate."

It was absurd, yet Howe was not only aware of the absurdity but of a tension suddenly and wonderfully relaxed. Now that the "attack" was on the table between himself and this strange boy, and subject to the boy's funny and absolutely certain contempt, the hidden force of his feeling was revealed to him in the very moment that it vanished. All unsuspected, there had been a film over the world, a transparent but discoloring haze of danger. But he had no time to stop over the brightened aspect of things. Tertan was going on. "I also am a man of letters. Putative."

"You have written a good deal?" Howe meant to be no more than polite, and he was surprised at the tenderness he heard in his words.

Solemnly the boy nodded, threw back the dank lock, and sucked in a deep, anticipatory breath. "First, a work of homiletics, which is a defense of the principles of religious optimism against the pessimism of Schopenhauer and the humanism of Nietzsche."

"Humanism? Why do you call it humanism?"

"It is my nomenclature for making a deity of man," Tertan replied negligently. "Then three fictional works, novels. And numerous essays in science, combating materialism. Is it your duty to read these if I bring them to you?"

Howe answered simply, "No, it isn't exactly

my duty, but I shall be happy to read them."

Tertan stood up and remained silent. He rested his bag on the chair. With a certain compunction—for it did not seem entirely proper that, of two men of letters, one should have the right to blue-pencil the other, to grade him or to question the quality of his "sentence structure"—Howe reached for Tertan's papers. But before he could take them up, the boy suddenly made his bow-to-Abelard, the stiff inclination of the body with the hands seeming to emerge from the scholar's gown. Then he was gone.

But after his departure something was still left of him. The timbre of his curious sentences, the downright finality of so quaint a phrase as "It is the inevitable fate" still rang in the air. Howe gave the warmth of his feeling to the new visitor who stood at the door announcing himself with a genteel clearing of the throat.

"Doctor Howe, I believe?" the student said. A large hand advanced into the room and grasped Howe's hand. "Blackburn, sir, Theodore Blackburn, vice-president of the Student Council. A great pleasure, sir."

Out of a pair of ruddy cheeks a pair of small eyes twinkled good-naturedly. The large face, the large body were not so much fat as beefy and suggested something "typical"—monk, politician, or innkeeper.

Blackburn took the seat beside Howe's desk. "I may have seemed to introduce myself in my public capacity, sir," he said. "But it is really as an individual that I came to see you. That is to say, as one of your students to be."

He spoke with an English intonation and he went on, "I was once an English major, sir."

For a moment Howe was startled, for the roast-beef look of the boy and the manner of his speech gave a second's credibility to one sense of his statement. Then the collegiate meaning of the phrase asserted itself, but some perversity made Howe say what was not really in good taste even with so forward a student, "Indeed? What regiment?"

Blackburn stared and then gave a little poufpouf of laughter. He waved the misapprehension away. "Very good, sir. It certainly is an ambiguous term." He chuckled in appreciation of Howe's joke, then cleared his throat to put it aside. "I look forward to taking your course in the romantic poets, sir," he said earnestly. "To me the romantic poets are the very crown of English literature."

Howe made a dry sound, and the boy, catching some meaning in it, said, "Little as I know them, of course. But even Shakespeare who is so dear to us of the Anglo-Saxon tradition is in a sense but the preparation for Shelley, Keats and Byron. And Wadsworth."

Almost sorry for him, Howe dropped his eyes. With some embarrassment, for the boy was not actually his student, he said softly, "Wordsworth."

"Sir?"

"Wordsworth, not Wadsworth. You said Wadsworth."

"Did I, sir?" Gravely he shook his head to rebuke himself for the error. "Wordsworth, of course—slip of the tongue." Then, quite in command again, he went on. "I have a favor to ask of you, Doctor Howe. You see, I began my college course as an English major,"—he smiled—"as I said."

"Yes?"

"But after my first year I shifted. I shifted to the social sciences. Sociology and government —I find them stimulating and very real." He paused, out of respect for reality. "But now I find that perhaps I have neglected the other side."

"The other side?" Howe said.

"Imagination, fancy, culture. A well-rounded man." He trailed off as if there were perfect understanding between them. "And so, sir, I have decided to end my senior year with your course in the romantic poets."

His voice was filled with an indulgence which Howe ignored as he said flatly and gravely, "But that course isn't given until the spring term."

"Yes, sir, and that is where the favor comes in. Would you let me take your romantic prose course? I can't take it for credit, sir, my program is full, but just for background it seems to me that I ought to take it. I do hope," he concluded in a manly way, "that you will consent."

"Well, it's no great favor, Mr. Blackburn. You can come if you wish, though there's not much point in it if you don't do the reading."

The bell rang for the hour and Howe got up.

"May I begin with this class, sir?" Blackburn's smile was candid and boyish.

Howe nodded carelessly and together, silently, they walked to the classroom down the hall. When they reached the door Howe stood back to let his student enter, but Blackburn moved adroitly behind him and grasped him by the arm to urge him over the threshold.

They entered together with Blackburn's hand firmly on Howe's biceps, the student inducting the teacher into his own room. Howe felt a surge of temper rise in him and almost violently he disengaged his arm and walked to the desk, while Blackburn found a seat in the front row and smiled at him.

II

The question was, At whose door must the tragedy be laid?

All night the snow had fallen heavily and only now was abating in sparse little flurries. The windows were valanced high with white. It was very quiet; something of the quiet of the world had reached the class, and Howe found that everyone was glad to talk or listen. In the room there was a comfortable sense of pleasure in being human.

Casebeer believed that the blame for the tragedy rested with heredity. Picking up the book he read, "The sins of the fathers are visited on their children." This opinion was received with general favor. Nevertheless, Johnson ventured to say that the fault was all Pastor Manders'[9] because the Pastor had made Mrs. Alving go back to her husband and was always hiding the truth. To this Hibbard objected with logic enough, "Well then, it was really all her husband's fault. He *did* all the bad things." DeWitt, his face bright with an impatient idea, said that the fault was all society's. "By society I don't mean upper-crust society," he said. He looked around a little defiantly, taking in any members of the class who might be members of upper-crust society. "Not in that sense. I mean the social unit."

Howe nodded and said, "Yes, of course."

"If the society of the time had progressed far enough in science," De Witt went on, "then there would be no problem for Mr. Ibsen to write about. Captain Alving plays around a little, gives way to perfectly natural biological urges, and he gets a social disease, a veneral disease. If the disease is cured, no problem. Invent salvarsan and the disease is cured. The problem of heredity disappears and li'l Oswald just doesn't get paresis. No paresis, no problem—no problem, no play."

This was carrying the ark into battle, and the class looked at De Witt with respectful curios-

[9] The play being discussed is *Ghosts* by Henrik Ibsen (1828–1906).

ity. It was his usual way and on the whole they were sympathetic with his struggle to prove to Howe that science was better than literature. Still, there was something in his reckless manner that alienated them a little.

"Or take birth-control, for instance," De Witt went on. "If Mrs. Alving had some knowledge of contraception, she wouldn't have had to have li'l Oswald at all. No li'l Oswald, no play."

The class was suddenly quieter. In the back row Stettenhover swung his great football shoulders in a righteous sulking gesture, first to the right, then to the left. He puckered his mouth ostentatiously. Intellect was always ending up by talking dirty.

Tertan's hand went up, and Howe said, "Mr. Tertan." The boy shambled to his feet and began his long characteristic gulp. Howe made a motion with his fingers, as small as possible, and Tertan ducked his head and smiled in apology. He sat down. The class laughed. With more than half the term gone, Tertan had not been able to remember that one did not rise to speak. He seemed unable to carry on the life of the intellect without this mark of respect for it. To Howe the boy's habit of rising seemed to accord with the formal shabbiness of his dress. He never wore the casual sweaters and jackets of his classmates. Into the free and comfortable air of the college classroom he brought the stuffy sordid strictness of some crowded, metropolitan high school.

"Speaking from one sense," Tertan began slowly, "there is no blame ascribable. From the sense of determinism, who can say where the blame lies? The preordained is the preordained and it cannot be said without rebellion against the universe, a palpable absurdity."

In the back row Stettenhover slumped suddenly in his seat, his heels held out before him, making a loud, dry, disgusted sound. His body sank until his neck rested on the back of his chair. He folded his hands across his belly and looked significantly out of the window, exasperated not only with Tertan, but with Howe, with the class, with the whole system designed to encourage this kind of thing. There was a certain insolence in the movement and Howe flushed. As Tertan continued to speak, Howe stalked casually toward the window and placed himself in the line of Stettenhover's vision. He stared at the great fellow, who pretended not to see him. There was so much power in the big body, so much contempt in the Greek-athlete face under the crisp Greek-athlete curls, that Howe felt almost physical fear. But at last Stettenhover admitted him to focus and under his disapproving gaze sat up with slow indifference. His eyebrows raised high in resignation, he began to examine his hands. Howe relaxed and turned his attention back to Tertan.

"Flux of existence," Tertan was saying, "produces all things, so that judgment wavers. Beyond the phenomena, what? But phenomena are adumbrated and to them we are limited."

Howe saw it for a moment as perhaps it existed in the boy's mind—the world of shadows which are cast by a great light upon a hidden reality as in the old myth of the Cave.[10] But the little brush with Stettenhover had tired him, and he said irritably, "But come to the point, Mr. Tertan."

He said it so sharply that some of the class looked at him curiously. For three months he had gently carried Tertan through his verbosities, to the vaguely respectful surprise of the other students, who seemed to conceive that there existed between this strange classmate and their teacher some special understanding from which they were content to be excluded. Tertan looked at him mildly, and at once came brilliantly to the point. "This is the summation of the play," he said and took up his book and read, " 'Your poor father never found any outlet for the overmastering joy of life that was in him. And I brought no holiday into his home, either. Everything seemed to turn upon duty and I am afraid I made your poor father's home unbearable to him, Oswald.' Spoken by Mrs. Alving."

Yes that was surely the "summation" of the play and Tertan had hit it, as he hit, deviously and eventually, the literary point of almost everything. But now, as always, he was wrapping it away from sight. "For most mortals," he said, "there are only joys of biological urgings, gross and crass, such as the sensuous Captain Alving. For certain few there are the transmutations beyond these to a contemplation of the utter whole."

Oh, the boy was mad. And suddenly the word, used in hyperbole, intended almost for the expression of exasperated admiration, became literal. Now that the word was used, it became simply apparent to Howe that Tertan was mad.

It was a monstrous word and stood like a

[10] Parable used by Plato (ca. 429–347 B.C.) in the *Republic*, Book VII.

bestial thing in the room. Yet it so completely comprehended everything that had puzzled Howe, it so arranged and explained what for three months had been perplexing him that almost at once its horror became domesticated. With this word Howe was able to understand why he had never been able to communicate to Tertan the value of a single criticism or correction of his wild, verbose themes. Their conferences had been frequent and long but had done nothing to reduce to order the splendid confusion of the boy's ideas. Yet, impossible though its expression was, Tertan's incandescent mind could always strike for a moment into some dark corner of thought.

And now it was suddenly apparent that it was not a faulty rhetoric that Howe had to contend with. With his new knowledge he looked at Tertan's face and wondered how he could have so long deceived himself. Tertan was still talking, and the class had lapsed into a kind of patient unconsciousness, a coma of respect for words which, for all that most of them knew, might be profound. Almost with a suffusion of shame, Howe believed that in some dim way the class had long ago had some intimation of Tertan's madness. He reached out as decisively as he could to seize the thread of Tertan's discourse before it should be entangled further.

"Mr. Tertan says that the blame must be put upon whoever kills the joy of living in another. We have been assuming that Captain Alving was a wholly bad man, but what if we assume that he became bad only because Mrs. Alving, when they were first married, acted toward him in the prudish way she says she did?"

It was a ticklish idea to advance to freshmen and perhaps not profitable. Not all of them were following.

"That would put the blame on Mrs. Alving herself, whom most of you admire. And she herself seems to think so." He glanced at his watch. The hour was nearly over. "What do you think, Mr. De Witt?"

De Witt rose to the idea; he wanted to know if society couldn't be blamed for educating Mrs. Alving's temperament in the wrong way. Casebeer was puzzled, Stettenhover continued to look at his hands until the bell rang.

Tertan, his brows louring in thought, was making as always for a private word. Howe gathered his books and papers to leave quickly. At this moment of his discovery and with the knowledge still raw, he could not engage himself with Tertan. Tertan sucked in his breath to prepare for speech and Howe made ready for the pain and confusion. But at that moment Casebeer detached himself from the group with which he had been conferring and which he seemed to represent. His constituency remained at a tactful distance. The mission involved the time of an assigned essay. Casebeer's presentation of the plea—it was based on the freshmen's heavy duties at the fraternities during Carnival Week—cut across Tertan's preparations for speech. "And so some of us fellows thought," Casebeer concluded with heavy solemnity, "that we could do a better job, give our minds to it more, if we had more time."

Tertan regarded Casebeer with mingled curiosity and revulsion. Howe not only said that he would postpone the assignment but went on to talk about the Carnival, and even drew the waiting constituency into the conversation. He was conscious of Tertan's stern and astonished stare, then of his sudden departure.

Now that the fact was clear, Howe knew that he must act on it. His course was simple enough. He must lay the case before the Dean. Yet he hesitated. His feeling for Tertan must now, certainly, be in some way invalidated. Yet could he, because of a word, hurry to assign to official and reasonable solicitude what had been, until this moment, so various and warm? He could at least delay and, by moving slowly, lend a poor grace to the necessary, ugly act of making his report.

It was with some notion of keeping the matter in his own hands that he went to the Dean's office to look up Tertan's records. In the outer office the Dean's secretary greeted him brightly, and at his request brought him the manila folder with the small identifying photograph pasted in the corner. She laughed. "He was looking for the birdie in the wrong place," she said.

Howe leaned over her shoulder to look at the picture. It was as bad as all the Dean's-office photographs were, but it differed from all that Howe had ever seen. Tertan, instead of looking into the camera, as no doubt he had been bidden, had, at the moment of exposure, turned his eyes upward. His mouth, as though conscious of the trick played on the photographer, had the sly superior look that Howe knew.

The secretary was fascinated by the picture.

"What a funny boy," she said. "He looks like Tartuffe!"[11]

And so he did, with the absurd piety of the eyes and the conscious slyness of the mouth and the whole face bloated by the bad lens.

"Is he *like* that?" the secretary said.

"Like Tartuffe? No."

From the photograph there was little enough comfort to be had. The records themselves gave no clue to madness, though they suggested sadness enough. Howe read of a father, Stanislaus Tertan, born in Budapest and trained in engineering in Berlin, once employed by the Hercules Chemical Corporation—this was one of the factories that dominated the sound end of the town—but now without employment. He read of a mother Erminie (Youngfellow) Tertan, born in Manchester, educated at a Normal School at Leeds, now housewife by profession. The family lived on Greenbriar Street which Howe knew as a row of once elegant homes near what was now the factory district. The old mansion had long ago been divided into small and primitive apartments. Of Ferdinand himself there was little to learn. He lived with his parents, had attended a Detroit high school and had transferred to the local school in his last year. His rating for intelligence, as expressed in numbers, was high, his scholastic record was remarkable, he held a college scholarship for his tuition.

Howe laid the folder on the secretary's desk. "Did you find what you wanted to know?" she asked.

The phrases from Tertan's momentous first theme came back to him. "Tertan I am, but what is Tertan? Of this time, of that place, of some parentage, what does it matter?"

"No, I didn't find it," he said.

Now that he had consulted the sad, half-meaningless record he knew all the more firmly that he must not give the matter out of his own hands. He must not release Tertan to authority. Not that he anticipated from the Dean anything but the greatest kindness for Tertan. The Dean would have the experience and skill which he himself could not have. One way or another the Dean could answer the question, "What is Tertan?" Yet this was precisely what he feared. He alone could keep alive—not forever but for a somehow important time—the question, "What is Tertan?" He alone could keep it still a question. Some sure instinct told

[11] The sanctimonious hypocrite in Moliere's comedy *Tartuffe*, first produced in 1667.

him that he must not surrender the question to a clean official desk in a clear official light to be dealt with, settled and closed.

He heard himself saying, "Is the Dean busy at the moment? I'd like to see him."

His request came thus unbidden, even forbidden, and it was one of the surprising and startling incidents of his life. Later when he reviewed the events, so disconnected in themselves, or so merely odd, of the story that unfolded for him that year, it was over this moment, on its face the least notable, that he paused longest. It was frequently to be with fear and never without a certainty of its meaning in his own knowledge of himself that he would recall this simple, routine request, and the feeling of shame and freedom it gave him as he sent everything down the official chute. In the end, of course, no matter what he did to "protect" Tertan, he would have had to make the same request and lay the matter on the Dean's clean desk. But it would always be a landmark of his life that, at the very moment when he was rejecting the official way, he had been, without will or intention, so gladly drawn to it.

After the storm's last delicate flurry, the sun had come out. Reflected by the new snow, it filled the office with a golden light which was almost musical in the way it made all the commonplace objects of efficiency shine with a sudden sad and noble significance. And the light, now that he noticed it, made the utterance of his perverse and unwanted request even more momentous.

The secretary consulted the engagement pad. "He'll be free any minute. Don't you want to wait in the parlor?"

She threw open the door of the large and pleasant room in which the Dean held his Committee meetings, and in which his visitors waited. It was designed with a homely elegance on the masculine side of the eighteenth-century manner. There was a small coal fire in the grate and the handsome mahogany table was strewn with books and magazines. The large windows gave on the snowy lawn, and there was such a fine width of window that the white casements and walls seemed at this moment but a continuation of the snow, the snow but an extension of casement and walls. The outdoors seemed taken in and made safe, the indoors seemed luxuriously freshened and expanded.

Howe sat down by the fire and lighted a cigarette. The room had its intended effect upon him. He felt comfortable and relaxed, yet nicely organized, some young diplomatic agent of the eighteenth century, the newly fledged Swift carrying out Sir William Temple's business.[12] The rawness of Tertan's case quite vanished. He crossed his legs and reached for a magazine.

It was that famous issue of *Life and Letters* that his idle hand had found and his blood raced as he sifted through it, and the shape of his own name, Joseph Howe, sprang out at him, still cabalistic in its power. He tossed the magazine back on the table as the door of the Dean's office opened and the Dean ushered out Theodore Blackburn.

"Ah, Joseph!" the Dean said.

Blackburn said, "Good morning, Doctor." Howe winced at the title and caught the flicker of amusement over the Dean's face. The Dean stood with his hand high on the door-jamb and Blackburn, still in the doorway, remained standing almost under the long arm.

Howe nodded briefly to Blackburn, snubbing his eager diference. "Can you give me a few minutes?" he said to the Dean.

"All the time you want. Come in." Before the two men could enter the office, Blackburn claimed their attention with a long full "er." As they turned to him, Blackburn said, "Can *you* give *me* a few minutes, Doctor Howe?" His eyes sparkled at the little audacity he had committed, the slightly impudent play with hierarchy. Of the three of them Blackburn kept himself the lowest, but he reminded Howe of his subaltern relation to the Dean.

"I mean, of course," Blackburn went on easily, "when you've finished with the Dean."

"I'll be in my office shortly," Howe said, turned his back on the ready "Thank you, sir," and followed the Dean into the inner room.

"Energetic boy," said the Dean. "A bit beyond himself but very energetic. Sit down."

The Dean lighted a cigarette, leaned back in his chair, sat easy and silent for a moment, giving Howe no signal to go ahead with business. He was a young Dean, not much beyond forty, a tall handsome man with sad, ambitious eyes. He had been a Rhodes scholar. His friends looked for great things from him, and it was generally said that he had notions of education

[12] Jonathon Swift (1667–1745), author of *Gulliver's Travels*, worked as secretary to Sir William Temple (1628–1699), English statesman and author, during the years 1689–1692 and 1696–1699.

which he was not yet ready to try to put into practice.

His relaxed silence was meant as a compliment to Howe. He smiled and said, "What's the business, Joseph?"

"Do you know Tertan—Ferdinand Tertan, a freshman?"

The Dean's cigarette was in his mouth and his hands were clasped behind his head. He did not seem to search his memory for the name. He said, "What about him?"

Clearly the Dean knew something, and he was waiting for Howe to tell him more. Howe moved only tentatively. Now that he was doing what he had resolved not to do, he felt more guilty at having been so long deceived by Tertan and more need to be loyal to his error.

"He's a strange fellow," he ventured. He said stubbornly, "In a strange way he's very brilliant." He concluded, "But very strange."

The springs of the Dean's swivel chair creaked as he came out of his sprawl and leaned forward to Howe. "Do you mean he's so strange that it's something you could give a name to?"

Howe looked at him stupidly. "What do you mean?" he said.

"What's his trouble?" the Dean said more neutrally.

"He's very brilliant, in a way. I looked him up and he has a top intelligence rating. But somehow, and it's hard to explain just how, what he says is always on the edge of sense and doesn't quite make it."

The Dean looked at him and Howe flushed up. The Dean had surely read Woolley on the subject of "the Howes" and the *tour d'ivresse*. Was that quick glance ironical?

The Dean picked up some papers from his desk, and Howe could see that they were in Tertan's impatient scrawl. Perhaps the little gleam in the Dean's glance had come only from putting facts together.

"He sent me this yesterday," the Dean said. "After an interview I had with him. I haven't been able to do more than glance at it. When you said what you did, I realized there was something wrong."

Twisting his mouth, the Dean looked over the letter. "You seem to be involved," he said without looking up. "By the way, what did you give him at mid-term?"

Flushing, setting his shoulders, Howe said firmly, "I gave him A-minus."

The Dean chuckled. "Might be a good idea

if some of our nicer boys went crazy—just a little." He said, "Well," to conclude the matter and handed the papers to Howe. "See if this is the same thing you've been finding. Then we can go into the matter again."

Before the fire in the parlor, in the chair that Howe had been occupying, sat Blackburn. He sprang to his feet as Howe entered.

"I said my office, Mr. Blackburn." Howe's voice was sharp. Then he was almost sorry for the rebuke, so clearly and naively did Blackburn seem to relish his stay in the parlor, close to authority.

"I'm in a bit of a hurry, sir," he said, "and I did want to be sure to speak to you, sir."

He was really absurd, yet fifteen years from now he would have grown up to himself, to the assurance and mature beefiness. In banks, in consular offices, in brokerage firms, on the bench, more seriously affable, a little sterner, he would make use of his ability to be administered by his job. It was almost reassuring. Now he was exercising his too-great skill on Howe. "I owe you an apology, sir," he said.

Howe knew that he did, but he showed surprise.

"I mean, Doctor, after your having been so kind about letting me attend your class, I stopped coming." He smiled in deprecation. "Extracurricular activities take up so much of my time. I'm afraid I undertook more than I could perform."

Howe had noticed the absence and had been a little irritated by it after Blackburn's elaborate plea. It was an absence that might be interpreted as a comment on the teacher. But there was only one way for him to answer. "You've no need to apologize," he said. "It's wholly your affair."

Blackburn beamed. "I'm so glad you feel that way about it, sir. I was worried you might think I had stayed away because I was influenced by—" he stopped and lowered his eyes.

Astonished, Howe said, "Influenced by what?"

"Well, by—" Blackburn hesitated and for answer pointed to the table on which lay the copy of *Life and Letters*. Without looking at it, he knew where to direct his hand. "By the unfavorable publicity, sir." He hurried on. "And that brings me to another point, sir. I am secretary of Quill and Scroll, sir, the student literary society, and I wonder if you would address us. You could read your own poetry, sir, and defend your own point of view. It would be very interesting."

It was truly amazing. Howe looked long and cruelly into Blackburn's face, trying to catch the secret of the mind that could have conceived this way of manipulating him, this way so daring and inept—but not entirely inept—with its malice so without malignity. The face did not yield its secret. Howe smiled broadly and said, "Of course I don't think you were influenced by the unfavorable publicity."

"I'm still going to take—regularly, for credit—your romantic poets course next term," Blackburn said.

"Don't worry, my dear fellow, don't worry about it."

Howe started to leave and Blackburn stopped him with, "But about Quill, sir?"

"Suppose we wait until next term? I'll be less busy then."

And Blackburn said, "Very good, sir, and thank you."

In his office the little encounter seemed less funny to Howe, was even in some indeterminate way disturbing. He made an effort to put it from his mind by turning to what was sure to disturb him more, the Tertan letter read in the new interpretation. He found what he had always found, the same florid leaps beyond fact and meaning, the same headlong certainty. But as his eye passed over the familiar scrawl it caught his own name, and for the second time that hour he felt the race of his blood.

"The Paraclete," Tertan had written to the Dean, "from a Greek word meaning to stand in place of, but going beyond the primitive idea to mean traditionally the helper, the one who comforts and assists, cannot without fundamental loss be jettisoned. Even if taken no longer in the supernatural sense, the concept remains deeply in the human consciousness inevitably. Humanitarianism is no reply, for not every man stands in the place of every other man for this other comrade's comfort. But certain are chosen out of the human race to be the consoler of some other. Of these, for example, is Joseph Barker Howe, Ph.D. Of intellects not the first yet of true intellect and lambent instructions, given to that which is intuitive and irrational, not to what is logical in the strict word, what is judged by him is of the heart and not the head. Here is one chosen, in that he chooses himself to stand in the place of another for comfort and consolation. To him more than another I give my gratitude, with all

respect to our Dean who reads this, a noble man, but merely dedicated, not consecrated. But not in the aspect of the Paraclete only is Dr. Joseph Barker Howe established, for he must be the Paraclete to another aspect of himself, that which is driven and persecuted by the lack of understanding in the world at large, so that he in himself embodies the full history of man's tribulations and, overflowing upon others, notably the present writer, is the ultimate end."

This was love. There was no escape from it. Try as Howe might to remember that Tertan was mad and all his emotions invalidated, he could not destroy the effect upon him of his student's stern, affectionate regard. He had betrayed not only a power of mind but a power of love. And, however firmly he held before his attention the fact of Tertan's madness, he could do nothing to banish the physical sensation of gratitude he felt. He had never thought of himself as "driven and persecuted" and he did not now. But still he could not make meaningless his sensation of gratitude. The pitiable Tertan sternly pitied him, and comfort came from Tertan's never-to-be-comforted mind.

III

In an academic community, even an efficient one, official matters move slowly. The term drew to a close with no action in the case of Tertan, and Joseph Howe had to confront a curious problem. How should he grade his strange student, Tertan?

Tertan's final examination had been no different from all his other writing, and what did one "give" such a student? De Witt must have his A, that was clear. Johnson would get a B. With Casebeer it was a question of a B-minus or a C-plus, and Stettenhover, who had been crammed by the team tutor to fill half a blue-book with his thin feminine scraw, would have his C-minus which he would accept with mingled indifference and resentment. But with Tertan it was not so easy.

The boy was still in the college process and his name could not be omitted from the grade sheet. Yet what should a mind under suspicion of madness be graded? Until the medical verdict was given, it was for Howe to continue as Tertan's teacher and to keep his judgment pedagogical. Impossible to give him an F: he had not failed. B was for Johnson's stolid mediocrity. He could not be put on the edge of passing with Stettenhover, for he exactly did not pass. In energy and richness of intellect he was perhaps even De Witt's superior, and Howe toyed grimly with the notion of giving him an A, but that would lower the value of the A De Witt had won with his beautiful and clear, if still arrogant, mind. There was a notation which the Registrar recognized—Inc., for Incomplete, and in the horrible comedy of the situation, Howe considered that. But really only a mark of M for Mad would serve.

In his perplexity, Howe sought the Dean, but the Dean was out of town. In the end, he decided to maintain the A-minus he had given Tertan at mid-term. After all, there had been no falling away from that quality. He entered it on the grade sheet with something like bravado.

Academic time moves quickly. A college year is not really a year, lacking as it does three months. And it is endlessly divided into units which, at their beginning, appear larger than they are—terms, half-terms, months, weeks. And the ultimate unit, the hour, is not really an hour, lacking as it does ten minutes. And so the new term advanced rapidly, and one day the fields about the town were all brown, cleared of even the few thin patches of snow which had lingered so long.

Howe, as he lectured on the romantic poets, became conscious of Blackburn emanating wrath. Blackburn did it well, did it with enormous dignity. He did not stir in his seat, he kept his eyes fixed on Howe in perfect attention, but he abstained from using his notebook, there was no mistaking what he proposed to himself as an attitude. His elbow on the writing-wing of the chair, his chin on the curled fingers of his hand, he was the embodiment of intellectual indignation. He was thinking his own thoughts, would give no public offense, yet would claim his due, was not to be intimidated. Howe knew that he would present himself at the end of the hour.

Blackburn entered the office without invitation. He did not smile; there was no cajolery about him. Without invitation he sat down beside Howe's desk. He did not speak until he had taken the blue-book from his pocket. He said, "What does this mean, sir?"

It was a sound and conservative student tactic. Said in the usual way it meant, "How

could you have so misunderstood me?" or "What does this mean for my future in the course?" But there were none of the humbler tones in Blackburn's way of saying it.

Howe made the established reply, "I think that's for you to tell me."

Blackburn continued icy. "I'm sure I can't, sir."

There was a silence between them. Both dropped their eyes to the blue-book on the desk. On its cover Howe had penciled: "F. This is very poor work."

Howe picked up the blue-book. There was always the possibility of injustice. The teacher may be bored by the mass of papers and not wholly attentive. A phrase, even the student's handwriting, may irritate him unreasonably. "Well," said Howe, "Let's go through it."

He opened the first page. "Now here: you write, 'In *The Ancient Mariner*, Coleridge lives in and transports us to a honey-sweet world where all is rich and strange, a world of charm to which we can escape from the humdrum existence of our daily lives, the world of romance. Here, in this warm and honey-sweet land of charming dreams we can relax and enjoy ourselves.' "

Howe lowered the paper and waited with a neutral look for Blackburn to speak. Blackburn returned the look boldly, did not speak, sat stolid and lofty. At last Howe said, speaking gently, "Did you mean that, or were you just at a loss for something to say?"

"You imply that I was just 'bluffing'?" The quotation marks hung palpable in the air about the word.

"I'd like to know. I'd prefer believing that you were bluffing to believing that you really thought this."

Blackburn's eyebrows went up. From the height of a great and firm-based idea he looked at his teacher. He clasped the crags for a moment and then pounced, craftily, suavely. "Do you mean, Doctor Howe, that there aren't two opinions possible?"

It was superbly done in its air of putting all of Howe's intellectual life into the balance. Howe remained patient and simple. "Yes, many opinions are possible, but not this one. Whatever anyone believes of *The Ancient Mariner*, no one can in reason believe that it represents a—a honey-sweet world in which we can relax."

"But that is what I *feel*, sir."

This was well-done, too. Howe said, "Look,

Mr. Blackburn. Do you really relax with hunger and thirst, the heat and the sea-serpents, the dead men with staring eyes, Life in Death and the skeletons? Come now, Mr. Blackburn."

Blackburn made no answer, and Howe pressed forward. "Now, you say of Wordsworth, 'Of peasant stock himself, he turned from the effete life of the salons and found in the peasant the hope of a flaming revolution which would sweep away all the old ideas. This is the subject of his best poems.'"

Beaming at his teacher with youthful eagerness, Blackburn said, "Yes, sir, a rebel, a bringer of light to suffering mankind. I see him as a kind of Prothemeus."

"A kind of what?"

"Prothemeus, sir."

"Think, Mr. Blackburn. We were talking about him only today and I mentioned his name a dozen times. You don't mean Prothemeus. You mean—" Howe waited, but there was no response.

"You mean Prometheus."

Blackburn gave no assent, and Howe took the reins. "You've done a bad job here, Mr. Blackburn, about as bad as could be done." He saw Blackburn stiffen and his genial face harden again. "It shows either a lack of preparation or a complete lack of understanding." He saw Blackburn's face begin to go to pieces and he stopped.

"Oh, sir" Blackburn burst out, "I've never had a mark like this before, never anything below a B, never. A thing like this has never happened to me before."

It must be true, it was a statement too easily verified. Could it be that other instructors accepted such flaunting nonsense? Howe wanted to end the interview. "I'll set it down to lack of preparation," he said. "I know you're busy. That's not an excuse, but it's an explanation. Now, suppose you really prepare, and then take another quiz in two weeks. We'll forget this one and count the other."

Blackburn squirmed with pleasure and gratitude. "Thank you sir. Your're really very kind, very kind."

Howe rose to conclude the visit. "All right, then—in two weeks."

It was that day that the Dean imparted to Howe the conclusion of the case of Tertan. It was simple and a little anti-climatic. A physician had been called in, and had said the word, given the name.

"A classic case, he called it," the Dean said. "Not a doubt in the world," he said. His eyes were full of miserable pity, and he clutched at a word. "A classic case, a classic case." To his aid and to Howe's there came the Parthenon and the form of the Greek drama, the Aristotelian logic, Racine and the Well-Tempered Clavichord, the blueness of the Aegean and its clear sky.[13] Classic—that is to say, without a doubt, perfect in its way, a veritable model, and, as the Dean had been told, sure to take a perfectly predictable and inevitable course to a foreknown conclusion.

It was not only pity that stood in the Dean's eyes. For a moment there was fear too. "Terrible," he said, "it is simply terrible."

Then he went on briskly. "Naturally, we've told the boy nothing. And, naturally, we won't. His tuition's paid by his scholarship, and we'll continue him on the rolls until the end of the year. That will be kindest. After that the matter will be out of our control. We'll see, of course, that he gets into the proper hands. I'm told there will be no change, he'll go on like this, be as good as this, for four to six months. And so we'll just go along as usual."

So Tertan continued to sit in Section 5 of English 1A, to his classmates still a figure of curiously dignified fun, symbol to most of them of the respectable but absurd intellectual life. But to his teacher he was now very different. He had not changed—he was still the greyhound casting[14] for the scent of ideas, and Howe could see that he was still the same Tertan, but he could not feel it. What he felt as he looked at the boy sitting in his accustomed place was the hard blank of a fact. The fact itself was formidable and depressing. But what Howe was chiefly aware of was that he had permitted the metamorphosis of Tertan from person to fact.

As much as possible he avoided seeing Tertan's upraised hand and eager eye. But the fact did not know of its mere factuality, it continued its existence as if it were Tertan, hand up and eye questioning, and one day it appeared in Howe's office with a document.

"Even the spirit who lives egregiously, above the herd, must have its relations with the fellowman," Tertan declared. He laid the document on Howe's desk. It was headed "Quill

---

[13] The Parthenon, the most celebrated example of Doric architecture, is a temple of Athena, built in the fifth century B.C.; Jean Baptiste Racine (1639–1699) was a famous French tragic poet; the *Well-tempered Clavichord* is a series of piano exercises by Johann Sebastian Bach (1685–1750).

[14] Hunting term; searching for a scent or trail.

and Scroll Society of Dwight College. Application for Membership."

"In most ways these are crass minds," Tertan said, touching the paper. "Yet as a whole, bound together in their common love of letters, they transcend their intellectual lacks since it is not a paradox that the whole is greater than the sum of its parts."

"When are the elections?" Howe asked.

"They take place tomorrow."

"I certainly hope you will be successful."

"Thank you. Would you wish to implement that hope?" A rather dirty finger pointed to the bottom of the sheet. "A faculty recommender is necessary," Tertan said stiffly, and waited.

"And you wish me to recommend you?"

"It would be an honor."

"You may use my name."

Tertan's finger pointed again. "It must be a written sponsorship, signed by the sponsor." There was a large blank space on the form under the heading, "Opinion of Faculty Sponsor."

This was almost another thing and Howe hesitated. Yet there was nothing else to do and he took out his fountain pen. He wrote, "Mr. Ferdinand Tertan is marked by his intense devotion to letters and by his exceptional love of all things of the mind." To this he signed his name, which looked bold and assertive on the white page. It disturbed him, the strange affirming power of a name. With a businesslike air, Tertan whipped up the paper, folding it with decision, and put it into his pocket. He bowed and took his departure, leaving Howe with the sense of having done something oddly momentous.

And so much now seemed odd and momentous to Howe that should not have seemed so. It was odd and momentous, he felt, when he sat with Blackburn's second quiz before him, and wrote in an excessively firm hand the grade of C-minus. The paper was a clear, an indisputable failure. He was carefully and consciously committing a cowardice. Blackburn had told the truth when he had pleaded his past record. Howe had consulted it in the Dean's office. It showed no grade lower than a B-minus. A canvass of some of Blackburn's previous instructors had brought vague attestations to the adequate powers of a student imperfectly remembered, and sometimes surprise that his abilities could be questioned at all.

As he wrote the grade, Howe told himself that his cowardice sprang from an unwillingness to have more dealings with a student he disliked. He knew it was simpler than that. He knew he feared Blackburn; that was the absurd truth. And cowardice did not solve the matter after all. Blackburn, flushed with a first success, attacked at once. The minimal passing grade had not assuaged his feelings and he sat at Howe's desk and again the blue-book lay between them. Blackburn said nothing. With an enormous impudence, he was waiting for Howe to speak and explain himself.

At last Howe said sharply and rudely, "Well?" His throat was tense and the blood was hammering in his head. His mouth was tight with anger at himself for his disturbance.

Blackburn's glance was almost baleful. "This is impossible, sir."

"But there it is," Howe answered.

"Sir?" Blackburn had not caught the meaning but his tone was still haughty.

Impatiently Howe said, "There it is, plain as day. Are you here to complain again?"

"Indeed I am, sir." There was surprise in Blackburn's voice that Howe should ask the question.

"I shouldn't complain if I were you. You did a thoroughly bad job on your first quiz. This one is a little, only a very little, better." This was not true. If anything, it was worse.

"That might be a matter of opinion, sir."

"It is a matter of opinion. Of my opinion."

"Another opinion might be different, sir."

"You really believe that?" Howe said.

"Yes." The omission of the "sir" was monumental.

"Whose, for example?"

"The Dean's for example." Then the fleshy jaw came forward a little. "Or a certain literary critic's, for example."

It was colossal and almost too much for Blackburn himself to handle. The solidity of his face almost crumpled under it. But he withstood his own audacity and went on. "And the Dean's opinion might be guided by the knowledge that the person who gave me this mark is the man whom a famous critic, the most eminent judge of literature in this country, called a drunken man. The Dean might think twice about whether such a man is fit to teach Dwight students."

Howe said in quiet admonition, "Blackburn, you're mad," meaning no more than to check the boy's extravagance.

But Blackburn paid no heed. He had another shot in the locker. "And the Dean might be guided by the information, of which I have evidence, documentary evidence,"—he slapped his breast pocket twice—"that this same person personally recommended to the college literary society, the oldest in the country, that he personally recommended a student who is crazy, who threw the meeting into an uproar—a psychiatric case. The Dean might take that into account."

Howe was never to learn the details of that "uproar." He had always to content himself with the dim but passionate picture which at that moment sprang into his mind, of Tertan standing on some abstract height and madly denouncing the multitude of Quill and Scroll who howled him down.

He sat quiet a moment and looked at Blackburn. The ferocity had entirely gone from the student's face. He sat regarding his teacher almost benevolently. He had played a good card and now, scarcely at all unfriendly, he was waiting to see the effect. Howe took up the blue-book and negligently sifted through it. He read a page, closed the book, struck out the C-minus and wrote an F.

"Now you may take the paper to the Dean," he said. "You may tell him that after reconsidering it, I lowered the grade."

The gasp was audible. "Oh, sir!" Blackburn cried. "Please!" His face was agonized. "It means my graduation, my livelihood, my future. Don't do this to me."

"It's done already."

Blackburn stood up. "I spoke rashly, sir, hastily. I had no intention, no real intention, of seeing the Dean. It rests with you—entirely, entirely. I *hope* you will restore the first mark."

"Take the matter to the Dean or not, just as you choose. The grade is what you deserve and it stands."

Blackburn's head dropped. "And will I be failed at mid-term, sir?"

"Of course."

From deep out of Blackburn's great chest rose a cry of anguish. "Oh, sir, if you want me to go down on my knees to you, I will, I will."

Howe looked at him in amazement.

"I will, I will. On my knees, sir. This mustn't, mustn't happen."

He spoke so literally, meaning so very truly that his knees and exactly his knees were involved and seeming to think that he was offering something of tangible value to his teacher, that Howe, whose head had become

icy clear in the nonsensical drama, thought, "The boy is mad," and began to speculate fantastically whether something in himself attracted or developed aberration. He could see himself standing absurdly before the Dean and saying, "I've found another. This time it's the vice-president of the Council, the manager of the debating team and secretary of Quill and Scroll."

One more such discovery, he thought, and he himself would be discovered! And there, suddenly, Blackburn was on his knees with a thump, his huge thighs straining his trousers, his hand outstretched in a great gesture of supplication.

With a cry, Howe shoved back his swivel chair and it rolled away on its casters half across the little room. Blackburn knelt for a moment to nothing at all, then got to his feet.

Howe rose abruptly. He said, "Blackburn, you will stop acting like an idiot. Dust your knees off, take your paper and get out. You've behaved like a fool and a malicious person. You have half a term to do a decent job. Keep your silly mouth shut and try to do it. Now get out."

Blackburn's head was low. He raised it and there was a pious light in his eyes. "Will you shake hands, sir?" he said. He thrust out his hand.

"I will not," Howe said.

Head and hand sank together. Blackburn picked up his blue-book and walked to the door. He turned and said, "Thank you, sir." His back, as he departed, was heavy with tragedy and stateliness.

IV

After years of bad luck with the weather, the College had a perfect day for Commencement. It was wonderfully bright, the air so transparent, the wind so brisk that no one could resist talking about it.

As Howe set out for the campus he heard Hilda calling from the back yard. She called, "Professor, professor," and came running to him.

Howe said, "What's this 'professor' business?"

"Mother told me," Hilda said. "You've been promoted. And I want to take your picture."

"Next year," said Howe. "I won't be a professor until next year. And you know better than to call anybody 'professor.' "

"It was just in fun," Hilda said. She seemed disappointed.

"But you can take my picture if you want. I won't look much different next year." Still, it was frightening. It might mean that he was to stay in this town all his life.

Hilda brightened. "Can I take it in this?" she said, and touched the gown he carried over his arm.

Howe laughed. "Yes, you can take it in this."

"I'll get my things and meet you in front of Otis," Hilda said. "I have the background all picked out."

On the campus the Commencement crowd was already large. It stood about in eager, nervous little family groups. As he crossed, Howe was greeted by a student, capped and gowned, glad of the chance to make an event for his parents by introducing one of his teachers. It was while Howe stood there chatting that he saw Tertan.

He had never seen anyone quite so alone, as though a circle had been woven about him to separate him from the gay crowd on the campus. Not that Tertan was not gay, he was the gayest of all. Three weeks had passed since Howe had last seen him, the weeks of examination, the lazy week before Commencement, and this was now a different Tertan. On his head he wore a panama hat, broad-brimmed and fine, of the shape associated with South American planters. He wore a suit of raw silk, luxurious, but yellowed with age and much too tight, and he sported a whangee cane.[15] He walked sedately, the hat tilted at a devastating angle, the stick coming up and down in time to his measured tread. He had, Howe guessed, outfitted himself to greet the day in the clothes of that ruined father whose existence was on record in the Dean's office. Gravely and arrogantly he surveyed the scene—in it, his whole bearing seemed to say, but not of it. With his haughty step, with his flashing eye, Tertan was coming nearer. Howe did not wish to be seen. He shifted his position slightly. When he looked again, Tertan was not in sight.

The chapel clock struck the quarter hour. Howe detached himself from his chat and hurried to Otis Hall at the far end of the campus. Hilda had not yet come. He went up into the high portico and, using the glass of

[15] Walking stick made from a plant similar to bamboo.

the door for a mirror, put on his gown, adjusted the hood on his shoulders and set the mortarboard on his head. When he came down the steps, Hilda had arrived.

Nothing could have told him more forcibly that a year had passed than the development of Hilda's photographic possessions from the box camera of the previous fall. By a strap about her neck was hung a leather case, so thick and strong, so carefully stitched and so molded to its contents that it could only hold a costly camera. The appearance was deceptive, Howe knew, for he had been present at the Aikens' pre-Christmas conference about its purchase. It was only a fairly good domestic camera. Still, it looked very impressive. Hilda carried another leather case from which she drew a collapsible tripod. Decisively she extended each of its gleaming legs and set it up on the path. She removed the camera from its case and fixed it to the tripod. In its compact efficiency the camera almost had a life of its own, but Hilda treated it with easy familiarity, looked into its eye, glanced casually at its gauges. Then from a pocket she took still another leather case and drew from it a small instrument through which she looked first at Howe, who began to feel inanimate and lost, and then at the sky. She made some adjustment on the instrument, then some adjustment on the camera. She swept the scene with her eye, found a spot and pointed the camera in its direction. She walked to the spot, stood on it and beckoned to Howe. With each new leather case, with each new instrument, and with each new adjustment she had grown in ease and now she said, "Joe, will you stand here?"

Obediently Howe stood where he was bidden. She had yet another instrument. She took out a tape-measure on a mechanical spool. Kneeling down before Howe, she put the little metal ring of the tape under the tip of his shoe. At her request, Howe pressed it with his toe. When she had measured her distance, she nodded to Howe who released the tape. At a touch, it sprang back into the spool. "You have to be careful if you're going to get what you want," Hilda said. "I don't believe in all this snap-snap-snapping," she remarked loftily. Howe nodded in agreement, although he was beginning to think Hilda's care excessive.

Now at last the moment had come. Hilda squinted into the camera, moved the tripod slightly. She stood to the side, holding the plunger of the shutter-cable. "Ready," she said. "Will you relax, Joseph, please?" Howe realized that he was standing frozen. Hilda stood poised and precise as a setter, one hand holding the little cable, the other extended with curled dainty fingers like a dancer's, as if expressing to her subject the precarious delicacy of the moment. She pressed the plunger and there was the click. At once she stirred to action, got behind the camera, turned a new exposure. "Thank you," she said. "Would you stand under that tree and let me do a character study with light and shade?"

The childish absurdity of the remark restored Howe's ease. He went to the little tree. The pattern the leaves made on his gown was what Hilda was after. He had just taken a satisfactory position when he heard in the unmistakable voice, "Ah, Doctor! Having your picture taken?"

Howe gave up the pose and turned to Blackburn who stood on the walk, his hands behind his back, a little too large for his bachelor's gown. Annoyed that Blackburn should see him posing for a character study in light and shade, Howe said irritably, "Yes, having my picture taken."

Blackburn beamed at Hilda. "And the little photographer?" he said. Hilda fixed her eyes on the ground and stood closer to her brilliant and aggressive camera. Blackburn, teetering on his heels, his hands behind his back, wholly prelatical and benignly patient, was not abashed at the silence. At last Howe said, "If you'll excuse us, Mr. Blackburn, we'll go on with the picture."

"Go right ahead, sir. I'm running along." But he only came closer. "Doctor Howe," he said fervently, "I want to tell you how glad I am that I was able to satisfy your standards at last."

Howe was surprised at the hard, insulting brightness of his own voice, and even Hilda looked up curiously as he said, "Nothing you have ever done has satisfied me, and nothing you could ever do would satisfy me, Blackburn."

With a glance at Hilda, Blackburn made a gesture as if to hush Howe—as though all his former bold malice had taken for granted a kind of understanding between himself and his teacher, a secret which must not be betrayed to a third person. "I only meant, sir," he said, "that I was able to pass your course after all."

Howe said, "You didn't pass my course. I passed you out of my course. I passed you without even reading your paper. I wanted to be sure the college would be rid of you. And when all the grades were in and I did read your paper, I saw I was right not to have read it first."

Blackburn presented a stricken face. "It was very bad, sir?"

But Howe had turned away. The paper had been fantastic. The paper had been, if he wished to see it so, mad. It was at this moment that the Dean came up behind Howe and caught his arm. "Hello, Joseph," he said. "We'd better be getting along, it's almost late."

He was not a familiar man, but when he saw Blackburn, who approached to greet him, he took Blackburn's arm, too. "Hello, Theodore," he said. Leaning forward on Howe's arm and on Blackburn's, he said, "Hello, Hilda dear." Hilda replied quietly, "Hello, Uncle George."

Still clinging to their arms, still linking Howe and Blackburn, the Dean said, "Another year gone, Joe, and we've turned out another crop. After you've been here a few years, you'll find it reasonably upsetting—you wonder how there can be so many graduating classes while you stay the same. But of course, you don't stay the same." Then he said, "Well," sharply, to dismiss the thought. He pulled Blackburn's arm and swung him around to Howe. "Have you heard about Teddy Blackburn?" he asked. "He has a job already, before graduation—the first man of his class to be placed." Expectant of congratulations, Blackburn beamed at Howe. Howe remained silent.

"Isn't that good?" the Dean said. Still Howe did not answer and the Dean, puzzled and put out, turned to Hilda. "That's a very fine-looking camera, Hilda." She touched it with affectionate pride.

"Instruments of precision," said a voice. "Instruments of precision." Of the three with joined arms, Howe was the nearest to Tertan, whose gaze took in all the scene except the smile and the nod which Howe gave him. The boy leaned on his cane. The broad-brimmed hat, canting jauntily over his eye, confused the image of his face that Howe had established, suppressed the rigid lines of the ascetic and brought out the baroque curves. It made an effect of preverse majesty.

?

"Instruments of precision," said Tertan for the last time, addressing no one, making a casual comment to the universe. And it occurred to Howe that Tertan might not be referring to Hilda's equipment. The sense of the thrice-woven circle of the boy's loneliness smote him fiercely. Tertan stood in majestic jauntiness, superior to all the scene, but his isolation made Howe ache with a pity of which Tertan was more the cause than the object, so general and indiscriminate was it.

Whether in his sorrow he made some unintended movement toward Tertan which the Dean checked, or whether the suddenly tightened grip on his arm was the Dean's own sorrow and fear, he did not know. Tertan watched them in the incurious way people watch a photograph being taken, and suddenly the thought that, to the boy, it must seem that the three were posing for a picture together made Howe detach himself almost rudely from the Dean's grasp.

"I promised Hilda another picture," he announced—needlessly, for Tertan was no longer there, he had vanished in the last sudden flux of visitors who, now that the band had struck up, were rushing nervously to find seats.

"You'd better hurry," the Dean said. "I'll go along, it's getting late for me." He departed and Blackburn walked stately by his side.

Howe again took his position under the little tree which cast its shadow over his face and gown. "Just hurry, Hilda, won't you?" he said. Hilda held the cable at arm's length, her other arm crooked and her fingers crisped. She rose on her toes and said "Ready," and pressed the release. "Thank you," she said gravely and began to dismantle her camera as he hurried off to join the procession.

The following questions focus on the theme in "Of This Time, of That Place," as an attempt to bring the individual into the social structure.

1 What does the camera symbolize at the beginning of the story? How does Trilling use this symbol at the story's end? What does this suggest about the modern conflict between scientific technology and the individual's struggle to be human? How does the camera reflect the underlying theme of the story?

2 Compare and contrast Tertan and Blackburn:
   a What does Tertan represent to Howe? What does Howe's response to Tertan reflect about his "inner" split? Why does Howe fail to resolve this?
   b What emotions do you detect in Howe regarding his attitude toward Tertan?
   c How does Howe leave Tertan? What does this suggest about the way Howe handles the making of a decision?
   d What does Blackburn represent to Howe? What does Howe's response to Blackburn reflect about his "inner" split? Does Howe resolve this? Explain!
   e What emotions do you detect in Howe regarding his attitude toward Blackburn? What emotions does he repress? What does this suggest?
   f Use the class discussion in the story to interpret Howe's attitude toward his students:
      (1) How does Howe relate to his students?
      (2) What "inner" conflicts emerge in this incident?
      (3) What is Howe's attitude toward power?
      (4) How does Howe view literature? Do his actions affirm or deny what he says? Explain!
      (5) How does Howe differ in this situation from his responses in dealing with the Dean? What does this suggest?

3 What image of education emerges in this story? How does this relate to your educational experiences? Have you ever had a teacher like Howe? Have you ever laughed at a student like Tertan? In what ways would you say that education has molded your concept of individuality? Explain!

Expressing Our Inner Experiences

These archetypes become universal patterns of behavior which may vary greatly in detail but not in basic pattern. C. G. Jung calls them "those images which give psychic contents form in order to express instinctual patterns of behavior." For example, when Oedipus says: "I must know who I am, and where I am from," he speaks of the universal quest found everywhere which expresses the human desire to give purpose and meaning to the life experience. The journey outward to find knowledge is synonymous with the journey inward to understand the self in relation to the world in which one lives. Archetypal images serve as a means to help us understand how the "outer" and "inner" journeys coincide to express what individuals might do so that they are not at variance within themselves. Two of the most common archetypal images to express what lies within us are the anima, the image of the woman who exists within the man, and the animus, the image of the man who exists within the woman.

SYMBOLIC REPRESENTATIONS
OF THE ANIMA

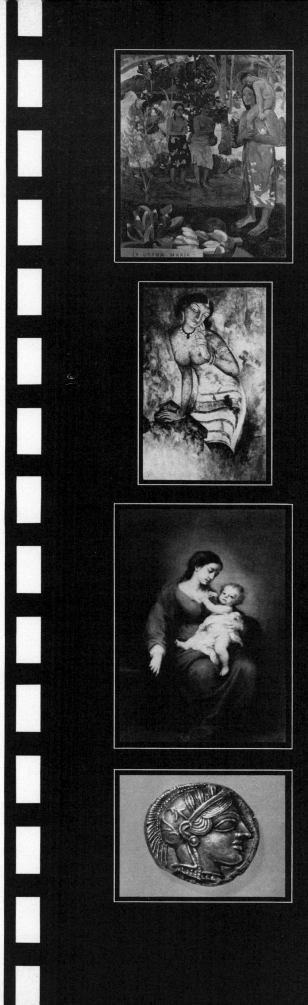

In this painting, Gaughin projects the primitive quality of the anima; the women appear as sensual but without knowledge of their sensual qualities. Eve before the fall is also a representative of this stage of the anima.

In this Ajanta painting we see the second stage of the anima in which the seductive powers of the beautiful woman are depicted. The young woman was sent by her father to lure the young Budda from his place of meditation. This is an archetypal representation of the temptress's use of sensuality as a means to distract the male from moral obligation.

In Murillo's painting of the Virgin and Child, we see the third stage of the anima. This symbolizes the benevolent qualities of the great mother. The dress of the Virgin is red, and this connects her with the eros or passion of the second stage of the anima.

Athena, the Greek goddess, symbolicly represents the fourth stage of the anima. She appears as a wise woman who also acts to save her city. She combines both physical strength and wisdom to blend the ideal qualities of both the anima and animus.

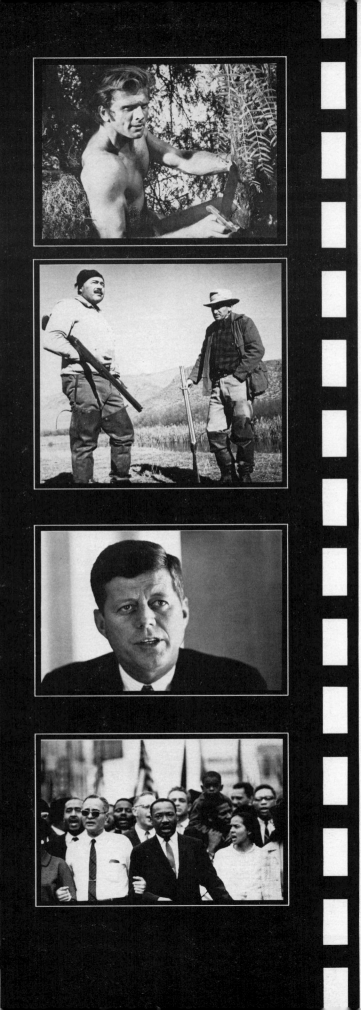

SYMBOLIC REPRESENTATIONS
OF THE ANIMUS

Tarzan is the symbol of the first stage of the animus. He symbolizes the man of physical strength who maintains his life through the development of his animal instincts.

Ernest Hemingway is a symbolic representation of the second stage of the animus. He is the romantic man of adventure who seeks danger in order to define himself as a hero in pursuit of a means to prove his abilities.

John Kennedy would symbolize the third stage of the animus. He represents the political leader who uses language to transform and lead his people to fulfill their destiny.

Martin Luther King symbolizes the fourth stage of the animus. He is the man of action who also searches for spiritual wisdom. At this stage both the spiritual qualities of the anima and the physical qualities of the animus blend to reveal the man who balances both the masculine and feminine within himself.

The Principal Archetypes

C. G. JUNG

The archetypes most clearly characterized from the empirical point of view are those which have the most frequent and the most disturbing influence on the ego. These are the *shadow,* the *anima,* and the *animus.* The most accessible of these, and the easiest to experience, is the shadow, for its nature can in large measure be inferred from the contents of the personal unconscious. The only exceptions to this rule are those rather rare cases where the positive qualities of the personality are repressed, and the ego in consequence plays an essentially negative or unfavorable role.

The shadow is a moral problem that challenges the whole ego personality, for no one can become conscious of the shadow without considerable moral effort. To become conscious of it involves recognizing the dark aspects of the personality as present and real. This act is an essential condition for any kind of self-knowledge, and it therefore, as a rule, meets with considerable resistance. Indeed, self-knowledge as a psychotherapeutic measure frequently requires much painstaking work extending over a long period.

Closer examination of the dark characteristics—that is, the inferiorities constituting the shadow—reveals that they have an *emotional* nature, a kind of *autonomy,* and accordingly an *obsessive* or, better, *possessive* quality. Emotion, incidentally, is not an activity of the individual but something that happens to him. Affects occur usually where adaptation is weakest, and at the same time they reveal the reason for its weakness, namely, a certain de-

gree of inferiority, and the existence of a lower level of personality. On this lower level with its uncontrolled or scarcely controlled emotions one behaves more or less like a primitive, who is not only the passive victim of his affects but also singularly incapable of moral judgment.

Although, with insight and good will, the shadow can to some extent be assimilated into the conscious personality, experience shows that there are certain features which offer the most obstinate resistance to moral control and prove almost impossible to influence. These resistances are usually bound up with *projections,* which are not recognized as such, and their recognition is a moral achievement beyond the ordinary. While some traits peculiar to the shadow can be recognized without too much difficulty as one's own personal qualities, in this case both insight and good will are unavailing because the cause of the emotion appears to lie, beyond all possibility of doubt, in the *other person.* No matter how obvious it may be to the neutral observer that it is a matter of projections, there is little hope that the subject will perceive this himself. He must be convinced that he throws a very long shadow before he is willing to withdraw his emotionally toned projections from their object. . . .

One might assume that projections like these, which are so very difficult if not impossible to dissolve, would belong to the realm of the shadow—that is, to the negative side of the personality. This assumption however becomes untenable after a certain point, because the symbols that then appear no longer refer to the same but to the opposite sex, in a man's case to a woman and vice versa. The source of projections is no longer the shadow—which is always of the same sex as the subject—but a contrasexual figure. Here we meet the *animus*

From "Aion: Contributions to the Symbolism of the Self" [1951] and "Psychological Aspects of the Mother Archetype" [1954], *The Collected Works of C. G. Jung,* translated from the German by R. F. C. Hull, New York, 1959, Vol. IX, part 2, pp. 8–9, 10–13, 13–14, 16, 19–20; part 1, pp. 80–84. Reprinted by permission of the Bollingen Foundation and Routledge & Kegan Paul Ltd.

of a woman and the *anima* of a man, two corresponding archetypes whose autonomy and unconsciousness explain the stubbornness of their projections. Though the shadow is a motif as well known to mythology as anima and animus, it represents first and foremost the personal unconscious, and its content can therefore be made conscious without too much difficulty. In this it differs from anima and animus, for whereas the shadow can be seen through and recognized fairly easily, the anima and animus are much further away from consciousness and in normal circumstances are seldom if ever realized. With a little self-criticism one can see through the shadow—so far as its nature is personal. But when it appears as an archetype, one encounters the same difficulties as with anima and animus. In other words, it is quite within the bounds of possibility for a man to recognize the relative evil of his nature, but it is a rare and shattering experience for him to gaze into the face of absolute evil. . . .

What, then, is this projection-making factor? The East calls it the "Spinning Woman"—Maya, who creates illusion by her dancing. Had we not long since known it from the symbolism of dreams, this hint from the Orient would put us on the right track: the enveloping, embracing, and devouring element points unmistakably to the mother,[1] that is, to the son's relation to the real mother, to her imago, and to the woman who is to become a mother for him. His Eros is passive like a child's; he hopes to be caught, sucked in, enveloped, and devoured. He seeks, as it were, the protecting, nourishing, charmed circle of the mother, the condition of the infant released from every care, in which the outside world bends over him and even forces happiness upon him. No wonder the real world vanishes from sight!

If this situation is dramatized, as the unconscious usually dramatizes it, then there appears before you on the psychological stage a man living regressively, seeking his childhood and his mother, fleeing from a cold cruel world which denies him understanding. Not infrequently a mother appears beside him who apparently shows not the slightest concern that her little son should become a man, but who, with tireless and self-immolating effort, neglects nothing that might hinder him from

[1] Here and in what follows, the word "mother" is not meant in the literal sense but as a symbol of everything that functions as a mother. (author's note)

growing up and marrying. You behold the secret conspiracy between mother and son, and how each helps the other to betray life.

Where does the guilt lie? With the mother, or with the son? Probably with both. The unsatisfied longing of the son for life and the world ought to be taken seriously. There is in him a desire to touch reality, to embrace the earth and fructify the field of the world. But he makes no more than a series of impatient beginnings, for his initiative as well as his staying power are crippled by the secret memory that the world and happiness may be had as a gift —from the mother. It makes demands on the masculinity of a man, on his ardor, above all on his courage and resolution, when it comes to throwing his whole being into the scales. For this he would need a faithless Eros, one capable of forgetting the mother and of hurting himself by deserting the first love of his life. The mother, foreseeing this danger, has carefully inculcated into him the virtues of faithfulness, devotion, loyalty, so as to protect him from the moral disruption which is the risk of every life adventure. He has learned these lessons only too well, and remains true to his mother, perhaps causing her the deepest anxiety (when, in her honor, he turns out to be a homosexual, for example) and at the same time affords her an unconscious satisfaction of a mythological nature, for in the relationship now reigning between them, there is consummated the immemorial and most sacred archetype of the marriage of mother and son.

At this level of the myth, which probably illustrates the nature of the collective unconscious better than any other, the mother is both old and young, Demeter and Persephone, and the son is spouse and sleeping infant all in one. The imperfections of real life, with its laborious adaptations and manifold disappointments, naturally cannot compete with such a state of indescribable fulfillment.

In the case of the son, the projection-making factor is identical with the *mother imago,* and this is consequently taken to be the real mother. The projection can only be dissolved when he comes to realize that in the realm of his psyche there exists an image of the mother and not only of the mother, but also of the daughter, the sister, the beloved, the heavenly goddess, and the earth spirit Baubo. Every mother and every beloved is forced to become the carrier and embodiment of this omnipresent and ageless image which corresponds to the deepest reality in a man. It is his own, this perilous image of Woman; she stands for the loyalty which in the interests of life he cannot always maintain; she is the vital compensation for the risks, struggles, sacrifices which all end in disappointment; she is the solace for all the bitterness of life. Simultaneously, she is the great illusionist, the seductress who draws him into life—not only into its reasonable and useful aspects but into its frightful paradoxes and ambivalences where good and evil, success and ruin, hope and despair counterbalance one another. . . .

The projection-making factor is the anima, or rather the unconscious as represented by the anima. Whenever she appears, in dreams, visions, and fantasies, she takes on personified forms, thus demonstrating that the factor she embodies possesses all the outstanding characteristics of a feminine being. She is not an invention of the conscious mind, but a spontaneous production of the unconscious. Nor is she a substitute figure for the mother. On the contrary, there is every likelihood that the numinous qualities which make the mother imago so dangerously powerful stem from the collective archetype of the anima, which is incarnated anew in every male child.

Since the anima is an archetype that is manifest in men, it is reasonable to suppose that an equivalent archetype must be present in women: for just as the man is compensated by a feminine element, so woman is compensated by a masculine one. . . . Just as the mother seems to be the first carrier of the projection-making factor for the son, so is the father for the daughter. . . . Woman is compensated by a masculine element and therefore her unconscious has, so to speak, a masculine imprint. This results in a considerable psychological difference between men and women, and accordingly I have called the projection-making factor in women the animus, which means reason or spirit. The animus corresponds to the paternal Logos just as the anima corresponds to the maternal Eros. It is far from my intention to give these two intuitive concepts too specific a definition. I use Eros and Logos merely as conceptual aids to describe the fact that woman's consciousness is characterized more by the connective quality of Eros than by the discrimination and cognition associated with Logos. In men, Eros, the function of relationship, is usually less developed than Logos. In women, on the other hand, Eros is an expres-

sion of their true nature, while their Logos is often only a regrettable accident. . . .

Like the anima, the animus too has a positive aspect. Through the figure of the father he expresses not only conventional opinion but—equally—what we call "spirit," philosophical or religious ideas in particular, or rather the attitude resulting from them. Thus the animus is a psychopomp, a mediator between the conscious and the unconscious and a personification of the latter. Just as the anima becomes, through integration, the Eros of consciousness, so the animus becomes a Logos; and in the same way that the anima gives relationship and relatedness to a man's consciousness, the animus gives woman's consciousness a capacity for reflection, deliberation, and self-knowledge. . . .

Not all the contents of the anima and animus are projected, however. Many of them appear spontaneously in dreams and so on, and many more can be made conscious through active imagination. In this way we find that thoughts, feelings, and affects are alive in us which we would never have believed possible in the figures of anima and animus. They personify those of its contents which, when withdrawn from projection, can be integrated into consciousness. To this extent, both figures represent *functions* which filter the contents of the collective unconscious through to the conscious mind. They appear or behave as such, however, only so long as the tendencies of the conscious and unconscious do not diverge too greatly. Should any tension arise, these functions, harmless till then, confront the conscious mind in personified form and behave rather like systems split off from the personality, or like part souls. This comparison is inadequate insofar as nothing previously belonging to the ego personality has split off from it; on the contrary, the two figures represent a disturbing accretion. The reason for their behaving in this way is that though the *contents* of anima and animus can be integrated, they themselves cannot, since they are archetypes. As such they are the foundation stones of the psychic structure, which in its totality exceeds the limits of consciousness and therefore can never become the object of direct cognition. The effects of anima and animus can indeed be made conscious, but they themselves are factors transcending consciousness and beyond the reach of perception and volition.

Like any other archetype, the mother archetype appears under an almost infinite variety of aspects. I mention here only some of the more characteristic. First in importance are the personal mother and grandmother, stepmother and mother-in-law; then any woman with whom a relationship exists, for example, a nurse or governess or perhaps a remote ancestress. Then there are what might be termed mothers in a figurative sense. To this category belongs the goddess, and especially the Mother of God, the Virgin, and Sophia. Mythology offers many variations of the mother archetype, as for instance the mother who reappears as the maiden in the myth of Demeter and Kore; or the mother who is also the beloved, as in the Cybele-Attis myth. Other symbols of the mother in a figurative sense appear in things representing the goal of our longing for redemption, such as Paradise, the Kingdom of God, the Heavenly Jerusalem. Many things arousing devotion or feelings of awe, as for instance the Church, university, city or country, Heaven, Earth, the woods, the sea or any still waters, matter even, the underworld and the moon, can be mother-symbols. The archetype is often associated with things and places standing for fertility and fruitfulness: the cornucopia, a plowed field, a garden. It can be attached to a rock, a cave, a tree, a spring, a deep well, or to various vessels such as the baptismal font, or to vessel-shaped flowers like the rose or the lotus. Because of the protection it implies, the magic circle or mandala can be a form of mother archetype. Hollow objects such as ovens and cooking vessels are associated with the mother archetype, and, of course, the uterus, *yoni,* and anything of a like shape. Added to this list there are many animals, such as the cow, hare, and helpful animals in general.

All these symbols can have a positive, favorable meaning or a negative, evil meaning. An ambivalent aspect is seen in the goddess of fate (Moira, Graeae, Norns). Evil symbols are the witch, the dragon (or any devouring and entwining animal, such as a large fish or a serpent), the grave, the sarcophagus, deep water, death, nightmares and bogies (Empusa, Lilith, etc.). This list is not, of course, complete; it presents only the most important features of the mother archetype.

The qualities associated with it are maternal solicitude and sympathy; the magic authority of the female; the wisdom and spiritual exaltation that transcend reason; any helpful instinct or impulse; all that is benign, all that cherishes and sustains, that fosters growth and fertility. The place of magic transformation and rebirth, together with the underworld and its inhabitants, are presided over by the mother. On the negative side the mother archetype may connote anything secret, hidden, dark; the abyss, the world of the dead, anything that devours, seduces, and poisons, that is terrifying and inescapable like fate. All these attributes of the mother archetype have been fully described and documented in my book *Symbols of Transformation.* There I formulated the ambivalence of these attributes as "the loving and the terrible mother." Perhaps the historical example of the dual nature of the mother most familiar to us is the Virgin Mary, who is not only the Lord's mother, but also, according to the medieval allegories, his cross. In India, "the loving and terrible mother" is the paradoxical Kali. Sankhya philosophy has elaborated the mother archetype into the concept of *prakrti* (matter) and assigned to it the three gunas or fundamental attributes: *sattva, rajas, tamas:* goodness, passion, and darkness. These are three essential aspects of the mother: her cherishing and nourishing goodness, her orgiastic emotionality, and her Stygian depths. The special feature of the philosophical myth, which shows Prakrti dancing before Purusha in order to remind him of "discriminating knowledge," does not belong to the mother archetype but to the archetype of the anima, which in a man's psychology invariably appears, at first, mingled with the mother-image.

Although the figure of the mother as it appears in folklore is more or less universal, this image changes markedly when it appears in the individual psyche. In treating patients one is at first impressed, and indeed arrested, by the apparent significance of the personal mother. This figure of the personal mother looms so large in all personalistic psychologies that, as we know, they never got beyond it, even in theory, to other important etiological factors. My own view differs from that of other medico-psychological theories principally in that I attribute to the personal mother only a limited etiological significance. That is to say, all those influences which the literature describes as being exerted on the children do not come from the mother herself, but rather from the archetype projected upon her, which gives her a mythological background and invests her with authority and numinosity.[2] The etiological and traumatic effects produced by the mother must be divided into two groups: (1) those corresponding to traits of character or attitudes actually present in the mother, and (2) those referring to traits which the mother only seems to possess, the reality being composed of more or less fantastic (i.e., archetypal) projections on the part of the child. Freud himself had already seen that the real etiology of neuroses does not lie in traumatic effects, as he at first suspected, but in a peculiar development of infantile fantasy. This is not to deny that such a development can be traced back to disturbing influences emanating from the mother. I myself make it a rule to look first for the cause of infantile neuroses in the mother, as I know from experience that a child is much more likely to develop normally than neurotically, and that in the great majority of cases definite causes of disturbances can be found in the parents, especially in the mother. The contents of the child's abnormal fantasies can be referred to the personal mother only in part, since they often contain clear and unmistakable allusions which could not possibly have reference to human beings. This is especially true where definitely mythological products are concerned, as is frequently the case in infantile phobias where the mother may appear as a wild beast, a witch, a specter, an ogre, a hermaphrodite, and so on. It must be borne in mind, however, that such fantasies are not always of unmistakably mythological origin, and, even if they are, they may not always be rooted in the unconscious archetype but may have been occasioned by fairy tales or accidental remarks. A thorough investigation is therefore indicated in each case. For practical reasons, such an investigation cannot be made so readily with children as with adults, who almost invariably transfer their fantasies to the physician during treatment—or, to be more precise, the fantasies transfer themselves to him automatically.

When that happens, nothing is gained by brushing them aside as ridiculous, for archetypes are among the inalienable assets of every psyche. They form the "treasure in the realm of shadowy thoughts" of which Kant spoke, and of which we have ample evidence in the countless treasure motifs of mythology. An archetype as such is in no sense just an annoying prejudice; it becomes so only when it is in the wrong place. In themselves, archetypal images are among the highest values of the human psyche; they have peopled the heavens of all races from time immemorial. To discard them as valueless would be a distinct loss. Our task is not, therefore, to deny the archetype, but to dissolve the projections, in order to restore their contents to the individual who has involuntarily lost them by projecting them outside himself.

[2] American psychology can supply us with any amount of examples. A blistering but instructive lampoon on this subject is Philip Wylie's *Generation of Vipers* (New York 1942). (author's note)

?

SYMBOLS OF TRANSFORMATION

This psychic life is the mind of our ancient ancestors, the way in which they thought and felt, the way in which they conceived of life and the world, of gods and human beings. The existence of these historical layers is presumably the source of the belief in reincarnation and in memories of past lives. As the body is a sort of museum of its phylogenetic history, so is the mind. There is no reason for believing that the psyche, with its peculiar structure, is the only thing in the world that has no history beyond its individual manifestation. Even the conscious mind cannot be denied a history extending over at least five thousand years. It is only individual ego-consciousness that has forever a new beginning and an early end. But the unconscious psyche is not only immensely old, it is also able to grow increasingly into an equally remote future. It forms, and is part of, the human species just as much as the body, which is also individually ephemeral, yet collectively of immeasurable duration.

To understand Jung's theory of archetypes, one needs to understand both the personal and collective unconscious. The symbols which reveal the psyche are viewed by Jung as the reconciliation of opposites. Thus to know good is to know evil, or to know the male is to know the female. The following questions are directed toward an understanding of the symbolic process.

1 The shadow: the symbol of the personal unconscious.
   a How does Jung describe the dark side of one's personality?
   b Give examples of the negative part of your personality.
   c How do we attach emotions to images which come from our shadow? What does this suggest about our unconscious?

   d How do we project our negative and positive shadows onto others? How is this form of projection a resistance to self-awareness?

2 The anima: the woman within the man.
   a How does Jung illustrate how the anima appears in the male psyche?
   b What are the images of woman which man seeks to capture?
   c How do men project their anima onto women?
   d What image of woman emerges from a study of *Playboy* magazine?

3 The animus: the man within the woman.
   a How does Jung illustrate how the animus appears in the female psyche?
   b What images of man appear in women?
   c How do women project these images onto men?
   d What image of man emerges from a study of *Cosmopolitan* magazine?

4 The mother archetype.
   a What levels of meaning does Jung attach to the mother archetype?
   b How does one know both the positive and negative aspects of the mother archetype?
   c What is the father archetype?
   d Select one of the creation myths and discuss the mother and father archetypes.

5 How do the animus and the anima appear in dreams?
   a The correlation between dreaming and the motion picture is very close; both project images onto flat surfaces. Select any film and interpret how the anima and animus project a cultural image of male and female.
   b How does Jung see myth as a projection of the collective unconscious? Discuss the implications of this concept.

THE METAMORPHOSIS

FRANZ KAFKA

1

As Gregor Samsa awoke one morning from uneasy dreams he found himself transformed in his bed into a gigantic insect. He was lying on his hard, as it were armor-plated, back and when he lifted his head a little he could see his dome-like brown belly divided into stiff arched segments on top of which the bed quilt could hardly keep in position and was about to slide off completely. His numerous legs, which were pitifully thin compared to the rest of his bulk, waved helplessly before his eyes.

What has happened to me, he thought. It was no dream. His room, a regular human bedroom, only rather too small, lay quiet between the four familiar walls. Above the table on which a collection of cloth samples was unpacked and spread out—Samsa was a commercial traveler—hung the picture which he had recently cut out of an illustrated magazine and put into a pretty gilt frame. It showed a lady, with a fur cap on and a fur stole, sitting upright and holding out to the spectator a huge fur muff into which the whole of her forearm had vanished!

Gregor's eyes turned next to the window, and the overcast sky—one could hear rain drops beating on the window gutter—made him quite melancholy. What about sleeping a little longer and forgetting all this nonsense, he thought, but it could not be done, for he was accustomed to sleep on his right side and in his present condition he could not turn himself over. However violently he forced himself towards his right side he always rolled on his back again. He tried it at least a hundred times, shutting his eyes to keep from seeing his struggling legs, and only desisted when he began to feel in his side a faint dull ache he had never experienced before.

Oh God, he thought, what an exhausting job I've picked on! Traveling about day in, day out. It's much more irritating work than doing the actual business in the office, and on top of that there's the trouble of constant

THE METAMORPHOSIS

traveling, of worrying about train connections, the bed and irregular meals, casual acquaintances that are always new and never become intimate friends. The devil take it all! He felt a slight itching up on his belly; slowly pushed himself on his back nearer to the top of the bed so that he could lift his head more easily; identified the itching place which was surrounded by many small white spots the nature of which he could not understand and made to touch it with a leg, but drew the leg back immediately, for the contact made a cold shiver run through him.

He slid down again into his former position. This getting up early, he thought, makes one quite stupid. A man needs his sleep. Other commercials live like harem women. For instance, when I come back to the hotel of a morning to write up the orders I've got, these others are only sitting down to breakfast. Let me just try that with my chief; I'd be sacked on the spot. Anyhow, that might be quite a good thing for me, who can tell? If I didn't have to hold my hand because of my parents I'd have given notice long ago, I'd have gone to the chief and told him exactly what I think of him. That would knock him endways from his desk! It's a queer way of doing, too, this sitting on high at a desk and talking down to employees, especially when they have to come quite near because the chief is hard of hearing. Well, there's still hope; once I've saved enough money to pay back my parents' debts to him—that should take another five or six years—I'll do it without fail. I'll cut myself completely loose then. For the moment, though, I'd better get up, since my train goes at five.

He looked at the alarm clock ticking on the chest. Heavenly Father! he thought. It was half-past six o'clock and the hands were quietly moving on, it was even past the half-hour, it was getting on toward a quarter to seven. Had the alarm clock not gone off? From the bed one could see that it had been properly set for four o'clock; of course it must have gone off. Yes, but was it possible to sleep quietly through that ear-splitting noise? Well, he had not slept quietly, yet apparently all the more soundly for that. But what was he to do now? The next train went at seven o'clock; to catch that he would need to hurry like mad and his samples weren't even packed up, and he himself wasn't feeling particularly fresh and active. And even if he did catch the train he wouldn't avoid a row with the chief, since the firm's porter would have been waiting for the five o'clock train and would have long since reported his failure to turn up. The porter was a creature of the chief's, spineless and stupid. Well, supposing he were to say he was sick? But that would be most unpleasant and would look suspicious, since during his five years' employment he had not been ill once. The chief himself would be sure to come with the sick-insurance doctor, would reproach his parents with their son's laziness and would cut all excuses short by referring to the insurance doctor, who of course regarded all mankind as perfectly healthy malingerers. And would he be so far wrong on this occasion? Gregor really felt quite well, apart from a drowsiness that was utterly superfluous after such a long sleep, and he was even unusually hungry.

As all this was running through his mind at top speed without his being able to decide to leave his bed—the alarm clock had just struck a quarter to seven—there came a cautious tap at the door behind the head of his bed. "Gregor," said a voice—it was his mother's—"it's a quarter to seven. Hadn't you a train to catch?" That gentle voice! Gregor had a shock as he heard his own voice answering hers, unmistakably his own voice, it was true, but with a persistent horrible twittering squeak behind it like an undertone, that left the words in their clear shape only for the first moment and then rose up reverberating round them to destroy their sense, so that one could not be sure one had heard them rightly. Gregor wanted to answer at length and explain everything, but in the circumstances he confined himself to saying: "Yes, yes, thank you, Mother, I'm getting up now." The wooden door between them must have kept the change in his voice from being noticeable outside, for his mother contented herself with this statement and shuffled away. Yet this brief exchange of words had made the other members of the family aware that Gregor was still in the house, as they had not expected, and at one of the side doors his father was already knocking, gently, yet with his fist. "Gregor, Gregor," he called, "what's the matter with you?" And after a little while he called again in a deeper voice: "Gregor! Gregor!" At the other side door his sister was saying in a low, plaintive tone: "Gregor? Aren't you well? Are you needing anything?" He answered them both at once: "I'm just ready," and did his best to make his voice sound as normal as possible by enunciating the words very clearly and leaving long pauses between them. So his father went back to his breakfast, but his sister whispered: "Gregor, open the door, do." However, he was not thinking of opening the door, and felt thankful for the prudent habit he had acquired in traveling of locking all doors during the night, even at home.

His immediate intention was to get up quietly without being disturbed, to put on his clothes and above all eat his breakfast, and only then to consider what else was to be done, since in bed, he was well aware, his mediations would come to no sensible conclusion. He remembered that often enough in bed he had felt small aches and pains, probably caused by awkward postures, which had proved purely imaginary once he got up, and he looked forward eagerly to seeing this morning's delusions gradually fall away. That the change in his voice was nothing but the precursor of a severe chill, a standing ailment of commercial travelers, he had not the least possible doubt.

To get rid of the quilt was quite easy; he had only to inflate himself a little and it fell off by itself. But the next move was difficult, especially because he was so uncommonly broad. He would have needed arms and hands to hoist himself up; instead he had only the numerous little legs which never stopped waving in all directions and which he could not control in the least. When he tried to bend one of them it was the first to stretch itself straight; and did he succeed at last in making it do what he wanted, all the other legs meanwhile waved the more wildly in a high degree of unpleasant agitation. "But what's the use of lying idle in bed," said Gregor to himself.

He thought that he might get out of bed with the lower part of his body first, but this lower part, which he had not yet seen and of which he could form no clear conception, proved too difficult to move; it shifted so slowly; and when finally, almost wild with annoyance, he gathered his forces together and thrust out recklessly, he had miscalculated the direction and bumped heavily against the lower end of the bed, and the stinging pain he felt informed him that precisely this lower part of his body was at the moment probably the most sensitive.

So he tried to get the top part of himself out first, and cautiously moved his head towards the edge of the bed. That proved easy enough, and despite its breadth and mass the bulk of his body at last slowly followed the movement of his head. Still, when he finally got his head free over the edge of the bed he felt too scared to go on advancing, for after all if he let himself fall in this way it would take a miracle to keep his head from being injured. And at all costs he must not lose consciousness now, precisely now; he would rather stay in bed.

But when after a repetition of the same efforts he lay in his former position again, sighing, and watched his little legs struggling against each other more wildly than ever, if that were possible, and saw no way of bringing any order into this arbitrary confusion, he told himself again that it was impossible to stay in bed and that the most sensible course was to risk everything for the smallest hope of getting away from it. At the same time he did not forget meanwhile to remind himself that cool reflection, the coolest possible, was much better than desperate resolves. In such moments he focused his eyes as sharply as possible on the window, but, unfortunately, the prospect of the morning fog, which muffled even the other side of the narrow street, brought him little encouragement and comfort. "Seven o'clock already," he said to himself when the alarm clock chimed again, "seven o'clock already and still such a thick fog." And for a little while he lay quiet, breathing lightly, as if perhaps expecting such complete repose to restore all things to their real and normal conditions.

But then he said to himself: "Before it strikes a quarter past seven I must be quite out of this bed, without fail. Anyhow, by that time someone will have come from the office to ask for me, since it opens before seven." And he set himself to rocking his whole body at once in a regular rhythm, with the idea of swinging it out of the bed. If he tipped himself out in that way he could keep his head from injury by lifting it at an acute angle when he fell. His back seemed to be hard and was not likely to suffer from a fall on the carpet. His biggest worry was the loud crash he would not be able to help making, which would probably cause anxiety, if not terror, behind all the doors. Still, he must take the risk.

When he was already half out of the bed— the new method was more a game than an effort, for he needed only to hitch himself across by rocking to and fro—it struck him how simple it would be if he could get help. Two strong people—he thought of his father and the servant girl—would be amply sufficient; they would only have to thrust their arms under his convex back, lever him out of the bed, bend down with their burden and then be patient enough to let him turn himself right over on to the floor, where it was to be hoped his legs would then find their proper function. Well, ignoring the fact that the doors were all locked, ought he really to call for help? In spite of his misery he could not suppress a smile at the very idea of it.

He had got so far that he could barely keep his equilibrium when he rocked himself strongly, and he would have to nerve himself very soon for the final decision since in five minutes' time it would be a quarter past seven—when the front door bell rang. "That's someone from the office," he said to himself, and grew almost rigid, while his little legs only jigged about all the faster. For a moment everything stayed quiet. "They're not going to open the door," said Gregor to himself, catching at some kind of irrational hope. But then of course the servant girl went as usual to the door with her heavy tread and opened it. Gregor needed only to hear the first good morning of the visitor to know immediately who it was—the chief clerk himself. What a fate, to be condemned to work for a firm where the smallest omission at once gave rise to the gravest suspicion! Were all employees in a body nothing but scoundrels, was there not among them one single loyal devoted man who, had he wasted only an hour

or so of the firm's time in a morning, was so tormented by conscience as to be driven out of his mind and actually incapable of leaving his bed? Wouldn't it really have been sufficient to send an apprentice to inquire—if any inquiry were necessary at all—did the chief clerk have to come and thus indicate to the entire family, an innocent family, that this suspicious circumstance could be investigated by no one less versed in affairs than himself? And more through the agitation caused by these reflections than through any act of will Gregor swung himself out of bed will all his strength. There was a loud thump, but it was not really a crash. His fall was broken to some extent by the carpet, his back, too, was less stiff than he thought, and so there was merely a dull thud, not so very startling. Only he had not lifted his head carefully enough and had hit it, he turned it and rubbed it on the carpet in pain and irritation.

"That was something falling down in there," said the chief clerk in the next room to the left. Gregor tried to suppose to himself that something like what had happened to him today might some day happen to the chief clerk; one really could not deny that it was possible. But as if in brusque reply to this supposition the chief clerk took a couple of firm steps in the next-door room and his patent leather boots creaked. From the right-hand room his sister was whispering to inform him of the situation: "Gregor, the chief clerk's here." "I know," muttered Gregor to himself; but he didn't dare to make his voice loud enough for his sister to hear it.

"Gregor," said his father now from the left-hand room "the chief clerk has come and wants to know why you didn't catch the early train. We don't know what to say to him. Besides, he wants to talk to you in person. So open the door, please. He will be good enough to excuse the untidiness of your room." "Good morning, Mr. Samsa," the chief clerk was calling amiably meanwhile. "He's not well," said his mother to the visitor, while his father was still speaking through the door, "he's not well, sir, believe me. What else would make him miss a train! The boy thinks about nothing but his work. It makes me almost cross the way he never goes out in the evenings; he's been here the last eight days and has stayed at home every single evening. He just sits there quietly at the table reading a newspaper or looking through railway timetables. The only amusement he gets is doing fretwork. For instance, he spent two or three evenings cutting out a little picture frame; you would be surprised to see how pretty it is; it's hanging in his room; you'll see it in a minute when Gregor opens the door. I must say I'm glad you've come, sir; we should never have got him to unlock the door by ourselves; he's so obstinate; and I'm sure he's unwell, though he wouldn't have it to be so this morning." "I'm just coming," said Gregor slowly and carefully, not moving an inch for fear of losing one word of the conversation. "I can't think of any other explanation, madam," said the chief clerk, "I hope it's nothing serious. Although on the other hand I must say that we men of business—fortunately or unfortunately—very often simply have to ignore any slight indisposition, since business must be attended to." "Well, can the chief clerk come in now?" asked Gregor's father impatiently, again knocking on the door. "No," said Gregor. In the left-hand room a painful silence followed this refusal, in the right-hand room his sister began to sob.

Why didn't his sister join the others? She was probably newly out of bed and hadn't even begun to put on her clothes yet. Well, why was she crying? Because he wouldn't get up and let the chief clerk in, because he was in danger of losing his job, and because the chief would begin dunning his parents again for the old debts? Surely these were things one didn't need to worry about for the present. Gregor was still at home and not in the least thinking of deserting the family. At the moment, true, he was lying on the carpet and no one who knew the condition he was in could seriously expect him to admit the chief clerk. But for such a small discourtesy, which could plausibly be explained away somehow later on, Gregor could hardly be dismissed on the spot. And it seemed to Gregor that it would be much more sensible to leave him in peace for the present than to trouble him with tears and entreaties. Still, of course, their uncertainty bewildered them all and excused their behavior.

"Mr. Samsa," the chief clerk called now in a louder voice, "what's the matter with you? Here you are, barricading yourself in your room, giving only 'yes' and 'no' for answers, causing your parents a lot of unnecessary trouble and neglecting—I mention this only in passing—neglecting your business duties in an incredible fashion. I am speaking here in the name of your parents and of your chief, and I beg you quite seriously to give me an immediate and precise explanation. You amaze me, you amaze me. I thought you were a quiet, dependable person, and now all at once you seem bent on making a disgraceful exhibition of yourself. The chief did hint to me early this morning a possible explanation of your disappearance—with reference to the cash payments that were entrusted to you recently—but I almost pledged my solemn word of honor that this could not be so. But now that I see how incredibly obstinate you are, I no longer have the slightest desire to take your part at all. And your position in the firm is not so unassailable. I came with the intention of telling you all this in private, but since you are wasting my time so needlessly I don't see why your parents shouldn't hear it too. For some time past your work has been most unsatisfactory; this is not the season of the year for a business boom, we admit that, but a season of the year for doing no business at all, that does not exist, Mr. Samsa, must not exist."

"But, sir," cried Gregor, beside himself and in his agitation forgetting everything else, "I'm just going to open the door this very minute. A slight illness, an attack of giddiness, has kept me from getting up. I'm still lying in bed. But I feel all right again. I'm getting out of bed now. Just give me a moment or two longer! I'm not quite so well as I thought. But I'm all right, really. How a thing like that can suddenly strike one down! Only last night I was quite well, my parents can tell you, or rather I did have a slight presentiment. I must have showed some sign of it. Why didn't I report it at the office! But one always thinks that an indisposition can be got over without staying in the house. Oh sir, do spare my parents! All that you're reproaching me with now has no foundation; no one has ever said a word to me about it. Perhaps you haven't looked at the last orders I sent in. Anyhow, I can still catch the eight o'clock train, I'm much the better for my few hours' rest. Don't let me detain you here, sir; I'll be attending to business very soon, and do be good enough to tell the chief so and to make my excuses to him!"

And while all this was tumbling out pell-mell and Gregor hardly knew what he was saying, he had reached the chest quite easily, perhaps because of the practice he had had in bed, and was now trying to lever himself upright by means of it. He meant actually to open the door, actually to show himself and speak to the chief clerk; he was eager to find out what the others, after all their insistence, would say at the sight of him. If they were horrified then the responsibility was no longer his and he could stay quiet. But if they took it calmly, then he had no reason either to be upset, and could really get to the station for the eight o'clock train if he hurried. At first he slipped down a few times from the polished surface of the chest, but at length with a last heave he stood upright; he paid no more attention to the pains in the lower part of his body, however they smarted. Then he let himself fall against the back of a near-by chair, and clung with his little legs to the edges of it. That brought him into control of himself again and he stopped speaking, for now he could listen to what the chief clerk was saying.

"Did you understand a word of it?" the chief clerk was asking; "surely he can't be trying to make fools of us?" "Oh dear," cried his mother, in tears, "perhaps he's terribly ill and we're tormenting him. Grete! Grete!" she called out then. "Yes Mother?" called his sister from the other side. They were calling to each other across Gregor's room. "You must go this minute for the doctor. Gregor is ill. Go for the doctor, quick. Did you hear how he was speaking?" "That was no human voice," said the chief clerk in a voice noticeably low beside the shrillness of the mother's. "Anna! Anna!" his father was calling through the hall to the kitchen, clapping his hands, "get a locksmith at once!" And the two girls were already running through the hall with a swish of skirts—how could his sister have got dressed so quickly?—and were tearing the front door open. There was no sound of its closing again; they had evidently left it open, as one does in houses where some great misfortune has happened.

But Gregor was now much calmer. The words he uttered were no longer understandable, apparently, although they seemed clear enough to him, even clearer than before, perhaps because his ear had grown accustomed to the sound of them. Yet at any rate people now believed that something was wrong with him, and were ready to help him. The positive certainty with which these first measures had been taken comforted him. He felt himself drawn once more into the human circle and hoped for great and remarkable results from both the doctor and the locksmith, without really distinguishing precisely between them.

To make his voice as clear as possible for the decisive conversation that was now imminent he coughed a little, as quietly as he could, of course, since this noise too might not sound like a human cough for all he was able to judge. In the next room meanwhile there was complete silence. Perhaps his parents were sitting at the table with the chief clerk, whispering, perhaps they were all leaning against the door and listening.

Slowly Gregor pushed the chair towards the door, then let go of it, caught hold of the door for support—the soles at the end of his little legs were somewhat sticky—and rested against it for a moment after his efforts. Then he set himself to turning the key in the lock with his mouth. It seemed, unhappily, that he hadn't really any teeth—what could he grip the key with?—but on the other hand his jaws were certainly very strong; with their help he did manage to set the key in motion, heedless of the fact that he was undoubtedly damaging them somewhere, since a brown fluid issued from his mouth, flowed over the key and dripped on the floor. "Just listen to that," said the chief clerk next door; "he's turning the key." That was a great encouragement to Gregor; but they should all have shouted encouragement to him, his father and mother too. "Go on, Gregor," they should have called out, "keep going, hold on to that key!" And in the belief that they were all following his efforts intently, he clenched his jaws recklessly on the key with all the force at his command. As the turning of the key progressed he circled round the lock, holding on now only with his mouth, pushing on the key, as required, or pulling it down again with all the weight of his body. The louder click of the finally yielding lock literally quickened Gregor. With a deep breath of relief he said to himself: "So I didn't need the locksmith," and laid his head on the handle to open the door wide.

Since he had to pull the door towards him, he was still invisible when it was really wide open. He had to edge himself slowly round the near half of the double door, and to do it very carefully if he was not to fall plump upon his back just on the threshold. He was still carrying out his difficult manoeuvre, with no time to observe anything else, when he heard the chief clerk utter a loud "Oh!"—it sounded like a gust of wind—and now he could see the man, standing as he was nearest to the door, clapping one hand before his open mouth and slowly backing away as if driven by some invisible steady pressure. His mother—in spite of the chief clerk's being there her hair was still undone and sticking up in all directions—first clasped her hands and looked at his father, then took two steps toward Gregor and fell on the floor among her outspread skirts, her face quite hidden on her breast. His father knotted his fist with a fierce expression on his face as if he meant to knock Gregor back into his room, then looked uncertainly round the living room, covered his eyes with his hands and wept till his great chest heaved.

Gregor did not go now into the living room, but leaned against the inside of the firmly shut wing of the door, so that only half his body was visible and his head above it bending sideways to look at the others. The light had meanwhile strengthened; on the other side of the street one could see clearly a section of the endlessly long, dark gray building opposite—it was a hospital—abruptly punctuated by its row of regular windows; the rain was still falling, but only in large singly discernible and literally singly splashing drops. The breakfast dishes were set out on the table lavishly, for breakfast was the most important meal of the day to Gregor's father, who lingered it out for hours over various newspapers. Right opposite Gregor on the wall hung a photograph of himself on military service, as a lieutenant, hand on sword, a carefree smile on his face, inviting one to respect his uniform and military bearing. The door leading to the hall was open, and one could see that the front door stood open too, showing the landing beyond and the beginning of the stairs going down.

"Well," said Gregor, knowing perfectly that he was the only one who had retained any composure, "I'll put my clothes on at once, pack up my samples and start off. Will you only let me go? You see, sir, I'm not obstinate, and I'm willing to work; traveling is a hard life, but I couldn't live without it. Where are you going, sir? To the office? Yes? Will you give a true account of all this? One can be temporarily incapacitated, but that's just the moment for remembering former services and bearing in mind that later on, when the incapacity has been got over, one will certainly work with all the more industry and concentration. I'm loyally bound to serve the chief, you know that very well. Besides, I have to provide for my parents and my sister. I'm in great difficulties,

but I'll get out of them again. Don't make things any worse for me than they are. Stand up for me in the firm. Travelers are not popular there, I know. People think they earn sacks of money and just have a good time. A prejudice there's no particular reason for revising. But you, sir, have a more comprehensive view of affairs than the rest of the staff, yes, let me tell you in confidence, a more comprehensive view than the chief himself, who, being the owner, lets his judgment easily be swayed against one of his employees. And you know very well that the traveler, who is never seen in the office almost the whole year round, can so easily fall a victim to gossip and ill luck and unfounded complaints, which he mostly knows nothing about, except when he comes back exhausted from his rounds, and only then suffers in person from their evil consequences, which he can no longer trace back to the original causes. Sir, sir, don't go away without a word to me to show that you think me in the right at least to some extent!"

But at Gregor's very first words the chief clerk had already backed away and only stared at him with parted lips over one twitching shoulder. And while Gregor was speaking he did not stand still one moment but stole away towards the door, without taking his eyes off Gregor, yet only an inch at a time, as if obeying some secret injunction to leave the room. He was already at the hall, and the suddenness with which he took his last step out of the living room would have made one believe he had burned the sole of his foot. Once in the hall he stretched his right arm before him towards the staircase, as if some supernatural power were waiting there to deliver him.

Gregor perceived that the chief clerk must on no account be allowed to go away in this frame of mind if his position in the firm were not to be endangered to the utmost. His parents did not understand this so well; they had convinced themselves in the course of years that Gregor was settled for life in this firm, and besides they were so preoccupied with their immediate troubles that all foresight had forsaken them. Yet Gregor had this foresight. The chief clerk must be detained, soothed, persuaded and finally won over; the whole future of Gregor and his family depended on it! If only his sister had been there! She was intelligent; she had begun to cry while Gregor was still lying quietly on his back. And no doubt the chief clerk, so partial to ladies, would have been guided by her; she would have shut the door of the flat and in the hall talked him out of his horror. But she was not there, and Gregor would have to handle the situation himself. And without remembering that he was still unaware what powers of movement he possessed, without even remembering that his words in all possibility, indeed in all likelihood, would again be unintelligible, he let go the wing of the door, pushed himself through the opening, started to walk towards the chief clerk, who was already ridiculously clinging with both hands to the railing of the landing; but immediately, as he was feeling for support, he fell down with a little cry upon all his numerous legs. Hardly was he down when he experienced for the first time this morning a sense of physical comfort; his legs had firm ground under them; they were completely obedient, as he noted with joy; they even strove to carry him forward in whatever direction he chose; and he was inclined to believe that a final relief from all his sufferings was at hand. But in the same moment as he found himself on the floor, rocking with suppressed eagerness to move, not far from his mother, indeed just in front of her, she, who had seemed so completely crushed, sprang all at once to her feet, her arms and fingers outspread, cried: "Help, for God's sake, help!" bent her head down as if to see Gregor better, yet on the contrary kept backing senselessly away; had quite forgotten that the laden table stood behind her; sat upon it hastily, as if in absence of mind, when she bumped into it; and seemed altogether unaware that the big coffee pot beside her was upset and pouring coffee in a flood over the carpet.

"Mother, Mother," said Gregor in a low voice, and looked up at her. The chief clerk, for the moment, had quite slipped from his mind; instead, he could not resist snapping his jaws together at the sight of the streaming coffee. That made his mother scream again, she fled from the table and fell into the arms of his father, who hastened to catch her. But Gregor had now no time to spare for his parents; the chief clerk was already on the stairs; with his chin on the banister he was taking one last backward look. Gregor made a spring, to be as sure as possible of overtaking him; the chief clerk must have divined his intention, for he leaped down several steps and vanished; he was still yelling "Ugh!" and it echoed through the whole staircase.

Unfortunately, the flight of the chief clerk seemed completely to upset Gregor's father, who had remained relatively calm until now, for instead of running after the man himself, or at least not hindering Gregor in his pursuit, he seized in his right hand the walking stick which the chief clerk had left behind on a chair, together with a hat and greatcoat, snatched in his left hand a large newspaper from the table and began stamping his feet and flourishing the stick and the newspaper to drive Gregor back into his room. No entreaty of Gregor's availed, indeed no entreaty was even understood, however humbly he bent his head his father only stamped on the floor the more loudly. Behind his father his mother had torn open a window, despite the cold weather, and was leaning far out of it with her face in her hands. A strong draught set in from the street to the staircase, the window curtains blew in, the newspapers on the table fluttered, stray pages whisked over the floor. Pitilessly Gregor's father drove him back, hissing and crying "Shoo!" like a savage. But Gregor was quite unpracticed in walking backwards, it really was a slow business. If he had only had a chance to turn round he could get back to his room at once, but he was afraid of exasperating his father by the slowness of such a rotation and at any moment the stick in his father's hand might hit him a fatal blow on the back or on the head. In the end, however, nothing else was left for him to do since to his horror he observed that in moving backwards he could not even control the direction he took; and so, keeping an anxious eye on his father all the time over his shoulder, he began to turn round as quickly as he could, which was in reality very slowly. Perhaps his father noted his good intentions, for he did not interfere except every now and then to help him in the manoeuvre from a distance with the point of the stick. If only he would have stopped making that unbearable hissing noise! It made Gregor quite lose his head. He had turned almost completely round when the hissing noise so distracted him that he even turned a little the wrong way again. But when at last his head was fortunately right in front of the doorway, it appeared that his body was too broad simply to get through the opening. His father, of course, in his present mood was far from thinking of such a thing as opening the other half of the door, to let Gregor have enough space. He had merely the fixed idea of driving Gregor back into his room as quickly as possible. He would never have suffered Gregor to make the circumstantial preparations for standing up on end and perhaps slipping his way through the door. Maybe he was now making more noise than ever to urge Gregor forward, as if no obstacle impeded him; to Gregor, anyhow, the noise in his rear sounded no longer like the voice of one single father; this was really no joke, and Gregor thrust himself—come what might—into the doorway. One side of his body rose up, he was tilted at an angle in the doorway, his flank was quite bruised, horrid blotches stained the white door, soon he was stuck fast and, left to himself, could not have moved at all, his legs on one side fluttered trembling in the air, those on the other were crushed painfully to the floor—when from behind his father gave him a strong push which was literally a deliverance and he flew far into the room, bleeding freely. The door was slammed behind him with the stick, and then at last there was silence.

2

Not until it was twilight did Gregor awake out of a deep sleep, more like a swoon than a sleep. He would certainly have waked up of his own accord not much later, for he felt himself sufficiently rested and well-slept, but it seemed to him as if a fleeting step and a cautious shutting of the door leading into the hall had aroused him. The electric lights in the street cast a pale sheen here and there on the ceiling and the upper surfaces of the furniture, but down below, where he lay, it was dark. Slowly, awkwardly trying out his feelers which he now first learned to appreciate, he pushed his way to the door to see what had been happening there. His left side felt like one single long, unpleasantly tense scar, and he had actually to limp on his two rows of legs. One little leg, moreover, had been severely damaged in the course of that morning's events—it was almost a miracle that only one had been damaged—and trailed uselessly behind him.

He had reached the door before he discovered what had really drawn him to it: the smell of food. For there stood a basin filled with fresh milk in which floated little sops of white bread. He could almost have laughed with joy, since he was now still hungrier than in the morning, and he dipped his head almost over the eyes straight into the milk. But soon in dis-

appointment he withdrew it again; not only did he find it difficult to feed because of his tender left side—and he could only feed with the palpitating collaboration of his whole body—he did not like the milk either, although milk had been his favorite drink and that was certainly why his sister had set it there for him, indeed it was almost with repulsion that he turned away from the basin and crawled back to the middle of the room.

He could see through the crack of the door that the gas was turned on in the living room, but while usually at this time his father made a habit of reading the afternoon newspaper in a loud voice to his mother and occasionally to his sister as well, not a sound was now to be heard. Well, perhaps his father had recently given up the habit of reading aloud, which his sister had mentioned so often in conversation and in her letters. But there was the same silence all around, although the flat was certainly not empty of occupants. "What a quiet life our family has been leading," said Gregor to himself, and as he sat there motionless staring into the darkness he felt great pride in the fact that he had been able to provide such a life for his parents and sister in such a fine flat. But what if all the quiet, the comfort, the contentment were now to end in horror? To keep himself from being lost in such thoughts Gregor took refuge in movement and crawled up and down the room.

Once during the long evening one of the side doors was opened a little and quickly shut again, later the other side door too; someone had apparently wanted to come in and then thought better of it. Gregor now stationed himself immediately before the living room door, determined to persuade any hesitating visitor to come in or at least to discover who it might be; but the door was not opened again and he waited in vain. In the early morning, when the doors were locked, they had all wanted to come in, now that he had opened one door and the other had apparently been opened during the day, no one came in and even the keys were on the other side of the doors.

It was late at night before the gas went out in the living room, and Gregor could easily tell that his parents and his sister had all stayed awake until then, for he could clearly hear the three of them stealing away on tiptoe. No one was likely to visit him, not until the morning, that was certain; so he had plenty of time to meditate at his leisure on how he was to arrange his life afresh. But the lofty, empty room in which he had to lie flat on the floor filled him with an apprehension he could not account for, since it had been his very own room for the past five years—and with a half-unconscious action, not without a slight feeling of shame, he scuttled under the sofa, where he felt comfortable at once, although his back was a little cramped and he could not lift his head up, and his only regret was that his body was too broad to get the whole of it under the sofa.

He stayed there all night, spending the time partly in a light slumber, from which his hunger kept waking him up with a start, and partly in worrying and sketching vague hopes, which all led to the same conclusion, that he must lie low for the present and, by exercising patience and the utmost consideration, help the family to bear the inconvenience he was bound to cause them in his present condition.

Very early in the morning, it was still almost night, Gregor had the chance to test the strength of his new resolutions, for his sister, nearly fully dressed, opened the door from the hall and peered in. She did not see him at once, yet when she caught sight of him under the sofa—well, he had to be somewhere, he couldn't have flown away, could he?—she was so startled that without being able to help it she slammed the door shut again. But as if regretting her behavior she opened the door again immediately and came in on tiptoe, as if she were visiting an invalid or even a stranger. Gregor had pushed his head forward to the very edge of the sofa and watched her. Would she notice that he had left the milk standing, and not for lack of hunger, and would she bring in some other kind of food more to his taste? If she did not do it of her own accord, he would rather starve than draw her attention to the fact, although he felt a wild impulse to dart out from under the sofa, throw himself at her feet and beg her for something to eat. But his sister at once noticed, with surprise, that the basin was still full, except for a little milk that had been spilt all around it, she lifted it immediately, not with her bare hands, true, but with a cloth and carried it away. Gregor was wildly curious to know what she would bring instead, and made various speculations about it. Yet what she actually did next, in the goodness of her heart, he could never have guessed at. To find out what he liked she brought him a whole selection of food, all set

out on an old newspaper. There were old, half-decayed vegetables, bones from last night's supper covered with a white sauce that had thickened; some raisins and almonds; a piece of cheese that Gregor would have called uneatable two days ago; a dry roll of bread, a buttered roll, and a roll both buttered and salted. Besides all that, she set down again the same basin, into which she had poured some water, and which was apparently to be reserved for his exclusive use. And with fine tact, knowing that Gregor would not eat in her presence, she withdrew quickly and even turned the key, to let him understand that he could take his ease as much as he liked. Gregor's legs all whizzed towards the food. His wounds must have healed completely, moreover, for he felt no disability, which amazed him and made him reflect how more than a month ago he had cut one finger a little with a knife and had still suffered pain from the wound only the day before yesterday. Am I less sensitive now? he thought, and sucked greedily at the cheese, which above all the other edibles attracted him at once and strongly. One after another and with tears of satisfaction in his eyes he quickly devoured the cheese, the vegetables and the sauce; the fresh food, on the other hand, had no charms for him, he could not even stand the smell of it and actually dragged away to some little distance the things he could eat. He had long finished his meal and was only lying lazily on the same spot when his sister turned the key slowly as a sign for him to retreat. That roused him at once, although he was nearly asleep, and he hurried under the sofa again. But it took considerable self-control for him to stay under the sofa, even for the short time his sister was in the room, since the large meal had swollen his body somewhat and he was so cramped he could hardly breathe. Slight attacks of breathlessness afflicted him and his eyes were starting a little out of his head as he watched his unsuspecting sister sweeping together with a broom not only the remains of what he had eaten but even the things he had not touched, as if these were now of no use to anyone, and hastily shoveling it all into a bucket, which she covered with a wooden lid and carried away. Hardly had she turned her back when Gregor came from under the sofa and stretched and puffed himself out.

In this manner Gregor was fed, once in the early morning while his parents and the servant girl were still asleep, and a second time after they had all had their midday dinner, for then his parents took a short nap and the servant girl could be sent out on some errand or other by his sister. Not that they would have wanted him to starve, of course, but perhaps they could not have borne to know more about his feeding than from hearsay, perhaps too his sister wanted to spare them such little anxieties wherever possible, since they had quite enough to bear as it was.

Under what pretext the doctor and the locksmith had been got rid of on that first morning Gregor could not discover, for since what he said was not understood by the others it never struck any of them, not even his sister, that he could understand what they said, and so whenever his sister came into his room he had to content himself with hearing her utter only a sigh now and then and an occasional appeal to the saints. Later on, when she had got a little used to the situation—of course she could never get completely used to it—she sometimes threw out a remark which was kindly meant or could be so interpreted. "Well, he liked his dinner today," she would say when Gregor had made a good clearance of his food; and when he had not eaten, which gradually happened more and more often, she would say almost sadly: "Everything's been left standing again."

But although Gregor could get no news directly, he overheard a lot from the neighboring rooms, and as soon as voices were audible, he would run to the door of the room concerned and press his whole body against it. In the first few days especially there was no conversation that did not refer to him somehow, even if only indirectly. For two whole days there were family consultations at every mealtime about what should be done; but also between meals the same subject was discussed, for there were always at least two members of the family at home, since no one wanted to be alone in the flat and to leave it quite empty was unthinkable. And on the very first of these days the household cook—it was not quite clear what and how much she knew of the situation—went down on her knees to his mother and begged leave to go, and when she departed, a quarter of an hour later, gave thanks for her dismissal with tears in her eyes as if for the greatest benefit that could have been conferred on her, and without any prompting swore a solemn oath that she would never say a single word to anyone about what had happened.

Now Gregor's sister had to cook too, helping her mother; true, the cooking did not amount to much, for they ate scarcely anything. Gregor was always hearing one of the family vainly urging another to eat and getting no answer but: "Thanks, I've had all I want," or something similar. Perhaps they drank nothing either. Time and again his sister kept asking his father if he wouldn't like some beer and offered kindly to go and fetch it herself, and when he made no answer suggested that she could ask the concierge to fetch it, so that he need feel no sense of obligation, but then a round "No" came from his father and no more was said about it.

In the course of that very first day Gregor's father explained the family's financial position and prospects to both his mother and his sister. Now and then he rose from the table to get some voucher or memorandum out of the small safe he had rescued from the collapse of his business five years earlier. One could hear him opening the complicated lock and rustling papers out and shutting it again. This statement made by his father was the first cheerful information Gregor had heard since his imprisonment. He had been of the opinion that nothing at all was left over from his father's business, at least his father had never said anything to the contrary, and of course he had not asked him directly. At that time Gregor's sole desire was to do his utmost to help the family to forget as soon as possible the catastrophe which had overwhelmed the business and thrown them all into a state of complete despair. And so he had set to work with unusual ardor and almost overnight had become a commercial traveler instead of a little clerk, with of course much greater chances of earning money, and his success was immediately translated into good round coin which he could lay on the table for his amazed and happy family. These had been fine times, and they had never recurred, at least not with the same sense of glory, although later on Gregor had earned so much money that he was able to meet the expenses of the whole household and did so. They had simply got used to it, both the family and Gregor; the money was gratefully accepted and gladly given, but there was no special uprush of warm feeling. With his sister alone had he remained intimate, and it was a secret plan of his that she, who loved music, unlike himself, and could play movingly on the violin, should be sent next year to study at the Conservatorium, despite the great expense that would entail, which must be made up in some other way. During his brief visits home the Conservatorium was often mentioned in the talks he had with his sister, but always merely as a beautiful dream which could never come true, and his parents discouraged even these innocent references to it; yet Gregor had made up his mind firmly about it and meant to announce the fact with due solemnity on Christmas Day.

Such were the thoughts, completely futile in his present condition, that went through his head as he stood clinging upright to the door and listening. Sometimes out of sheer weariness he had to give up listening and let his head fall negligently against the door, but he always had to pull himself together again at once, for even the slight sound his head made was audible next door and brought all conversation to a stop. "What can he be doing now?" his father would say after a while, obviously turning towards the door, and only then would the interrupted conversation gradually be set going again.

Gregor was now informed as amply as he could wish—for his father tended to repeat himself in his explanations, partly because it was a long time since he had handled such matters and partly because his mother could not always grasp things at once—that a certain amount of investments, a very small amount it was true, had survived the wreck of their fortunes and had even increased a little because the dividends had not been touched meanwhile. And besides that, the money Gregor brought home every month—he had kept only a few dollars for himself—had never been quite used up and now amounted to a small capital sum. Behind the door Gregor nodded his head eagerly, rejoiced at this evidence of unexpected thrift and foresight. True, he could really have paid off some more of his father's debts to the chief with this extra money, and so brought much nearer the day on which he could quit his job, but doubtless it was better the way his father had arranged it.

Yet this capital was by no means sufficient to let the family live on the interest of it; for one year, perhaps, or at the most two, they could live on the principal, that was all. It was simply a sum that ought not to be touched and should be kept for a rainy day; money for living expenses would have to be earned. Now his father was still hale enough but an old man, and he had done no work for the past five years and could not be expected to do much; during these five years, the first years of leisure in his laborious though unsuccessful life, he had grown rather fat and become sluggish. And Gregor's old mother, how was she to earn a living with her asthma, which troubled her even when she walked through the flat and kept her lying on a sofa every other day panting for breath beside an open window? And was his sister to earn her bread, she who was still a child of seventeen and whose life hitherto had been so pleasant, consisting as it did in dressing herself nicely, sleeping long, helping in the housekeeping, going out to a few modest entertainments and above all playing the violin? At first whenever the need for earning money was mentioned Gregor let go of his hold on the door and threw himself down on the cool leather sofa beside it, he felt so hot with shame and grief.

Often he just lay there the long nights through without sleeping at all, scrabbling for hours on the leather. Or he nerved himself to the great effort of pushing an armchair to the window, then crawled up over the window sill and, braced against the chair, leaned against the window panes, obviously in some recollection of the sense of freedom that looking out of a window always used to give him. For in reality day by day things that were even a little way off were growing dimmer to his sight; the hospital across the street, which he used to execrate for being all too often before his eyes, was now quite beyond his range of vision, and if he had not known that he lived in Charlotte Street, a quiet street but still a city street, he might have believed that his window gave on a desert waste where gray sky and gray land blended indistinguishably into each other. His quick-witted sister only needed to observe twice that the armchair stood by the window; after that whenever she had tidied the room she always pushed the chair back to the same place at the window and even left the inner casements open.

If he could have spoken to her and thanked her for all she had to do for him, he could have borne his ministrations better; as it was, they oppressed him. She certainly tried to make as light as possible of whatever was disagreeable in her task, and as time went on she succeeded, of course, more and more, but time brought more enlightenment to Gregor too. The very way she came in distressed him. Hardly was she in the room when she rushed to the window, without even taking time to shut the door, careful as she was usually to shield the sight of Gregor's room from the others, and as if she were almost suffocating tore the casements open with hasty fingers, standing then in the open draught for a while even in the bitterest cold and drawing deep breaths. This noisy scurry of hers upset Gregor twice a day; he would crouch trembling under the sofa all the time, knowing quite well that she would certainly have spared him such a disturbance had she found it at all possible to stay in his presence without opening the window.

On one occasion, about a month after Gregor's metamorphosis, when there was surely no reason for her to be still startled at his appearance, she came a little earlier than usual and found him gazing out of the window, quite motionless, and thus well placed to look like a bogey. Gregor would not have been surprised had she not come in at all, for she could not immediately open the window while he was there, but not only did she retreat, she jumped back as if in alarm and banged the door shut; a stranger might well have thought that he had been lying in wait for her there meaning to bite her. Of course he hid himself under the sofa at once, but he had to wait until midday before she came again, and she seemed more ill at ease than usual. This made him realize how repulsive the sight of him still was to her, and that it was bound to go on being repulsive, and what an effort it must have cost her not to run away even from the sight of the small portion of his body that stuck out from under the sofa. In order to spare her that, therefore, one day he carried a sheet on his back to the sofa—it cost him four hours' labor —and arranged it there in such a way as to hide him completely, so that even if she were to bend down she could not see him. Had she considered the sheet unnecessary, she would certainly have stripped it off the sofa again, for it was clear enough that this curtaining and confining of himself was not likely to conduce to Gregor's comfort, but she left it where it was, and Gregor even fancied that he caught a thankful glance from her eye when he lifted the sheet carefully a very little with his head to see how she was taking the new arrangement.

For the first fortnight his parents could not bring themselves to the point of entering his room, and he often heard them expressing their appreciation of his sister's activities, whereas formerly they had frequently scolded her for being as they thought a somewhat useless daughter. But now, both of them often waited outside the door, his father and his mother, while his sister tidied his room, and as soon as she came out she had to tell them exactly how things were in the room, what Gregor had eaten, how he had conducted himself this time and whether there was not perhaps some slight improvement in his condition. His mother, moreover, began relatively soon to want to visit him, but his father and sister dissuaded her at first with arguments which Gregor listened to very attentively and altogether approved. Later, however, she had to be held back by main force, and when she cried out: "Do let me in to Gregor, he is my unfortunate son! Can't you understand that I must go to him?" Gregor thought that it might be well to have her come in, not every day, of course, but perhaps once a week; she understood things, after all, much better than his sister, who was only a child despite the efforts she was making and had perhaps taken on so difficult a task merely out of childish thoughtlessness.

Gregor's desire to see his mother was soon fulfilled. During the daytime he did not want to show himself at the window, out of consideration for his parents, but he could not crawl very far around the few square yards of floor space he had, nor could he bear lying at rest all during the night, while he was fast losing any interest he had ever taken in food, so that for mere recreation he had formed the habit of crawling crisscross over the walls and ceiling. He especially enjoyed hanging suspended from the ceiling; it was much better than lying on the floor; one could breathe more freely; one's body swung and rocked lightly; and in the almost blissful absorption induced by this suspension it could happen to his own surprise that he let go and fell plump on the floor. Yet he now had his body much better under control than formerly, and even such a big fall did him no harm. His sister at once remarked the new distraction Gregor had found for himself —he left traces behind him of the sticky stuff on his soles wherever he crawled—and she got the idea in her head of giving him as wide a field as possible to crawl in and of removing the pieces of furniture that hindered him, above all the chest of drawers and the writing desk. But that was more than she could manage all by herself; she did not dare ask her father to help her; and as for the servant girl, a young creature of sixteen who had had the courage to stay on after the cook's departure, she could not be asked to help, for she had begged as an especial favor that she might keep the kitchen door locked and open it only on a definite summons; so there was nothing left but to apply to her mother at an hour when her father was out. And the old lady did come, with exclamations of joyful eagerness, which, however, died away at the door of Gregor's room. Gregor's sister, of course, went in first, to see that everything was in order before letting his mother enter. In great haste Gregor pulled the sheet lower and rucked it more in folds so that it really looked as if it had been thrown accidentally over the sofa. And this time he did not peer out from under it; he renounced the pleasure of seeing his mother on this occasion and was only glad that she had come at all. "Come in, he's out of sight," said his sister, obviously leading her mother in by the hand. Gregor could now hear the two women struggling to shift the heavy old chest from its place, and his sister claiming the greater part of the labor for herself, without listening to the admonitions of her mother who feared she might overstrain herself. It took a long time. After at least a quarter of an hour's tugging his mother objected that the chest had better be left where it was, for in the first place it was too heavy and could never be got out before his father came home, and standing in the middle of the room like that it would only hamper Gregor's movements, while in the second place it was not at all certain that removing the furniture would be doing a service to Gregor. She was inclined to think to the contrary; the sight of the naked walls made her own heart heavy, and why shouldn't Gregor have the same feeling, considering that he had been used to his furniture for so long and might feel forlorn without it. "And doesn't it look," she concluded in a low voice—in fact she had been almost whispering all the time as if to avoid letting Gregor, whose exact whereabouts she did not know, hear even the tones of her voice, for she was convinced that he could not understand her words—"doesn't it look as if we were showing him, by taking away his furniture, that we have given up hope of his ever getting better and are just leaving him coldly to himself? I think it would be best to keep his room exactly as it has always been, so that when he

comes back to us he will find everything unchanged and be able all the more easily to forget what has happened in between."

On hearing these words from his mother Gregor realized that the lack of all direct human speech for the past two months together with the monotony of family life must have confused his mind, otherwise he could not account for the fact that he had quite earnestly looked forward to having his room emptied of furnishing. Did he really want his warm room, so comfortably fitted with old family furniture, to be turned into a naked den in which he would certainly be able to crawl unhampered in all directions but at the price of shedding simultaneously all recollection of his human background? He had indeed been so near the brink of forgetfulness that only the voice of his mother, which he had not heard for so long, had drawn him back from it. Nothing should be taken out of his room; everything must stay as it was; he could not dispense with the good influence of the furniture on his state of mind; and even if the furniture did hamper him in his senseless crawling round and round, that was no drawback but a great advantage.

Unfortunately his sister was of the contrary opinion; she had grown accustomed, and not without reason, to consider herself an expert in Gregor's affairs as against her parents, and so her mother's advice was now enough to make her determined on the removal not only of the chest and the writing desk, which had been her first intention, but of all the furniture except the indispensable sofa. This determination was not, of course, merely the outcome of childish recalcitrance and of the self-confidence she had recently developed so unexpectedly and at such cost; she had in fact perceived that Gregor needed a lot of space to crawl about in, while on the other hand he never used the furniture at all, so far as could be seen. Another factor might have been also the enthusiastic temperament of an adolescent girl, which seeks to indulge itself on every opportunity and which now tempted Grete to exaggerate the horror of her brother's circumstances in order that she might do all the more for him. In a room where Gregor lorded it all alone over empty walls no one save herself was likely ever to set foot.

And so she was not to be moved from her resolve by her mother, who seemed moreover to be ill at ease in Gregor's room and therefore unsure of herself, was soon reduced to silence and helped her daughter as best she could to push the chest outside. Now, Gregor could do without the chest, if need be, but the writing desk he must retain. As soon as the two women had got the chest out of his room, groaning as they pushed it, Gregor stuck his head out from under the sofa to see how he might intervene as kindly and cautiously as possible. But as bad luck would have it, his mother was the first to return, leave Grete clasping the chest in the room next door where she was trying to shift it all by herself, without of course moving it from the spot. His mother however was not accustomed to the sight of him, it might sicken her and so in alarm Gregor backed quickly to the other end of the sofa, yet could not prevent the sheet from swaying a little in front. That was enough to put her on the alert. She paused, stood still for a moment and then went back to Grete.

Although Gregor kept reassuring himself that nothing out of the way was happening, but only a few bits of furniture were being changed round, he soon had to admit that all this trotting to and fro of the two women, their little ejaculations and the scraping of furniture along the floor affected him like a vast disturbance coming from all sides at once, and however much he tucked in his head and legs and cowered to the very floor he was bound to confess that he would not be able to stand it for long. They were clearing his room out; taking away everything he loved; the chest in which he kept his fret saw and other tools was already dragged off; they were now loosening the writing desk which had almost sunk into the floor, the desk at which he had done all his homework when he was at the commercial academy, at the grammar school before that, and, yes, even at the primary school—he had no more time to waste in weighing the good intentions of the two women, whose existence he had by now almost forgotten, for they were so exhausted that they were laboring in silence and nothing could be heard but the heavy scuffling of their feet.

And so he rushed out—the women were just leaning against the writing desk in the next room to give themselves a breather—and four times changed his direction, since he really did not know what to rescue first, then on the wall opposite, which was already otherwise cleared, he was struck by the picture of the lady muffled in so much fur and quickly crawled up to it and pressed himself to the glass, which was

a good surface to hold on to and comforted his hot belly. This picture at least, which was entirely hidden beneath him, was going to be removed by nobody. He turned his head towards the door of the living room so as to observe the women when they came back.

They had not allowed themselves much of a rest and were already coming; Grete had twined her arm round her mother and was almost supporting her. "Well, what shall we take now?" said Grete, looking round. Her eyes met Gregor's from the wall. She kept her composure, presumably because of her mother, bent her head down to her mother, to keep her from looking up, and said, although in a fluttering, unpremeditated voice: "Come, hadn't we better go back to the living room for a moment?" Her intentions were clear enough to Gregor, she wanted to bestow her mother in safety and then chase him down from the wall. Well, just let her try it! He clung to his picture and would not give it up. He would rather fly in Grete's face.

But Grete's words had succeeded in disquieting her mother, who took a step to one side, caught sight of the huge brown mass on the flowered wallpaper, and before she was really conscious that what she saw was Gregor screamed in a loud, hoarse voice: "Oh God, oh God!" fell with outspread arms over the sofa as if giving up and did not move. "Gregor!" cried his sister, shaking her fist and glaring at him. This was the first time she had directly addressed him since his metamorphosis. She ran into the next room for some aromatic essence with which to rouse her mother from her fainting fit. Gregor wanted to help too—there was still time to rescue the picture—but he was stuck fast to the glass and had to tear himself loose; he then ran after his sister into the next room as if he could advise her, as he used to do; but then had to stand helplessly behind her; she meanwhile searched among various bottles and when she turned round started in alarm at the sight of him; one bottle fell on the floor and broke; a splinter of glass cut Gregor's face and some kind of corrosive medicine splashed him; without pausing a moment longer Grete gathered up all the bottles she could carry and ran to her mother with them; she banged the door shut with her foot. Gregor was now cut off from his mother, who was perhaps nearly dying because of him; he dared not open the door for fear of frightening away his sister, who had to stay with her mother; there was nothing he could do but wait; and harassed by self-reproach and worry he began now to crawl to and fro, over everything, walls, furniture and ceiling, and finally in his despair, when the whole room seemed to be reeling round him, fell down on to the middle of the big table.

A little while elapsed, Gregor was still lying there feebly and all around was quiet, perhaps that was a good omen. Then the doorbell rang. The servant girl was of course locked in her kitchen, and Grete would have to open the door. It was his father. "What's been happening?" were his first words; Grete's face must have told him everything. Grete answered in a muffled voice, apparently hiding her head on his breast: "Mother had been fainting, but she's better now. Gregor's broken loose." "Just what I expected," said his father, "just what I've been telling you, but you women would never listen." It was clear to Gregor that his father had taken the worst interpretation of Grete's all too brief statement and was assuming that Gregor had been guilty of some violent act. Therefore Gregor must now try to propitiate his father, since he had neither time nor means for an explanation. And so he fled to the door of his own room and crouched against it, to let his father see as soon as he came in from the hall that his son had the good intention of getting back into his room immediately and that it was not necessary to drive him there, but that if only the door were opened he would disappear at once.

Yet his father was not in the mood to perceive such fine distinctions. "Ah!" he cried as soon as he appeared, in a tone which sounded at once angry and exultant. Gregor drew his head back from the door and lifted it to look at his father. Truly, this was not the father he had imagined to himself; admittedly he had been too absorbed of late in his new recreation of crawling over the ceiling to take the same interest as before in what was happening elsewhere in the flat, and he ought really to be prepared for some changes. And yet, and yet, could that be his father? The man who used to lie wearily sunk in bed whenever Gregor set out on a business journey; who welcomed him back of an evening lying in a long chair in a dressing gown; who could not really rise to his feet but only lifted his arms in greeting, and on the rare occasions when he did go out with his family, on one or two Sundays a year and on high holidays, walked between Gregor and his mother, who were slow walkers anyhow, even more slowly than they did, muffled in his old greatcoat, shuffling laboriously forward with the help of his crook-handled stick which he set down most cautiously at every step and, whenever he wanted to say anything, nearly always came to a full stop and gathered his escort around him? Now he was standing there in fine shape; dressed in a smart blue uniform with gold buttons, such as bank messengers wear; his strong double chin bulged over the stiff high collar of his jacket; from under his bushy eyebrows his black eyes darted fresh and penetrating glances; his onetime tangled white hair had been combed flat on either side of a shining and carefully exact parting. He pitched his cap, which bore a gold monogram, probably the badge of some bank, in a wide sweep across the whole room on to a sofa and with the tail-ends of his jacket thrown back, his hands in his trouser pockets, advanced with a grim visage towards Gregor. Likely enough he did not himself know what he meant to do; at any rate he lifted his feet uncommonly high, and Gregor was dumbfounded at the enormous size of his shoe soles. But Gregor could not risk standing up to him, aware as he had been from the very first day of his new life that his father believed only the severest measures suitable for dealing with him. And so he ran before his father, stopping when he stopped and scuttling forward again when his father made any kind of move. In this way they circled the room several times without anything decisive happening, indeed the whole operation did not even look like a pursuit because it was carried out so slowly. And so Gregor did not leave the floor, for he feared that his father might take as a piece of peculiar wickedness any excursion of his over the walls or the ceiling. All the same, he could not stay this course much longer, for while his father took one step he had to carry out a whole series of movements. He was already beginning to feel breathless, just as in his former life his lungs had not been very dependable. As he was staggering along, trying to concentrate his energy on running, hardly keeping his eyes open; in his dazed state never even thinking of any other escape than simply going forward; and having almost forgotten that the walls were free to him, which in this room were well provided with finely carved pieces of furniture full of knobs and crevices—suddenly something lightly flung landed close behind him and rolled before him. It was an apple; a second apple followed immediately; Gregor came to a stop in alarm; there was no point in running on, for his father was determined to bombard him. He had filled his pockets with fruit from the dish on the sideboard and was now shying apple after apple, without taking particularly good aim for the moment. The small red apples rolled about the floor as if magnetized and cannoned into each other. An apple thrown without much force grazed Gregor's back and glanced off harmlessly. But another following immediately landed right on his back and sank in; Gregor wanted to drag himself forward, as if this startling, incredible pain could be left behind him; but he felt as if nailed to the spot and flattened himself out in a complete derangement of all his senses. With his last conscious look he saw the door of his room being torn open and his mother rushing out ahead of his screaming sister, in her underbodice, for her daughter had loosened her clothing to let her breathe more freely and recover from her swoon, he saw his mother rushing toward his father, leaving one after another behind her on the floor her loosened petticoats, stumbling over her petticoats straight to his father and embracing him, in complete union with him—but here Gregor's sight began to fail—with her hands clasped round his father's neck as she begged for her son's life.

3

The serious injury done to Gregor, which disabled him for more than a month—the apple went on sticking in his body as a visible reminder, since no one ventured to remove it—seemed to have made even his father recollect that Gregor was a member of the family, despite his present unfortunate and repulsive shape, and ought not to be treated as an enemy, that, on the contrary, family duty required the suppression of disgust and the exercise of patience, nothing but patience.

And although his injury had impaired, probably for ever, his powers of movement, and for the time being it took him long, long minutes to creep across his room like an old invalid—there was no question now of crawling up the wall—yet in his own opinion he was sufficiently compensated for this worsening of his condition by the fact that towards evening the living-room door, which he used to watch intently for an hour or two beforehand, was always thrown open, so that lying in the darkness of his room, invisible to the family, he could see them all at the lamp-lit table and listen to their talk, by general consent as it were, very different from his earlier eavesdropping.

True, their intercourse lacked the lively character of former times, which he had always called to mind with a certain wistfulness in the small hotel bedrooms where he had been wont to throw himself down, tired out, on damp bedding. They were now mostly very silent. Soon after supper his father would fall asleep in his armchair; his mother and sister would admonish each other to be silent; his mother, bending low over the lamp, stitched at fine sewing for an underwear firm; his sister, who had taken a job as a salesgirl, was learning shorthand and French in the evenings on the chance of bettering herself. Sometimes his father woke up, and as if quite unaware that he had been sleeping said to his mother: "What a lot of sewing you're doing today!" and at once fell asleep again, while the two women exchanged a tired smile.

With a kind of mulishness his father persisted in keeping his uniform on even in the house; his dressing gown hung uselessly on its peg and he slept fully dressed where he sat, as if he were ready for service at any moment and even here only at the beck and call of his superior. As a result, his uniform, which was not brand-new to start with, began to look dirty, despite all the loving care of the mother and sister to keep it clean, and Gregor often spent whole evenings gazing at the many greasy spots on the garment, gleaming with gold buttons always in a high state of polish, in which the old man sat sleeping in extreme discomfort and yet quite peacefully.

As soon as the clock struck ten his mother tried to rouse his father with gentle words and to persuade him after that to get into bed, for sitting there he could not have a proper sleep and that was what he needed most, since he had to go on duty at six. But with the mulishness that had obsessed him since he became a bank messenger he always insisted on staying longer at the table, although he regularly fell asleep again and in the end only with the greatest trouble could be got out of his armchair and into his bed. However insistently Gregor's mother and sister kept urging him with gentle reminders, he would go on slowly shaking his head for a quarter of an hour, keeping his eyes shut, and refuse to get to his feet. The mother plucked at his sleeve, whispering endearments in his ear, the sister left her lessons to come to her mother's help, but Gregor's father was not to be caught. He would only sink down deeper in his chair. Not until the two women hoisted him up by the armpits did he open his eyes and look at them both, one after the other, usually with the remark: "This is a life. This is the peace and quiet of my old age." And leaning on the two of them he would heave himself up, with difficulty, as if he were a great burden to himself, suffer them to lead him as far as the door and then wave them off and go on alone, while the mother abandoned her needlework and the sister her pen in order to run after him and help him farther.

Who could find time, in this overworked and tired-out family, to bother about Gregor more than was absolutely needful? The household was reduced more and more; the servant girl was turned off; a gigantic bony charwoman with white hair flying round her head came in morning and evening to do the rough work; everything else was done by Gregor's mother, as well as great piles of sewing. Even various family ornaments, which his mother and sister used to wear with pride at parties and celebrations, had to be sold, as Gregor discovered of an evening from hearing them all discuss the prices obtained. But what they lamented most was the fact they could not leave the flat which was much too big for their present circumstances, because they could not think of any way to shift Gregor. Yet Gregor saw well enough that consideration for him was not the main difficulty preventing the removal, for they could have easily shifted him in some suitable box with a few air holes in it; what really kept them from moving into another flat was rather their own complete hopelessness and the belief that they had been singled out for a misfortune such as had never happened to any of their relations or acquaintances. They fulfilled to the uttermost all that the world demands of poor people, the father fetched breakfast for the small clerks in the bank, the mother devoted her energy to making underwear for strangers, the sister trotted to and fro behind the counter at the behest of customers, but more than this they had not the strength to do. And the wound in Gregor's back began to nag at him

afresh when his mother and sister, after getting his father into bed, came back again, left their work lying, drew close to each other and sat cheek by cheek; when his mother, pointing towards his room, said: "Shut that door now, Grete," and he was left again in darkness, while next door the women mingled their tears or perhaps sat dry-eyed staring at the table.

Gregor hardly slept at all by night or by day. He was often haunted by the idea that next time the door opened he would take the family's affairs in hand again just as he used to do; once more, after this long interval, there appeared in his thoughts the figures of the chief and the chief clerk, the commercial travelers and the apprentices, the porter who was so dull-witted, two or three friends in other firms, a chambermaid in one of the rural hotels, a sweet and fleeting memory, a cashier in a milliner's shop, whom he had wooed earnestly but too slowly—they all appeared, together with strangers or people he had quite forgotten, but instead of helping him and his family they were one and all unapproachable and he was glad when they vanished. At other times he would not be in the mood to bother about his family, he was only filled with rage at the way they were neglecting him, and although he had no clear idea of what he might care to eat he would make plans for getting into the larder to take the food that was after all his due, even if he were not hungry. His sister no longer took thought to bring him what might especially please him, but in the morning and at noon before she went to business hurriedly pushed into his room with her foot any food that was available, and in the evening cleared it out again with one sweep of the broom, heedless of whether it had been merely tasted, or—as most frequently happened—left untouched. The cleaning of his room, which she now did always in the evenings, could not have been more hastily done. Streaks of dirt stretched along the walls, here and there lay balls of dust and filth. At first Gregor used to station himself in some particularly filthy corner when his sister arrived, in order to reproach her with it, so to speak. But he could have sat there for weeks without getting her to make any improvements; she could see the dirt as well as he did, but she had simply made up her mind to leave it alone. And yet, with a touchiness that was new to her, which seemed anyhow to have infected the whole family, she jealously guarded her claim to be the sole caretaker of Gregor's room. His mother once subjected his room to a thorough cleaning, which was achieved only by means of several buckets of water—all this dampness of course upset Gregor too and he lay widespread, sulky and motionless on the sofa—but she was well punished for it. Hardly had his sister noticed the changed aspect of his room that evening than she rushed in high dudgeon into the living room and, despite the imploringly raised hands of her mother, burst into a storm of weeping, while her parents—her father had of course been startled out of his chair—looked on at first in helpless amazement; then they too began to go into action; the father reproached the mother on his right for not having left the cleaning of Gregor's room to his sister; shrieked at the sister on his left that never again was she to be allowed to clean Gregor's room; while the mother tried to pull the father into his bedroom, since he was beyond himself with agitation; the sister, shaken with sobs, then beat upon the table with her small fists; and Gregor hissed loudly with rage because not one of them thought of shutting the door to spare him such a spectacle and so much noise.

Still, even if the sister, exhausted by her daily work, had grown tired of looking after Gregor as she did formerly, there was no need for his mother's intervention or for Gregor's being neglected at all. The charwoman was there. This old widow, whose strong bony frame had enabled her to survive the worst a long life could offer, by no means recoiled from Gregor. Without being in the least curious she had once by chance opened the door of his room and at the sight of Gregor, who, taken by surprise, began to rush to and fro although no one was chasing him, merely stood there with her arms folded. From that time she never failed to open his door a little for a moment, morning and evening, to have a look at him. At first she even used to call him to her, with words which apparently she took to be friendly, such as: "Come along, then, you old dung beetle!" or "Look at the old dung beetle, then!" To such allocutions Gregor made no answer, but stayed motionless where he was, as if the door had never been opened. Instead of being allowed to disturb him so senselessly whenever the whim took her, she should rather have been ordered to clean out his room daily, that charwoman! Once, early in the morning—heavy rain was lashing on the windowpanes, perhaps a sign that spring was on the way—

Gregor was so exasperated when she began addressing him again that he ran at her, as if to attack her, although slowly and feebly enough. But the charwoman instead of showing fright merely lifted high a chair that happened to be beside the door, and as she stood there with her mouth wide open it was clear that she meant to shut it only when she brought the chair down on Gregor's back. "So you're not coming any nearer?" she asked, as Gregor turned away again, and quietly put the chair back into the corner.

Gregor was now eating hardly anything. Only when he happened to pass the food laid out for him did he take a bit of something in his mouth as a pastime, kept it there for an hour at a time and usually spat it out again. At first he thought it was chagrin over the state of his room that prevented him from eating, yet he soon got used to the various changes in his room. It had become a habit in the family to push into his room things there was no room for elsewhere, and there were plenty of these now, since one of the rooms had been let to three lodgers. These serious gentlemen—all three of them with full beards, as Gregor once observed through a crack in the door—had a passion for order, not only in their own room but, since they were now members of the household, in all its arrangements, especially in the kitchen. Superfluous, not to say dirty, objects they could not bear. Besides, they had brought with them most of the furnishings they needed. For this reason many things could be dispensed with that it was no use trying to sell but that should not be thrown away either. All of them found their way into Gregor's room. The ash can likewise and the kitchen garbage can. Anything that was not needed for the moment was simply flung into Gregor's room by the charwoman, who did everything in a hurry; fortunately Gregor usually saw only the object, whatever it was, and the hand that held it. Perhaps she intended to take the things away again as time and opportunity offered, or to collect them until she could throw them all out in a heap, but in fact they just lay wherever she happened to throw them, except when Gregor pushed his way through the junk heap and shifted it somewhat, at first out of necessity, because he had not room enough to crawl, but later with increasing enjoyment, although after such excursions, being sad and weary to death, he would lie motionless for hours. And since the lodgers often ate their supper at home in the common living room, the living-room door stayed shut many an evening, yet Gregor reconciled himself quite easily to the shutting of the door, for often enough on evenings when it was opened he had disregarded it entirely and lain in the darkest corner of his room, quite unnoticed by the family. But on one occasion the charwoman left the door open a little and it stayed ajar even when the lodgers came in for supper and the lamp was lit. They set themselves at the top end of the table where formerly Gregor and his father and mother had eaten their meals, unfolded their napkins and took knife and fork in hand. At once his mother appeared in the other doorway with a dish of meat and close behind his sister with a dish of potatoes piled high. The food steamed with a thick vapor. The lodgers bent over the food set before them as if to scrutinize it before eating, in fact the man in the middle, who seemed to pass for an authority with the other two, cut a piece of meat as it lay on the dish, obviously to discover if it were tender or should be sent back to the kitchen. He showed satisfaction, and Gregor's mother and sister, who had been watching anxiously, breathed freely and began to smile.

The family itself took its meals in the kitchen. None the less, Gregor's father came into the living room before going into the kitchen and with one prolonged bow, cap in hand, made a round of the table. The lodgers all stood up and murmured something in their beards. When they were alone again they ate their food in almost complete silence. It seemed remarkable to Gregor that among the various noises coming from the table he could always distinguish the sound of their masticating teeth, as if this were a sign to Gregor that one needed teeth in order to eat, and that with toothless jaws even of the finest make one could do nothing. "I'm hungry enough," said Gregor sadly to himself, "but not for that kind of food. How these lodgers are stuffing themselves, and here am I dying of starvation!"

On that very evening—during the whole of his time there Gregor could not remember ever having heard the violin—the sound of violin-playing came from the kitchen. The lodgers had already finished their supper, the one in the middle had brought out a newspaper and given the other two a page apiece, and now they were leaning back at ease reading and smoking. When the violin began to play they pricked up their ears, got to their feet, and went on tiptoe to the hall door where they stood huddled together. Their movements must have been heard in the kitchen, for Gregor's father called out: "Is the violin-playing disturbing you, gentlemen? It can be stopped at once." "On the contrary," said the middle lodger, "could not Fräulein Samsa come and play in this room, beside us, where it is much more convenient and comfortable?" "Oh certainly," cried Gregor's father, as if he were the violin-player. The lodgers came back into the living room and waited. Presently Gregor's father arrived with the music stand, his mother carrying the music and his sister with the violin. His sister quietly made everything ready to start playing; his parents, who had never let rooms before and so had an exaggerated idea of the courtesy due to lodgers, did not venture to sit down on their own chairs; his father leaned against the door, the right hand thrust between two buttons of his livery coat, which was formally buttoned up; but his mother was offered a chair by one of the lodgers and, since she left the chair just where he had happened to put it, sat down in a corner to one side.

Gregor's sister began to play; the father and mother, from either side, intently watched the movements of her hands. Gregor, attracted by the playing, ventured to move forward a little until his head was actually inside the living room. He felt hardly any surprise at his growing lack of consideration for the others; there had been a time when he prided himself on being considerate. And yet just on this occasion he had more reason than ever to hide himself, since owing to the amount of dust which lay thick in his room and rose into the air at the slightest movements, he too was covered with dust; fluff and hair and remnants of food trailed with him, caught on his back and along his sides; his indifference to everything was much too great for him to turn on his back and scrape himself clean on the carpet, as once he had done several times a day. And in spite of his condition, no shame deterred him from advancing a little over the spotless floor of the living room.

To be sure, no one was aware of him. The family was entirely absorbed in the violin-playing; the lodgers, however, who first of all had stationed themselves, hands in pockets, much too close behind the music stand so that they could all have read the music, which must have bothered his sister, had soon retreated to the window, half-whispering with downbent heads, and stayed there while his father turned an anxious eye on them. Indeed, they were making it more than obvious that they had been disappointed in their expectation of hearing good or enjoyable violin-playing, that they had had more than enough of the performance and only out of courtesy suffered a continued disturbance of their peace. From the way they all kept blowing the smoke of their cigars high in the air through nose and mouth one could divine their irritation. And yet Gregor's sister was playing so beautifully. Her face leaned sideways, intently and sadly her eyes followed the notes of music. Gregor crawled a little farther forward and lowered his head to the ground so that it might be possible for his eyes to meet hers. Was he an animal, that music had such an effect upon him? He felt as if the way were opening before him to to the unknown nourishment he craved. He was determined to push forward till he reached his sister, to pull at her skirt and so let her know that she was to come into his room with the violin, for no one here appreciated her playing as he would appreciate it. He would never let her out of his room, at least, not so long as he lived; his frightful appearance would become, for the first time, useful to him; he would watch all the door of his room at once and spit at intruders; but his sister should need no constraint, she should stay with him of her own free will; she should sit beside him on the sofa, bend down her ear to him and hear him confide that he had had the firm intention of sending her to the Conservatorium, and that, but for this mishap, last Christmas—surely Christmas was long past?—he would have announced it to everybody without allowing a single objection. After this confession his sister would be so touched that she would burst into tears, and Gregor would then raise himself to her shoulder and kiss her on the neck, which, now that she went to business, she kept free of any ribbon or collar.

"Mr. Samsa!" cried the middle lodger, to Gregor's father, and pointed, without wasting any more words, at Gregor, now working himself slowly forwards. The violin fell silent, the middle lodger first smiled to his friends with a shake of the head and then looked at Gregor again. Instead of driving Gregor out, his father seemed to think it more needful to begin by soothing down the lodgers, although they were not at all agitated and apparently found Gregor more entertaining than the violin-playing. He hurried towards them and, spreading out his arms, tried to urge them back into their own room and at the same time to block their view of Gregor. They now began to be really a little angry, one could not tell whether because of the old man's behavior or because it had just dawned on them that all unwittingly they had such a neighbor as Gregor next door. They demanded explanations of his father, they waved their arms like him, tugged uneasily at their beards, and only with reluctance backed towards their room. Meanwhile Gregor's sister, who stood there as if lost when her playing was so abruptly broken off, came to life again, pulled herself together all at once after standing for a while holding violin and bow in nervelessly hanging hands and staring at her music, pushed her violin into the lap of her mother who was still sitting in her chair fighting asthmatically for breath, and ran into the lodgers' room to which they were now being shepherded by her father rather more quickly than before. One could see the pillows and blankets on the beds flying under her accustomed fingers and being laid in order. Before the lodgers had actually reached their room she had finished making the beds and slipped out.

The old man seemed once more to be so possessed by his mulish self-assertiveness that he was forgetting all the respect he should show to his lodgers. He kept driving them on and driving them on until in the very door of the bedroom the middle lodger stamped his foot loudly on the floor and so brought him to a halt. "I beg to announce," said the lodger, lifting one hand and looking also at Gregor's mother and sister, "that because of the disgusting conditions prevailing in this household and family"—here he spat on the floor with emphatic brevity—"I give you notice on the spot. Naturally I won't pay you a penny for the days I have lived here, on the contrary I shall consider bringing an action for damages against you, based on claims—believe me—that will be easily susceptible of proof." He ceased and stared straight in front of him, as if he expected something. In fact his two friends at once rushed into the breach with these words: "And we too give notice on the spot." On that he seized the door-handle and shut the door with a slam.

Gregor's father, groping with his hands, staggered forward and fell into his chair; it looked as if he were stretching himself there for his ordinary evening nap, but the marked jerkings of his head, which was as if uncontrollable, showed that he was far from asleep. Gregor had simply stayed quietly all the time on the spot where the lodgers had espied him. Disappointment at the failure of his plan, perhaps also the weakness arising from extreme hunger, made it impossible for him to move. He feared, with a fair degree of certainty, that at any moment the general tension would discharge itself in a combined attack upon him, and he lay waiting. He did not react even to the noise made by the violin as it fell off his mother's lap from under her trembling fingers and gave out a reasonant note.

"My dear parents," said his sister, slapping her hand on the table by way of introduction, "things can't go on like this. Perhaps you don't realize that, but I do. I won't utter my brother's name in the presence of this creature, and so all I say is: we must try to get rid of it. We've tried to look after it and to put up with it as far as is humanly possible, and I don't think anyone could reproach us in the slightest."

"She is more than right," said Gregor's father to himself. His mother, who was still choking for lack of breath, began to cough hollowly into her hand with a wild look in her eyes.

His sister rushed over to her and held her forehead. His father's thoughts seemed to have lost their vagueness at Grete's words, he sat more upright, fingering his service cap that lay among the plates still lying on the table from the lodgers' supper, and from time to time looked at the still form of Gregor.

"We must try to get rid of it," his sister now said explicitly to her father, since her mother was coughing too much to hear a word, "it will be the death of both of you, I can see that coming. When one has to work as hard as we do, all of us, one can't stand this continual torment at home on top of it. At least I can't stand it any longer." And she burst into such a passion of sobbing that her tears dropped on her mother's face, where she wiped them off mechanically.

"My dear," said the old man sympathetically, and with evident understanding, "but what can we do?"

Gregor's sister merely shrugged her shoulders to indicate the feeling of helplessness that had now overmastered her during her weeping fit, in contrast to her former confidence.

"If he could understand us," said her father, half questioningly; Grete, still sobbing, vehemently waved a hand to show how unthinkable that was.

"If he could understand us," repeated the old man, shutting his eyes to consider his daughter's conviction that understanding was impossible, "then perhaps we might come to some agreement with him. But as it is—"

"He must go," cried Gregor's sister, "that's the only solution, Father. You must try to get rid of the idea that this is Gregor. The fact that we've believed it for so long is the root of all our trouble. But how can it be Gregor? If this were Gregor, he would have realized long ago that human beings can't live with such a creature, and he'd have gone away on his own accord. Then we wouldn't have any bother, but we'd be able to go on living and keep his memory in honor. As it is, this creature persecutes us, drives away our lodgers, obviously wants the whole apartment to himself and would have us all sleep in the gutter. Just look, Father," she shrieked all at once, "he's at it again!" And in the access of panic that was quite incomprehensible to Gregor she even quitted her mother, literally thrusting the chair from her as if she would rather sacrifice her mother than stay so near to Gregor, and rushed behind her father, who also rose up, being simply upset by her agitation, and half-spread his arms out as if to protect her.

Yet Gregor had not the slightest intention of frightening anyone, far less his sister. He had only begun to turn round in order to crawl back to his room, but it was certainly a startling operation to watch, since because of his disabled condition he could not execute the difficult turning movements except by lifting his head and then bracing it against the floor over and over again. He paused and looked round. His good intentions seemed to have been recognized; the alarm had only been momentary. Now they were all watching him in melancholy silence. His mother lay in her chair, her legs stiffly out stretched and pressed together, her eyes almost closing for sheer weariness; his father and his sister were sitting beside each other, his sister's arm around the old man's neck.

Perhaps I can go on turning round now, thought Gregor, and began his labors again. He could not stop himself from panting with the effort, and had to pause now and then to take breath. Nor did anyone harass him, he was left entirely to himself. When he had completed the turn-round he began at once to crawl straight back. He was amazed at the distance separating him from his room and could not understand how in his weak state he had managed to accomplish the same journey so recently, almost without remarking it. Intent on crawling as fast as possible, he barely noticed that not a single word, not an ejaculation from his family, interfered with his progress. Only when he was already in the doorway did he turn his head round, not completely, for his neck muscles were getting stiff, but enough to see that nothing had changed behind him except that his sister had risen to her feet. His last glance fell on his mother, who was not quite overcome by sleep.

Hardly was he well inside his room when the door was hastily pushed shut, bolted and locked. The sudden noise in his ear startled him so much that his little legs gave beneath him. It was his sister who had shown such haste. She had been standing ready waiting and had made a light spring forward, Gregor had not even heard her coming, and she cried "At last!" to her parents as she turned the key in the lock.

"And what now?" said Gregor to himself, looking round in the darkness. Soon he made the discovery that he was now unable to stir a limb. This did not surprise him, rather it seemed unnatural that he should ever actually have been able to move on these feeble little legs. Otherwise he felt relatively comfortable. True, his whole body was aching, but it seemed that the pain was gradually growing less and would finally pass away, the rotting apple in his back and the inflamed area around it, all covered with soft dust, already hardly troubled him. He thought of his family with tenderness and love. The decision that he must disappear was one that he held to even more strongly than his sister, if that were possible. In this state of vacant and peaceful meditation he remained until the tower clock struck three in the morning. The first broadening of light in the world outside the window entered his consciousness once more. Then his head sank to the floor of its own accord and from his nostrils came the last faint flicker of his breath.

When the charwoman arrived early in the morning—what between her strength and her impatience she slammed all the doors so loudly, never mind how often she had been begged not to do so, that no one in the whole apartment could enjoy any quiet sleep after her arrival—she noticed nothing unusual as she took her customary peep into Gregor's room. She thought he was lying motionless on purpose, pretending to be in the sulks; she credited him with every kind of intelligence. Since she happened to have the long-handled broom in her hand she tried to tickle him up with it from the doorway. When that too produced no reaction she felt provoked and poked at him a little harder, and only when she had pushed him along the floor without meeting any resistance was her attention aroused. It did not take her long to establish the truth of the matter, and her eyes widened, she let out a whistle, yet did not waste much time over it but tore open the door of the Samsas' bedroom and yelled into the darkness at the top of her voice: "Just look at this, it's dead; it's lying here dead and done for!"

Mr. and Mrs. Samsa started up in their double bed and before they realized the nature of the charwoman's announcement had some difficulty in overcoming the shock of it. But then they got out of bed quickly, one on either side, Mr. Samsa throwing a blanket over his shoulders, Mrs. Samsa in nothing but her nightgown; in this array they entered Gregor's room. Meanwhile the door of the living room opened, too, where Grete had been sleeping since the advent of the lodgers; she was completely dressed as if she had not been to bed, which seemed to be confirmed also by the paleness of her face. "Dead?" said Mrs. Samsa, looking questioningly at the charwoman, although she could have investigated for herself, and the fact was obvious enough without investigation. "I should say so," said the charwoman, proving her words by pushing Gregor's corpse a long way to one side with her broomstick. Mrs. Samsa made a movement as if to stop her, but checked it. "Well," said Mr. Samsa, "now thanks be to God." He crossed himself, and the three women followed his example. Grete, whose eyes never left the corpse, said: "Just see how thin he was. It's such a long time since he's eaten anything. The food came out again just as it went in." Indeed, Gregor's body was completely flat and dry, as could only now be seen when it was no longer supported by the legs and nothing prevented one from looking closely at it.

"Come in beside us, Grete, for a little while," said Mrs. Samsa with a tremulous smile, and

Grete, not without looking back at the corpse, followed her parents into their bedroom. The charwoman shut the door and opened the window wide. Although it was so early in the morning a certain softness was perceptible in the fresh air. After all, it was already the end of March.

The three lodgers emerged from their room and were surprised to see no breakfast; they had been forgotten. "Where's our breakfast?" said the middle lodger peevishly to the charwoman. But she put her finger to her lips and hastily, without a word, indicated by gestures that they should go into Gregor's room. They did so and stood, their hands in the pockets of their somewhat shabby coats, around Gregor's corpse in the room where it was now fully light.

At that the door of the Samsas' bedroom opened and Mr. Samsa appeared in his uniform, his wife on one arm, his daughter on the other. They all looked a little as if they had been crying; from time to time Grete hid her face on her father's arm.

"Leave my house at once!" said Mr. Samsa, and pointed to the door without disengaging himself from the women. "What do you mean by that?" said the middle lodger, taken somewhat aback, with a feeble smile. The two others put their hands behind them and kept rubbing them together, as if in gleeful expectation of a fine set-to in which they were bound to come off the winners. "I mean just what I say," answered Mr. Samsa, and advanced in a straight line with his two companions towards the lodger. He stood his ground at first quietly, looking at the floor as if his thought were taking a new pattern in his head. "Then let us go, by all means," he said, and looked up at Mr. Samsa as if in a sudden access of humility he were expecting some renewed sanction for this decision. Mr. Samsa merely nodded briefly once or twice with meaning eyes. Upon that the lodger really did go with long strides into the hall, his two friends had been listening and had quite stopped rubbing their hands for some moments and now went scuttling after him as if afraid that Mr. Samsa might get into the hall before them and cut them off from their leader. In the hall they all three took their hats from the rack, their sticks from the umbrella stand, bowed in silence and quitted the apartment. With a suspiciousness which proved quite unfounded Mr. Samsa and the two women followed them out to the landing; leaning over the banister they watched the three figures slowly but surely going down the long stairs, vanishing from sight at a certain turn of the staircase on every floor and coming into view again after a moment or so; the more they dwindled, the more the Samsa family's interest in them dwindled, and when a butcher's boy met them and passed them on the stairs coming up proudly with a tray on his head, Mr. Samsa and the two women soon left the landing and as if a burden had been lifted from them went back into their apartment.

They decided to spend this day in resting and going for a stroll; they had not only deserved such a respite from work, but absolutely needed it. And so they sat down at the table and wrote three notes of excuse, Mr. Samsa to his board of management, Mrs. Samsa to her employer and Grete to the head of her firm. While they were writing, the charwoman came in to say that she was going now, since her morning's work was finished. At first they only nodded without looking up, but as she kept hovering there they eyed her irritably. "Well?" said Mr. Samsa. The charwoman stood grinning in the doorway as if she had good news to impart to the family but meant not to say a word unless properly questioned. The small ostrich feather standing upright on her hat, which had annoyed Mr. Samsa ever since she was engaged, was waving gaily in all directions. "Well, what is it then?" asked Mrs. Samsa, who obtained more respect from the charwoman than the others. "Oh," said the charwoman, giggling so amiably that she could not at once continue, "just this, you don't need to bother about how to get rid of the thing next door. It's been seen to already." Mrs. Samsa and Grete bent over their letters again, as if preoccupied; Mr. Samsa, who perceived that she was eager to begin describing it all in detail, stopped her with a decisive hand. But since she was not allowed to tell her story, she remembered the great hurry she was in, being obviously deeply huffed: "Bye, everybody," she said, whirling off violently, and departed with a frightful slamming of doors.

"She'll be given notice tonight," said Mr. Samsa, but neither from his wife nor his daughter did he get any answer, for the charwoman seemed to have shattered again the composure they had barely achieved. They rose, went to the window and stayed there, clasping each other tight. Mr. Samsa turned in his chair to look at them and quietly observed them for a little. Then he called out: "Come along, now, do. Let bygones be bygones. And you might have some consideration for me." The two of them complied at once, hastened to him, caressed him and quickly finished their letters.

Then they all three left the apartment together, which was more than they had done for months, and went by train into the open country outside the town. The tram, in which they were the only passengers, was filled with warm sunshine. Leaning comfortably back in their seats they canvassed their prospects for the future, and it appeared on closer inspection that these were not at all bad, for the jobs they had got, which so far they had never really discussed with each other, were all three admirable and likely to lead to better things later on. The greatest immediate improvement in their condition would of course arise from moving to another house; they wanted to take a smaller and cheaper but also better situated and more easily run apartment than the one they had, which Gregor had selected. While they were thus conversing, it struck both Mr. and Mrs. Samsa, almost at the same moment, as they became aware of their daughter's increasing vivacity, that in spite of all the sorrow of recent times, which had made her cheeks pale, she had bloomed into a pretty girl with a good figure. They grew quieter and half unconsciously exchanged glances of complete agreement, having come to the conclusion that it would soon be time to find a good husband for her. And it was like a confirmation of their new dreams and excellent intentions that at the end of their journey their daughter sprang to her feet first and stretched her young body.

Life is a continual distraction which does not allow
us to reflect on that from which we are distracted.
                                    Franz Kafka

In "The Metamorphosis" Franz Kafka invites us to view the world of a human form from the perspective of an insect. The transformation begins at this point. We see Gregor struggle to balance the contradictions between his "inner" and "outer" worlds in order to break the barriers of time and space. The story is divided into three sections. The first part illustrates Gregor's relation to his profession. At this point in the story Kafka introduces the transformation of modern man from human form into an object. As we watch the insect plead with his boss to remain a salesman, we are aware of Gregor's fight for dignity in the modern world which turns man into a part of an assembly line. The second section, which begins a day later, reveals Gregor's relation to his family. This part is representative of the "creation myths" at the beginning of this chapter. Here we view man as a puny insect pleading for divine intervention. The scene in which the Father throws the apple at the insect reveals Gregor's attempt to find paradise lost. We see Gregor's awareness of man's fall from innocence. Kafka introduces the theme of innocence versus experience as a means to reflect on what brings about the "metamorphosis" of Gregor Samsa. On another level, we might view Gregor's relation with his sister as a reversal of the fairy tale "Beauty and the Beast." Again the hoped-for transformation does not "free" Gregor from his imprisonment. The last section (the time between the second and third parts is indefinite) reveals Gregor's relation to himself. At one moment in this pitiful story, we view Gregor as a human form moved by the music which he describes as "an unknown nourishment." This symbol brings Gregor to face what he has done to bring about his imprisonment. He might have developed his creative side, rather than become a "thing" working as a traveling salesman. The story is rich in meanings because of Kafka's ability to depict a world in which an unknown power invades our imaginations. The inability to find empirical evidence to validate or invalidate this invasion leads the Samsa family to attempt to come to terms with this occurrence: "Even the unusual must have its limits." The story's ending brings the Samsa family "outside" where they see Grete moving into sexual bloom. This ending suggests the movement away from the insect whose death may have brought about this transition. Perhaps Grete is the one who undergoes a metamorphosis; she changes in the story while Gregor regresses into ultimate withdrawal

The following questions focus on Kafka's story as transformation of "inner" time and space to reveal the animal as man.

1 What does the first line suggest? How does Kafka use Gregor's room to reveal the "inner" world of his man turned animal? What symbols does Gregor focus on in his room? What does the picture above his dresser suggest? How does the glass in this picture separate and frustrate Gregor? What does this reveal about Gregor's chastity? Is this what he wants to keep? Explain!

2 Describe Gregor's family as the mirror of his transformation: How does the father represent the symbol of authority? How does the insect learn to see the father's weakness? In what ways does the father resemble Gregor's strengths and weaknesses? What does the mother represent to Gregor? How is her voice the man's delight and the insect's repulsion? What does this suggest about Gregor's dual feelings toward his mother? What does Grete represent to Gregor? Is she his other half? Develop your ideas on how Kafka blends the brother and sister together! Why does the family accept Gregor's transformation as a matter of fact? How does this reveal how they deal with the transformation of life and death?

3 To understand the relation of Gregor and Grete, we need to focus on the patterns of identification established within the family romance. In what ways does the relation between the brother and sister mirror that of the father and mother? Is the theme of incest present? Discuss the implications of this possibility.
a How would Freud's essay in this chapter cast light on Gregor's actions in the story?
   (1) Is Gregor a victim of the Oedipus Complex? Explain!
   (2) Is his guilt a disguise for aggression? Does this suggest that Gregor's struggle is between the life force, eros, and the death force, thanatos? Explain!
b How would Jung's discussion of the

anima help clarify the relation between Gregor and Grete? How does Gregor express his anima?

4 How is Gregor depicted in relationship to his social environment? What social attitudes emerge in the story? How does the family respond to social pressure? How is Gregor's position in opposition to his desire to create music? What does this suggest? How do the guests function in the story? What role does money play in Gregor's transformation process?
a The story of creation which appears in Genesis is an attempt to transform human beings from the world of nature. Compare and contrast Kafka's vision of man transformed into an insect with the story in Genesis. Does Gregor attempt to reconcile the differences between the human and the spiritual? Explain!
b Use Eliade's essay on "Modern Man's Need to Understand the Rites of Passage" to interpret the initiation ceremony in Kafka's story.
   (1) What "second birth" does Gregor undergo? What test must he complete in order to bring this about? What does this suggest about Kafka's desire to explain a world devoid of spiritual meaning?
   (2) Is Gregor's death a "transition to a higher mode of being"? How does this explain the differences between primitive and modern man? Is Gregor a representation of the modern individual lost in profane time? Explain!

5 Discuss the ending of the story. What does it mean to be an "untouchable"? Who are the untouchables in the story? How does Kafka resolve the conflict between time and space for Gregor Samsa? In what ways do you feel modern individuals have lost touch with nature? Do you think Grete will end as Gregor does? Is there any evidence to suggest this? Why are the parents aware of her growing sexual maturity? What does this suggest about their values?

FERN HILL

DYLAN THOMAS

Now as I was young and easy under the apple
  boughs
About the lilting house and happy as the grass was
  green,
    The night above the dingle starry,
      Time let me hail and climb
    Golden in the heydays of his eyes,
And honored among wagons I was prince of the
  apple towns
And once below a time I lordly had the trees and
  leaves
      Trail with daisies and barley
    Down the rivers of the windfall light.

And as I was green and carefree, famous among the
  barns
About the happy yard and singing as the farm was
  home,
    In the sun that is young once only,
      Time let me play and be
    Golden in the mercy of his means,
And green and golden I was huntsman and herds-
  man, the calves
Sang to my horn, the foxes on the hills barked clear
  and cold,
      And the sabbath rang slowly
    In the pebbles of the holy streams.

All the sun long it was running, it was lovely, the
  hay
Fields high as the house, the tunes from the chimneys, it was air
    And playing, lovely and watery
      And fire green as grass.
    And nightly under the simple stars
As I rode to sleep the owls were bearing the farm
  away.
All the moon long I heard, blessed among stables,
  the night-jars
    Flying with the ricks, and the horses
      Flashing into the dark.

And then to awake, and the farm, like a wanderer
  white
With the dew, come back, the cock on his shoulder:
  it was all
    Shining, it was Adam and maiden,
      The sky gathered again
    And the sun grew round that very day.
So it must have been after the birth of the simple
  light
In the first, spinning place, the spellbound horses
  walking warm
    Out of the whinnying green stable
      On to the fields of praise.

And honored among foxes and pheasants by the
  gay house
Under the new made clouds and happy as the heart
  was long,
    In the sun born over and over,
      I ran my heedless ways,
    My wishes raced through the house high hay
And nothing I cared, at my sky blue trades, that
  time allows
In all his tuneful turning so few and such morning
  songs
    Before the children green and golden
      Follow him out of grace,

Nothing I cared, in the lamb white days, that time
  would take me
Up to the swallow thronged loft by the shadow of
  my hand,
    In the moon that is always rising,
      Nor that riding to sleep
    I should hear him fly with the high fields
And wake to the farm forever fled from the childless
  land.
Oh as I was young and easy in the mercy of his
  means,
      Time held me green and dying
    Though I sang in my chains like the sea.

?

"Fern Hill" brings this chapter full circle as a metaphorical expression of what happens to those who encounter the wheel of time. As one enters into the magical landscape of Dylan Thomas's world, the reader begins a journey back into the remembrance of childhood. The poet uses language to weave his web around the symbol of time as a connecting link between the present and past. Dust is scattered over the memory of youth as we descend into a world where innocence becomes experience and life becomes death. Time which begins as a friend ends as our enemy. One is reminded of T. S. Eliot's statement that it is only in time and through it that we escape from it. For Thomas this period of transition makes possible the reflections of the golden age of childhood as seen from the shadowy sorrows of maturity. The celebration of these moments are sung "on to the fields of praise" in the world of art. But, finally, even the sunflower becomes weary of time. What begins with "time allows" ends with "time held" as the cycle of the poem and of life draws to a close. During the journey the poet and the reader reexperience that primal scene in Paradise. The poet, like God, banishes us from Eden as he shuts the gates because time leads us "out of grace." We know that the eaten apple, if green, will bring discomfort, and, if golden, will bring discord. It is only the "tuneful turning" of time which sings the praise of what was. The sun is the measure of all that was, is, and will be. We must be satisfied with our knowledge that this is all the light there is. To understand Thomas's vision of time, the following questions focus on the symbolic meaning of the poem.

1 Discuss the ambiguity of the first phrase: "Now as I was young...". What mood does this create for the poem? How does Thomas transform a world for the boy in the apple tree?

2 How does the poet bring together the creation of the world with the child's understanding of life on a farm? What image of nature emerges in this poem? Select one of the myths of creation and compare and contrast the myth's vision of nature with Thomas's.

3 How does Thomas use the images of light and dark to reveal the movement from innocence to experience? When the boy awakens, what insight does he attain? What has he lost? Does Thomas balance these two points of view? Explain!

4 How does Thomas use the colors of green and gold as symbolic representations of the life and death forces? What do these symbols suggest about the regeneration of life? How does Thomas's view of this opposition between life and death contrast with Hawthorne's in "My Kinsman, Major Molineaux"?

5 With what image of time are we left at the poem's close? Explain: "Time held me green and dying/Though I sang in my chains like the sea." How does your view of time compare with Thomas's? Has the modern individual become the slave of time in order to escape knowledge and remain innocent? What knowledge do we seek to avoid? Explain!

6 How would Jung interpret this poem as an expression of Thomas's anima? Explain how time represents the contradiction between the male and female force at work in human beings.

SEPARATION

The Tree of Forgiveness

In the painting by Dürer shown here, Adam and Eve appear as the archetypal representatives of the way the first man and woman moved from ignorance to knowledge. The incident in Eden provided them with the means to accept and understand human consciousness. But they choose to deny, rather than affirm, what they saw. The fig leaf became their symbolic cover, but the moment they put on the fig leaf we know that they know. Deception becomes possible only when we choose to deny what is. Adam and Eve use their fig leaves to protect the illusion that there are no differences between men and women. This leads to a confusion between the sexes and makes separation, rather than union, the goal of love.

The contradictions between male and female begin at the point of separation, and yet...
"The two shall be as one flesh."

VI

THE LOVERS.

Metaphor divides
where it unites,
and we divided
are united,
and so we are,
we find,
our first company
in the universe.

Jean Pumphrey

The transition from boy to man and girl to woman begins with the awareness of the differences between males and females. The sexes are separate—sometimes they oppose each other, sometimes they seek to dominate each other—but always both are necessary for the life process to continue. The rites of passage which brings about the union of these two opposite elements in nature reveals how cultures attempt to explain the unity of these two sexes in one person. Some interpreters of the Garden of Eden myth contend that since Eve was taken from Adam's body, Adam must have originally incorporated both sexes, and the fall occurred when the two were separated. In Greek mythology, Hermes and Aphrodite had a child who had the characteristics of both sexes; they called their child Hermaphrodite. The major god of the Zulu's, Awonawilona, began as both male and female and had to separate into two sexes in order for creation to begin. In Hindu mythology, Siva and his wife often appear united in one body in statues. The left half is female and the right half male. The point of separation marks the first awakening to human consciousness. The contradictions between the two sexes lead to an understanding of the illusions and truths surrounding this complex process.

to keep the universe in motion

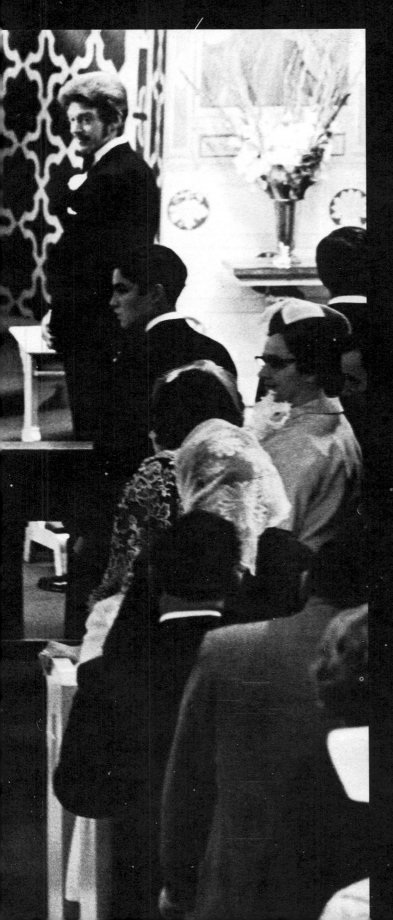

It is well for a man not to touch a woman. But because of the temptation to immorality, each man should have his own wife and each woman her own husband. The husband should give to his wife her conjugal rights, and likewise the wife to her husband. For the wife does not rule over her own body, but the husband does; likewise the husband does not rule over his own body, but the wife does.

I Corinthians 7:1–4

Marriage is neither merely a matter of love, as claimed by some, nor merely an economic institution, as claimed by others. It is the form into which sexual needs were forced by the socioeconomic processes.

Wilhelm Reich

The Transfer
In the picture shown here, the marriage ceremony is the ritual enactment of the rites of passage which unite the male and female. The father kisses his daughter before he gives her to the groom. The priest awaits the couple to formally bless this union. The bride wears white to symbolize her innocence, and after the ceremony friends and relatives will throw rice at the couple to wish them fertility in their marriage. In each of the myths which follow, the explanation of the movement from innocence to experience is used as a means to explain the contradictions between the male and female.

What is needed for sexual harmony is not refinement in technique, rather, on the foundation of the moment's erotic charm, a mutual generosity of body and soul.

Simone de Beauvoir

"Did you know that a woman can now have children without a man?"
"But what on earth for?"
"You can apply ice to a woman's ovaries, for instance. She can have a child. Men are no longer necessary to humanity."
At once Ella laughs, and with confidence. "But what woman in her senses would want ice applied to her ovaries instead of a man?"

The Golden Notebook
Doris Lessing

The contradictions between the male and the female

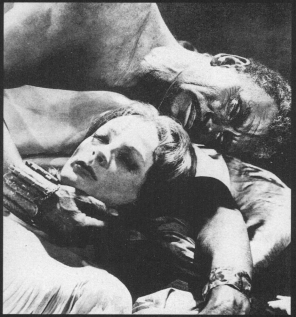

In the first picture from the play *The Storm*, we see the male clinging to the female for help. Both appear frightened, but she appears to be comforting him; they look as if they have just eaten from the "Tree Of Knowledge." Each serves as the other's fig leaf: The woman masks her fear by clutching at the man; the man masks his fear by clinging to the woman. This allows each to see the other without focusing on his or her private fears. The second picture is from Sir Lawrence Oliver's production of *Othello*. This is the final scene in which Othello, after murdering Desdemona because of his suspicions, murders himself when he discovers that his jealousy was based on false assumptions. His inability to accept his guilt and her innocence brings about the death of both lovers. The price for Adam and Eve in knowing the difference between "good and evil" is death; Othello and Desdemona resemble this archetypal pair as they find union only in death.

The first step on the path from child to adult

In the beginning there is unity. Every image is pregnant with meaning. The world often appears as a magical garden filled with wonder and delight. All elements coexist in harmony. But with the separation of night from day comes the movement toward independence and self-liberation. To take this first step is to experience the anxiety that accompanies separation. The primary impressions are stamped on the brain to form the molds which set the life patterns in motion. During this time of transition, each individual moves toward consciousness while experiencing the desire to remain in a world where there is no separation. This dual response also accompanies the division of male from female and female from male. The ritual of marriage functions as a means to help individuals through this crisis. The myths which depict this original action illustrate the separation and union of the World Parents. The movement toward consciousness is characterized by the domination of the masculine principle as a guide to understanding. The opposite pole is represented by the female which represents the unconscious force in the history of human evolution. Both of these forces coexist; the attempt of one to dominate the other ends not in union but in disharmony. The following myths are illustrations of the first encounter between the archetypal representatives of male and female.

As light filters through the trees, the garden symbolizes the environment of the first womb. Neither the man nor the woman knew what it meant to be naked. When their eyes were opened they hid, not just from a god, but from each other as well. The lesson in this story provides us with a means to understand the pursuit of illusion as a means to protect us against the possibilities of differences between the sexes.

ADAM AND EVE: EXPOSURE IN A GARDEN

HEBREW

You shall not eat of the fruit of the tree which is in the midst of the garden, neither shall you touch it, least you die.

Genesis

The Lord God took the man and put him in the Garden of Eden to till it and keep it. And the Lord God commanded the man saying, "You may freely eat of every tree of the garden; but of the tree of knowledge of good and evil you shall not eat, for in the day that you eat of it you shall die."

Then the Lord God said, "It is not good that the man should be alone; I will make him a helper fit for him." So out of the ground the Lord God formed every beast of the field and every bird of the air, and brought them to the man to see what he would call them; and whatever the man called every living creature, that was its name. The man gives names to all cattle, and to the birds of the air, and to every beast of the field; but for the man there was not found a helper fit for him. So the Lord God caused a deep sleep to fall upon the man, and while he slept he took one of his ribs and closed up its place with flesh; and the rib which the Lord God had taken from the man he made into a woman and brought her to the man. Then the man said, "This at last is bone of my bones and flesh of my flesh; she shall be called Woman, because she was taken out of Man."

Therefore a man leaves his father and his mother and cleaves to his wife, and they become one flesh. And the man and his wife were both naked, and were not ashamed.

Now the serpent was more subtle than any other wild creature that the Lord God had made. He said to the woman, "Did God say, 'You shall not eat of any tree of the garden'?" And the woman said to the serpent, "We may eat of the fruit of the trees of the garden; but God said, 'You shall not eat of the fruit of the tree which is in the midst of

the garden, neither shall you touch it, lest you die.'" But the serpent said to the woman, "You will not die. For God knows that when you eat of it your eyes will be opened, and you will be like God, knowing good and evil." So when the woman saw that the tree was good for food, and that it was a delight to the eyes, and that the tree was to be desired to make one wise, she took of its fruit and ate; and she also gave some to her husband, and he ate. Then the eyes of both were opened, and they knew that they were naked; and they sewed fig leaves together and made themselves aprons.

And they heard the sound of the Lord God walking in the garden in the cool of the day, and the man and his wife hid themselves from the presence of the Lord God among the trees of the garden. But the Lord God called to the man, and said to him, *"Where are you?"* And he said, "I heard the sound of thee in the garden, and I was afraid, because I was naked, and I hid myself." He said, *"Who told you that you were naked? Have you eaten of the tree of which I commanded you not to eat?"* The man said, "The woman whom thou gavest to be with me, she gave me fruit of the tree, and I ate." Then the Lord God said to the woman, *"What is this that you have done?"* The woman said, "The serpent beguiled me, and I ate." The Lord God said to the serpent,

"Because you have done this,
cursed are you above all cattle;
and above all wild animals,
upon your belly you shall go,
and dust you shall eat
all the days of your life.
I will put enmity between you and
the woman,
and between your seed and her
seed;

he shall bruise your head,
and you shall bruise his heel."
To the woman he said,
"I will greatly multiply your pain in
childbearing;
yet your desire shall be for your
husband,
and he shall rule over you."
And to Adam he said,
"Because you have listened to the
voice of your wife,
and have eaten of the tree of
which I commanded you,
'You shall not eat of it,'
cursed is the ground because of
you;
in toil you shall eat of it all the
days of your life;
thorns and thistles it shall bring
forth to you;
and you shall eat the plants of the
field.
In the sweat of your face you shall
eat bread
till you return to the ground, for
out of it you were taken;
you are dust,
and to dust you shall return."

The man called his wife's name Eve, because she was the mother of all living. And the Lord God made for Adam and for his wife garments of skins, and clothed them.

Then the Lord God said, "Behold, the man has become like one of us, knowing good and evil; and now, lest he put forth his hand and take also of the tree of life, and eat, and live forever"—therefore the Lord God sent him forth from the Garden of Eden, to till the ground from which he was taken. He drove out the man; and at the east of the Garden of Eden he placed the cherubim, and a flaming sword which turned every way, to guard the way to the tree of life.

Genesis 2:15–25, 3:1–24

SATI AND SIVA: THE FIRST LOVE WILL REAPPEAR IN OTHER FORMS

HINDU

When creation was completed, two pairs of the divine trinity, Brahma and his wife, Sarasvati, and Vishnu and his wife, Lakshmi, were working hard in their roles as creators and preservers of the world. But high on a lofty mountain in the Himalayas, Siva sat alone meditating, refusing to become involved in the affairs of the world. Brahma and Vishnu became worried. Siva's role as destroyer of the old and worn-out was essential to the functioning of the world. If he could not be induced to take a wife and assume his job as destroyer, the world would stagnate and turn into a hugh trash pile.

Sarasvati and Lakshmi looked eagerly for woman who would be worthy of being Siva's partner. Only Makashakti, the Great Mother herself, could fulfill the role. So at the urging of the four great gods, the Great Mother incarnated herself as Sati, the daughter of the sage Dakshi. Knowing from the time of her birth that she was destined to be the wife of Siva, she devoted herself to the practice of yoga and to agonizing austerities so that she might be worthy of him.

But Sati's father disliked Siva, for he was thin and pale from his life of yoga and wore beggar's rags and dead men's bones. Dakshi was angry that his daughter was imitating Siva in meditation and austerities. Perhaps, he thought, if she were married and had a family she would act more normal. So all of the handsome and wealthy men in the country were invited to Dakshi's home so Sati could choose a husband. Sati walked unhappily through the ranks of brave princes decked in gold and jewels and found none that appealed to her. For hours she walked among the men, carrying the wreath she was to give to the man she chose, and at last her father and all of the suitors became tired of her procrastination.

"There is no one else coming," her father said angrily. "So hurry up and make your choice. You are embarrassing me before the most powerful men in the country!"

In desperation Sati threw the wreath into the air and cried, "Siva, take me, for I will have no other!"

And the great miracle occurred. The powerful yogi left his spot on the mountain and took the wreath and his bride.

Now that Siva had found a woman he could love, he became the most devoted of husbands, and the couple spent the years in lovemaking and sharing together in meditation.

But Sati was not quite Siva's equal in meditation, and occasionally she became tired and would slip off to rest. One day she was feeling very playful so she skipped up behind Siva and put her hands over his eyes. Immediately the world plunged into darkness. Horrified, Sati started to take her hands off, but before she could, a third eye suddenly appeared in Siva's forehead. It gave off such tremendous power that all of the forests were burned black.

Sati fell down weeping over the horrible ruin that her joke had caused, and Siva, who could not bear her tears, gave the trees back their life and caused new leaves to spring on their branches. But the third eye which appeared in his forehead remained to give him power.

After several years, Sati's father planned a great festival and invited all of the gods except Siva and Sati. Sati and Siva were both furious at this insult, and they decided to go anyway. When they arrived at the festival, they found a great fire burning which Dakshi had built for the renewing of the universe. Without warning, Sati rushed into the middle of the gathering and, before the eyes of all the horrified spectators, cast herself into the fire!

Siva ran after her, but he was too late. All he took out of the fire was a blackened body. Crazed with grief, he began dancing a dance of grief. Over the heavens and through the mountains he danced with the charred body of his beloved, and as he danced, the tides and the winds began to beat in time to the rhythm of Siva's feet. Brahma watched aghast as Siva's dance of mourning began to slowly evolve into the dance of destruction which would end the created world and cause all to be absorbed into the World Spirit.

But it was not time for the world to end. Vishnu, the preserver, had to stop the crazed Siva. Vishnu rushed after Siva and began to cut the charred body of Sati into thousands of pieces, dropping them in the various parts of India. By now Siva was so involved in his dance that he did not even notice, until as last Sati was gone. Siva suddenly realized that his beloved had disappeared, and turned around to face the sorrowful Vishnu.

"You cannot stop the world because you have lost your wife," Vishnu said. "You know that she is immortal and will reappear in another form."

Siva did not reply, but stopped his dance and returned to his long-interrupted meditations on the mountains.

Sati, Parvati, and Kali. Siva can appear in only one form, but woman is so many-faceted and confusing that it seems impossible to express all of her confusing and conflicting attributes in one person.

After many years, Siva was again needed in the world and so Sati was reborn as Parvati. Again she grew to womanhood knowing that she was Siva's intended, but having already known his love, she did not think that she would need to meditate to gain power over him. So she grew up a beautiful and talented girl, but Siva showed no interest in her. Parvati and the gods used every trick they could think of to attract Siva's attention, but he might as well have been blind. He apparently did not even know that she existed.

Finally, in despair, the gods called Kama, the god of love. Kama shot an arrow at Siva, but Siva was so angry at being disturbed that he turned the full force of his third eye on Kama and burned him to a crisp.

Now the gods were really upset, and Parvati was so worried that she began to undergo the most extreme penances possible. She vowed not to eat and to lie in ice water and torture herself until Siva would marry her.

Siva finally awakened from his meditation and finally noticed the beautiful girl who was rapidly becoming emaciated from her self-tortures. So he took the form of Brahma and went down to talk to her.

"Why are you destroying your beautiful body?" he asked.

"So that I will be worthy of my Lord Siva," was her reply.

"Worthy of him?" laughed Siva in Brahma's form. "He is old, ugly, and bad-tempered, and he spends all of his time in cemeteries. What do you want with him?"

But Parvati put her hands over her ears and refused to listen to anything against Siva. Then Siva appeared to her in his own form and married her.

Parvati and Siva again spent many years in conjugal bliss, but Siva's spouse had to assume still other forms in order to assist him in all his jobs. Siva's primary role is the destruction of the old universe, and when she helps him with this task, Sati/Parvati appears as Kali, a terrible form wearing a necklace of skulls and drinking blood.

Kali first appeared to kill the demon Raktavira, who was so powerful that every drop of his blood that was shed would produce thousands of new demons. To save the world from his cruelty, Kali killed him and drank his blood as it fell. But from this combat she gained a love of blood and destruction.

As Kali, she dances with Siva to bring in the end of the age. But so excited she is by blood and destruction that she sometimes tries to start the dance too early. One time she began the great dance of destruction long before its time. Already she had slaughtered all of the evil demons and was ready to start on the gods. Siva rushed to her in desperation to stop her, but she was so crazed that she didn't even see him. Soon she was dancing on top of Siva himself, and only then did she come to her senses. Contrite after this treatment of her lover, she now waits patiently with Siva for the day of destruction to come at the proper time.

THE BUYING OF LOVE TO EASE THE PAIN OF LONELINESS

SWAHILI

There was once a young man whose parents died and left him a hundred cattle. He was lonely after the death of his parents, so he decided to get married. He went to his neighbors and asked them to help him find a wife.

Soon one of the neighbors came to tell him that he had found the most beautiful girl in the country for him to marry. "The girl is very good and wise and beautiful, and her father is very wealthy," he said. "Her father owns six thousand cattle."

The young man became very excited when he heard about this girl. But then he asked, "How much is the bride price?"

"The father wants a hundred cattle," was the reply.

"A hundred cattle! That is all I have. How will we be able to live?" replied the young man.

"Well, make up your mind. I have to take an answer to the father soon," said the neighbor.

The young man thought, "I cannot live without this girl." So he said, "Go and tell the father that I want to marry his daughter."

So the two were married. But after they returned home, they quickly ran out of food, and the young man had to herd cattle for a neighbor to get anything to eat. What he got was not very much for a young lady who was used to eating well and living in style.

One day as the young wife was sitting outside the house, a strange man came by and was struck by her beauty. He decided to try to seduce her and sent a message to her. The young wife told him that she could not make up her mind and he would have to come back later.

Several months later, the girl's father came to visit. She was very upset because she did not have any-thing to feed him. But on that same day, the seducer came back. So the young wife told the seducer that she would give in to his requests if he would bring her some meat to cook for her father.

Soon the seducer returned with the meat and the girl went inside to cook it. Her husband returned, and he and her father sat down to eat and have a good time. The seducer was standing outside listening. Soon he became angry and went inside to see what was happening. The young husband, who was hospitable, invited him in.

The young wife then brought in the meat and said, "Eat, you three fools."

"Why do you call us fools?" the three men said all together.

"Well, Father," the girl replied. "You are a fool because you sold something precious for something worthless. You had only one daughter and traded her for a hundred cattle when you already had six thousand."

"You are right," said her father. "I was a fool."

"As for you, husband," she went on. "You inherited only a hundred cattle and you went and spent them all on me, leaving us nothing to eat. You could have married another woman for ten or twenty cows. That is why you were a fool."

"And why am I a fool?" asked the seducer.

"You are the biggest fool of all. You thought you could get for one piece of meat what had been bought for a hundred cattle."

At that, the seducer ran away as fast as he could. Then the father said, "You are a wise daughter. When I get home, I will send your husband three hundred cattle so that you can live in comfort."

THE ROSE OF SHARON

I am the rose of Sharon, the lily of the valleys.
As the lily among thorns, so is my love among the daughters.
As the apple tree among the trees of wood, so is my beloved among the sons. I sat down under his shadow with great delight, and his fruit was sweet to my taste.
He brought me to the banqueting house, and his banner over me was love.
Stay me with flagons, comfort me with apples: for I am sick of love.
His left hand is under my head, and his right hand doth embrace me.
My beloved spake, and said unto me, Rise up, my love, my fair one, and come away.
For, lo, the winter is past, the rain is over and gone: the flowers appear on the earth: the time of the singing of birds is come, and the voice of the turtle is heard in our land;
The fig tree puttest forth her green figs, and the vines with the tender grape gave a good smell. Arise, my love, my fair one, and come away.

Song of Solomon (2:1–6, 10–13)

THE WOMAN MUST KNOW HER PLACE

IBIBIAN (AFRICA)

There was once a man who had a very beautiful daughter named Nkoyo. But she was also very spoiled and disobedient and refused to marry any of the fine young men her father found for her.

One day a skull from the Bush of Ghosts heard of Nkoyo's beauty and decided he wanted to marry her. However, he knew that she would not marry a skull, so he went to all of his friends and borrowed various parts of the body. He chose only those parts of the body that were most perfect and handsome, borrowing a face from one friend and arms from another. By the time he was ready to visit Nkoyo, he had the most handsome body in the country.

As soon as he got to town, Nkoyo heard about the handsome stranger, and the moment she caught sight of him she fell in love with him. Her parents did not want her to marry a stranger, but she was so insistent that they finally gave in. As soon as they were married, the skull said, "I must be returning to my home in a far country and Nkoyo must come with me."

Nkoyo's father took her aside and said, "I still do not like the looks of this man, but you must go with your husband. Let me give you one piece of advice, though. Do not be as disobedient and stubborn in your new home as you have been here."

At first Nkoyo enjoyed the journey, but as they approached the Bush of Ghosts, she became rather apprehensive. At last they came to the home of one of the skull's friends from whom he had borrowed his arms. The skull said, "We must stop **here** to return something I have borrowed."

Nkoyo was very frightened when her husband returned without arms. But she was more frightened when they stopped at the next house and returned his feet, then his legs, then his torso, and finally his face, and she discovered that her handsome husband was only a skull.

There was no way of escape. The unhappy girl had to go with the husband she had chosen. At last they arrived at his home, and Nkoyo found that she had to take care of the skull's invalid mother.

By now Nkoyo was sorry that she had been so willful and remembered her father's advice. So she was a very obedient wife and took very good care of her mother-in-law.

One day the grateful mother-in-law came to Nkoyo quietly. "I have heard a rumor," she said, "that the people of the Bush of Ghosts have heard that a living person is here. They are planning to come tonight to kill you and eat you. But since you have been so good to me, I will help you escape to your parents' home. However, I will only let you go if you will promise never to be disobedient again. I hope you have learned by now that good looks and love are very fleeting."

Nkoyo eagerly promised that she would never again disobey her parents, and her mother-in-law called up a wind which blew her back to her home.

The whole town rejoiced at Nkoyo's return for they had learned that her husband was a skull. As for Nkoyo, she married the man her parents had chosen for her and became known throughout the village as the model of an obedient wife.

PANDORA:
THE BEARER
OF EVIL

GREEK

"Prometheus has destroyed us," Zeus confided morosely to Hephaestus. "He has made man too powerful by giving him the gift of fire and the skill to use it to make weapons. Our little creature is likely to destroy us someday."

"There must be some way we could make him weaker," Hephaestus replied. And for a long time the two gods pondered the problem. Then Hera, Zeus' quarrelsome wife, walked by the door and Zeus snapped his fingers with glee.

"I know," he said, "let's make a woman for man!"

Hephaestus, the master craftsman, immediately set to work and soon fashioned a beautiful woman out of clay. The gods, who were delighted with Zeus' scheme, gave her all of their gifts of beauty, charm, and grace, but also filled her with lies, treachery, and deceit. They also gave her an urn filled with all the diseases, natural calamities, and evils that could plague mankind and warned her never to look inside it. Then they dressed her in beautiful clothes and sent her to Epimetheus, his brother, because Prometheus had already been bound on Mount Caucasus in punishment for giving man fire.

Epimetheus was true to his name "Afterthought" and did not even think once before accepting this beautiful woman from his enemy.

Pandora had scarcely entered her new home before she was overcome with curiosity about the mysterious urn which she had been warned not to open. She tried hard to busy herself entertaining her new husband and decorating the house, but the strange urn was never out of her thoughts for more than a few minutes.

At last, one day when Epimetheus was gone, Pandora could not restrain herself any longer. She went into the room with the urn and picked it up, thinking she would only take a little peek.

But as soon as the lid was off, a horrible cloud of noisy, evil beings flew up into the air and scattered over the whole earth. Pandora clapped the lid back on immediately, but it was too late. All of man's miseries had been let loose on the world.

But there was something else in the urn. Pandora could hear a fluttering against the walls. Again her curiosity overcame her and she decided that surely nothing worse could happen, so she opened the lid again.

A small, butterfly-like being that fluttered out and rested on her shoulder emerged. It was hope, one final gift of the gods. But whether it was good or evil, man has not yet decided.

?

In these mythical encounters between the first man and woman, we see the way the male and female transform the other's view of a world. The initiation into the roles underlying the relation of a man and a woman is rich with archetypal symbolism. Each myth depicts the way the individuals must first separate from a family, and the test they must undergo before gaining status as adults. The polarization of the sexes reveals the way the two may be united or divided. The patterns reveal how images of the male and female emerge in symbolic enactments of the world parents. Interpret the myths from the following perspectives:

1 The patterns of separation from the world parents.
   a What is the relation of the male to his mother? How is he separated from her? What is the relation of the male to his father? Does he accept or reject the father as an authority figure?
   b What is the relation of the female to her father? Does she accept his as an authority figure? What is the relation of the female to other females? What does this suggest about the woman's relation to her mother?
   c In which myths are the first man and woman exiled from their environment? What does this suggest about the pattern of family behavior? In which of these myths is punishment linked to this exile? In which of these myths is acceptance back into the family the end result of action? How is this action linked to an understanding of the life and death force?

2 The emergence of a male pattern from the world parents.
   a How do the males appear in these various myths?
   b How does the male act when he first encounters the female?
   c What tests must the male undergo to attain the female?
   d What is the function of pain for the male in these myths?
   e In which of these myths does the male fail to accept what he knows? What does this suggest?
   f How does the male attain love in these myths?
   g What is the relation of punishment to love for the male in these myths?
   h What synthesis of the male archetype emerges from this first encounter with a world?

3 The emergence of a female pattern from the world parents.
   a How does the female appear in these various myths?
   b How does the female act when she first encounters the male?
   c In which of these myths must the female undergo a test to attain the male?
   d In which of these myths does the female work with the male? What does this suggest?
   e In which myths are beauty and youth important to the female?
   f How does the female attain love in these myths?
   g In which of these myths must the female acquiesce to someone else?
   h What synthesis of the female archetype emerges from the female's encounter with a world?

THE box is open

All we did was eat an apple?

The modern confusion begins.

The reward for Knowledge: Punishment

For Blake, God punishes man for "following his energies." As a result of this primal action, we create a belief in the possibility of innocence which for Blake is "contrary" to experience. Experience leads us to doubt, and because of this we become incapable of bringing together spiritual and physical love. The inability of men and women to express love for one another is a theme which appears in both "London" and "The Garden of Love."

LONDON

WILLIAM BLAKE

I wander through each charter'd street,
Near where the charter'd Thames does flow,
And mark in every face I meet
Marks of weakness, marks of woe.

In every cry of every Man,
In every Infant's cry of fear,
In every voice, in every ban
The mind-forg'd manacles I hear.

How the chimney-sweeper's cry
Every black'ning church appals;
And the hapless soldier's sigh
Runs in blood down palace walls.

But most through midnight streets I hear
How the youthful harlot's curse
Blasts the new-born infant's tear,
And blights with plagues the marriage hearse.

THE GARDEN OF LOVE

WILLIAM BLAKE

I went to the Garden of Love,
And saw what I never had seen:
A Chapel was built in the midst,
Where I used to play on the green.

And the gates of this Chapel were shut,
And "Thou shalt not" writ over the door;
So I turn'd to the Garden of Love
That so many sweet flowers bore;

And I saw it was filled with graves,
And tomb-stones where flowers should be;
And Priests in black gowns were walking their
    rounds,
And binding with briars my joys & desires.

William Blake's vision focuses on man's perversion of the Christian principle of love. Blake contends that Christ preached "free" love, and that man has perverted and distorted this vision. The result of this distortion is the creation of a modern hell. Blake echoes the saying of one of Dostoevski's characters: "Fathers and teachers I ponder 'What is hell?' I maintain that it is the suffering of being unable to love." Both of Blake's poems deal with this contradiction.

1 In both "London" and "The Garden of Love" what image of civilized man emerges?

2 How have institutions contributed to man's imprisonment? What has this done to man's emotions? What part did religion play in the degradation of love? Why is there a chapel in the "garden of love"? How does this connect the poem to the myth of the Garden of Eden?

3 In "London" what does Blake mean by "the youthful harlot's curse"? Why would a man go to a prostitute? What does this suggest about a culture's social values?

4 What kills the baby? How does this plague destroy the marriage? What is Blake's view of marriage? What has happened to love because of these restrictions?

5 How does "Thou shalt not" express what has happened to love? What do the priests do in "The Garden of Love"? What does this suggest?

6 To what degree has Christianity influenced our construct of love? Discuss the implications of this idea.

THE SEPARATION OF THE WORLD PARENTS

ERICH NEUMANN

Space only came into being when, as the Egyptian myth puts it, the god of the air, Shu, parted the sky from the earth by stepping between them. Only then, as a result of his light-creating and space-creating intervention, was there heaven above and earth below, back and front, left and right—in other words, only then was space organized with reference to an ego.

Originally there were no abstract spatial components; they all possessed a magical reference to the body, had a mythical, emotional character, and were associated with gods, colors, meanings, allusions. Gradually, with the growth of consciousness, things and places were organized into an abstract system and differentiated from one another; but originally thing and place belonged together in a continuum and were fluidly related to an ever-changing ego. In this inchoate state there was no distinction between I and You, inside and outside, or between men and things, just as there was no clear dividing line between man and the animals, man and man, man and the world. Everything participated in everything else, lived in the same undivided and overlapping state in the world of the unconscious as in the world of dreams. Indeed, in the fabric of images and symbolic presences woven by dreams, a reflection of this early situation still lives on in us, pointing to the original promiscuity of human life.

Not only space but time and the passage of time are oriented by the mythical space picture, and this formative capacity to orient oneself by the sequence of light and darkness, thus widening the scope of consciousness and one's grasp of reality, extends from the phasal organization of primitive society, with its division into age groups, to the modern "psychology of life's stages." In practically all cultures, therefore, the division of the world into four, and the opposition of day and night, play an extremely important part. Because light, consciousness, and culture are made possible only

by the separation of the World Parents, the original uroboros dragon often appears as the chaos dragon. From the standpoint of the orderly light-and-day world of consciousness, all that existed before was night, darkness, chaos, tohubohu. The inward as well as the outward development of culture begins with the coming of light and the separation of the World Parents. Not only do day and night, back and front, upper and lower, inside and outside, I and You, male and female, grow out of this development of opposites and differentiate themselves from the original promiscuity, but opposites like "sacred" and "profane," "good" and "evil," are now assigned their place in the world.

The embedding of the germinal ego in the uroboros corresponds sociologically to the state in which collective ideas prevailed, and the group and group consciousness were dominant. In this state the ego was not an autonomous, individualized entity with a knowledge, morality, volition, and activity of its own; it functioned solely as part of the group, and the group with its superordinate power was the only real subject.

The emancipation of the ego, when the "son" establishes itself as an ego and separates the World Parents, is accomplished on several different levels.

The fact that, at the beginning of conscious development, everything is still interfused, and that each archetypal stage of transformation such as the separation of the World Parents always reveals to us different levels of action, with different effects and values, makes the task of presentation extraordinarily difficult.

The experience of "being different," which is the primary fact of nascent ego consciousness and which occurs in the dawnlight of discrimination, divides the world into subject and object; orientation in time and space succeeds man's vague existence in the dim mists of prehistory and constitutes his early history.

Besides disentangling itself from its fusion with nature and the group, the ego, having now opposed itself to the nonego as another datum of experience, begins simultaneously to constellate its independence of nature as independence of the body. Later we shall have to come back to the question of how the ego and consciousness experience their own reality by distinguishing themselves from the body. This is one of the fundamental facts of the human mind and its discovery of itself as something distinct from nature. Early man is in the same case as the infant and small child: his body and his "inside" are part of an alien world. The acquisition of voluntary muscular movement, i.e., the fact that the ego discovers, in its own "person," that its conscious will can control the body, may well be the basic experience at the root of all magic. The ego, having its seat, as it were, in the head, in the cerebral cortex, and experiencing the nether regions of the body as something strange to it, an alien reality, gradually begins to recognize that essential portions of this nether corporeal world are subject to its will and volition. It discovers that the "sovereign power of thought" is a real and actual fact: the hand in front of my face, and the foot lower down, do what I will. The obviousness of these facts should not blind us to the enormous impression which this very early discovery must make, and unquestionably has made, on every infantile ego nucleus. If technics are an extension of the "tool" as a means for dominating the world around us, then the tool in its turn is nothing but an extension of the voluntary musculature. Man's will to dominate nature is but an extension and projection of that fundamental experience of the ego's potential power over the body, discovered in the voluntariness of muscular movement.

Opposition between ego and body is, as we have said, an original condition. Containment in the uroboros and its supremacy over the ego mean, on the bodily level, that ego and consciousness are at the outset continually at the mercy of the instincts, impulses, sensations, and reactions deriving from the world of the body. To begin with, this ego, existing first as a point and then as an island, knows nothing of itself and consequently nothing of its difference. As it grows stronger, it detaches itself more and more from the world of the body. This leads finally, as we know, to a state of systematized ego consciousness where the entire

bodily realm is to a large extent unconscious, and the conscious system is split off from the body as the representative of unconscious processes. Though the split is not in effect so drastic as this, the illusion of it is so powerful and so real for the ego that the body region and the unconscious can only be rediscovered with a great effort. In yoga, for instance, a strenuous attempt is made to reconnect the conscious mind with the unconscious bodily processes. This exercise may, if overdone, lead to illness, but in itself it is quite sensible.

In the beginning, the realm of ego consciousness and the spiritual and psychic realm are indissolubly united with the body. Instinct and volition are as little divided as instinct and consciousness. Even in modern man, depth psychology has found that the division which has resulted between these two spheres in the course of cultural development—for their mutual tensions constitute what we call culture—is largely an illusion. The activity of instinct lies behind actions which the ego coordinates with its sphere of decision and volition, and to an even higher degree instincts and archetypes are at the back of our conscious attitudes and orientations. But, whereas in modern man there is at any rate the possibility of decision and conscious orientation, the psychology of archaic man and of the child is marked by a mingling of these spheres. Volitions, moods, emotions, instincts, and somatic reactions are still for all practical purposes fused together. The same applies to the original ambivalence of affects, which are later resolved into antithetical positions. Love and hate, joy and sorrow, pleasure and pain, attraction and repulsion, yes and no, are at first juxtaposed and interfused, and do not possess the antithetical character they subsequently appear to have.

The stage of separation of the World Parents which initiates the independence of the ego and consciousness by giving rise to the principle of opposites is therefore also the stage of increasing masculinity. Ego consciousness stands in manly opposition to the feminine unconscious. This strengthening of consciousness is borne out by the laying down of taboos and of moral attitudes which delimit the conscious from the unconscious by substituting knowing action for unwitting impulse. The meaning of ritual, irrespective of the useful effects which primitive man expects from it, lies precisely in strengthening the conscious system. The magical forms by means of which archaic man comes to terms with his surroundings are, all other considerations apart, anthropocentric systems of world domination. In his rituals he makes himself the responsible center of the cosmos; on him depends the rising of the sun, the fertility of crops, and all the doings of the gods. These projections and the various procedures by which the Great Individuals distinguish themselves from the herd as chiefs, medicine men, or divine kings, and the demons, spirits, and gods are crystallized out from a welter of indeterminate "powers," we know to be expressions of a centering process that imposes order upon the chaos of unconscious events and leads to the possibility of conscious action. Although nature and the unconscious are ordinarily experienced by primitive man as a field of unseen forces which leave no room for chance, life remains chaotic for the germinal ego, dark and impenetrable, so long as no orientation is possible with regard to these forces. But orientation comes through ritual, through the subjugation of the world by magic, which imposes world order. Even though this order is different from the kind we impose, the connection between our conscious order and the magical order of early man can be proved at all points. The important thing is that consciousness as the acting center precedes consciousness as the cognitive center, in the same way as ritual precedes myth, or magic ceremonial and ethical action precede the scientific view of the world and anthropological knowledge.

The center common to conscious action through the will and to conscious knowledge through cognition is, however, the ego. From being acted upon by external forces, it develops slowly into the agent, just as it ascends from the state of being overpowered by revealed knowledge into the light of conscious knowledge. Once again, this process is first accomplished not in the collective parts of the group, but only in the great, i.e., differentiated, individuals who are the representative bearers of the group's consciousness. They are the institutional forerunners and leaders whom the group follows. The ritual marriage between fructifier and earth goddess, between king and queen, becomes the model for all marriages between members of the collective. The immortal soul of the divine king Osiris becomes the immortal soul of each and every Egyptian, even as Christ the Saviour becomes the Christ-soul of every Christian, the self within us. In

the same way, the function of the chief, which is to will and to decide, becomes the model for all subsequent acts of free will in the ego of the individual; and the law-making function, originally attributed to God and later to the mana personality, has in modern man become his inner court of conscience.

Then follows the fragmentation of archetypes and the separation of the personal "good" side of the Mother figure from her transpersonal, negative side, or vice versa. The child's fear and feeling of being threatened does not derive from the traumatic character of the world, for no trauma exists under normal human conditions or even under primitive ones; it comes rather from the "night space," or, to be more precise, it arises when the ego steps forth from this night space. The germinal ego consciousness then experiences the overwhelming impact of the world-and-body stimulus, either directly or in projection. The importance of family relationships lies precisely in the fact that the personal figures of the environment who are the first form of society must be able, as soon as the ego emerges from the primary security of the uroboric state, to offer it the secondary security of the human world.

This development is paralleled by the exhaustion of emotional components and the outgrowing of the early accentuation of the body, and this in turn leads to the gradual building up of a superego through the demands and prohibitions of the environment.

Another general feature of conscious development, namely the deflation of the unconscious, can be traced in the normal growth of the child, when the primordial, unconscious world of childhood, the world of dream and fairy tale, and also of children's drawings and children's games, fades in increasing measure before the reality of the external world. The libido accruing from the activated unconscious is now employed to build up and extend the conscious system. The implementation of this process marks the transition from playing to learning. School in our culture is the architect whom the collective has commissioned to erect, systematically, a bastion between the deflated unconscious and a consciousness orientated towards collective adaptation.

The patriarchal line of conscious development with its watchword "Away from the Mother-world! Forward to the Father-world!" is enjoined upon male and female alike, although they may follow it in different ways. To be a mother's darling is a sign of not having accomplished the initial dragon fight which brings infancy to a close. This failure makes entry into school and the world of other children impossible, just as failure in the rites of initiation at puberty precludes entry into the adult world of men and women.

We come now to the formation of those components of personality whose discovery we owe to the analytical psychology of Jung: the persona, the anima and animus figures, and the shadow. They are produced by the differentiation processes we have already described, which occur during the first half of life. In all of them, personalistic and individual features are combined with archetypal and transpersonal ones, and the personality components which ordinarily exist in the structure of the psyche as potential psychic organs now become amalgamated with the fateful, individual variants realized by the individual in the course of his development.

The development of the persona is the outcome of a process of adaptation that suppresses all individually significant features and potentialities, disguising and repressing them in favor of collective factors, or those deemed desirable by the collective. Here again, wholeness is exchanged for a workable and successful sham personality. The "inner voice" is stifled by the growth of a superego, of conscience, the representative of collective values. The voice, the individual experience of the transpersonal, which is particularly strong in childhood, is renounced in favor of conscience. When paradise is abandoned, the voice of God that spoke in the Garden is abandoned too, and the values of the collective, of the fathers, of law and conscience, of the current morality, etc., must be accepted as the supreme values in order to make social adaptation possible.

Whereas the natural disposition of every individual inclines him to be physically and psychically bisexual, the differential development of our culture forces him to thrust the contrasexual element into the unconscious. As a result, only those elements which accord with the outward characteristics of sex and which conform to the collective valuation are recognized by the conscious mind. Thus "feminine" or "soulful" characteristics are considered undesirable in a boy, at least in our culture. Such a one-sided accentuation of one's specific sexuality ends by constellating the contrasexual

element in the unconscious, in the form of the anima in men and the animus in women, which, as part souls, remain unconscious and dominate the conscious-unconscious relationship. This process has the support of the collective, and sexual differentiation, precisely because the repression of the contrasexual element is often difficult, is at first accompanied by typical forms of animosity towards the opposite sex. This development, too, follows the general principle of differentiation which presupposes the sacrifice of wholeness, here represented by the figure of the hermaphrodite.

Progression through the archetypal phases, the patriarchal orientation of consciousness, the formation of the superego as the representative of collective values within the personality, the existence of a collective value-canon, all these things are necessary conditions of normal, ethical development. If any one of these factors is inhibited, developmental disturbances result. A disturbance of the first two factors, which are specifically psychic, leads to neuroticism; a disturbance of the other two, which are cultural, expresses itself more in social maladjustment, delinquency, or criminality.

The average child not only survives this process of uprooting, but derives from it an enhanced inner tension. Relative loss of unity, polarization into two psychic systems, insulation of the inner world and the building up of authorities within the personality may be productive of conflict, but they cannot be said to lay the foundations of any neurotic development. They are on the contrary normative, and it is their absence, or rather their incompleteness, that leads to illness.

A certain one-sidedness of development favorable to consciousness is largely characteristic of our specifically Western psychic structure, which therefore includes conflict and sacrifice from the start. At the same time, however, such a structure has the innate capacity to make the conflict fruitful and to endow the sacrifice with a meaning. Centroversion expresses itself in the psyche as a striving for wholeness which, as life goes on, balances the one-sidedness of the first half by a compensatory development during the second half. The tensional conflict between conscious and unconscious, provided that the natural compensatory tendencies of the unconscious are at work, leads to a steady growth of personality; and, with an intensification of the conscious-unconscious relationship in such a maturing personality, the original conflict is replaced by an ever richer and more complete synthesis.

But, to begin with, the differentiation and division which we found to be necessary in the development of mankind are also necessary for the individual, who in his own development retraces the old paths that mankind has trod. The tension arising from his inner psychic polarization forms the personality's energy potential and relates him to the world in two ways.

As ego consciousness increases there is a progressive transference of libido to the world, a cumulative "investment" of it in external objects. This transference of libido derives from two sources: on the one hand from the application of conscious interest by the ego, and on the other hand from the projection of unconscious contents. Whenever the energy-charge of unconscious contents becomes excessive, they discharge themselves from the unconscious and are projected. They now approach the conscious mind as world-animating images, and the ego experiences them as contents of that world. In this way projection results in an intensified fixation to the world and to the carriers of the projection.

This process is particularly noticeable in puberty. Activation of the unconscious, which at this period occurs as a parallel symptom to psychophysical change, manifests itself in the increased activity of the collective unconscious and of the archetypes; it far exceeds the activation of the sexual sphere, and its manifestations consist not only in the danger of invasion, as evidenced by the frequency of psychoses at this period, but more particularly in a newly fledged and passionate interest in everything suprapersonal, in ideas and ideals of universal import, which many people evince only at this period of heightened activity in the collective unconscious. Puberty is further characterized by a change of emotional tone, a feeling for life and the world more akin to the universal oneness of the dawn man than to the mood of the modern adult. This lyrical animation and the relatively frequent emergence of mythological motifs in the dreams and poetic compositions of this period are typical symptoms of the activation of the collective unconscious layer.

But since the compensatory working of consciousness is also heightened in puberty, it is only with markedly introverted or creative natures that there is any direct perception of the movement in the unconscious. Generally it passes off behind the dividing wall between the ego and the unconscious, and only faint radiations reach the conscious mind. Besides radiating out into interest and feeling, the activated unconscious also makes itself felt through "fascinating" projections which initiate and guarantee the next stage of normal development.

The most important projections at this period are of the anima or animus, the contrasexual imagos lying dormant in the unconscious, which now become activated. These glamorous images are projected into the world and sought there, thus constellating the problem of a partner, the main theme during the first half of life.

In "The Separation of the World Parents" Erich Neumann contends that the energy we attach to the opposite sex is charged with the emotions characterized by our awareness of the existence of opposites. Originally, there was no abstract separation between the individual and his world. The author links the growth of consciousness to the development of a masculine orientation of the world development. The suppression of the negative, or dark, side of our personality becomes embodied in the collective unconscious which Neumann describes as feminine in principle. The following questions are directed toward an understanding of the images contained within the figures of the anima and animus.

1 How does Neumann illustrate the original world picture? What myths reveal this picture before the separation of the world parents?

2 How does Neumann relate "being different" to the development of consciousness? How does Sati in the Hindu myth illustrate this principle?

3 Why does Neumann contend that the body is the root of all magic? How does the body appear in the Ibibian myth? In the myth of Adam and Eve?

4 How does the ego work in opposition to the body? In the Garden of Eden myth, what does consciousness of good and evil do to Adam and Eve?

5 How does the separation from the first family give rise to the principle of opposites? In the Hindu myth, how is this principle illustrated?

6 What do the positive and negative elements reveal about the mother and father in the Garden of Eden myth?

7 How does ritual strengthen the development of consciousness?

8 Why is the development of the persona an outgrowth of the process of adaption? In which myths must individuals learn to adapt?

9 How do individuals learn to transfer energy onto members of the opposite sex? What does this suggest about the male's attitude toward the female, and the female's attitude toward the male?

10 What activates the anima and the animus during puberty? How does this illustrate the rites of passage during this stage of development?

Looking at some Reflections...

Valentino symbolizes the romantic man of action. Millions of women projected onto him their animus. His pursuit of women and their capture combine to make him appear as the illusion of perfection. Valentino represents some of the contradictions which cause confusion between the ideal and the real.

THE BIRTHMARK

NATHANIEL HAWTHORNE

In the latter part of the last century there lived a man of science, an eminent proficient in every branch of natural philosophy, who not long before our story opens had made experience of a spiritual affinity more attractive than any chemical one. He had left his laboratory to the care of an assistant, cleared his fine countenance from the furnace smoke, washed the stain of acids from his fingers, and persuaded a beautiful woman to become his wife. In those days when the comparatively recent discovery of electricity and other kindred mysteries of Nature seemed to open paths into the region of miracle, it was not unusual for the love of science to rival the love of woman in its depth and absorbing energy. The higher intellect, the imagination, the spirit, and even the heart might all find their congenial aliment in pursuits which, as some of their ardent votaries believed, would ascend from one step of powerful intelligence to another, until the philosopher should lay his hand on the secret of creative force and perhaps make new worlds for himself. We know not whether Aylmer possessed this degree of faith in man's ultimate control over Nature. He had devoted himself, however, too unreservedly to scientific studies ever to be weaned from them by any second passion. His love for his young wife might prove the stronger of the two; but it could only be by intertwining itself with his love of science, and uniting the strength of the latter to his own.

Such a union accordingly took place, and was attended with truly remarkable consequences and a deeply impressive moral. One day, very soon after their marriage, Aylmer sat gazing at his wife with a trouble in his countenance that grew stronger until he spoke.

"Georgiana," said he, "has it never occurred to you that the mark upon your cheek might be removed?"

"No, indeed," said she, smiling; but perceiving the seriousness of his manner, she blushed deeply. "To tell you the truth it has been so often called a charm that I was simple enough to imagine it might be so."

"Ah, upon another face perhaps it might," replied her husband; "but never on yours. No, dearest Georgiana, you came so nearly perfect from the hand of Nature that this slightest possible defect, which we hesitate whether to term a defect or a beauty, shocks me, as being the visible mark of earthly imperfection."

"Shocks you, my husband!" cried Georgiana, deeply hurt; at first reddening with momentary anger, but then bursting into tears. "Then why did you take me from my mother's side? You cannot love what shocks you!"

To explain this conversation it must be mentioned that in the centre of Georgiana's left cheek there was a singular mark, deeply interwoven, as it were, with the texture and substance of her face. In the usual state of her complexion—a healthy though delicate bloom—the mark wore a tint of deeper crimson, which imperfectly defined its shape amid the surrounding rosiness. When she blushed it gradually became more indistinct, and finally vanished amid the triumphant rush of blood that bathed the whole cheek with its brilliant glow. But if any shifting motion caused her to turn pale there was the mark again, a crimson stain upon the snow, in what Aylmer sometimes deemed an almost fearful distinctness. Its shape bore not a little similarity to the human hand, though of the smallest pygmy size. Georgiana's lovers were wont to say that some fairy at her birth hour had laid her tiny hand upon the infant's cheek, and left this impress there in token of the magic endowments that were to give her such sway over all hearts. Many a desperate swain would have risked life for the privilege of pressing his lips to the mysterious hand. It must not be concealed, however, that the impression wrought by this fairy sign manual varied exceedingly, according to the difference of temperament in the beholders. Some fastidious persons—but they were exclusively of her own sex—affirmed that the bloody hand, as they chose to call it, quite destroyed the effect of Georgiana's beauty, and rendered her countenance even hideous. But it would be as reasonable to say that one of those small blue stains which sometimes occur in the purest statuary marble would convert the Eve of Powers to a monster. Masculine observers, if the birthmark did not heighten their admiration, contented themselves with wishing it away, that the world might possess one living specimen of ideal loveliness without the semblance of a flaw. After his marriage—for he thought little or nothing of the matter before—Aylmer discovered that this was the case with himself.

Had she been less beautiful—if Envy's self could have found aught else to sneer at—he might have felt his affection heightened by the prettiness of this mimic hand, now vaguely portrayed, now lost, now stealing forth again and glimmering to and fro with every pulse of emotion that throbbed within her heart; but seeing her otherwise so perfect, he found this one defect grow more and more intolerable with every moment of their united lives. It was the fatal flaw of humanity which Nature, in one shape or another, stamps ineffaceably on all her productions, either to imply that they are temporary and finite, or that their perfection must be wrought by toil and pain. The crimson hand expressed the ineludible gripe in which mortality clutches the highest and purest of earthly mould, degrading them into kindred with the lowest, and even with the very brutes, like whom their visible frames return to dust. In this manner, selecting it as the symbol of his wife's liability to sin, sorrow, decay, and death, Aylmer's sombre imagination was not long in rendering the birthmark a frightful object, causing him more trouble and horror than ever Georgiana's beauty, whether of soul or sense, had given him delight.

At all the seasons which should have been their happiest, he invariably and without intending it, may, in spite of a purpose to the contrary, reverted to this one disastrous topic. Trifling as it at first appeared, it so connected itself with innumerable trains of thought and modes of feeling that it became the central point of all. With the morning twilight Aylmer opened his eyes upon his wife's face and recognized the symbol of imperfection; and when they sat together at the evening hearth his eyes wandered stealthily to her cheek, and beheld, flickering with the blaze of the wood fire, the spectral hand that wrote mortality where he would fain have worshipped. Georgiana soon learned to shudder at his gaze. It needed but a glance with the peculiar expression that his face often wore to change the roses of her cheek into a deathlike paleness, amid which the crimson hand was brought strongly out, like a bas-relief by ruby on the whitest marble.

Late one night when the lights were growing dim, so as hardly to betray the strain on the poor wife's cheek, she herself, for the first time, voluntarily took up the subject.

"Do you remember, my dear Aylmer," said she, with a feeble attempt at a smile, "have you any recollection of a dream last night about this odious hand?"

"None! none whatever!" replied Aylmer, starting; but then he added, in a dry, cold tone, affected for the sake of concealing the real depth of his emotion, "I might well dream of it; for before I fell asleep it had taken a pretty firm hold of my fancy."

"And you did dream of it?" continued Georgiana, hastily; for she dreaded lest a gush of tears should interrupt what she had to say. "A terrible dream! I wonder that you can forget it. Is it possible to forget this one expression?—'It is in her heart now; we must have it out!' Reflect, my husband; for by all means I would have you recall that dream."

The mind is in a sad state when Sleep, the all-involving, cannot confine her spectres within the dim region of her sway, but suffers them to break forth, affrighting this actual life with secrets that perchance belong to a deeper one. Aylmer now remembered his dream. He had fancied himself with his servant Aminadab, attempting an operation for the removal of the birthmark; but the deeper went the knife, the deeper sank the hand, until at length its tiny grasp appeared to have caught hold of Georgiana's heart; whence, however, her husband was inexorably resolved to cut or wrench it away.

When the dream had shaped itself perfectly in his memory, Aylmer sat in his wife's presence with a guilty feeling. Truth often finds its way to the mind close muffled in robes of sleep, and then speaks with uncompromising directness of matters in regard to which we practise an unconscious self-deception during our waking moments. Until now he had not been aware of the tyrannizing influence acquired by one idea over his mind, and of the lengths which he might find in his heart to go for the sake of giving himself peace.

"Aylmer," resumed Georgiana, solemnly, "I know not what may be the cost to both of us to rid me of this fatal birthmark. Perhaps its removal may cause cureless deformity; or it may be the stain goes as deep as life itself. Again: do we know that there is a possibility, on any terms, of unclasping the firm gripe of this little hand which was laid upon me before I came into the world?"

"Dearest Georgiana, I have spent much thought upon the subject," hastily interrupted Aylmer. "I am convinced of the perfect practicability of its removal."

"If there be the remotest possibility of it," continued Georgiana, "let the attempt be made at whatever risk. Danger is nothing to me; for life, while this hateful mark makes me the object of your horror and disgust—life is a burden which I would fling down with joy. Either remove this dreadful hand, or take my wretched life! You have deep science. All the world bears witness of it. You have achieved great wonders.

Cannot you remove this little, little mark, which I cover with the tips of two small fingers? Is this beyond your power, for the sake of your own peace, and to save your poor wife from madness?"

"Noblest, dearest, tenderest wife," cried Aylmer, rapturously, "doubt not my power. I have already given this matter the deepest thought—thought which might almost have enlightened me to create a being less perfect than yourself. Georgiana, you have led me deeper than ever into the heart of science. I feel myself fully competent to render this dear cheek as faultless as its fellow; and then, most beloved, what will be my triumph when I shall have corrected what Nature left imperfect in her fairest work! Even Pygmalion, when his sculptured woman assumed life, felt not greater ecstasy than mine will be."

"It is resolved, then," and Georgiana, faintly smiling. "And, Aylmer, spare me not, though you should find the birthmark take refuge in my heart at last."

Her husband tenderly kissed her cheek—her right cheek—not that which bore the impress of the crimson hand.

The next day Aylmer apprised his wife of a plan that he had formed whereby he might have opportunity for the intense thought and constant watchfulness which the proposed operation would require; while Georgiana, likewise, would enjoy the perfect repose essential to its success. They were to seclude themselves in the extensive apartments occupied by Aylmer as a laboratory, and where, during his toilsome youth, he had made discoveries in the elemental powers of Nature that had roused the admiration of all the learned societies in Europe. Seated calmly in this laboratory, the pale philosopher had investigated the secrets of the highest cloud region and of the profoundest mines; he had satisfied himself of the causes that kindled and kept alive the fires of the volcano; and had explained the mystery of fountains, and how it is that they gush forth, some so bright and pure, and others with such rich medicinal virtues, from the dark bosom of the earth. Here, too, at an earlier period, he had studied the wonders of the human frame, and attempted to fathom the very process by which Nature assimilates all her precious influences from earth and air, and from the spiritual world, to create and foster man, her masterpiece. The latter pursuit, however, Aylmer had long laid aside in unwilling recognition of the truth—against which all seekers sooner or later stumble—that our great creative Mother, while she amuses us with apparently working in the broadest sunshine, is yet severely careful to keep her own secrets, and, in spite of her pretended openness, shows us nothing but results. She permits us, indeed, to mar, but seldom to mend, and, like a jealous patentee, on no account to make. Now, however, Aylmer resumed these half-forgotten investigations; not, of course, with such hopes or wishes as first suggested them; but because they involved much physiological truth and lay in the path of his proposed scheme for the treatment of Georgiana.

As he led her over the threshold of the laboratory, Georgiana was cold and tremulous. Aylmer looked cheerfully into her face, with intent to reassure her, but was so startled with the intense glow of the birthmark upon the whiteness of her cheek that he could not restrain a strong convulsive shudder. His wife fainted.

"Aminadab! Aminadab!" shouted Aylmer, stamping violently on the floor.

Forthwith there issued from an inner apartment a man of low stature, but bulky frame, with shaggy hair hanging about his visage, which was grimed with the vapors of the furnace. This personage had been Aylmer's underworker during his whole scientific career, and was admirably fitted for that office by his great mechanical readiness, and the skill with which, while incapable of comprehending a simple principle, he executed all the details of his master's experiments. With his vast strength, his shaggy hair, his smoky aspect, and the indescribable earthiness that incrusted him, he seemed to represent man's physical nature; while Aylmer's slender figure, and pale, intellectual face, were no less apt a type of the spiritual element.

"Throw open the door of the boudoir, Aminadab," said Aylmer, "and burn a pastil."

"Yes, master," answered Aminadab, looking intently at the lifeless form of Georgiana; and then he muttered to himself, "If she were my wife, I'd never part with that birthmark."

When Georgiana recovered consciousness she found herself breathing an atmosphere of penetrating fragrance, the gentle potency of which had recalled her from her deathlike faintness. The scene around her looked like enchantment. Aylmer had converted those smoky, dingy, sombre rooms, where he had spent his brightest years in recondite pursuits, into a series of beautiful apartments not unfit to be the secluded abode of a lovely woman. The walls were hung with gorgeous curtains, which imparted the combination of grandeur and grace that no other species of adornment can achieve; and as they fell from the ceiling to the floor, their rich and ponderous folds, concealing all angles and straight lines, appeared to shut in the scene from infinite space. For aught Georgiana knew, it might be a pavilion among the clouds. And Aylmer, excluding the sunshine, which would have interfered with his chemical process, had supplied its place with perfumed lamps, emitting flames of various hue, but all uniting in a soft, impurpled radiance. He now knelt by his wife's side, watching her earnestly, but without alarm; for he was confident in his science, and felt that he could draw a magic circle round her within which no evil might intrude.

"Where am I? Ah, I remember," said Georgiana, faintly; and she placed her hand over her cheek to hide the terrible mark from her husband's eyes.

"Fear not, dearest!" exclaimed he. "Do not shrink from me! Believe me, Georgiana, I even rejoice in this single imperfection, since it will be such a rapture to remove it."

"Oh, spare me!" sadly replied his wife. "Pray do not look at it again. I never can forget that convulsive shudder."

In order to soothe Georgiana, and, as it were, to release her mind from the burden of actual things, Aylmer now put in practice some of the light and playful secrets which science had taught him among its profounder lore. Airy figures, absolutely bodiless ideas, and forms of unsubstantial beauty came and danced before her, imprinting their momentary footsteps on beams of light. Though she had some indistinct idea of the method of these optical phenomena, still the illusion was almost perfect enough to warrant the belief that her husband possessed sway over the spiritual world. Then again, when she felt a wish to look forth from her seclusion, immediately, as if her thoughts were answered, the procession of external existence flitted across a screen. The scenery and the figures of actual life were perfectly represented, but with that bewitching, yet indescribable difference which always makes a picture, an image, or a shadow so much more attractive than the original. When wearied of this, Aylmer bade her cast her eyes upon a vessel containing a quantity of earth. She did so, with little interest at first; but was soon startled to perceive the germ of a plant shooting upward from the soil. Then came the slender stalk; the leaves gradually unfolded themselves; and amid them was a perfect and lovely flower.

"It is magical!" cried Georgiana. "I dare not touch it."

"Nay, pluck it," answered Aylmer—"pluck it, and inhale its brief perfume while you may. The flower will wither in a few moments and leave nothing save its brown seed vessels; but thence may be perpetuated a race as ephemeral as itself."

But Georgiana had no sooner touched the flower than the whole plant suffered a blight, its leaves turning coalblack as if by the agency of fire.

"There was too powerful a stimulus," said Aylmer, thoughtfully.

To make up for this abortive experiment, he proposed to take her portrait by a scientific process of his own invention. It was to be effected by rays of light striking upon a polished plate of metal. Georgiana assented; but, on looking at the result, was affrighted to find the features of the portrait blurred and indefinable; while the minute figure of a hand appeared where the cheek should have been. Aylmer snatched the metallic plate and threw it into a jar of corrosive acid.

Soon, however, he forgot these mortifying failures. In the intervals of study and chemical experiment he came to her flushed and exhausted, but seemed invigorated by her presence, and spoke in glowing language of the resources of his art. He gave a history of the long dynasty of the alchemists, who spent so many ages in quest of the universal solvent by which the golden principle might be elicited from all things vile and base. Aylmer appeared to believe that, by the plainest scientific logic, it was altogether within the limits of possibility to discover this long-sought medium; "but," he added, "a philosopher who should go deep enough to acquire the power would attain too lofty a wisdom to stoop to the exercise of it." Not less singular were his opinions in regard to the elixir vitæ. He more than intimated that it was at his option to concoct a liquid that should prolong life for years, perhaps interminably; but that it would produce a discord in Nature which all the world, and chiefly the quaffer of the immortal nostrum, would find cause to curse.

"Aylmer, are you in earnest?" asked Georgiana, looking at him with amazement and fear. "It is terrible to possess such power, or even to dream of possessing it."

"Oh, do not tremble, my love," said her husband. "I would not wrong either you or myself by working such inharmonious effects upon our lives; but I would have you consider how tri-fling, in comparison, is the skill requisite to remove this little hand."

At the mention of the birthmark, Georgiana, as usual, shrank as if a redhot iron had touched her cheek.

Again Aylmer applied himself to his labors. She could hear his voice in the distant furnace room giving directions to Aminadab, whose harsh, uncouth, misshapen tones were audible in response, more like the grunt or growl of a brute than human speech. After hours of absence, Aylmer reappeared and proposed that she should now examine his cabinet of chemical products and natural treasures of the earth. Among the former he showed her a small vial, in which, he remarked, was contained a gentle yet most powerful fragrance, capable of impregnating all the breezes that blow across a kingdom. They were of inestimable value, the contents of that little vial; and, as he said so, he threw some of the perfume into the air and filled the room with piercing and invigorating delight.

"And what is this?" asked Georgiana, pointing to a small crystal globe containing a gold-colored liquid. "It is so beautiful to the eye that I could imagine it the elixir of life."

"In one sense it is," replied Aylmer; "or, rather, the elixir of immortality. It is the most precious poison that ever was concocted in this world. By its aid I could apportion the lifetime of any mortal at whom you might point your finger. The strength of the dose would determine whether he were to linger out years, or drop dead in the midst of a breath. No king on his guarded throne could keep his life if I, in my private station, should deem that the welfare of millions justified me in depriving him of it."

"Why do you keep such a terrific drug?" inquired Georgiana in horror.

"Do not mistrust me, dearest," said her husband, smiling; "its virtuous potency is yet greater than its harmful one. But see! here is a powerful cosmetic. With a few drops of this in a vase of water, freckles may be washed away as easily as the hands are cleansed. A stronger infusion would take the blood out of the cheek, and leave the rosiest beauty a pale ghost."

"Is it with this lotion that you intend to bathe my cheek?" asked Georgiana, anxiously.

"Oh, no," hastily replied her husband; "this is merely superficial. Your case demands a remedy that shall go deeper."

In his interviews with Georgiana, Aylmer generally made minute inquiries as to her sensations and whether the confinement of the rooms and the temperature of the atmosphere agreed with her. These questions had such a particular drift that Georgiana began to conjecture that she was already subjected to certain physical influences, either breathed in with the fragrant air or taken with her food. She fancied likewise, but it might be altogether fancy, that there was a stirring up of her system—a strange, indefinite sensation creeping through her veins, and tingling, half painfully, half pleasurably, at her heart. Still, whenever she dared to look into the mirror, there she beheld herself pale as a white rose and with the crimson birthmark stamped upon her cheek. Not even Aylmer now hated it so much as she.

To dispel the tedium of the hours which her husband found it necessary to devote to the processes of combination and analysis, Georgiana turned over the volumes of his scientific library. In many dark old tomes she met with chapters full of romance and poetry. They were the works of philosophers of the middle ages, such as Albertus Magnus, Cornelius Agrippa, Paracelsus, and the famous friar who created the prophetic Brazen Head. All these antique naturalists stood in advance of their centuries, yet were imbued with some of their credulity, and therefore were believed, and perhaps imagined themselves to have acquired from the investigation of Nature a power above Nature, and from physics a sway over the spiritual world. Hardly less curious and imaginative were the early volumes of the Transactions of the Royal Society, in which the members, knowing little of the limits of natural possibility, were continually recording wonders or proposing methods whereby wonders might be wrought.

But to Georgiana the most engrossing volume was a large folio from her husband's own hand, in which he had recorded every experiment of his scientific career, its original aim, the methods adopted for its development, and its final success or failure, with the circumstances to which either event was attributable. The book, in truth, was both the history and emblem of his ardent, ambitious, imaginative, yet practical and laborious life. He handled physical details as if there were nothing beyond them; yet spiritualized them all, and redeemed himself from materialism by his strong and eager aspiration towards the infinite. In his grasp the veriest clod of earth assumed a soul. Georgiana, as she read, reverenced Aylmer and loved him more profoundly than ever, but with a less entire dependence on his judgment than heretofore. Much as he had accom-

plished, she could not but observe that his most splendid successes were almost invariably failures, if compared with the ideal at which he aimed. His brightest diamonds were the merest pebbles, and felt to be so by himself, in comparison with the inestimable gems which lay hidden beyond his reach. The volume, rich with achievements that had won renown for its author, was yet as melancholy a record as ever mortal hand had penned. It was the sad confession and continual exemplification of the shortcomings of the composite man, the spirit burdened with clay and working in matter, and of the despair that assails the higher nature at finding itself so miserably thwarted by the earthly part. Perhaps every man of genius in whatever sphere might recognize the image of his own experience in Aylmer's journal.

So deeply did these reflections affect Georgiana that she laid her face upon the open volume and burst into tears. In this situation she was found by her husband.

"It is dangerous to read in a sorcerer's books," said he with a smile, though his countenance was uneasy and displeased. "Georgiana, there are pages in that volume which I can scarcely glance over and keep my senses. Take heed lest it prove as detrimental to you."

"It has made me worship you more than ever," said she.

"Ah, wait for this one success," rejoined he, "then worship me if you will. I shall deem myself hardly unworthy of it. But come, I have sought you for the luxury of your voice. Sing to me, dearest."

So she poured out the liquid music of her voice to quench the thirst of his spirit. He then took his leave with a boyish exuberance of gayety, assuring her that her seclusion would endure but a little longer, and that the result was already certain. Scarcely had he departed when Georgiana felt irresistibly impelled to follow him. She had forgotten to inform Aylmer of a symptom which for two or three hours past had begun to excite her attention. It was a sensation in the fatal birthmark, not painful, but which induced a restlessness throughout her system. Hastening after her husband, and intruded for the first time into the laboratory.

The first thing that struck her eye was the furnace, that hot and feverish worker, with the intense glow of its fire, which by the quantities of soot clustered above it seemed to have been burning for ages. There was a distilling apparatus in full operation. Around the room were retorts, tubes, cylinders, crucibles, and other apparatus of chemical research. An electrical machine stood ready for immediate use. The atmosphere felt oppressively close, and was tainted with gaseous odors which had been tormented forth by the processes of science. The severe and homely simplicity of the apartment, with its naked walls and brick pavement, looked strange, accustomed as Georgiana had become to the fantastic elegance of her boudoir. But what chiefly, indeed almost solely, drew her attention, was the aspect of Aylmer himself.

He was pale as death, anxious and absorbed, and hung over the furnace as if it depended upon his utmost watchfulness whether the liquid which it was distilling should be the draught of immortal happiness or misery. How different from the sanguine and joyous mien that he had assumed for Georgiana's encouragement!

"Carefully now, Aminadab; carefully, thou human machine; carefully, thou man of clay!" muttered Aylmer, more to himself than his assistant. "Now, if there be a thought too much or too little, it is all over."

"Ho! ho!" mumbled Aminadab. "Look, master! look!"

Aylmer raised his eyes hastily, and at first reddened, then grew paler than ever, on beholding Georgiana. He rushed towards her and seized her arm with a grip that left the print of his fingers upon it.

"Why do you come hither? Have you no trust in your husband?" cried he, impetuously. "Would you throw the blight of that fatal birthmark over my labors? It is not well done. Go, prying woman, go!"

"Nay, Aylmer," said Georgiana with the firmness of which she possessed no stinted endowment, "it is not you that have a right to complain. You mistrust your wife; you have concealed the anxiety with which you watch the development of this experiment. Think not so unworthily of me, my husband. Tell me all the risk we run, and fear not that I shall shrink; for my share in it is far less than your own."

"No, no. Georgiana!" said Aylmer, impatiently; "it must not be."

"I submit," replied she calmly. "And, Aylmer, I shall quaff whatever draught you bring me; but it will be on the same principle that would induce me to take a dose of poison if offered by your hand."

"My noble wife," said Aylmer, deeply moved, "I knew not the height and depth of your nature until now. Nothing shall be concealed. Know, then, that this crimson hand, superficial as it seems, has clutched its grasp into your being with a strength of which I had no previous conception. I have already administered agents powerful enough to do aught except to change your entire physical system. Only one thing remains to be tried. If that fail us we are ruined."

"Why did you hesitate to tell me this?" asked she.

"Because, Georgiana," said Aylmer, in a low voice, "there is danger."

"Danger? There is but one danger—that this horrible stigma shall be left upon my cheek!" cried Georgiana. "Remove it, remove it, whatever be the cost, or we shall both go mad!"

"Heaven knows your words are too true," said Aylmer, sadly. "And now, dearest, return to your boudoir. In a little while all will be tested."

He conducted her back and took leave of her with a solemn tenderness which spoke far more than his words how much was now at stake. After his departure Georgiana became rapt in musings. She considered the character of Aylmer, and did it completer justice than at any previous moment. Her heart exulted, while it trembled, at his honorable love—so pure and lofty that it would accept nothing less than perfection nor miserably make itself contented with an earthlier nature than he had dreamed of. She felt how much more precious was such a sentiment than the meaner kind which would have borne with the imperfection for her sake, and have been guilty of treason to holy love by degrading its perfect idea to the level of the actual; and with her whole spirit she prayed that, for a single moment, she might satisfy his highest and deepest conception. Longer than one moment she well knew it could not be; for his spirit was ever on the march, ever ascending, and each instant required something that was beyond the scope of the instant before.

The sound of her husband's footsteps aroused her. He bore a crystal goblet containing a liquor colorless as water, but bright enough to be the draught of immortality. Aylmer was pale; but it seemed rather the consequence of a highly wrought state of mind and tension of spirit than of fear or doubt.

"The concoction of the draught has been perfect," said he, in answer to Georgiana's look. "Unless all my science have deceived me, it cannot fail."

"Save on your account, my dearest Aylmer," observed his wife, "I might wish to put off this birthmark of mortality by relinquishing mortality itself in preference to any other mode. Life is but a sad possession to those who have attained precisely the degree of moral advancement at which I stand. Were I weaker and blinder it might be happiness. Were I stronger, it might be endured hopefully. But, being what I find myself, methinks I am of all mortals the most fit to die."

"You are fit for heaven without tasting death!" replied her husband. "But why do we speak of dying? The draught cannot fail. Behold its effect upon this plant."

On the window seat there stood a geranium diseased with yellow blotches, which had overspread all its leaves. Aylmer poured a small quantity of the liquid upon the soil in which it grew. In a little time, when the roots of the plant had taken up the moisture, the unsightly blotches began to be extinguished in a living verdure.

"There needed no proof," said Georgiana, quietly.

"Give me the goblet. I joyfully stake all upon your word."

"Drink, then, thou lofty creature!" exclaimed Aylmer, with fervid admiration. "There is no taint of imperfection on thy spirit. Thy sensible frame, too, shall soon be all perfect."

She quaffed the liquid and returned the goblet to his hand.

"It is grateful," said she with a placid smile. "Methinks it is like water from a heavenly fountain; for it contains I know not what of unobtrusive fragrance and deliciousness. It allays a feverish thirst that had parched me for many days. Now, dearest, let me sleep. My earthly senses are closing over my spirit like the leaves around the heart of a rose at sunset."

She spoke the last words with a gentle reluctance, as if it required almost more energy than she could command to pronounce the faint and lingering syllables. Scarcely had they loitered through her lips ere she was lost in slumber. Aylmer sat by her side, watching her aspect with the emotions proper to a man the whole value of whose existence was involved in the process now to be tested. Mingled with this mood, however, was the philosophic investigation characteristic of the man of science. Not the minutest symptom escaped him. A heightened flush of the cheek, a slight irregularity of breath, a quiver of the eyelid, a hardly perceptible tremor through the frame—such were the details which as the moments passed, he wrote down in his folio volume. Intense thought had set its stamp upon every previous page of that volume, but the thoughts of years were all concentrated upon the last.

While thus employed, he failed not to gaze often at the fatal hand, and not without a shudder. Yet once, by a strange and unaccountable impulse, he pressed it with his lips. His spirit recoiled, however, in the very act; and Georgiana, out of the midst of her deep sleep, moved uneasily and murmured as if in remonstrance. Again Aylmer resumed his watch. Nor was it without avail. The crimson hand, which at first had been strongly visible upon the marble paleness of Georgiana's cheek now grew more faintly outlined. She remained not less pale than ever; but the birthmark, with every breath that came and went, lost somewhat of its former distinctness. Its presence had been awful; its departure was more awful still. Watch the stain of the rainbow fading out the sky, and you will know how that mysterious symbol passed away.

"By Heaven! it is well-nigh gone!" said Aylmer to himself, in almost irrepressible ecstasy. "I can scarcely trace it now. Success! success! And now it is like the faintest rose color. The lightest flush of blood across her cheek would overcome it. But she is so pale!"

He drew aside the window curtain and suffered the light of natural day to fall into the room and rest upon her cheek. At the same time he heard a gross, hoarse chuckle, which he had long known as his servant Aminadab's expression of delight.

"Ah, clod; ah, earthly mass!" cried Aylmer, laughing in a sort of frenzy, "you have served me well! Matter and spirit—earth and heaven—have both done their part in this! Laugh, thing of the senses! You have earned the right to laugh."

These exclamations broke Georgiana's sleep. She slowly unclosed her eyes and gazed into the mirror which her husband had arranged for that purpose. A faint smile flitted over her lips when she recognized how barely perceptible was now that crimson hand which had once blazed forth with such disastrous brilliancy as to scare away all their happiness. But then her eyes sought Aylmer's face with a trouble and anxiety that he could by no means account for.

"My poor Aylmer!" murmured she.

"Poor? Nay, richest, happiest, most favored!" exclaimed he. "My peerless bride, it is successful! You are perfect!"

"My poor Aylmer," she repeated, with a more than human tenderness, "you have aimed loftily;

you have done nobly. Do not repent that with so high and pure a feeling, you have rejected the best the earth could offer. Aylmer, dearest Aylmer, I am dying!"

Alas! it was too true! The fatal hand had grappled with the mystery of life, and was the bond by which an angelic spirit kept itself in union with a mortal frame. As the last crimson tint of the birthmark—that sole token of human imperfection—faded from her cheek, the parting breath of the now perfect woman passed into the atmosphere, and her soul, lingering a moment near her husband, took its heavenward flight.

Then a hoarse, chuckling laugh was heard again! Thus ever does the gross fatality of earth exult in its invariable triumph over the immortal essence which, in this dim sphere of half development, demands the completeness of a higher state. Yet, had Aylmer reached a profounder wisdom, he need not thus have flung away the happiness which would have woven his mortal life of the selfsame texture with the celestial. The momentary circumstance was too strong for him; he failed to look beyond the shadowy scope of time, and, living once for all in eternity, to find the perfect future in the present.

?

Cultural recognition of the movement from non-sexual to sexual is accomplished through the ritual of marriage. This ritual is a rite of passage which makes possible the union of the couple and perpetuation of the group. The Garden of Eden myth connects this process to an awareness of good and evil. Both Adam and Eve refuse to accept this knowledge. The fig leaf becomes the symbol which allows them to pursue the illusion of innocence. This theme is illustrated in Hawthorne's story "The Birthmark." Aylmer's desire to find perfection becomes the fig-leaf symbol which allows him to remove himself from his actions. The images in the story connect the archetypal moment of Adam and Eve to the relation between Aylmer and Georgiana. The following questions focus on this parallel.

1 What image is suggested by the title "The Birthmark"? How does this connect the individual to a social world? How does the birthmark relate to the concept of original sin? What does this suggest?

2 Compare and contrast Hawthorne's view of nature with the view of nature in the Garden of Eden myth. How does the laboratory resemble the garden?

3 What is the function of science in the story? How does this relate to the knowledge of good and evil? Does this divide the intellect from the emotions? Does this divide the male from the female? Why? Does this become Aylmer's sin of pride?

4 What archetypal image of the male emerges from this story?

5 What archetypal image of the female emerges from this story?

6 What is Aylmer unable to express? What is Georgiana unable to express? Why do they hide from what we see in the story?

7 How does the story's ending resemble the ending in the Garden of Eden myth?

8 Discuss Hawthorne's vision of the pursuit of perfection. What does he view as the deadliest form of human guilt? What is his comment on the social man? How does he depict love between men and women? What does the story suggest about separation and union?

PATTERNS OF ROMANTIC LOVE

ALBERT ELLIS

During a rite of passage, individuals were instructed in those mythical secrets which gave purpose and meaning to their tribe. This meant a study of the traditions which explained their behavioral patterns. One of the most powerful symbols which molds behavior in Western civilization is the tradition of romantic love. The concept of love transforms individuals to such a degree that it has been linked to a guide establishing the moral behavior of individuals; to a source of energy which brings intense pain and pleasure; to a platonic ideal based on spiritual love and trust, and to an erotic form which often motivates the life of an individual without the individual's awareness. The roles of males and females differ in attempting to reach this illusive concept of romantic love. If we understand the evolution of this process, perhaps we might gain insight into what shapes and molds our destiny.

The pattern of courtship in American and in practically all of Western civilized society is . . . that of the Sex Tease. In following this pattern, the modern woman, whether she consciously knows it or not, is forcibly striving to do two major things: First, to make herself appear infinitely sexually desirable—but finally approachable only in legal marriage. Second, to use sex as bait and therefore to set it up as something special. If she gives in too easily to sex pleasure, she loses her favorite man-conquering weapon. Hence she must retain sexuality on a special plane, and dole it out only under unusual conditions.

The idealized aspect of this philosophy of let-us-women-stick-together-and-only-employ-sex-for-special-baiting-purposes is what we usually call romantic love. For at the very core of modern romance is a tight rope tautly stretched between, and uneasily dividing as well as soldering, gratified and ungratified, over- and under-evaluated sexuality. Where non-romantic types of love prevail—as they do in numerous primitive, peasant, and Eastern cultures—sex is either enjoyed for its own sake or is hedged in by practical (socio-economic, status-giving, marital, or other) restrictions. Where romance is the rule, sex is virtually never enjoyed for itself. It is invariably hemmed in by idealistic, non-practical love restrictions. Romanticism, hand in hand with the sex tease game of American courtship, often plays up the verbal and plays down the active expression of human sexuality.

To understand modern romantic love, we should first know a little about its origins and history. Although the history of love may be traced to the beginnings of mankind, romantic love seems to have been born in Western Europe during the Middle Ages. It is, as Finck has pointed out, "A modern sentiment, less than a thousand years old."[1]

[1] Henry T. Finck, *Romantic Love and Personal Beauty.* New York: Macmillan, 1887, p. 1.

The so-called Dark Ages which preceded the twelfth century was an epoch of acute socio-economic, religious, philosophic, and esthetic rigidity. The individual of the day was born into a world which, to the largest possible extent, predetermined his work, his thoughts, and even his emotions. Against this church-bound and custom-ridden condition of living, romanticisim was something of a reflexive, and certainly a healthy, rebellion.

Like most rebellious movements, however, romantic love at first tended to take to extremes its floutings of the established social order. Thus, where the amorous ideal had emphasized sexual fidelity, *courtoisie* love frequently glorified adultery. Where eighth century love was based on patriarchal traditions, tenth century troubadours extolled woman-centered, female-worshipping *amour*. Where the priests preached divine love, the courtiers deified human love. Where Christianized conjugality was truly coffined, cabined, and confined, romantic love emphasized freedom of choice—and of parting. As Denis de Rougement has observed: "The cultivation of passionate love began in Europe as a reaction to Christianity (and in particular to its doctrine of marriage) by people whose spirit, whether naturally or by inheritance, was still pagan."[2]

Just as an insurgent political group will often, both prior and subsequent to its victory, take over many of the trappings of the vested interests it is undermining, romantic love borrowed from the Christianized version of love that preceded it. It preempted many of the mystical, irrational, evangelical aspects of early Christianity. Fighting the restrictions imposed by a mighty religion, it eventually became almost a religion in its own right.

It should be noted that man achieves so-called free will almost in direct inverse ratio to his becoming a socialized human being. The mere fact that one has, and early in one's life is raised by, duly conditioned and biased parents reduces one's possible free will to meagre amounts; the fact that one, additionally, is raised among hundreds of other human beings, and among humans who have a long history and an intrenched culture, further reduces one's potential free will to near-zero

[2] Denis de Rougemont, *Love in the Western World.* New York: Harcourt, Brace, 1940, p. 70; G. R. Taylor, *Sex in History.* New York: Vanguard, 1955.

proportions. Romanticism, therefore, by very virtue of its being a philosophy with quite well-defined rules of the game of living, eventually leads to virtually as much restriction and human determination as do medieval or other non-romantic philosophies. To be human is to be, in one degree or another, predetermined in one's thoughts, feelings, actions. One mainly has a choice of what *kind* of determination one will live by. And even that choice is largely chimerical: since, as it for example happened, early Christianity and its heir-apparent, medievalism, actually determined most of the trappings of the romantic revolt that followed. Small wonder was it, then, that soon after its inception romantic love blanketed itself in religiosity and traditionalism.

Again, although romantic love was in part a reaction against the sexual repressiveness of early Christianity, it quickly took on so many characteristics of the Christianized love that it was trying to replace that, in its own right, it became antisexual. As Emil Lucka observed: "As time went on the barrier errected between true spiritual love and insidious sensuality became more and more clearly defined; the former pervaded the erotic emotion of the whole period. Parallel with chaste love, sensuality continued to exist as something contemptible, unworthy of a noble mind." The cycle, curiously enough, was then complete: romantic love, which originated as a revolt against Christian antisexuality, soon was conquered by its victim: so that, at least in some of its extreme manifestations, it became itself a bulwark against pagan sensuality.

Three notable facts, however, kept the antisexual elements of medieval romantic love within the bounds of practicality and sanity. In the first place, it was not, when it first originated, a mass phenomenon. The troubadours and their ladies followed the romantic patterns, to be sure. But the peasants, foot-soldiers, common tradesmen and artisans, and other members of the community tended to remain scrupulously orthodox. In the second place, while the troubadours and lords maintained romantic attachments to the ladies of the day, these were invariably adulterous, and not marital, attachments. Marriages, at this time, were socio-economically arranged, and had little or nothing to do with love either in their courtship or post-courtship stages. In the third place, although the troubadours and courtiers could fall romantically in love with their ladies, they also could, and invariably did, find plenty of girls from the peasant and other classes with whom they could roll in the hay. They could therefore well afford to use love as a special ritual for the unattainable lady while they used sex as a pleasant pastime and an essential ingredient of their relations with women of the lower classes.

Medieval romanticism was in several ways an exceptionally class-limited form of love; and it hardly interfered with sex activity, which the courtier could always have, practically for the asking, with a wife, prostitute, or girl of the lower classes for whom he had very frank sex desire and, usually, no romantic love whatever. Under such conditions, the courtier could easily build love into a mystical, religious, anti-sexual emotion—while he was gaily, and quite unromantically, fulfilling his sexual needs at the same time.

Up until the twentieth century, vestiges of this medieval pattern of romantic love have persisted. Although the nineteenth century male was supposed to show some degree of romantic love for his wife, several non-romantic aspects of sex and marriage also were so widespread in the 1800's as to be virtually socially sanctioned. Males of the upper class in Europe and America frequently had their regular mistresses; while lower class males often frequented brothels. Marriages, particularly among the gentry, were often arranged by parents, or at least had to be entered into with parental permission; and in a country like the United States, where the frontier still existed and where women tended to bear several children and to work just as hard as their husbands, there was relatively little opportunity for romantic love in marriage, even when some measure of it existed in courtship.

Only in our own day, for the first time in history, has romantic love become ubiquitous. Whereas our forefathers expected only relatively few gentlemen and gentlewomen to love romantically, we expect every male and female to do so. There are several reasons why romantic attitudes have become so democratized today. For one thing, romantic love is facilitated by small families, by weakened religiosity, by the freedom of women, and by social mobility, all of which are considerably more prevalent today than they were a century or more ago. For another thing, modern living arrangements and technological inventions (such as kitchenettes, automobiles, and birth control appliances) make it easy for households to be moved and for families to break up, and this in turn favors romantic views of love. Our present concepts of individual freedom, democracy, and personal adventurousness also encourage romanticism. Finally, we have literally taken up the cudgels for romantic love and actually preach its precepts in our schools, fiction, drama, movies, and television performances. "Romantic love is to a large extent a convention developed by society,"[3] and in our own society we have deliberately adopted this convention and promulgated it with a vengeance.

All love is not, of course, romantic love. Love itself consists of any kind of more or less intense emotional attraction to or involvement with another. It includes many different types and degrees of affection, such as conjugal love, parental love, familial love, religious love, love of humanity, love of animals, love of things, self-love, sexual love, obsessive-compulsive love, etc. Although *romantic* has become, in our day, virtually a synonym for *loving,* romantic love is actually a special type of love, and has several distinguishing features.

A summary description of the characteristics of romantic love—or more accurately of the romantic lover—will help clarify. The romantic lover is unrealistic: he over-evaluates and fictionalizes his beloved. He is verbal and esthetic about his love. As Tolstoy remarked of the lovers of his day, "Many people's love would be instantly annihilated if they could not speak of it in French."[4] He is aggressively individualistic: he insists, utterly, on his own romantic love choice, and on all but absolute lack of restraint in that choice. This aspect of romantic love was taken so seriously by the famous Comtesse de Champagne's twelfth century Court of Love that it held, in one of its decisions, that "love cannot extend its rights over two married persons. For indeed lovers grant each other all, mutually and freely, without being constrained by any motive of necessity, whereas husband and wife are holden, by their

[3] Arthur Garfield Hays, in V. F. Calverton and Samuel D. Schmalhausen, *Sex in Civilization.* New York: Macaulay, 1929, p. 219.
[4] Leo Tolstoy, in Frederick W. Morton, *Love in Epigram,* Chicago: McClurg, 1899.

duty, to submit their wills to each other and to refuse each other nothing."[5]

The romantic lover, furthermore, frequently is in love with love rather than with his beloved; and he may well repeat, with Elizabeth Barrett Browning, "If thou must love me, let it be for naught except for love's sake only." He is monopolistic, in that he normally devotes himself to one paramount love object. As Folsom has noted, "Romantic love is intensely monagamous *at any one time.* Yet, essentially, its loyalty is to *love* rather than to a person."[6]

The romantic lover is demanding: he wishes to be loved, in his turn, by his beloved; to be loved madly, completely, monopolistically; and for himself, rather than for his position and accomplishments. He is perfectionistic: he strives for not merely a fine, good, lasting, happy relationship with his beloved, but for the finest, greatest, most lasting, most ecstatic amour.

The romantic lover is, as we previously noted, antisexual. He acknowledges the value of sexuality only when it is linked to love. He is sentimental and tends to overact and overstate the greatness of his love. He is passionate and intense: he is supposed to love madly and to be violently in love, rather than affectionately loving.

The romantic lover is changeable, and frequently goes from one violent passion to another. He is jealous, often intensely so, of his beloved. He tends to emphasize physical attractiveness above all else. Finally, in today's world, the romantic lover invariably stresses marrying only for love, and is likely to believe that one should never remain married when love dies. For him, too, the death of love from his marriage tends to become sufficient license for every sort of adultery. In the high name of romantic love, he is free to pursue his true passion at any cost.

The romantic lover believes, in sum, two basic propositions which Ernest W. Burgess lists as follows: "1. That the highest personal happiness comes from marriage based upon romantic love. 2. That love and marriage are essentially personal and private and are,

perhaps, even more than other aspects of life, to be controlled by the individual himself."[7]

This, in general is what the romantic lover is; or, in other words, these may be said to be the *facts* of romantic love. Even more interesting, however, are some of the current American beliefs and attitudes—or folklore—concerning love. For several main tenets about romantic amour are constantly being drilled into the eyes and ears of the American public; and, apparently, some measure of belief in these tenets ultimately comes to be held by this public. Our mass media are full of assertions, implicit and explicit, about the nature of romantic love, some of which we shall now document.

1 *Romantic love is a feeling that takes you unawares, at first sight or a reasonable facsimile thereof, and quickly cooks your goose.*

a.   "The first time I saw her, I knew that this was the woman for whom I would live or die."—Play broadcast over Columbia Broadcasting System.

b.   Some enchanted evening, if you see a stranger in a crowded room, and know she's your true love, you had better immediately *fly* to her side, and make her your own, unless you want to dream out the rest of your life alone.—Song, "Some Enchanted Evening," from *South Pacific.*

2 *When once you really and truly fall in love, your emotion is deathless, and not even complete rejection by your beloved will serve to make you fall out of love again.*

a.   "At last" Jerry knew and understood the meaning of loving her, of knowing that nothing could ever wholly alter the need of her that had become a part of him."
—Novel, *The Lonely.*

b.   "I made a declaration of my undying love. I would not, could not, ever love anyone else but her. It was impossible, unthinkable . . . Love like this was immortal."
—Autobiography, *The Seven Storey Mountain.*

3 *Romantic love is more than welcome at any age, and oldsters, as well as youngsters, should hasten to let themselves fall in love.*

a.   "Love has no age limit. The intelligent world is coming to realize that strong and fervent love, instead of blooming only during

[5] Comtesse de Champagne, in De Stendhal, *On Love.* New York: Liveright, 1947; Alan Watts, *Nature, Man and Woman.* New York: Pantheon, 1958; R. H. Robbins, "Courts of Love." *Sexology,* 1962, 28, 392–396.

[6] Joseph K. Folsom, *The Family.* New York: Harper, 1935, p. 74.

[7] Ernest W. Burgess, "Sociological Aspects of Sex Life of the Unmarried Adult," in Ira S. Wile, *Sex Life of the Unmarried Adult.* New York: Vanguard, 1934, pp. 153–154.

youth, often waits until maturity to reach its greatest ardor." —Article in *New Physical Culture*.

b. It is only natural for a woman in her sixties to want a romantic love and marriage. —Comic strip in the *New York Post*.

4 *Romantic love, when it is reciprocated and fulfilled, leads to unalloyed, ecstatic happiness.*

a. "Give me your love! And make life divine!"—Song, "Give Me Your Hand."

b. When you find love, you'll "find your happy, happy time."—Film, *The Inspector General*.

5 *When romantic love is unrequited, or when one's lover deserts, it is the most painful, agonizing feeling possible.*

a. "Nothing ever had hurt so much in all her life [as her boyfriend being out with another girl], and yet she didn't want to cry. She wanted just one thing: she wanted to be dead." —Story in *McCall's*.

b. "I lay on my bed, or sat in the armchair at the foot of the bed. I clutched in my hands one of Mino's jackets which I had found hanging up, and every now and again I kissed it passionately or bit it to calm my restlessness. Even when mother forced me to eat something, I ate with one hand only and continued to grip the jacket convulsively in the other hand. Mother wanted to put me to bed on the second night and I let her undress me passively. But when she tried to take the jacket from me, I gave such a shrill scream that she was terrified." —Novel, *The Woman of Rome*.

6 *Romantic love is a completely irrational, illogical feeling that makes lovers do the maddest things.*

"When people are in love, their minds cease to function properly." —Novel, *The Woman of Rome*.

7 *Romantic love is worth making any sacrifice for, and the greater the sacrifice the greater, presumably, the love.*

a. " 'You'll fail if you stick to me now,' Frankie warned her. 'I'd rather fail with you than make it without you, Frankie.' "—Novel, *The Man with the Golden Arm*.

b. It is perfectly natural for a great ballet dancer to sacrifice her career, and finally her life, for her husband. —Film, *The Red Shoes*.

8 *True love is utterly monogamous, and once you fall in love—honest and truly—you* can never love another—even though your beloved is worthless, unloving, or already married.

a. "If I ever love again, it will be you." —Song, "If I Ever Love Again."

b. "Love tends to produce a feeling of oneness, and genuine love is centered only on one person." —Article in *Your Marriage*.

9 *Romantic love is an all-important emotion, without which life is dull, pitiful, and meaningless.*

a. "Suppose we could not love, dear; imagine ourselves as neither living nor dead." —Poem in *Wake*.

b. "We both knew that our getting married was the whole point of our lives." —Story in *True Experiences*.

10 *Love has the power of life and death over men and women and can make them do, or not do, almost anything.*

a. Even though a man has had several paralytic strokes and though neurologists have given him a short time to live, his wife's love can keep him alive and well indefinitely. —Article in *True Experiences*.

b. Love will redeem a man and change his entire character and existence; lack of love will literally drive a woman crazy. —Play, *The Madwoman of Chaillot*.

11 *Love transforms sexuality and makes it truly good. Sex without love is nasty and worthless.*

a. A woman whose husband even hints that she can be physically attracted to a man whom she does not love should leave that husband immediately. —Novel, *The Long Love*.

b. A normal, healthy man cannot possibly have sex relations with a girl without coming to love her. —Article in *Reader's Digest*.

12 *A true lover gives in completely to his beloved, and becomes entirely subservient to her wishes and whims.*

a. "She belonged to Jerry, everything she was—her thoughts, her person, her mind, her heart, the deep, swelling buds of womanhood that were bursting within her—awake, asleep, living, dying, breathing, walking, wherever she might be, to the ends of time, she belonged to him." —Novel, *The Lonely*.

b. "All right, Jack, I'll go away with you— I'll do anything you want me to." —Film, *All the King's Men*.

13 *There may be many types of love, but there is only one* true *love, which is easily* *recognizable. When you really and truly love—*

    a.   "you join your whole destiny to that of your beloved." —Story in *Cosmopolitan*.

    b.   "you want to be with your beloved *every* evening." —Article in *Your Marriage*.

    c.   "you never doubt your love."—Story in *Love Novels Magazine*.

It might be thought that, as the years go by and Americans presumably become more sophisticated in regard to sex-love matters, the super-romantic depictions that are common in our mass media would significantly decrease. If so, the decline in romanticism is not yet evident. A review of American love attitudes in the 1960's quickly turned up the following typical examples of extreme romanticism:

From the song, *I'll Always Love You:* "Day after day I'll always love you—live just to say I'll always love you."

From a play by William Inge in *Esquire:* "I get disgusted with myself sometimes, after he treats me bad, and promise myself I'm never going to have anything more to do with him, but . . . when he comes to me and puts his arms around me, I . . . can't help myself. I fall in love all over again. And that's the way it goes."

From a story in *Alfred Hitchcock's Mystery Magazine:* "I told her I'd be an angel or anything else she wanted me to be. I was in love with Martha, faithfully, slavishly, completely, hopelessly."

Although the best-selling novels of the 1960's are distinctly more sexually liberal and semi-pornographic than those of the 1950's, their apotheosizing of highly romantic love has, curiously enough, not been dimmed a whit by their increased sexualization. Thus, in Ruark's *Poor No More,* the ultra-sophisticated Susan Strong falls madly in love with the old roué, Craig Price, at first sight; and when he later treats her cruelly in almost every possible way she still insists on returning to him "because I love you because I can't help it, and I want to love you all my life, you miserable, stupid, arrogant, prideful, dishonest son of a bitch!"

In Nevil Shute's *On the Beach,* the hero, Dwight, refuses to get entangled with a most lovely girl, because he must remain true to his dead wife and children. In Costain's *Darkness and the Dawn,* Nicolan falls in love with Ildico when she is five years old and continues to love her "all my life."

From the foregoing data, it may clearly be seen that romantic love, in today's America, is continually touted, over evaluated, and deified. It is not merely a cardinal value of our culture; it almost *is* our culture. Amour is taken to such ultra-romantic extremes that we easily find examples in our mass media, of the most exaggerated, distorted, and often downright silly manifestations of heterosexual affectability.

The impression could easily be given, from the material thus far presented in this chapter, that romanticism monopolizes our contemporary philosophies of love and marriage. This is not entirely true: since dissident, non-romantic voices are also heard from time to time. A *Modern Bride* writer, for example, tells us that "we are hampered by ideas of love that represent a combination of infantile and adolescant patterns, instead of those appropriate to a grown-up." In a tale in *Gay Love Stories* the heroine says: "I—don't want romance or glamour—I want—genuine affection, tenderness . . ." In an article in the magazine, *Wake*, we are informed that mature love is selfless and does not demand super-romantic requitement. An *American Sociological Review* article by William L. Kolb points out that our society puts considerable pressure on young people not to marry just for love, but for more logical, socio-economic reasons. Even some of our popular jokes contain unromantic implications, as this one from *Joke Parade:* "A young woman wrote in her diary, after the loss of her husband, 'My sorrow is more than I can bear.' Several months later, leafing through the diary she came to the entry, paused, and then added the word 'alone.' "

Despite these criticisms of romantic love, and for all the jokes current about it, the fact remains that our mass media overwhelmingly favor the belief that romantic amour is incredibly delightful, delicious, and delectable and that a life not rooted in romantic affection is detestable, deleterious, and damnably dull. While not even a dozen non-romantic or anti-romantic views were found in the course of surveying literally hundreds of mass media outlets, several hundred distinctly romantic attitudes were uncovered.

The ubiquity of ultra-romantic philosophies in our mass media, particularly when combined with the unromantic and often harsh realities of modern life, leads to serious (conscious and unconscious) conflicts and disturbances on the part of virtually all the members of our society. Some of the reasons for these conflicts and disturbances are as follows:

1   Romanticism is, almost by definition, passionately untrammeled and unrestricted. But our courtship customs . . . are normally hemmed in by many practical and non-romantic considerations. Consequently, the swain who is romantically enamored of his girl friend must almost necessarily encounter parental objections, financial difficulties, sexual tabus, and other limitations. It may therefore be predicted that, quite aside from his girlfriend's reacting negatively to him, most of his romantic attachments will never get the chance to bud or will be cruelly nipped before they have consequentially flowered. Although the sex tease of courtship which is prevalent in our society nicely dovetails with romanticism's anti-sexuality, our other courtship restrictions are mainly antithetical to romance: they, to some extent, encourage romantic dreams—but savagely combat the fulfillment of these dreams.

2   The kind of romantic love which is enthusiastically espoused by our mass media is based on many assumptions which, ordinarily, are not sustained by the realities of either living or loving. Thus, it is assumed that romantic love does not change; but, on the contrary, it most often does. It is assumed that romantic love survives the lover's aging processes and the beloved's loss of youth and beauty; but, most frequently, it does not. It is assumed that it is easy to tell "true love" from "infatuation"; which, of course, it isn't. It is assumed that romantic love brings nothing but ecstatic joy; when, actually, it often brings worry, responsibility, loss of independence, and all kinds of anguish. It is assumed that having steady sex relations with one's beloved will make one romantically love her more; when, in point of fact, it frequently makes one love her less. It is assumed that if a pair of romantic lovers have children, their offspring will help increase their mutual ardor; when, in numerous instances, children seriously sabotage romantic ardor. Similarly, numerous other assumptions about romantic love are made in our popular publications and productions which, in reality, are distinctly false.

Consequently, the utter, terrible disillusionment of many or most romantic lovers becomes eventually assured.

3   Romanticism, again almost by definition, implies a considerable degree of fiction, of facing away from instead of toward reality. The romantic lover exaggerates, overestimates, sees his beloved as she really is not. But life, particularly in our technologically influenced world, is hardly fictional; and adjustment to life, as we psychologists have been stressing for years, means full acceptance of reality. Neurosis, in the last analysis, invariably includes a considerable degree of failure to recognize reality. If, then, romantic love also includes a failure to recognize reality, we should expect it importantly to overlap with neurosis at several points. This means that we, on the one hand, are trying to raise our children to be realistic and, on the other hand, to be non-realistic—that is, romantic. Not only, then, are we directly raising them to be at least semi-neurotic, but we are heading them for a virtually irreconcilable conflict between their romantic and non-romantic aspirations: which conflict, in its turn, is only likely to intensify their neurosis.

4   Many romantic ideals, such as those concerned with purity, dedication, holy affection, and the deification of physical beauty, supply us with perfectionistic goals which will inevitably be unachievable by most of us, and will lead to grim disappointment and disillusionment. The result, particularly where sexuality is at issue, is likely to be neurotic and psychotic feelings of dirtiness, failure, guilt, inadequacy, profanation of what is considered to be holy, and so on. Human happiness, as has long been known, is a ratio between what people expect and what they get from life. When their expectations are ultra-romantic, and hence unrealistic, failure to achieve their level of aspiration must inevitably ensue: with consequent unhappiness and a tendency toward emotional disturbance.

5   Romantic love, in our culture, is supposed to lead to engagement and marriage; but its tenets, actually, are largely opposed to the type of marriage which exists among us. Normal marriage has numerous socio-economic aspects which are antithetical to the maintenance of romantic (though not necessarily other types of) love. Thus, married couples must be concerned about purchases, repairs, sickness, insurance, child care, enter-

tainment, business success, in-laws, relatives, friends, education, cooking, cleaning, shopping, mending, sleeping facilities, and hundreds of other practical aspects of modern living which are utterly nonromantic and which tend to restrict emotional outpourings of a romantic nature.

Romanticism, moreover, puts a premium on intense amative *feelings:* which are notoriously changeable and fleeting. Romantic courtship usually follows a highly erratic pattern, and includes considerable affectional promiscuity. Romantic marriage, quite logically, tends to follow this same pattern and to result in numerous separations and divorces—at which our society hardly looks with equanimity.

Marriage usually becomes a relatively calm, steady relationship that is not too demanding emotionally: since few married couples have available a great reserve of sustained, intense emotional energy. But romanticism, as Gross has pointed out, demands "constant and unequivocal demonstrations of affection."[8] An individual who is raised to crave romantic love is rarely content with anything but the sustained emotional intensity which is thoroughly non-indigenous to everyday marital domesticity. Hence the almost inevitable dissatisfaction of the arch romanticist who marries.

Romantic love, again, is partly based on the sexual teasing and blocking of modern courtship. Its very intensity, to a large extent, grows out of the generous promises combined with the niggardly actualities of sex fulfillment which exist during the courtship stages. When, after marriage, the sex blockings of the courtship days are necessarily removed, the intensity of romantic love which partly stemmed from these blockings may easily fade; and the result is a relatively (romantically) loveless marriage—which, by the very premises of romanticism, is considered to be worthless and must be broken up.

Romantic love, because it is an idealized, perfectionist emotion, particularly thrives on intermittent rather than steady association between two lovers. During courtship, fellows and girls see each other for relatively few hours per week, when they are well-rested, well-fed, and well-accoutered for having a good time. On such a basis, they are at their best and their handsomest or loveliest,

[8] Llewellyn Gross, "A Belief Pattern Scale for Measuring Attitudes Toward Romanticism." *American Sociological Review,* 1944, 9, 463–472.

and can reasonably well live up to perfectionist ideals. Marriage, however, invariably means domesticity: meaning a constant, more or less monotonous, living together on an hour after hour, year after year basis. This type of domesticity, probably, is as well designed to sabotage romantic love as is any other mode of social living. Indeed, if romantic lovers wanted, with perfect logic, to induce their passions to endure for a maximum period of time, they might well ban, under almost any circumstances, marital domesticity. But, in our society, they do just the opposite: they, as it were, condemn themselves to living under the same roof, for perhaps forty or fifty years, with their beloveds. The result, in terms of their own romantic ideals, is almost invariably frightful.

6 Romantic love, in our culture, is essentially opposed to the other modes of love which we also, in one way or another, espouse. It is particularly opposed to conjugal or familial love which our religious institutions and (increasingly) our schools are continually upholding. Moreover, most of our married women, once they see that their early romantic love for their husbands does not last, tend to raise their sons and daughters, and particularly perhaps the former, in a Momistic, family-tied manner that brooks little romantic opposition. Mother-centered sons are not encouraged to fall madly in love with the girl next door; and many of them, in point of fact, are raised so that they cannot possibly romantically love anyone. When, because of the pressurizing and pulling influences of their culture (particularly, the novels, films, and television shows of this culture), they do become romantically attached to a woman, they are almost automatically propelled right into the center of a bitter struggle for their souls between their mother and their wife. Since romanticism, with its unrealistic idealizations and demands, can afford no such struggle, it usually gets the worst of the conflict, and the consequent wrestle with reality is often agonizing.

7 Of the several possible logical culminations of romantic love that theoretically may, and presumably should, occur, virtually none are consciously permitted to occur; so that its usual end is desultory, unplanned, and heartbreaking. Some of the possible logical culminations of romantic love are these:

a. Romantic love may, under some circumstances, be sustained by severely limiting the period of its expression. Thus, Somerset

Maugham has the heroine of his play, *The Constant Wife*, declare that she is going off to stay with her lover only for a period of six weeks: "Because I'm putting a limit to our love it may achieve the perfection of something that is beautiful and transitory."[9]

b. Romantic love may flower indefinitely if lovers consciously become varietists and change their individual partners while continuing their romantic patterns of attachment.

c. Romantic lovers may, quite logically, engage in plural love affairs and thus, by having two or more romantic partners simultaneously, avoid much of the monotony and domesticity which normally dooms romanticism.

d. Romantic lovers may keep their love alive by consciously renouncing its fruition. Thus, Ibsen has his lovers in *Love's Comedy* break with each other just as they are about to marry, with the heroine ecstatically removing her engagement ring, casting it into the fjord, and exclaiming to her lover: "Now for this earthly life I have forgone thee,—But for the life eternal I have won thee!"[10] George Moore, in his *Memoirs of My Dead Life,* Andre Gide in *Strait is the Gate,* Walter Van Tilburg Clark in *The City of Trembling Leaves,* and Ben Hecht in *Erik Dorn* solve the problem of longevity of romantic love in precisely the way Ibsen solved it in *Love's Comedy.*[11] Theophile Gautier, in *Mlle. de Maupin,* gives one of the best summaries of this renunciation philosophy by having his heroine write a farewell letter to her lover in this wise: "You believe, perhaps, that I do not love you because I am leaving you. Later, you will recognize the truth of the contrary. Had I valued you less, I should have remained, and would have poured out to you the insipid beverage to the dregs. Your love would soon have died of weariness; after a time you would have quite forgotten me, and, as you read over my name on the list of your conquests, would have asked yourself: 'Now, who the deuce was she?' I have at least the satisfaction of thinking that you will re-member me sooner than another. Your unsated desire will again spread its wings to fly to me; I shall ever be to you something desirable to which your fancy will love to return, and I hope that in the arms of the mistresses you may have, you will sometimes think of the unrivalled night you spent with me."[12]

e. Romantic love, most logically perhaps, may be ended in the most drastic of all human acts: death. As Emil Lucka has pointed out: "One thing is certain: the great love cannot find its consummation on earth . . . The love-death is the last and inevitable conclusion of reciprocal love which knows no value but itself, and is resolved to face eternity, so that no alien influence shall reach it."[13] Denis de Rougemont concurs: "The mystic lovers in the Romance are compelled to pursue the *intensification* of passion, not its fortunate appeasement. The keener their passion, the more it can detach them from created things, the more readily do they feel that they are on the way to attaining the death in *endura* which they desire."[14]

Of these logical, or romantically self-consistent, ways of bringing romantic love to a climax, none are consciously espoused by any number of lovers in our culture: for the good reason that the general marital philosophy of our society is quite opposed to such acts as lovers limiting the period of their love, becoming varietists, engaging in plural affairs, consciously renouncing their loves, or arranging a suicide pact with their beloveds. Instead, we espouse what might be called the most illogical climax to romantic courtship and love: consummation. For sexual and marital consummation indubitably, in the vast majority of instances, maims, bloodies, and finally kills romanticism until it is deader than—well, yesterday's romance. Noting this, the famous troubadour Peiral maintained that "I cannot believe that a true lover can continue to love after he has received the last favor."[15]

The pernicious and widespread effects of our romantic ideologies may perhaps be illustrated by considering ten patients I have seen at the beginning of one of my regular work weeks. Patient No. 1, a 23 year old girl, keeps

[9] Somerset Maugham, *The Constant Wife.* New York: Doubleday, 1932.

[10] Henrik Ibsen, *Love's Comedy.* New York: Willey Book, 1911, pp. 470–71.

[11] George Moore, *Memoirs of My Dead Life.* London: Heinemann, 1921, p. 72; Andre Gide, *Strait is the Gate.* New York: Knopf, 1936, pp. 187–89; Walter Van Tilburg Clark, *The City of Trembling Leaves.* New York: Random House, 1945, p. 395; Ben Hecht, *Erik Dorn.* New York: Modern Library, 1930, p. 130.

[12] Theophile Gautier, *Mlle. de Maupin.* New York: Three Pay Sales Co., 1900, p. 223.

[13] Emil Lucka, *Eros.* New York: Putnam, 1915.

[14] Denis de Rougemont, *op. cit.,* pp. 123–24.

[15] Pieral the Troubadour, quoted in Emil Lucka, *op. cit.,* p. 129.

contending that she does not want to marry; actually, she has highly romantic ideals of marriage that aggravate her general feelings of inadequacy, so that she deems herself unworthy of ever acquiring the ideal type of partner she would like to marry; hence her stated lack of desire for the marital state. Patient No. 2, a 28 year old male, is living with a girl for whom he has considerable affection, but whom he will not consider marrying because, in some respects, she does not live up to his ideal of a tall, slim, beautiful, unearthly creature. Patient No. 3 has left his wife because, among other things, she has never lived up to his notion of romantic love during their twenty years of married life. Patient No. 4 has turned to homosexuality because, after twelve years of marriage, he still feels guilty about engaging in various non-coital sex activities with his wife (who is quite willing to engage in these activities) while he does not feel guilty, or as guilty, about engaging in these same activities with other males. Patient No. 5 feels that his wife does not love him because she is too close to her mother. Patient No. 6 cannot live comfortably with her husband, who she admits is a fine person and a good companion, because she is madly infatuated with another man who she says is quite inferior to him. Patient No. 7 has no special problems in relation to romantic love. Patient No. 8 cannot put his heart into sex relations with his wife, with whom he says he wants to keep living, because he feels that their marriage got off on the wrong foot when they married for practical, utterly non-romantic reasons. Patient No. 9 keeps falling intensely in love with males to whom she is absolutely afraid, because of fears that they may reject her, to show any indication of her feeling, and with whom she normally parts long before any chance for real intimacy arises between them. Patient No. 10, while saying that she would marry almost any normal male who loved her and wanted to marry her, actually goes with literally scores of boyfriends every year, most of whom she soon rejects because they do not live up to her impossibly romantic, perfectionist notions.

So it goes with most of my patients, particularly my female patients: although romantic aspirations and ideals are not necessarily their main source of difficulty and disturbance, romanticism is definitely one of the chief reasons for their being considerably more un-

happy and maladjusted than they would be had they more realistic goals of love and marriage. Similarly, I am sure, if we had adequate statistics on the place of romanticism in the causation of modern neurosis, we would find literally millions of instances where romantic ideologies have caused or abetted emotional disturbance.

Psychologists, psychiatrists, social workers, and marriage counselors rarely, alas, keep the kind of statistics which would be most helpful in gauging just how much maladjustment results from the inculcation in our populace of super-romantic ideals. Many case histories and clinical observations, however, have been published in regard to this point. Alfred Adler, for example, shows how a person who invents a "romantic, ideal, or unattainable love . . . can thus luxuriate in [his] feelings without the necessity of approaching a partner in reality."[16] Karen Horney demonstrates how romantic, over-evaluated love may be made "a screen for satisfying wishes that have nothing to do with it . . . made an illusion by our expecting much more of it than it can possibly fulfil."[17] John Levy points out how an individual's romantically expecting too much from marriage inevitably leads to a "universal feeling of disillusionment about marriage."[18] W. Beran Wolfe contends that "romanticism is the sexual life of the adolescent. When practiced by mature men and women it reaps a narrow horizon, a high degree of subjectivity, a desire to be pampered, to be treated like a prince or a princess."[19] Sandor Ferenczi notes that a full appreciation of reality is lacking in persons who remain fixated at the romantic stage of love.[20] Freud stresses the fact that extreme romanticism may lead to masochistic submissiveness to the love partner and to actual sexual perversion.[21] Lorine Pruette discusses a number of the childish marital attitudes to

[16] Alfred Adler, What Life Should Mean to You. Boston: Little Brown, 1931, pp. 275–76.

[17] Karen Horney, The Neurotic Personality of Our Time. New York: Norton, 1937, p. 387.

[18] John Levy and Ruth Munroe, The Happy Family. New York: Knopf, 1938, p. 66.

[19] W. Beran Wolfe, How to Be Happy Though Human. New York: Farrar and Rinehart, 1931, p. 261.

[20] Sandor Ferenczi, Further Contributions to the Theory and Technique of Psychoanalysis. New York: Basic Books, 1952.

[21] Sigmund Freud, Group Psychology and the Analysis of the Ego. London: International Psychoanalytic Press, 1922.

which romantic ideologies may lead.[22] Theodore Reik and Edmund Bergler show how unrealistic love attitudes, sparked by literary productions, result in many sorts of neurotic phenomena.[23]

Sociologists and anthropologists, on the basis of their studies, have also consistently demonstrated the pernicious effects of ultra-romantic attitudes. Ray E. Baber has pointed out that "the fact that so frequently the response satisfactions in the early years of marriage do not come up to expectation is due to social misguidance. The literature of love has brought into being a cult of romance that dominates the thinking of both old and young, though not in exactly the same way. It is a wishful cult, ignoring the basic realities of life and building its castles in the clouds of fancy, where none but knights and ladies, princes and princesses exist."[24] J. B. Lichtenberger has noted that "we have here, in the perversion of the concept of the marriage of true affection and in the over-emphasis upon the romantic element, one of the obvious causes of the increases of divorces . . . Romantic love as the exclusive basis of marriage is hopelessly inadequate. Even connubial love can flourish only in a congenial atmosphere and often is killed by antagonisms which arise from other sources."[25] Sumner and Keller contended that it is romantic influences "which bring men and women up to matrimony with false and impossible notions and prepare them for speedy disillusionment, misery, divorce, a new attempt to reach the impossible, and so on."[26] Similar realistic observations on the effects of romanticisms have been made by many other outstanding sociological thinkers, including Folsom,[27] Green, Gross, Groves and Groves, Landis, MacIver, Mowrer, and Schmiedeler.[28]

This is not to gainsay romanticism's many valuable aspects: the democracy of choice, the freedom from restraint, the aspirations to high-level individualism, the frank avowal of hedonism, the glorious potentialities for human ecstasy, and the indubitable other benefits that it valiantly espouses. As Vernon Grant points out,[29] the amorous emotion has many lovely sensual and esthetic elements. Ortega y Gasset and Sorokin[30] have also emphasized its advantages. The conclusion is factually and clinically inevitable, however, that romantic love, in its present form, is a very mixed blessing. Unless it evolves (as, fortunately, Ellis' discussion of romantic love touches on the archetypal symbols of love which are alive in our imagination today. He states:

. . . although romantic aspirations and ideals are not necessarily the main source of difficulty and disturbance, romanticism is definitely one of the chief reasons for their being considerably more unhappy and maladjusted than they would be had they had more realistic goals of love and marriage.

[22] Lorine Pruette, *The Parent and the Happy Child*. New York: Holt, 1932, p. 9.

[23] Theodore Reik, *A Psychologist Looks at Love*. New York: Rinehart, 1945, p. 67; Theodore Reik, *Love and Lust*. New York: Straus, 1958; Edmund Bergler, "Further Contributions to the Psychoanalysis of Writers," *Psychoanalytic Review*, 1948, 35, 33–50.

[24] Ray E. Baber, *Marriage and the Family*. New York: McGraw-Hill, 1939, p. 203; Crane Brinton, *A History of Western Morals*. New York: Braziller, 1959.

[25] J. B. Lichtenberg, *Divorce*. New York: Whittlesey House, 1931, p. 345.

[26] William Graham Sumner and Albert G. Keller, *The Science of Society*. New Haven: Yale Univ. Press, 1927, p. 2049.

[27] Joseph K. Folsom, *The Family and Democratic Society*. New York: Harpers, 1950.

[28] Arnold W. Green, "Social Values and Psychotherapy," *Journal of Personality*, 1946, 14, 19–228; Llewellyn Gross, *op. cit.*, p. 469; Ernest Groves and Gladys Groves, "The Case for Monogamy," in W. F. Bigelow, *The Good Housekeeping Marriage Book*. New York: Prentice Hall, 1938, p. 157; Paul H. Landis, "Control of the Romantic Impulse Through Education," *School and Society*, 1936, 213; R. M. MacIver, *Society*. New York: Long and Smith, 1932, p. 145; Ernest R. Mowrer, *Family Disorganization*. Chicago: Univ. Chicago Press, 1927, p. 162; Edgar Schmiedeler, *An Introductory Study of the Family*. New York: Century, 1930, p. 169.

[29] Vernon W. Grant, *The Psychology of Sexual Emotion*. New York: Longmans, Green, 1957.

[30] Jose Ortega y Gasset, *On Love*. New York: Meridian Books, 1960; Pitirim A. Sorokin, *The Ways and Power of Love*. Boston: Beacon, 1954.

The author links contemporary problems with a past that is often not understood by the contemporary individual. His essay explains the Christian influence on love, and goes on to explore the metamorphosis of love through the centuries. The following questions focus on Ellis' discussion as a means to understand the archetypal symbols which express romantic love.

1   Explain this statement: "Romantic love is to a large extent a convention developed by society." How does this relate to the social, moral, and political goals of a culture?

2   How would you relate Ellis' concept of "the sex tease" to Adam and Eve's actions in the Garden of Eden myth?

3   Discuss Ellis' emphasis of romantic love in contemporary America: How does the mass media influence our attitudes toward love? How is sex related to love in contemporary life? In what basic ways does modern love differ from medieval love? Select a film and discuss the way Ellis would interpret the concept of romantic love in that film.

4   Do these patterns of love create fantasies which drive us away from reality? Explain what mythical encounters between the world parents support or refute this concept.

5   How does Ellis' view of love and death compare and contrast with Hawthorne's view in "The Birthmark"?

6   What image of the male and female emerges from Ellis' discussion of romantic love?

7   Ellis contends that romantic love is a "mixed blessing." Discuss the implications of this statement from the following perspectives:
    a   The view of love developed in the story of Sati and Siva.
    b   Erich Neumann's concept of projection and identification with the love object.
    c   Your views on this complex process of romantic love.

The image of the Male and Female in America

In these pictures, we see the American male and female regressed to the role of boy and girl in order to avoid confronting who they are. In the first picture, W. C. Fields appears as the "naughty" boy. His counterpart is Mae West; she is the "bad" girl who is reformed before the film is over. Each of these characters is trapped in the illusions of a child who is nonsexual except in play. Fields and West add a touch of humor in the search of male and female in America. In the second picture, Mickey Rooney and Judy Garland appear as America's sweethearts. These two never grow up because they appear as the perfect brother and sister. They also are nonsexual. In fact, Judy Garland as the friend of Mickey Rooney often helps him straighten out his love life. Rooney is the young idealist who seeks approval from his father, the judge. In the third picture from *It Happened One Night*, Clark Gable and Claudette Colbert appear as the representatives of a sophisticated man and a spoiled little girl who meet, fight, and then find romance. Gable does not take advantage of Miss Colbert. The couple spend most of their energy on the chase. The film is directed toward the one night which will make them a man and woman joined in sexual union. The illusion that is created reveals how much energy is put into the moments leading up to their first sexual encounter. The ending reveals the male and female as a boy and girl attempting to gain approval for their actions. In the last picture *For Whom The Bell Tolls*, Gary

the American Dream Couple

Cooper is the symbolic representation of the strong, silent man of action. He must always appear to be in control, for weakness is linked to the feminine. Here he appears to be non-involved with the woman, but her arms encircle his waist to reveal his vulnerability. His counterpart is Ingrid Bergman. She appears helpless but strong. She is holding on to him as a means of support. Each assumes a mask which prevents them from moving together as interdependent. Both use fig leafs as a means to preserve their illusion of independence for the male and dependence for the female. Gary Cooper and Ingrid Bergman are symbols which express the rigidity of the American dream couple who fail to go beyond their fantasy of life. They do not become part of their experience, and death for Cooper makes union impossible in this film. Margaret Mead discusses the way the social roles of American man and woman prevent them from accepting the other as an equal.

MALE AND FEMALE IN AMERICA: TO BOTH THEIR OWN   MARGARET MEAD

We have seen how children of each sex learn, from their own bodies and the way in which others respond to their bodies, that they are male and female. And we have seen that each sex position can be stated as the surer one, with the other sex a pallid or compensatory or imperfect version of the other. We have seen that the girl may feel herself an incomplete person and spend her life trying to imitate male achievements, and that equally the boy may feel himself incomplete and spend his life in symbolic and far-fetched imitations of the girl's maternity. Each sex may be distorted by the presence of the other sex, or it may be given a fuller sense of sex membership. Either solution is possible, neither is inevitable. If parents define one child as less complete, less potentially gifted, with less right to be free, less claim to love and protection, or less a source of pride to themselves than the other, the child of that sex will, in many cases, feel envy. If society defines each sex as having inalienable and valuable qualities of its own but does not relate those qualities to the reproductive differences between the sexes, then each sex may be proud and strong, but some of the values that come from sex contrast will be lacking. If women are defined without reference to their maternity, men may find that their own masculinity seems inadequate, because its continuance into paternity will also lose definition. And if men are defined in terms of paternity rather than as lovers, women will find that their own capacities of wifehood have been muted in favour of their capacities for motherhood.

Externally at some given period of history and in some set of social arrangements it may often look as if one sex gained and the other lost, but such gains and losses must in the end be temporary. To the extent that women are denied the right to use their minds, their sons suffer as well as their daughters. An over-emphasis on the importance of virility will in the end make the lives of men as instrumental as an over-emphasis on their merely reproductive functions makes the lives of women. If our analysis is deep enough and our time-perspective long enough, if we hold in mind all the various possibilities that other cultures hint at or fully embody, it is possible to say that to the extent that either sex is disadvantaged, the whole culture is poorer, and the sex that, superficially, inherits the earth, inherits only a very partial legacy. The more whole the culture, the more whole each member, each man, each woman, each child will be. Each sex is shaped from birth by the presence and the behaviour of both sexes, and each sex is dependent upon both. The myths that conjure up islands of women who live all alone without men always contain, and rightly, some flaw in the picture. A one-sex world would be an imperfect world, for it would be a world without a future. Only a denial of life itself makes it possible to deny the interdependence of the sexes. Once that interdependence is recognized and traced in minute detail to the infant's first experience of the contrast between the extra roughness of a shaven cheek and a deeper voice and his mother's softer skin and higher voice, any program which claims that the wholeness of one sex can be advanced without considering the other is automatically disallowed. Isolated consideration of the position of women becomes as essentially one-sided as the isolated consideration of the position of men. We must think instead of how to live in a two-sex world so that each sex will benefit at every point from each expression of the presence of two sexes.

To insist on building a world in which both sexes benefit does not mean that we glow over or deny the differential vulnerability of either sex, the learnings that are harder for boys, the learnings that are harder for girls, the periods of greater physical vulnerability for one sex than the other. This does not mean that we deny that when both sexes are cared for more by the mother than by the father, the learnings will be different as the boy accepts a first-beloved person who is unlike himself and the girl one who is like herself, as each lives out its first warm contacts with the world with eager little mouths that for one will remain a prototype of adult relationships, but for the other will be reversed. Nor does it mean that we fail to recognize the period when the little girl's sex membership is so much less explicit than the little boy's that while he is proudly, exhibitionistically sure of his masculinity, she has to ignore what seems like a deficiency in herself in favour of a promised future maternity. It means recognizing that training to control elimination, to plan, to respond, to inhibit, appropriately, in terms of time and place, has a different impact on the boy and on the girl. It does mean that we also recognize that as both children seize on the behaviour of grown men and women to give them clues as to what their future rôles will be, the conspicuousness of pregnancy to which the girl can look forward overshadows the paternal rôle that is so much harder for a small boy's imagination to follow through. As the girl is left vulnerable to any cultural arrangements that seem to deny her some freedom—the right to use her mind or her body in some way that is permitted to a boy—so the boy is left vulnerable to cultural arrangements that spur him on to efforts that may be beyond his strength, if achievement is defined as necessary to validate an otherwise imperfect maleness.

Giving each sex its due, a full recognition of its special vulnerabilities and needs for protection, means looking beyond the superficial resemblances during the period of later childhood, when both boys and girls, each having laid many of the problems of sex adjustment aside, seem so eager to learn, and so able to learn the same things. Paced too closely together, with a school system that closes its eyes to the speed with which the girls are outdistancing the boys in height, and the greater ease that girls have in learning certain kinds of lessons, both boys and girls may be injured during this period, the boy given a fear of the superiority of the girl, the girl given a fear of being superior to the boy. Each fear is deeply detrimental to the full development of each sex later, but it operates differently, making the boy angry and grudging about achievement in women, making the girl frightened and deprecatory about her own gifts. At puberty, there is again a difference. The girl's attainment of puberty is definite and clear. Only cultural arrangements which insist that chronological age is more important than maturity, or which fail to recognize that late maturation is as normal as early, can make the girl as doubtful

of herself and of her full sex membership as is the boy as he responds to the less sure, less definite signs of his own puberty.

As young adults ready for a full sex relationship, both boy and girl are limited by the irrevocability of a full sex experience for a woman as compared with that of a man. This irrevocability of the severed hymen often stays the man's spontaneity as greatly as it does the girl's. Then in the full sex relationship there is again a shift. The man may live over again phantasies of re-entering his mother's body, but the woman must accept her obligation to herself, the willingness to become a body in which new life is sheltered. However, once she has borne a child, her full sex membership, her ability to conceive and carry and bear another human being, is assured and can never be taken away from her. The male who has impregnated a female is given no such full assurance; his paternity remains to the end inferential, his full sex membership has to be referred again and again to continual potency rather than to past paternity. And with advancing years, the woman faces a moment when giving up her productive maternity will occur as irrevocably and unmistakably as the beginning was once signalled at menarche. But the male's loss of his potential paternity, like the diminution of his potency, is gradual, indefinite, reversible. It has neither the quality of a single devastating event, which is the way women often experience the menopause, nor the possibility of a peaceful acceptance of a consummated step in life, which is also possible to women. He keeps the rewards and the psychological hazards that go with a less punctuated ageing process.

Our tendency at present is to minimize all these differences in learning, in rhythm, in type and timing of rewards, and at most to try to obliterate particular differences that are seen as handicaps on one sex. If boys are harder to train, train them harder; if girls grow faster than boys, separate them, so the boys won't be damaged; if women have a little less strength than men, invent machines so that they can still do the same work. But every adjustment that minimizes a difference, a vulnerability, in one sex, a differential strength in the other, diminishes their possibility of complementing each other, and corresponds—symbolically—to sealing off the constructive receptivity of the female and the vigorous outgoing constructive activity of the male, muting them both in the end to a duller version of human life, in which each is denied the fullness of humanity that each might have had. Guard each sex in its vulnerable moments we must, protect and cherish them through the crises that at some times are so much harder for one sex than for the other. But as we guard, we may also keep the differences. Simply compensating for differences is in the end a form of denial.

But if each sex is to realize sex membership fully, each boy and each girl must also feel as a whole human being. We are human beings first, and while sex membership very quickly overrides race feeling, so that boys of a race that assumes itself superior will express themselves as more willing to be males of the "inferior" race than to be females in their own, people do not similarly choose not to be human. The most boldly swaggering male would be staggered by the choice of keeping his masculinity at the price of becoming a lion or a stag, the most deeply maternal female would not elect to be turned into a ewe or a doe rather than lose her femininity. Humanity at any price, but please God, a human being of my own sex, fully, sums up the approach that men and women make in every culture in the world. We may bring them up to wish they had been born a member of the other sex, and so impair forever their full and happy functioning, but even so they would not barter away their humanity. Yet we have seen how damaging to full sex membership can be some of the conventions by which each society has differentiated the sexes. Every known society creates and maintains artificial occupational divisions and personality expectations for each sex that limit the humanity of the other sex. One form that these distinctions take is to deny the range of difference among the members of one sex, and so insist that all men should be taller than all women, so that any man who is shorter than any woman is less a man. This is the simplest form of a damaging conventionalization. But there are a thousand others, rooted in our failure to recognize the great variety of human beings who are now mingled and mated in one great mélange that includes temperamental contrasts as great as if the rabbit mated with the lion and sheep with leopards. Characteristic after characteristic in which the differences within a sex are so great that there is enormous overlapping are artificially assigned as masculine or feminine. Hairiness may be repudiated by both sexes and men forced to shave their beards and women to shave their legs and armpits; hairiness may be a proof of maleness, so that women

shave their heads and men wear false curls. Shaving takes time, the male who has no beard feels unmanned, the woman who has three hairs between her breasts may be taken for a witch, and even so adjustment to such stereotypes does relatively much less harm than when personality differences are assigned in the same way. If initiative is limited to one sex, especially in sex relationships themselves, a great number of marriages will be distorted and often destroyed, to the extent that the one to whose sex initiative is forbidden is the one of that particular pair who is able to initiate, and so either refrains from the relationship or conceals and manipulates and falsifies it. As with initiative, so with responsiveness. Each sex is capable of taking certain kinds and certain types of initiative, and some individuals in each sex in relation to some individuals of the other sex, at certain times, in certain places, should, if they are to act as whole individuals, be initiating regardless of their sex, or be responsive regardless of their sex. If the stereotypes forbid this, it is hazardous for each to do so. We may go up the scale from simple physical differences through complementary definitions that overstress the rôle of sex difference and extend it inappropriately to other aspects of life, to stereotypes of such complex activities as those involved in the formal use of the intellect, in the arts, in government, and in religion.

In all these complex achievements of civilization, those activities which are mankind's glory, and upon which depends our hope of survival in this world that we have built, there has been this tendency to make artificial distinctions that limit an activity to one sex, and by denying the actual potentialities of human beings limit not only both men and women, but also equally the development of the activity itself. Singing may be taken as a very simple example. There are societies in which nobody sings in anything but a flat, rhythmic, dull chant. Significantly enough, Manus, which is built on the duller similarities of men and women, is such a society. There are societies in which women sing, and men sing falsetto. There have probably been societies in which men sang and only woman who could sing alto were allowed to sing. There are societies that wished to achieve the full beauty of a chorus which spanned the possibilities of the human voice, but in linking religion and music together also wished to ban women, as unsuited for an active rôle in the church, from the choir.

Boys' voices provide an apparently good substitute. So also do eunuchs, and so in the end we may have music modelled on a perfect orchestration of men and women's voices, but at the price of the exclusion of women and the castration of men.

Throughout history, the more complex activities have been defined and re-defined, now as male, now as female, now as neither, sometimes as drawing equally on the gifts of both sexes, sometimes as drawing differentially on both sexes. When an activity to which each could have contributed—and probably all complex activities belong in this class—is limited to one sex, a rich differentiated quality is lost from the activity itself. Once a complex activity is defined as belonging to one sex, the entrance of the other sex into it is made difficult and compromising. There is no heavy taboo in Bali against a woman if she wishes, or a man if he wishes, practising the special arts of the other sex. But painting in Bali has been a male art. When a gifted little adolescent girl in the village of Batoean, where there were already some sixty young men experimenting with the modern innovation of painting on paper, tried a new way of painting—by setting down what she saw rather than painting conventional stylized representations of the world—the boy artists derided and discouraged her until she gave up and made poor imitations of their style. The very difference in sex that made it possible for her to see a little differently, and so make an innovation, also made her so vulnerable that her innovation could be destroyed. Conversely, the entrance of one sex into the activities of the other if the other has less prestige may be simply destructive. In ancient Samoa, the women made lovely bark-cloth, pressing out the fluctuating, beautifully soft lines against mats on which the pattern was sewed in coconut-leaf riblets. When iron tools were introduced, the men, because men were defined as the carvers, learned to carve wooden pattern-boards that were stronger and easier to work with than the old fragile mats. But the designs, made for an art for which they had no feeling, suffered, became stiff and dull, and even the women's attempt to get some freedom back into the designs by painting imitations rather than using the boards failed.

In religion we find the same gamut. Religious experience and religious leadership may be permitted to one sex alone, and the periodic outbreak of vision in the wrong sex may be penalized. A woman may be branded as a witch, a man as an invert. The whole picture may become so confused between real gift and social definition of sex rôle that we get the final institutionalized patterns that confuse sex inversion, transvestitism, and religious function, as among some Siberian tribes. It is always possible for society to deny to one sex that which both sexes are able to do; no human gift is strong enough to flower fully in a person who is threatened with loss of sex membership. The insistence on limiting a two-sex potentiality to one sex results in the terrible tragedies of wrong definition of one's own sex in the man who becomes a homosexual because of the way in which society defines his desire to paint or to dance, or in the woman who becomes a homosexual because she likes to ride horses, or use a slide-rule. If the interest the other sex takes in a one-sex activity is strong enough, then the intruders may win, as men have been largely driven from teaching in the schools of the United States. Or even more peculiar things may happen. In some particular place and time a developing medical practice may include obstetrics within the proper sphere of the doctor. Those male physicians who have had the strongest interest in the reproductive capacities of women may gravitate initially towards obstetrics and pediatrics. So also may females whose interest in medicine has been defined as male. There may come to be a group of practitioners that includes males who have been very strongly influenced by their conceptions of what a female rôle is, and females who are strongly repelled by their conceptions of the limitations of the female rôle. Together they may shape medical practice into strange forms in which the women who might make a contribution from a first-hand knowledge of femininity are silent, and the men are left freer to follow their phantasies than they would have been had there been no women among them. Such a development may sometimes finally include a determination to indoctrinate women in "natural child-birth," in fact to return to them the simple power of bearing their own children, which in the course of a most devoted but one-sided development of medicine has practically been taken away from them.

I have elaborated this particular example in some detail, because no matter with what goodwill we may embark on a program of actually rearing both men and women to make their full and special contributions in all the complex processes of civilization—medicine and law, education and religion, the arts and sciences—the task will be very difficult. Where an occupation or an art is defined as feminine, the males who are attracted to it are either already in some way injured or may be injured if they try to practise it. If simple social definition does not set them to doubting their manhood, the very feminine rules and procedures of the occupation itself may so befuddle and exasperate them that they inevitably do not do different and good work, but similar and worse work, than the women who are already there. When an occupation is defined as masculine, the women who first enter it will be similarly handicapped.[1] They may have entered it out of a simple drive to act like a male, to compete with males, to prove that they are as good as males. Such a drive, compensatory and derivative rather than primary, will blur their vision and make clumsy fingers that should be deft as they try to act out the behaviour of the other sex, deemed so desirable. Or if they enter the occupation not out of any desire to compete with men, but out of simple primary motivations, of curiosity or a desire to create or to participate in some activity that is fascinating in itself, they too, like the men who enter occupations in which women have set the style, will find themselves handicapped at every turn by a style that has been completely set by the other sex. As the member of another culture fumbles and stumbles in a different land, with hand stretched out for a door-knob that is not there, a foot raised for a step that is missing, an appetite that rises insistently at an hour when there is no food, and an ear trained to wake to sounds that are never heard in these strange streets, so the immigrant coming into an occupation that has been the sole preserve of the other sex will stumble and fumble and do less than is in him or her to do. How can such an immigrant compete with those whose upbringing fits them to find their way, effortlessly, gracefully, with never a false step or a wasted motion? Whether it be the arts or the sciences, the whole pattern of thought, the whole symbolic system within which the novice must work, facilities every step taken by the expected sex, obstructs every step taken by the unexpected sex. These same one-sex patterns also restrict the sex that practises them the longer they are practised by one sex alone, and not made new by the interwoven imaginations of both. It may even be that one

[1] Mead, Margaret, "Cultural Aspects of Women's Vocational Problems in Post World War II," *Journal of Consulting Psychology*, vol. 10, 1946, pp. 23–28.

of the explanations which lie behind the decline of great periods of civilized activity, when philosophies fail, arts decline, and religions lose their vigour, may be found to be a too rigid adherence to the insights and the gifts of one sex. The higher the development of some faculty of creativeness that has been defined as rigidly male or rigidly female, the more the personality of the practitioner is split, and the deeper the danger that the personal life of mating and parenthood, which must be keyed to the presence of the other sex, may be divorced from the creative life of thought and action. This may in turn result in a secondary solution, such as the split in Greek society between the uneducated wife and the sophisticated mistress; it may push a large part of society towards celibacy or homosexuality, simply because a heterosexual relationship involves unbearable complications. The deeper the commitment to a creative activity becomes, be it government or science, industry or the arts, religion or exploration, the more the participating individuals will seek wholeness in it, and the more they will be vulnerable if the activity itself is one that only partially expresses our full two-sexed humanity.

There is likewise the very simple consideration that when we have no indication that intelligence is limited to one sex, any occupational restriction that prevents gifted women from exercising their gifts leaves them, and also the world that is sorely in need of every gift, the poorer. I have not put this consideration first, because there is still the possibility that the world might lose more by sacrificing sex differentiation than it would lose by limiting the exercise of that intelligence to certain ways of life. It is of very doubtful value to enlist the gifts of women if bringing women into fields that have been defined as male frightens the men, unsexes the women, muffles and distorts the contribution the women could make, either because their presence excludes men from the occupation or because it changes the quality of the men who enter it. There is slight gain if the struggle the intruders have to go through limits any primary feminine contribution they could make. It can be cogently argued that the profession of education —which should be by both sexes for both sexes —has lost as much if not more than it has gained as men departed not only from the primary grades, where the special gifts of women were badly needed, but from the higher grades, where boys have suffered because taught only by women. Men teachers took refuge in the universities, where they jealously guard their departments against the entrance of any woman into fields where women's insights are needed. Such sequence can well make one pause, and suggest that the cure is often worse than the disease.

This is more likely to be so whenever women's abilities are seen quantitatively in relation to men's.[2] The phrasing is then that there are many women who are as bright or brighter, as strong or stronger, as good or better organizers, than men. Crusades based on the rights of women to enter any field are likely to recoil upon themselves. The entrance of women is defined as competitive, and this is dangerous, whether the competition be expressed in the Soviet woman railroad engineer's plaint that women are allowed to run only engines on freight trains, or in the devastating antagonisms that are likely to occur in America, where it is so hard to forgive any person who wins in the same race, although so easy to acclaim success in races one has not entered. Almost every excursion of American women into fields that women had never, or at least not for many epochs, entered has been phrased in just these competitive terms. How dangerous it is can be measured in many ways: by the big poster advertisements on the Pacific coast in the spring of 1948, which advertised bread with a girl wielding the bat and the boy behind her holding the catcher's mit; by the "Here's How" in the New York subway, in which a text that describes the wedding-ring as a sign of subjection is illustrated by a *male* in evening-dress putting a ring on his *own* third finger. It is folly to ignore the signs which warn us that the present terms of which women are lured by their own curiosities and drives developed under the same educational system as boys, or forced by social conditions that deny homes and children to many women—a fourth of American women reach the menopause having borne no children[3]—are bad for both men and women. We have to count very carefully what gains there are, what possibilities there are of drawing rapidly enough upon the sensitivities of both men and women to right the balance and still go on.

There will be very great temptations in America to right the balance rudely, to tighten the lines against the continued entrance of women into these new fields, rather than to change the nature of that entrance. To the extent that we do go backwards we lose an opportunity to make the social inventions that will make it possible for women to contribute as much to civilization as they now contribute to the continuance of the race. As matters now stand and have stood through history, we have drawn on the gifts of men in both ways, and on the gifts of women almost entirely in one way. From each sex, society has asked that they so live that others may be born, that they cherish their masculinity and femininity, discipline it to the demands of parenthood, and leave new lives behind them when they die. This has meant that men had to be willing to choose, win, and keep women as lovers, protect and provide for them as husbands, and protect and provide for their children as fathers. It has meant that women have had to be willing to accept men as lovers, live with them as wives, and conceive, bear, feed, and cherish their children. Any society disappears which fails to make these demands on its members and to receive this much from them.

But from men, society has also asked and received something more than this. For thousands of generations men have been asked to do something more than be good lovers and husbands and fathers, even with all that that involved of husbandry and organization and protection against attack. They have been asked to develop and elaborate, each in terms of his own ability, the structure within which the children are reared, to build higher towers, or wider roads, to dream new dreams and see new visions, to penetrate ever farther into the secrets of nature, to learn new ways of making life more human and more rewarding. And within the whole adventure there has been a silent subtle division of labour, which had its roots perhaps in a period of history when the creativeness of bearing children outweighted in splendour every act that men performed, however they danced and pantomimed their pretence that the novices were really their children after all. In this division of labour, there was the assumption that bearing children is enough for the women, and in the rest of the task all the elaborations belong to men. This assumption becomes the less tenable the more men succeed in those elaborations which they have taken on themselves. As a civilization becomes complex, human life is defined in individual terms as well as in the service of

[2] The best summary of this approach to sex differences may be found in Seward, George H., *Sex and Social Order*, McGraw-Hill, New York and London, 1946.

[3] Ogburn, W. F., "Who Will Be Who in 1980," *New York Times Magazine*, May 30, 1948, p. 23.

the race, and the great structures of law and government, religion and art and science, become something highly valued for themselves. Practised by men, they become indicators of masculine humanity, and men take great pride in these achievements. To the extent that women are barred from them, women become less human. An illiterate woman is no less human than an illiterate man. As long as few men write and most men cannot, a woman may suffer no loss in her sense of herself. But when writing becomes almost universal—access to books, increased precision of thought, possibilities of communication—then if women cannot learn to write because they are women, they lose in stature, and the whole subtle process begins by which the wholeness of both sexes is undermined. When the woman's sense of loss of participation is compensated for by other forms of power, by the iron will of the mother-in-law who has been the docile, home-bound wife—as in China and Japan—then the equilibrating pattern may take the form of covert distortions of human relationships that may persist over centuries. When women's sense of impaired participation in society is expressed directly, in rebellion against the restrictions that it has placed on her, we may find instead the sort of freedom for women that occurred just before the break-down of the Roman Empire, or in the goals of the women's movement of the last century. But whatever the compensatory adjustment within the society, women's belief in their own power to contribute directly to human culture will be subtly and deeply impaired, and men's isolation, either covertly threatened or openly attacked, in a world that they have built alone will increase.

If we once accept the premise that we can build a better world by using the different gifts of each sex, we shall have two kinds of freedom, freedom to use untapped gifts of each sex, and freedom to admit freely and cultivate in each sex their special superiorities. We may well find that there are certain fields, such as the physical sciences, mathematics, and instrumental music, in which men by virtue of their sex, as well as by virtue of their qualities as specially gifted human beings, will always have that razor-edge of extra gift which makes all the difference, and that while women may easily follow where men lead, men will always make the new discoveries. We may equally well find that women, through the learning involved in maternity, which once experienced can be taught more easily to all

women, even childless women, than to men, have a special superiority in those human sciences which involve that type of understanding which until it is analyzed is called intuition. If intuition is based, as it seems to be, upon an ability to recognize the difference from the self rather than upon one to project the self in building a construct or a hypothesis, it may well be that the greatest intuitive gifts will be found among women. Just as for endless ages men's mathematical gifts were neglected and people counted one, two, two and one, and a dog, or were limited to counting on the fingers of their hands, so women's intuitive gifts have lain fallow, uncultivated, uncivilized.

Once it is possible to say it is as important to take women's gifts and make them available to both men and women, in transmittable form, as it was to take men's gifts and make the civilization built upon them available to both men and women, we shall have enriched our society. And we shall be ready to synthesize both kinds of gifts in the sciences, which are now sadly lop-sided with their far greater knowledge of how to destroy than of how to construct, far better equipped to analyze the world of matter into which man can project his intelligence than the world of human relations, which requires the socialized use of intuition. The mother who must learn that the infant who was but an hour ago a part of her body is now a different individual, with its own hungers and its own needs, and that if she listens to her own body to interpret the child, the child will die, is schooled in an irreplaceable school. As she learns to attend to that different individual, she develops a special way of thinking and feeling about human beings. We can leave these special learnings at the present level, or convert them into a more elaborate part of our civilization. Already the men and women who are working together in the human sciences are finding the greatly increased understanding that comes from the way in which their insights complement each other. We are learning that we pay different prices for our insights: for instance, to understand the way a culture socializes children a man must return in imagination to childhood, but a woman has also another and different path, to learn to understand the mothers of these children. Yet both are necessary, and the skill of one sex gives only a partial answer. We can build a whole society only by using both the gifts special to each sex and those shared by both sexes—by using the gifts of the whole of humanity.

Every step away from a tangled situation, in which moves and counter-moves have been made over centuries, is a painful step, itself inevitably imperfect. Here is a vicious circle to which it is not possible to assign either a beginning or an end, in which men's over-estimation of women's rôles, or women's over-estimation of men's rôles, leads one sex or the other to arrogate, to neglect, or even to relinquish part of our so dearly won humanity. Those who would break the circle are themselves a product of it, express some of its defects in their very gesture, may be only strong enough to challenge it, not able actually to break it. Yet once identified, once analyzed, it should be possible to create a climate of opinion in which others, a little less the product of the dark past because they have been reared with a light in their hand that can shine backwards as well as forwards, may in turn take the next step. Once by recognizing that each change in human society must be made by those who carry in every cell of their bodies the very reason why the change is necessary can we school our hearts to the patience to build truly and well, recognizing that it is not only the price, but also the glory, of our humanity that civilization must be built by human beings.

Margaret Mead states, "Each sex is shaped from birth by the presence and behavior of both sexes, and each sex is dependent on the other." Her essay focuses on what happens when this balance is not maintained. She discusses how a "one-sex pattern" leads to a denial of life. The following questions focus on Mead's contention that each sex should be fully realized for its own unique qualities.

1 According to Mead, what forces shape and mold the male and female?

2 What do we need to do to build a world in which both sexes benefit?

3 What are the special "vulnerabilities" of each sex? Does the Garden of Eden myth affirm or deny this "vulnerability"?

4 What does Mead suggest that we do to minimize the difference between the sexes? Does the Hindu myth of Siva and Sati minimize the differences? What does this suggest?

5 How might each sex be fully recognized? In which of the myths does this occur? Explain what this implies about the relations between men and women.

6 How do the achievements of civilization make an artificial distinction between the sexes? In which myths do you see this artificial distinction?

7 What happens to cultures which practice a "one-sex pattern"? Compare and contrast the Swahili and the Ibibian myths as examples of the "one-sex pattern" orientation.

8 How does competition influence American attitudes toward woman? Does this contribute to the exclusion of women from society? Does this make women appear less than human? How might one interpret Hawthorne's "The Birthmark" from the point of view of competition between the sexes?

9 What is necessary for each sex to learn about being a whole human being?

10 Compare and contrast Mead's essay with Ellis' essay. What patterns emerge from our understanding of the complexities which define the male and female?

Isn't there an easier way to earn my Canadian Club?

No.

A reward for men. A delight for women. Smooth as the wind. Mellow as sunshine. Friendly as laughter. The whisky that's bold enough to be lighter than them all.

Exploitation of the Fig Leaf

NATURAL MENTHOL for the taste of Springtime.

NATURAL MENTHOL. Not the artificial kind. That's what gives Salem a taste that's never harsh or hot. That's why Salem always tastes Springtime fresh.

1 How does each of these advertisements use the myths of male and female to manipulate people into buying their products?

2 What does each advertisement symbolize about the relation between males and females?

3 In each of the advertisements, who is innocent and who is guilty?

4 Have the men and women in these two advertisements moved from asexual to sexual knowledge? Explain.

5 How would Mead see these advertisements as an expression of the American male's and female's identities?

Changing Faces of Women

In the first frame, we see the pioneer woman as a symbol of the woman who undertook a heroic quest in order to find a new way of life. Her "rite of passage" began with her separation from her homeland. To survive in the new world, she often had to foresake the traditional role assigned to women. This lead her to establish a code of ethics founded on strength and one's ability to face adversity with independence.

In the second frame, we see the American woman as she is initiated into the ritual of motherhood. Although she represents the traditional values, of home and family, the American woman has not been limited to this role alone. Modern technology combined with the spirit of adventure has made it possible for her to continue the woman's need to be a complete person.

In the third frame, we see a modern woman who has been transformed to experience and express a new dimension of consciousness. Her quest is in the political arena. She combines the strength and wisdom of her mother and grandmother to demonstrate that she also has a "right" to confront injustice in the modern world.

The Changing Woman

NAVAJO

In the great desert of multicolored sand stood the Mountain-Around-Which-Moving-Was-Done, and at the foot of this great mountain was found a baby girl.

First Man and First Woman found the child when the earth was still unformed and incomplete. They took her home with them and raised her carefully, and the gods smiled on her and loved her. As she grew into womanhood, the world itself reached maturity as the mountains and valleys were all put into the proper places.

At last she was grown and the world was complete, and to celebrate her becoming a woman, the gods gave her a Blessing Way, Walking-into-Beauty. Songs and chants were sung to her, and her body was shaped with a sacred stick so that it would grow strong and beautiful. Each morning of the ceremony, she ran to greet the sun as it arose. The sacred ceremony was preserved and it is now given to all Navajo girls when they reach adulthood.

But the young girl did not stay the same. Each winter she became withered and white-haired, just as the earth became bare and snow-covered. But each spring as the colors of life grew back on the land, the colors of youth and beauty appeared in her cheeks and in her hair. So she is called Changing Woman, or "A Woman She Becomes Time and Again."

The sun fell in love with Changing Woman, but she did not know what to do with him. So she went to First Woman for advice. On the advice of First Woman, she met the sun and he made love to her. Nine months later, twin sons were born to her and she raised them with love and care. For monsters had now appeared in the world, and the people were being destroyed. Changing Woman hoped her sons could save the world from the monsters.

When the twin boys were grown, Changing Woman sent them to the sun, their father, to get power from him so that they could fight the monsters. After undergoing severe tests by their father, the boys returned and destroyed all of the monsters.

Now the world was complete and the monsters were dead. It was a perfect place for people, but there were very few left. Changing Woman pondered over this problem, and at last she took two baskets of corn. One was of white corn and one was of yellow corn. From the white cornmeal she shaped a man and from the yellow cornmeal she shaped a woman.

And so the earth was populated again, a changing world and a beautiful world—the world of Changing Woman.

KATE MILLETT

FROM "THEORY OF SEXUAL POLITICS"

ANTHROPOLOGICAL: MYTH AND RELIGION

Evidence from anthropology, religious and literary myth all attests to the politically expedient character of patriarchal convictions about women. One anthropologist refers to a consistent patriarchal strain of assumption that "woman's biological differences set her apart . . . she is essentially inferior," and since "human institutions grow from deep and primal anxieties and are shaped by irrational psychological mechanisms . . . socially organized attitudes toward women arise from basic tensions expressed by the male."[1] Under patriarchy the female did not herself develop the symbols by which she is described. As both the primitive and the civilized worlds are male worlds, the ideas which shaped culture in regard to the female were also of male design. The image of women as we know it is an image created by men and fashioned to suit their needs. These needs spring from a fear of the "otherness" of woman. Yet this notion itself presupposes that patriarchy has already been established and the male has already set himself as the human norm, the subject and referent to which the female is "other" or alien. Whatever its origin, the function of the male's sexual antipathy is to provide a means of control over a subordinate group and a rationale which justifies the inferior station of those in a lower order, "explaining" the oppression of their lives.

The feeling that woman's sexual functions are impure is both worldwide and persistent. One sees evidence of it everywhere in literature, in myth, in primitive and civilized life. It is striking how the notion persists today. The event of menstruation, for example, is a largely clandestine affair, and the psycho-social effect of the stigma attached must have great effect of the female ego. There is a large anthropological literature on menstrual taboo; the practice of isolating offenders in huts at the edge of the village occurs throughout the primitive world. Contemporary slang denominates menstruation as "the curse." There is considerable evidence that such discomfort as women suffer during their period is often likely to be psychosomatic, rather than physiological, cultural rather than biological, in origin. That this may also be true to some extent of labor and delivery is attested to by the recent experiment with "painless childbirth." Patriarchal circumstances and beliefs seem to have the effect of poisoning the female's own sense of physical self until it often truly becomes the burden it is said to be.

Primitive peoples explain the phenomenon of the female's genitals in terms of a wound, sometimes reasoning that she was visited by a bird or snake and mutilated into her present condition. Once she was wounded, now she bleeds. Contemporary slang for the vagina is "gash." The Freudian description of the female genitals is in terms of a "castrated" condition. The uneasiness and disgust female genitals arouse in patriarchal societies is attested to through religious, cultural, and literary proscription. In preliterate groups fear is also a factor, as in the belief in a castrating *vagina dentata*. The penis, badge of the male's superior status in both preliterate and civilized patriarchies, is given the most crucial significance, the subject both of endless boasting and endless anxiety.

Nearly all patriarchies enforce taboos against women touching ritual objects (those of war or religion) or food. In ancient and preliterate societies women are generally not permitted to eat with men. Women eat

[1] H. R. Hays, *The Dangerous Sex, the Myth of Feminine Evil* (New York: Putnam, 1964). Much of my summary in this section is indebted to Hays's useful assessment of cultural notions about the female.

apart today in a great number of cultures, chiefly those of the Near and Far East. Some of the inspiration of such custom appears to lie in fears of contamination, probably sexual in origin. In their function of domestic servants, females are forced to prepare food, yet at the same time may be liable to spread their contagion through it. A similar situation obtains with blacks in the United States. They are considered filthy and infectious, yet as domestics they are forced to prepare food for their queasy superiors. In both cases the dilemma is generally solved in a deplorably illogical fashion by segregating the act of eating itself, while cooking is carried on out of sight by the very group who would infect the table. With an admirable consistency, some Hindu males do not permit their wives to touch their food at all. In nearly every patriarchal group it is expected that the dominant male will eat first or eat better, and even where the sexes feed together, the male shall be served by the female.[2]

All patriarchies have hedged virginity and defloration in elaborate rites and interdictions. Among preliterates virginity presents an interesting problem in ambivalence. On the one hand, it is, as in every patriarchy, a mysterious good because a sign of property received intact. On the other hand, it represents an unknown evil associated with the mana of blood and terrifyingly "other." So auspicious is the event of defloration that in many tribes the owner-groom is willing to relinquish breaking the seal of his new possession to a stronger or older personality who can neutralize the attendant dangers.[3] Fears of defloration appear to originate in a fear of the alien sexuality of the female. Although any physical suffering endured in defloration must be on the part of the female (and most societies cause her—bodily and men-

tally—to suffer anguish), the social interest, institutionalized in patriarchal ritual and custom, is exclusively on the side of the male's property interest, prestige, or (among preliterates) hazard.

Patriarchal myth typically posits a golden age before the arrival of women, while its social practices permit males to be relieved of female company. Sexual segregation is so prevalent in patriarchy that one encounters evidence of it everywhere. Nearly every powerful circle in contemporary patriarchy is a men's group. But men form groups of their own on every level. Women's groups are typically auxiliary in character, imitative of male efforts and methods on a generally trivial or ephemeral plane. They rarely operate without recourse to male authority, church or religious groups appealing to the superior authority of a cleric, political groups to male legislators, etc.

In sexually segregated situations the distinctive quality of culturally enforced temperament becomes very vivid. This is particularly true of those exclusively masculine organizations which anthropology generally refers to as men's house institutions. The men's house is a fortress of patriarchal association and emotion. Men's houses in preliterate society strengthen masculine communal experience through dances, gossip, hospitality, recreation, and religious ceremony. They are also the arsenals of male weaponry.

David Riesman has pointed out that sports and some other activities provide males with a supportive solidarity which society does not trouble to provide for females.[4] While hunting, politics, religion, and commerce may play a role, sport and warfare are consistently the chief cement of men's house comradery. Scholars of men's house culture from Hutton Webster and Heinrich Schurtz to Lionel Tiger tend to be sexual patriots whose aim is to justify the apartheid

the institution represents.[5] Schurtz believes an innate gregariousness and a drive toward fraternal pleasure among peers urges the male away from the inferior and constricting company of women. Notwithstanding his conviction that a mystical "bonding instinct" exists in males, Tiger exhorts the public, by organized effort, to preserve the men's house tradition from its decline. The institution's less genial function of power center within a state of sexual antagonism is an aspect of the phenomenon which often goes unnoticed.

The men's houses of Melanesia fulfill a variety of purposes and are both armory and the site of masculine ritual initiation ceremony. Their atmosphere is not very remote from that of military institutions in the modern world: they reek of physical exertion, violence, the aura of the kill, and the throb of homosexual sentiment. They are the scenes of scarification, headhunting celebrations, and boasting sessions. Here young men are to be "hardened" into manhood. In the men's houses boys have such low status they are often called the "wives" of their initiators, the term "wife" implying both inferiority and the status of sexual object. Untried youths become the erotic interest of their elders and betters, a relationship also encountered in the Samurai order, in oriental priesthood, and in the Greek gymnasium. Preliterate wisdom decrees that while inculcating the young with the masculine ethos, it is necessary first to intimidate them with the tutelary status of the female. An anthropologist's comment on Melanesian men's houses is applicable equally to Genet's underworld, or Mailer's U. S. Army: "It would seem that the sexual brutalizing of the young boy and the effort to turn him into a woman both enhances the older warrior's desire of power, gratifies his sense of hostility toward the maturing male competitor, and eventually, when he takes him into the male group, strengthens the male solidarity in its symbolic attempt to do without women."[6] The

---

[2] The luxury conditions of the "better" restaurant affords a quaint exception. There not only the cuisine but even the table service is conducted by males, at an expense commensurate with such an occasion.

[3] See Sigmund Freud, *Totem and Taboo*, and Ernest Crawley, *The Mystic Rose* (London, Methuen, 1902, 1927).

[4] David Riesman, "Two Generations," in *The Woman in America*, edited by Robert Lifton (Boston, Beacon, 1967). See also James Coleman, *The Adolescent Society.*

[5] Heinrich Schurtz, *Altersklassen und Männerbünde* (Berlin, 1902) and Lionel Tiger, *op. cit.*

[6] Hays, *The Dangerous Sex*, p. 56.

derogation of feminine status in lesser males is a consistent patriarchal trait. Like any hazing procedure, initiation once endured produces devotees who will ever after be ardent initiators, happily inflicting their own former sufferings on the newcomer.

The psychoanalytic term for the generalized adolescent tone of men's house culture is "phallic state." Citadels of virility, they reinforce the most saliently power-oriented characteristics of patriarchy. The Hungarian psychoanalytic anthropologist Géza Róheim stressed the patriarchal character of men's house organization in the preliterate tribes he studied, defining their communal and religious practices in terms of a "group of men united in the cult of an object that is a materialized penis and excluding the women from their society."[7] The tone and ethos of men's house culture is sadistic, power-oriented, and latently homosexual, frequently narcissistic in its energy and motives.[8] The men's house inference that the penis is a weapon, endlessly equated with other weapons, is also clear. The practice of castrating prisoners is itself a comment on the cultural confusion of anatomy and status with weaponry. Much of the glamorization of masculine comradery in warfare originates in what one might designate as "the men's house sensibility." Its sadistic and brutalizing aspects are disguised in military glory and a particularly cloying species of masculine sentimentality. A great deal of our culture partakes of this tradition, and one might locate its first statement in Western literature in the heroic intimacy of Patroclus and Achilles. Its development can be traced through the epic and the saga to the chanson de geste. The tradition still flourishes in war novel and movie, not to mention the comic book.

Considerable sexual activity does take place in the men's house, all of it, needless to say, homosexual. But the taboo against homosexual behavior (at least among equals) is almost universally of far stronger force than the impulse and tends to effect a rechanneling of the libido into violence. This association of sexuality and violence is a particularly militaristic habit of mind.[9] The negative and militaristic coloring of such men's house homosexuality as does exist, is of course by no means the whole character of homosexual sensibility. Indeed, the warrior caste of mind with its ultravirility, is more *incipiently* homosexual, in its exclusively male orientation, than it is *overtly* homosexual. (The Nazi experience is an extreme case in point here.) And the heterosexual role-playing indulged in, and still more persuasively, the contempt in which the younger, softer, or more "feminine" members are held, is proof that the actual ethos is misogynist, or perversely rather than positively heterosexual. The true inspiration of men's house association therefore comes from the patriarchal situation rather than from any circumstances inherent in the homo-amorous relationship.

If a positive attitude toward heterosexual love is not quite, in Seignebos' famous dictum, the invention of the twelfth century, it can still claim to be a novelty. Most patriarchies go to great length to exclude love as a basis of mate selection. Modern patriarchies tend to do so through class, ethnic, and religious factors. Western classical thought was prone to see in heterosexual love either a fatal stroke of ill luck bound to end in tragedy, or a contemptible and brutish consorting with inferiors. Medieval opinion was firm in its conviction that love was sinful if sexual, and sex sinful if loving.

Primitive society practices its misogyny in terms of taboo and mana which evolve into explanatory myth. In historical cultures, this is transformed into ethical, then literary, and in the modern period, scientific rationalizations for the sexual politic. Myth is, of course, a felicitous advance in the level of propaganda, since it so often bases its arguments on ethics or theories of origins. The two leading myths of Western culture are the classical tale of Pandora's box and the Biblical story of the Fall. In both cases earlier mana concepts of feminine evil have passed through a final literary phase to become highly influential ethical justifications of things as they are.

Pandora appears to be a discredited version of a Mediterranean fertility goddess, for in Hesiod's *Theogony* she wears a wreath of flowers and a sculptured diadem in which are carved all the creatures of land and sea.[10] Hesiod ascribes to her the introduction of sexuality which puts an end to the golden age when "the races of men had been living on earth free from all evils, free from laborious work, and free from all wearing sickness."[11] Pandora was the origin of "the damnable race of women—a plague which men must live with."[12] The introduction of what are seen to be the evils of the male human condition came through the introduction of the female and what is said to be her unique product, sexuality. In *Works and Days* Hesiod elaborates on Pandora and what she represents—a perilous temptation with "the mind of a bitch and a thievish nature," full of "the cruelty of desire and longings that wear out the body," "lies and cunning words and a deceitful soul," a snare sent by Zeus to be "the ruin of men."[13]

[7] Géza Róheim, "Psychoanalysis of Primitive Cultural Types," *International Journal of Psychoanalysis* Vol. XIII London, 1932.

[8] All these traits apply in some degree to the bohemian circle which Miller's novels project, the Army which never leaves Mailer's consciousness, and the homosexual subculture on which Genet's observations are based. Since these three subjects of our study are closely associated with the separatist men's house culture, it is useful to give it special attention.

[9] Genet demonstrates this in *The Screens;* Mailer reveals it everywhere.

[10] Wherever one stands in the long anthropologists' quarrel over patriarchal versus matriarchal theories of social origins, one can trace a demotion of fertility goddesses and their replacement by patriarchal deities at a certain period throughout ancient culture.

[11] Hesiod, *Works and Days*, translated by Richmond Lattimore (University of Michigan, 1959), p. 29.

[12] Hesiod, *Theogony*, translated by Norman O. Brown (Indianapolis, Liberal Arts Press, 1953), p. 70.

[13] Hesiod, *Work and Days*, phrases from lines 53–100. Some of the phrases are from Lattimore's translation, some from A. W. Mair's translation (Oxford, 1908).

Patriarchy has God on its side. One of its most effective agents of control is the powerfully expeditious character of its doctrines as to the nature and origin of the female and the attribution to her alone of the dangers and evils it imputes to sexuality. The Greek example is interesting here: when it wishes to exalt sexuality it celebrates fertility through the phallus; when it wishes to denigrate sexuality, it cites Pandora. Patriarchal religion and ethics tend to lump the female and sex together as if the whole burden of the onus and stigma it attaches to sex were the fault of the female alone. Thereby sex, which is known to be unclean, sinful, and debilitating, pertains to the female, and the male identity is preserved as a human, rather than a sexual one.

The Pandora myth is one of two important Western archetypes which condemn the female through her sexuality and explain her position as her well-deserved punishment for the primal sin under whose unfortunate consequences the race yet labors. Ethics have entered the scene, replacing the simplicities of ritual, taboo, and mana. The more sophisticated vehicle of myth also provides official explanations of sexual history. In Hesiod's tale, Zeus, a rancorous and arbitrary father figure, in sending Epimetheus evil in the form of female genitalia, is actually chastising him for adult heterosexual knowledge and activity. In opening the vessel she brings (the vulva or hymen, Pandora's "box") the male satisfies his curiosity but sustains the discovery only by punishing himself at the hands of the father god with death and the assorted calamities of postlapsarian life. The patriarchal trait of male rivalry across age or status line, particularly those of powerful father and rival son, is present as well as the ubiquitous maligning of the female.

The myth of the Fall is a highly finished version of the same themes. As the central myth of the Judeo-Christian imagination and therefore of our immediate cultural heritage, it is well that we appraise and acknowledge the enormous power it still holds over us even in a rationalist era which has long ago given up literal belief in it while maintaining its emotional assent intact.[14] This mythic version of the female as the cause of human suffering, knowledge, and sin is still the foundation of sexual attitudes, for it represents the most crucial argument of the patriarchal tradition in the West.

The Israelites lived in a continual state of war with the fertility cults of their neighbors; these latter afforded sufficient attraction to be the source of constant defection, and the figure of Eve, like that of Pandora, has vestigial traces of a fertility goddess overthrown. There is some, probably unconscious, evidence of this in the Biblical account which announces, even before the narration of the fall has begun—"Adam called his wife's name Eve; because she was the mother of all living things." Due to the fact that the tale represents a compilation of different oral traditions, it provides two contradictory schemes for Eve's creation, one in which both sexes are created at the same time, and one in which Eve is fashioned later than Adam, an afterthought born from his rib, peremptory instance of the male's expropriation of the life force through a god who created the world without benefit of female assistance.

The tale of Adam and Eve is, among many other things, a narrative of how humanity invented sexual intercourse. Many such narratives exist in preliterate myth and folk tale. Most of them strike us now as delightfully funny stories of primal innocents who require a good deal of helpful instruction to figure it out. There are other major themes in the story: the loss of primeval simplicity, the arrival of death, and the first conscious experience of knowledge. All of them revolve about sex. Adam is forbidden to eat of the fruit of life or of the knowledge of good and evil, the warning states explicitly what should happen if he tastes of the latter: "in that day that thou eatest thereof thou shalt surely die." He eats but fails to die (at least in the story), from which one might infer that the serpent told the truth.

But at the moment when the pair eat of the forbidden tree they awake to their nakedness and feel shame. Sexuality is clearly involved, though the fable insists it is only tangential to a higher prohibition against disobeying orders in the matter of another and less controversial appetite—one for food. Róheim points out that the Hebrew verb for "eat" can also mean coitus. Everywhere in the Bible "knowing" is synonymous with sexuality, and clearly a product of contact with the phallus, here in the fable objectified as a snake. To blame the evils and sorrows of life—loss of Eden and the rest—on sexuality, would all too logically implicate the male, and such implication is hardly the purpose of the story, designed as it is expressly in order to blame all this world's discomfort on the female. Therefore it is the female who is tempted first and "beguiled" by the penis, transformed into something else, a snake. Thus Adam has "beaten the rap" of sexual guilt, which appears to be why the sexual motive is so repressed in the Biblical account. Yet the very transparency of the serpent's universal phallic value shows how uneasy the mythic mind can be about its shifts. Accordingly, in her inferiority and vulnerability the woman takes and eats, simple carnal thing that she is, affected by flattery even in a reptile. Only after this does the male fall, and with him, humanity—for the fable has made him the racial type, whereas Eve is a mere sexual type and, according to tradition, either expendable or replaceable. And as the myth records the original sexual adventure, Adam was seduced by woman, who was seduced by a penis. "The woman whom thou gavest to be with me, she gave me of the fruit and I did eat" is the first man's defense. Seduced by the phallic snake, Eve is

---

[14] It is impossible to assess how deeply embedded in our consciousness is the Eden legend and how utterly its patterns are planted in our habits of thought. One comes across its tone and design in the most unlikely places, such as Antonioni's film *Blow-Up*, to name but one of many striking examples. The action of the film takes place in an idyllic garden, loaded with primal overtones largely sexual, where, prompted by a tempter with a phallic gun, the female again betrays the male to death. The photographer who witnesses the scene reacts as if he were being introduced both to the haggard knowledge of the primal scene and original sin at the same time.

convicted for Adam's participation in sex.

Adam's curse is to toil in the "sweat of his brow," namely the labor the male associates with civilization. Eden was a fantasy world without either effort or activity, which the entrance of the female, and with her sexuality, has destroyed. Eve's sentence is far more political in nature and a brilliant "explanation" of her inferior status. "In sorrow thou shalt bring forth children. And thy desire shall be to thy husband. And he shall rule over thee." Again, as in the Pandora myth, a proprietary father figure is punishing his subjects for adult heterosexuality. It is easy to agree with Róheim's comment on the negative attitude the myth adopts toward sexuality: "Sexual maturity is regarded as a misfortune, something that has robbed mankind of happiness . . . the explanation of how death came into the world."

What requires further emphasis is the responsibility of the female, a marginal creature, in bringing on this plague, and the justice of her suborned condition as dependent on her primary role in this original sin. The connection of woman, sex, and sin constitutes the fundamental pattern of western patriarchal thought thereafter.

Before a man gets married, he's like a tree in the forest. He stands there, independent, an entity unto himself. And then he's chopped down. His branches are cut off—he's stripped of his bark—and he's thrown into the river with the rest of the logs. Then this tree is taken to the mill—and when it comes out it's no longer a tree. It's the vanity table, the breakfast nook, the baby crib, and the newspaper that lines the family garbage can.

Rock Hudson in *Pillow Talk*

GIVE HER A PATTERN

D. H. LAWRENCE

The real trouble about women is that they must always go on trying to adapt themselves to men's theories of women, as they always have done. When a woman is thoroughly herself, she is being what her type of man wants her to be. When a woman is hysterical it's because she doesn't quite know what to be, which pattern to follow, which man's picture of woman to live up to.

For, of course, just as there are many men in the world, there are many masculine theories of what women should be. But men run to type, and it is the type, not the individual, that produces the theory, or "ideal" of woman. Those very grasping gentry, the Romans, produced a theory or ideal of the matron, which fitted in very nicely with the Roman property lust. "Cæsar's wife should be above suspicion."—So Cæsar's wife kindly proceeded to be above it, no matter how far below it the Cæsar fell. Later gentlemen like Nero produced the "fast" theory of woman, and later ladies were fast enough for everybody. Dante arrived with a chaste and untouched Beatrice, and chaste and untouched Beatrices began to march self-importantly through the centuries. The Renaissances discovered the learned woman, and learned women buzzed mildly into verse and prose. Dickens invented the child-wife, so child-wives have swarmed ever since. He also fished out his version of the chaste Beatrice, a chaste but marriageable Agnes. George Eliot imitated this pattern, and it became confirmed. The noble woman, the pure spouse, the devoted mother took the field, and was simply worked to death. Our own poor mothers were this sort. So we younger men, having been a bit frightened of our noble mothers, tended to revert to the child-wife. We weren't very inventive. Only the child-wife must be a boyish little thing—that was the new touch we added. Because young men are definitely frightened of the real female. She's too risky a quantity. She is too untidy, like David's Dora. No, let her be a boyish little thing, it's safer. So a boyish little thing she is.

There are, of course, other types. Capable men produce the capable woman ideal. Doctors produce the capable nurse. Business men produce the capable secretary. And so you get all sorts. You can produce the masculine sense of honor (whatever that highly mysterious quantity may be) in women, if you want to.

There is, also, the eternal secret ideal of men —the prostitute. Lots of women live up to this ideal just because men want them to.

And so, poor woman, destiny makes away with her. It isn't that she hasn't got a mind— she has. She's got everything that man has. The only difference is that she asks for a pattern. Give me a pattern to follow! That will always be woman's cry. Unless of course she has already chosen her pattern quite young, then she will declare she is herself absolutely, and no man's idea of women has any influence over her.

Now the real tragedy is not that women ask and must ask for a pattern of womanhood. The tragedy is not, even, that men give them such abominable patterns, child-wives, little-boy-baby-face girls, perfect secretaries, noble spouses, self-sacrificing mothers, pure women who bring forth children in virgin coldness, prostitutes who just make themselves low, to please the men; all the atrocious patterns of womanhood that men have supplied to woman; patterns all perverted from any real natural fullness of a human being. Man is willing to accept woman as an equal, as a man in skirts, as an angel, a devil, a baby-face, a machine, an instrument, a bosom, a womb, a pair of legs, a servant, an encyclopædia, an ideal or an obscenity; the one thing he won't accept her as, is a human being, a real human being of the feminine sex.

And, of course, women love living up to strange patterns, weird patterns—the more uncanny the better. What could be more uncanny than the present pattern of the Eton-boy girl with flower-like artificial complexion? It is just weird. And for its very weirdness women like living up to it. What can be more gruesome than the little-boy-baby-face pattern? Yet the girls take it on with avidity.

But even that isn't the real root of the tragedy.

The absurdity, and often, as in the Dante-Beatrice business, the inhuman nastiness of the pattern—for Beatrice had to go on being chaste and untouched all her life, according to Dante's pattern, while Dante had a cozy wife and kids at home—even that isn't the worst of it. The worst of it is, as soon as a woman has really lived up to the man's pattern, the man dislikes her for it. There is intense secret dislike for the Eton-young-man girl, among the boys, now that she is actually produced. Of course, she's very nice to show in public, absolutely the thing. But the very young men who have brought about her production detest her in private and in their private hearts are appalled by her.

When it comes to marrying, the pattern goes all to pieces. The boy marries the Eton-boy girl, and instantly he hates the *type*. Instantly his mind begins to play hysterically with all the other types, noble Agneses, chaste Beatrices, clinging Doras and lurid *filles de joie*. He is in a wild welter of confusion. Whatever pattern the poor woman tries to live up to, he'll want another. And that's the condition of modern marriage.

Modern woman isn't really a fool. But modern man is. That seems to me the only plain way of putting it. The modern man is a fool, and the modern young man a prize fool. He makes a greater mess of his women than men have ever made. Because he absolutely doesn't know *what* he wants her to be. We shall see the changes in the woman-pattern follow one another fast and furious now, because the young men hysterically don't know what they want. Two years hence women may be in crinolines—there was a pattern for you!—or a bead flap, like naked negresses in mid-Africa—or they may be wearing brass armor, or the uniform of the Horse Guards. They may be anything. Because the young men are off their heads, and don't know what they want.

The women aren't fools, but they *must* live up to some pattern or other. They *know* the men are fools. They don't really respect the pattern. Yet a pattern they must have, or they can't exist.

Women are not fools. They have their own logic, even if it's not the masculine sort. Women have the logic of emotion, men have the logic of reason. The two are complementary and mostly in opposition. But the woman's logic of emotion is no less real and inexorable than the man's logic of reason. It only works differently.

And the woman never really loses it. She may spend years living up to a masculine pattern.

But in the end, the strange and terrible logic of emotion will work out the smashing of that pattern, if it has not been emotionally satisfactory. This is the partial explanation of the astonishing changes in women. For years they go on being chaste Beatrices or child-wives. Then on a sudden—bash! The chaste Beatrice becomes something quite different, the child-wife becomes a roaring lioness! The pattern didn't suffice, emotionally.

Whereas men are fools. They are based on a logic of reason, or are supposed to be. And then they go and behave, especially with regard to women, in a more-than-feminine unreasonableness. They spend years training up the little-boy-baby-face type, till they've got her perfect. Then the moment they marry her, they want something else. Oh, beware, young women, of the young men who adore you! The moment they've got you they'll want something utterly different. The moment they marry the little-boy-baby face, instantly they begin to pine for the noble Agnes, pure and majestic, or the infinite mother with deep bosom of consolation, or the perfect business woman, or the lurid prostitute on black silk sheets; or, most idiotic of all, a combination of all the lot of them at once. And that is the logic of reason! When it comes to women, modern men are idiots. They don't know what they want, and so they never want, permanently, what they get. They want a cream cake that is at the same time ham and eggs and at the same time porridge. They are fools. If only women weren't bound by fate to play up to them!

For the fact of life is that women *must* play up to man's pattern. And she only gives her best to a man when he gives her a satisfactory pattern to play up to. But today, with a stock of ready-made, worn-out idiotic patterns to live up to, what can women give to men but the trashy side of their emotions? What could a woman possibly give to a man who wanted her to be a boy-baby face? What could she possibly give him but the dribblings of an idiot?—And, because women aren't fools, and aren't fooled even for very long at a time, she gives him some nasty cruel digs with her claws, and makes him cry for mother dear!—abruptly changing his pattern.

Bah! men are fools. If they want anything from women, let them give women a decent, satisfying idea of womanhood—not these trick patterns of washed-out idiots.

The changing role of woman is characterized from different perspectives: (1) D. H. Lawrence develops a view of woman created by a male-oriented world; (2) Kate Millett concerns herself with the way the male initiation ceremony uses symbols to deny the presence of women in order to overcome their fear of the female. The following questions link these points of view with the myths of "The Changing Woman" and "Pandora: The Bearer of Evil":

1 What patterns do men use to define women, according to D. H. Lawrence? What has this done to the male? To the female? Would Pandora fit the mold suggested by Lawrence?

2 Compare Lawrence's point of view with Millett's: What patterns emerge from the symbols which are used to define men and women according to the two authors?

3 According to Millett how do myths distort the view of a woman? What is the function of initiation ceremonies for men? Do you agree or disagree with Millett's contention that these rites imply male homosexuality? Explain!

4 How would Pandora illustrate the way men see women? Compare the story of Pandora with the Navajo myth.

5 How does Millett interpret the Garden of Eden myth? Do you agree or disagree with her interpretation? What evidence is there in the contemporary world to either refute or support Millett's interpretation?

6 Do these myths, according to Millett, create a negative attitude toward the sexual differences?

7 How would Ellis interpret Millett's view of the modern world? Would Mead agree that there has been a "one-sex pattern" created by men? Would she agree or disagree with Millett's view of women? To what extent do you agree or disagree with Millett's view of male and female?

"OK, then—if it makes you feel like a man, leave it on . . . leave it on!"

1 **What changes do you see depicted in (1) the cartoon and (2) the picture of the woman and the men? How do these changes reflect a rite of passage?**

2 **How would Millett interpret these images of men and women?**

3 **What myths, that you have read, would explain (1) the man's need to prove his masculinity; (2) the woman's response to the demonstration she encounters; and (3) the men demonstrating?**

In the picture at the left, the woman looks disapprovingly at the men who are demonstrating for equal rights for homosexuals. For this woman, as well as for many like her, the world consists of two categories; "good and evil." The "good" act according to her norm, and the "evil" act differently. To perpetuate their point of view, these individuals want to see "evil" punished immediately. This simplistic moral view of absolutes often prevents human beings from seeing the multilevels of meaning which operate as human beings interact. For example, a young businessman may be walking down Wall Street as a group of protesters are demonstrating against the war in Vietnam. The demonstrators use language which seems indecent to this man. He forgets about the war as he becomes angry with their language. These individuals long to return to a world where Eden is not lost, and God is present because Adam and Eve deny that they know the difference between good and evil. This illusion often destroys the possibility for understanding and identifying with the world in which we live. The works of D. H. Lawrence abound in attacks against a system of "good and evil" which denies our primary, instinctive feelings. Lawrence uses sexual relations as a metaphor to link man with nature. In a letter to a friend, Lawrence wrote, "I am a profoundly religious man." But his religion is different from the Judeo-Christian ethic. For Lawrence, sex reveals the god of mystery which flows through man's blood. The social and political values of the writer are demonstrated as his characters either accept or reject the responsibility for the emotions connected to their sexual impulses. In "The Prussian Officer" (see below) Lawrence weaves the tale of a young man who undergoes a rite of passage from innocence to experience. Through a series of tests, the young orderly is presented with the choice of responding with his mental consciousness, his ability to rationalize what he does, or his blood consciousness, his emotional nature which propels him to act. The antagonist in the story is the Captain who represents the ambiguity between "pleasure and shame" which the young man wants to repress. The ritual murder of the Captain transforms the orderly from youth to man. Each man has attempted to repress what he feels. This leads to a denial of the nature which exists within. They become compulsively manipulated by the illusion of control which appears in the urge toward violence. The Captain's brutal treatment of the orderly leads to a chain of actions which ends with the orderly asserting that he must kill the Captain in order to survive. The hidden force within the story is this very problem: Each man struggles with a desire to use mental consciousness as a deterrent to accepting a consciousness of the blood. The orderly wants to passively act out his desires, but he learns that this is an illusion. He runs from the knowledge of good and evil as he seeks an Eden where nature invokes the innocence of all who seek perfection. Lawrence ends his tale in the death of both to reveal that within these men there are demons which are neither good nor evil. The orderly is liberated from his search for power in a world of absolutes. The military code of ethics fails to provide him with a fig leaf to cover his illusions. He fails to accept responsibility for his actions. This leads to a denial of identification between the men and with nature as well. The orderly seeks a union with the mountains, but he has contracted the black plague from the Captain. Lawrence criticizes the concept of "original sin" as a symbolic means to deny our participation in the circumstances of life. Each human being is subject to an order which is mysterious, and those who seek to find simple answers end in destroying the risk of being one of nature's works of imperfection.

THE PRUSSIAN OFFICER

D. H. LAWRENCE

1

They had marched more than thirty kilometers since dawn, along the white, hot road where occasional thickets of trees threw a moment of shade, then out into the glare again. On either hand, the valley, wide and shallow, glittered with heat; dark green patches of rye, pale young corn, fallow and meadow and black pine woods spread in a dull, hot diagram under a glistening sky. But right in front the mountains ranged across, pale blue and very still, snow gleaming gently out of the deep atmosphere. And towards the mountains, on and on, the regiment marched between the rye fields and the meadows, between the scraggy fruit trees set regularly on either side the high road. The burnished, dark green rye threw off a suffocating heat, the mountains drew gradually nearer and more distinct. While the feet of the soldiers grew hotter, sweat ran through their hair under their helmets, and their knapsacks could burn no more in contact with their shoulders, but seemed instead to give off a cold, prickly sensation.

He walked on and on in silence, staring at the mountains ahead, that rose sheer out of the land, and stood fold behind fold, half earth, half heaven, the heaven, the barrier with slits of soft snow, in the pale, bluish peaks.

He could now walk almost without pain. At the start, he had determined not to limp. It had made him sick to take the first steps, and during the first mile or so, he had compressed his breath, and the cold drops of sweat had stood on his forehead. But he had walked it off. What were they after all but bruises! He had looked at them, as he was getting up: deep bruises on the backs of his thighs. And since he had made his first step in the morning, he had been conscious of them, till now he had a tight hot place in his chest, with suppressing the pain, and holding himself in. There seemed no air when he breathed. But he walked almost lightly.

The Captain's hand had trembled at taking his coffee at dawn: his orderly saw it again. And he saw the fine figure of the Captain wheeling on horseback at the farmhouse ahead, a handsome figure in pale blue uniform with facings of scarlet, and the metal gleaming on the black helmet and the sword-scabbard, and dark streaks of sweat coming on the silky bay horse. The orderly felt he was connected with that figure moving so suddenly on horseback: he followed it like a shadow, mute and inevitable and damned by it. And the officer was always aware of the tramp of the company behind, the march of his orderly among the men.

The Captain was a tall man of about forty, gray at the temples. He had a handsome, finely knit figure, and was one of the best horsemen in the West. His orderly, having to rub him down, admired the amazing riding muscles of his loins.

For the rest, the orderly scarcely noticed the officer any more than he noticed himself. It was rarely he saw his master's face: he did not look at it. The Captain had reddish-brown, stiff hair, that he wore short upon his skull. His mustache was also cut short and bristly over a full, brutal mouth. His face was rather rugged, the cheeks thin. Perhaps the man was the more handsome for the deep lines of his face, the irritable tension of his brow, which gave him the look of a man who fights with life. His fair eyebrows stood bushy over light blue eyes that were always flashing with cold fire.

He was a Prussian aristocrat, haughty and overbearing. But his mother had been a Polish countess. Having made too many gambling debts when he was young, he had ruined his prospects in the army, and remained an infantry captain. He had never married: his position did not allow of it, and no woman had ever moved him to it. His time he spent riding —occasionally he rode one of his own horses at the races—and at the officers' club. Now and then he took himself a mistress. But after such an event, he returned to duty with his brow still more tense, his eyes still more hostile and irritable. With the men, however, he was merely impersonal, though a devil when roused; so that, on the whole, they feared him, but had no great aversion from him. They accepted him as the inevitable.

To his orderly he was at first cold and just and indifferent: he did not fuss over trifles. So that his servant knew practically nothing about him, except just what orders he would give, and how he wanted them obeyed. That was quite simple. Then the change gradually came.

The orderly was a youth of about twenty-two, of medium height, and well built. He had strong, heavy limbs, was swarthy, with a soft, black, young mustache. There was something altogether warm and young about him. He had firmly marked eyebrows over dark, expressionless eyes, that seemed never to have thought, only to have received life direct through his senses and acted straight from instinct.

Gradually the officer had become aware of his servant's young, vigorous, unconscious presence about him. He could not get away from the sense of the youth's person, while he was in attendance. It was like a warm flame upon the older man's tense, rigid body, that had become almost unliving, fixed. There was something so free and self-contained about him, and something in the young fellow's movement, that made the officer aware of him. And this irritated the Prussian. He did not choose to be touched into life by his servant. He might easily have changed his man, but he did not. He now very rarely looked direct at his orderly, but kept his face averted, as if to avoid seeing him. And yet as the young soldier moved unthinking about the apartment, the elder watched him, and would notice the movement of his strong young shoulders under the blue cloth, the bend of his neck. And it irritated him. To see the soldier's young, brown, shapely peasant's hand grasp the loaf or the wine-bottle sent a flash of hate or of anger through the elder man's blood. It was not that the youth was clumsy: it was rather the blind, instinctive sureness of movement of an unhampered young animal that irritated the officer to such a degree.

Once, when a bottle of wine had gone over, and the red gushed out on to the tablecloth, the officer had started up with an oath, and his eyes, bluey like fire, had held those of the confused youth for a moment. It was a shock for the young soldier. He felt something sink deeper, deeper into his soul, where nothing had ever gone before. It left him rather blank and wondering. Some of his natural completeness in himself was gone, a little uneasiness took its place. And from that time an undiscovered feeling had held between the two men.

Henceforward the orderly was afraid of really meeting his master. His subconsciousness remembered those steely blue eyes and the harsh brows, and did not intend to meet them again. So he always stared past his master, and avoided him. Also, in a little anxiety, he waited for the three months to have gone, when his time would be up. He began to feel a constraint in the Captain's presence, and the soldier even more than the officer wanted to be left alone, in his neutrality as servant.

He had served the Captain for more than a year, and knew his duty. This he performed easily, as if it were natural to him. The officer and his commands he took for granted, as he took the sun and the rain, and he served as a matter of course. It did not implicate him personally.

But now if he were going to be forced into a personal interchange with his master he would be like a wild thing caught; he felt he must get away.

But the influence of the young soldier's being had penetrated through the officer's stiffened discipline, and perturbed the man in him. He, however, was a gentleman, with long, fine hands and cultivated movements, and was not going to allow such a thing as the stirring of his innate self. He was a man of passionate temper, who had always kept himself suppressed. Occasionally there had been a duel, an outburst before the soldiers. He knew himself to be always on the point of breaking out. But he kept himself hard to the idea of the Service. Whereas the young soldier seemed to live out his warm, full nature, to give it off in his very movements, which had a certain zest, such as wild animals have in free movement. And this irritated the officer more and more.

In spite of himself, the Captain could not regain his neutrality of feeling towards his orderly. Nor could he leave the man alone. In spite of himself, he watched him, gave him sharp orders, tried to take up as much of his time as possible. Sometimes he flew into a rage with the young soldier, and bullied him. Then the orderly shut himself off, as it were out of earshot, and waited, with sullen, flushed face, for the end of the noise. The words never pierced to his intelligence. He made himself, protectively, impervious to the feelings of his master.

He had a scar on his left thumb, a deep seam going across the knuckle. The officer had long suffered from it, and wanted to do something to it. Still it was there, ugly and brutal on the young, brown hand. At last the Captain's reserve gave way. One day, as the orderly was smoothing out the tablecloth, the officer pinned down his thumb with a pencil, asking:

"How did you come by that?"

The young man winced and drew back at attention.

"A wood ax, Herr Hauptmann," he answered.

The officer waited for further explanation. None came. The orderly went about his duties. The elder man was sullenly angry. His servant avoided him. And the next day he had to use all his will power to avoid seeing the scarred thumb. He wanted to get hold of it and—A hot flame ran in his blood.

He knew his servant would soon be free, and would be glad. As yet, the soldier had held himself off from the elder man. The Captain grew madly irritable. He could not rest when the soldier was away, and when he was present, he glared at him with tormented eyes. He hated those fine, black brows over the unmeaning, dark eyes, he was infuriated by the free movement of the handsome limbs, which no military discipline could make stiff. And he became harsh and cruelly bullying, using contempt and satire. The young soldier only grew more mute and expressionless.

"What cattle were you bred by, that you can't keep straight eyes? Look me in the eyes when I speak to you."

And the soldier turned his dark eyes to the other's face, but there was no sight in them: he stared with the slightest possible cast, holding back his sight, perceiving the blue of his master's eyes, but receiving no look from them. And the elder man went pale, and his reddish eyebrows twitched. He gave his order, barrenly.

Once he flung a heavy military glove into the young soldier's face. Then he had the satisfaction of seeing the black eyes flare up into his own, like a blaze when straw is thrown on a fire. And he had laughed with a little tremor and a sneer.

But there were only two months more. The youth instinctively tried to keep himself intact: he tried to serve the officer as if the latter were an abstract authority and not a man. All his instinct was to avoid personal contact, even definite hate. But in spite of himself the hate grew, responsive to the officer's passion. However, he put it in the background. When he had left the Army he could dare acknowledge it. By nature he was active, and had many friends. He thought what amazing good fellows they were. But, without knowing it, he was alone. Now this solitariness was intensified. It would carry him through his term. But the officer seemed to be going irritably insane, and the youth was deeply frightened.

The soldier had a sweetheart, a girl from the mountains, independent and primitive. The two walked together, rather silently. He went with her, not to talk, but to have his arm round her, and for the physical contact. This eased him, made it easier for him to ignore the Captain; for he could rest with her held fast against his chest. And she, in some unspoken fashion, was there for him. They loved each other.

The Captain perceived it, and was mad with irritation. He kept the young man engaged all the evenings long, and took pleasure in the dark look that came on his face. Occasionally, the eyes of the two men met, those of the younger sullen and dark, doggedly unalterable, those of the elder sneering with restless contempt.

The officer tried hard not to admit the passion that had got hold of him. He would not know that his feeling for his orderly was anything but that of a man incensed by his stupid, perverse servant. So, keeping quite justified and conventional in his consciousness, he let the other thing run on. His nerves, however, were suffering. At last he slung the end of a belt in his servant's face. When he saw the youth start back, the pain-tears in his eyes and the blood on his mouth, he had felt at once a thrill of deep pleasure and of shame.

But this, he acknowledged to himself, was a thing he had never done before. The fellow was too exasperating. His own nerves must be going to pieces. He went away for some days with a woman.

It was a mockery of pleasure. He simply did not want the woman. But he stayed on for his time. At the end of it, he came back in an agony of irritation, torment, and misery. He rode all the evening, then came straight in to supper. His orderly was out. The officer sat with his long, fine hands lying on the table, perfectly still, and all his blood seemed to be corroding.

At last his servant entered. He watched the strong, easy young figure, the fine eyebrows, the thick black hair. In a week's time the youth had got back his old well-being. The hands of the officer twitched and seemed to be full of mad flame. The young man stood at attention, unmoving, shut off.

The meal went in silence. But the orderly seemed eager. He made a clatter with the dishes.

"Are you in a hurry?" asked the officer, watching the intent, warm face of his servant. The other did not reply.

"Will you answer my question?" said the Captain.

"Yes, sir," replied the orderly, standing with his pile of deep Army plates. The Captain waited, looked at him, then asked again:

"Are you in a hurry?"

"Yes, sir," came the answer, that sent a flash through the listener.

"For what?"

"I was going out, sir."

"I want you this evening."

There was a moment's hesitation. The officer had a curious stiffness of countenance.

"Yes, sir," replied the servant, in his throat.

"I want you tomorrow evening also—in fact, you may consider your evenings occupied, unless I give you leave."

The mouth with the young mustache set close.

"Yes, sir," answered the orderly, loosening his lips for a moment.

He again turned to the door.

"And why have you a piece of pencil in your ear?"

The orderly hesitated, then continued on his way without answering. He set the plates in a pile outside the door, took the stump of pencil from his ear, and put it in his pocket. He had been copying a verse for his sweetheart's birthday card. He returned to finish clearing the table. The officer's eyes were dancing, he had a little, eager smile.

"Why have you a piece of pencil in your ear?" he asked.

The orderly took his hands full of dishes. His master was standing near the great green stove, a little smile on his face, his chin thrust forward. When the young soldier saw him his heart suddenly ran hot. He felt blind. Instead of answering, he turned dazedly to the door.

As he was crouching to set down the dishes, he was pitched forward by a kick from behind. The pots went in a stream down the stairs, he clung to the pillar of the banisters. And as he was rising he was kicked heavily again, and again, so that he clung sickly to the post for some moments. His master had gone swiftly into the room and closed the door. The maid-servant downstairs looked up the staircase and made a mocking face at the crockery disaster.

The officer's heart was plunging. He poured himself a glass of wine, part of which he spilled on the floor, and gulped the remainder, leaning against the cool, green stove. He heard his man collecting the dishes from the stairs. Pale, as if intoxicated, he waited. The servant entered again. The Captain's heart gave a pang, as of pleasure, seeing the young fellow bewildered and uncertain on his feet, with pain.

"Schöner!" he said.

The soldier was a little slower in coming to attention.

"Yes, sir!"

The youth stood before him, with pathetic young mustache, and fine eyebrows very distinct on his forehead of dark marble.

"I asked you a question."

"Yes, sir."

The officer's tone bit like acid.

"Why had you a pencil in your ear?"

Again the servant's heart ran hot, and he could not breathe. With dark, strained eyes, he looked at the officer, as if fascinated. And he stood there sturdily planted, unconscious. The withering smile came into the Captain's eyes, and he lifted his foot.

"I—I forgot it—sir," panted the soldier, his dark eyes fixed on the other man's dancing blue ones.

"What was it doing there?"

He saw the young man's breast heaving as he made an effort for words.

"I had been writing."

"Writing what?"

Again the soldier looked him up and down. The officer could hear him panting. The smile came into the blue eyes. The soldier worked his dry throat, but could not speak. Suddenly the smile lit like a flame on the officer's face, and a kick came heavily against the orderly's thigh. The youth moved a pace sideways. His face went dead, with two black staring eyes.

"Well?" said the officer.

The orderly's mouth had gone dry, and his tongue rubbed in it as on dry brown-paper. He worked his throat. The officer raised his foot.

The servant went stiff.

"Some poetry, sir," came the crackling, unrecognizable sound of his voice.

"Poetry, what poetry?" asked the Captain with a sickly smile.

Again there was the working in the throat. The Captain's heart had suddenly gone down heavily, and he stood sick and tired.

"For my girl, sir," he heard the dry, inhuman sound.

"Oh!" he said, turning away. "Clear the table."

"Click!" went the soldier's throat; then again, "click!" and then the half-articulate:

"Yes, sir."

The young soldier was gone, looking old, and walking heavily.

The officer, left alone, held himself rigid, to prevent himself from thinking. His instinct warned him that he must not think. Deep inside him was the intense gratification of his passion, still working powerfully. Then there was a counteraction, a horrible breaking down of something inside him, a whole agony of reaction. He stood there for an hour motionless, a chaos of sensations, but rigid with a will to keep blank his consciousness, to prevent his mind grasping. And he held himself so until the worst of the stress had passed, when he began to drink, drank himself to an intoxication, till he slept obliterated. When he woke in the morning he was shaken to the base of his nature. But he had fought off the realization of what he had done. He had prevented his mind from taking it in, had suppressed it along with his instincts, and the conscious man had nothing to do with it. He felt only as after a bout of intoxication, weak, but the affair itself all dim and not to be recovered. Of the drunkenness of his passion he successfully refused remembrance. And when his orderly appeared with coffee, the officer assumed the same self he had had the morning before. He refused the event of the past night—denied it had ever been—and was successful in his denial. He had not done any such thing—not he himself. Whatever there might be lay at the door of a stupid, insubordinate servant.

The orderly had gone about in a stupor all the evening. He drank some beer because he was parched, but not much, the alcohol made his feeling come back, and he could not bear it. He was dulled, as if nine-tenths of the ordinary man in him were inert. He crawled about disfigured. Still, when he thought of the kicks, he went sick, and when he thought of the threat of more kicking, in the room afterwards, his heart went hot and faint, and he panted, remembered the one that had come. He had been forced to say, "For my girl." He was much too done even to want to cry. His mouth hung slightly open, like an idiot's. He felt vacant, and wasted. So, he wandered at his work, painfully, and very slowly and clumsily, fumbling blindly with the brushes, and finding it difficult, when he sat down, to summon the energy to move again. His limbs, his jaw, were slack and nerveless. But he was very tired. He got to bed at last, and slept inert, relaxed, in a sleep that was rather stupor than slumber, a dead night of stupefaction shot through with gleams of anguish.

In the morning were the maneuvers. But he woke even before the bugle sounded. The painful ache in his chest, the dryness of his throat, the awful steady feeling of misery made his eyes come awake and dreary at once. He knew, without thinking, what had happened. And he knew that the day had come again, when he must go on with his round. The last bit of darkness was being pushed out of the room. He would have to move his inert body and go on. He was so young, and had known so little trouble, that he was bewildered. He only wished it would stay night, so that he could lie still, covered up by the darkness. And yet nothing would prevent the day from coming, nothing would save him from having to get up and saddle the Captain's horse, and make the Captain's coffee. It was there, inevitable. And then, he thought, it was impossible. Yet they would not leave him free. He must go and take the coffee to the Captain. He was too stunned to understand it. He only knew it was inevitable—inevitable, however long he lay inert.

At last, after heaving at himself, for he seemed to be a mass of inertia, he got up. But he had to force every one of his movements from behind, with his will. He felt lost, and dazed, and helpless. Then he clutched hold of the bed, the pain was so keen. And looking at his thighs, he saw the darker bruises on his swarthy flesh and he knew that, if he pressed one of his fingers on one of the bruises, he should faint. But he did not want to faint—he did not want anybody to know. No one should ever know. It was between him and the Captain. There were only the two people in the world now—himself and the Captain.

Slowly, economically, he got dressed and forced himself to walk. Everything was obscure, except just what he had his hands on. But he managed to get through his work. The very pain revived his dull senses. The worst remained yet. He took the tray and went up to the Captain's room. The officer, pale and heavy, sat at the table. The orderly, as he saluted, felt himself put out of existence. He stood still for a moment submitting to his own nullification—then he gathered himself, seemed to regain himself, and then the Captain began to grow vague, unreal, and the younger soldier's heart beat up. He clung to this situation —that the Captain did not exist—so that he himself might live. But when he saw his officer's hand tremble as he took the coffee, he felt everything falling shattered. And he went away, feeling as if he himself were coming to pieces, disintegrated. And when the Captain was there on horseback, giving orders, while he himself stood, with rifle and knapsack, sick with pain, he felt as if he must shut his eyes— as if he must shut his eyes on everything. It was only the long agony of marching with a parched throat that filled him with one single, sleep-heavy intention; to save himself.

2

He was getting used even to his parched throat. That the snowy peaks were radiant among the sky, that the whity-green glacier-river twisted through its pale shoals, in the valley below, seemed almost supernatural. But he was going mad with fever and thirst. He plodded on uncomplaining. He did not want to speak, not to anybody. There were two gulls, like flakes of water and snow, over the river. The scene of green rye soaked in sunshine came like a sickness. And the march continued, monotonously, almost like a bad sleep.

At the next farmhouse, which stood low and broad near the high road, tubs of water had been put out. The soldiers clustered round to drink. They took off their helmets, and the steam mounted from their wet hair. The Captain sat on horseback, watching. He needed to see his orderly. His helmet threw a dark shadow over his light, fierce eyes, but his mustache and mouth and chin were distinct in the sunshine. The orderly must move under the presence of the figure of the horseman. It was not that he was afraid, or cowed. It was as if he were disemboweled, made empty, like an empty shell.

He felt himself as nothing, a shadow creeping under the sunshine. And, thirsty as he was, he could scarcely drink, feeling the Captain near him. He would not take off his helmet to wipe his wet hair. He wanted to stay in shadow, not to be forced into consciousness. Starting, he saw the light heel of the officer prick the belly of the horse; the Captain cantered away, and he himself could relapse into vacancy.

Nothing, however, could give him back his living place in the hot, bright morning. He felt like a gap among it all. Whereas the Captain was prouder, overriding. A hot flash went through the young servant's body. The Captain was firmer and prouder with life, he himself was empty as a shadow. Again the flash went through him, dazing him out. But his heart ran a little firmer.

The company turned up the hill, to make a loop for the return. Below, from among the trees, the farm-bell clanged. He saw the laborers, mowing barefoot at the thick grass, leave off their work and go downhill, their scythes hanging over their shoulders, like long, bright claws curving down behind them. They seemed like dream-people, as if they had no relation to himself. He felt as in a blackish dream: as if all the other things were there and had form, but he himself was only a consciousness, a gap that could think and perceive.

The soldiers were tramping silently up the glaring hillside. Gradually his head began to revolve, slowly, rhythmically. Sometimes it was dark before his eyes, as if he saw this world through a smoked glass, frail shadows and unreal. It gave him a pain in his head to walk.

The air was too scented, it gave no breath. All the lush green-stuff seemed to be issuing its sap, till the air was deathly, sickly with the smell of greenness. There was the perfume of clover, like pure honey and bees. Then there grew a faint acrid tang—they were near the beeches; and then a queer clattering noise, and a suffocating, hideous smell; they were passing a flock of sheep, a shepherd in a black smock, holding his crook. Why should the sheep huddle together under this fierce sun? He felt that the shepherd would not see him, though he could see the shepherd.

At last there was the halt. They stacked rifles in a conical stack, put down their kit in a scattered circle around it, and dispersed a little, sitting on a small knoll high on the hillside. The chatter began. The soldiers were steaming with heat, but were lively. He sat still, seeing the blue mountains rising upon the land, twenty kilometers away. There was a blue fold in the ranges, then out of that, at the foot, the broad, pale bed of the river, stretches of whity-green water between pinkish-gray shoals among the dark pine woods. There it was, spread out a long way off. And it seemed to come down-hill, the river. There was a raft being steered, a mile away. It was a strange country. Nearer, a red-roofed, broad farm with white base and square dots of windows crouched beside the wall of beech foliage on the wood's edge. There were long strips of rye and clover and pale green corn. And just at his feet, below the knoll, was a darkish bog, where globe flowers stood breathless still on their slim stalks. And some of the pale gold bubbles were burst, and a broken fragment hung in the air. He thought he was going to sleep.

Suddenly something moved in the colored mirage before his eyes. The Captain, a small, light-blue and scarlet figure, was trotting evenly between the strips of corn, along the level brow of the hill. And the man making flag-signals was coming on. Proud and sure moved the horseman's figure, the quick, bright thing, in which was concentrated all the light of this morning, which for the rest lay a fragile, shin-ing shadow. Submissive, apathetic, the young soldier sat and stared. But as the horse slowed to a walk, coming up the last steep path, the great flash flared over the body and soul of the orderly. He sat waiting. The back of his head felt as if it were weighted with a heavy piece of fire. He did not want to eat. His hands trem-bled slightly as he moved them. Meanwhile the officer on horseback was approaching slowly and proudly. The tension grew in the orderly's soul. Then again, seeing the Captain ease him-self on the saddle, the flash blazed through him.

The Captain looked at the patch of light blue and scarlet, and dark heads, scattered closely on the hillside. It pleased him. The command pleased him. And he was feeling proud. His orderly was among them in common subjec-tion. The officer rose a little on his stirrups to look. The young soldier sat with averted, dumb face. The Captain relaxed on his seat. His slim-legged, beautiful horse, brown as a beech nut, walked proudly uphill. The Captain passed into the zone of the company's atmosphere: a hot smell of men, sweat, of leather. He knew it very well. After a word with the lieutenant, he went a few paces higher, and sat there, a dom-inant figure, his sweat-marked horse swishing its tail, while he looked down on his men, on his orderly, a nonentity among the crowd.

The young soldier's heart was like fire in his chest, and he breathed with difficulty. The offi-cer, looking downhill, saw three of the young soldiers, two pails of water between them, staggering across a sunny green field. A table had been set up under a tree, and there the slim lieutenant stood, importantly busy. Then the Captain summoned himself to an act of courage. He called his orderly.

The flame leapt into the young soldier's throat as he heard the command, and he rose blindly, stifled. He saluted, standing below the officer. He did not look up. But there was the flicker in the Captain's voice.

"Go to the inn and fetch me . . ." the officer gave his commands. "Quick!" he added.

At the last word, the heart of the servant leapt with a flash, and he felt the strength come over his body. But he turned in mechan-ical obedience, and set off at a heavy run downhill, looking almost like a bear, his trou-sers bagging over his military boots. And the officer watched this blind, plunging run all the way.

But it was only the outside of the orderly's body that was obeying so humbly and mechan-ically. Inside had gradually accumulated a core into which all the energy of that young life was compact and concentrated. He executed his commission, and plodded quickly back uphill. There was a pain in his head, as he walked, that made him twist his features unknowingly. But hard there in the center of his chest was himself, himself, firm, and not to be plucked to pieces.

The Captain had gone up into the wood. The orderly plodded through the hot, powerfully smelling zone of the company's atmosphere. He had a curious mass of energy inside him now. The Captain was less real than himself. He approached the green entrance to the wood. There, in the halfshade, he saw the horse standing, the sunshine and the flickering shadow of leaves dancing over his brown body. There was a clearing where timber had lately been felled. Here, in the gold-green shade be-side the brilliant cup of sunshine, stood two figures, blue and pink, the bits of pink showing out plainly. The Captain was talking to his lieu-tenant.

The orderly stood on the edge of the bright clearing, where great trunks of trees, stripped and glistening, lay stretched like naked, brown-skinned bodies. Chips of wood littered the trampled floor, like splashed light, and the bases of the felled trees stood here and there, with their raw, level tops. Beyond was the brilliant, sunlit green of a beech.

"Then I will ride forward," the orderly heard his Captain say. The lieutenant saluted and strode away. He himself went forward. A hot flash passed through his belly, as he tramped towards his officer.

The Captain watched the rather heavy figure of the young soldier stumble forward, and his veins, too, ran hot. This was to be man to man between them. He yielded before the solid, stumbling figure with bent head. The orderly stooped and put the food on a level-sawn tree-base. The Captain watched the glistening, sun-inflamed, naked hands. He wanted to speak to the young soldier, but could not. The servant propped a bottle against his thigh, pressed open the cork, and poured out the beer into the mug. He kept his head bent. The Captain accepted the mug.

"Hot!" he said, as if amiably.

The flame sprang out of the orderly's heart, nearly suffocating him.

"Yes, sir," he replied, between shut teeth.

And he heard the sound of the Captain's drinking and he clenched his fists, such a strong torment came into his wrists. Then came the faint clang of the closing of the pot-lid. He looked up. The Captain was watching him. He glanced swiftly away. Then he saw the officer stoop and take a piece of bread from the tree-base. Again the flash of flame went through the young soldier, seeing the stiff body stoop beneath him, and his hands jerked. He looked away. He could feel the officer was nervous. The bread fell as it was being broken. The officer ate the other piece. The two men stood tense and still, the master laboriously chewing his bread, the servant staring with averted face, his fist clenched.

Then the young soldier started. The officer had pressed open the lid of the mug again. The orderly watched the lid of the mug, and the white hand that clenched the handle, as if he were fascinated. It was raised. The youth followed it with his eyes. And then he saw the thin, strong throat of the elder man moving up and down as he drank, the strong jaw working. And the instinct which had been jerking at the young man's wrist suddenly jerked free. He jumped, feeling as if it were rent in two by a

strong flame.

The spur of the officer caught in a tree-root, he went down backwards with a crash, the middle of his back thudding sickeningly against a sharp-edged tree-base, the pot flying away. And in a second the orderly, with serious, earnest young face, and underlip between his teeth, had got his knee in the officer's chest and was pressing the chin backward over the farther edge of the tree-stump, pressing, with all his heart behind in a passion of relief, the tension of his wrists exquisite with relief. And with the base of his palms he shoved at the chin, with all his might. And it was pleasant, too, to have that chin, that hard jaw already slightly rough with beard, in his hands. He did not relax one hair's breadth, but, all the force of all his blood exulting in his thrust, he shoved back the head of the other man, till there was a little "cluck" and a crunching sensation. Then he felt as if his head went to vapor. Heavy convulsions shook the body of the officer, frightening and horrifying the young soldier. Yet it pleased him, too, to repress them. It pleased him to keep his hands pressing back the chin, to feel the chest of the other man yield in expiration to the weight of his strong, young knees, to feel the hard twitchings of the prostrate body jerking his own whole frame, which was pressed down on it.

But it went still. He could look into the nostrils of the other man, the eyes he could scarcely see. How curiously the mouth was pushed out, exaggerating the full lips, and the mustache bristling up from them. Then, with a start, he noticed the nostrils gradually filled with blood. The red brimmed, hesitated, ran over, and went in a thin trickle down the face to the eyes.

It shocked and distressed him. Slowly, he got up. The body twitched and sprawled there, inert. He stood and looked at it in silence. It was a pity *it* was broken. It represented more than the thing which had kicked and bullied him. He was afraid to look at the eyes. They were hideous now, only the whites showing, and the blood running to them. The face of the orderly was drawn with horror at the sight. Well, it was so. In his heart he was satisfied. He had hated the face of the Captain. It was extinguished now. There was a heavy relief in the orderly's soul. That was as it should be. But he could not bear to see the long, military body lying broken over the tree-base, the fine fingers crisped. He wanted to hide it away.

Quickly, busily, he gathered it up and pushed it under the felled tree-trunks, which rested their beautiful, smooth length either end on logs. The face was horrible with blood. He covered it with the helmet. Then he pushed the limbs straight and decent, and brushed the dead leaves off the fine cloth of the uniform. So, it lay quite still in the shadow under there. A little strip of sunshine ran along the breast, from a chink between the logs. The orderly sat by it for a few moments. Here his own life also ended.

Then, through his daze, he heard the lieutenant, in a loud voice, explaining to the men outside the wood, that they were to suppose the bridge on the river below was held by the enemy. Now they were to march to the attack in such and such a manner. The lieutenant had no gift of expression. The orderly, listening from habit, got muddled. And when the lieutenant began it all again he ceased to hear.

He knew he must go. He stood up. It surprised him that the leaves were glittering in the sun, and the chips of wood reflecting white from the ground. For him a change had come over the world. But for the rest it had not—all seemed the same. Only he had left it. And he could not go back. It was his duty to return with the beer-pot and the bottle. He could not. He had left all that. The lieutenant was still hoarsely explaining. He must go, or they would overtake him. And he could not bear contact with any one now.

He drew his fingers over his eyes, trying to find out where he was. Then he turned away. He saw the horse standing in the path. He went up to it and mounted. It hurt him to sit in the saddle. The pain of keeping his seat occupied him as they cantered through the wood. He would not have minded anything, but he could not get away from the sense of being divided from the others. The path led out of the trees. On the edge of the wood he pulled up and stood watching. There in the spacious sunshine of the valley soldiers were moving in a little swarm. Every now and then, a man harrowing on a strip of fallow shouted to his oxen, at the turn. The village and the white-towered church was small in the sunshine. And he no longer belonged to it—he sat there, beyond, like a man outside in the dark. He had gone out from everyday life into the unknown, and he could not, he even did not want to go back.

Turning from the sun-blazing valley, he rode deep into the wood. Tree-trunks, like people standing gray and still, took no notice as he went. A doe, herself a moving bit of sunshine and shadow, went running through the flecked shade. There were bright green rents in the foliage. Then it was all pine wood, dark and cool. And he was sick with pain, he had an intolerable great pulse in his head, and he was sick. He had never been ill in his life. He felt lost, quite dazed with all this.

Trying to get down from the horse, he fell, astonished at the pain and his lack of balance. The horse shifted uneasily. He jerked its bridle and sent it cantering jerkily away. It was his last connection with the rest of things.

But he only wanted to lie down and not be disturbed. Stumbling through the trees, he came on a quiet place where beeches and pine trees grew on a slope. Immediately he had lain down and closed his eyes, his consciousness went racing on without him. A big pulse of sickness beat in him as if throbbed through the whole earth. He was burning with dry heat. But he was too busy, too tearingly active in the incoherent race of delirium to observe.

3

He came to with a start. His mouth was dry and hard, his heart beat heavily, but he had not the energy to get up. His heart beat heavily. Where was he?—the barracks—at home? There was something knocking. And, making an effort, he looked round—trees, and litter of greenery, and reddish, bright, still pieces of sunshine on the floor. He did not believe he was himself, he did not believe what he saw. Something was knocking. He made a struggle towards consciousness, but relapsed. Then he struggled again. And gradually his surroundings fell into relationship with himself. He knew, and a great pang of fear went through his heart. Somebody was knocking. He could see the heavy, black rags of a fir tree overhead. Then everything went black. Yet he did not believe he had closed his eyes. He had not. Out of the blackness sight slowly emerged again. And someone was knocking. Quickly, he saw the blood-disfigured face of his Captain, which he hated. And he held himself still with horror. Yet, deep inside him, he knew that it was so, the Captain should be dead. But the physical delirium got hold of him. Someone was knocking. He lay perfectly still, as if dead with fear. And he went unconscious.

When he opened his eyes again, he started, seeing something creeping swiftly up a tree-trunk. It was a little bird. And the bird was whistling overhead. Tap-tap-tap—it was the small, quick bird rapping the tree-trunk with its beak, as if its head were a little round hammer. He watched it curiously. It shifted sharply, in its creeping fashion. Then, like a mouse, it slid down the bare trunk. Its swift creeping sent a flash of revulsion through him. He raised his head. It felt a great weight. Then, the little bird ran out of the shadow across a still patch of sunshine, its little head bobbing swiftly, its white legs twinkling brightly for a moment. How neat it was in its build, so compact, with pieces of white on its wings. There were several of them. They were so pretty—but they crept like swift, erratic mice, running here and there among the beechmast.

He lay down again exhausted, and his consciousness lapsed. He had a horror of the little creeping birds. All his blood seemed to be darting and creeping in his head. And yet he could not move.

He came to with a further ache of exhaustion. There was the pain in his head, and the horrible sickness, and his inability to move. He had never been ill in his life. He did not know where he was or what he was. Probably he had got sunstroke. Or what else?—he had silenced the Captain forever—some time ago—oh, a long time ago. There had been blood on his face, and his eyes had turned upwards. It was all right, somehow. It was peace. But now he had got beyond himself. He had never been here before. Was it life, or not life? He was by himself. They were in a big, bright place, those others, and he was outside. The town, all the country, a big bright place of light: and he was outside, here, in the darkened open beyond, where each thing existed alone. But they would all have to come out there sometime, those others. Little, and left behind him, they all were. There had been father and mother and sweetheart. What did they all matter? This was the open land.

He sat up. Something scuffled. It was a little, brown squirrel running in lovely, undulating bounds over the floor, its red tail completing the undulation of its body—and then, as it sat up, furling and unfurling. He watched it, pleased. It ran on again, friskily, enjoying itself. It flew wildly at another squirrel, and they were chasing each other, and making little scolding, chattering noises. The soldier wanted to speak to them. But only a hoarse sound came out of his throat. The squirrels burst away—they flew up the trees. And then he saw the one peeping round at him, halfway up a tree-trunk. A start of fear went through him, though, insofar as he was conscious, he was amused. It still stayed, its little, keen face staring at him halfway up the tree-trunk, its little ears pricked up, its clawy little hands clinging to the bark, its white breast reared. He started from it in panic.

Struggling to his feet, he lurched away. He went on walking, walking, looking for something—for a drink. His brain felt hot and inflamed for want of water. He stumbled on. Then he did not know anything. He went unconscious as he walked. Yet he stumbled on, his mouth open.

When, to his dumb wonder, he opened his eyes on the world again, he no longer tried to remember what it was. There was thick, golden light behind golden-green glitterings, and tall gray-purple shafts, and darknesses farther off, surrounding him, growing deeper. He was conscious of a sense of arrival. He was amid the reality, on the real, dark bottom. But there was the thirst burning in his brain. He felt lighter, not so heavy. He supposed it was newness. The air was muttering with thunder. He thought he was walking wonderfully swiftly and was coming straight to relief—or was it to water?

Suddenly he stood still with fear. There was a tremendous flare of gold, immense—just a few dark trunks like bars between him and it. All the young level wheat was burnished gold glaring on its silky green. A woman, full-skirted, a black cloth on her head for head-dress, was passing like a block of shadow through the glistening, green corn, into the full glare. There was a farm, too, pale blue in shadow, and the timber black. And there was a church spire, nearly fused away in the gold. The woman moved on, away from him. He had no language with which to speak to her. She was the bright, solid unreality. She would make a noise of words that would confuse him, and her eyes would look at him without seeing him. She was crossing there to the other side. He stood against a tree.

When at last he turned, looking down the long, bare grove whose flat bed was already filling dark, he saw the mountains in a wonder-light, not far away, and radiant. Behind the soft, gray ridge of the nearest range the further mountains stood golden and pale gray, the snow all radiant like pure, soft gold. So still, gleaming in the sky, fashioned pure out of the ore of the sky, they shone in their silence. He stood and looked at them, his face illuminated. And like the golden, lustrous gleaming of the snow he felt his own thirst bright in him. He stood and glazed, leaning against a tree. And then everything slid away into space.

During the night the lightning fluttered perpetually, making the whole sky white. He must have walked again. The world hung livid round him for moments, fields a level sheen of gray-green light, trees in dark bulk, and the range of clouds black across a white sky. Then the darkness fell like a shutter, and the night was whole. A faint flutter of a half-revealed world, that could not quite leap out of the darkness! —Then there again stood a sweep of pallor for the land, dark shapes looming, a range of clouds hanging overhead. The world was a ghostly shadow, thrown for a moment upon the pure darkness, which returned ever whole and complete.

And the mere delirium of sickness and fever went on inside him—his brain opening and shutting like the night—then sometimes convulsions of terror from something with great eyes that stared round a tree—then the long agony of the march, and the sun decomposing his blood—then the pang of hate for the Captain, followed by a pang of tenderness and ease. But everything was distorted, born of an ache and resolving into an ache.

In the morning he came definitely awake. Then his brain flamed with the sole horror of thirstiness! The sun was on his face, the dew was steaming from his wet clothes. Like one possessed, he got up. There, straight in front of him, blue and cool and tender, the mountains ranged across the pale edge of the morning sky. He wanted them—he wanted them alone —he wanted to leave himself and be identified with them. They did not move, they were still and soft, with white, gentle markings of snow. He stood still, mad with suffering, his hands crisping and clutching. Then he was twisting in a paroxysm on the grass.

He lay still, in a kind of dream of anguish. His thirst seemed to have separated itself from him, and to stand apart, a single demand. Then the pain he felt was another single self. Then there was the clog of his body, another separate thing. He was divided among all kinds of separate beings. There was some strange, agonized connection between them, but they were drawing further apart. Then they would all split. The sun, drilling down on him, was drilling through the bond. Then they would all fall, fall through the everlasting lapse of space. Then again, his consciousness reasserted itself. He roused on to his elbow and stared at the gleaming mountains. There they ranked, all still and wonderful between earth and heaven. He stared till his eyes went black, and the mountains, as they stood in their beauty, so clean and cool, seemed to have it, that which was lost in him.

4

When the soldiers found him, three hours later, he was lying with his face over his arm, his black hair giving off heat under the sun. But he was still alive. Seeing the open, black mouth[1] the young soldiers dropped him in horror.

He died in the hospital at night, without having seen again.

The doctors saw the bruises on his legs, behind, and were silent.

The bodies of the two men lay together, side by side, in the mortuary, the one white and slender, but laid rigidly at rest, the other looking as if every moment it must rouse into life again, so young and unused, from a slumber.

[1] Black mouth: a symptom of bubonic plague.

The following questions focus on the theme in "The Prussian Officer" of a young man's initiation into an adult world which prevents him from maintaining the illusion of innocence in light of what he does.

1   How does Lawrence use nature to depict the antagonism between the Captain and the orderly? What attracts and repels each man to the other? What tests does the Captain give the orderly? How does this lead each man to seek the neutrality of his role? What does this suggest about the use of mental consciousness as a means to deny blood consciousness? Do the roles of master–slave inhibit individuals from accepting a link with nature? What does Lawrence imply about roles as a means to deny what we feel? Explain whether this illusion is an actuality in the story.

2   How does Lawrence use the concept of the unconscious and the conscious as a metaphor for the contradictions which exist in each character? How does each act committed deny what each man thinks? What split within each man does this provoke? Explain how this split leads to the violence which erupts in the story!

3   What is the function of women in the story? How does the Captain's attitude toward women differ from the orderly's? Is this a result of the male-dominated world of the military? Use Kate Millett's essay to discuss the way each of these men is manipulated by the myths of masculinity.

4   What is the function of the Captain's murder in the story? Is this a ritual killing of authority? What myths in Chapter 1 reveal a pattern similar to this murder? How would Erich Neumann's essay, in Chapter 1, shed light on this act as a symbolic gesture of the son to remove the world parents?

5   Why does the orderly run from the sight of blood? What fear does this suggest? In mounting the Captain's horse, the orderly completes the transference of power from one generation to the next: why does he run from this? Use the Garden of Eden myth to interpret the orderly's refusal to accept the knowledge of his actions.

6   How does Lawrence use nature to contrast with the orderly as he attempts to run from himself? What does Lawrence do to create the impression that the orderly seeks to control a power within? How does this struggle reveal to us his primitive impulses? Is the orderly struggling to be a Christ symbol who restores the balance between "heaven and hell" which was destroyed by Adam and Eve in Eden? Explain!

7   What does the story suggest about the movement from asexual to sexual knowledge? What sexual attitudes and feelings underlie the actions in the story? How does the orderly assert himself against a male-dominated world? How does each character express the contradiction between the desire for power and the illusion of innocence? How does the ending reveal the perversion between pain and pleasure? What images of love emerge in this story? What does Lawrence suggest about man's attempt to bring about his own destruction? Why does this destruction deny the flow of energy between man and nature? Explain!

a   Use Mead to interpret this story as a reflection of the roles which prevent the male and female from accepting one another!

b   Use Lawrence's essay to interpret his story. To what extent does his essay validate or invalidate the story's point of view? Explain the difference between the essay and fiction in making a statement about the human attempt to deny the process of life!

Being a woman is to perceive the indignity and inequality which corrode the human situation, is to act with compassion and involvement to find solutions which are born of a fusion of the mind and heart to ensure that, instead of confrontation and conflict, there is understanding and enrichment.

Indira Gandhi

"Woman" is a very old word . . . existed ever since the world has existed. She is the basis of the world. I wish she would take the mission more seriously—because it's not as easy as it looks. It's not made only of wonderful times. It's mainly made of unseen hard work—woman's kind of work, which is sustaining. There's no applause, no glory . . . if she can manage to make her husband somewhat happy and bring up her children the proper way—and make them honorable citizens—then the future of the world is in her hands. Woman's mission is a silent one—but the basis of humanity is on her back. We women have the world in our hands. Our greatest power is in being woman—woman, woman, woman.

Maria Callas

In the film *A Star Is Born* Judy Garland appears as a woman who succeeds as a man fails. And yet the film attempts to perpetuate the illusion that both the man and woman are innocent of the events which lead up to the man's suicide. Judy Garland and James Mason both desperately need each other, but union is not possible in a world where success and love are not permitted. In F. Scott Fitzgerald's story "Babylon Revisited," the theme of death as a punishment for love also appears, but in this story the woman dies instead of the man. We see the Garden of Eden motif repeated as characters attempt to appear innocent rather than experience their involvement with each other. Death is the result of love, but in both cases the surviving partner attempts to restore the harmony which existed before the relation.

A Repeat Performance

BABYLON REVISITED

"And where's Mr. Campbell?" Charlie asked.

"Gone to Switzerland. Mr. Campbell's a pretty sick man, Mr. Wales."

"I'm sorry to hear that. And George Hardt?" Charlie inquired.

"Back in America, gone to work."

"And where is the Snow Bird?"[2]

"He was in here last week. Anyway, his friend, Mr. Schaeffer, is in Paris."

Two familiar names from the long list of a year and a half ago. Charlie scribbled an address in his notebook and tore out the page.

"If you see Mr. Schaeffer, give him this," he said. "It's my brother-in-law's address. I haven't settled on a hotel yet."

He was not really disappointed to find Paris was so empty. But the stillness in the Ritz bar was strange and portentous. It was not an American bar any more—he felt polite in it, and not as if he owned it. It had gone back into France. He felt the stillness from the moment he got out of the taxi and saw the doorman, usually in a frenzy of activity at this hour, gossiping with a *chasseur*[3] by the servants' entrance.

Passing through the corridor, he heard only a single, bored voice in the once-clamorous women's room. When he turned into the bar he travelled the twenty feet of green carpet with his eyes fixed straight ahead by old habit; and then, with his foot firmly on the rail, he turned and surveyed the room, encountering only a single pair of eyes that fluttered up from a newspaper in the corner. Charlie asked for the head bar-man, Paul, who in the latter days of the bull market had come to work in his own custom-built car—disembarking, however, with due nicety at the nearest corner. But Paul was at his country house today and Alix giving him information.

"No, no more," Charlie said. "I'm going slow these days."

Alix congratulated him: "You were going pretty strong a couple of years ago."

"I'll stick to it all right," Charlie assured him. "I've stuck to it for over a year and a half now."

[1] First published in the *Saturday Evening Post* for February 21, 1931, and collected in *Taps at Reveille* (1935), the last of the author's volumes to appear before his death. The story represents the final stage of his criticism of the generation of which he had become a symbol.

[2] Slang for one addicted to (or sometimes peddling) "snow," *i.e.*, cocaine or heroin.

[3] Liveried footman or porter.

"How do you find conditions in America?"

"I haven't been to America for months. I'm in business in Prague, representing a couple of concerns there. They don't know about me down there."

Alix smiled.

"Remember the night of George Hardt's bachelor dinner here?" said Charlie. "By the way, what's become of Claude Fessenden?"

Alix lowered his voice confidentially: "He's in Paris, but he doesn't come here any more. Paul doesn't allow it. He ran up a bill of thirty thousand francs, charging all his drinks and his lunches, and usually his dinner, for more than a year. And when Paul finally told him he had to pay, he gave him a bad check."

Alix shook his head sadly.

"I don't understand it, such a dandy fellow. Now he's all bloated up—" He made a plump apple of his hands.

Charlie watched a group of strident queens installing themselves in a corner.

"Nothing affects them," he thought. "Stocks rise and fall, people loaf or work, but they go on forever." The place oppressed him. He called for the dice and shook with Alix for the drink.

"Here for long, Mr. Wales?"

"I'm here for four or five days to see my little girl."

"Oh-h! You have a little girl?"

Outside, the fire-red, gas-blue, ghost-green signs shone smokily through the tranquil rain. It was late afternoon and the streets were in movement; the *bistros* gleamed. At the corner of the Boulevard des Capucines he took a taxi. The Place de la Concorde moved by in pink majesty; they crossed the logical Seine, and Charlie felt the sudden provincial quality of the left bank.

Charlie directed his taxi to the Avenue de l'Opéra, which was out of his way. But he wanted to see the blue hour spread over the magnificent façade, and imagine that the cab horns, playing endlessly the first few bars of *La Plus que Lente*,[4] were the trumpets of the Second Empire. They were closing the iron grill in front of Brentano's Bookstore, and people were already at dinner behind the trim little bourgeois hedge of Duval's. He had never eaten at a really cheap restaurant in Paris. Five-course dinner, four francs fifty, eighteen cents, wine included. For some odd reason he wished that he had.

[4] A slow waltz by Debussy. It was a fad for taxicabs to carry horns playing scraps of familiar music.

As they rolled on to the Left Bank and he felt its sudden provincialism, he thought, "I spoiled this city for myself. I didn't realize it, but the days came along one after another, and then two years were gone, and everything was gone, and I was gone."

He was thirty-five, and good to look at. The Irish mobility of his face was sobered by a deep wrinkle between his eyes. As he rang his brother-in-law's bell in the Rue Palatine, the wrinkle deepened till it pulled down his brows; he felt a cramping sensation in his belly. From behind the maid who opened the door darted a lovely little girl of nine, who shrieked "Daddy!" and flew up, struggling like a fish, into his arms. She pulled his head around by one ear and set her cheek against his.

"My old pie," he said.

"Oh, daddy, daddy, daddy, daddy, dads, dads, dads!"

She drew him into the salon, where the family waited, a boy and girl his daughter's age, his sister-in-law and her husband. He greeted Marion with his voice pitched carefully to avoid either feigned enthusiasm or dislike, but her response was more frankly tepid, though she minimized her expression of unalterable distrust by directing her regard toward his child. The two men clasped hands in a friendly way and Lincoln Peters rested his for a moment on Charlie's shoulder.

The room was warm and comfortably American. The three children moved intimately about, playing through the yellow oblongs that led to other rooms; the cheer of six o'clock spoke in the eager smacks of the fire and the sounds of French activity in the kitchen. But Charlie did not relax; his heart sat up rigidly in his body and he drew confidence from his daughter, who from time to time came close to him, holding in her arms the doll he had brought.

"Really extremely well," he declared in answer to Lincoln's question. "There's a lot of business there that isn't moving at all, but we're doing even better than ever. In fact, damn well. I'm bringing my sister over from America next month to keep house for me. My income last year was bigger than it was when I had money. You see, the Czechs——"

His boasting was for a specific purpose; but after a moment, seeing a faint restiveness in Lincoln's eye, he changed the subject:

"Those are fine children of yours, well brought up, good manners."

"We think Honoria's a great little girl too."

Marion Peters came back from the kitchen. She was a tall woman with worried eyes, who had once possessed a fresh American loveliness. Charlie had never been sensitive to it and was always surprised when people spoke of how pretty she had been. From the first there had been an instinctive antipathy between them.

"Well, how do you find Honoria?" she asked.

"Wonderful. I was astonished how much she's grown in ten months. All the children are looking well."

"We haven't had a doctor for a year. How do you like being back in Paris?"

"It seems very funny to see so few Americans around."

"I'm delighted," Marion said vehemently. "Now at least you can go into a store without their assuming you're a millionaire. We've suffered like everybody, but on the whole it's a good deal pleasanter."[5]

"But it was nice while it lasted," said Charlie. "We were a sort of royalty, almost infallible, with a sort of magic around us. In the bar this afternoon"—he stumbled, seeing his mistake—"there wasn't a man I knew."

She looked at him keenly. "I should think you'd have had enough of bars."

"I only stayed a minute. I take one drink every afternoon, and no more."

"Don't you want a cocktail before dinner?" Lincoln asked.

"I take only one drink every afternoon, and I've had that."

"I hope you keep to it," said Marion.

Her dislike was evident in the coldness with which she spoke, but Charlie only smiled; he had larger plans. Her very aggressiveness gave him an advantage, and he knew enough to wait. He wanted them to initiate the discussion of what they knew had brought him to Paris.

At dinner he couldn't decide whether Honoria was most like him or her mother. Fortunate if she didn't combine the traits of both that had brought them to disaster. A great wave of protectiveness went over him. He thought he knew what to do for her. He believed in character; he wanted to jump back a whole generation and trust in character again as the eternally valuable element. Everything else wore out.

He left soon after dinner, but not to go home. He was curious to see Paris by night with clearer and more judicious eyes than those of other days. He brought a *strapontin*[6] for the Casino and watched Josephine Baker[7] go through her chocolate arabesques.

After an hour he left and strolled toward Montmartre, up the Rue Pigalle into the Place Blanche. The rain had stopped and there were a few people in evening clothes disembarking from taxis in front of cabarets, and *cocottes*[8] prowling singly or in pairs, and many Negroes. He passed a lighted door from which issued music, and stopped with the sense af familiarity; it was Bricktop's, where he had parted with so many hours and so much money. A few doors farther on he found another ancient rendezvous and incautiously put his head inside. Immediately an eager orchestra burst into sound, a pair of professional dancers leaped to their feet and a maître d'hôtel[9] swooped toward him, crying, "Crowd just arriving, sir!" But he withdrew quickly.

"You have to be damn drunk," he thought.

Zelli's was closed, the bleak and sinister cheap hotels surrounding it were dark; up in the Rue Blanche there was more light and a local, colloquial French crowd. The Poet's Cave[10] had disappeared, but the two great mouths of the Café of Heaven and the Café of Hell still yawned— even devoured, as he watched, the meager contents of a tourist bus—a German, a Japanese, and an American couple who glanced at him with frightened eyes.

So much for the effort and ingenuity of Montmartre.[11] All the catering to vice and waste was on an utterly childish scale, and he suddenly realized the meaning of the word "dissipate"— to dissipate into thin air; to make nothing out of something. In the little hours of the night every move from place to place was an enormous human jump, an increase of paying for the privilege of slower and slower motion.

He remembered thousand-franc notes given to an orchestra for playing a single number, hundred-franc notes tossed to a doorman for calling a cab.

But it hadn't been given for nothing.

It had been given, even the most wildly

[5] The American stock market crashed in 1929; when depression hit Paris, about two years later, the larger American colony had vanished.

[6] A low-priced jump seat that opens down into the aisle.

[7] Josephine Baker, talented American Negro entertainer, became a spectacular feature of Parisian night life in the late twenties.

[8] Prostitutes.

[9] Headwaiter.

[10] In Paris, *cave* (literally, "wine vault") was widely used to designate a cabaret below the sidewalk level.

[11] During the twenties Montmartre, a quarter of Paris, had become the international center of Bohemianism.

squandered sum, as an offering to destiny that he might not remember the things most worth remembering, the things that now he would always remember—his child taken from his control, his wife escaped to a grave in Vermont.

In the glare of a *brasserie* a woman spoke to him. He bought her some eggs and coffee, and then, eluding her encouraging stare, gave her a twenty-franc note and took a taxi to his hotel.

II

He woke up on a fine fall day—football weather. The depression of yesterday was gone and he liked the people on the streets. At noon he sat opposite Honoria at Le Grand Vatel, the only restaurant he could think of not reminiscent of champagne dinners and long luncheons that began at two and ended in a blurred and vague twilight.

"Now, how about vegetables? Oughtn't you to have some vegetables?"

"Well, yes."

"Here's *épinards* and *chou-fleur* and carrots and *haricots*."[12]

"I'd like *chou-fleur*."

"Wouldn't you like to have two vegetables?"

"I usually have only one at lunch."

The waiter was pretending to be inordinately fond of children. "*Qu'elle est mignonne, la petite! Elle parle exactement comme une française*."[13]

"How about dessert? Shall we wait and see?"

The waiter disappeared. Honoria looked at her father expectantly.

"What are we going to do?"

"First, we're going to that toy store in the Rue Saint-Honoré and buy you anything you like. And then we're going to the vaudeville at the Empire."

She hesitated. "I like it about the vaudeville, but not the toy store."

"Why not?"

"Well, you brought me this doll." She had it with her. "And I've got lots of things. And we're not rich any more, are we?"

"We never were. But today you are to have anything you want."

"All right," she agreed resignedly.

When there had been her mother and a French nurse he had been inclined to be strict; now he

[12] The French words mean "spinach," "cauliflower," "beans."

[13] She is charming, the little one! She speaks precisely like a French girl.

extended himself, reached out for a new tolerance; he must be both parents to her and not shut any of her out of communication.

"I want to get to know you," he said gravely. "First let me introduce myself. My name is Charles J. Wales, of Prague."

"Oh, daddy!" her voice cracked with laughter.

"And who are you, please?" he persisted, and she accepted a rôle immediately: "Honoria Wales, Rue Palatine, Paris."

"Married or single?"

"No, not married. Single."

He indicated the doll. "But I see you have a child, madame."

Unwilling to disinherit it, she took it to her heart and thought quickly: "Yes, I've been married, but I'm not married now. My husband is dead."

He went on quickly, "And the child's name?"

"Simone. That's after my best friend at school."

"I'm very pleased that you're doing so well at school."

"I'm third this month," she boasted. "Elsie"—that was her cousin—"is only about eighteenth, and Richard is about at the bottom."

"You like Richard and Elsie, don't you?"

"Oh, yes. I like them all right."

Cautiously and casually he asked: "And Aunt Marion and Uncle Lincoln—which do you like best?"

"Oh, Uncle Lincoln, I guess."

He was increasingly aware of her presence. As they came in, a murmur of "... adorable" followed them, and now the people at the next table bent all their silences upon her, staring as if she were something no more conscious than a flower.

"Why don't I live with you?" she asked suddenly. "Because mamma's dead?"

"You must stay here and learn more French. It would have been hard for daddy to take care of you so well."

"I don't really need much taking care of any more. I do everything for myself."

Going out of the restaurant, a man and a woman unexpectedly hailed him.

"Well, the old Wales!"

"Hello there, Lorraine ... Dunc."

Sudden ghosts out of the past: Duncan Schaeffer, a friend from college. Lorraine Quarles, a lovely, pale blonde of thirty; one of a crowd who had helped them make months into days in the lavish times of three years ago.

"My husband couldn't come this year," she

said, in answer to his question. "We're poor as hell. So he gave me two hundred a month, and told me I could do my worst on that. . . . This your little girl?"

"What about coming back and sitting down?" Duncan asked.

"Can't do it." He was glad for an excuse. As always, he felt Lorraine's passionate, provocative attraction, but his own rhythm was different now.

"Well, how about dinner?" she asked.

"I'm not free. Give me your address and let me call you."

"Charlie, I believe you're sober," she said judicially. "I honestly believe he's sober, Dunc. Pinch him and see if he's sober."

Charlie indicated Honoria with his head. They both laughed.

"What's your address?" said Duncan skeptically.

He hesitated, unwilling to give the name of his hotel.

"I'm not settled yet. I'd better call you. We're going to see the vaudeville at the Empire."

"There! That's what I want to do," Lorraine said. "I want to see some clowns and acrobats and jugglers. That's just what we'll do, Dunc."

"We've got to do an errand first," said Charlie. "Perhaps we'll see you there."

"All right, you snob. . . . Good-by, beautiful little girl."

"Good-by."

Honoria bobbed politely.

Somehow, an unwelcome encounter. They liked him because he was functioning, because he was serious; they wanted to see him, because he was stronger than they were now, because they wanted to draw a certain sustenance from his strength.

At the Empire, Honoria proudly refused to sit upon her father's folded coat. She was already an individual with a code of her own, and Charlie was more and more absorbed by the desire of putting a little of himself into her before she crystallized utterly. It was hopeless to try to know her in so short a time.

Between the acts they came upon Duncan and Lorraine in the lobby where the band was playing.

"Have a drink?"

"All right, but not up at the bar. We'll take a table."

"The perfect father."

Listening abstractedly to Lorraine, Charlie watched Honoria's eyes leave their table, and

he followed them wistfully about the room, wondering what they saw. He met her glance and she smiled.

"I liked that lemonade," she said.

What had she said? What had he expected? Going home in a taxi afterward, he pulled her over until her head rested against his chest.

"Darling, do you ever think about your mother?"

"Yes, sometimes," she answered vaguely.

"I don't want you to forget her. Have you got a picture of her?"

"Yes, I think so. Anyhow, Aunt Marion has. Why don't you want me to forget her?"

"She loved you very much."

"I loved her too."

They were silent for a moment.

"Daddy, I want to come and live with you," she said suddenly.

His heart leaped; he had wanted it to come like this.

"Aren't you perfectly happy?"

"Yes, but I love you better than anybody. And you love me better than anybody, don't you, now that mummy's dead?"

"Of course I do. But you won't always like me best, honey. You'll grow up and meet somebody your own age and go marry him and forget you ever had a daddy."

"Yes, that's true," she agreed tranquilly.

He didn't go in. He was coming back at nine o'clock and he wanted to keep himself fresh and new for the thing he must say then.

"When you're safe inside, just show yourself in that window."

"All right. Good-by, dads, dads, dads, dads."

He waited in the dark street until she appeared, all warm and glowing, in the window above and kissed her fingers out into the night.

III

They were waiting. Marion sat behind the coffee service in a dignified black dinner dress that just faintly suggested mourning. Lincoln was walking up and down with the animation of one who had already been talking. They were as anxious as he was to get into the question. He opened it almost immediately:

"I suppose you know what I want to see you about—why I really came to Paris."

Marion played with the black stars on her necklace and frowned.

"I'm awfully anxious to have a home," he continued. "And I'm awfully anxious to have Honoria in it. I appreciate you taking in Honoria for her mother's sake, but things have changed now"—he hesitated and then continued more forcibly—"changed radically with me, and I want to ask you to reconsider the matter. It would be silly for me to deny that about three years ago I was acting badly——"

Marion looked up at him with hard eyes.

"—But all that's over. As I told you, I haven't had more than a drink a day for over a year, and I take that drink deliberately, so that the idea of alcohol won't get too big in my imagination. You see the idea?"

"No," said Marion succinctly.

"It's a sort of stunt I set myself. It keeps the matter in proportion."

"I get you," said Lincoln. "You don't want to admit it's got any attraction for you."

"Something like that. Sometimes I forget and don't take it. But I try to take it. Anyhow, I couldn't afford to drink in my position. The people I represent are more than satisfied with what I've done, and I'm bringing my sister over from Burlington to keep house for me, and I want awfully to have Honoria too. You know that even when her mother and I weren't getting along well we never let anything that happened touch Honoria. I know she's fond of me and I know I'm able to take care of her—well, there you are. How do you feel about it?"

He knew that now he would have to take a beating. It would last an hour or two hours, and it would be difficult, but if he modulated his inevitable resentment to the chastened attitude of the reformed sinner, he might win his point in the end.

Keep your temper, he told himself. You don't want to be justified. You want Honoria.

Lincoln spoke first: "We've been talking it over ever since we got your letter last month. We're happy to have Honoria here. She's a dear little thing, and we're glad to be able to help her, but of course that isn't the question——"

Marion interrupted suddenly. "How long are you going to stay sober, Charlie?" she asked.

"Permanently, I hope."

"How can anybody count on that?"

"You know I never did drink heavily until I gave up business and came over here with nothing to do. Then Helen and I began to run around with——"

"Please leave Helen out of it. I can't bear to hear you talk about her like that."

He stared at her grimly; he had never been certain how fond of each other the sisters were in life.

"My drinking only lasted about a year and a half—from the time we came over until I—collapsed."

"It was time enough."

"It was time enough," he agreed.

"My duty is entirely to Helen," she said. "I try to think what she would have wanted me to do. Frankly, from the night you did that terrible thing you haven't really existed for me. I can't help that. She was my sister."

"Yes."

"When she was dying she asked me to look out for Honoria. If you hadn't been in a sanitarium then, it might have helped matters."

He had no answer.

"I'll never in my life be able to forget the morning when Helen knocked at my door, soaked to the skin and shivering, and said you'd locked her out."

Charlie gripped the sides of the chair. This was more difficult than he expected: he wanted to launch out into a long expostulation and explanation, but he only said: "The night I locked her out—" and she interrupted, "I don't feel up to going over that again."

After a moment's silence Lincoln said: "We're getting off the subject. You want Marion to set aside her legal guardianship and give you Honoria. I think the main point for her is whether she has confidence in you or not."

"I don't blame Marion," Charlie said slowly, "but I think she can have entire confidence in me. I had a good record up to three years ago. Of course, it's within human possibilities I may go wrong again. But if we wait much longer I'll lose Honoria's childhood and my chance for a home." He shook his head. "I'll simply lose her, don't you see?"

"Yes, I see," said Lincoln.

"Why didn't you think of all this before?" Marion asked.

"I suppose I did, from time to time, but Helen and I were getting along badly. When I consented to the guardianship, I was flat on my back in a sanitarium, and the market had cleaned me out. I knew I'd acted badly, and I thought if it would bring any peace to Helen, I'd agree to anything. But now it's different. I'm functioning, I'm behaving damn well, so far as——"

"Please don't swear at me," Marion said.

He looked at her, startled. With each remark the force of her dislike became more and more apparent. She had built up all her fear of life into one wall and faced it toward him. This trivial reproof was possibly the result of some trouble with the cook several hours before. Charlie became increasingly alarmed at leaving Honoria in this atmosphere of hostility against himself; sooner or later it would come out, in a word here, a shake of the head there, and some of that distrust would be irrevocably implanted in Honoria. But he pulled his temper down out of his face and shut it up inside him; he had won a point, for Lincoln realized the absurdity of Marion's remark, and asked her lightly since when she had objected to the word "damn."

"Another thing," Charlie said: "I'm able to give her certain advantages now. I'm going to take a French governess to Prague with me. I've got a lease on a new apartment——"

He stopped, realizing that he was blundering. They couldn't be expected to accept with equanimity the fact that his income was again twice as large as their own.

"I suppose you can give her more luxuries than we can," said Marion. "When you were throwing away money we were living along watching every ten francs. . . . I suppose you'll start doing it again."

"Oh, no," he said. "I've learned. I worked hard for ten years, you know—until I got lucky in the market, like so many people. Terribly lucky. It didn't seem any use working any more, so I quit. It won't happen again."

There was a long silence. All of them felt their nerves straining, and for the first time in a year Charlie wanted a drink. He was sure now that Lincoln Peters wanted him to have his child.

Marion shuddered suddenly; part of her saw that Charlie's feet were planted on the earth now, and her own maternal feeling recognized the naturalness of his desire; but she had lived for a long time with a prejudice—a prejudice founded on a curious disbelief in her sister's happiness, which, in the shock of one terrible night, had turned to hatred for him. It had all happened at a point in her life where the discouragement of ill health and adverse circumstances made it necessary for her to believe in tangible villainy and a tangible villain.

"I can't help what I think!" she cried out suddenly. "How much you were responsible for Helen's death. I don't know. It's something you'll have to square with your own conscience."

An electric current of agony surged through him; for a moment he was almost on his feet, an unuttered sound echoing in his throat. He hung on to himself for a moment, another moment.

"Hold on there," said Lincoln uncomfortably.

"I never thought you were responsible for that."

"Helen died of heart trouble," Charlie said dully.

"Yes, heart trouble." Marion spoke as if the phrase had another meaning for her.

Then, in the flatness that followed her outburst, she saw him plainly and she knew he had somehow arrived at control over the situation. Glancing at her husband, she found no help from him, and as abruptly as if it were a matter of no importance, she threw up the sponge.

"Do what you like!" she cried, springing up from her chair. "She's your child. I'm not the person to stand in your way. I think if it were my child I'd rather see her——" She managed to check herself. "You two decide it. I can't stand this. I'm sick. I'm going to bed."

She hurried from the room; after a moment Lincoln said:

"This has been a hard day for her. You know how strongly she feels——" His voice was almost apologetic: "When a woman gets an idea in her head."

"Of course."

"It's going to be all right. I think she sees now that you—can provide for the child, and so we can't very well stand in your way or Honoria's way."

"Thank you, Lincoln."

"I'd better go along and see how she is."

"I'm going."

He was still trembling when he reached the street, but a walk down the Rue Bonaparte to the quais set him up, and as he crossed the Seine, fresh and new by the quai lamps, he felt exultant. But back in his room he couldn't sleep. The image of Helen haunted him. Helen whom he had loved so until they had senselessly begun to abuse each other's love, tear it into shreds. On that terrible February night that Marion remembered so vividly, a slow quarrel had gone on for hours. There was a scene at the Florida, and then he attempted to take her home, and then she kissed young Webb at a table; after that there was what she had hysterically said. When he arrived home alone he turned the key in the lock in wild anger. How could he know she would arrive an hour later alone, that there would be a snowstorm in which she wandered about in slippers, too confused to find a taxi? Then the aftermath, her escaping pneumonia by a miracle, and all the attendant horror. They were "reconciled," but that was the beginning of the end, and Marion, who had seen with her own eyes and who imagined it to be one of many scenes from her sister's martyrdom, never forgot.

Going over it again brought Helen nearer, and in the white, soft light that steals upon half sleep near morning he found himself talking to her again. She said that he was perfectly right about Honoria and that she wanted Honoria to be with him. She said she was glad he was being good and doing better. She said a lot of other things—very friendly things—but she was in a swing in a white dress, and swinging faster and faster all the time, so that at the end he could not hear clearly all that she said.

IV

He woke up feeling happy. The door of the world was open again. He made plans, vistas, futures for Honoria and himself, but suddenly he grew sad, remembering all the plans he and Helen had made. She had not planned to die. The present was the thing—work to do, and some one to love. But not to love too much, for he knew the injury that a father can do to a daughter or a mother to a son by attaching them too closely; afterward, out in the world, the child would seek in the marriage partner the same blind tenderness and, failing probably to find it, turn against love and life.

It was another bright, crisp day. He called Lincoln Peters at the bank where he worked and asked if he could count on taking Honoria when he left for Prague. Lincoln agreed that there was no reason for delay. One thing—the legal guardianship. Marion wanted to retain that a while longer. She was upset by the whole matter, and it would oil things if she felt that the situation was still in her control for another year. Charlie agreed, wanting only the tangible, visible child.

Then the question of a governess. Charlie sat in a gloomy agency and talked to a cross Bernaise and to a buxom Breton peasant, neither of whom he could have endured. There were others whom he would see tomorrow.

He lunched with Lincoln Peters at Griffons, trying to keep down his exultation.

"There's nothing quite like your own child," Lincoln said. "But you understand how Marion feels too."

"She's forgotten how hard I worked for seven year there," Charlie said. "She just remembers one night."

"There's another thing," Lincoln hesitated. "While you and Helen were tearing around Europe throwing money away, we were just getting along. I didn't touch any of the prosperity because I never got ahead enough to carry anything but my insurance. I think Marion felt there was some kind of injustice in it—you not even working toward the end, and getting richer and richer."

"It went just as quick as it came," said Charlie.

"Yes, a lot of it stayed in the hands of *chasseurs* and saxophone players and maîtres d'hôtel —well, the big party's over now. I just said that to explain Marion's feeling about those crazy years. If you drop in about six o'clock tonight before Marion's too tired, we'll settle the details on the spot."

Back at his hotel, Charlie found a *pneumatique*[14] that had been redirected from the Ritz bar where Charlie had left his address for the purpose of finding a certain man.

Dear Charlie:

You were so strange when we saw you the other day that I wondered if I did something to offend you. If so, I'm not conscious of it. In fact, I have thought about you too much for the last year, and it's always been in the back of my mind that I might see you if I came over here. We *did* have such good times that crazy spring, like the night you and I stole the butcher's tricycle, and the time we tried to call on the president and you had the old derby rim and the wire cane. Everybody seems so old lately, but I don't feel old a bit. Couldn't we get together some time today for old time's sake? I've got a vile hang-over for the moment, but will be feeling better this afternoon and will look for you about five in the sweet-shop at the Ritz.

Always devotedly,
Lorraine.

His first feeling was one of awe that he had actually, in his mature years, stolen a tricycle and pedalled Lorraine all over the Étoile[15] between the small hours and dawn. In retrospect it was a nightmare. Locking out Helen didn't fit in with any other act of his life, but the tricycle incident did—it was one of many. How many weeks or months of dissipation to arrive at that condition of utter irresponsibility?

He tried to picture how Lorraine had appeared to him then—very attractive; Helen was unhappy about it, though she said nothing. Yesterday, in the resturant, Lorraine had seem trite, blurred, worn away. He emphatically did not want to see her, and he was glad Alix had not given away his hotel address. It was a relief to

[14] A message; originally one delivered by pneumatic tube.

[15] An open square in Paris, site of the Arc de Triomphe.

think, instead, of Honoria, to think of Sundays spent with her and of saying good morning to her and of knowing she was there in his house at night, drawing her breath in the darkness.

At five he took a taxi and bought presents for all the Peters—a piquant cloth doll, a box of Roman soldiers, flowers for Marion, big linen handkerchiefs for Lincoln.

He saw, when he arrived in the apartment, that Marion had accepted the inevitable. She greeted him now as though he were a recalcitrant member of the family, rather than a menacing outsider. Honoria had been told she was going; Charlie was glad to see that her tact made her conceal her excessive happiness. Only on his lap did she whisper her delight and the question "When?" before she slipped away with the other children.

He and Marion were alone for a minute in the room, and on an impulse he spoke out boldly:

"Finally quarrels are bitter things. They don't go according to any rules. They're not like aches or wounds; they're more like splits in the skin that won't heal because there's not enough material. I wish you and I could be on better terms."

"Some things are hard to forget," she answered. "It's a question of confidence." There was no answer to this and presently she asked, "When do you propose to take her?"

"As soon as I can get a governess. I hoped the day after tomorrow."

"That's impossible. I've got to get her things in shape. Not before Saturday."

He yielded. Coming back into the room, Lincoln offered him a drink.

"I'll take my daily whisky," he said.

It was warm here, it was a home, people together by a fire. The children felt very safe and important; the mother and father were serious, watchful. They had things to do for the children more important than his visit here. A spoonful of medicine was, after all, more important than the strained relations between Marion and himself. They were not dull people, but they were very much in the grip of life and circumstances. He wondered if he couldn't do something to get Lincoln out of his rut at the bank.

A long peal at the door-bell; the *bonne à tout faire*[16] passed through and went down the corridor. The door opened upon another long ring, and then voices, and the three in the salon looked up expectantly; Richard moved to bring the corridor within his range of vision, and Marion rose. Then the maid came back along

[16] Maid of all work.

the corridor, closely followed by the voices, which developed under the light into Duncan Schaeffer and Lorraine Quarles.

They were gay, they were hilarious, they were roaring with laughter. For a moment Charlie was astounded; unable to understand how they had ferreted out the Peters' address.

"Ah-h-h!" Duncan wagged his finger roguishly at Charlie. "Ah-h-h!"

They both slid down another cascade of laughter. Anxious and at a loss, Charlie shook hands with them quickly and presented them to Lincoln and Marion. Marion nodded, scarcely speaking. She had drawn back a step toward the fire; her little girl stood beside her, and Marion put an arm about her shoulder.

With growing annoyance at the intrusion, Charlie waited for them to explain themselves. After some concentration Duncan said:

"We came to invite you out to dinner. Lorraine and I insist that all this shishi business 'bout your address got to stop."

Charlie came closer to them, as if to force them backward down the corridor.

"Sorry, but I can't. Tell me where you'll be and I'll phone you in half an hour."

This made no impression. Lorraine sat down suddenly on the side of a chair, and focussing her eyes on Richard, cried, "Oh, what a nice little boy! Come here, little boy." Richard glanced at his mother, but did not move. With a perceptible shrug of her shoulders, Lorraine turned back to Charlie:

"Come and dine. Sure your cousins won' mine. See you so sel'om. Or solemn."

"I can't," said Charlie sharply. "You two have dinner and I'll phone you."

Her voice became suddenly unpleasant. "All right, we'll go. But I remember once when you hammered on my door at four A.M. I was enough of a good sport to give you a drink. Come on, Dunc." Still in slow motion, with blurred, angry faces, with uncertain feet, they retired along the corridor.

"Good night," Charlie said.

"Good night!" responded Lorraine emphatically.

When he went back into the salon Marion had not moved, only now her son was standing in the circle of her other arm. Lincoln was still swinging Honoria back and forth like a pendulum from side to side.

"What an outrage!" Charlie broke out. "What an absolute outrage!"

Neither of them answered. Charlie dropped into an armchair, picked up his drink, set it down again and said:

"People I haven't seen for two years having the colossal nerve——"

He broke off. Marion had made the sound "Oh!" in one swift, furious breath, turned her body from him with a jerk and left the room.

Lincoln set down Honoria carefully.

"You children go in and start your soup," he said, and when they obeyed, he said to Charlie:

"Marion's not well and she can't stand shocks. That kind of people make her really physically sick."

"I didn't tell them to come here. They wormed your name out of somebody. They deliberately——"

"Well, it's too bad. It doesn't help matters. Excuse me a minute."

Left alone, Charlie sat tense in his chair. In the next room he could hear the children eating, talking in monosyllables, already oblivious to the scene between their elders. He heard a murmur of conversation from a farther room and then the ticking bell of a telephone receiver picked up, and in a panic he moved to the other side of the room and out of earshot.

In a minute Lincoln came back. "Look here, Charlie. I think we'd better call off dinner for tonight. Marion's in bad shape."

"Is she angry with me?"

"Sort of," he said, almost roughly. "She's not strong and——"

"You mean she's changed her mind about Honoria."

"She's pretty bitter right now. I don't know. You phone me at the bank tomorrow."

"I wish you'd explain to her I never dreamed these people would come here. I'm just as sore as you are."

"I couldn't explain anything to her now."

Charlie got up. He took his coat and hat and started down the corridor. Then he opened the door of the dining room and said in a strange voice, "Good night, children."

Honoria rose and ran around the table to hug him.

"Good night, sweetheart," he said vaguely, and then trying to make his voice more tender, trying to conciliate something, "Good night, dear children."

V

Charlie went directly to the Ritz bar with the furious idea of finding Lorraine and Duncan, but they were not there, and he realized that in any case there was nothing he could do. He had not touched his drink at the Peters', and now he ordered a whisky-and-soda. Paul came over to say hello.

"It's a great change," he said sadly. "We do about half the business we did. So many fellows I hear about back in the States lost everything, maybe not in the first crash, but then in the second. Your friend George Hardt lost every cent, I hear. Are you back in the States?"

"No, I'm in business in Prague."

"I heard that you lost a lot in the crash."

"I did," and he added grimly, "but I lost everything I wanted in the boom."

"Selling short?"

"Something like that."

Again the memory of those days swept over him like a nightmare—the people they had met travelling; the people who couldn't add a row of figures or speak a coherent sentence. The little man Helen had consented to dance with at the ship's party, who had insulted her ten feet from the table; the women and girls carried screaming with drink or drugs out of public places . . . the men who locked their wives out in the snow, because the snow of '29 wasn't real snow. If you didn't want it to be snow, you just paid some money.

He went to the phone and called the Peters apartment; Lincoln answered.

"I called up because this thing is on my mind. Has Marion said anything definite?"

"Marion's sick," Lincoln answered shortly. "I know this thing isn't altogether your fault, but I can't have her go to pieces about it. I'm afraid we'll have to let it slide for six months; I can't take the chance of working her up to this state again."

"I see."

"I'm sorry, Charlie."

He went back to his table. His whisky glass was empty, but he shook his head when Alix looked at it questioningly. There wasn't much he could do now except send Honoria some things; he would send her a lot of things tomorrow. He thought rather angrily that this was just money—he had given so many people money. . . .

"No, no more," he said to another waiter. "What do I owe you?"

He would come back some day; they couldn't make him pay forever. But he wanted his child, and nothing was much good now, beside that fact. He wasn't young any more, with a lot of nice thoughts and dreams to have by himself. He was absolutely sure Helen wouldn't have wanted him to be so alone.

1931, 1935

?

In "Babylon Revisited" F. Scott Fitzgerald illustrates what separates and divides individuals from one another. The story includes an attempt to recreate the past. Fitzgerald directs our attention to the contradiction between innocence and guilt. Charles struggles to understand this contradiction. To do this, he must experience the "I" in relation to his actions. The story deals with the individual's search to avoid or accept responsibility for his or her actions.

1 What image of the male and female emerge in this story? What does Charles want from Helen? What does Helen want from Charles? How does Charles' battle with Helen's sister reflect his "inner" conflict? What is the purpose of the little girl in the story? Does Charles want to find the child within? Explain!

2 How might someone be innocent and guilty at the same time? Explain this contradiction in the story! How does this contradiction connect Charles and Helen to Adam and Eve?

3 Does alcohol represent a fig leaf for Charles and Helen? How does the use of this symbol cause Charles to be divided from himself? In what ways is this division similar to the division between male and female? In what ways does the use of alcohol reveal the preference of fantasy over reality? What does this suggest about the illusion of escape?

4 Is despair a way of maintaining innocence? Is the union that Charles seeks impossible? What motivates his actions? Does the ending of the story resemble the ending in the Garden of Eden myth?

5 How does "Babylon Revisited" sum up this chapter:

a How do the myths of male and female reappear in the story?

b How would Erich Neumann's concept of projection and object-choice explain the unconscious desires of Charles and Helen?

c Is there a "birthmark" in this story? Does Charles or Helen have this mark? Discuss the implications of this concept.

d How would Ellis characterize Charles' romantic illusions?

e In what ways do both Charles and Helen reflect the competitive drive discussed by Margaret Mead?

f How would Blake interpret love in this story?

g Would D. H. Lawrence agree that the men have created patterns for the women in this story?

h Would Kate Millett see Charles as a man who had not yet undergone his initiation ceremony? Does Charles doubt his role as a male? Are Helen, Marion, and the daughter victims of symbols created by men to explain innocence and guilt?

i In what ways does this story re-create the atmosphere of the modern world where the old values no longer seem to have meaning?

j Is union possible in a world which seeks separation between the sexes?

3 RITES OF

INITIATION: A SECOND BIRTH

A SCARLET LETTER ABOUT MARY MAGDALENE

JULIA RANDALL

If I asked you to look out
The back window, where the crumbs are spread,
And asked you who was king
Of the sparrows, you would say the red
Bird, not a sparrow, and not because
He has manners, or is larger than them all.
He is not more virtuous:
He is more beautiful.

It is hard to conceive
A god irrational as man,
But we believe
In the image, patch it as we can.
We fall in love
Not with the best or brightest in the nest
Of reason, but some light in the heart's cave.

And that, perhaps, my dear, is how we save
Ourselves. How after a life of sin,
We say "I love you," and we enter in
Unworthy, to the kingdom which he made,
Where weak are strong, whores maid,
And oily love announces: I obeyed
Necessity, who blessed me.
God possessed me.

The theme of rebirth is illustrated for the male in "The Bridge of Dread" and for the female in "A Scarlet Letter about Mary Magdalene." Both poems focus on the individual's quest for identity. Each poem depicts what steps must be completed before one undergoes an initiation rite transforming the individual from one state of being to the next. The following questions discuss how these poems deal with the hero's and temptress's rites of passage.

1   Discuss what opposites must be reconciled by the protagonist in "The Bridge of Dread." What forces are exerted to move him into action? What does this suggest? What tests must he undergo before he crosses the bridge? What happens to him after he crosses? What image of the male hero emerges in Muir's vision?

2   Discuss what opposites must be reconciled by Magdalene in order to accomplish her transformation from whore to virgin. What attitudes toward males and females emerge as Randall illustrates this transformation? How does "necessity" change the past of this woman? What does the last line of the poem reveal? What image of the temptress emerges in Randall's vision? In what ways do these poets differ in their exploration of the male's and female's transformation into hero and temptress? Explain!

INITIATION: A SECOND BIRTH

Hero as Warrior

In Goya's depiction of *The Execution of May 3rd* we see a man's courage tested as he dies to affirm a belief in his convictions. Often the death of a hero is associated with his courageous struggle to fight for ideals which are important for the survival of the collective.

Botticelli's *Birth of Venus* illustrates the birth of a woman who symbolically expresses the goddess of love.

To move from adolescence to adulthood, individuals must often undergo a series of ordeals which symbolically depict their second birth as men or women. In primitive societies, this change was celebrated by an initiation ceremony which was also linked to the culture's fertility rites. The ability to overcome obstacles which threatened to destroy the individual was symbolically connected to the birth process which ensured the continuation of the group. Those who became the models for others to follow became the archetypal representatives of the initiation myths which narrated the tribe's folklore. For the males, the warrior hero expressed the individual's struggle to fight against any force which threatened to prevent him from completing his quest. For the females, the temptress expressed the woman who held the power to unlock the secrets surrounding the mysteries of life and death. These initiation tales closely resemble the formula for rites of passage: separation, initiation, and return.

Voices that tell what it means to be HUMAN

A hero ventures forth from the world of common day into a region of supernatural wonder: fabulous forces are there encountered and a decisive victory is won: the hero comes back from this mysterious adventure with the power to bestow boons on his fellow man.

Joseph Campbell, *The Hero with a Thousand Faces*

THE BRIDGE OF DREAD

EDWIN MUIR

But when you reach the Bridge of Dread
Your flesh will huddle into its nest
For refuge and your naked head
Creep in the casement of your breast,

And your great bulk grow thin and small
And cower within its cage of bone,
While dazed you watch your footsteps crawl
Toadlike across the leagues of stone.

If they come, you will not feel
About your feet the adders slide,
For still your head's demented wheel
Whirls on your neck from side to side

Searching for danger. Nothing there.
And yet your breath will whistle and beat
As on you push the stagnant air
That breaks in rings about your feet

Like dirty suds. If there should come
Some bodily terror to that place,

Great knotted serpents dread and dumb,
You would accept it as a grace.

Until you see a burning wire
Shoot from the ground. As in a dream
You'll wonder at that flower of fire,
That weed caught in a burning beam.

And you are past. Remember then,
Fix deep within your dreaming head
Year, hour or endless moment when
You reached and crossed the Bridge of Dread.

In popular myths of all cultures, the temptress is the irresistible woman who is the highest prize and ultimate destruction of man.

A SCARLET LETTER ABOUT MARY MAGDALENE

JULIA RANDALL

If I asked you to look out
The back window, where the crumbs are spread,
And asked you who was king
Of the sparrows, you would say the red
Bird, not a sparrow, and not because
He has manners, or is larger than them all.
He is not more virtuous:
He is more beautiful.

It is hard to conceive
A god irrational as man,
But we believe
In the image, patch it as we can.
We fall in love
Not with the best or brightest in the nest
Of reason, but some light in the heart's cave.

And that, perhaps, my dear, is how we save
Ourselves. How after a life of sin,
We say "I love you," and we enter in
Unworthy, to the kingdom which he made,
Where weak are strong, whores maid,
And oily love announces: I obeyed
Necessity, who blessed me.
God possessed me.

The theme of rebirth is illustrated for the male in "The Bridge of Dread" and for the female in "A Scarlet Letter about Mary Magdalene." Both poems focus on the individual's quest for identity. Each poem depicts what steps must be completed before one undergoes an initiation rite transforming the individual from one state of being to the next. The following questions discuss how these poems deal with the hero's and temptress's rites of passage.

1   Discuss what opposites must be reconciled by the protagonist in "The Bridge of Dread." What forces are exerted to move him into action? What does this suggest? What tests must he undergo before he crosses the bridge? What happens to him after he crosses? What image of the male hero emerges in Muir's vision?

2   Discuss what opposites must be reconciled by Magdalene in order to accomplish her transformation from whore to virgin. What attitudes toward males and females emerge as Randall illustrates this transformation? How does "necessity" change the past of this woman? What does the last line of the poem reveal? What image of the temptress emerges in Randall's vision? In what ways do these poets differ in their exploration of the male's and female's transformation into hero and temptress? Explain!

I rescued men from shattering destruction that would have carried them to Hades house; and therefore I am tortured on this rock, a bitterness to suffer, and a pain to pitiful eyes, I gave to mortal man a precedence over myself in pity.

Aeschylus, *Prometheus Bound*

All initiations aim to safeguard the individual against the annihilating powers of the grave, of the devouring feminine.

Erich Neumann

The Search for Self-Expression

A Test to Extend beyond the Reach of Mortals...

When individuals undergo a transition from
one stage of existence to the next, they often
see revealed the unknown possibilities of the
human imagination. To be "twice born" expresses the way the individual makes the transition which enables him or her to have a vocation within the tribe. A rite of passage in the
Barundi of Tanganyika expresses the way an individual becomes a priest or priestess through
the following ritual. To be called to this role,
one has to (1) be chosen by inheritance or or-
dination; (2) receive the sacred spear from his
or her father or mother; (3) receive a sudden
calling or be struck by thunder. The ceremony
which initiates the individual is as follows:

> During one of the "ceremonies of the spear"
> a boy or girl will rise suddenly and stand op-
> posite the officiating kiranga or, rather, opposite
> the sacred spear; he or she will head toward
> the kiranga and look at him fiercely with all
> the energy of their being until he or she begins
> to tremble and finally faint, as if dead.... The
> person who has fainted is laid on a mat and
> carried into a house to sleep for three or four
> days. When the person comes to, he or she is
> henceforth a sacred priest or priestess-spouse
> of the god. Neighbors are called: "the cere-
> mony of the spear" is performed; and the new
> kiranga presides and officiates for the first time.

—from *Rites of Passage*, Arnold Van Gennep

THE SECRETS OF MANHOOD

In the olden days, a young man was taken into the forest to learn the secrets of manhood before he could be initiated into the adult life of the tribe. During this time he could have nothing at all to do with women.

One day a young girl named Alabe accidentally discovered the young men performing their secret rituals in the sacred forest. Terrified of discovery, she quickly hid behind a bush, but being a woman, she could not resist the desire to see what was going on. One of the young men she saw was so handsome that she immediately fell in love with him.

So instead of running away, she stayed and watched the handsome young man all day. That night as the young men lay down to sleep, Alabe noticed where her favorite was and crept up beside him.

The young man woke up, startled to find a woman by his side. "What are you doing here?" he asked. "Don't you know that it is forbidden for women to be here?"

Alabe just laughed. "I don't easily give up on something I have set my mind on," she boasted. "And now I have set my mind on you." And she began to embrace him passionately.

Soon the young man stopped protesting and began to return her kisses.

He became more and more passionate, but suddenly his body shook all over and he fell back stiff and dead. Alabe cried out in alarm, and the other young men came running and caught her.

The chief of the sacred forest called upon the gods to restore the young man's life. Soon he received a message from the gods and called all of the people of the village together to hear it. He said, "The gods have told me how to save this boy's life. We are to build a huge bonfire and throw a lizard into the middle of it. If someone will rush into the fire and rescue the lizard, he will save the life of the young man."

So the people built a huge bonfire and the chief threw the lizard in. The young man's mother first rushed at the fire, but she could not stand the heat and fell back. The boy's father tried also, but failed.

At last Alabe said, "It is because of me that the young man is dead, so it is up to me to rescue him." With that, she rushed into the center of the fire and brought out the lizard. Then the young man came to life again.

But the people decided that Alabe's evil was too great to be forgiven and threw her back into the center of the still raging flames.

AFRICAN

THE MARINES: AN INITIATION INTO MANHOOD

The marine must be separated from his culture, taught how to be a combat soldier, and then returned in his new role to the community. The marine becomes a recruit who is propelled through a training center as a rite of passage in order to fit the mold. First his civilian clothes must be removed; his hair is shorn to baldness; and he is conducted naked through a delousing chamber, at the opposite end of which he is given "shots" and an issue of clothing. His "new" role begins with the tearing down of all his connections with that which previously defined his individuality. In *Identity and Anxiety*, A. J. Vidich and M. R. Stein discuss what next happens to the marine:

To be a Marine was to be a man, and to be a Marine-man, it was necessary to have had the combat experience. The combat role was held up as the major area of self-fulfillment. In line with this, training included the inculcation of new definitions of masculinity, a feature perhaps more necessary in Marine training, since the recruit tended to bring with him a conventional civilian conception of himself as a strong he-man type; many were athletes and some were top collegiate athletes. The civilian self-conception of he-man and athlete was broken down in training by the techniques of physical hazing and rifle calisthenics, wherein the recruit had to accept the hazing mutely and without self-defense and allow himself to be physically taxed in ways to which he was unaccustomed. Frequently the heroic athlete was selected as the specific object of hazing to the point of collapse, thereby standing as an example to all others of the inadequacy of civilian forms of manliness.

The valued form of manliness found a focus in adeptness in the use of the rifle. A small man with supple muscles could frequently sustain 500 rifle push-ups better than the muscle-bound athlete. In such instances, he would be held up as an example of physical virtuosity. Dropping a rifle or having a dirty one was cause for punishment and humiliation. Disciplinary action, in cases of breach of respect for, or lack of proper care of, the rifle, took the form of requiring the offender to sleep with his "piece," the other term by which the weapon is known in military terminology. In Marine Corps culture, the "piece" was the pre-eminent symbol of masculinity; having to sleep with it introduced a confusion of symbols and cast aspersion on the masculine identity of the degraded victim.

The image of combat experience that had been built up emphasized the theme that hated caste etiquette was dropped in favor of frontline comradeship. In combat, moreover, the soldier could affirm a self-respecting masculinity. Combat men were looked up to by all, especially in the training camp itself where they were accorded special deference well beyond their nominal rank. In combat, the restoration of self-esteem could be found and a manly self acted out. . . .

The enlisted man, then, accepts caste and chicken because that's the way the "social system" works, and the officer enjoys his caste privileges without pangs of conscience. At this stage, both the officer and the enlisted man resolve caste tension by ignoring social reality, through the technique of conceiving their combat-selves to be their true selves. This dynamic was so compelling that it frequently led the soldier to exaggerate his combat experience, and, in some cases, to falsely claim combat experience.

The capacity to achieve an identity rested on the ability to ignore immediate experience and to construct, each according to his situation, a self-image sufficiently serviceable that it would sustain the motivation to act his part. The civilian self was dissolved, at least for the duration, and in its place was substituted a highly plastic military identity that in some way enabled the soldiers to think of themselves as soldiers and to fight. The soldier seems to develop a capacity to dissolve himself in a situation and then to find a self consistent with it. . . .

The major mechanism of self-defense for the soldier is to entertain those preferred self-images that allow him to act, irrespective of the consistency, or lack of it, between reality and the preferred image sustained by illusion. Since there seems to be no one self-image that can consistently integrate immediate experi-ence, the soldier's self exists in shifting and disparate layers of consciousness, which parallel similar dynamics in the community as a whole. The civilian past, the defeated self of the training period, the magnified or falsified self of combat, and above all, the future-civilian self all combine in various ways to produce a workable self-mechanism. The capacity to live with self depends upon capacity to live in a world of multiple realities and multiple self-consciousness. The consciousness that falls victim to each new situation constitutes the dissolution of identity in the military community.

The civilian becomes a soldier as he identifies with masculine symbols. The rifle connects him to the male-dominated world and excludes any feminine traits from the world of the marine. The creed which accompanies the marine's association with the rifle is as follows:

This is my rifle. There are many like it, but this one is mine.

My rifle is my best friend. It is my life. I must master it as I master my life.

My rifle, without me, is useless. Without my rifle, I am useless. I must fire my rifle true. I must shoot straighter than my enemy who is trying to kill me. I must shoot him before he shoots me. I will. . . .

My rifle and myself know that what counts in this war is not the rounds we fire, the noise of our burst, nor the smoke we make. We know that it is the hits that count. We will hit. . . .

My rifle is human, even as I, because it is my life. Thus, I will learn it as a brother. I will learn its weaknesses, its strengths, its parts, its accessories, its sights, and its barrel. I will keep my rifle clean and ready, even as I am clean and ready. We will become part of each other. We will. . . .

Before God I swear this creed. My rifle and myself are the defenders of my country. We are the masters of our enemy. We are the saviors of my life.

So be it, until victory is America's and there is no enemy, but Peace!

United States Marine Corps, Parris Island, S.C., 1966

?

If the recruit is successful, he is reborn as a marine and a man. In "The Secrets of Manhood" and "The Marines: An Initiation into Manhood," the road of trials is seen as a prologue to a new way of understanding the adult's birth into a society. The following questions focus on the patterns which emerge from these three perspectives:

1 "The Secrets of Manhood"
  a What must the young man learn before he will be recognized as an adult?
  b Why is he forbidden to have anything to do with women? What does this suggest?
  c What image of the woman emerges from this myth? How does she tempt the man from his quest? Why does she bring about both his death and rebirth? What does this suggest about her secret powers?

  d What image of the male emerges from this tale?
  e Has the male crossed Edwin Muir's "The Bridge of Dread"? Explain.

2 "The Marines: An Initiation into Manhood"
  a What concept of manliness emerges from this discussion?
  b How is the civilian transformed into a soldier?
  c Discuss the significance of the rifle.
  d How does "The Marine: An Initiation into Manhood" differ from "The Secrets of Manhood"?
  e In what ways does the marine undergo a rite similar to that which the young man undergoes in "The Secrets of Manhood"?
  f Does the marine learn anything about "The Bridge of Dread" as described in Muir's poem? Explain why or why not.

Seperation—
Initiation—
Return

The standard saga itself may be formulated according to the following outline: The hero is the child of most distinguished parents, usually the son of a king. His origin is preceded by difficulties, such as continence, prolonged barrenness, or secret intercourse of the parents due to external prohibition or obstacles. During or before the pregnancy, there is a prophecy, in the form of a dream or oracle, cautioning against his birth, and usually threatening danger to the father (or his representative). As a rule, he is surrendered to the water, in a box. He is then saved by animals, or by lowly people (shepherds), and is suckled by a female animal or by an humble woman. After he has grown up, he finds his distinguished parents, in a highly versatile fashion. He takes his revenge on his father, on the one hand, and is acknowledged, on the other. Finally he achieves rank and honors.

—from "The Myth of the Birth of the Hero,"
Otto Rank

In dealing with symbols and myths from far away, we are really conversing with ourselves—with a part of ourselves, however, which is as unfamiliar to our conscious being as the interior of the earth to the students of geology. Hence the mythical tradition provides us with a sort of map for exploring and ascertaining contents of our own inner being to which we consciously feel only scantily related.

Heinrich Zimmer

These social beliefs and values have a universal significance to the members of a culture because the basic emotional structure of each person is largely acquired and formed in childhood from his earliest intimate experiences as a new member of society. Each growing individual sees, feels, and hears beliefs and values not as abstract concepts and principles but as integral, personal parts of loved or disliked persons whom he experiences through social and personal interaction. . . . Abstract principles, precepts, and moral judgments are consequently more easily felt and understood, and more highly valued, when met in a human being endowed with a symbolic form that expresses them. Obviously the "hero" is ideally suited to this role.

Wloly D. Warner

. . . the essential meaning of the journey of the hero which I consider the pivotal myth that unites the spiritual adventure of ancient heroes with the modern search for meaning. As always, the hero must venture forth from the world of common-sense consciousness into a region of supernatural wonder. There he encounters fabulous forces—demons and angels, dragons and helping spirits. After a fierce battle he wins a decisive victory over the powers of darkness. Then he returns from his mysterious adventure with the gift of knowledge of fire, which he bestows on his fellow man.

Joseph Campbell

A mixture of Ecstasy and Danger

The warrior-hero must be able to meet any dangers which befall him. He is often aided by some mysterious source of strength. In the pictures below, we see the warrior-hero appear as an archetypal representative of the initiate who will be transformed as a result of his battles.

Gilgamish, the Babylonian warrior, must prove his physical strength by testing his powers against the lion who is often depicted as the king of beasts. This symbolic struggle reveals man's need to overcome the beast within.

The hero myth often demonstrates how individuals affirm victory over their adversaries by proving their physical strength. The athlete is a manifestation of the hero archetype. In this picture, "Statute of an Athlete" (Roman copy of a Greek statute), we see how the Greeks viewed victory. The boy in the picture wears the fillet on his head to symbolize his victory, but notice how modestly he inclines his head. For the Greeks, modesty must accompany victory. The boy is not shy about being nude, but he must not suffer from an excess of pride, i.e., hubris. His modern counterpart would be shy about being nude but would blatantly display his victory.

Samson, the Hebrew warrior, is betrayed by a woman. Delilah saps his strength by cutting off his hair. This serves as a symbolic warning to the warrior: the male must be aware of the woman's power to disarm him.

GILGAMISH

Into the Temple where his mother dwelt Gilgamish went, and when she saw by the look upon his face that he was bent upon going on some strange journey or upon doing some terrifying deed, his mother cried out to Shamash, the Sun God, asking him why he had given her son a heart that could never keep still. And Gilgamish, hearing her cry, said to her, "Peace, O woman! I am Gilgamish, and it must be that I shall see everything, learn everything, understand everything." Then his mother said to him, "These longings are yours, O Gilgamish, because not all of you is mortal. Two-thirds of your flesh is as the flesh of the Gods and only one-third is as the flesh of men. And because of the God's flesh that is on you, you must be always daring, always restless. But yet, O my son, you have not immortal life. You must die because a part of you is man. Yea, Gilgamish, even you must die, and go down into the House of Dust."

And Gilgamish, hearing his mother say this, groaned loudly, terribly; the tears flowed down his cheeks; no word that was said to him might content him. He groaned, he wept, even although in the courts of the Temple he heard the women sing:

> Who is splendid among men,
> Who is glorious among heroes?

And answer back, one to the other:

> Gilgamish is splendid among men,
> Gilgamish is glorious among heroes.

In a while he rose up and he said, "O Ninsunna, O my mother, what is it to die?"

Then Ninsunna, his mother, made answer, and said, "It is to go into the abode out of which none ever returns: it is to go into the dark abyss of the dread Goddess, Irkalla. They who dwell there are without light; the beings that are there eat of the dust and feed on the mud." So his mother said, and Gilgamish, the great king, groaned aloud, and the tears flowed down his face.

Gilgamish dwelt in Erech, and was king over the people there. The works that he did in Erech were mighty, surpassing the works of men. He built walls round the city that were an hundred cubits in thickness and in height over a hundred cubits. He built towers that were higher than any that men had builded before. He built great ships that went upon the great sea. All these things he did because Gilgamish had a restless heart. But the people of Erech groaned because of the labours he laid upon them; they groaned and sent up prayers to the Gods.

The Gods harkened to the prayers of the people of Erech; they said in the Council of the Gods, "Behold, Gilgamish lays upon the people labours that crush them. The life goes out of them, and they no longer can offer sacrifice to the Gods. He lays these labours upon them because he alone is mighty in the world. But if we make one who is mightier than he, Gilgamish will be abashed when he sees that one, and no longer will he think that he is lord of all; then will he not engage in labours that give his people no rest."

The Gods called upon the Goddess Aruru. And Aruru considered in her heart how she would make one who was mightier than Gilgamish. Thereafter she washed her hands and she took clay and mixed her spittle into it. And Aruru made a being, a living male creature that was in the likeness of the God Anu. His body was covered all over with hair so that he appeared to be clothed in leaves. The Gods named him Enkidu, and they gave him the wild places of the earth for his portion.

And Enkidu, mighty in stature, invincible in strength, lived in these wild places. Gilgamish passed through the land he dwelt in, but saw him not. Gilgamish passed through the land to make war upon Khumbaba who dwelt in the country where the forests of cedars are. Those who went with him were struck with awe when they saw the cedars in their height and in their closeness of growth together; they were worn out because of their journey and the fear that possessed them, and they prayed to the Gods to deliver them from under the hand of a king who had a heart that was so restless. They came upon Khumbaba whose voice was like the roar of a storm, whose breath was like a gale of wind. They fought the armies of Khumbaba, these soldiers of Gilgamish, and Gilgamish himself fought Khumbaba and with his own hand slew him. And then Gilgamish and his army passed through the country where Enkidu maintained himself, but they saw not Enkidu. And Enkidu, mighty in stature, invincible in strength, drank the water that the wild cattle drank and ate the herbs that the gazelles lived on; he was a friend to the wild beasts and he knew not the faces of men.

Now when Gilgamish returned to Erech, his city, after having overthrown Khumbaba, he heard the women in his palace sing:

Who is splendid among men,
Who is glorious among heroes?

And he heard the women answer back, one to the other:

Gilgamish is splendid among men,
Gilgamish is glorious among heroes.

But he remembered what had been told him about the House of Dust and the Abyss of the Goddess Irkala; he groaned, and the tears coursed down his face.

Below the forest of cedars dwelt a hunter, a young man who dug pits and laid nets for the wild beasts that were upon the mountains. One day, expecting to find many wild beasts in his pits and his nets, he went to them, but behold! the pits he had digged were filled up and the nets he had laid were torn; also the prey had been taken out of the nets and the pits. Then the young man, the hunter, went up the mountain, and coming nigh a pit he had made he watched, for he saw something at the pit. He saw the shoulders and the head of a man. And he watched the man come out of the pit, and he had upon his shoulders a gazelle that had fallen into it. And behold! the man went to where a company of gazelles stood waiting, and they were not fearful of the man. He laid down the gazelle he carried, and the gazelle joined the company of gazelles. Then the man went back and filled up the pit with earth, and went with great strides towards the forest. The young man, the hunter, saw that he was all naked and covered with hair; and that the hair on his head was long and like a woman's. The hunter was affrighted, and he went from the place. He came upon others of the pits he had digged, and they were all filled up; there was no creature near any of them nor was there one under any of the nets he had laid.

Then was the hunter made anxious. He said within himself, "What shall become of me? I till no land, and I know of no way of living save by my nets and my pits! But if the creatures that have been snared are taken out of my pits and from under my nets, what shall I do to find food for myself and my parents?" He wept as he spoke thus to himself, and, carrying no beast, he went back to the hut where his father was.

His father heard what the young man said and considered it. "This is one who is friendly to the beasts and knows not the faces of men," he said. "What he has done he will do again and yet again, and there will be no prey left for us in the pits or under the nets. Therefore, we must have him led away from this place. Often have you brought beasts to the Temple in Erech to be sacrificed there to Anu and Ishtar and the rest of the Gods. Go to that city and into the place of the mighty Gilgamish, and have those in the Temple give you a woman of the Temple to go with you. And when the one who has not seen the faces of men sees the face of the woman of the Temple, and sees her take off her veil, he will be amazed; he will go to the woman of the Temple, and she will speak with him and will draw him from this place."

The young man, the hunter, did as his father instructed him: he went into Erech, the city that Gilgamish ruled over, and he went within the Temple. He spoke to Ninsunna, the mother of Gilgamish. And having heard what he had to tell, the mother of Gilgamish brought to him a woman of the Temple; she put the woman's hand in the hunter's hand, and the young man brought the woman out of that place and into the mountainous region where he had looked upon Enkidu.

It was then that Ishtar the Goddess stood before Gilgamish in her terrible beauty. She said unto him, "Thou, O Gilgamish, shalt be my man; I shall be thy woman. Thou shalt come into my house, and those who sit upon the thrones shall kiss thy feet. Gifts from the mountain and the lowland shall be laid before thee. I shall make to be harnessed for thee a chariot of lapis-lazuli and gold; the wheels of it shall be gold and the horns upon it shall be precious stones. Thou shalt harness to it mighty horses; they shall prance proudly; there shall be no horses like unto the horses that shall be under thy yoke. All these things shall be for thee when, with perfume of cedar upon thee, thou shalt come into my house."

Gilgamish made answer to the Goddess; in wrath he spoke to Ishtar, the Beautiful One, the Terrible One, answering her: "Thy lovers have perished. Thy love is like to a door that letteth in the storm. Thy love is like a fortress that falls upon and crushes the warrior within it. The lover of thy youth, Tammuz, even he, was destroyed; destroyed are all the men whom thou hadst to do with. The creatures who come under thine influence rejoice, but they rejoice for a while only: the wing of the bird is broken through thee; the lion is destroyed; the horse is driven to death. Thou sayst thou lovest me, Ishtar. Loved by thee I should fare as they have fared."

When Ishtar heard the words that Gilgamish spoke she was filled with wrath. She left the place where he was. She meditated evil against him. In a while she made a fire-breathing bull and sent it down into Erech to destroy Gilgamish and Gilgamish's people.

The young man, the hunter, went back into the mountain regions where he had digged pits before and spread his nets. He brought the woman of the Temple with him. He made her to sit nigh the place where the wild beasts came to drink; he bade her draw to her the wild man if he should come to drink with the beasts.

Then the hunter went away. The Temple woman sat by the pool, plaiting the tresses of her hair. One by one the beasts came to drink, but finding there the scent of a human creature they went away.

At last Enkidu, the wild man, came down to the pool. He did not have the power of scent that the beasts had. He went into the drinking-place and he filled his palms with water, and he raised them up to his mouth, and he drank. The Temple woman saw him there in his great stature, with the hair on his head long and flowing as if it were a woman's, and the hair on his skin making him look as if he were dressed in leaves. She called out; she spoke, and Enkidu heard her voice.

He saw her; she held her arms out to him; she took off her veil. Then Enkidu was astonished. He went towards her, and she took his hand, and she led him away. He came under the spell of the Temple woman's beauty; he would not leave her, but stayed where she stayed at the edge of the forest. On the sixth day he rose up and went away from where she stayed. His heart had become hungry to look upon the wild beasts whose friend he had been. He went towards where the companies of gazelles were. The gazelles fled from him. He went to where the wild cattle grazed, and the wild cattle fled as soon as he came near to them. He went to where the panthers were, and the panthers bounded away when he came near to them. Then Enkidu was sore in his heart. He cried out, "Why do my friends, the beasts, forsake me?" He did not know that the beasts had wind of another human creature in the wind that was from him. Wherever he went the beasts fled from him. Then Enkidu was made ashamed; his knees gave way under him; he swooned away from shame.

When he rose up again he went back to where the Temple woman stayed, and the beasts still fled before him. The Temple woman waited for him; she smiled upon him; she held out her arms to him, and spoke flattering words to him. He stayed with her and she spoke to him of Erech, and of the Temple, and of Gilgamish the Mighty. At last she led him with her to Erech, Gilgamish's city.

It was then that Gilgamish had his struggle with the fire-breathing bull that Ishtar, in her anger, had sent against him and his people. Multitudes of the inhabitants of the city had been destroyed by the bull. Gilgamish—even he—was not able to prevail against the Bull of Heaven. He lodged an arrow in the neck of the bull. Still it came on against him, and Gilgamish had to flee from before it.

And the bull came upon the way along which Enkidu was coming with the woman of the Temple. He laid his hands against the front of the bull, and held it. Then Gilgamish came and delivered mighty blows between its horns and its neck, and when the bull would have trampled upon him, Enkidu, with his mighty strength, pulled it backwards. Gilgamish with Enkidu attacked the bull again. Long they fought against the fury of the fire-breathing bull, but at length the two of them slew Ishtar's mighty creature.

The Goddess appeared upon the battlements and cursed them for having destroyed the Bull of Heaven. And Enkidu, fearless before Gods and before men, tore the flesh from the side of the bull and threw it at the feet of Ishtar. The Goddess and all the women of the Temple made lamentations over the portion of the bull that had been flung up to them.

But Gilgamish called together the people of the city. He showed them the creature that had been slain. They looked, and they marvelled at the size of the horns, for they were horns that could hold six measures of oil. Gilgamish took the horns of the Bull of Heaven to the Temple of God Lugalbanda, and he hung them before the seat of the God. He made friends with Enkidu. And he and Enkidu went down to the river Euphrates, and there they washed, and they came back and they stood in the market-place. All men marvelled at the stature and power of these two, Gilgamish and Enkidu. Gilgamish took Enkidu to his palace; he gace him the raiment of a king to put on; he gave him a chair, and he had him sit on his left side; he gave him food fit for the Gods to eat, and wine fit for a king to drink. These two mighty men became friends, and they loved each other exceedingly.

Together Gilgamish and Enkidu hunted; together they made war; the lion and the panther of the desert fell to their bows and spears. And at last the people of Erech had rest from their labours, for no longer did Gilgamish make them weary raising great buildings, and they had peace, for no longer did he bring them to make war upon the people of far lands.

A time came when Enkidu longed for the life of the forest. Thither he went. And Gilgamish, when he knew that his friend has gone from Erech, put on coarse attire; he arrayed himself in the skin of a lion, and he pursued Enkidu. And Enkidu was glad because of this, for he knew that his friend, the noble Gilgamish, would not forsake him. Together they lived in the forest; they hunted together and they became more and more dear to each other.

Later Enkidu had a dream that terrified him. He dreamt that there were thunderings in the heavens and quakings in the earth. He dreamt that a being came before him and gripped him in talons that were the talons of an eagle, and carried him down into a dread abyss. There Enkidu saw creatures that had been kings when they were upon the earth; he saw shadowy beings offering sacrifices to the Gods. He saw in the House of Dust priests and magicians and prophets dwelling. He saw there Bêlit-sêri who writes down the deeds done upon the earth.

Enkidu was terrified; he knew not the meaning of the dream that had come to him. To Ninsunna he went, and he told her his dream. She wept when she heard him tell it. But she would not tell him the meaning that it had.

Thereafter Enkidu lay down on the well-decked bed that Gilgamish, his friend, had given him. He groaned upon his bed. Gilgamish came to comfort him, but Enkidu, although he had joy of Gilgamish's coming, could not banish from his heart the thing that had been shown him in his dream. For ten days he lay upon his bed with Gilgamish beside him. In two days more his sickness became more grievous. Then Enkidu lay silent, and Ninsunna said to her son, "Now is Enkidu dead."

Long gazed Gilgamish upon Enkidu, his friend in the palace, his companion in the hunt upon the mountains and in the forest, his brave ally in his fight against the Bull of Heaven. Long gazed Gilgamish upon his friend lying there. Then Gilgamish said:

"What kind of sleep is this that is upon thee?
"Thou starest out blankly and hearest me not.
"Shall this sleep be upon Gilgamish also? Shall I lie down and be as Enkidu?
"Sorrow hath entered into my soul.
"Because of the fear of death that hath come upon me my heart is restless; I shall go; I shall wander through the lands."

Then Gilgamish touched the breast of his friend, and he found that the heart in his breast was still. Tenderly, as though leaving it over a bridge, Gilgamish laid the covering over Enkidu. He turned away; he roared in his grief as a lion or as a lioness robbed of her young. And when his roarings had ceased, his mother said to him, "What dost thou desire, my son, and what is it that will quiet the grief and the restlessness that are in thine heart?"

Gilgamish said to her, "My desire is to escape death which hath taken hold of Enkidu, my friend."

His mother said, "Only one hath escaped death; the one is Uta-Napishtim the Remote, thine ancestor."

THE DEATH OF HECTOR

HOMER

Safe back in Troy, but all a-tremble like fright-ened fawns, the Trojans leant on the battle-ments, slaking their thirst and cooling their sweaty limbs. The Greek army advanced with raised shields, but found no opponents still facing them on the plain: except Hector the Bright-Helmed alone, whom Destiny compelled to post himself in front of the Scaean Gate.

Thereupon Phoebus Apollo called over his shoulder to Achilles the Swift-Footed: 'Why blindly neglect your task of harrying the Tro-jans, to pursue an Immortal? They have now retired behind their walls, while you wander along Xanthus' riverbank. And your exertions are futile: I never die!'

Choking with anger, Achilles replied: 'Archer Apollo, most mischievous of gods, what a mean trick to play! But for this, I should have rolled many Trojans in the dust before they hurtled through that Gate. You have light-heartedly robbed me of renown, safe in the knowledge that I cannot exact vengenance—as I should certainly do, had I the power.'

Achilles darted away at full speed, as if he were a proud, victorious chariot-horse. Old King Priam soon observed him: his armour blazing like Sirius, harbinger of fevers, the evil star (also called Orion's Hound) which dom-inates the night sky in harvest time. Priam uttered a yell, drubbed on his head, and waved wildly to catch the attention of Hector, who stood below, prepared for stern combat.

Homer, "The Death of Hector," from Book 22, *The Anger of Achilles, Homer's Iliad*, Robert Graves, trans. (1959).

'Hector, sweet son,' he cried, gesticulating, 'I beg you not to remain there, alone and un-supported! Achilles is far stronger than you, and knows no mercy; he will cut your life short. Ah, that the gods felt as little love for him as I do! Then he would die on the spot, leaving dogs and vultures to ease my heart of its pain. He has robbed me of a dozen splendid sons, by killing them or selling them into slavery abroad. And now I miss two more among those who have just returned: Lycaon and Polydorus, my sons by Laothoë, pearl of women! They may of course be captured. In that case I could offer as ransom part of her dowry, which Altes paid me in bronze and gold. But if they are dead, she and I will be past consolation. Nevertheless, dear Hector, none of my subjects, whether men or women, will feel their loss deeply, so long as you sur-vive.

'Back, back! Inside! Protect us! Would you let Achilles triumph over your helpless and unfortunate old father, who can yet suffer agonies of grief before Zeus, Son of Cronus, brings him to a miserable end? Fearful horrors must first appal these eyes: sons butchered, daughters dragged into captivity, palace sacked, infant grandchildren dashed against stones, daughters-in-law outraged by the evil Greek soldiery. And last of all they will kill me: some-one will hack or thrust me down in yonder palace gateway, and the hounds lying there will greedily tear my flesh—the very hounds that I fed at table and trained as watch-dogs. A young man fallen in battle undergoes no humiliation, even if his body be mangled, and left stark naked; but when a white-headed, white-bearded veteran has his secret parts ripped off by dogs, that is a shocking and pitiable sight indeed!'

Though Priam might pull his hair out by the roots, he could not weaken Hector's resolution. Queen Hecuba also wept, undoing her upper garment and displaying a wrinkled breast. 'Hector, my child,' she wailed, 'I charge you by this breast which once gave you suck, to do as your father orders! Achilles is ruthless, and if he kills you there, Andromache and I will be denied the poor solace of weeping over your dead body—carried off to the Greek camp for dogs to tear.'

The old couple continued their lamentations, imploring Hector to come back and organize the city's resistance; but he calmly awaited Achilles, who was bounding towards him on his powerful legs.

> A serpent, coiled in a dark den,
>   That has on noxious herbage supped
> Conceives a hatred of all men
>   (Such poisons can the soul corrupt),
> And, glowering rage, resolves to lie
> In ambush for a passer-by.

With equal resolution, though less venomous feelings, Hector leaned his polished shield against a buttress of the tower. He thought unhappily: 'If I do as my parents ask, Polydamas will blame me for having disregarded his advice. I should have listened when he begged me to lead the army home before Achilles could destroy it. But now that we are ruined by my obstinate folly, I am ashamed to face the lords and ladies of Troy. And some churl is bound to mutter: "Hector's vainglory was our downfall." That I could not bear; so I must either kill Achilles, or else die gloriously. Yet, another alternative offers: to remove my helmet, lay it on the ground, lean my spear beside this shield, and meet him with a peace proposal. I might say: "We will restore Helen and her entire fortune (Paris' theft of which caused the war) to King Agamemnon and his brother Menelaus; we will, moreover, divide the city's own treasures into halves, and give you one of them as a condition of your raising the siege." Then I should have to make the Royal Council swear that no valuables would be concealed or withheld from the common stock. Impossible! If I went forward unarmed, Achilles would doubtless disregard the overture and fell me

ruthlessly, as though I were a woman. This is no occasion for whispered agreements, such as a girl might exchange with a gallant from the shelter of a rock or an oak-tree. We must fight, and let Zeus choose between us.'

Achilles was almost upon Hector, brandishing the dreadful lance. He resembled the formidable God of War, and his bronze armour flashed like a bonfire, or a sunrise. Hector, aghast at the sight, turned and fled.

> The mountain falcon, mighty-winged and
>   swooping from above
> With screams of rage, hotly pursues a terror-
>   smitten dove.

Going at a great speed close under the walls, Hector flashed by Priam's look-out tower and the wind-blown fig-tree which had taken root on the western curtain; then along a wagon track towards two neighbouring sources of the Scamander—one so hot that it smoked, as if heated by a furnace; the other as cold as snow, hail or ice, even in summer. Near them stood a pair of massive troughs used by Trojan housewives and girls when they washed their fine linen—in days of peace.

Hector ran past these troughs, with Achilles in fierce pursuit. A desperate struggle, since the runners were contending not for the carcase of a sacrificial beast, or an ox-hide, or any such ordinary prize; but for Hector's life! Yet it did recall a chariot-race, where a tripod or a woman-slave is the prize and competing teams wheel rapidly at the stadium's goal-posts; because Hector kept his lead and drew Achilles three times round the whole circuit of walls.

All the Olympians sat watching in a rapt silence, finally broken by Zeus himself. 'Alas,' he sighed, 'how sad to see a man whom I love chased around his own city walls! Hector has burned me countless sacrifices on the spurs of Ida and at the Trojan Citadel—beautiful thigh-bones wrapped in prime fat. Come, friends, your advice! Is this brave fellow to be rescued from Achilles, or shall I let him die?'

'Father Zeus, Lord of the Lightning and the Dark Storm Cloud,' Athene the Owl-Eyed cried. 'What is this? Would you dare rescue a mortal from the fate to which he has long ago been destined? Do as you please, of course, but without our approval.'

'Dear child,' Zeus answered, 'you must not take me too seriously. I am very well disposed to you. There will be no interference with your schemes.'

So Athene flew down from Olympus and found the rival champions once more circling the walls.

> A hound pursues a brocket stag
> Through glen and glade, nor does he flag
> But onward yelping goes;
> For though his prey may halt beside
> A bramble bush and seek to hide,
> The hound can trust his nose.

Hector's tactics were to make for the battlements covering the Dardanian Gate, where his comrades would send a volley of spears at Achilles; but whenever he approached it, Achilles always spurted, took the inside berth, and forced him towards the plain.

> Often in dream I chase a fleeing man,
> Eager to catch and kill him if I can;
> Yet there's no finish, struggle how we may:
> I cannot reach him, nor he get away.

Here the case was similar, because Apollo so strengthened Hector's lungs and legs that even the Swift-Footed failed to overhaul him. Nevertheless, Achilles tossed his head as a sign that no Greek must steal the triumph by aiming at Hector as he rushed past.

When they came to the troughs in their fourth circuit, Zeus grasped his golden balance and laid a lot in each of its pans—one for Achilles, one for Hector—and poised them carefully. Hector's lot sank down; at which token of doom, Apollo abandoned him to his fate.

Athene thereupon revealed herself to Achilles, crying: 'Glorious son of Peleus, Zeus' favourite! Together we will kill Hector, despite his valour, and drag his corpse victoriously to your camp. This time he cannot escape us, even if Apollo should fall grovelling at the knees of Zeus the Shield-Bearer and plead his cause in desperation. So halt and recover your breath; I shall induce Hector to make a stand!''

Grateful for the respite, Achilles paused, leaning on his long lance; while Athene, disguised as Hector's brother Deiphobus, ran on shouting in his familiar loud voice: 'Dear brother, you are being roughly handled! Stop, and let us face Achilles, you and I; then he will be battling against odds.'

'Deiphobus!' exclaimed Hector. 'Always the best of brothers to me—which is natural, because we have the same father and mother—and never more welcome than now! So you alone dared venture to my aid!'

'Yes, brother,' answered Athene, 'although our parents and friends all begged me to remain on the battlements—they are terrified of Achilles—compassion and grief proved too strong, and here I come! We must fight like heroes; it will soon be seen whether Achilles can kill us and carry our blood-stained spoils back to his ship, or whether, contrariwise, you can destroy him.'

Tricked by Athene's ruse, Hector strode towards Achilles. When within casting distance, he announced: 'Son of Peleus, after three circuits of my father's city I have resolved to stand fast, and engage you in mortal combat. Yet first we should swear on oath—solemnly calling on our gods to witness it—that whichever of us, by Zeus' permission, kills and despoils the other, will abstain from maltreating the corpse and convey it to his own people for burial.'

Achilles replied grimly: 'Dare you bargain with me, madman? If man meets lion, or wolf meets sheep, what chance of agreement can there be? We shall never clasp hands in friendship, nor even in ratification of a pledge. The sole feeling we share is pure hatred; and one of us two must surely fall, his lifeblood glutting the implacable God of War. Now summon all your skill to fight and die like a hero, since no escape is left. I am promised victory by Pallas Athene, and I will make you pay in full for the bitter grief that you have caused me and mine!'

Poising his great lance, Achilles hurled at Hector, who crouched low, letting it whizz over his head and plunge into the earth beyond.

'A miss!' Hector cried. 'You are mistaken. Zeus cannot have told you of my doom! Nor will your smooth tongue and crooked speech scare me into turning about and exposing my kidneys. Should Heaven grant you the upper hand, I shall die from a thrust through the lungs as I charge. But beware! May my spear-blade skewer your flesh, and free Troy of the worst terror that this war has brought upon her!'

His hurtling spear struck the centre of Achilles' shield, but rebounded harmlessly. Angered and discouraged by his ill-success, that being the only spear he carried, Hector cried: 'Quick, Deiphobus, lend me yours!' No answer came and, glancing behind him, he found that Deiphobus had vanished. Then he understood. 'Alas,' he thought, 'Heaven has led me to the slaughter! That was Athene's work. She disguised herself as Deiphobus, who is still watching from the battlements. I am trapped. Zeus and his son Apollo, though careful of my life until today, must have staged this scene long ago. Yet I will not die without first performing a feat of arms to stir the hearts of all posterity.'

He drew his huge, sharp, heavy broadsword, brandished it, gathered himself, and ran at Achilles as a soaring eagle swoops at a lamb or cowering hare on the plain beneath. How was he to know that Athene had covertly pulled the famous lance from the ground and restored it to the grasp of his opponent? In an ectasy of rage, Achilles leaped to the encounter, shield lifted and golden plumes waving.

> Darkly, darkly falls the night.
> One fair star is burning bright:
> HESPERUS his name, and he
> Rivals all the stars that be.

Starlight flashed at Achilles' lance-point, as he planned a mortal thrust against some vulnerable part of Hector's body.

The suit of proof armour, however, won from the corpse of Patroclus, afforded him complete protection, except that it lacked a gorget. Achilles took aim at Hector's bare neck, the most dangerous spot of all, drove the lance clean through, and sent him crashing to the dust.

'Aha, Hector!' Achilles exulted. 'You thought yourself safe when you stole these arms from Patroclus! Did it never cross your mind that his brother-in-arms, a far doughtier antagonist, might be serving in the same camp? At last I am avenged! At last I can give Patroclus a splendid funeral, while leaving you to the dogs and carrion-birds.'

Hector whispered in reply—for the lance had not severed his windpipe: 'Son of Peleus, I beseech you by everything that you hold dearest—your life, your strength, your parents—spare my corpse! King Priam and Queen Hecuba will ransom it at a noble price; grant me decent burial among my people!'

'Scoundrel!' was Archilles' harsh answer. 'I despise these idle appeals to life, strength and parents. If only my stomach did not revolt against such a diet, I would carve your raw flesh into gobbets and swallow them—a fitting punishment for the wrong you did me! Ransom? I should scorn ten or twenty times what your family might tender. Even if King Priam came out here himself, with a pair of scales, eager to pay me the weight of your body in gold, I should laugh at him. No: Queen Hecuba shall never have the solace of lamenting

at the bier on which she has laid you! Nothing in the world can keep the carrion-birds from tearing at your belly, or the dogs from crunching your bones!'

Hector spoke his dying words: 'Now I know you; now I see clearly! Fate forbids me to melt a heart of iron, yet beware: my ghost will draw down the wrath of Heaven on your head—when Paris, aided by Phoebus Apollo, destroys you at yonder Gate.'

The shadow of Death touched Hector, life left him, and a ghost fled to the kingdom of Hades, bewailing his lost youth and vigour.

'Die, then!' Achilles stormed. 'And I am ready to meet my own doom as soon as Zeus and his fellow-Immortals give the order.'' He freed the lance, and stooped to unbuckle Hector's blood stained armour.

A crowd of Greeks ran up, noisily admiring the corpse's muscular perfection. None failed to plunge a sword or spear into it, and the jest went round: 'He is much easier to handle today than yesterday, when he fired our fleet!'

Achilles stripped Hector to the buff, rose, and began a speech: 'Princes and Councillors, since by the gods' help we are rid of a champion who did us more harm than all the rest of Priam's brood together, we should probe the city's defences without delay. Perhaps the loss of their commander-in-chief will induce these Trojans to capitulate . . .'

Suddenly Achilles broke off. 'Alas!' he exclaimed. 'What am I saying? Patroclus' corpse still lies stretched unburied on his brier, and so long as I breathe and move, I cannot forget him. No, no! Though every other ghost in Hades' kingdom forgets his fallen comrades, yet I shall always be faithful to my love, even in the grave. Enough, friends! Sing me a paean of victory, while I haul this carrion to the camp. We have won great glory: we have slain Prince Hector, to whom the Trojans paid almost divine honours.'

Achilles set himself to outrage the corpse: having slit the tendon of each foot from heel to ankle, he looped a rawhide thong through the holes and bound both ends to his chariot-tail. Then he mounted, flung the spoils of battle beside him, lashed Xanthus and Balius to a gallop. Away they flew, and Hector's corpse trailed after them, churning up the dust, his dark, flowing locks dishevelled, and his once glorious features begrimed with filth of the battlefield. Such was the fate ordained for him by Zeus: to have his body desecrated in full sight of his fellow-citizens.

RAMA...
A Holy Name

Rama, Rama, Rama, Rama, Rama, Rama.

So meditating on the holy name of Rama, Valmiki composed the sacred poem, the *Ramayana*, even before Rama himself was born.

Rama was not an ordinary prince, for he was the avatar, or incarnation, of the god Vishnu, come to earth to save the world from the demon Ravana.

But he appeared to be a fairly normal person when he was born the son of King Dasaratha. While he was still quite young, the sage Viswamitra appeared before King Dasaratha and requested that Rama and Lakshmana, one of his brothers, come with him to keep the demons away from the temple where he and other sages were trying to sacrifice.

The king did not want to send his young sons off, but Rama and Lakshmana insisted that they were eager to try their strength, so they followed the sage. The next day as the sages began their sacrifices, the demons again attacked them. But this time Rama and Lakshmana fought them off with their bow and arrow, and the sages could then sacrifice in peace.

While the young men were there, they heard that the Swayamwara of the beautiful daughter of King Janaka was to be held. A Swayamwara was a means by which a lady would choose a husband for herself, and both Rama and Lakshmana decided to try their luck.

Rama was immediately struck by the beauty of Sita and fell in love with her. He was pleased when he discovered that the task she had set for the men to prove themselves was to string a bow which Siva had given to King Janaka. Rama, who was already famous as an archer, easily bent the great bow and claimed Sita for his bride. So the two brothers returned home proudly with Sita.

But good fortune did not await them at home. Kaikeyi, Rama's father's third wife, was jealous of Rama's success and knew that he would soon be appointed heir to the throne. Her own son, Bharata, being younger than Rama and the son of the third wife, had no claim to the throne. But she had a claim on the king. Once she had saved his life on the battlefield and he had promised to grant her two favors. Now she was ready to ask for them.

"Dasaratha," she said one day as he was relaxing in her chamber. "Do you remember the time I saved your life during battle?"

"Of course I remember," replied Dasaratha. "And I also remember that I offered to grant you two boons which you have not yet used."

"I am now ready to ask those boons," replied Kaikeyi. "The first boon is that my son Bharata be named heir to the throne. And the second boon is that Rama be banished from the kingdom for fourteen years."

King Dasaratha wept when he heard her requests. He hated the

thought of losing Rama as his heir, but he could not go back on his word. When the king announced that Rama was to be banished, Sita, his wife, insisted on going with him. "A wife's place is with her husband," she said. "And whether his home is a palace or a hovel, she must be beside him."

Rama knew that she was right, and he was glad for her company. His brother Lakshmana also insisted that he be allowed to go with him. So the three of them found a small but comfortable cave in the forest and prepared to stay for fourteen years.

Bharata had been away when all of this happened and knew nothing of his mother's request. When he returned he found that his father had died from grief and that he himself was to be crowned king. He refused to accept the kingdom won so unfairly and set out to find Rama. After months of searching in the forest, he found Rama and said, "I have come to beg forgiveness for what my mother has done and to ask you to return to the city as king."

But Rama replied, "My father made a vow, and it is my duty to fulfill it. I will not return until the fourteen years are up."

When Bharata realized that he could never persuade Rama to return, he asked, "Then give me your sandals that I can take them back and set them upon the throne. They will serve as a reminder that you are the real king and I am only serving as your regent until you return in fourteen years." Rama complied, and Bharata returned sadly to the capital. Lakshmana, Sita, and Rama remained in the forest living a blissful and idyllic life.

However, their peace did not last long, for the demoness Surpanakha came into the forest one day and saw the two handsome young men. She was determined to marry one of them, but Rama pointed out that he was already married. Lakshmana, even though he was not married, would have nothing to do with her. At last, enraged, Surpanakha attacked Sita, and Lakshmana angrily drew his sword and cut off her nose, ears, and breasts.

Furious, she flew to her brother, the demon Ravana, on his island fortress.

"See how I have been treated," she cried, showing his whole court her mutilated face. "You must avenge me!"

"Who has done this to you?" asked Ravana.

"The brothers Rama and Lakshmana," she replied.

Ravana's court advisers immediately warned him that he must have nothing to do with these two, that Rama was the most powerful archer in the world and seemed to be blessed with supernatural power.

But this challenge only whetted Ravana's appetite.

"Besides," said Surpanakha, "the best way to get revenge would be to steal Rama's wife, Sita. Then he would die of a broken heart. And Sita would be a good addition to your collection of beautiful young maidens."

So Ravana sent one of his men disguised as a golden deer that grazed close by the cave of Rama and Sita.

Looking out the opening of the cave, Sita was delighted by the beautiful animal and asked Rama to get it for her.

"I am afraid that there is something magic about it," Rama replied.

"Oh, please," begged Sita. "It is the most beautiful thing I have seen since we left the city."

Realizing how much Sita had suffered by following him into exile, Rama agreed. "All right, if it is a real deer I will bring it to you alive. If it is an evil spirit, I can kill it and bring you the hide."

Swiftly Rama started after the deer, but it darted away easily, staying far in front of him. For several hours he followed the deer that teasingly stayed just in sight but too far away for him to catch. As they came to a ridge on a strange mountain, Rama realized how far he had traveled, and suddenly he knew that the strange deer must be a trick to lure him away from Sita. Very worried, he quickly drew an arrow and shot the mysterious deer straight through the heart. But with its dying breath, the deer cried loudly. "Help, Lakshmana! I am dying! Save me!"

Back in their cave, Lakshmana heard what he thought was his brother's cry for help and, forgetting his duty to protect Sita, rushed toward the sound of the cry.

As soon as he was gone, the demon Ravana, in the form of a hermit, appeared to Sita and forced her to show him hospitality by going into the cave to fix him something to eat. As soon as she was inside he assumed his horrible form, a ten-headed demon, and imprisoned her. Sita screamed in terror, but he put one of his thousand hands over her mouth, and with another grabbed her hair and dragged her off in his chariot.

Hearing Sita's scream, Rama and Lakshmana rushed back to their home, but they could find no trace of her. They knew that she must have been carried off by a terrible demon but had no idea where to begin looking. As the two brothers were still searching their cave in despair, a huge vulture fell from the sky to their feet. Rama rushed to the giant bird and saw that he had been wounded in several spots and was near to death.

"Sita has been captured by Ravana," the great bird gasped. "I tried to rescue her but failed. He has imprisoned her on his island." As soon as he had whispered these words, the vulture died. Rama felt a strange recognition of this bird, but he could not yet know that he was an incarnation of the god Vishnu and the vulture was an incarnation of his sacred mount, Garuda.

Meanwhile, Ravana had carried Sita to his island fortress where he put her in his harem. He planned to make her another of his wives, but she refused to have anything to do with him, even when he threatened to kill and eat her if she would not yield to him. Finally he told her she had a year to make up her mind and then she must either marry him or die.

Rama and Lakshmana despaired of ever rescuing Sita, for they had discovered that Ravana was the most powerful of all the demons and had dared to threaten the gods themselves. He seemed almost invincible, for he had the promise of Indra that he could not be killed by any god.

While Rama and Lakshmana were traveling toward Ravana's island and trying to think up a plan to attack him, they found a monkey who was in distress. He was the king of monkeys and had been forced out of his kingdom. Rama and Lakshmana, deciding that his cause was just, helped him to regain his throne, and the grateful monkey king offered his army and his general Hanuman to Rama to assist him in his struggle.

Hanuman, who had magical powers, proved a very valuable ally. First he went on a spy mission to Ravana's home where he found Sita weeping in a garden. Comforting her, he told her of Rama's plans. Then he mischievously began destroying Ravana's city—tearing up trees, pulling down buildings, and knocking over the towers. The furious Ravana sent his whole army after him, but the agile monkey mocked them from the tops of trees and towers as he continued his destruction. At last, however, he was caught, and Ravana decreed that his soldiers should burn him by tying oily rags to his tail.

Hanuman pretended to be terrified by this edict and moaned and wailed as the rags were tied and lighted. But then he grew to a giant size and dashed to the sea, setting the whole city on fire with his burning tail as he went.

When Hanuman returned from his spy mission, Rama and the rest of the monkeys marched to the seashore across from Ravana's island.

"Part for us, so we can cross to Ravana's island," Rama cried to the ocean. But the ocean replied, "We cannot disobey the laws of nature for you. You must use other means. If you will build a causeway, though, we will be careful not to disturb it."

So Rama and the monkeys built a great causeway to Ravana's island. As Ravana and his men watched their progress, his advisers urged the great demon to return Sita so they would not all be killed. But he would not listen to them. His pride was so great that he felt he was invincible. Certainly he was not afraid of a few men and an army of monkeys!

At last Rama and his monkey army reached Ravana's city, and a great battle raged for many days. At last all of the demons except Ravana were killed, and Rama engaged him in single combat. Ravana, who had not bothered to ask Indra to make him invincible against mere men, was certainly a powerful adversary. He had ten heads, and when one was cut off, another grew in its place. But Rama also had a powerful weapon, the Astra, the sacred weapon of Brahma, and when he threw it, it landed in Ravana's heart and killed him.

Finally Sita was freed and joyfully rushed into Rama's arms. But Rama held her at arm's length.

"You have been defiled by another man," said Rama sadly. "I can no longer consider you my wife."

Sita was stunned. "But Rama," she pled. "He never came near me."

Rama was adamant. "I will continue to take care of you, but I will never touch you again," he said and turned to walk away.

"Wait!" Sita cried and her voice was terrible. "Lakshmana," she ordered, "bring wood and build a fire. I call on the gods to prove my innocence!"

A huge fire was built right in the middle of the battlefield and when the flames were towering high above the heads of the men, Sita threw herself on it. Immediately the flames formed themselves into the shape of a god, lifted Sita from the ground, and set her down in front of Rama.

Rama embraced her joyfully, for the gods had now shown that he could accept her without damaging his self-respect. So Rama and Sita and Lakshmana returned to their home, where Bharata still waited with Rama's sandals on the throne. Amid the rejoicing of all the people, Rama assumed the throne and ruled well for many years.

But the couple's troubles were still not over. After several years rumors began to fly around the capital that Sita had been unfaithful with Ravana. Since no one there had seen Sita's trial by fire except Rama and Lakshmana, there was no one who could vindicate her, and at last Rama decided to send her into exile.

Sita started off on her journey, thinking that she would visit the cave where she and Rama had been in exile together so many years before. But on the way she came to the ashram of the sage Valmiki, who had all this time been composing a great poem, *The Ramayana*, not yet knowing whether his hero had even been born. He greeted Sita very warmly and begged her to stay there. Sita was very glad to find a kind home, for she was pregnant and in a few months born twin boys, Kusa and Lava.

As the boys grew up, Valmiki taught them *The Ramayana*, which he was still composing. At last a great ceremony was held in Rama's king-

dom, and Valmiki sent Kusa and Lava, who had now learned the whole poem, to participate in it. While the ceremony was going on, the two voices were suddenly heard reciting the great poem. Rama and all of his men were thrilled by it and called the boys to them. For days and days the whole city sat spellbound listening to the tremendous epic, and when it was finished they all sat in silence.

At last Rama asked, "Who are you and where did you learn this poem?"

"Our mother is Sita, and our father is a great king, but we do not know him," the boys replied.

Then Rama wept and gathered them to him. "Go get Sita and bring her to me," he begged Lakshmana. "I want her here whatever the rumors may say."

So Sita again was returned to Rama, but this time she refused to accept a man who had twice accused her of unfaithfulness.

"Mother Earth," she cried. "If I have been pure, take me unto yourself!" And before the startled eyes of the crowd, the earth opened and Sita disappeared into it.

Rama went mad with rage and despair. He cried to the earth to give him back his wife. His friends feared that he would take his own life. But suddenly Brahma himself appeared to him.

"Have you become so wrapped up in the world of illusion that you have forgotten who you are? You are the great Lord Vishnu and this body you are in is only a temporary form you assumed in order to destroy Ravana. This woman you called Sita was an incarnation of your eternal wife Lakshmi and she awaits you in your heavenly home."

Rama was once again at peace, and a short time afterward he walked into the River Sarayu and disappeared from the earth to the heavens where as Vishnu he continues to watch over the world and wait for another time when he must come to earth again to save it from destruction.

? The preceding myths illustrate the warrior hero's struggle to define the relation of death to life. In each of these myths individuals come face to face with death in order to save the energy of life. Each individual must prove the limits of his endurance as he tests his courage in the battle for his life and the life of his group. What charges these encounters with meaning is the nobility of purpose underlying the heroes' quest. Gilgamish completes his task, but suffers the loss of his friend, Enkidu. Hector fails to save Troy, but in confronting his mortality, suffers a noble failure. Rama seeks to understand the wisdom of unity which connects death to life through the process of reincarnation. The following questions focus on initiation into the ruling class of a male-oriented culture. The hero's journey is a rite of passage to test his courage of spirit and nobility of purpose.

1 Understanding the separation:
  a In which myths does the father appear, either as a spirit or a father of the hero, to illustrate what expectations he demands of the son? How does this bridge the generation gap between father and son? What does this suggest about the transfer of power?

  b In which of the myths is the hero helped by his mother or a mother goddess? In which of the myths is the hero hindered by a mother symbol? What does this suggest about the relation between the mother and son?

  c Discuss the opponents of Gilgamish, Hector, and Rama. How do they differ? How can they be compared? What is the relation between the opponent and the survival of a culture? In defeating the opponent, does the hero identify with the symbolic father of the culture? What does this suggest about the struggle of the hero and the eventual outcome of his quest?

2 Understanding the Initiation:
  a In which of the myths is the hero's quest a struggle with the morality of his own existence? Explain the implications of this concept!

  b In which of the myths does the hero seek a hidden treasure?

  c What restrictions or taboos are placed on the heroes of these myths? In which myths are there magical symbols to help the hero? What is the source of this magic?

d Compare and contrast the way the hero receives help from a friend in each of the myths. In which of the myths does the help come from a sisterlike symbol? In which myths does this help come from another male? Develop the implications of this process.

e In which myths does the hero fail? Discuss his failure and what this reveals about strength and weakness among males!

f Discuss the ways each of the heroes attempts to win personal honor and glory. How is this struggle linked to the hero's sacrifice of his personal glory in favor of the need to save the collective?

g How does the hero respond to danger?

3 Understanding the return:

a What insight does the hero provide us with regarding man's ability to test his endurance against the forces of destruction?

b What insight about nature emerges from the hero's battle?

c How does the hero's task reinforce the male authority within a culture?

d What image of woman emerges from these mythical encounters?

e What questions underlie the mythical separation, initiation, and return?

f How do each of these myths illustrate the hero's role in the rejuvenation of the collective? What does this suggest about fertility, e.g., the ritual of birth, as an underlying metaphor?

g In which of the myths is aggression and force the most important value illustrated? Develop the idea that this suggests!

h Which of the heroes brings us to see (1) what is necessary for man to adapt to an "outside" world and (2) what "inner" realization the hero attains from his journey?

i What conflicts are resolved? What conflicts are not resolved by these heroes?

j In what ways does the hero's adventure transform his society? What conclusions would you draw about the hero's initiation into a world?

What is being sacrificed?

In these pictures of the initiation ceremonies of the Australian aborigines, we see the way a boy becomes a man in the tribe. A symbolic sacrifice is usually required. This often is performed in the ritual of male circumcision.

The four stages of an initiation ceremony:

The boys are placed under blankets to symbolically depict their death. The child must die in order for the man to be born.

They are removed from under the blankets and held by the men of the tribe for the actual operation. The letting of blood is used to symbolize the individual's willingness to endure physical pain, and this is also a sacrificial offering to the god to protect the individual from harm.

The boys are given men's conical hats to symbolize their new status within the community.

They are removed from the tribe in order to be purified and to receive instructions in the tribal secrets.

SYMBOLIC WOUNDS

BRUNO BETTELHEIM

One other aspect of this study of puberty rites should be mentioned. In my work with asocial children, delinquents, schizophrenics, and severe neurotics, I have come to see that types of behavior which appear as expressions of the most violent hostility, of "the id in the raw," are actually frantic efforts by the ego to regain rational control over a total personality overwhelmed by irrational instinctual forces. This is by no means a new observation—on the contrary, it is an accepted view of schizophrenia.

A different perspective on human nature might emerge if this view found wider application as a heuristic hypothesis. Much that leads us to doubt man's humanity might then look like efforts—sometimes violent, desperate, and often unsuccessful—to affirm his humanity despite powerful instinctual pressure. For example, I hope to show how likely it is that certain initiation rites originate in the adolescent's attempts to master his envy of the other sex, or to adjust to the social role prescribed for his sex and give up pregenital, childish pleasures. If this effort succeeds, it permits the sexes to live together more satisfactorily. But even when such integrative efforts do not succeed, they stand for a position purpose, in contrast to the negativism ascribed to them in current psychoanalytic theory.

I think the prevailing psychoanalytic opinion on circumcision and puberty rites represents an unbalanced view of the nature of human beings. It seems at least partly the result of viewing social institutions as expressing mainly destructive or irrational instinctual tendencies. This was perhaps necessary at the start of psychoanalysis, when entrenched denial of instinctual tendencies had to be counteracted. But it is a one-sided view and applies only part of the theoretic framework of psychoanalysis to the study of human nature. It reflects early theory concerned mainly with the id, and not the ego psychology which has lately come to stand in the center of psychoanalytic speculation. Ego and superego are not "mere" superstructures built upon the "only reality" of the id. The human personality results from the continuous interplay of all three institutions of the mind. Social phenomena must reflect not only one institution, the id (in this case the castrating father), but also the superego and, most of all, the ego. Social institutions are indeed ego creations—the superego and id can only act upon the world through the ego.

I think that the functional anthropologist who asks what is the purpose of initiation for the well-being of society, though he may give a too-rational answer, has put the question correctly. We cannot be satisfied with an explanation that accounts solely for the destructive, sex-inhibiting, anxiety-evoking aspects of a great social institution, even if these play an important part. I am profoundly impressed with the great measure to which initiation rites seem to arise from efforts to integrate, rather than to discharge, asocial instinctual tendencies.

Our wish to think well of man has played many tricks on scientific accuracy, and this study was not begun in defense of man's dignity. But in my work with children I have learned that while little good results from an unjustly high opinion of persons and motives, much and serious damage may result from an unwarrantedly low opinion. If the latter prevails, valiant ego attempts at integration (which may be recognized in initiation rites despite some of the features so astonishing to civilized persons) may be misinterpreted as barely controlled aggression acted out. I think in our discussion of initiation and circumcision we have been far too engrossed in what looks like destruction (damage to the genitals) and have overlooked the more hidden fascination with pregnancy and birth. It may be that what has been linked narrowly and pessimistically with castration, truly a destruction of life, will come to be seen as resulting rather from the most constructive desires, those concerned with progeny, with new life.

That such views were in the air when I wrote this book may be seen from the fact that only a year later E. Neumann remarked:

"When we look for the psychological conditions that must have given rise to the initiation of adolescents, to the various secret rites, and to segregation, we find nothing of the sort in the normal male development; while the mysterious occurrence of menstruation or pregnancy and the dangerous episode of childbearing make it necessary for the inexperienced woman to be initiated by those who are informed in these matters. The monthly 'segregation' in the closed (i.e., taboo) sacral female precinct is only a logical continuation of the initiation that has occurred in this place at the first menstruation.

Childbearing occurs in this same precinct, which is the natural, social, and psychological center of the female group, ruled over by the old, experienced woman."[1]

His views are based on such reasoning as:

"The earliest sacred precinct of the primordial age was probably that in which women gave birth. . . . Not only is the place of childbearing the sacral place of female life in early and primitive cultures; obviously it also stands at the center of all cults that are dedicated to the Great Goddess as the goddess of birth, fertility—and death. In Malekula, for example, the name 'birth enclosure' is given both to the fence within which women give birth and to the one surrounding the site where the male mysteries of rebirth are solemnized."[2]

It is hoped that this excursion into the far distant past and into the lives of preliterate people living today may hold something of value to the social scientist as well as the clinician, both laboring in the present and in our own complex society for the well-being of modern, civilized man. Indeed, it was while working with modern schizophrenic children that I made the observations that aroused my interest in preliterate man and eventually led me back in my thinking to our own society. . . .

I do not attempt to establish the following hypotheses as valid, but only to show that they are just as reasonable, or more so, than current

[1] E. Neumann, *The Great Mother*, (New York, Panethon Books Inc., 1955), p. 290.
[2] *Ibid.*, p. 159.

psychoanalytic theories on initiation. They need to be tested by field studies which may validate some, cause others to be discarded or radically modified.

1. Initiation rites, including circumcision, should be viewed within the context of fertility rites.
2. Initiation rites of both boys and girls may serve to promote and symbolize full acceptance of the socially prescribed sexual role.
3. One purpose of male initiation rites may be to assert that men, too, can bear children.
4. Through subincision men try to acquire sexual apparatus and functions equivalent to women's.
5. Circumcision may be an effort to prove sexual maturity or may be a mutilation instituted by women, or both.
6. The secrecy surrounding male initiation rites may serve to disguise the fact that the desired goal is not reached.
7. Female circumcision may be partly the result of men's ambivalence about female sex functions and partly a reaction to male circumcision.

No single set of theories can cover more than the essence of initiation rites, because by now they are infinitely varied in form, in content, and origin. Many ritual details are explainable only by conditions that prevail in the society they occur in. One great advantage of the accepted psychoanalytic theory is that it seems to account for all initiation rites simply, concisely, and universally. But this, it appears, is also the root of its major shortcomings. Because in order to maintain such economy and elegance, certain facts have been forced to fit the theory and others neglected.

Later, in presenting data supporting my hypotheses,* my goal is limited. The anthropological field observations are so numerous that it would take a lifetime to evaluate them. I have found no data in the field observations or in the psychoanalytical literature to contradict my hypotheses. Where contradictions seem to exist, they are traceable not to original source material but to how it was interpreted, and these I have felt free to disregard.

At this point the question may be asked: How is one to justify basing initiation-rite theory on

* In which I shall not follow the above sequence because that would mean tiresome repetition of points that apply to more than one hypothesis.

observations of twentieth-century schizoid or schizophrenic children—and conversely, interpreting the behavior of such children in terms of the actions of preliterate people at puberty? Indeed, such a procedure is not certainly valid, having more the character of an *argumentum ad judicium*. Therefore, although some of my next comments follow a precedent set by Freud, they should not be swallowed whole.

Freud introduced his anthropological speculations by remarking that the psychic life of the so-called savage and semisavage races "assumes a peculiar interest for us, for we can recognize in their psychic life a well-preserved, early stage of our own development."[3] This I consider doubtful, since I do not believe that ontogeny simply repeats phylogeny. But when Freud goes on to say that "Comparison of the psychology of primitive races . . . with the psychology of the neurotic . . . will reveal numerous points of correspondence," then he refers to heuristically valid hypotheses of comparative psychology, except that I do not believe they should be restricted to neurotics, but extended to the psychology of all persons. Still, it is on the basis of his remarks that interpretations of childhood experiences have since been used freely to support speculations about primitive behavior and vice versa.

Here, one might even speculate that if preliterate peoples had personality structures as complex as those of modern man, if their defenses were as elaborate and their consciences as refined and demanding, if the dynamic interplay between ego, superego, and id were as intricate, and if their egos were as well adapted to meet and change external reality—they would have developed societies as complex as ours, although probably different. Their societies, however, have remained small and relatively ineffective in coping with the external environment. It may be that one of the reasons for this is their tendency to try to solve problems by autoplastic rather than alloplastic manipulation; that is, by altering their bodies or behavior instead of the physical environment.

Two very thoughtful reviewers[4] took strong exception to these remarks, one called them a delusional statement, while the other felt repelled by my speculations. Though I have given

[3] S. Freud, *Totem and Taboo*, Basic Writings, p. 807.

[4] Aberle, *loc. cit.*; and Schneider [Book review of *Symbolic Wounds*], *American Anthropologist*, 57 (1955), pp. 390–392.

the matter considerable thought I see no reason to change them save to label any remarks more clearly as speculation. Still, the reader is warned that at least two scholars were convinced that I am here in error.

My reason for not heeding their criticism is that I do not claim that preliterate people cannot have as complex personalities as modern man, but only that they do not. I do not doubt their potentialities; on the contrary, my whole thesis is based on the conviction that fundamentally we are all more or less alike. It is exactly because I believe that our potentialities differ but little, that there must be some other reason why different groups of men have developed differently. Why indeed should some groups have questioned the human condition, tried to understand themselves, the world and each other, and in the process of their quest, built complex edifices, changing themselves, external nature, and their societies on the basis of greater rational understanding? Why should one group of men, over the years, small step by small step, have created modern society, modern science, and modern technology, and another group, for a similar period of time, remained relatively stationary under conditions such as those of the Australian aborigines? If this difference is not to be found in the one group's development of an ever more complex personality structure on a basis common to both, then I would like to be told what else accounts for the difference. Otherwise, we return to the belief in a basic difference of intellectual endowment between different groups of man, a belief that I hope has been relegated to those prejudices we outgrew as we developed rationally and in the complexity of our personality structure.

Since my comments were misunderstood by two separate scholars, the burden of defense rests with me. Unfortunately I can again do no better than an argument *ad judicium*, because this is an issue where knowledge is lacking, though we continue to penetrate our ignorance. For obvious reasons the following example is taken from the relationship of parent and child which looms so large in this book.

In settings more primitive than ours, sex may be less shrouded in secrecy, but everything else is more shrouded in permanent ignorance. This ignorance may take the form of uncertainty about how a child is conceived or what causes the sequence of seasons or of rain in dry countries, so important for the regeneration of plants and with it the availability of food (for without sufficient rain, the child in more primitive societies may go hungry for a year or even starve). The modern child may know much less about sex than his preliterate counterpart and much less about where his sustenance actually comes from. After all, the modern city child knows that despite the stories we read him, the farmer does not give us our food since we buy it at the supermarket for money. But by what secret manipulations his parents manage to assure a recurring supply of this money—that is a much greater unknown to him than is food gathering to the Australian aboriginal child. Thus the modern city child actually knows less, is surrounded by many more mysteries he will have to penetrate. But he knows, and here's the rub, that potentially he can know the true cause of impregnation, of how money is earned, and why the farmer is willing to sell food for money. It is this conviction—that you can know as soon as you have acquired enough knowledge—that gives such great impetus to the modern child to develop what I call a complex personality structure. No such powerful appeal to develop his ratiocination is made to the preliterate child. And since one of the secrets the child is most curious about, sex and intercourse, is no secret to him, a great stimulus to find out about secrets in general is lacking. As for the modern child, his wish to unravel it may create the desire to unravel other secrets, too. Such a desire is supported by the conviction of society (including the mass media) that through higher learning all secrets can become known. And this, particularly if the child has learned what lies behind the great secret of sex, may give him the courage to explore many others on his own.

Observations such as this one are what led me to connect complex society with complex personality structure, including complex psychological defenses, and defenses against them. They led me to assume that while in primitive society more of the basic facts are known to the child, this knowledge removes an impetus to develop a very complex personality structure. In short, I believe that primitive children could develop personalities as complex as ours, but their conditions of life give them little reason to do so.

Roheim has said without qualification that the Australian's culture is autoplastic.[5] (He did not,

[5] Roheim, *Australian Totemism* (London: George Allen and Unwin, 1925), p. 221.

however, apply the concept to circumcision.) In our own society we may see a small child frustrated in his efforts to master a toy or a situation, hit himself or bang his head against the floor; he does not stop to reason out if the frustration began in the external world or in his emotions. Similarly, persons in preliterate societies often act as if external reality can be met only by resignation or by doing something with or to their bodies. Further, the small child tries to become like his mother, not by adopting her way of behaving or trying to live by her values, but by wearing her clothes. In the same way some preliterate peoples tend to copy externals rather than internalize less visible characteristics. When men by subincision make themselves *resemble* women, the obvious reason is that they are trying to *be* women. Only if the data themselves rule out such an interpretation must we search for another.

Another indication of the relatively undeveloped state of the primitive's ego is that the superego seems at times extremely cruel and at other times hardly able to assert itself. How valid such comparisons may be is, of course, not established. But if the theory of comparative immaturity, of a relatively poor personality integration is correct, then the net result may be that the barriers against expression of certain tendencies are low. Thus in preliterate cultures a person might act out freely what in Western man would be taken for signs of personality disintegration; he may ritualize desires that in "normal" persons in our culture must be deeply repressed or else integrated and sublimated, that can at most be expressed only in fantasy.

I was further guided by the assumption that motivations which in "normal" persons are unconscious are often expressed openly by schizophrenic adults, and that "normal" children show behavior that in "normal" adults remains hidden. Therefore it seemed reasonable to conclude that the content of the unconscious is apt to be most visible in the behavior (and statements) of schizophrenic children. Fenichel,[6] as a matter of fact, goes so far as to say that "in schizophrenia 'the unconscious is conscious,'" and in all probability this is even truer of schizophrenic children than of schizophrenic adults.

Although psychoanalytic theory holds that the unconscious remains relatively or wholly un-

[6] S. Ferenczi, "An 'Anal Hollow-Penis' in Women," *Further Contributions to the Theory and Technique of Psychoanalysis* (London: Hogarth Press, 1950), p. 450.

touched by the process of civilization, I am not convinced. Only a full study of the unconscious of preliterate peoples would permit definite opinions on the matter. What I do believe is that if persons in entirely different settings develop similar types of behavior in response to a like challenge (in this case the onset of puberty), they are motivated by similar desires; this seems the more likely if the known facts should support rather than contradict such notions. Still our children's behavior can only suggest a review of our theories on the motives of preliterates: it does not tell us what these motives are.

One cannot, for example, ignore the fact that the boys at the Orthogenic School suffered from sex fears that were probably much stronger than those of preliterate adolescents, and that this affected their motives.

The desires and motives of the boy who so warmly praised the advantages of circumcision were very different from those of the two who joined the secret society. His case does not permit unequivocal inferences, because, first, he was living among boys who had been circumcised since infancy, and, second, painful adhesions interfered with full functioning of the penis. From this we cannot draw conclusions about the emotions of boys in preliterate societies toward circumcision, if they are not suffering from adhesions. What his behavior does show is that living among circumcised men may make circumcision appear very desirable, and this condition obtains in most societies that include circumcision among their initiation rites.

As for the anthropological literature on initiation, while it supports some of my conjectures about the children's behavior, it supports them only equivocally. There is no easy parallel between the behavior of youngsters in our highly civilized twentieth-century—children who have grown up in a more or less patriarchal and sex-repressive society—and that of children reared in a society granting relatively great, often full, sexual freedom. Symptoms cannot justifiably be compared out of context, particularly when they originate in vastly different social and psychological fields. So here, too, while my experience led me to challenge the accepted interpretations of certain aspects of initiation rites, and to elaborate and qualify others, it offered mainly the stimulus to investigate further.

Some Initial Comparisons

What, then, were the points of resemblance between the study of initiation as reported by field workers and the examination of the conduct of our children?

The first point of resemblance was that through their planned secret society these four pubertal children, like the novice at initiation, tried to move themselves by a magical act once and for all out of childhood into adulthood. For the girls this required that they find ways to accept the feminine role, a task that first menstruation often suddenly and traumatically imposes on the maturing girl. To make at least this aspect of femininity—the one of most concern at the moment—more acceptable, they created a situation in which menstruation was no longer a liability of their sex alone. If this also made the boys more similar to themselves, they might seem less fearsome, less different and strange.

Other attitudes toward menstruation can also be explained in part by the search for ways of accepting the feminine role. Viewing menstruation not as something debilitating but as something that confers extraordinary magic powers may make genital sexuality more acceptable. The new power again makes men seem less enviable and dangerous and sexual intercourse with them less hazardous. All of which makes it easier for girls to give up the pregenital, pre-Oedipal strivings that Freud was the first to recognize, calling it the child's polymorphous-perverse disposition.[7]

Retaining soiled sanitary pads, etc., may represent a desire to retain proof that sexual maturity has been reached; where it results from the contrary wish to remain a child, then menstruation is viewed as disgusting.

Another point of resemblance is the woman's desire for male genitals which is seen in both initiation rites and in our children's behavior. The girl who pulled at her skin in the genital region hoped to develop a penis. She did not, however, give up either her vagina or the future ability to bear children, which she frequently acted out. Unlike the four adolescent children, she was not motivated toward greater sex maturity or adult independence. Her actions, like those of the younger boys, originated in the desire to find fulfillment in both sexes, either simultaneously or in rapid succession. She reminded me of those African girls who, at about the same age, manipulate the clitoris or labia or both so that they become enlarged and pendent (I am tempted to say) like a penis. This distortion of

[7] S. Freud, *Aus den Anfängen der Psychoanalyse* (London: Imago Publishing Co., 1950), pp. 54–55.

the female genitals is required by tribal custom among several peoples. At present it is not imposed by men but is insisted upon by women, contrary to some widely held notions. The field reports do not suggest that the little girls conform to custom unwillingly.

The opposite of this is extirpation of the clitoris, an operation that forms part of the initiation rites of girls in several tribes. Although excision is usually performed by women and not by men, the general assumption is that the custom is forced on women by men. The desires of our little boys indeed suggest that some men would excise part of the female sex organs if not prevented. But the example of the girl who had to prevent herself from tearing off her own clitoris raises a doubt as to whether even this far-reaching mutilation may not also be reinforced in part by spontaneous desires in women.

The "initiation" ritual of our adolescents, specifically the required cutting of the boys' genitals, was originated by a girl. It remains to be seen whether the rites of preliterate people in which an analogous operation on the male genital takes place may have similar origins.

The delusional relating of menstruation to the penis, as demonstrated by one of our girls, parallels certain beliefs of Australians regarding the subincised penis. Just as this girl fantasied that in menstruation she acquired a penis, so the Australian aborigines believe that in bleeding from their penes they acquire vulvas. Though no direct connection exists, the two types of behavior seem to express parallel unconscious tendencies.

Our boys, like their preliterate counterparts, seemed to want proof as definite as menstruation that they, too, had reached sexual maturity. They may also have tried to lessen their anxiety about women by pleasing or submitting to them. The act by which they hoped to do this was important in itself, since it would reproduce in them something similar to menstruation; this, they may also have felt, would give them a better understanding of women's sexuality. For the boy who wished for circumcision, the circumcised penis with the now permanently freed glans may have served as well as menstruation to assure him that his sexual maturity had been attained.

Parallel to women's envy is the desire of men to possess female genitals in addition to their own. The boys who wished this so intensely were considerably younger than the adolescent boys who took part in the "initiation" plans.

But the age difference may not be specially significant, since we have observed similar desires, though less frankly expressed, in adolescent boys. The egos of the two younger boys were undeveloped, and they were much more primitive in their reactions than the four adolescents. Unrelated, utterly unable to form attachments to adults or other children, they could not act purposefully or even play for any length of time. No force would have been needed to make them change their bodies and acquire vaginal-like openings. If we had not restrained them, they might well have experimented along the lines of subincision.

These boys were less concerned than the adolescents with sexual maturity and menstruation. They wished to be of both sexes; to have vaginas like—hence to *be* like—the powerful, feared, loved, and hated women. Concomitant with this desire was the powerful urge to extirpate women's sex organs. Thus the desire to possess a vagina may represent identification with women, while the wish to excise it seems to result from the hatred and anxiety generated by women and from the desire to overpower them.

The rituals of many preliterate peoples seem to represent a gratification of both these desires: Through subincision men operate on the penis so that it comes to resemble the vulva. In the so-called circumcision of girls the clitoris and sometimes the labia are excised.

Still another point of resemblance lies in the desire of males to bear children and to participate in other female functions. The boys' hostile feelings toward women's genitalia were violent and destructive, rather than constructive. The desire to bear children is more positive; it may be viewed as constructive even when expressed by boys and combined with an envy of women because they can do so. Though few boys go so far as to act out pregnancy, we have several times observed it. But the re-enactment of childbirth is a very nearly universal feature of initiation rites and "pregnant" boys are to be seen at Hallowe'en.

Our children's Hallowe'en costumes suggest a final area of resemblance to initiation rites, since masquerading as a person of the other sex, or at least wearing their clothes, is part of numerous rites. Among some tribes transvestism occurs only on very special occasions. Among others, initiation customs not only permit but require it.

Transvestism seems another indication of the pervading desires of both men and women to share the sexual functions and social role of the other sex. It also seems to assure the child that with the reaching of sexual maturity not all of his desire to share the prerogatives and pleasures of the other sex must be given up once and for all. Dressing up at Hallowe'en in the clothes of the other sex seems not only to represent the wish to play the other sex's role; it is also reassurance that from time to time this will be permitted. Thus the overmasculine boys who disguise themselves so well as women can occasionally show openly the degree to which their masculine assertion is a defense against strong wishes to be feminine. The behavior of those very unintegrated children who wish to have both male and female sexual organs takes forms that are socially less acceptable. Their desires seem to reveal not only their infantile refusal to commit themselves to any definite sexual role, but their envy of anyone who can do so. Yet even their behavior has integrative connotations, to the extent that it lessens their envy and permits them to live in peace with themselves. Still their way of doing it is obviously destructive and cannot lead to higher integration. . . .

Initiation as a Learning Experience

Because many puberty rites include both circumcision and the teaching of tribal lore, circumcision is interpreted as ensuring obedience to tribal precepts through the threat of castration. This explanation seems to represent *post hoc, ergo propter hoc* reasoning, making causal connections where no causal relations exist. Moreover, such an interpretation cannot cover all initiation rites, not even all that include circumcision, because in many tribes no explicit teaching takes place.

There is even reason to doubt that learning or teaching, whether in regard to the incest taboo or to tribal lore, is an intrinsic feature of initiation. From his comparative study of tribal initiation, Loeb[8] found four essential elements in the rites. He does not include the teaching of precepts among them.

In reading anthropological accounts, one is struck in many cases with how little, or what insignificant, teaching and learning actually oc-

[8] E. M. Loeb, "Tribal Initiation and Secret Societies," *University of California Publications in American Archaeology and Ethnology,* XXV (1929), pp. 249–250.

curs (unless one considers the acting out of instinctual tendencies as chiefly a learning experience).

At least a few field workers have concluded that the teaching occurs more in the minds of white observers than in the experience of those who take part in the rituals. Firth, for example, observed: "But of explicit instruction in tribal lore and manners there is usually, I think, less than is imagined, and what is given is by no means a primary feature . . . the insistence on the educative aspect of initiation comes, I fancy, from the attempt to justify rites which on first observation were described as being cruel, barbarous, degraded, and meriting abolition. When it was learnt, as in Australia, that moral and religious instruction was imparted at this time, this was grasped as an argument in favour, and sometimes exaggerated."[9]

This suggests that to view initiation rites as an educational (or superego-enforcing) experience may be a defensive reaction by which observers protect themselves against an experience that evokes quite a bit of anxiety.

I believe that deep emotional needs of both initiators and initiates, not the desire to teach and to learn, find some degree of satisfaction in initiation rites. But even if we accept for the moment the theory that an important lesson is taught, it does not follow that the experience is therefore entirely progressive or entirely inhibiting.

Among anthropologists, initiation rites are considered predominantly progressive phenomena. To the psychoanalyst, they can easily be considered either regressive or id-motivated. Probably they are all of this. Some parts of the rituals, such as learning tribal customs, may have mainly progressive meanings and accord with ego and superego strivings. Others, such as subincision, may be the result of a "regressive" breaking through of pregenital desires and serve mainly to satisfy id strivings. Still others may be both at once.

If, as I believe, man's envy of the other sex is a major factor, the participant may well act out such "regressive" tendencies; but where the ceremonies result in a better adjustment to his own sex role, this constitutes an integrative, progressive aspect. This explanation in terms of motivation and function, if valid, suggests that attempts to explain the rites on a unilateral basis are again too narrow.

[9] R. Firth, *We, the Tikopia* (London: George Allen and Unwin, Ltd., 1936), p. 466.

Almost any central institution of society, while it may serve the needs or desires of one sex more than the other, must to some degree satisfy certain needs of the other sex in order to survive permanently. Those satisfactions need not be primary or basic, but may be the consequence of custom. For example, certain passive desires may be activated in women who begin to live in a patriarchal society. But once aroused, they need to be satisfied. That such a society frustrates many of women's active desires goes without saying. Still, it could not have continued to do so had it not also met some of women's passive wishes.

An institution such as adolescent circumcision may well satisfy the hostile desires of a few (elders or women), but it must also satisfy certain needs of many more. The adolescent's masochism, or his wish to identify with women or with adult men, may be among them. Obviously an institution may serve the constructive desires of one group and the destructive desires of another; may serve the ego tendencies of some persons, the id desires of others, and the superego demands of a third group; may serve the conscious needs of one group and the unconscious, repressed needs of another.

It seems to me that examination of any human institution must begin with the *a priori* assumption that in some way it serves all parts of the society. Only after this assumption has been proven false is it safe to conclude that the institution benefits only one segment. The idea that both male and female initiation ceremonies (rituals worldwide in extent and going back many generations in time) have to do mainly or only with the interests of males, or of the small group of male elders, seems to violate this premise.

Yet much as anthropological and psychoanalytic interpretations of initiation rites differ, both agree that the purpose is to enforce what might be called superego demands. The question remains of what id and ego reactions are evoked.

Let us consider first those who do the initiating. Psychoanalytic theory gives full recognition to the instinctual desires of the older men in shaping the rituals, perhaps overestimating their importance. In assuring their own sexual ascendency, the elders combine hostility and superego strivings, the first by inhibiting their sons as potential sexual rivals, the second by teaching of tribal lore, assuring obedience to tradition. The actions of the elders are thus at the same time under the influence of both institutions of the mind: id and superego; indeed, they must be, since these men act as human beings, and human beings can never at any one time be motivated by only a single institution.

But what about those who are initiated? What are the positive appeals to their instincts in ceremonies that supposedly make such strong demands on their superegos or on their ability to integrate experiences? According to some students, these lie in the fact that the youngsters gain sexual freedom through initiation. But among the peoples who have developed the most elaborate initiation rites, children enjoy such freedom all their lives, and the rites can add nothing in this respect.

An analysis of the rituals makes it doubtful that only superego demands that are not equally id-motivated in both initiator and initiate are created or met in the young. There seems little reason to conclude that two sets of motivations —one in those who initiate and an entirely different one in those they initiate—are at work in a ritual that so successfully binds people together; psychoanalytic evidence suggests that the opposite is more probable.*[10]

Even the simplest anthropological explanation of the rites as a learning experience presupposes cooperation. But psychological investigations have shown convincingly that learning is only effective and lasting if the learner cooperates for his own motives. What is difficult and frustrating can only be surmounted by strong positive motivation. It may simply be a desire to master the content, or to pacify the superego and ego (which tell the student that the experience is necessary, despite id resistance), or to please a parent or teacher, or to gain status, etc. When the student is forced to learn against his resistance, the results may be diametrically opposite to the teacher's intentions.

In our highly organized society, in which the feelings and doings of adults and children are widely separated, it is true that teachers often teach children who are reluctant to learn. But even here the most successful teaching takes place when teacher and student are moved by

the parallel desire to transmit and receive, or even better, to share a common experience. These successful teaching experiences have positive connotations to both teacher and learner, and offer id, ego, and superego satisfactions to both at the same time. The most successful teaching of all occurs when both teacher and student are urged on by a similar, often unconscious, desire to master a common problem.

Psychoanalysis has also shown that parental efforts to impose cleanliness (for instance) will lead to very different results in learning and personality formation, depending on what the child brings to it in terms of expectations, past experience, etc.; whether he cooperates to please a loved parent or whether he refuses to defy a hated one. Precepts that are forcefully imposed by elders on the relatively helpless infant may lead to a host of different learnings and results —ranging from utter submission to total resistance, not to speak of an immense variety of sublimations and reaction formations.

In view of this it is unlikely that a series of supposedly traumatic experiences to which a number of adolescents are subjected against their wishes will lead to the uniform results desired by their elders. If the single result of the supposed trauma of circumcision is that the boys come to fear and obey tribal elders and to avoid incest, we might reasonably expect that toilet training should cause all children to become identically trained and compulsively clean. The more logical conclusion is that externally imposed ritual traumata should bring at least as varied results in primitive youngsters as externally imposed habits of cleanliness brings in our children. Probably the results would be even more varied, since initiation takes place when the child is older.

If, on the other hand, initiation is not entirely adult-imposed, if it partly satisfies important strivings of adolescents, then we can understand how the shared experience might produce similar results. In modern society, adolescents beset by common instinctual strivings try to be like one another, often in defiance of adults. Though comparisons between primitive society and our own are more suggestive than convincing, they may still serve to make a point that seems valid and significant for both.

Individuals seem to react dissimilarly to outside-imposed control of instinctual tendencies (as in toilet training); but when they react spontaneously and as a group to the problem of finding instinctual satisfaction, then individual de-

* Freud, in discussing the ritual defloration of girls, says that "Primitive custom appears to accord some recognition to the existence of the early sexual wish [of the girls] by assigning the duty of defloration to an elder, a priest, or a holy man, that is, to a father-substitute." Thus he recognizes the possibility that such rituals are id-motivated in the adolescent girl, that this rite may be as much desired by the girls as by those who perform it.

[10] S. Freud, "The Taboo of Virginity," Collected Papers, IV, p. 229.

velopment seems to be strikingly similar. If initiation were forcibly imposed on the adolescents, it would not lead to uniform consequences; if, on the other hand, it was even partially desired by both initiates and initiators, if it was a response to essentially similar strivings of the young, then the results might be relatively uniform.

Initiates, and possibly the initiators too, may feel basically ambivalent about specific rituals such as circumcision. Social pressure and approval may then lead to the more or less full satisfaction of one part of the ambivalent desire, and the token satisfaction, suppression, integration, or sublimation of the other.

To use again the example of teaching cleanliness: The human infant seems to have little interest in becoming clean. His ambivalence about toilet training results from outside influences—that is, the wish to please the parent is placed in opposition to the child's own natural inclinations. But in initiation, I believe, the ambivalence is inherently the adolescent's. He himself wishes to be grown up and also to be a child (to retain his own sex and to enjoy prerogatives of the other sex, etc.). But he also wishes to free himself of this inner ambivalence. In addition, social custom tells him which of its aspects he may satisfy and how he may deal with the others. Because adult demands and the youngster's inner wishes thus unfold in somewhat parallel fashion, the result may be more or less uniform for the group.

Considering these everyday observations on learning situations, perhaps we come to initiation rites with an extraneous frame of reference when we assume that an unwilling learner meets an overpowering, threatening, inimical teacher. This seems particularly misleading in the case of preliterate societies where the interests and activities of child and adult are so little differentiated. . . .

Behind many human rituals lies an interest in fertility, both the fertility of human beings and of their sources of food. And indeed, the economic and social well-being of any people depends on the regeneration of its food supply. In preliterate societies that have no means of rational control over their animal, plant, or human fertility, its people tend to rely on magico-religious ceremonial to affect it.

The society we are here most concerned with, that of the Australian aborigines, represents a cultural stage that predates the beginning of

animal breeding or agriculture; both of these techniques presuppose a concentrated interest in fertility, with first the desire, and later the ability, to assure procreation. Nevertheless, the Australians are very much concerned with procreation, and much of their ritual centers around it. "The Aborigine has no granaries, but he has, if we may use the term, these 'spiritual' storehouses, in that they insure him against starvation, and give him a sense of security and confidence in regard to his food-supply for the coming year."[11] The story the aborigines tell is as follows: "As the totemic ancestors passed through the country they felt stones or sometimes a tree, each of which is supposed to contain the *gunin* of some animal, bird, fish, reptile, tuber, and so on. . . . By rubbing one of these or striking it with brushes and uttering a spell, the *gunin* will go forth and cause the species with which it is associated to multiply."[12]

This is evidence both of the resources and desires of a surviving preliterate people in relation to fertility. We have less exact but suggestive evidence that paleolithic man was likewise concerned with procreation. But the subject of greatest interest here is not merely whether and to what degree religious rites were connected in early times with a desire for abundance of animals and men—and hence with procreation and childbirth—but whether this function was thought to be female or male. In the Old Testament, where a male God promises to make males numerous as the stars, it was clearly a male function. Sometimes it is assumed that the rites of the early hunters were masculine in nature, and that the feminine element came only with agriculture. There is indeed ample evidence that, with the development of agriculture, women came to play a very important role in fecundity ceremonies. It was believed that the livelihood of the tribes depended on women and on the rites they performed; that without these, no crops would grow.

In recent years, ever more abundant evidence comes to light suggesting that even in the days of the earliest hunters man's mind was concerned not only with conjuring up the animals he hunted for food but also with magically increasing their number. It seems, for example, that we shall have to revise our earlier notions of the meaning of paleolithic cave paintings of animals and of so-called hunting scenes. Originally these paintings were thought to represent

[11] Kaberry, *op. cit.*, p. 203.
[12] *Ibid.*

magic efforts to assure good hunting of the animals depicted. Now it is believed that, possibly in association with rituals, they were efforts to stimulate animal procreation. Raphael, for example, says that among the main purposes of the paintings "besides the magic of hunting there was the magic fertility."[13] He also discusses drawings in which "animals pictured one inside the other may represent pregnancy."

These relatively recent analyses do not settle the question of whether any ceremonies—increase or otherwise—were performed, and if so, whether they were performed by men or by women. Beyond this remains the incontrovertible fact of the paintings' location. Since these hunters lived in caves, it is natural that the paintings should be found on cave walls. But the caves contain rooms that are easily accessible, as well as others that can only be reached with great difficulty; and it was the latter that the artists generally chose. Many authors have commented with surprise on the fact that the paintings are so commonly located in almost inaccessible places. In reading their reports, I was most impressed by the tortuous paths leading to the pictures, by the fact that they are hidden behind serious obstacles and often cannot be reached except by crawling through narrows.

Levy,[14] for example, speaks of "the formidable nature" of the long, narrow, slippery corridors, often crossed by waterfalls, and the chimneys that must be negotiated to reach the halls of the pictures. To illustrate: The chamber of Clotilde can only be approached on hands and knees. At one point the passage to Font-de-Gaune becomes a tunnel through which a large person can pass only with great difficulty. To reach La Pasiega the visitor passes through a manhole below which a river runs, and the painted animals can only be seen above the precipices that border it. Levy and others insist that if the purpose of the paintings had been simply to assure success in hunting (not to speak of "pure" artistic creation), their placement at such inaccessible locations would remain incomprehensible. Many who have explored them have concluded that their location must have had a specific purpose. As Marett[15] said, no one would dream of hedging round a mere picture gallery with such trying turnstiles.

[13] M. Raphael, *Prehistoric Cave Paintings* (Washington, D.C.: Pantheon Books, 1945), pp. 5–6.
[14] G. R. Levy, *The Gate of Horn* (London: Faber and Faber, 1946), pp. 11–12.
[15] R. R. Marett, *The Threshold of Religion* (2nd ed.; London: Methuen & Co., 1914). p. 218.

All this suggests to me one possibility: that an effort was made to reproduce the setting in which procreation takes place. If so, then to crawl through narrow, wet channels on entering may have represented how access is gained to the secret place of procreation; on leaving, the process of birth might have been reenacted symbolically. The paintings were therefore executed at places that may have been viewed as representing the womb, where animals come into existence. So it is possible that early man was creating a new animal, the painted one, in a place which to him represented the womb, so that the real animal might be induced to do likewise.

This interpretation of the cave paintings' location has not been suggested, to my knowledge, by those who have written about them, but Levy at least sees a definite and close connection between the pictures, the rituals of early man, and their emphasis on birth, death, and rebirth. She stresses how often gravid female figures can be found among the remnants of the same paleolithic culture in the same places, and notes that many of these figures and other female symbols are found lying face downward. She suggests that some significance may have been attached, even before the beginnings of agriculture, to contact with the earth—that, in fact, the cave had already become "a Mother."

Among modern preliterate people, Levy stresses the importance of the ritual re-enactment of traveling a long, winding path, and how important are the experiences that can only be had in caves. Speaking about the Australian aborigines, and quoting Spencer and Gillen, she says:

"In the well-known ceremony for the propagation of the witchetty-grub, the winding march is taken to the sacred caves in which stones have been deposited to represent this insect and her eggs. After contact has been established, first between the stones and their own persons, later with the sacred rock . . . they return to enter the cave-like 'chrysalis' which has meanwhile been constructed at the camp. . . . From this they emerge singing the re-born grub. . . .[16]

"This applies equally to the initiation ceremonies of the boys and girls, whose period of seclusion seems to have been passed in the bush, with the exception of novice magicians who repaired to a cave for their sleep of death and rebirth."[17]

[16] Levy, *op. cit.*, p. 27.
[17] *Ibid.*, pp. 36–37.

Levy leaves little doubt that these caves represent the womb in which the initiates are born again. I shall not follow much further her speculations on the connection between a mother goddess and the pregnant female figures, beyond the following quotations:

"It does appear possible, indeed, that on all the continents where later civilizations did not influence her development, the 'Mother Goddess' disappeared from the religious system, as her images disappeared from the Magdalenian hearths. In South Eastern Europe, on the other hand, in the North African hinterland and Western Asia, the great discoveries of the succeeding eras, especially the domestication of animals and the cultivation of corn, imparted to this conception an increasingly deep significance. . . ."[18]

"The little statues of mammoth ivory, stone, or conglomerate, represent in general an upright woman with small featureless bent head and feeble arms usually laid upon her huge breasts, with very wide or deep hips, loins and abdomen, and legs dwindling to small or nonexistent feet. . . .

"Some cult of human fertility is indicated, which was brought into touch with the rites for animal reproduction in the caves. This cult appears, on the evidence of the statuettes, to have originated among the Aurignacians of Eastern Europe and spread westward, where the figures are found in smaller numbers, occasionally possessing great formal artistry."[19]

The importance of the gravid female figures is further emphasized by the face that no male figures have been found. This is consistent with Braidwood's findings in the excavation of the village of Jarmo, which he considers the earliest permanent settlement of man; at Jarmo there was a combination of a hunting and agricultural setting, a community in transition toward what Braidwood calls "incipient agriculture and animal domestication."[20] There, too, gravid female figures are among the predominant ritual artifacts, the most characteristic being "a seated pregnant woman with rather fat buttocks—probably a 'mother goddess' symbol of fertility." No male or phallic figures were discovered.

We have no evidence that paleolithic man practiced circumcision, as the modern hunters

and food gatherers of Australia do. But evidence from prehistory does indicate that the earliest man had a deep and abiding interest in fertility, and that if he had a ritual life, the ceremony of increase was probably its most essential part. Great effort went into the creation of pregnant female figures of the Venus of Willendorf type.

In Australian aboriginal society a relationship clearly exists between the rites of fertility and initiation. In mythical times, according to Strehlow,[21] they were not separated at all, there being only one great series of ceremonies to initiate the young and to assure totemic increase. In modern times, during the initiation of aboriginal boys, various totemistic ceremonies take place to assure an abundance of food animals. Seemingly more important even than circumcision or subincision is the fact that for the first time boys are permitted to witness the fertility ceremonies. Thus the puberty rites of boys among these people is an initiation into the secret of how to influence magically the increase of food animals and edible fruits.

On these occasions, men decorate themselves (i.e., change themselves symbolically) to represent the animal they wish to procreate abundantly; it seems plausible that the changes they make on their own bodies have the same purpose—to assure their own fertility. The difference is that the change into the animal is only temporary, the decorations being discarded or washed off after the ceremony is over, while the changes made on their penes are permanent. The fact that among certain Australian tribes the initiation ceremony always takes place before harvest may also be significant. Thus the puberty rite is probably meant to assure procreation of the human animal, while other increase rites, from the *intichiuma* of the Australians to the buffalo dances of the Sioux, encourage the multiplication of food animals.

If we are allowed to draw inferences from some modern preliterate societies to paleolithic man, available evidence would justify the conclusion that increase rites were the most important ceremonies of the earliest human societies and that initiation ceremonies may be mainly special subforms.*

[18] *Ibid.*, p. 53.

[19] *Ibid.*, pp. 55–57.

[20] R. J. Braidwood, "From Cave to Village," *Scientific American*, CLXXXVII, 4 (1952), 64, and private communication.

[21] C. Strehlow, *Die Aranda und Loritja Stämme in Zentral Australien* (Frankfurt am Main: Joseph Baer & Co., 1910), p. 2.

* By the time anthropologists came to observe these rites, their order of importance may have become reversed, with initiation rites the more widespread and elaborate, until they could well be regarded as the central rites of primitive society. Here the relative im-

During the ceremonies of the Uli cult of New Ireland (neither an initiation ritual nor an initiation society) elaborate male figures called Ulis are carved. They are powerfully proportioned, bearded figures, whose oversized breasts and phalli express the power of fertility, the cult which they serve. They are not viewed as hermaphroditic; on the contrary, they are considered the more male because they also possess female sex powers and characteristics. The ceremonies in which these figures were used sometimes lasted a year, and included dances in which the men tied carved female breasts around their chests. These rites were extremely sacred and all females were excluded from them. Uli figures were never discarded, but were carefully preserved for future ceremonies. Nevermann says that both the Uli figures and the dances seem to have originated in a fertility cult, and Krämer[22] adds that the oversized breasts and phallus express the great power of fecundity. Thus men have used other methods than manipulation of the penis by which to claim a greater share in procreation.

Certain of the Goulbourn Islanders who have had considerable contact with white civilization and have come to understand a little better the male contribution to procreation, have evolved an interesting variation of the mother goddess. The Berndts,[23] in discussing the fertility goddess and main deity of these tribes (who practice neither circumcision nor subincision), report that the beliefs and ceremonies surrounding her are less vivid than elsewhere, rituals and beliefs connected with the snake having been superimposed. At this moment, the religious beliefs of these tribes may thus be in transition. The predominance of a female fertility goddess may be giving way to the predominance of a male (or bisexual) fertility symbol. The original concept of the fertility goddess, however, is neither lost nor seriously obscured. One of the central rites of this transitional cult is the re-enactment of the fight for predominance between the male and the female principle. The female tries to assert her superiority, but the male deity, by means of a phallic symbol, succeeds in taking revenge on her. Still, many details emphasize that the ritual was, and still is, closely related to the mother goddess. For example:

"At Goulbourn Island the sacred ground is the body of the Mother, and the 'outside' (secular) name of the 'u:ba:r [phallic symbol] is 'kamo:mo, which is the ordinary word for a mother. It is said that she comes out when she hears it is ceremonial time; her spirit enters the 'u:ba:r, which is made and erected . . . for the purpose, and she 'talks'—that is, the beating of the 'u:ba:r. She is calling for everybody to come, but only the men can enter her presence and her body. . . . Should the beating [of the 'u:ba:r] be stopped, her spirit will go also and the ritual will lose its potency; she maintains the essence of sanctity, and gives the participants power to perform their ritual actions and dancing. It is she who attends to the increase of the natural species."[24]

Even in the snake ritual, therefore, everything depends on the female fertility goddess. While this ritual may illustrate a transition from a maternal to a phallic religion, under the influence of a growing knowledge of procreation, we are here mainly concerned with developments that may have taken place before such masculine gods appeared. Phallicism does not seem to exist in a society such as that of the Australians who believe that the man's contribution to procreation lies only in "finding" the spirit child, and his "making a way" for the child to be born. It should be stressed once more that their ritual life must be understood in terms of their utter dependence on the chance multiplication of their food sources; animals are not abundant, and the people lack the knowledge needed for agriculture or animal husbandry. Thus their concern with fertility is almost inevitable.

Whether or not there is an intrinsic link between castration and circumcision, they are now so closely connected in the thinking of many persons that a discussion of puberty rites must also consider castration. As an institution, castration appeared comparatively late in history, among relatively sophisticated peoples. It was then performed by the castrate to please, or to make himself more like, an overpowering mother figure.

Historical reviews tell us little about whether, or how commonly, castration actually took place

portance of rituals merely followed the development of society. In our own society, for example, fertility seems again to be the most elaborate ritual of our private lives. According to religious precepts and the official moral code, procreation must not occur without marriage. Thus, at least in official doctrine, our principal ritual is concerned with procreation, if not with fertility.

[22] A. Krämer, *Die Malanggane von Tombara* (München: Georg Müller, 1925), pp. 60–61.

[23] Berndt and Berndt, *Sexual Behavior*, p. 110.

[24] *Ibid.*, p. 127.

in preliterate society. Browe[25] and others believe that the custom probably originated with the Hittites and spread first to the Semitic and then to other Asian and European civilizations. Like other authors, including Weigert-Vowinkel, Browe stresses the practice of castration among the priests of the mother goddesses as part of their rites. Compared with this ritual castration in the service of a female deity, castration as a punishment inflicted by men on men for religious reasons, or by law, is a comparatively late institution. In the Middle Ages it was part of the talion law, with no special sexual connotations. Among the Germans at this period it was a punishment for sacreligious acts, but only as part of total dismemberment.

In combat or war, however, castration appears in much earlier times as the toll exacted by the victor from his defeated enemy. In Egypt this form of it was known in both religious and military practice; witness the eternal fight between Horus and Set in which Horus castrated Set for tearing out Horus' eye. Similar tales of castrating the vanquished occur in other mythologies, particularly the Greek. The victor's main purpose was to gain for himself the masculine power of his victim.

In Egypt, killing and castrating the conquered in war was later supplemented by the custom of creating eunuchs who could act as servants, especially in the harem. Similarly, the Persians under Darius castrated the handsomest boys after the conquests of Chios, Lesbos, and Tenedos, and then used them as eunuchs or for homosexual pleasure. In the Western Hemisphere, castration was known at least to the Carib-speaking natives of the Antilles. According to Roth, they "practised it on their boy prisoners, who were subsequently fattened for the table."[26] Castration in later times, for artistic purposes (to retain high adult voices in the papal choir) is of little interest here.

Thus the known history of the castration of men by men, though meager, shows no connection with age-grading ceremonies at puberty and no direct connection with jealousy between father and son or with any psychological motives connected with the Oedipal situation or the in-

cest taboo. Speculation based on these connections remain unsupported by factual evidence.

The story of castration in the service of the great maternal deities is different. There we are in no doubt that the mother goddess required emasculation as the price of grace.[27] Weigert-Vowinkel has summarized for us Daly's analysis of Hindu mythology as it pertains to the castration complex. In it she refers to the "flood of uncontrollable fear" of the castrating maternal divinity which permeates that literature. She suggests that conflicts characterized by the castration theme, which were also prominent in the myths of the Trobrianders, may be typical of matriarchal societies, the myths having been invented after the rites, to explain them.

Of the rites of the maternal deities, those of Cybele are perhaps the best known. They tell us that "... at the peak of exaltation on *deis sanguinis*, March 24, every one of the Galloi [priests of Cybele] voluntarily castrated himself by cutting off the entire genitals with a consecrated stone knife.... The use of bronze or iron was forbidden for this act. Women who dedicated themselves to the goddess in like manner cut off one or both breasts."[28] Even in ancient times it was assumed that the command to use only stone implements for self-mutilation testified to the great antiquity of the practice.

Here too, self-mutilation was not restricted to one sex, just as male circumcision is often paralleled by the manipulation and mutilation of female organs. The Cybele rites reflect deviate tendencies in both men and women; either an inordinate desire to be, or an extreme fear of, the opposite sex. Still, mutilation of the men was much more severe than that of women; the male sacrificed his primary sex characteristics, the female only the secondary ones.

During the course of the rites "... the flood of orgiastic emotion even spread to the onlookers and they, too, castrated themselves. With their genitals in their hands, the worshippers ran through the streets and threw them into some house, from which they then received women's clothing, according to custom."[29] Considering what the castrates received for the gift of their genitals, it seems legitimate to infer

[25] Browe, *op. cit.*, p. 63.

[26] W. E. Roth, "An Introductory Study of the Arts, Crafts, and Customs of the Guiana Indians," *38th Annual Report of the Bureau of American Ethnology... 1916–1917* (Washington: Government Printing Office, 1924), pp. 417, 591.

[27] E. Weigert-Vowinkel, "The Cult and Mythology of the Magna Mater from the Standpoint of Psychoanalysis," *Psychiatry*, I (1938), pp. 348–349.

[28] *Ibid.*, p. 352.

[29] *Ibid.*, p. 353.

that they threw them to or at women, who, in return, gave them female garments.*

Once the devotees of the mother goddess were castrated, their genitals and masculine clothing were carried into the bridal chamber of Cybele. Thereafter, they wore only women's clothing, were anointed and wore their hair long. Latin and Greek writers usually speak of them in the feminine gender.

This example of ritual castration, and many others not mentioned here, indicates that it was exacted by maternal figures as a sign of devotion and submission on the part of their male followers and particularly of the priests who were closest in their service. Of women, other signs of devotion were required; only the priests had to approximate the other sex in attire and behavior. Their becoming "female" after self-mutilation had no counterpart in what was expected of women serving the goddess.† The fact that the mutilation was self-chosen and self-inflicted suggests that the psychological motivation came from deeper layers of the personality than would be true if it were imposed by others. It also indicates that men were ready and willing to become "female" in order to share women's superior powers. . . .

If the basic purpose of male initiation were to teach tribal lore or to ritualize maturity, it would be easy to see why it should be marked by elaborate ceremonies intended to give it special dignity and impressiveness. But if these were its only purposes, it is hard to find a plausible reason for its being shrouded in secrecy and forbidden to women and children. Tribal lore would be more effectively taught if every member of the community were instructed repeatedly, and from childhood. A deep impression can be made when the entire population takes part in or observes a ceremony, as in inaugurations or coronations. If secrecy is used for greater impressiveness there must be particular reasons that make secrecy more effective than wide public participation.

Sometimes the purpose of secrecy is to keep a magic power from the hands of unbelievers, or from enemies who may use it for sorcery. But in many cases it is intended to make those excluded think that initiates have superior powers.

Accepting for the moment my interpretation of initiation rites, it may be inferred that the act of birth is kept as great a secret from men as the act of initiation is from women. This indeed appears to be the case. Among the Australian aborigines, little ceremonial secrecy accompanies first menstruation or the so-called initiation of women; but childbirth rituals are so secret that they evaded the attention of most observers.

It may also be that the androcentric bias of male observers was reinforced by the reluctance of aboriginal women to let any man learn of this, their greatest secret. In any case, we owe most of our knowledge of these rituals to women investigators, and even Kaberry[30] reported that she found it harder to get an account of the childbirth songs from the women than to discuss initiation with men. She lived with the natives for seven months before she finally heard the first of these songs, although she had previously seen a women's secret corroboree.

"Now although the men know some of the details of childbirth . . . still they are ignorant of those songs which are sacred . . . [and] which for all their simplicity are fraught with the power that they possess by virtue of their supernatural origin. In so far as they are commands which appear to achieve their result automatically, they may be considered magical; but their efficacy is attributed to the fact that they were first uttered by the female totemic ancestors.

---

* Fantasies about similar acts occur today. The wish that a man should cut off his genitals and throw them to a woman was expressed by a schizoid pubertal girl living at the Orthogenic School. She had only recently begun to menstruate when one day, in a public park near the School, she observed a man in the bushes who was urinating, or exposing himself to her, or both. Turning to her woman counselor and another girl she said with great glee, "He'll cut off his penis and throw it at us." Fantasies about boys who are turned into girls and then have to wear female clothing are so common among neurotic children, both boys and girls, that they need hardly be mentioned. While such ideas reflect castration anxiety, they originate in even earlier experiences, . . .

† In this context, but without wishing to speculate too far, I should like to point out that it was approximately in the geographical area where the mother goddesses were worshipped that the use of harem eunuchs was widespread. The explanation generally given is that eunuchs are safe as harem servants because they cannot have sexual relations with the women in their care. But if this were the only reason, one might ask why female servants were not used. Although it is perhaps far-fetched, the possibility might be considered that this custom was a remnant of the rites of the mother goddess. It might also be based partly on the women's desire to have subservient to them men who had first been deprived of their male sexuality. The castrated priests of Cybele were, after all, as much servants of the mother goddess as eunuchs were the servants of women in the harem.

[30] Kaberry, op. cit., p. 241.

They have the same sanctions as the increase ceremonies, . . . the cult totems, subincision and circumcision."[31]

The extreme secrecy of male initiation rites and childbirth ritual therefore suggests that they may be parallel phenomena; the parallel between male and female initiation seems external and nonessential by comparison.

On the other hand, while men speak of the secret of women and mean their sex apparatus and functions, women do not make a similar association to the secret of men. They may even scoff at the very idea of men's secrets. Berndt,[32] in discussing the origin of the Australian Kunapipi rites, refers to one of the myths that tells how originally the men "had nothing: no sacred objects, no sacred ceremonies, the women had everything."[33] So one day the men stole the women's sacred objects and took them back to their own camp. The mythical Wawilak sisters, on finding that their sacred objects had disappeared, decided that perhaps it was just as well the men had taken them, since men could now carry out most of the ritual for them while they busied themselves chiefly with raising families and collecting food.

Or as one of Berndt's present-day informants told him: " 'But really we have been stealing what belong to them (the women), for it is mostly all woman's business; and since it concerns them it belongs to them. Men have nothing to do really, except copulate, it belongs to the women. All that belonging to those *Wawilak*, the baby, the blood, the yelling, their dancing, all that concerns the women; but every time we have to trick them. Women can't see what men are doing, although it really is their own business, but we can see their side . . . in the beginning we had nothing, because men had been doing nothing; we took these things from the women.' "[34]

Summarizing the question of why men and not women now act out these fertility rites, Berndt concludes that women "know that the rituals are principally concerned with peculiarly feminine functions and that men are carrying out the more strenuous features of ceremonial life. 'These rituals,' said one informant, 'are just like a man copulating with a woman, he does all the hard working so that the women can carry out the really important business of child-

birth.' This may be a one-sided attitude, but it does adequately express local native reasoning in this matter."

I cannot accept the obvious rationalization as to the cause of the division of labor. I suggest that the main reason for the existence of the rites is the men's desire for an equally important "business."[35]

The Need for Secrecy

Other rituals go beyond a mere simple assertion that men have significant secrets. They are found in cultures as diverse as the preliterate African and highly civilized Greek, and include the long series of rites claiming the rebirth of initiates by men. Rites that claim occurrences contrary to nature, but that cannot demonstrate those events, must be kept secret. Otherwise the participants cannot tell themselves that such events have in fact taken place. Moreover, secrecy protects the believer against the doubt of sceptics who are kept from collecting evidence that might destroy the belief. Since initiation rites serve purposes that can be achieved only in symbol but not in reality, its fictions must be hidden if the devotees are to enjoy the psychological benefits of symbolic achievement. Secrecy is thus necessary for the continuing satisfaction of the needs of the believers.

Among some peoples, women may be killed even today for observing these rites. The Poro society's method of dealing with a woman who spies on the men shows it is her ability to reveal the secrets to others, rather than her own presence or knowledge, that destroys the power of initiation. Such a woman is not necessarily killed; she is often permitted to live in the initiation hut and to observe the ceremonies freely. But once initiation is over, she must remain mute for the rest of her life. If she should ever break down and talk, even if only in a dream, she is immediately killed by a member of the society.

My views are not new. Lowie,[36] for example, has expressed them in regard to the secrecy of the bull-roarer,* the swinging of which accom-

[31] *Ibid.*, pp. 244–245.

[32] Berndt, *Kunapipi*, p. 8.

[33] *Ibid.*

[34] *Ibid.*, p. 55.

[35] *Ibid.*, p. 58.

[36] R. H. Lowie, *Primitive Society* (New York: Boni and Liveright, 1920), pp. 265–266.

* The bull-roarer is made of a small, flat piece of wood or stone, carved or otherwise decorated with sacred designs. Through a hole in one end a string is passed; swung rapidly it makes a booming, humming noise. In many ceremonies bull-roarers are swung, and it is maintained that the noise so produced is the voice of certain spirits.

panies the most sacred ceremonies of the Australians. Women and children are taught to regard the curious buzzing noise of the bull-roarer as the voice of a spirit that presides over the ceremony. But one of the secrets revealed to initiates, with great emphasis on the necessity of hiding it from the women, is the true nature of the bull-roarer and how men came to possess it.

The everyday behavior of children offers parallel observations that suggest further explanation of the nature of this secrecy. Children often claim to possess secret knowledge, just because they feel so lacking in knowledge. A child will boast of some special piece of information which he does not have or which is as commonplace as the whirling of a flat stick (like the bull-roarer). Under no circumstances will he reveal the secret, since its only purpose is to give him status in the eyes of another person. By inventing a secret language, for example, and using it in the presence of a parent or older sibling whom the child considers superior to himself, he tries to convince the other person as well as himself that he is not inferior since he has certain important abilities or knowledge.

Blackwood[37] too thinks that the main purpose of the male secret societies is to hoodwink the women. The men do not hesitate to kill a few boys in order to convince the women that all have been killed and that men have brought some of them back to life. This parallels the myth of the bull-roarer in which they killed all the women to keep them from telling that the bull-roarer was stolen by men. The men even cut down groves of areca palms, although the areca nut is a highly prized delicacy, to show women the power and malignancy of the male ghosts who kill their sons. Like the neurotic who will readily destroy important possessions to keep his unrealistic defenses intact, these men destroy the cherished palm trees to impress the women more thoroughly with the power to create life.

The writer on female initiation finds relatively little material to work on. Partly because most investigators have been men, and partly because male rites are more prominant, the literature on female initiation is thin. But, on one point, female rites offer better evidence than male. In the myths explaining boys' rituals it is said that manipulation of the male genital was once performed by women; but in present practice the actual interference is nearly always performed by men. In the manipulation of the female sex organs, on the other hand, certain rites were and are performed by men and certain others by women. Thus in girls' rites we may find a clue to which types of manipulation are imposed by the other sex (and possibly why) and which are self-chosen or suggested and imposed by persons of the same sex on each other.

Comparing manipulation of the female sex apparatus by men and by women, it can be seen that, by and large, manipulation by men is destructive, showing an aggressive enmity that is most readily explained by fear or envy. Manipulation by women, on the other hand, results more often than not in greater sex enjoyment and in an extension of the sex apparatus that makes the existing organs more like those of men. That the labia, as Herskovits[38] points out, become by artificial manipulation more muscular, harder, less flexible, is to make them more like the erect penis.

These practices, no less than the rites of boys, suggest again that the human being's envy of the other sex leads to the desire to acquire similar organs, and to gain power and control over the genitals of the other sex.

[37] B. Blackwood, *Both Sides of Buka Passage* (New York: Oxford University Press, 1935), p. 244.

[38] *Ibid.*, p. 245.

In "Symbolic Wounds" Bruno Bettelheim discusses the way initiation ceremonies reveal the basic fears which emanate from the male's envy of the female and the female's envy of the male. The author contends that in prior times these ceremonies enabled individuals to express deep emotional needs. These rites made it easier to understand the differences "between the biological and social roles according to nature and the norms of society." The young were motivated by their desire to integrate opposites within their character, and to be recognized as adult members of their society. Bettelheim focuses on the male's need to affirm his maturity by undergoing a ritual which entails the shedding of blood. He concurs with Margaret Mead that women, because of menstruation, do not need as elaborate a ceremony as men. Bettelheim contends that this conflict appears in modern children who suffer from psychological maladjustment.

1 Discuss Bettelheim's hypothesis of sexual envy between the sexes. How well does he document his thesis? In what ways does he fail to prove his thesis? In which of the warrior myths do you detect sexual envy of the opposite sex? Explain! In a discussion do men and women resent or defend any allusion that they might have traits of the opposite sex? Is this more prevalent among men or women? What does this suggest? You might use Bettelheim's contention that men envy women having babies.

2 How does Bettelheim connect the initiation ceremony to the individual psyche? How does the adolescent of today affirm or deny Bettelheim's point of view? How does Bettelheim relate the psyche's needs to social pressure? In which of the warrior myths does the hero learn to adapt to social pressure? Explain!

3 Discuss Bettelheim's view that underlying the initiation ceremony is the need to understand the process of fertility. What is the purpose of ritualizing fertility? In which of the warrior myths does the hero struggle with the problem of procreation (continuing the life of the group)? In the spring of the year, what evidence is there that we still have remnants of fertility rites?

4 What does Bettelheim mean by ritual surgery? In which of the warrior myths do you see evidence of symbolic castration? Who is responsible for this? Discuss the implications of your answer.

5 Do you agree that the initiation ceremony is more important for males than females? In which of the warrior myths is the hero attempting to define himself apart from females?

6 How do men know in the modern world whether they have reached sexual maturity? What are the implications of this complex process? Does this cause anxiety and mistrust between men and women? Explain!

7 What insights into adolescent behavior does one gain from Bettelheim's discussion? How does this essay help one to better understand the complexities which exist between males and females during adolescence?

8 How does this essay reveal:
a the adolescent's need to be separated from the family?
b the adolescent's need to be recognized as an adult?
c the need for males and females to find analogies which will help them understand their opposites?

Hero as Antihero

In these pictures from the films of Humphrey Bogart, we see emerge the rites-of-passage pattern: separation, initiation, and return. In the first scene from *Casablanca*, Bogart, the American exile, finally decides to fight against Nazism after trying to remain noninvolved. The appearance of Ingrid Bergman brings Bogart to his initiation; she helps Bogart become a man. He allows her to go, but his return reveals an acceptance of the ideals of brotherhood. In the second scene from *To Have and Have Not*, Bogart is once again an exile acting only for himself. Lauren Bacall helps initiate him into the role of manhood. During their first meeting, Miss Bacall looks toward Bogart to light her cigarette. He sizes her up and decides to toss her the matches instead. Each character is on familiar ground; he will act with her only as an equal. In this film, both Bogart and Bacall emerge as a man and woman capable of existing in a hostile world where corruption seems to outweigh ideals. In the last scene from *The African Queen*, Bogart again is separated from those who fight to stop the Nazis. This time Katherine Hepburn helps Bogart through his difficult separation and "second birth" as a man. In this case Bogart has passion and ideals. In his films, Bogart appears as an antihero; unlike Gilgamesh or Achilles, he is a loner. He is more in the tradition of Hector. Bogart fights even though corruption still exists. He makes his existential choice to be a man with the help of those women who pledge him their loyalty; he is a representation of the American male who fights to protect his woman.

THE THREE-DAY BLOW

ERNEST HEMINGWAY
from *In Our Time*

The rain stopped as Nick turned into the road that went up through the orchard. The fruit had been picked and the fall wind blew through the bare trees. Nick stopped and picked up a Wagner apple from beside the road, shiny in the brown grass from the rain. He put the apple in the pocket of his Mackinaw coat.

The road came out of the orchard on to the top of the hill. There was the cottage, the porch bare, smoke coming from the chimney. In back was the garage, the chicken coop and the second-growth timber like a hedge against the woods behind. The big trees swayed far over in the wind as he watched. It was the first of the autumn storms.

As Nick crossed the open field above the orchard the door of the cottage opened and Bill came out. He stood on the porch looking out.

"Well, Wemedge," he said.

"Hey, Bill," Nick said, coming up the steps.

They stood together, looking out across the country, down over the orchard, beyond the road, across the lower fields and the woods of the point to the lake. The wind was blowing straight down the lake. They could see the surf along Ten Mile point.

"She's blowing," Nick said.

"She'll blow like that for three days," Bill said.

"Is your dad in?" Nick said.

"No. He's out with the gun. Come on in."

Nick went inside the cottage. There was a big fire in the fireplace. The wind made it roar. Bill shut the door.

"Have a drink?" he said.

He went out to the kitchen and came back with two glasses and a pitcher of water. Nick reached the whisky bottle from the shelf above the fireplace.

"All right?" he said.

"Good," said Bill.

They sat in front of the fire and drank the Irish whisky and water.

"It's got a swell, smoky taste," Nick said, and looked at the fire through the glass.

"That's the peat," Bill said.

"You can't get peat into liquor," Nick said.

"That doesn't make any difference," Bill said.

"You ever seen any peat?" Nick asked.

"No," said Bill.

"Neither have I," Nick said.

His shoes, stretched out on the hearth, began to steam in front of the fire.

"Better take your shoes off," Bill said.

"I haven't got any socks on."

"Take them off and dry them and I'll get you some," Bill said. He went upstairs into the loft and Nick heard him walking about overhead. Upstairs was open under the roof and was where Bill and his father and he, Nick, sometimes slept. In back was a dressing room. They moved the cots back out of the rain and covered them with rubber blankets.

Bill came down with a pair of heavy wool socks.

"It's getting too late to go around without socks," he said.

"I hate to start them again," Nick said. He pulled the socks on and slumped back in the chair, putting his feet up on the screen in front of the fire.

"You'll dent in the screen," Bill said. Nick swung his feet over to the side of the fireplace.

"Got anything to read?" he asked.

"Only the paper."

"What did the Cards do?"

"Dropped a double header to the Giants."

"That ought to cinch it for them."

"It's a gift," Bill said. "As long as McGraw can buy every good ball player in the league there's nothing to it."

"He can't buy them all," Nick said.

"He buys all the ones he wants," Bill said. "Or he makes them discontented so they have to trade them to him."

"Like Heinie Zim," Nick agreed.

"That bonehead will do him a lot of good." Bill stood up.

"He can hit," Nick offered. The heat from the fire was baking his legs.

"He's a sweet fielder, too," Bill said. "But he loses ball games."

"Maybe that's what McGraw wants him for," Nick suggested.

"Maybe," Bill agreed.

"There's always more to it than we know about," Nick said.

"Of course. But we've got pretty good dope for being so far away."

"Like how much better you can pick them if you don't see the horses."

"That's it."

Bill reached down the whisky bottle. His big hand went all the way around it. He poured the whisky into the glass Nick held out.

"How much water?"

"Just the same."

He sat down on the floor beside Nick's chair.

"It's good when the fall storms come, isn't it?" Nick said.

"It's swell."

"It's the best time of year," Nick said.

"Wouldn't it be hell to be in town?" Bill said.

"I'd like to see the World Series," Nick said.

"Well, they're always in New York or Philadelphia now," Bill said. "That doesn't do us any good."

"I wonder if the Cards will ever win a pennant?"

"Not in our lifetime," Bill said.

"Gee, they'd go crazy," Nick said.

"Do you remember when they got going that once before they had the train wreck?"

"Boy!" Nick said, remembering.

Bill reached over to the table under the window for the book that lay there, face down, where he had put it when he went to the door. He held his glass in one hand and the book in the other, leaning back against Nick's chair.

"What are you reading?"

"Richard Feverel."

"I couldn't get into it."

"It's all right," Bill said. "It ain't a bad book, Wemedge."

"What else have you got I haven't read?" Nick asked.

"Did you read the Forest Lovers?"

"Yup. That's the one where they go to bed every night with the naked sword between them."

"That's a good book, Wemedge."

"It's a swell book. What I couldn't ever understand was what good the sword would do. It would have to stay edge up all the time because if it went over flat you could roll right over it and it wouldn't make any trouble."

"It's a symbol," Bill said.

"Sure," said Nick, "but it isn't practical."

"Did you ever read Fortitude?"

"It's fine," Nick said. "That's a real book. That's where his old man is after him all the time. Have you got any more by Walpole?"

"The Dark Forest," Bill said. "It's about Russia."

"What does he know about Russia?" Nick asked.

"I don't know. You can't ever tell about those guys. Maybe he was there when he was a boy. He's got a lot of dope on it."

"I'd like to meet him," Nick said.

"I'd like to meet Chesterton," Bill said.

"I wish he was here now," Nick said. "We'd take him fishing to the 'Voix tomorrow."

"I wonder if he'd like to go fishing," Bill said.

"Sure," said Nick. "He must be about the best guy there is. Do you remember the *Flying Inn?*"

> Thank him for his kind intentions;
> Go and pour them down the sink.' "
> " 'If an angel out of heaven
> Gives you something else to drink,

"That's right," said Nick. "I guess he's a better guy than Walpole."

"Oh, he's a better guy, all right," Bill said.

"But Walpole's a better writer."

"I don't know," Nick said. "Chesterton's a classic."

"Walpole's a classic, too," Bill insisted.

"I wish we had them both here," Nick said. "We'd take them both fishing to the 'Voix tomorrow."

"Let's get drunk," Bill said.

"All right," Nick agreed.

"My old man won't care," Bill said.

"Are you sure?" said Nick.

"I know it," Bill said.

"I'm a little drunk now," Nick said.

"You aren't drunk," Bill said.

He got up from the floor and reached for the whisky bottle. Nick held out his glass. His eyes fixed on it while Bill poured.

Bill poured the glass half full of whisky.

"Put in your own water," he said. "There's just one more shot."

"Got any more?" Nick asked.

"There's plenty more but dad only likes me to drink what's open."

"Sure," said Nick.

"He says opening bottles is what makes drunkards," Bill explained.

"That's right," said Nick. He was impressed. He had never thought of that before. He had always thought it was solitary drinking that made drunkards.

"How is your dad?" he asked respectfully.

"He's all right," Bill said. "He gets a little wild sometimes."

"He's a swell guy," Nick said. He poured water into his glass out of the pitcher. It mixed slowly with the whisky. There was more whisky than water.

"You bet your life he is," Bill said.

"My old man's all right," Nick said.

"You're damn right he is," said Bill.

"He claims he's never taken a drink in his life," Nick said, as though announcing a scientific fact.

"Well, he's a doctor. My old man's a painter. That's different."

"He's missed a lot," Nick said sadly.

"You can't tell," Bill said. "Everything's got its compensations."

"He says he's missed a lot himself," Nick confessed.

"Well, dad's had a tough time," Bill said.

"It all evens up," Nick said.

They sat looking into the fire and thinking of this profound truth.

"I'll get a chunk from the back porch," Nick said. He had noticed while looking into the fire that the fire was dying down. Also he wished to show he could hold his liquor and be practical. Even if his father had never touched a drop Bill was not going to get him drunk before he himself was drunk.

"Bring one of the big beech chunks," Bill said. He was also being consciously practical.

Nick came in with the log through the kitchen and in passing knocked a pan off the kitchen table. He laid the log down and picked up the pan. It had contained dried apricots, soaking in water. He carefully picked up all the apricots off the floor, some of them had gone under the stove, and put them back in the pan. He dipped some more water onto them from the pail by the table. He felt quite proud of himself. He had been thoroughly practical.

He came in carrying the log and Bill got up from the chair and helped him put it on the fire.

"That's a swell log," Nick said.

"I'd been saving it for the bad weather," Bill said. "A log like that will burn all night."

"There'll be coals left to start the fire in the morning," Nick said.

"That's right," Bill agreed. They were conducting the conversation on a high plane.

"Let's have another drink," Nick said.

"I think there's another bottle open in the locker," Bill said.

He kneeled down in the corner in front of the locker and brought out a square-faced bottle.

"It's Scotch," he said.

"I'll get some more water," Nick said. He went out into the kitchen again. He filled the pitcher with the dipper dipping cold spring water from the pail. On his way back to the living room he passed a mirror in the dining room and looked in it. His face looked strange. He smiled at the face in the mirror and it grinned back at him. He winked at it and went on. It was not his face but it didn't make any difference.

Bill had poured out the drinks.

"That's an awfully big shot," Nick said.

"Not for us, Wemedge," Bill said.

"What'll we drink to?" Nick asked, holding up the glass.

"Let's drink to fishing," Bill said.

"All right," Nick said. "Gentlemen, I give you fishing."

"All fishing," Bill said. "Everywhere."

"Fishing," Nick said. "That's what we drink to."

"It's better than baseball," Bill said.

"There isn't any comparison," said Nick. "How did we ever get talking about baseball?"

"It was a mistake," Bill said. "Baseball is a game for louts."

They drank all that was in their glasses.

"Now let's drink to Chesterton."

"And Walpole," Nick interposed.

Nick poured out the liquor. Bill poured in the water. They looked at each other. They felt very fine.

"Gentlemen," Bill said, "I give you Chesterton and Walpole."

"Exactly, gentlemen," Nick said.

They drank. Bill filled up the glasses. They sat down in the big chairs in front of the fire.

"You were very wise, Wemedge," Bill said.

"What do you mean?" asked Nick.

"To bust off that Marge business," Bill said.

"I guess so," said Nick.

"It was the only thing to do. If you hadn't, by now you'd be back home working trying to get enough money to get married."

Nick said nothing.

"Once a man's married he's absolutely bitched," Bill went on. "He hasn't got anything more. Nothing. Not a damn thing. He's done for. You've seen the guys that get married."

Nick said nothing.

"You can tell them," Bill said. "They get this sort of fat married look. They're done for."

"Sure," said Nick.

"It was probably bad busting it off," Bill said. "But you always fall for somebody else and then it's all right. Fall for them but don't let them ruin you."

"Yes," said Nick.

"If you'd have married her you would have had to marry the whole family. Remember her mother and that guy she married."

Nick nodded.

"Imagine having them around the house all the time and going to Sunday dinners at their house, and having them over to dinner and her telling Marge all the time what to do and how to act."

Nick sat quiet.

"You came out of it damned well," Bill said. "Now she can marry somebody of her own sort and settle down and be happy. You can't mix oil and water and you can't mix that sort of thing any more than if I'd marry Ida that works for Strattons. She'd probably like it, too."

Nick said nothing. The liquor had all died out of him and left him alone. Bill wasn't there. He wasn't sitting in front of the fire or going fishing tomorrow with Bill and his dad or anything. He wasn't drunk. It was all gone. All he knew was that he had once had Marjorie and that he had lost her. She was gone and he had sent her away. That was all that mattered. He might never see her again. Probably he never would. It was all gone, finished.

"Let's have another drink," Nick said.

Bill poured it out. Nick splashed in a little water.

"If you'd gone on that way we wouldn't be here now," Bill said.

That was true. His original plan had been to go down home and get a job. Then he had planned to stay in Charlevoix all winter so he could be near Marge. Now he did not know what he was going to do.

"Probably we wouldn't even be going fishing tomorrow," Bill said. "You had the right dope, all right."

"I couldn't help it," Nick said.

"I know. That's the way it works out," Bill said.

"All of a sudden everything was over," Nick said. "I don't know why it was. I couldn't help it. Just like when the three-day blows come now and rip all the leaves off the trees."

"Well, it's over. That's the point," Bill said.

"It was my fault," Nick said.

"It doesn't make any difference whose fault it was," Bill said.

"No, I suppose not," Nick said.

The big thing was that Majorie was gone and that probably he would never see her again. He had talked to her about how they would go to Italy together and the fun they would have.

Places they would be together. It was all gone now.

"So long as it's over that's all that matters," Bill said. "I tell you, Wemedge, I was worried while it was going on. You played it right. I understand her mother is sore as hell. She told a lot of people you were engaged."

"We weren't engaged," Nick said.

"It was all around that you were."

"I can't help it," Nick said. "We weren't."

"Weren't you going to get married?" Bill asked.

"Yes. But we weren't engaged," Nick said.

"What's the difference?" Bill asked judicially.

"I don't know. There's a difference."

"I don't see it," said Bill.

"All right," said Nick. "Let's get drunk."

"All right," Bill said. "Let's get really drunk."

"Let's get drunk and then go swimming," Nick said.

He drank off his glass.

"I'm sorry as hell about her but what could I do?" he said. "You know what her mother was like!"

"She was terrible," Bill said.

"All of a sudden it was over," Nick said. "I oughtn't to talk about it."

"You aren't," Bill said. "I talked about it and now I'm through. We won't ever speak of it again. You don't want to think about it. You might get back into it again."

Nick had not thought about that. It had seemed so absolute. That was a thought. That made him feel better.

"Sure," he said. "There's always that danger."

He felt happy now. There was not anything that was irrevocable. He might go into town Saturday night. Today was Thursday.

"There's always a chance," he said.

"You'll have to watch yourself," Bill said.

"I'll watch myself," he said.

He felt happy. Nothing was finished. Nothing was ever lost. He would go into town on Saturday. He felt lighter, as he had felt before Bill started to talk about it. There was always a way out.

"Let's take the guns and go down to the point and look for your dad," Nick said.

"All right."

Bill took down the two shotguns from the rack on the wall. He opened a box of shells. Nick put on his Mackinaw coat and his shoes. His shoes were stiff from the drying. He was still quite drunk but his head was clear.

"How do you feel?" Nick asked.

"Swell. I've just got a good edge on." Bill was buttoning up his sweater.

"There's no use getting drunk."

"No. We ought to get outdoors."

They stepped out the door. The wind was blowing a gale.

"The birds will lie right down in the grass with this," Nick said.

They struck down toward the orchard.

"I saw a woodcock this morning," Bill said.

"Maybe we'll jump him," Nick said.

"You can't shoot in this wind," Bill said.

Outside now the Marge business was no longer so tragic. It was not even very important. The wind blew everything like that away.

"It's coming right off the big lake," Nick said.

Against the wind they heard the thud of a shotgun.

"That's dad," Bill said. "He's down in the swamp."

"Let's cut down that way," Nick said.

"Let's cut across the lower meadow and see if we jump anything," Bill said.

"All right," Nick said.

None of it was important now. The wind blew it out of his head. Still he could always go into town Saturday night. It was a good thing to have in reserve.

THE BENCH

RICHARD RIVE

"We form an integral part of a complex society, a society in which a vast proportion of the population is denied the very basic right of existence, a society that condemns a man to an inferior position because he has the misfortune to be born black, a society that can only retain its precarious social and economic position at the expense of an enormous oppressed mass!"

The speaker paused for a moment and sipped some water from a glass. Karlie's eyes shone as he listened. Those were great words, he thought, great words and true. Karlie sweated. The hot November sun beat down on the gathering. The trees on the Grand Parade in Johannesburg afforded very little shelter and his handkerchief was already soaked where he had placed it between his neck and his shirt collar. Karlie stared around him at the sea of faces. Every shade of color was represented, from shiny ebony to the one or two whites in the crowd. Karlie stared at the two detectives who were busily making shorthand notes of the speeches, then turned to stare back at the speaker.

"It is up to us to challenge the right of any group who willfully and deliberately condemn a fellow group to a servile position. We must challenge the right of any people who see fit to segregate human beings solely on grounds of pigmentation. Your children are denied the rights which are theirs by birth. They are segregated educationally, socially, economically. . . ."

Ah, thought Karlie, that man knows what he is speaking about. He says I am as good as any other man, even a white man. That needs much thinking. I wonder if he means I have the right to go to any bioscope, or eat in any restaurant, or that my children can go to a white school. These are dangerous ideas and need much thinking. I wonder what Ou Klaas would say to this. Ou Klaas said that God made the white man and the black man separately, and the one must always be "baas" and the other "jong." But this man says different things and somehow they ring true.

Karlie's brow was knitted as he thought. On the platform were many speakers, both white and black, and they were behaving as if there were no differences of color among them. There was a white woman in a blue dress offering

Nxeli a cigarette. That never could have happened at Bietjiesvlei. Old Lategan at the store there would have fainted if his Annatjie had offered Witbooi a cigarette. And Annatjie wore no such pretty dress.

These were new things and he, Karlie, had to be careful before he accepted them. But why shouldn't he accept them? He was not a colored man any more, he was a human being. The last speaker had said so. He remembered seeing pictures in the newspapers of people who defied laws which relegated them to a particular class, and those people were smiling as they went to prison. This was a queer world.

The speaker continued and Karlie listened intently. He spoke slowly, and his speech was obviously carefully prepared. This is a great man, thought Karlie.

The last speaker was the white lady in the blue dress, who asked them to challenge any discriminatory laws or measures in their own way. Why should she speak like that? She could go to the best bioscopes and swim at the best beaches. Why she was even more beautiful than Annatjie Lategan. They had warned him in Bietjiesvlei about coming to the city. He had seen the skollies in District Six and he knew what to expect there. Hanover Street held no terrors for him. But no one had told him about this. This was new, this set one's mind thinking, yet he felt it was true. She had said one should challenge. He, Karlie, would astound old Lategan and Van Wyk at the Dairy Farm. They could do what they liked to him after that. He would smile like those people in the newspapers.

The meeting was almost over when Karlie threaded his way through the crowd. The words of the speakers were still milling through his head. It could never happen in Bietjiesvlei. Or could it? The sudden screech of a car pulling to a stop whirled him back to his senses. A white head was thrust angrily through the window.

"Look where you're going, you black bastard!"

Karlie stared dazedly at him. Surely this white man never heard what the speakers had said. He could never have seen the white woman offering Nxeli a cigarette. He could never imagine the white lady shouting those words at him. It would be best to catch a train and think these things over.

He saw the station in a new light. Here was a mass of human beings, black, white and some brown like himself. Here they mixed with one another, yet each mistrusted the other with an unnatural fear, each treated the other with sus-

picion, moved in a narrow, haunted pattern of its own. One must challenge these things the speaker had said . . . in one's own way. Yet how in one's own way? How was one to challenge? Suddenly it dawned upon him. Here was his challenge! *The bench.* The railway bench with "Europeans Only" neatly painted on it in white. For one moment it symbolized all the misery of the plural South African society.

Here was his challenge to the rights of a man. Here it stood. A perfectly ordinary wooden railway bench, like hundreds of thousands of others in South Africa. His challenge. That bench now had concentrated in it all the evils of a system he could not understand and he felt a victim of. It was the obstacle between himself and humanity. If he sat on it, he was a man. If he was afraid he denied himself membership as a human being in a human society. He almost had visions of righting this pernicious system, if he only sat down on that bench. Here was his chance. He, Karlie, would challenge.

He seemed perfectly calm when he sat down on the bench, but inside his heart was thumping wildly. Two conflicting ideas now throbbed through him. The one said, "I have no right to sit on this bench." The other was the voice of a new religion and said, "Why have I no right to sit on this bench?" The one voice spoke of the past, of the servile position he had occupied on the farm, of his father, and his father's father who were born black, lived like blacks and died like mules. The other voice spoke of new horizons and said: "Karlie, you are a man. You have dared what your father and your father's father would not have dared. You will die like a man."

Karlie took out a cigarette and smoked. Nobody seemed to notice his sitting there. This was an anticlimax. The world still pursued its monotonous way. No voice had shouted, "Karlie has conquered!" He was a normal human being sitting on a bench in a busy station, smoking a cigarette. Or was this his victory: the fact that he was a normal human being? A well-dressed white woman walked down the platform. Would she sit on the bench? Karlie wondered. And then that gnawing voice, "You should stand and let the white woman sit!" Karlie narrowed his eyes and gripped tighter at his cigarette. She swept past him without the slightest twitch of an eyelid and continued walking down the platform. Was she afraid to challenge—to challenge his right to be a human being? Karlie now felt tired. A third conflicting idea was now creeping in, a compensatory idea which said, "You sit on this bench because you are tired; you are tired therefore you sit." He would not move because he was tired, or was it because he wanted to sit where he liked?

People were now pouring out of a train that had pulled into the station. There were so many people pushing and jostling one another that nobody noticed him. This was his train. It would be easy to step into the train and ride off home, but that would be giving in, suffering defeat, refusing the challenge, in fact admitting that he was not a human being. He sat on. Lazily he blew the cigarette smoke into the air, thinking. . . . His mind was away from the meeting and the bench: he was thinking of Bietjiesvlei and Ou Klaas, how he had insisted that Karlie should come to Cape Town. Ou Klaas would suck on his pipe and look so quizzically at one. He was wise and knew much. He had said one must go to Cape Town and learn the ways of the world. He would spit and wink slyly when he spoke of District Six and the women he knew in Hanover Street. Ou Klaas knew everything. He said God made us white or black and we must therefore keep our places.

"Get off this seat!"

Karlie did not here the gruff voice. Ou Klaas would be on the land now waiting for his tot of cheap wine.

"I said get off the bench, you swine!!" Karlie suddenly whipped back to reality. For a moment he was going to jump up, then he remembered who he was and why he was sitting there. He suddenly felt very tired. He looked up slowly into a very red face that stared down at him.

"Get up!" it said. "There are benches down there for you."

Karlie looked up and said nothing. He stared into a pair of sharp, gray, cold eyes.

"Can't you hear me speaking to you? You black swine!"

Slowly and deliberately Karlie puffed at the cigarette. This was his test. They both stared at each other, challenged with the eyes, like two boxers, each knowing that they must eventually trade blows yet each afraid to strike first.

"Must I dirty my hands on scum like you?"

Karlie said nothing. To speak would be to break the spell, the supremacy he felt was slowly gaining.

An uneasy silence, then: "I will call a policeman rather than soil my hands on a Hotnot like you. You can't even open up your black jaw when a white man speaks to you."

Karlie saw the weakness. The white man was afraid to take action himself. He, Karlie, had won the first round of the bench dispute.

A crowd had now collected.

"Afrika!" shouted a joker.

Karlie ignored the remark. People were now milling around him, staring at the unusual sight of a black man sitting on a white man's bench. Karlie merely puffed on.

"Look at the black ape. That's the worst of giving these Kaffirs enough rope."

"I can't understand it. They have their own benches!"

"Don't get up! You have every right to sit there!"

"He'll get up when a policeman comes!"

"After all why shouldn't they sit there?"

"I've said before, I've had a native servant once, and a more impertinent . . ."

Karlie sat and heard nothing. Irresolution had *now* turned to determination. Under no condition was he going to get up. They could do what they liked.

"So, this is the fellow, eh! Get up there! Can't you read?"

The policeman was towering over him. Karlie could see the crest on his buttons and the wrinkles in his neck.

"What is your name and address! Come on!"

Karlie still maintained his obstinate silence. It took the policeman rather unawares. The crowd was growing every minute.

"You have no right to speak to this man in such a manner!" It was the white lady in the blue dress.

"Mind your own business! I'll ask your help when I need it. It's people like you who make these Kaffirs think they're as good as white men. Get up, you!" The latter remark was addressed to Karlie.

"I insist that you treat him with proper respect."

The policeman turned red.

"This . . . this . . ." He was lost for words.

"Kick up the Hotnot if he won't get up!" shouted a spectator. Rudely a white man laid hands on Karlie.

"Get up, you bloody bastard!" Karlie turned to resist, to cling to the bench, his bench. There was more than one man pulling at him. He hit out wildly and then felt a dull pain as somebody rammed a fist into his face. He was bleeding now and wild-eyed. He would fight for it. The constable clapped a pair of handcuffs on him and tried to clear a way through the crowd.

Karlie still struggled. A blow or two landed on him. Suddenly he relaxed and slowly struggled to his feet. It was useless to fight any longer. Now it was his turn to smile. He had challenged and won. Who cared the rest?

"Come on, you swine!" said the policeman forcing Karlie through the crowd.

"Certainly!" said Karlie for the first time. And he stared at the policeman with all the arrogance of one who dared sit on a "European bench."

?

In Hemingway's "The Three-Day Blow" Nick Adams goes through a rite of passage which transforms him from boy to man. Nick learns of the divisions which exist within himself and in his culture. Nature is the metaphor which provides Nick with the knowledge that nothing is permanent: "The wind blows everything . . . away." In "The Bench" Richard Rive introduces his character to a culture which denies him both as a man and a human being. Both of these stories illustrate the theme of initiation. Each character crosses a threshold into an unknown territory in order to affirm that each is a self in contact with a world. The following questions focus on what each story reveals about rites of passage.

1 Compare and contrast the social conflict in "The Three-Day Blow" with the social conflict in "The Bench": What pressures are exerted on Nick? What pressures are exerted on Karlie? What values are explored in Nick's discussion with Bill? What values are explored in Karlie's struggle to get his bench?

2 What test does Nick undergo? How does his dialogue with Bill reveal this test? What test does Karlie undergo? How does the speaker at the beginning of the story reveal this test? What does this suggest about language?

3 Compare and contrast the ways Nick and Karlie relate to their respective fathers: What evidence of a generation gap between the fathers and sons is there? What does this suggest about the assertion of manhood?

4 What is the function of women in each of the stories? How does Marge represent a possible danger for Nick? How does the white woman in the train station represent danger for Karlie? How would Bettelheim interpret these two events?

5 What magical symbols appear in these stories? How do these symbols help or hinder the characters' responses to various situations?

6 How do both of the stories reveal the concept of death? Does this relate to the rebirth of the boy as a man? Explain!

7 Compare and contrast the endings in the stories: How does Nick learn to deal with his conflicts? How does Karlie learn to deal with his conflicts? What is the difference between Karlie's knowledge and Nick's knowledge of a culture? How do both of these stories relate to the "inner" awareness of the individual as well as the adaption to a culture that neither boy created?

The Sea Separates Men from Culture

The sea often symbolizes man's chance to escape from the confinement of cultural patterns of living. At sea there are no women, and men prove their masculinity by enduring the fate which awaits them. The sea also can become a substitute for liberation. In Tennyson's poem, the hero wants to relive his past as a means to escape the present.

ULYSSES

ALFRED, LORD TENNYSON

It little profits that an idle king,
By this still hearth, among these barren crags,
Matched with an aged wife, I mete and dole
Unequal laws unto a savage race,
That hoard, and sleep, and feed, and know not me.
I cannot rest from travel: I will drink
Life to the lees: all times I have enjoyed
Greatly, have suffered greatly, both with those
That loved me, and alone; on shore, and when
Through scudding drifts the rainy Hyades
Vext the dim sea: I am become a name;
For always roaming with a hungry heart
Much have I seen and known; cities of men
And manners, climates, councils, governments,

Myself not least, but honored of them all;
And drunk delight of battle with my peers,
Far on the ringing plains of windy Troy.
I am a part of all that I have met;
Yet all experience is an arch wherethro'
Gleams that untraveled world, whose margin fades
For ever and for ever when I move.
How dull it is to pause, to make an end,
To rust unburnished, not to shine in use!
As though to breathe were life. Life piled on life
Were all too little, and of one to me
Little remains: but every hour is saved
From that eternal silence, something more,
A bringer of new things; and vile it were
For some three suns to store and hoard myself,
And this gray spirit yearning in desire
To follow knowledge like a sinking star,
Beyond the utmost bound of human thought.

This is my son, mine own Telemachus,
To whom I leave the scepter and the isle—
Well-loved of me, discerning to fulfill

This labor, by slow prudence to make mild
A rugged people, and through soft degrees
Subdue them to the useful and the good.
Most blameless is he, centered in the sphere
Of common duties, decent not to fail
In offices of tenderness, and pay
Meet adoration to my household gods,
When I am gone. He works his work, I mine.

There lies the port; the vessel puffs her sail:
There gloom the dark broad seas. My mariners,
Souls that have toiled, and wrought, and thought
  with me—
That ever with a frolic welcome took
The thunder and the sunshine, and opposed
Free hearts, free foreheads—you and I are old;
Old age hath yet his honor and his toil.
Death closes all: but something ere the end,
Some work of noble note, may yet be done,
Not unbecoming men that strove with Gods.
The lights begin to twinkle from the rocks;
The long day wanes: the slow moon climbs: the deep
Moans round with many voices. Come, my friends.

'T is not too late to seek a newer world.
Push off, and sitting well in order smite
The sounding furrows; for my purpose holds
To sail beyond the sunset, and the baths
Of all the western stars, until I die.
It may be that the gulfs will wash us down:
It may be we shall touch the Happy Isles,
And see the great Achilles, whom we knew.
Though much is taken, much abides; and though
We are not now that strength which in old days
Moved earth and heaven, that which we are, we are;
One equal temper of heroic hearts,
Made weak by time and fate, but strong in will
To strive, to seek, to find, and not to yield.

In *The Odyssey* Homer weaves the story of Ulysses, the legendary King of Ithaca. After 10 years at the siege of Troy, Ulysses set sail for home, but he incurred the wrath of the god of the sea. He was subjected to the storms and vicissitudes of the water which forced him to wander for another 10 years. Ulysses explored the Mediterranean world before returning home to his wife, son, and followers in Ithaca. In *The Divine Comedy* Dante presents us with another picture of Ulysses who wanted to continue his travels "to follow virtue and knowledge." Tennyson uses both of these versions of the Greek warrior-hero. We see Ulysses at an advanced age about to start on his final voyage which might bring him to the Happy Isles, the Greek version of Paradise. There he would be in the company of another great warrior, Achilles. The poem bridges three dimensions of time and space to reveal the way man attempts to go beyond what is known in order to understand the process of transformation.

The poem begins in the present, but the metaphor of travel soon brings the aged warrior into his past to establish a frame of reference to help him understand the purpose of life.

1   What scene does Tennyson set in the poem's introduction? What is Ulysses' attitude toward his wife? What does he mean when he says the "people know me not"? Why is he separate from his surroundings? What does Tennyson suggest about the differences between the life of a warrior-adventurer and the ruler of a culture?

2   Why does Ulysses want to look beyond the "sunset"? Does he want to recapture his past? Why? How does his past life reveal his attitude toward his present situation? What is his attitude toward Telemachus? How does the rivalry between father and son in *Ulysses* differ from the rivalry between the fathers and sons in "The Three-Day Blow" and "The Bench"?

3   What attitudes toward life does Ulysses symbolically represent? How does Tennyson relate the past to death? What rite of passage is being enacted in this poem?

The desire for travel maintains the possibility of a future. Tennyson connects this metaphor to explain how the warrior hero yields to the natural forces which balance life and death.

1   Why does Tennyson have Ulysses say: " 'T is not too late to seek a newer world"? What world is he seeking? How is this final journey described? How does this journey differ from his initial journey to Troy? What does this suggest about the need to repeat patterns of behavior?

2   How would Bettelheim interpret Ulysses' need for another initiation ceremony? Does Ulysses' desire for travel reveal the male's desire to remain apart from the female?

3   How does Ulysses differ from Gilgamish and Hector?

4   What does Ulysses reveal about modern man's plight to know and understand his maturity? How does Ulysses reflect the spirit of man's need to act out his dreams?

The Hero Today

JOSEPH CAMPBELL

There is no final system for the interpretation of myths, and there will never be any such thing. Mythology is like the god Proteus, "the ancient one of the sea, whose speech is sooth." The god "will make assay, and take all manner of shapes of things that creep upon the earth, of water likewise, and of fierce fire burning."[1]

The life-voyager wishing to be taught by Proteus must "grasp him steadfastly and press him yet the more," and at length he will appear in his proper shape. But this wily god never discloses even to the skillful questioner the whole content of his wisdom. He will reply only to the question put to him, and what he discloses will be great or trivial, according to the question asked. "So often as the sun in his course stands high in mid heaven, then forth from the brine comes the ancient one of the sea, whose speech is sooth, before the breath of the West Wind he comes, and the sea's dark ripple covers him. And when he is got forth, he lies down to sleep in the hollow of the caves. And around him the seals, the brood of the fair daughter of the brine, sleep all in a flock, stolen forth from the grey sea water, and bitter is the scent they breathe of the deeps of the salt sea."[2] The Greek warrior-king Menelaus, who was guided by a helpful daughter of this old sea-father to the wild lair, and instructed by her how to wring from the god his response, desired only to ask the secret of his own personal difficulties and the whereabouts of his personal friends. And the god did not disdain to reply.

Mythology has been interpreted by the modern intellect as a primitive, fumbling effort to explain the world of nature (Frazer); as a production of poetical fantasy from prehistoric times, misunderstood by succeeding ages (Müller); as a repository of allegorical instruction, to shape the individual to his group (Durkheim): as a group dream, symptomatic of archetypal urges within the depths of the human psyche (Jung); as the traditional vehicle of man's profoundest metaphysical insights (Coomaraswamy); and as God's Revelation to His children (the Church). Mythology is all of these. The various judgments are determined by the viewpoints of the judges. For when scrutinized

Sean Connery portrays the man of action as James Bond, the modern version of the warrior-hero. Bond's actions have no consequences in the "real" world, but his actions allow the audience to vicariously participate in fantasy.

[1] *Odyssey*, IV, 401, 417–418, translation by S. H. Butcher and Andrew Lang (London, 1879).
[2] *Ibid.*, IV, 400–406.

in terms not of what it is but of how it functions, of how it has served mankind in the past, of how it may serve today, mythology shows itself to be as amenable as life itself to the obsessions and requirements of the individual, the race, the age.

In his life-form the individual is necessarily only a fraction and distortion of the total image of man. He is limited either as male or as female; at any given period of his life he is again limited as child, youth, mature adult, or ancient; furthermore, in his life-role he is necessarily specialized as craftsman, tradesman, servant, or thief, priest, leader, wife, nun, or harlot; he cannot be all. Hence, the totality—the fullness of man—is not in the separate member, but in the body of the society as a whole; the individual can be only an organ. From his group he has derived his techniques of life, the language in which he thinks, the ideas on which he thrives; through the past of that society descended the genes that built his body. If he presumes to cut himself off, either in deed or in thought and feeling, he only breaks connection with the sources of his existence.

The tribal ceremonies of birth, initiation, marriage, burial, installation, and so forth, serve to translate the individual's life-crises and life-deeds into classic, impersonal forms. They disclose him to himself, not as this personality or that, but as the warrior, the bride, the widow, the priest, the chieftain; at the same time rehearsing for the rest of the community the old lesson of the archetypal stages. All participate in the ceremonial according to rank and function. The whole society becomes visible to itself as an imperishable living unit. Generations of individuals pass, like anonymous cells from a living body; but the sustaining, timeless form remains. By an enlargement of vision to embrace this superindividual, each discovers himself enhanced, enriched, supported, and magnified. His role, however unimpressive, is seen to be intrinsic to the beautiful festival-image of man—the image, potential yet necessarily inhibited, within himself.

Social duties continue the lesson of the festival into normal, everyday existence, and the individual is validated still. Conversely, indifference, revolt—or exile—break the vitalizing connectives. From the standpoint of the social unit, the broken-off individual is simply nothing—waste. Whereas the man or woman who can honestly say that he or she has lived the role—whether that of priest, harlot, queen, or slave—*is* something in the full sense of the verb *to be*.

Rites of initiation and installation, then, teach the lesson of the essential oneness of the individual and the group; seasonal festivals open a larger horizon. As the individual is an organ of society, so is the tribe or city—so is humanity entire—only a phase of the mighty organism of the cosmos.

It has been customary to describe the seasonal festivals of so-called native peoples as efforts to control nature. This is a misrepresentation. There is much of the will to control in every act of man, and particularly in those magical ceremonies that are thought to bring rain clouds, cure sickness, or stay the flood; nevertheless, the dominant motive in all truly religious (as opposed to black-magical) ceremonial is that of submission to the inevitables of destiny—and in the seasonal festivals this motive is particularly apparent.

No tribal rite has yet been recorded which attempts to keep winter from descending; on the contrary: the rites all prepare the community to endure, together with the rest of nature, the season of the terrible cold. And in the spring, the rites do not seek to compel nature to pour forth immediately corn, beans, and squash for the lean community; on the contrary: the rites dedicate the whole people to the work of nature's season. The wonderful cycle of the year, with its hardships and periods of joy, is celebrated and delineated, and represented as continued in the life-round of the human group.

Many other symbolizations of this continuity fill the world of the mythologically instructed community. For example, the clans of the American hunting tribes commonly regarded themselves as descended from half-animal, half-human, ancestors. These ancestors fathered not only the human members of the clan, but also the animal species after which the clan was named; thus the human members of the beaver clan were blood cousins of the animal beavers, protectors of the species and in turn protected by the animal wisdom of the wood folk. Or another example: The hogan, or mud hut, of the Navahos of New Mexico and Arizona, is constructed on the plan of the Navaho image of the cosmos. The entrance faces east. The eight sides represent the four directions and the points between. Every beam and joist corresponds to an element in the great hogan of the all-embracing earth and sky. And since the soul of man itself is regarded as identical in form with the universe, the mud hut is a representation of the basic harmony of man and world, and a reminder of the hidden life-way of perfection.

But there is another way—in diametric opposition to that of social duty and the popular cult. From the standpoint of the way of duty, anyone in exile from the community is a nothing. From the other point of view, however, this exile is the first step of the quest. Each carries within himself the all; therefore it may be sought and discovered within. The differentiations of sex, age, and occupation are not essential to our character, but mere costumes which we wear for a time on the stage of the world. The image of man within is not to be confounded with the garments. We think of ourselves as Americans, children of the twentieth century, Occidentals, civilized Christians. We are virtuous or sinful. Yet such designations do not tell what it is to be man, they denote only the accidents of geography, birth-date, and income. What is the core of us? What is the basic character of our being?

The asceticism of the medieval saints and of the yogis of India, the Hellenistic mystery initiations, the ancient philosophies of the East and of the West, are techniques for the shifting of the emphasis of individual consciousness away from the garments. The preliminary meditations of the aspirant detach his mind and sentiments from the accidents of life and drive him to the core. "I am not that, not that," he meditates: "not my mother or son who has just died; my body, which is ill or aging; my arm, my eye, my head; not the summation of all these things. I am not my feeling; not my mind; not my power of intuition." By such meditations he is driven to his own profundity and breaks through, at last, to unfathomable realizations. No man can return from such exercises and take very seriously himself as Mr. So-and-so of Such-and-such a township, U.S.A.—society and duties drop away. Mr. So-and-so, having discovered himself big with man, becomes indrawn and aloof.

This is the stage of Narcissus looking into the pool, of the Buddha sitting contemplative under the tree, but it is not the ultimate goal; it is a requisite step, but not the end. The aim is not to see, but to realize that one *is*, that essence; then one is free to wander as that es-

sence in the world. Furthermore: the world too is of that essence. The essence of oneself and the essence of the world: these two are one. Hence separateness, withdrawal, is no longer necessary. Wherever the hero may wander, whatever he may do, he is ever in the presence of his own essence—for he has the perfected eye to see. There is no separateness. Thus, just as the way of social participation may lead in the end to a realization of the All in the individual, so that of exile brings the hero to the Self in all.

Centered in this hub-point, the question of selfishness or altruism disappears. The individual has lost himself in the law and been reborn in identity with the whole meaning of the universe. For Him, by Him, the world was made. "O Mohammed," God said, "hadst thou not been, I would not have created the sky."

The democratic ideal of the self-determining individual, the invention of the power-driven machine, and the development of the scientific method of research, have so transformed human life that the long-inherited, timeless universe of symbols has collapsed. In the fateful, epoch-announcing words of Nietzsche's Zarathustra: "Dead are all the gods." One knows the tale; it has been told a thousand ways. It is the hero-cycle of the modern age, the wonderstory of mankind's coming to maturity. The spell of the past, the bondage of tradition, was shattered with sure and mighty strokes. The dream-web of myth fell away; the mind opened to full waking consciousness; and modern man emerged from the ancient ignorance, like a butterfly from its cocoon, or like the sun at dawn from the womb of mother night.

It is not only that there is no hiding place for the gods from the searching telescope and microscope; there is no such society any more as the gods once supported. The social unit is not a carrier of religious content, but an economic political organization. Its ideals are not those of the hieratic pantomime, making visible on earth the forms of heaven, but of the secular state, in hard and unremitting competition for material supremacy and resources. Isolated societies, dream-bounded within a mythologically charged horizon, no longer exist except as areas to be exploited. And within the progressive societies themselves, every last vestige of the ancient human heritage of ritual, morality, and art is in full decay.

The problem of mankind today, therefore, is precisely the opposite to that of men in the comparitively stable periods of those great co-ordinating mythologies which now are known as lies. Then all meaning was in the group, in the great anonymous forms, none in the self-expressive individual; today no meaning is in the group—none in the world: all is in the individual. But there the meaning is absolutely unconscious. One does not know toward what one moves. One does not know by what one is propelled. The lines of communication between the conscious and the unconscious zones of the human psyche have all been cut, and we have been split in two.

The hero-deed to be wrought is not today what it was in the century of Galileo. When then there was darkness, now there is light; but also, where light was, there now is darkness. The modern hero-deed must be that of questing to bring to light again the lost Atlantis of the coordinated soul.

Obviously, this work cannot be wrought by turning back, or away, from what has been accomplished by the modern revolution; for the problem is nothing if not that of rendering the modern world spiritually significant—or rather (phrasing the same principle the other way around) nothing if not that of making it possible for men and women to come to full human maturity through the conditions of contemporary life. Indeed, these conditions themselves are what have rendered the ancient formulae ineffective, misleading, and even pernicious. The community today is the planet, not the bounded nation; hence the patterns of projected aggression which formerly served to co-ordinate the in-group now can only break it into factions. The national idea, with the flag as totem, is today an aggrandizer of the nursery ego, not the annihilator of an infantile situation. Its parody-rituals of the parade ground serve the ends of Holdfast, the tyrant dragon, not the God in whom self-interest is annihilated. And the numerous saints of this anticult—namely the patriots whose ubiquitous photographs, draped with flags, serve as official icons—are precisely the local threshold guardians (our demon Sticky-hair) whom it is the first problem of the hero to surpass.

Nor can the great world religions, as at present understood, meet the requirement. For they have become associated with the cause of the factions, as instruments of propaganda and self-congratulation. (Even Buddhism has lately suffered this degradation, in reaction to the lessons of the West.) The universal triumph of the secular state has thrown all religious organizations into such a definitely secondary, and finally ineffectual, position that religious pantomine is hardly more today than a sanctimonious exercise for Sunday morning, whereas business ethics and patriotism stand for the remainder of the week. Such a monkey-holiness is not what the functioning world requires; rather, a transmutation of the whole social order is necessary, so that through every detail and act of secular life the vitalizing image of the universal god-man who is actually immanent and effective in all of us may be somehow made known to consciousness.

And this is not a work that consciousness itself can achieve. Consciousness can no more invent, or even predict, an effective symbol than foretell or control tonight's dream. The whole thing is being worked out on another level, through what is bound to be a long and very frightening process, not only in the depths of every living psyche in the modern world, but also on those titanic battlefields into which the whole planet has lately been converted. We are watching the terrible clash of the Symplegades, through which the soul must pass—identified with neither side.

But there is one thing we may know, namely, that as the new symbols become visible, they will not be identical in various parts of the globe; the circumstances of local life, race, and tradition must all be compounded in the effective forms. Therefore, it is necessary for men to understand, and be able to see, that through various symbols the same redemption is revealed. "Truth is one," we read in the Vedas; "the sages call it by many names." A single song is being inflected through all the colorations of the human choir. General propaganda for one or another of the local solutions, therefore, is superfluous—or much rather, a menace. The way to become human is to learn to recognize the lineaments of God in all of the wonderful modulations of the face of man.

With this we come to the final hint of what the specific orientation of the modern hero-task must be, and discover the real cause for the disintegration of all of our inherited religious formulae. The center of gravity, that is to say, of the realm of mystery and danger has definitely shifted. For the primitive hunting peoples of those remotest human millenniums when the sabertooth tiger, the mammoth, and the lesser presences of the animal kingdom were the primary manifestations of what was alien—the source at once of danger, and of sustenance—the great human problem was to become linked psychologically to the task of sharing the wilderness with these beings. An unconscious identification took place, and this was finally rendered conscious in the half-human, half-animal figures of the mythological totem-ancestors. The animals became the tutors of humanity. Through acts of literal imitation—such as today appear only on the children's playground (or in the madhouse)—an effective annihilation of the human ego was accomplished and society achieved a cohesive organization. Similarly, the tribes supporting themselves on plantfood became cathected to the plant; the life-rituals of planting and reaping were identified with those of human procreation, birth, and progress to maturity. Both the plant and the animal worlds, however, were in the end brought under social control. Whereupon the great field of instructive wonder shifted—to the skies—and mankind enacted the great pantomine of the sacred moon-king, the sacred sun-king, the hieratic, planetary state, and the symbolic festivals of the world-regulating spheres.

Today all of these mysteries have lost their force; their symbols no longer interest our psyche. The notion of a cosmic law, which all existence serves and to which man himself must bend, has long since passed through the preliminary mystical stages represented in the old astrology, and is now simply accepted in mechanical terms as a matter of course. The descent of the Occidental sciences from the heavens to the earth (from seventeenth-century astronomy to nineteenth-century biology), and their concentration today, at last, on man himself (in twentieth-century anthropology and psychology), mark the path of a prodigious transfer of the focal point of human wonder. Not the animal world, not the plant world, not the miracle of the spheres, but man himself is now the crucial mystery. Man is that alien presence with whom the forces of egoism must come to terms, through whom the ego is to be crucified and resurrected, and in whose image society is to be reformed. Man, understood however not as "I" but as "Thou": for the ideals and temporal institutions of no tribe, race, continent, social class, or century, can be the measure of the inexhaustible and multifariously wonderful divine existence that is the life in all of us.

The modern hero, the modern individual

who dares to heed the call and seek the mansion of that presence with whom it is our whole destiny to be atoned, cannot, indeed must not, wait for his community to cast off its slough of pride, fear, rationalized avarice, and sanctified misunderstanding. "Live," Nietzsche says, "as though the day were here." It is not society that is to guide and save the creative hero, but precisely the reverse. And so every one of us shares the supreme ordeal—carries the cross of the redeemer—not in the bright moments of his tribes great victories, but in the silences of his personal despair.

?

In "The Hero Today" Joseph Campbell uses the dream as a metaphor to illustrate the way human beings balance the contradictions between the individual and society. For Campbell, the personal dream merges with the collective dream in those myths which reveal a culture's view of the world. In primitive times during a rite of passage, man was supplied with the necessary symbols which made it possible for the human spirit to move forward. For modern man the world no longer seems to be filled with awe and wonder. Campbell traces this loss to that point when symbols began to lose meaning for our psyches. The initiation theme is a reflection of the hero's struggle for self. Campbell believes that this quest is synonymous with a person's attempt to bridge the differences between the individual and the collective in order to fully develop human potential. Campbell illustrates the following basic pattern underlying all heroic journals: (1) The hero's separation from a society. (2) A test to be performed in which the hero must overcome obstacles. These obstacles are a reflection of "inner" conflicts. For Campbell, the battleground illustrates the evolution of the human psyche. (3) The hero's return with some insight that had hitherto not been known to the collective. The hero's adventure is an archetypal quest which reveals how "the whole society becomes visible to itself as an imperishable living unit." The following questions focus on the hero's struggle for consciousness from both a primitive and modern point of view.

1 Discuss the problems facing the modern life voyager. How does Campbell relate the need for understanding myths to the need for understanding the human desire to express its full potential?

2 How did the initiation ceremony help the individual to adapt to changing patterns during the stages of life? How did the individual merge with the collective? How do modern individuals escape the feeling of alienation from each other?

3 Relate the epic of Gilgamish to Campbell's discussion of the need for the hero to be separate from his society. How does Nick's separation in "The Three-Day Blow" differ from Gilgamish's separation from society?

4 Does Tennyson's Ulysses fear the collective? Explain how the individual affirms himself in spite of the pressure from a group.

5 What image of primitive man emerges in the myth of Rama? How would Campbell interpret this as part of the collective dream of India? How does Karlie in "The Bench" rise above the modern community in order to affirm his identity? Would Campbell say that Karlie has fulfilled the task of the modern hero? Explain!

6 Discuss Campbell's contention that there is a breakdown of universal symbols from the following perspectives:
a How has science helped bring about this breakdown?
b To what degree have religious symbols lost their meaning?
c What does Campbell suggest the modern hero do to heal this split between society and the individual?

Who am I?

The Actor as Hero

These are the faces of mock heroes: the actor pretending to be a hero or heroine. They present us with illusions about the world as it is and create for us a "pseudoreality." If we identify with these individuals, we accept the group's image of a hero. In "Television and the American Character" Dr. Glynn discusses the way television has influenced our identity. The psychiatrist contends that ours has become a passive-dependent culture in which individuality is traded for an illusion of satisfaction.

The Mass Man as Hero

The new sophisticate is not castrated by society but, like Origen, is self-castrated. Sex and the body are for him not something to be and live out, but tools to be cultivated like a TV announcer's voice. And like all genuine Puritans (very passionate men underneath) the new sophisticate does it by devoting himself passionately to the moral principle of dispersing all passion, loving everybody until love has no power left to scare anyone. He is deathly afraid of his passions unless they are kept under leash, and the theory of total expression is precisely his leash. His dogma of liberty is his repression; and his principle of full libidinal health, full sexual satisfaction, are his puritanism and amount to the same thing as his New England forefathers' denial of sex. The first Puritans repressed sex and were passionate; our new man represses passion and is sexual. Both have the purpose of holding back the body, both are ways of trying to make nature a slave. The modern man's rigid principle of full freedom is not freedom at all but a new straitjacket, in some ways as compulsive as the old. He does all this because he is afraid of his body and his compassionate roots in nature, afraid of the soil and his procreative power. He is our latter-day Baconian devoted to gaining power over nature, gaining knowledge in order to get more power. And you gain power over sexuality (like working the slave until all zest for revolt is squeezed out of him) precisely by the role of full expression. Sex becomes our tool like the caveman's wheel, crowbar, or adz. Sex, the new machine, the Machina Ultima.

Rollo May

Playboy really feeds on the existence of a repressed fear of involvement with women, which for various reasons is still present in many otherwise adult Americans. So *Playboy's* version of sexuality grows increasingly irrelevant as authentic sexual maturity is achieved.

The male identity crisis to which *Playboy* speaks has at its roots a deeply set fear of sex, a fear that is uncomfortably combined with fascination. *Playboy* strives to resolve this antinomy by reducing the proportions of sexuality, its power and its passion, to a packageable consumption item. Thus in *Playboy's* iconography the nude woman symbolizes total sexual accessibility but demands nothing from the observer. "You drive it—it doesn't drive you." The terror of sex, which cannot be separated from its ecstasy, is dissolved. But this futile attempt to reduce the *mysterium tremendum* of the sexual fails to solve the problem of being a man. For sexuality is the basic form of all human relationship, and therein lies its terror and its power.

Harvey Cox

For James Bond is the Renaissance man in mid-century guise, lover, warrior, connoisseur. He fights the forces of darkness, speaks for the sanitary achievements of the age, enjoys hugely the fruits of the free enterprise economy. He lives the dreams of countless drab people, his gun ready, his honor intact, his morals loose: the hero of our anxiety-ridden, mythless age: the savior of our culture.

George Grella

TELEVISION AND THE AMERICAN CHARACTER— A PSYCHIATRIST LOOKS AT TELEVISION

EUGENE DAVID GLYNN, M.D.

To consider television as a shaping force on the American character, the attempt must be made to study it so far as possible purely as a form. Content and quality vary in a very great range, and while of great importance in the immediate and particular effects upon the viewer, there is a structure inherent in the very medium of television which must be seen completely in itself. It is this basic form which exerts the greatest influence upon the shaping of character when character is considered as the long-term expectations and responses of a person; automatic, repetitive, more or less conscious. This molding is almost completely outside of the awareness of the viewer. The customary repeated experience of television structures the viewer's whole idea of the world and his relation to it. It is here that permanent responses to television lie; it is here that character is formed, for these attitudes are what the viewer then takes into the rest of his experience.

What attitudes toward the world and what expectations of it does television bring about?

Certain types of adult illness—particularly the depressions, the oral character neuroses, the schizophrenias —and the use they make of television can be most valuable here. Those traits that sick adults now satisfy by television can be presumed to be those traits which children, exposed to television from childhood (infancy, really!), and all through the char-

acter forming years, may be expected to develop. Consider these actual clinical examples.

A twenty-five-year-old musician, daughter of an adoring, constantly present, constantly acting mother, quarrels with her parents and gives up her own quite busy professional life. She turns to the television set, and soon is spending ten to twelve hours a day watching it, constantly sitting before it, transfixed, drinking beer or eating ice cream, lost and desperate if the set is turned off. Making a joke one day, she said, "Boy, I don't know what I would do for a mother if that tube ever burned out." This girl, of real intellectual attainment, was completely indifferent as to what the programs actually were. A fifty-five-year-old man, hugely obese, all his life close to his three older sisters, who took care of him, becomes depressed after the death of one of them. His only activity for many months is to watch television, looking for interesting programs, but settling for anything. The staff of a hospital for schizophrenic adolescent girls finds that these girls, insatiable in their demands, and yet themselves incapable of sustaining activity, want nothing so much as to be allowed endless hours of television. Without it they are soon noisy, unruly and frequently destructive. Significantly, the only other control of these girls is an adult who constantly directs them or organizes their entertainment for them.

These examples could be multiplied endlessly. They all demonstrate quite clearly the special set of needs television satisfies, needs centering around the wish for someone to care, to nurse, to give comfort and solace. Adults, by their very age and status, can scarcely hope to find someone to take on this role, once their own mothers give it up. These infantile longings can be satisfied only symbolically, and how readily the television set fills in. Warmth, sound, constancy, availability, a steady giving without ever a demand for return, the encouragement to complete passive surrender and envelopment—all this and active fantasy besides. Watching these adults, one is deeply impressed by their acting out with the television set of their unconscious longings to be infants in mother's lap.

These, then, are traits television can so easily satisfy in adults, or foster in children; traits of passivity, receptiveness, being fed, taking in and absorbing what is offered. Activity, self-reliance, and aggression are notably absent. A great deal of activity and aggression may be present, but they are deceptive, for the demands and even rages are not to be doing, but to be getting. Very much energy can be spent, not in constructive accomplishment, but in trying to reestablish or keep a dependent relationship. The image is evident; the relationship clearly established. The musician's joke went to the core, for these are the relationships of a child to its mother; the relationship of a very young child who lives literally on its mother's bounty: her food, her warmth, her knowledge. This is the age described in Freudian psychology as the oral age; the age of intake and being fed, when the mouth is the vital organ in relation to the world. The extensions of this include such things as taking in the sound of others' voices through the ears or of absorbing others' ideas, as can easily be seen. The underlying pattern in whatever symbolic form is worked out will relate it to this oral character orientation: the counting on someone else to supply satisfaction and security rather than oneself. Typical, too, of this character structure are the intensity with which needs are felt, the poor tolerance of frustration and delay, the demand for immediate satisfaction. The television set is easily and agreeably a mother to whom the child readily turns with the same expectations as to her.

These traits, of course, are inherent in all spectator participation, be it sport or art or reading. What is crucially important about television is its ubiquitousness: there is so much television, so early, so steadily; five-year-olds watch television as a matter of course, and, increasingly, so do three-year-olds and even two-year-olds. Television at this age can, in the limited experience of the child, only be seen as a mother-substitute or a mother-extension. These needs of the child should be outgrown, and his relationship to his mother changed. Basically, this growth depends in great part on the mother's attitude toward the child; her encouraging him to greater activity and self-reliance, the lessening of her feeding functions. It is of the greatest importance in character formation that the child can now have these infantile wishes and needs satisfied by the always available television set. Indeed, to continue enjoying television,

it becomes necessary these traits remain prominent. The danger is here: the passive dependent oral character traits become fixed. There are endless differences between children playing tag or cops and robbers and watching even the most action-filled Western; even between walking to the movies once a week and just switching on television by reaching out.

Hence, the chief effect of television is passivity and dependence in multiple shapes and forms. The world supplies and the individual feasts. In opposition to the point of view here expressed, the claim is made that aggression is not so much inhibited by television as displaced; that dormant aggressive forces are stimulated in the viewer, and that these forces result in increased activity of many kinds in other spheres. Similarly, television may release many new forces, aggressive or constructive in a direct way. This type of effect, however, depends almost entirely on the content of the particular program. Television might indeed arouse the viewer to extreme activity, but only by the portrayal of specific situations or specific messages. For example, some juvenile delinquency might be shaped by a television crime program, or a tree planting program be inspired. Again, attitudes toward parents, toward husbands and wives, toward social groups, attitudes which could lead to action of a most constructive kind can certainly be caused or influenced by television, but this, however, must always be specifically dependent on the content of the program. Action so aroused does not produce a characterological basis for further activity. The underlying structure, even here, is clear, for the stimulus to action, be it aggressive or sexual, comes from without. Deep characterological attitudes toward parents or family might be shaped, but only by specific propaganda content to programs.

The picture of the American character which emerges has a familiar look, for many students in the field have pointed out that the new American character is one of conformity; the search is for security, not glory, comfort in the group, not individual prominence. The whole present concept of the welfare state illustrates this. Americans today must be much more responsible to their society, much more aware of their group, much more conforming; the non-entrepreneur is rapidly becoming the necessary American character. It must look outside itself constantly for orientation so as to smoothly fit in. Television is simultaneously the result of and the instrument for producing the character needed to live in much of the current American world. To be responsive to and dependent on television, well trained in this, is to be able to live much more easily in our society.

There are other aspects of television's influence. It is used, certainly, in every hospital and in every institution as an extremely effective non-chemical sedative. An interesting parallel has been pointed out recently. It is well-known that fixing on a moving visual stimulus inhibits motor activity. The prime example of this is the situation in hypnosis, and the concentration and stillness of television watchers certainly is reminiscent of the hypnotized. Television-addiction certainly exists, and bears an immediate relation to the drug addicts, those who search for, in pills, what they once found in mother's milk. A forty-four-year-old salesman, a chronic alcoholic, tried to give up liquor. Every night he came home and watched television, "drinking it in" (his words) until he fell asleep before the set. Once off the wagon, he gave up television, too.

How lulling television can be has been widely observed. Most homes soon give in to the temptation of using television to keep the children quiet and out of mischief. It does this, but in a way much different from playing games.

Marriage after marriage is preserved by keeping it drugged on television; television is used quite consistently to prevent quarreling from breaking out by keeping people apart. This points up a somewhat less obvious side of watching television: its schizoid-fostering aspects. Television seems to be a social activity, an activity performed by many people together. Actually, though, it smothers contact, really inhibiting interpersonal exchange. A group watching television is frequently a group of isolated people, not in real exchange at all. Television viewers are given to solitary pleasures, not the social ones. Children and adolescents frequently revert to thumb-sucking while watching; how much eating and drinking goes on before the set! The complaint is common enough today that social visiting has lost its social, conversational, engaged side.

There are two more important aspects of television to consider: its stimulation and its fantasy. The question can only be asked at this point, for the television generation is not yet adolescent: what will be the result of such constant stimulation from such early ages? Will it result in the need for ever increasing stimulation as the response to the old stimulus becomes exhausted? In the early 1940s a radio program which created national interest and caused great excitement was "Take It or Leave It," with its climax of the $64.00 Question. This year (1955) television's greatest success has been the $64,000 Question. Discount the monetary inflation of the past ten years. What is left is a vivid figure of how much more it takes to excite. The Lone Ranger served as a radio hero for well over ten years; Davy Crockett, a hero of almost mythic proportions, lasted less than one year. What way can stimulation be continuously increased? As the responses are exhausted, will television move toward increasing violence, as the movies have? Similarly, it is too soon to know what children so massively exposed to sex on television will consider exciting and sex-stimulating as adults. A critical question is raised here: is television ultimately blunting and destructive of sensibility?

Then too, one wonders: Will reality match up to the television fantasies this generation has been nursed on? These children are in a peculiar position; experience is exhausted in advance. There is little they have not seen or done or lived through, and yet this is second-hand experience. When the experience itself comes, it is watered down, for it has already been half lived, but never truly felt. The fate of Emma Bovary may become the common fate. This has always been a "disease" of the literary sensibility and of the romantics, but will this become a mass characteristic?

A word of balance should be put in here. The television generation will not be a completely infantile one, for there are many other forces at work, including the normal growth potentials of the human being. The point here is just to isolate the lines of television's influence. At the same time, equally inherent in its nature, television can be a growth-promoting experience, an enriching force of the most tremendous power.

Horizons have been greatly expanded: millions of people have seen the ballet, have travelled to distant lands, have explored some of the country's best museums; experiences they could never have in their own lifetimes. Television has taken its viewers into the United Nations, into the meetings of Congressional investigating committees. It has led a mass audience into intimate active participation in the political heart of the country in a way never dreamed possible. The range here is without bounds. Television can produce a people wider in knowledge, more alert and aware of the world, prepared to be much more actively interested in the life of their times. Television can be the great destroyer of provincialism. Television can produce a nation of people who really live in the world, not in just their own hamlets. It is here that the great opportunity of educational television lies.

Educational television must be acutely aware of its own nature. By being very conscious of its particular character shaping potential, it can counteract it by extremely careful attention to content. It is always a difficult task for the teacher to liberate his pupil; educational television must remember how many more times difficult it is for it. It must find ways to encourage active audience participation; programs which will not satiate but stimulate its viewers, programs which will leave its audience eager to do and to try. Cooking instruction programs are an example here. Techniques will have to be worked out for educational television for showing, not a baseball game, but how to pitch a curved ball; for sending its audience on nature hunts, into club activity, to the library for books. Being aware of the dependent relationship in its audience, television must look for ways to undo it—the problem of any teacher or parent.

With this orientation, television can overcome the dangers pointed out and find its way to being highly growth-promoting. Otherwise it will find itself degraded into an instrument for the shaping of a group man: dependent, outward seeking, the natural foil of any authoritarianism, be it left or right.

?

The hero of the modern world is often a celluloid-created version of the warrior who pretends to be authentic. In his essay, Glynn demonstrates that the process of watching television tends to make individuals become "passive-dependent" members of the group. The author contends that Americans remain in an arrested stage of infancy, and that they prefer to have a breast, i.e., television, than to venture forth and act. The photographer captures a moment in time, leaving us with appearance as a measure for our actions. Unlike Hamlet, we cannot say, "I know not seems. Nay, it is." This split over the confusion between appearance and "reality" brings us back to Plato's cave. This rite of passage seems to be a regressive step to capture something that never was. The following questions focus on the modern attempt to live in a "psuedoreality."

1 Discuss Glynn's view that television fulfills a psychological need in modern man. What does he mean when he calls this time "an age of intake"? What attitudes and expectations about the world are conveyed to us through television? Do you agree or disagree with Glynn's contention that television functions as a breast? You might use *Playboy* as a metaphor to validate your point of view.

2 Is watching television a social activity? Explain! Select a detective program which appears on television. Discuss whether the hero fulfills the audience's expectation of the image of a mock hero. How would this hero differ from David or Hector? How would Glynn relate the hero to a "passive-dependent" American? Does he seem to be more than human? How important is technology to him? Would Campbell interpret the detective as an individual or as one who gives in to social pressure? Explain!

Temptress: Victim or Executioner?

The stereotype is the Eternal Feminine. She is the Sexual Object sought by all men, and by all women. She is of neither sex, for she herself has no sex at all.
Germaine Greer

In Greece the sirens' haunting song which no man could resist, and which led all who heard it to their death.

Hidden behind the rocks of the Rhine, Lorelei dangled her long locks to lure the sailors to their deaths.

In the painting by Allori shown here, we see illustrated the dual function of woman. The artist brings the mother and daughter together to symbolize woman as the mother who is the lifegiver and the daughter who is lifetaker. The young woman in the painting holds the head of her victim. She has the power either to bestow pleasure or to bring about the man's destruction. It is woman who tempts man away from his spiritual quest, and it is woman who is the prize of this quest.

DEIDRE OF THE SORROWS

IRISH MYTH

"Woe to this child," prophesied the soothsayer at Deirdre's birth, "for she shall be the ruin of all Ireland and the death of its three greatest heroes."

The tiny baby was so sweet and innocent that Felimid could almost laugh at these dire predictions. But his friends believed strongly in the soothsayer and at their urgings, Felimid sent his small daughter and a faithful nurse to live in a remote, isolated forest where she could never possibly have any effect on the fate of Ireland. So Deirdre grew up into the most beautiful woman of Ireland without ever seeing the face of a man. But word of her beauty leaked out of the forest and came to the castle of King Conchobar, who decided that if her beauty matched her reputation, he would marry her himself.

So the king sent for Deirdre and found that she was even more beautiful than he had imagined. But Deirdre was not at all impressed with Conchobar, for he was old and ugly, and although Deirdre had not seen many men in her secluded life, she was sure there had to be something better than this! That night Deirdre dreamed of a young and handsome man with hair like the raven, flesh like the snow, and cheeks as red as berries. "A man like that I could love," she thought.

The next day the king asked her to marry him. Deirdre replied that she was too young to be married, and begged the king to let her live in the forest for another year until she was old enough. The king was satisfied with her answer, and Deirdre and her nurse returned to the forest.

Deirdre thought little of the king she was betrothed to and instead spent all of her time dreaming of the man with the raven hair and cheeks like berries. The nurse listened to her musings in fear and worry. At last she said, "Deirdre, you must quit dreaming of a man like this, for I know one who fits the description. He is Naois, the son of Usnach, and I am sure that he is the man of the prophecy, for he and his two brothers are the greatest heroes of all Ireland. If you ever meet him, you will bring death to him and ruin to all of Ireland."

It was only a few days later that Deirdre heard a hunting horn. She ran to the window just in time to see three handsome men ride by, and one of them had hair like the raven, flesh like the snow, and cheeks as red as berries. "It is Naois," she cried.

"Don't be a fool," cried her nurse, struggling to hold Deirdre. "Let him go."

But Deirdre pulled free from the nurse and ran out into the forest after the three huntsmen. "Naois," she cried. "Don't leave me!"

"I heard something call," said Naois. "Let's go back."

"It was only the wind," said his two brothers, Ainle and Arden.

But again the call came. "Naois! Come back!"

"Don't go," said Arden. "I am afraid that this voice will bring evil."

But Naois could not resist the sweet voice he heard, and rode back toward the sound. As he came out of the forest onto a grassy knoll beside a stream he saw the most beautiful woman in the world.

"Who are you?" he asked in awe. "Are you a woman or a fairy?"

"I am Deirdre," she replied.

Naois was struck with horror when he heard her name, for he, too, had heard the prophecy about Deirdre and he knew that she was betrothed to the king. But as he looked into her eyes, he knew that neither death, nor banishment, nor disloyalty could keep him from loving her.

When Ainle and Arden found their brother, he and Deirdre were already deep in a kiss of love. The two looked at each other in despair, for they knew that the prophecy meant their undoing as well as Naois's, but it took them only a minute to decide that they would never desert their brother.

Knowing that King Conchobar would never allow his beloved to marry another, the three brothers fled with Deirdre to another country. For several years they lived in peace, but they were all lonely for their homeland.

One day a messenger from King Conchobar arrived, bringing an invitation to the four of them to come to a feast. Hoping that this meant the end of their exile, the four young people eagerly accepted and returned to their beloved Ireland.

King Conchobar, too, hoped that they could return in peace, but he was not strong enough to look on the beauty of Deirdre knowing she belonged to another man. As soon as he saw her, he went into a jealous rage and ordered his men to attack the sons of Usnach.

But not all of his men were willing to follow their king in this unjust attack, for many were friends of Naois. So the forces of Ireland fought against each other and in the dreadful battle, Naois, Ainle, and Arden were all killed.

A large grave was dug so that the three brothers could be buried together. "Dig it wider," said Deirdre, as she stood beside the open grave and sang a death chant. "Dig it wide, for I must have room beside my beloved."

And as soon as the grave was finished, Deirdre stepped into the tomb, lay down beside her beloved Naois, and died.

The
Goddess

of
Fertility

Isis appears as the archetypal woman of sensuality who holds the power of life and death within her body. She is one of the reasons men want to enslave women. The male is afraid that he might be caught by the irresistable power of the Eternal Female.

ISIS, THE GODDESS OF FERTILITY

EGYPTIAN MYTH

In the myth of Isis, the transition from a matriarchal world to a patriarchal world is symbolized in the relationship of Isis to her brother-husband Osiris. Isis helps her loved one, Osiris, reign over Egypt, while her brother Sêth and her sister Nephthys live in the desert. Sêth wants to overthrow his brother and become King of Egypt. During the reign of Isis and Osiris the land was fertile. Everywhere there was to be seen vine, grain, and flowers. Sêth was angry when he saw the success of Isis and Osiris. Many times Sêth plotted against Osiris, but it was always Iris who watched with care over her husband-brother. She helped him rule and was responsible for preventing his death. Sêth conceived of a plan which would destroy Osiris. One day he took the measurement of Osiris's body—he took the measurement from his shadow—and he made a chest that was the exact size of Osiris.

Soon, at the time before the season of drought, Sêth gave a banquet, and to that banquet he invited all the children of Earth and the Sky. To that banquet came Thout, the Wise One, and Nephthys, the wife of Sêth, and Sêth himself, and Isis, and Osiris. And where they sat at banquet they could see the chest that Sêth had made—the chest made of fragrant and diversified woods. All admired that chest. Then Sêth, as though he would have them enter into a game, told all of them that he would give the chest to the one whose body fitted most closely in it. The children of Qêb and Nut went and laid themselves in the chest that Sêth had made: Sêth went and laid himself in it, Nephthys went and laid herself in it, Thout went and laid himself in it, Isis went and laid herself in it. All were short; none laid in the chest, but left a space above his or her head.

Then Osiris took the crown off his head and laid himself in the chest. His form filled it in its length and its breadth. Isis and Nephthys and Thout stood above where he lay, looking down upon Osiris, so resplendent of face, so perfect of limb, and congratulating him upon coming into possession of the splendid chest that Sêth had made. Sêth was not beside the chest then. He shouted, and his attendants to the number of seventy-two came into the banquetting hall. They placed the heavy cover upon the chest; they hammered nails into it; they soldered it all over with melted lead. Nor could Isis, nor Thout, nor Nephthys break through the circle that Sêth's attendants made around the chest. And they, having nailed the cover down, and having soldered it, took up the sealed chest, and, with Sêth going before them, they ran with it out of the hall.

Isis and Nephthys and Thout ran after those who bore the chest. But the night was dark, and these three children of Qêb and Nut were separated, one from the other, and from Sêth and his crew. And these came to where the river was, and they flung the sealed chest into the river. Isis, and Thout, and Nephthys, following the tracks that Sêth and his crew had made, came to the river bank when it was daylight, but by that time the current of the river had brought the chest out into the sea.

Isis followed along the bank of the river, lamenting for Osiris. She came to the sea, and she crossed over it, but she did not know where to go to seek for the body of Osiris. She wandered through the world, and where she went bands of children went with her, and they helped her in her search.

The chest that held the body of Osiris had drifted in the sea. A flood had cast it upon the land. It has lain in a thicket of young trees. A tree, growing, had lifted it up. The branches of the tree wrapped themselves around it; the bark of the tree spread itself around it; at last the tree grew there, covering the chest with its bark.

The land in which this happened was Byblos. The king and queen of the city, Melquart and Astarte, heard of the wonderful tree, the branches and bark of which gave forth a fragrance. The king had the tree cut down; its branches were trimmed off, and the tree was set up as a column in the king's house. And then Isis, coming to Byblos, was told of the wonderful tree that grew by the sea. She was told of it by a band of children who came to her. She came to the place: she found that the tree had been cut down and that its trunk was now set up as a column in the king's house.

She knew from what she heard about the wonderful fragrance that was in the trunk and branches of the tree that the chest she was seeking was within it. She stayed beside where the tree had been. Many who came to that place saw the queenly figure that, day and night, stood near where the wonderful tree had been. But none who came near was spoken to by her. Then the queen, having heard about the stranger who stood there, came to her. When she came near, Isis put her hand upon her head, and thereupon a fragrance went from Isis and filled the body of the queen.

The queen would have this majestical stranger go with her to her house. Isis went. She nursed the queen's child in the hall in which stood the column that had closed in it the chest which she sought.

She nourished the queen's child by placing her finger in its mouth. At night she would strip wood from the column that had grown as a tree, and throw the wood upon the fire. And in this fire she would lay the queen's child. The fire did not injure it at all; it burned softly around the child. Then Isis, in the form of a swallow, would fly around the column, lamenting.

One night the queen came into the hall where her child was being nursed. She saw no nurse there; she saw her child lying in the fire. She snatched the child up, crying out. Then Isis spoke to the queen from the column on which, in the form of a swallow, she perched. She told the queen that the child would have gained immortality had it been suffered to lie for a night and another night longer within the fire made from the wood of the column. Now it would be long-lived, but not immortal. And she revealed her own divinity to the queen, and claimed the column that had been made from the wonderful tree.

The king had the column taken down; it was split open, and the chest which Isis had sought for so long and with so many lamentations was within it. Isis wrapped the chest in linen, and it was carried for her out of the king's house. And then a ship was given to her, and on that ship, Isis, never stirring from beside the chest, sailed back to Egypt.

And coming into Egypt she opened the chest, and took the body of her lord and husband out of it. She breathed into his mouth, and, with the motion of her wings (for Isis, being divine, could assume wings), she brought life back to Osiris. And there Osiris and Isis lived together.

But one night Sêth, as he was hunting gazelles by moonlight, came upon Osiris and Isis sleeping. Fiercely he fell upon his brother; he tore his body into fourteen pieces. Then, taking the pieces that were the body of Osiris, he scattered them over the land.

Death had come into the land from the time Osiris had been closed in the chest through the cunning of Sêth; war was in the land; men always had arms in their hands. No longer did music sound, no longer did men and women talk sweetly and out of the depths of their feelings. Less and less did grain, and fruit-trees, and the vine flourish. The green places everywhere were giving way to the desert. Sêth was triumphant; Thout and Nephthys cowered before him.

And all the beauty and all the abundance that had come from Rê would be destroyed if the pieces that had been the body of Osiris were not brought together once more. So Isis sought for them, and Nephthys, her sister, helped her in her seeking. Isis, in a boat that was made of reeds, floated over the marshes, seeking for the pieces. One, and then another, and then another was found. At last she had all the pieces of his torn body. She laid them together on a floating island, and reformed them. And as the body of Osiris was formed once more, the wars that men were waging died down; peace came; grain, and the vine, and the fruit-trees grew once more.

And a voice came to Isis and told her that Osiris lived again, but that he lived in the Underworld where he was now the Judge of the Dead, and that through the justice that he meted out, men and women had life immortal. And a child of Osiris was born to Isis: Horus he was named. Nephthys and the wise Thout guarded him on the floating island where he was born. Horus grew up, and he strove against the evil power of Sêth. In battle he overcame him, and in bonds he brought the evil Sêth, the destroyer of his father, before Isis, his mother. Isis would not have Sêth slain: still he lives, but now he is of the lesser Gods, and his power for evil is not so great as it was in the time before Horus grew to be the avenger of his father.

Avenging Osiris links Horus to the father and brings to pass the patriarchal dominance over Egypt. But it is Isis who symbolizes the bridge which makes this possible. She will also be the mother of Horus' four sons. Isis is the goddess of fertility who represents the multilevels of meaning underlying the matriarchal dominance. She is sister-wife, mother-wife, and life-giver who enters the land of the dead to reassemble her dead brother-husband. She holds the keys to the secrets of life and death.

The temptress symbolizes the goddess of fertility and is often associated with the powers assigned to the moon. She is also the goddess of love for her province is the human heart. She is often portrayed as holding in her hands the power of life and death. Deirdre and Isis are archetypal representations of the temptress' ability to control the destiny of an individual's lifespan. She often appears as mother and daughter, linking her to the concept of the eternally young woman. This also reveals her connection to the moon. Mircea Eliade states, "The moon is the first creature to die; but also the first to live again." The temptress appears; she increases her seductive appeal; the power wanes after the male has succumbed to her charms; she often disappears and, then, reappears as a renewed woman to fully live again. The moon is her metaphor; Isis symbolically appears as daughter, sister, wife, and mother to the men in her life. The energy contained within this cluster of symbols illustrates the temptress as goddess of fertility: she brings about birth, death, and rebirth. The moon's dark side is the energy underlying her power. The males she meets are attracted to her through their unconscious association with the anima. She may appear benign and helpful, but she also may become terrifying. The fertility cults associated with the temptress are often closely linked to the "sacred prostitutes" of antiquity. They remained vestal virgins in the service of the father-god, but their allegiance was always to the mother. Their virginity was maintained, not because they did not have sexual relations, but because they never became the captive-bride of a male. This process became identified with female initiation rites which existed outside the laws and taboos of the male's world. The temptress undergoes a rite of passage to mark her maturity as a woman. The blood which is shed in her name by males relates this ancient rite to the female's entrance into puberty at the point of menstruation. The following questions focus on the temptress and the ritual of initiation which accompanies her change from girl to woman.

1 Understanding her separation:
   a Compare and contrast the way Deirdre and Isis are separated from the collective. Describe the physical setting of their separation. In what ways do you see symbols of fertility associated with this locale? Discuss the reasons each is not part of the group. What "secret" powers does each seem to possess?
   b In which of the two stories does the temptress have difficulties with other members of her family? What is the basis of Deirdre's conflict with the King? Is he a father symbol? What quarrels does Isis have with Sêth? Why does she go to the land of the dead?
   c What is the source of Deirdre's and Isis' power? How does each use symbols to bring about magical transformations? In which of the myths is the temptress taught the means to fulfill her mission?

2 Understanding her initiation:
   a What test does Deirdre encounter after her separation? Why is she feared? How does Isis act to bring about Osiris' rebirth? How important are the males' functions in directing their actions? In which of these myths does the temptress bring about the failure of the hero? Discuss the implications of her ability

to remain in touch with the fertile powers of nature.
   b In which of these myths does the temptress appear evil? Discuss the way she symbolizes this negative force on her victims. In which myths does the temptress also appear "good"? What does this suggest about her ability to adapt to the male world?
   c What sacrifices are reported in these myths? Is the temptress the executioner of this sacrifice? Is she the victim? What is revealed about the emotions of the temptress? Is she independent? Explain! In which of the myths does the temptress overpower males? How does the temptress attest to her ability to be mature in a male-oriented culture? Discuss the marriage of Isis to her son. Why does Deirdre choose death over life? Does she fail or succeed in fulfilling her test?

3 Understanding her return:
   a What must the woman accept before she returns to the group? Discuss the transformation of the temptress as a sister who helps the male overcome his destruction. What insights about the potential power of the temptress do we gain from her role?
   b What "inner" realization about being a woman do we see in these myths? Do these women reflect the female's desire not to be the captive of the male? Explain!
   c What conflict does the temptress resolve? What conflicts does she fail to resolve? Discuss the contradictions between these two points of view.
   d What do these myths suggest about the relation of the temptress to the hero? Compare and contrast Deirdre with Hector; Isis with Rama. What differences and similarities are there about those human beings who choose to be individuals?

THE SHE-WOLF

GIOVANNI VERGA

She was tall, thin; she had the firm and vigorous breasts of the olive-skinned—and yet she was no longer young; she was pale, as if always plagued by malaria, and in that pallor, two enormous eyes, and fresh red lips which devoured you.

In the village they called her the She-wolf, because she never had enough—of anything. The women made the sign of the cross when they saw her pass, alone as a wild bitch, prowling about suspiciously like a famished wolf; with her red lips she sucked the blood of their sons and husbands in a flash, and pulled them behind her skirt with a single glance of those devilish eyes, even if they were before the altar of Saint Agrippina. Fortunately, the She-wolf never went to church, not at Easter, not at Christmas, not to hear Mass, not for confession.—Father Angiolino of Saint Mary of Jesus, a true servant of God, had lost his soul on account of her.

Maricchia, a good girl, poor thing, cried in secret because she was the She-wolf's daughter, and no one would marry her, though, like every other girl in the village, she had her fine linen in a chest and her good land under the sun.

One day the She-wolf fell in love with a handsome young man who had just returned from the service and was mowing hay with her in the fields of the notary; and she fell in love in the strongest sense of the word, feeling the flesh afire beneath her clothes; and staring him in the eyes, she suffered the thirst one has in the hot hours of June, deep in the plain. But he went on mowing undisturbed, his nose bent over the swaths.

"What's wrong, Pina?" he would ask.

In the immense fields, where you heard only the crackling flight of the grasshoppers, as the sun hammered down overhead, the She-wolf gathered bundle after bundle, and sheaf after sheaf, never tiring, never straightening up for an instant, never raising the flask to her lips, just to remain at the heels of Nanni, who mowed and mowed and asked from time to time:

"What is it you want, Pina?"

One evening she told him, while the men were dozing on the threshing floor, tired after the long day, and the dogs were howling in the vast, dark countryside.

"It's you I want. You who're beautiful as the sun and sweet as honey. I want you!"

"And I want your daughter, instead, who's a maid," answered Nanni laughing.

The She-wolf thrust her hands into her hair, scratching her temples, without saying a word, and walked away. And she did not appear at the threshing floor any more. But she saw Nanni again in October, when they were making olive oil, for he was working near her house, and the creaking of the press kept her awake all night.

"Get the sack of olives," she said to her daughter, "and come with me."

Nanni was pushing olives under the millstone with a shovel, shouting "Ohee" to the mule, to keep it from stopping.

"You want my daughter Maricchia?" Pina asked him.

"What'll you give your daughter Maricchia?" answered Nanni.

"She has all her father's things, and I'll give her my house too; as for me, all I need is a little corner in the kitchen, enough for a straw mattress."

"If that's the way it is, we can talk about it at Christmas," said Nanni.

Nanni was all greasy and filthy, spattered with oil and fermented olives, and Maricchia didn't want him at any price. But her mother grabbed her by the hair before the fireplace, muttering between her teeth:

"If you don't take him, I'll kill you!"

The She-wolf was almost sick, and the people were saying that when the devil gets old he becomes a hermit. She no longer roamed here and there, no longer lingered at the doorway, with those bewitched eyes. Whenever she fixed them on his face, those eyes of hers, her son-in-law began to laugh and pulled out the scapular of the Virgin to cross himself. Maricchia stayed at home nursing the babies, and her mother went into the fields to work with the men, and just like a man too, weeding, hoeing, feeding the animals, pruning the vines, despite the northeast and levantine winds of January or the August sirocco, when the mules' heads drooped and the men slept face down along the wall, on the north side. "In those hours between nones and vespers when no good woman goes roving around," * Pina was the only living soul to be seen wandering in the countryside, over the burning stones of the paths, through the scorched stubble of the immense fields that became lost in the suffocating heat, far, far away toward the foggy Etna, where the sky was heavy on the horizon.

"Wake up!" said the She-wolf to Nanni, who was sleeping in the ditch, along the dusty hedge, his head on his arms. "Wake up. I've brought you some wine to cool your throat."

Nanni opened his drowsy eyes wide, still half asleep, and finding her standing before him, pale, with her arrogant breasts and her coal-black eyes, he stretched out his hands gropingly.

"No! no good woman goes roving around in the hours between nones and vespers!" sobbed Nanni, throwing his head back into the dry grass of the ditch, deep, deep, his nails in his scalp. "Go away! go away! don't come to the threshing floor again!"

The She-wolf was going away, in

fact, retying her superb tresses, her gaze bent fixedly before her as she moved through the hot stubble, her eyes as black as coal.

But she came to the threshing floor again, and again than once, and Nanni did not complain. On the contrary, when she was late, in the hours between nones and vespers, he would go and wait for her at the top of the white, deserted path, with his forehead bathed in sweat; and he would thrust his hands into his hair, and repeat every time:

"Go away! go away! don't come to the threshing floor again!"

Maricchia cried night and day, and glared at her mother, her eyes burning with tears and jealousy, like a young she-wolf herself, every time she saw her come, mute and pale, from the fields.

"Vile, vile mother!" she said to her. "Vile mother!"

"Shut up!"

"Thief! Thief!"

"Shut up!"

"I'll go to the Sergeant, I will!"

"Go ahead!"

And she really did go, with her babies in her arms, fearing nothing, and without shedding a tear, like a madwoman, because now she too loved that husband who had been forced on her, greasy and filthy, spattered with oil and fermented olives.

The Sergeant sent for Nanni; he threatened him even with jail and the gallows. Nanni began to sob and tear his hair; he didn't deny anything, he didn't try to clear himself.

"It's the temptation!" he said. "It's the temptation of hell!"

He threw himself at the Sergeant's feet begging to be sent to jail.

"For God's sake, Sergeant, take me out of this hell! Have me killed, put me in jail; don't let me see her again, never! never!"

"No!" answered the She-wolf instead, to the Sergeant. "I kept a little corner in the kitchen to sleep in, when I gave him my house as dowry. It's my house. I don't intend to leave it."

Shortly afterward, Nanni was kicked in the chest by a mule and was at

the point of death, but the priest refused to bring him the Sacrament if the She-wolf did not go out of the house. The She-wolf left, and then her son-in-law could also prepare to leave like a good Christian; he confessed and received communion with such signs of repentance and contrition that all the neighbors and the curious wept before the dying man's bed.—And it would have been better for him to die that day, before the devil came back to tempt him again and creep into his body and soul, when he got well.

"Leave me alone!" he told the She-wolf. "For God's sake, leave me in peace! I've seen death with my own eyes! Poor Maricchia is desperate. Now the whole town knows about it! If I don't see you it's better for both of us . . ."

And he would have liked to gouge his eyes out not to see those of the She-wolf, for whenever they peered into his, they made him lose his body and soul. He did not know what to do to free himself from the spell. He paid for Masses for the souls in purgatory and asked the priest and the Sergeant for help. At Easter he went to confession, and in penance he publicly licked more than four feet of pavement, crawling on the pebbles in front of the church—and then, as the She-wolf came to tempt him again:

"Listen!" he said to her. "Don't come to the threshing floor again; if you do, I swear to God, I'll kill you!"

"Kill me," answered the She-wolf, "I don't care; I can't stand it without you."

As he saw her from the distance, in the green wheat fields, Nanni stopped hoeing the vineyard, and went to pull the ax from the elm. The She-wolf saw him come, pale and wild-eyed, with the ax glistening in the sun, but she did not fall back a single step, did not lower her eyes; she continued toward him, her hands laden with red poppies, her black eyes devouring him.

"Ah! damn your soul!" stammered Nanni.

* An old Sicilian proverb, which refers to the hours of the early afternoon, when the Sicilian countryside lies motionless under a scorching sun and no person would dare walk on the roads. Those hours are traditionally believed to be under the spell of malignant spirits.

In "The She-Wolf" Verga spins a tale of the temptress who struggles to make captive the male whom she needs to fulfill her desires. She is an "outsider." The rules of the group do not seem to relate to her sense of time and place. The male she selects is both attracted and repulsed by her, and he attempts to make her the culprit who forces him to do what he does not want to do. Verga's woman is a modern temptress who is animal and woman. The following questions focus on the she-wolf as a metaphor of the male and female's struggle to go beyond illusion.

1   What is implied by the title? In the first paragraph of the story, how does Verga's description of the woman depict her as a beast of prey? What does this suggest about the male's view of the female?

2   Why are the people concerned that "she never had enough of anything"? What projections are they directing toward the she-wolf? What does this suggest about their fears of her "secret powers"?

3   Describe the she-wolf's relation with her daughter. Does the daughter's "goodness" cast light on the mother's "evilness"? What does this suggest about the split between mother and daughter?

4   How does Verga bring in fertility symbols to describe the setting where the she-wolf meets Nanni? Does Nanni want to be seduced by the she-wolf? How does Nanni divide the mother and daughter? Why does the she-wolf threaten her daughter if she does not marry Nanni?

5   What does Nanni reveal about himself when he goes to the sergeant for help? What does this suggest about the male's need to impose laws on the female's passions? Is Nanni afraid of castration from the she-wolf? Or is he afraid of his own feelings? Explain!

6   Why is Nanni punished for his transgression? Does this encounter prevent him from seeing the she-wolf? Why does he seek religious advice? Does this help him against the she-wolf's powers? Why does he go to confession at Easter? What ritual is associated with Easter?

7   Discuss Verga's point of view in the conclusion of the story. Does Nanni use his ax? What does this suggest? What enables the she-wolf to be confident? Why does Nanni say: "Ah! damn your soul"? Who is damned, the she-wolf or Nanni? Why does he stammer? Does this suggest his failure to express his emotions? Explain the significance of this. Does this reveal the way the male projects his sexual desires onto the temptress?

8   Discuss the she-wolf as an archetypal representative of the temptress. What insights are revealed about the she-wolf's desire to be in control of her destiny? Does she resemble Deirdre? Isis? Explain!

The Dream Factory creates the cult of the Sex Goddess

In the twentieth century, Hollywood uses the fatal woman to project an image of feminine sexuality. From Theda Bara to Marilyn Monroe, who is pictured above, the sex goddess is the temptress whose domain is the realm of love. The men who come in contact with her often have to battle against all odds to win her approval. The sex goddesses are members of a cult which brings together both the executioner and victim in one symbol.

John Gilbert once whispered to Greta Garbo, "There is mystery in you." Garbo represents the fatal woman who projects the illusion of an enigmatic woman. Miss Garbo used this image to separate herself from anyone who tried to decode her secrets. The price she paid for her pedestal was a life aloof from others. The sex goddess often becomes the victim of her own desires. Jean Harlow tells Clark Gable, "I want to be free, be gay and have fun. Life's short, but I want to live while I am alive." Miss Harlow symbolized the good-bad girl of the 1930s. She used her body to project the erotic force of energy, but she was always a good sport in her relationships with men. Miss Harlow died

at the peak of her career. The aggressive part of Jean Harlow was captured by Mae West who said, "Do you have a pistol in your pocket, or are you just glad to see me?" She was a parody of the fatal woman. It could be said that Miss West was vulgar because she made fun of sex. She acted the aggressive side of the woman who strove to be independent of the rules of society.

Marilyn Monroe, the angel of sex, combined the characteristics of Garbo, Harlow, and West. She appeared innocent in her approach to men and, like Garbo, she appeared to be aloof from her sex appeal. Miss Monroe once walked off a set because a director told her to look sexy. She was like Harlow in her attempt to live life to gain satisfaction from her experiences. Possessing the humor of West, she, too, could be vulgar without appearing sexual. Marilyn Monroe said, "I want everybody to see my body." She symbolized the little, frightened girl exposing herself to an indifferent world. She used comedy to deflect from her power as a sex symbol. Her life revealed the breaking of a woman's spirit.

THE AWFUL FATE

PARKER TYLER

What, by virtue of the movies, is a sex goddess? It is easy to point, say, to Sophia Loren, imagine her quite naked (as may be done without the camera's assistance) and have the right answer. But Miss Loren's case is relatively simple and unaffected. The matter, with regard to the movies' history of sex, is too complex for mere pointing. The sex goddess's mutation, starting with the celebrated Vampire, is something to arrest and fascinate movie buffs and other susceptible scholars. Its ups and downs, turnabouts and triumphs, take on cosmic dimensions. Going in as straight a line as possible from Theda Bara to Greta Garbo, one's wits are staggered by so vast a change visible in one stroke of the imagination—and that stroke takes us only to 1941. . . . Technically, Garbo is a direct descendant of her distant Hollywood predecessor: the fatal Queen of Love and Ruler of Man which a sex goddess is—or was—supposed to be.

I change the tense and *there's* the rub. For whatever reasons, a sharp decline of divine dimensions in nominal sex goddesses has come about; it is as if 'sex' and 'goddess' were terms that, idiomatically, no longer agreed. Take the case of one who bore a notable physical resemblance to Sophia Loren, Jane Russell, a goddess ephemeral and now long extinct. Miss Russell was two great breasts mounted upon a human pedestal with a doll's head to top it off. Besides being no actress at all (which Loren, after all, *is*), Russell was hardly a sound recipe for a sex goddess. Her peculiar weakness may have lain in the very fact that a California judge, passing on the claim that her film, *The Outlaw,* was obscene owing largely to her salient and partly exposed mammary equipment, decided that anything God-given, such as breasts, could not be 'obscene.' Goddesses, by definition, *are* beyond the law. But voluptuous breasts are but the window-dressing of sex divinity. Jane represented one of the last historic efforts to invent a great personality on the basis of sex-appeal alone.

Plausibly, the physical dimensions of sex goddesses first tended to be ample. Theda Bara had a maternal figure. She was, in fact, remarkably like a suburban housewife circa World War I, bitten by the glamor bug into imagining herself supreme seductress of men, and by some weird turn of fate succeeding at it. Today, an Elizabeth Taylor also succeeds though *her* proportions and personality start by being those of the reigning office minx, from whom neither president of the company nor errand boy is safe. By another weird turn of fate we get instead, in this actress, a universal Miss Sexpot—for a sex goddess, one is obliged to call that a comedown. Nowadays sex-goddessing is more a trade than something, as it were, acquired by divine privilege. Another Italian star, Gina Lollobrigida, oddly resembles Miss Taylor although she is better-looking. Lollobrigida is simply Sophia Loren seen a few paces further off: a sort of reproduction in minor scale. But big and beautiful as La Loren is, we must face the fact that sheer majesty in the female body has become, historically, badly compromised as a glamor asset. Being a sex goddess has nothing whatever to do with the sexual act as such. Getting laid is a strictly human, quite unglamorous occupation.

Mediating between Bara and Garbo, Mae West turned up as an eccentric, utterly unexpected manifestation of sex divinity. Like the old gods of the Greek plays, she appeared with the primal authority of 'Here I am!' Part of the majesty of Mae's corseted figure, hefty of hip and bosom, was its anachronism: she duplicated the physical image of the late nineteenth-century stage, where even chorus girls were girthy. The very pathos of distance helped make West a goddess, and historic. I confess to having been, in 1944, the first to describe what her style owed to the female impersonator: just about everything basic. A true parody of sex divinity, Mae was the opposite of the classic Vampire because she aimed at being both funny and good-natured: qualities more plebeian than royal or divine.

The movie canon of the teens and twenties had it that personified sex-appeal was a destroyer of men. Hence the Vampire embodied irresistible sexual evil. She was no laughing matter till time gave us the modern perspective, in which she's little *but* that. Vintage eroticism, regally portrayed by beautiful ladies throughout the twenties, automatically evokes titters when seen today. Mae West's sudden greatness was to have introduced a *deliberately* comic parody of the sex goddess. Her unique blend of sexiness and vulgar comedy, in other words, was the screen's first sterling brand of conscious sex camp. Other brands developed but these were the cynical farcing of tired-out actresses who had never quite believed in their own eroticism. Mae *did* believe in hers. That was the wonder of the spectacle she made. Few others actually did—probably not even her leading men! What

her public believed in was the raw, happy camp of it. That incredible nasality, that incredible accent!

Garbo is virtually unique among the remoter goddesses because, even in some of her earlier roles (such as that in *Romance*), she can still be taken seriously. And yet even Garbo is not foolproof against the sensibility of what once a very few called, and now the world calls, camp. (Camp, one must note, is a proved culture virus affecting non-deviates as well as deviates.) Seeing Greta gotten up as an innocent country girl in *The Torrent*, one understands better that creeping parody of passion that meant her downfall in *Two-Faced Woman*, her last picture. The 'two-faced' was painfully exact. A split personality may have suited the being termed by Robert Graves the Triple Goddess of archaic times on earth. But for our times, even one extra personality makes *The Divine Woman* (the title of a Garbo film) into a schizophrenic with professional delusion-of-grandeur. Film myths of the making and unmaking of a star began to appear as early as the thirties and their climax, in the sixties, was explicitly labelled *The Goddess*—no accident that an actress with superficial sex-appeal and no real ability, Kim Stanley, was featured in it.

The sex goddess, supposedly, satisfies a basic human need: she would and should be the sanctified, superhuman symbol of bedroom pleasure, and bedroom pleasure as such seems here to stay. Europe, however, held a more tangible appreciation of sex as sex. Thus, a Brigitte Bardot came as no surprise at all. This legitimate goddess, after fifteen years' hard labor, has faded. Yet while she was at her international peak (somewhat pre-Loren), she had the simplicity and stark presence natural to erotic greatness. B. B., with canonic plenitude up front, facile nudity and long, tumbling blonde hair, was an impressive paradox: a cheerful Magdalene. Repentance and guilt were alien to her if only because her assets (like Jane Russell's before her) were so unmistakably Godgiven. Unworldly innocence imparted to B. B.'s sexiness a gay pathos; worldly sophistication imparted to Mae West's a more complex gaiety, a more complex pathos. B. B. was a symbol that implied nothing but reality, Mae a reality that implied nothing but a symbol . . .

When the self-farcing tendency began overtaking stars and films in the late fifties and sixties, even bouncy B. B. began parodying her rather down-to-earth divinity. As of now, screen nudity (to take sex at its simplest) has begun to be so proliferant as to look common. Arty, self-conscious, coyly denuding camera shots of the sexual clutch (one has had to creep up on body-candor in movies) has become, by 1969, a cliché. Sex goddesses inevitably were victimized by the big breakthrough toward sexual realism. Currently, we are down to the nitty-gritty of the postures, the pantings, the in-plain-view of sex —down, in other words, to its profanity, including the garniture of those four-letter words. The sex goddesses have become sitting ducks for the exploding peephole of a film frame. In *La Dolce Vita* (1960), Fellini's genius for casting cannily registered the fatal downwardness then true of sex-goddessing. We found a perfect big-blonde-goddess type, Anita Ekberg, playing a parody movie star with a bust like a titaness, a baby voice and the courage of Minnie Mouse.

Sexy even so? Well, yes. Fellini pressed some delicate poetry no less than some satire from the combination of Miss Ekberg's shape, poundage and sweet, naïve femininity. Yet when, in the film, her husband whacks her for moonlighting with Mastroianni and she slinks off to bed, La Ekberg is just another silly woman—and 'divine' only as a young man's midnight fancy. Even when she had answered in kind to the baying of neighborhood dogs, it was more a chorus than a command: the gorgeous bitch fled in an auto when the baying became serious. Fellini thereby branded the explicit profession of sex goddess a benignly comic fraud. Whyever should sex goddesses have fallen so low as to be 'caught out' like that? The way they were caught out is clear enough: their regal posture was shown as an imposture: a fabricated illusion based on physical pretensions and almost nothing else. The method was to expose the base fleshly mechanism behind a grand illusion. In Hollywood, both sex goddesses and other stars were, it seemed, manufactured. Essentially, the goddesses had been lovely hoaxes foisted upon a naïve, gullible and dated public of both sexes: the gaga identifiers (female) and the gasping adorers (male).

It is a pause-giving irony that the truly great among sex goddesses were the first to show glaring symptoms of the decline and fall of the movie line. Was there something too *façade-like* about the Very Greats? Gazing back, one can detect one of the handsomest, Nita Naldi (who played opposite Valentino in *Blood and Sand*), unable to be anything from head to foot but a striking mask. In the teens and early twenties,

statuesque feminine fulsomeness was still bona fide; it was the sweet and pure star actresses who were petite. Today, like Bara, Naldi must seem a rather puffy anachronism; if not downright absurd, at least strangely pathetic—a period clotheshorse, stunning but quite without humor. And take Mae West as a 'mask' rather than a comedienne: physically she seems made from a mold, as if her whole body were a layer of simulated flesh about an inch thick, with nothing whatever inside. It took wit, humor and an interesting face to make La West a real 'divine woman.'

Historically, humor came into Hollywood supersex with the later twenties in the personnel of Flaming Youth: chiefly the 'It Girl,' Clara Bow. And then, of course, came Jean Harlow, who created a totally new standard for sex goddesses. Jean was a sacred-whore type whose unabashed vulgarity (even as West's) was integral with the spell she cast. Yet a few veils of illusion had been brutally torn off: evidently the sex goddess was no lady if, as Harlow, she could be a downright slut. Nobody sensed it then, I think, but a great symbol was being debunked. There could be no question about *Harlow's* real fleshliness, all over and through and through, if only because nothing seemed to exist between her and her filmy dresses but a little perspiration.

Like Mae, Jean was funny—more professionally and seriously so than Clara Bow, who was only a rampaging teenager with sex-appeal; essentially, that is, Clara was *decent*. Both West and Harlow let a certain middle-class decency (allied with basic chastity) simply go by the board. Both gloried in being, at least potentially, unchaste. They weren't exactly prostitutes (or but rarely) yet that they exploited sex professionally hit one between the eyes. They were Gimme Girls as much as Glamor Girls and quite beyond morality in those vocations. It would be humanly unnatural should beautiful ladies, every bare inch of them, cease to be darlings of the camera's eye. But capitalized Lust is either a mad holiday or a deadly sin. Once, being a sex goddess was to skip all mundane considerations and assume that Lust meant Glorious Aphrodite. In the movies' advanced age (they are well over seventy), sex and other sorts of violence keep the film cameras grinding. But make no mistake: the goddessing of movie sex, subtly and brutally too, has met an awful fate.

In West, parody was a divine she-clown act; in Harlow, sex bloomed miraculously, nakedly, gaudily from the gutter. *The Queen*, a documentary about classy transvestites competing for the title of Miss All-American, offers (at the moment I write) the most eloquent evidence anywhere that sex-goddessing can still be taken seriously. Yet among those to whom queendom is synonymous with homosexuality, the divinity of sex as a public symbol carries a necessary irony and a necessary narrowness. 'Harlow' has become a sort of trade name among professional transvestites. The winner of the contest in *The Queen* calls himself just Harlow, and one of Andy Warhol's home-made films is titled *Harlot* because it features an Underground transvestite's camp act in a blonde wig.

This 'superstar,' Mario Montez, has attached the name of a minor sex goddess (extinct) who was lately honored with an Underground cult: Maria Montez. The camp symbolism of the Warhol film, whose action takes place entirely on and about a couch where four people are grouped—two young men, a 'lesbian' and 'Harlow'—is to have Montez extract first one banana then another from various caches and munch them deliberately, in voluptuous leisure, for about an hour. This is the principal 'action.' Get the picture? If you do, you qualify for the Underground sex scene. It's this way: one is to imagine a camp queen of sex, even when genuinely female, not with an adoring male crawling up her knees, but an adored male with *her* crawling up *his* knees. In her early days, Garbo herself used to slither over her men like a starved python. But she was only combating Old Man Morality: her erotic power, and its authenticity, were never in question.

Today everything is in question about the sex goddess but the blunt mechanism any woman offers a man. Personally, I find the progressive demoralization of the s. g. in females rather desperately saddening. Two acting celebrities, Bette Davis and Tallulah Bankhead (while neither was ever a sex goddess), have parodied neurotic and unconsciously funny females so often and so emphatically that they represent an historic attack on high feminine seductiveness. Sex-parody became, rather early, an integral part of Miss Davis' style till it exploded in her 100 per cent camp films, *Whatever Happened to Baby Jane?* and *Hush, Hush, Sweet Charlotte*. The aging Miss Bankhead's failure as a serious actress was suavely turned into success on the radio as a bass-voiced caricature. In the movies, finally, Bankhead followed suit to *Hush, Hush, Sweet Charlotte* with *Die, Die, My Darling*

(Ugh!). Yet she (a handsome woman in her own right) had once in her career, if transiently, vied with Garbo.

We find a rich clue to the fate of the sex goddesses if we look at the way classic beauty currently serves movie sex. If the physical proportions and personalities of Sophia Loren and Anita Ekberg lend themselves easily to light sex-comedy with a wedge of farce and satire, the face and figure of Ursula Andress (taken in themselves) have a pure, invulnerable classic beauty. In the nineteenth century and the first quarter of the twentieth, Ursula would have been destined as a sex goddess of real if removed divinity, surrounded with protocol and awe, a queen of fashion as of sex. On looks and style alone, Andress would do as well in society as in the acting profession. But what, alas! was her fate? To be an ultra-classy foil for a James Bond—a lesbianlike Pussy Galore! A 'destroyer of men,' by all means, but stamped with the comic-strip sensibility (see *Modesty Blaise*, et al.) that informs all Pop versions of camp sex.

The newest archetype of the sex goddess, robbing her of her former dignity and classic authority, inhabits the comic strip itself, where Barbarella (played by Jane Fonda) has been enshrined as the supreme Vinyl Girl of sex-appeal. Fundamentally, she is the oldtime serial queen, *rediviva*. Remember that serials (take *The Perils of Pauline*) were always animated comic strips with real performers. Even more significantly, there has been the completely nude Phoebe Zeit-Geist, the comicstrip heroine introduced by the Evergreen Review. Like a metaphysical idea, Phoebe seemed not to know what clothes are. Her sole function, naked and attractive as she was, was to be camp sacrificial victim *in perpetuo* for the historic villains and most grandiose, come-lately freaks of comicstripdom (for more clarification of this theme, consult the well-thumbed dictionary of sado-masochism at your local library).

Maybe no fate is really awful so long as, like Phoebe's, it's also fun. Yet the point is erotically disputable. To those tending to think the female sex represents a supreme power, like antiquity's Ruler of Men, the latterday Pop versions of sex goddesses partake more of existential gloom than existential fun. The 'fun' is slightly sick. Shouldn't the put-it-on-the-line psychology of sex-presentation be left for the hardcore geeks in the audience? Actually the transvestites, with their delusions of reincarnating extinct sex goddesses, are truer queens of beauty and sex than

Ursula Andress—who looks more and more as if she had been cut out of cardboard and achieved her classic volumes by courtesy of 3-D (flesh-tones by Technicolor). I, for one, think it an awful fate that the grand profession of sex-goddessing should have sunk to the petty profession of sex-shoddessing. The robotizing trend of female charms (against which only that cartoon pair of *Playboy* tits seems holding out) must not be underrated. Think, ladies and gentlemen! The supreme goal of male propulsion, as foreseen in *2001: a Space Odyssey*, is a geometric black slab with unproved sexual capacities. Theda Bara would, tacitly, be more negotiable than that; and shapelier.

Come to think of it, Marilyn Monroe came along in those fidgety fifties and altered the whole set-up. There was something genuine about her, and really pathetic, as if she were all too human to exercise the great craft of queening it for the tradition. We know what finally happened to her. Maybe she was the last 'goddess' actually seeming to be made out of flesh rather than foamrubber: something to sleep *with*, not *on*. And that was probably her fatal mistake. Goddesses are to be slept *about*.

Parker Tyler's essay focuses on Hollywood's version of the temptress: the sex goddess. These women appear as symbolic representations of the mysterious woman's power over men. The initiation for the sex goddess is a test to be performed on the battleground of love. Tyler contends that from Theda Bara to Marilyn Monroe certain women have captured the imagination of the moviegoing audience. He believes that current movies are lacking in a form in which the sex goddess can act out her role. The demise of the sex goddess, Tyler believes, is revealed in the transvestite's enactment of love on the screen, and, in *2001: A Space Odyssey*, where she becomes a marble slab. He concludes with a statement about Marilyn Monroe which reveals her as a woman composed of flesh and blood. Tyler believes that Monroe ends alone because of her desire to be a woman rather than a goddess. Perhaps because she played the role, Marilyn Monroe was set apart from a male-dominant world. The following questions link the sex goddess to the temptress.

1 How does Tyler compare and contrast Garbo as the queen of love with Mae West as a parody of the woman? How do both of these women represent aspects of the temptress' image? What needs do both of these women fulfill? What attitudes about the nature of women are reflected in the images surrounding these two women? How would Mae West relate to Isis?

2 What image of the temptress emerges in Tyler's discussion of Jean Harlow? How is she the temptress as a representation of the unchaste woman? Would she be described in antiquity as one of the "sacred prostitutes"?

3 What characteristics does Tyler contend define a sex goddess? What sex goddess in the contemporary world has any of these characteristics? How does the sex goddess seduce her lovers?

4 Discuss Tyler's view of the presence of a contemporary sex goddess or lack of one. Is there a loss of illusion surrounding the sex goddess? What does this suggest about the temptress in the modern world?

5 In Tyler's view of the sex goddess, do you see any representations of Isis? Deirdre? Explain!

6 Select a contemporary sex goddess and discuss the way she either affirms or denies Tyler's theory. What kind of symbolic status is associated with her image? Is she an independent woman? What is known about her relations with men? Is she much-married and much-divorced? Explain why so many of these women marry so often. Does this reflect the concept of the "vestal virgins" of antiquity?

THE MYSTERIES OF WOMAN

M. ESTHER HARDING

The fertilizing power of the moon was symbolized by its light. But this "symbolizing" was no abstract intellectualized concept. To antique man, as to the primitives, the light of the moon was its fertilizing power. Moonlight falling on a woman as she slept might in very fact generate new life in her, an actual flesh-and-blood child. And so we find that the light of the moon is, as it were, tended or encouraged by lights on earth. Torches, candles, and fires are burned in honor of the moon and are used as fertilizing magic, being carried, for example, round the newly seeded fields to aid the germination of the grain, just as Hecate's torches were carried around the freshly sown fields, long ago in Greece, to promote their fertility.

This idea of the fertilizing power of the moon being actually fire is a very common one. It is thought that this power can be hidden in wood or tree where it lies sleeping in latent form, and can be drawn out again by rubbing, the primitive way of producing fire. The Huitoto, for instance, say that fire was first obtained from the moon by a woman. And there is another primitive myth, which states that an old woman probably the moon herself, who is so often called the Old Woman, made the first fire by rubbing her genitals, while in the Vedic hymns of a far higher culture, Agni, the fire spirit, is also regarded as being hidden in the sacred wood, from which he is born again through rubbing the fire stick.

The Moon Goddess was, indeed, thought of as being actually the fire or the light of the moon, which could lie latent in wood. This is attested by the legend that Orestes brought the worship of the great goddess to Italy, after slaying King Thoas, by concealing her image in a bundle of faggots, which he took with him. Thus the goddess was, as it were, the flame latent in the bundle, waiting to be brought to life again by certain rituals. In Italy they named her Diviana, which means *The* Goddess, a name that is more familiar to us in its shortened form of Diana. For Diana, the Huntress, was none other than the Moon Goddess, Mother of all animals. She is shown in her statues crowned with the crescent and carrying a raised torch. The Latin word for torch or candle is *vesta,* and Diana was also known as Vesta. So that the bundle of faggots, in which she came from Greece, was really an unlighted torch. In her temple a perpetual fire was kept burning and her chief festival was called the Festival of Candles or of

Torches. It was celebrated on August the fifteenth when her groves shone with a multitude of torches. This day is still celebrated as a Festival of Candles, but the torches are no longer lighted in Rome for Diana, but for the Virgin Mary. It is the day of her Assumption. On this day of Diana's old festival it is Mary who is carried to the heavens above, to reign there as Queen of Heaven.

Another ancient festival of candles celebrated long ago for a moon goddess is now repeated on the same date, February the second, for the Virgin Mary, Moon of our Church, as the Fathers call her. This is the Festival of Candlemas. It corresponds in date and customs to the Celtic Holy Day of St. Bride or St. Brigit. St. Brigit is the Christianized form of the ancient Celtic goddess Bridgit or Brigentis, a triune moon goddess whose worship was at one time very widespread. On February the first, as today in the Catholic Church at the Festival of Candlemas, the new fire was kindled and blessed.

A feast of lamps was also celebrated at Sais in Egypt in honor of Isis-Net. The ceremony took place in an under-chapel beneath the temple. Lamps were carried in procession around the coffin of Osiris, for it was by the power of light, symbolizing the life-giving power of the moon, that Isis could rekindle life in the dead Osiris.

Another custom in regard to the tendance of fire is of interest here. A perpetual fire was kept burning at Tara, the seat of the ancient Irish kings. On Midsummer Eve the fire was extinguished and was rekindled the following day, on the Feast of Beltane, which was originally a moon, not a sun, festival. On taboo days sacred fires are usually extinguished, signifying that then the deity has gone to the underworld. In the Catholic Church, for instance, the light which burns before the altar is quenched on Good Friday, when Christ has left the earth and descended into Hades, and is relighted on Easter Saturday. In the Eastern or Greek church the coming of the new light is one of the most important ceremonials of the year. Pilgrims congregate in Jerusalem in order to be present at the kindling of the new fire and to take home a taper lighted from the sacred flame. At the special morning service the archimandrite goes apart and remains in communion with God until the new fire is miraculously kindled. It is a rebirth of the light, symbolizing the return

of Christ from the underworld, where in striking resemblance to the moon deities of an earlier time, he remained after his death, preaching to the souls in Hades.

In Babylon and in the Jewish law it was prescribed that there should be no fires kindled on the Sabbath, the Nefast, or taboo day. This ordinance, as we have seen, was connected with the belief that the Moon Goddess was under a menstrual taboo at that time. Similarly the tribes of the Orinoco also put out their fires during an eclipse of the moon, which is to them an inauspicious day.

The sacred fire was conceived of quite definitely as the spark or power of fertility. In the north of England, for instance, Candlemas used to be called The Wives Feast Day because it was regarded as a fertility festival. An interesting custom which survived in Scotland till as late as the end of the seventeenth century, bears witness to this fact. On Candlemas Eve a sheaf of oats was dressed in women's clothing. This "woman" was laid in what was called "Brigid's bed," and a wooden club was placed beside her. The women of the village sat up and kept a torch burning in the room all night long.[1] This drama was clearly a fertility rite. For "Brigid" refers to the Celtic goddesses who were known as the Three Brigids representing the three phases of the moon. So on the festival night the moon's fertilizing power, its light, was symbolized and invoked by the torch that was kept burning beside the corn woman in her union with the wooden pole, symbol of the phallus. The custom seems to say that the corn woman could not give rise to a new harvest unless she were energized by a sacred marriage blessed by the fertilizing power of the moon.

In many places a perpetual sacred fire was kept burning in the temple of the moon goddess, guarded and tended by a group of priestesses dedicated to its service. They were usually called Vestal Priestesses after the Vestal Virgins who tended the perpetual fire in the temple of the goddess Vesta in Rome. They did not marry, except under certain ritual conditions, but in some cases, they were considered to be "wives" of the king, although they were still called virgin, and not infrequently the king owed his pre-eminence to the fact that he was so "married" to a Vestal

[1] T. Banes, "Candlemas," *Hastings Encyclopaedia of Religion and Ethics* (New York and Edinburgh, 1909), III, 192.

Priestess. This was the case in Rome, and indeed, many of the early kings were sons of Vestal Virgins. Frazer notes that at her consecration each girl received the name of Amata, or beloved, which was the title of the wife of the legendary King Latinus.[2] In many places these priestesses were sacred harlots, who gave themselves to strangers and to the male worshippers of the Goddess. The term virgin was thus clearly used in its original sense of unmarried. For these women were pledged to the service of the Goddess, their sex, their attraction, their love, were not to be used for their own satisfaction or for the ordinary purposes of human life. They could not unite themselves to a husband, for their woman's nature was dedicated to a higher purpose, that of bringing the fertilizing power of the Goddess into effective contact with the lives of human beings.

Closely associated with the symbol of the fire, maintained in the temples of the Moon Goddess, to embody or represent her power of perpetual fertility, are to be found certain explicitly phallic objects which were venerated side by side with the Goddess herself. In Rome, for instance, in the temple of the goddess Vesta, a god, Pales, or Pallas, was also worshipped. He seems to have been identical with Priapus, and was represented by a phallic image. These two together formed the deity Pabulum which is Food.[3] The union of the moon goddess and the phallic image recalls the Scottish Candlemas custom of Brigid's Bed mentioned above, which was intended to secure a good supply of food.

The phallic god, Pallas, was not considered to be a rival deity but rather the associate of the Goddess. Each carried the symbol of fertility, but only when they were united in their functions was the "mystery" fulfilled. A similar connection existed in the case of other moon goddesses. For instance, the lover of Selene was Pan, and there has recently been discovered at the Acropolis, a tunnel leading from the temple of Aphrodite down to the temple of Eros which is below it. It is believed that at night a maiden descended by this tunnel carrying sacred objects. The visit doubtless represented a sacred union or marriage between Eros and Aphrodite.

[2] J. G. Frazer, "The Magic Art and the Evolution of Kings," *The Golden Bough*, Part I (New York, 1917), II, 197.

[3] Briffault, *The Mothers* (New York, 1927), III, 18.

Now these three gods, Priapus, Pan, and Eros, are all phallic or erotic gods. They do not carry the same significance as Tammuz, Adonis, and Attis, who are vegetation gods. Hence, when they are worshipped in company with the moon goddesses, their rites do not signify the fertilizing power of the moon married to the fruitfulness of earth, but rather the union of the masculine essence or principle with the feminine power.

This same idea that the divine power is manifested through the union of male and female is expressed in a symbol which is sometimes found representing the goddess Cybele, who was one form of the Magna Dea. She is represented as a lunar crescent in perpetual union with the sun. A similar symbol is found in Celebes in modern times. There an ithyphallic[4] god is worshipped as the supreme deity. He, like Pallas in the temple of Vesta, is served by priestesses. His supreme revelation is in the form of a symbol of the lingam and yoni (male and female genitalia) in contact. His chief festival is held at the first full moon after Ramadan. His connection with moon worship is established by this date, for Ramadan is the fast of lamentation for Tammuz, son of Ishtar, who died and went to the underworld. The festival of the phallic god of Celebes proclaims that God is manifested anew at the first full moon, in the *union* of the male and female power. God is not here represented as existing either in the erect phallus, or in the all embracing woman, but he shines out, comes into manifest being, in the *moment* of union, in the act through which tension is released and energy put forth.

To symbolize this truth of God as manifest, potent, in the union of male and female, the union, that is, of masculine and feminine principles, women, at their initiation into the mysteries of the Great Goddess, sacrificed their virginity in the temple, by entering into a *hieros gamos,* or sacred marriage, which was consummated sometimes with the priest, as representative of the phallic power of the god, sometimes with the phallic image itself, and sometimes with any stranger who might be spending the night in the temple precincts.

In this transition of the partner to the *hieros gamos* we see clearly the attempt to make of the act an impersonal ritual. At first it was the priest, who was not considered to be a man

[4] Ithyphallic is a Greek word meaning "with erect penis."

like other men, but was believed to be an incarnation of the god; he was recognized as functioning only in his office. In other cases the image of the phallus of the god was used. This rite was entirely without personal connotation. When the "stranger" enacted the part of the priest or the god, too, the impersonality of the situation was evident. The rite was performed by two people who had never seen each other before and would in all probability never see each other again. Indeed the regulations prescribed that the stranger should depart before daylight. In this way the nonpersonal, or divine aspect of the rite was impressed upon the participants.

It seems to have been a quite general custom for the moon goddess to be served by virgin priestesses, who were hierodules, or sacred prostitutes. In the temples of Ishtar, they were called Joy-maidens, and the term Ishtaritu, used to describe them, is the equivalent of the Greek hierodule meaning sacred prostitute. In some places these priestesses had sexual congress only with the man who impersonated the moon god, like the Vestal Virgins who were considered to be wives of the kings. But more often the sacred marriage could take place with any male worshipper or initiate who sought for union with the goddess. A sacred marriage of this kind probably formed part of the initiation of men to the mysteries of the goddess.

The priestesses were usually dedicated to the service of the Goddess for life. They remained in the sanctuary and performed the sexual rites, as they were prescribed, in addition to their other functions of tending the sacred flame and performing the water rites. They did not enter into secular marriages. They were virgins. But in addition to these sacred harlots, other women who were not pledged to a religious life were required to prostitute themselves once in their lifetime in the temple.

In his *History* Herodotus writes: "The worst Babylonian custom is that which compels every woman of the land once in her life to sit in the temple of love and have intercourse with some stranger . . . the men pass and make their choice. It matters not what be the sum of money; the woman will never refuse, for that were a sin, the money being by this act made sacred. After their intercourse she has made herself holy in the sight of the goddess and goes away to her home; and thereafter there is no bribe however great that will get

her. So then the women that are tall and fair are soon free to depart, but the uncomely have long to wait because they cannot fulfill the law; for some of them remain for three years or four. There is a custom like to this in some parts of Cyprus."

The custom of religious prostitution was practiced particularly by the royal women of Greece and Asia Minor. The king was then regarded as an incarnation of the god, and his sisters and daughters, by becoming priestesses and mating with him, relived with him the myth of the union of Aphrodite and Adonis. For the mating of the god and goddess was "deemed essential to the propagation of animals and plants, each in their several kind; and further, the fabulous union of the divine pair was simulated and as it were, multiplied on earth by the real though temporary, union of the human sexes at the sanctuary of the goddess for the sake of thereby ensuring the fruitfulness of the ground and the increase of man and beast."[5] In Babylon also the daughters of noble families prostituted themselves in the temple of Anahita, the Mazdian moon goddess, dedicating, as it were, the first fruits of their womanhood to her.

In later times in Greece, when the social feeling against promiscuous sexual relations, at least for women, was more developed, women who went to the temple of the goddess to perform the ancient ceremony, were allowed to sacrifice their hair instead of their virginity as a sort of symbolic surrender of their womanhood to her. But on the occasion of the ceremonial they still spent the night in the temple, a vivid reminder of the origin of the ritual.

In the worship of Cybele, whose symbol of the crescent moon was often shown in perpetual union with the sun, the initiate recited the following confession which is recorded by Clement of Alexandria.

> I have eaten from the timbrel,
> I have drunk from the cymbal,
> I have borne the sacred vessel,
> I have entered into the bridal chamber.

The first two lines obviously refer to a communion meal. That which was eaten was in all probability a cake or barley meal or of some other grain. This symbolized the body of the god, son of the mother; the drink was probably

[5] Frazer, *op. cit.*, Part IV, I, 39.

either of wine or of blood, or of wine as the symbol of blood. The Moon God was believed to have taught the knowledge of the vine as well as how to grow grain. He *was* the fruit of the corn and in some cases was also considered to be himself the fruit of the vine, his blood being the wine. Or perhaps the drink may be considered to be the Soma drink, wine of the gods, which was brewed from the moon tree and whose earthly counterpart was an intoxicating drink variously called "soma," "hoama," or "moly." The third line "I have borne the sacred vessel" refers to the carrying of the *kernos* which was a vase or bowl divided into many separate compartments, intended to contain different fruits and grains. In the center was a candle or torch representing the light of fertility whose power caused the fruits of the earth to grow. The initiant carried the sacred vessel, thus enacting the part of priest or priestess. The vase or vessel represented the womb of the Great Mother, giver of all life and increase, and was frequently used as a symbol or emblem of the goddess herself. The Virgin Mary for instance is called the Holy Vase, recipient of the fertilizing power of the Holy Spirit, from which Christ was born. Isis was symbolized by the vase of water, where the water was the fertilizing power of Osiris caught and contained in the Vase of Isis, by which it was brought into manifestation in material form, namely the whole of nature.

In this confession the initiant declares: "I have borne the sacred vessel, I have become the recipient of the creative power of god." And the confession ends with the statement: "I have entered into the bridal chamber."

This was evidently a deeply significant experience. The concreteness with which it was enacted may repel us with our conscious morality and our rationalistic attitude but we cannot fail to appreciate the sincerity of those who took part in the ceremonial. To them it was in very truth a *hieros gamos,* a sacred marriage. In it they dedicated their most precious function, namely their reproductive power, to the goddess and avowed that for them spiritual fulfillment, attained through union with the godhead, was more important than biological satisfaction or ordinary human love.

It may seem strange at first sight that women should be required to sacrifice or give up their virginity to the goddess of love. It might be expected that she would bestow upon her worshippers gifts enhancing their attraction for men instead of demanding the sacrifice of their feminine function in her service. Frazer raises this problem and in answer to it he says: "The gods stood as much in need of their worshippers as the worshippers in need of them."[6] The goddess, the all-powerful deity of fertility, represents the creative power which resides in all female things and this power is renewed by the service rendered her in the *hieros gamos,* for as women sacrifice or give up the personal use and control of their feminine power to her, her divine power is enhanced, it shines forth anew. These things are not easy to express in words, they are more feelings than concepts, nor can they be grasped rationally, but we can perhaps intuitively sense something of this kind as being the essence or significance of the experience which lay behind the confession: "I have borne the sacred vessel. I have entered the bridal chamber." Nevertheless the *relation* which the ancients sought to establish between men and the gods they themselves called The Mysteries. The experience *is* a mystery which can be understood only when it is recognized that the "gods" are not beings external to man but are rather psychological forces or principles which have been projected and personified in "the gods." They overshadow man, but their roots are buried in the hidden depths of the human psyche.

In the mysteries, the chief priestess who impersonated the Moon Goddess, herself, was "married," once a year, to a man impersonating the male principle, the Priapic God. While the mystery was enacted in the holy place, the worshippers kept vigil in the temple. At the consummation of the rite attendant priestesses came forth from the sacred shrine bearing the new Sacred Fire which had just been born through the renewal of the power of the goddess, and from the new fire the household fires of all the worshippers were relighted. This rite recalls the similar ceremony performed to this day on Easter Saturday in Jerusalem.

The priestesses of the Moon Goddess in addition to performing those offices which represented the goddess in her fertilizing and life-giving activities, had also to impersonate her in her dark and destructive aspect. The Vestal Virgins, it will be recalled, threw twenty-four manikins into the Tiber each year, and infant

[6] *Ibid.,* Part I, I, 31.

sacrifices were regularly performed in honor of, certainly, some forms of the goddess. It is recorded, for instance, that around the sacred stone which represented the goddess Astarte, hundreds of skeletons of human infants have been found. She was the goddess of untrammelled sexual love and first-born children and animals were sacrificed to her.

The chief priestess of the Celtic moon goddess were required to act as executioner whenever a human sacrifice was made. She had to kill the victim with her own hands. After a battle, for instance, the prisoners were so sacrificed, their heads being cut off, while they were held over a silver cauldron in which the blood was caught. One of the cauldrons was discovered in Jutland and is now in the Museum at Copenhagen. It is embossed with figures which not only show scenes of battle but also depict the Moon Goddess and the sacrificial ceremonial.

The silver vessel was called the Cauldron of Regeneration. It is the cauldron of the Moon Goddess who was the giver of fertility and of love. The blood poured into it must have formed a regenerating drink, or possibly bath. It is also recorded that the cauldron must be boiled until it yielded "three drops of the grace of inspiration," so that it is also the cauldron of inspiration, giving a drink like the soma mentioned earlier. MacCulloch informs us that this Celtic cauldron is probably the forerunner of the Holy Grail of the Arthurian Legends. He says: "Thus in the Grail there was a fusion of the magic cauldron of Celtic paganism and the sacred chalice of Christianity, with the products made mystic and glorious in the most wonderful manner."[7]

The Grail is a mysterious symbol. It is sometimes spoken of as a Chalice in which a spear, perpetually dripping blood, is thrust; and sometimes as a stone: or again as a food-bearing dish. It is always associated with a king who is either dead or mortally ill. This king is called the Fisher. His country, like himself, is sick, dried up, barren. It is called the Wastelands. In this old Celtic legend we have elements that correspond to important details in the myths of other moon deities.[8] The lands are waste because the Moon God has gone to the underworld and the moisture that he alone can bring is withdrawn. The chalice containing blood is the sacrificial cauldron of the Celtic moon goddess. To drink from that vessel bestows regeneration, renewal, perhaps immortality. As stone, the Grail is obviously a symbol for the Moon Mother herself, who, in many ancient religions, as we saw above, was worshipped under the form of a stone or cone. As food-bearing dish, the Grail is the symbol of the Goddess of Agriculture and of Plenty. In the Celtic version, the Fisher King, guardian of the Grail, suffers perpetual sickness, being neither dead nor alive, but suspended in a halfstate between life and death, until the mystery of the Grail should be revealed to a mortal man, who has achieved that illumination through his courage and endurance. Then the Fisher King will be restored to life and the Wastelands will become fertile once more.

Such is the legend of the Grail and, as Jessie Weston points out, it is clearly the story of an initiation.[9] The ordeal always requires that the hero shall ask a certain question: namely "What do these things mean and whom do they serve?" Failure to do so means that the mysteries continue in their eternal round, but no one is served thereby, and the lands remain waste. But if the question *is* asked and the meaning is made conscious, then the spell is broken, the king is healed and peace and plenty are restored to the lands.

There is a very interesting variant of these archetypal happenings recorded in the story of Isis, where Maneros, the Fisher, falls into the sea and is drowned. In this legend the reason why the Fisher is dead, or mortally sick, is recounted. In the Grail legends this point is never made very clear, though in Wagner's *Parsifal,* his condition is ascribed to his failure to keep his vow of chastity. Maneros fell overboard because of his inability to endure the sight of Isis' grief over the dead Osiris; he could not stand the "awe of the Goddess."

Other examples of a Cauldron of Regeneration are to be found in the cauldron of the Alchemists and the cauldron of the Chinese

[7] J. A. MacCulloch, *The Religion of the Ancient Celts* (Edinburgh, 1911), p. 383. *See also* J. A. MacCulloch, "The Abode of the Blest," Hastings' *Encyclopaedia of Religion and Ethics* (New York and Edinburgh, 1909), II, 694.

[8] In the Arthurian cycle, recorded by Chrétien de Troyes and in *The Mabinogion*, the old Celtic legend has been "Christianized." Thus the grail represents the chalice used at the Last Supper, and the spear dripping blood is the one used by Longinus to pierce the side of Christ. These sacred objects were believed to have been carried to Britain by Joseph of Arimathea and housed at Glastonbury.

[9] Jessie L. Weston, *The Quest of the Holy Grail* (London, 1913).

and Hindu philosophies. In all these instances the cauldron is believed to have power to change the base material into the spiritual, the mortal into the immortal. It brewed the drink of immortality and of spiritual regeneration, and also the drink of inspiration. However, it could be used to brew "medicine," magic, powerful stuff, which was not beneficial but harmful. Just as the witches of the Middle Ages and of folklore were said to brew love potions, or fertility medicine for the fields or for barren women; or might instead produce baleful effects such as storms, illness, and fits, or even death. One reason for the extraordinary persistence of the witch cults in the Middle Ages, a persistence which survived wholesale massacre, burnings, and torturings, was doubtless that the women who took part in them really believed that the fertility of the countryside depended on their activities. Their religion had an extraordinary hold upon them. Its symbols must have sprung from a very deep level of the unconscious, for, as the records of the witch trials bear witness, they inspired hundreds of simple countrywomen to face a horrible death without flinching.[10]

The sexual rites of the witches carried the significance of a union with the divine power as well as being a magic rite to secure fertility. But as the religion had already been superseded by Christianity its symbols had dropped into the unconscious and appeared from there in negative form. The phallic god in the witch cults was not Bright Son of the Moon Mother, but was the Son of Darkness, the Devil. His rites, however, were still carried out at the new and full moon. The witch rites also included a *hieros gamos,* a sexual union either with a man who impersonated the devil, or more often with the image of a phallus. These rites correspond to those practiced in the ancient mysteries of the Moon Goddess.

The Moon Goddess was attended primarily by priestesses; but she also had priests attached to her temple. Like the priestesses they also took upon themselves vows which were not required of the ordinary man, nor even of the initiate who was not a priest. The ordinary man restored to the temple of the goddess to take part in the *hieros gamos,* perhaps once in his life, at his initiation. It was a sacrament of union with the divine feminine nature and was also a ritual for the renewal of his powers of fertility. But the priests who were vowed to the service of the goddess for life, had a characteristic which seems very strange in the devotees of a goddess of fertility and in a temple where the phallic emblem is so directly venerated. These priests were eunuchs, or they were treated in some way as women, for instance they had long hair and women's clothes.

In certain tribes the priests of the moon wore feminine garb habitually, in others they wore masculine clothes when serving the male powers of nature, but feminine ones when serving the female powers; as Adolph Bastian reports, they learned "the idea of sex change from the Moon."[11]

The outstanding example of the ancient moon goddesses being served by eunuch priests is to be found in the worship of Phrygian Cybele. The emasculated men who were dedicated to her worship were considered to be incarnations of her son Attis, who was himself a moon god, wearing the crescent as a crown and in typical fashion, both son and lover of his mother, the Moon Goddess, Cybele.

The myth of Attis relates that he was about to wed the king's daughter when his mother, or his grandmother, who was in love with him, struck him mad. Attis, in madness, or ecstasy, castrated himself before the Great Goddess. Annually in a worship dating from 900 B.C., on March the twenty-fourth, Cybele's grief for her son is celebrated. The lamentation for Attis recalls the grief of Ishtar for Tammuz and of Aphrodite for Adonis.

But in the worship of Cybele a special element was given great prominence. The third day of the festival was called the *Dies Sanguinis.* In it the emotional expression of grief for Attis reached its height. Singing and wailing intermingled and the emotional abandon rose to orgiastic heights. Then in a religious frenzy young men began to wound themselves with knives; some even performed the final sacrifice, castrating themselves before the image of the goddess and throwing the bloody parts upon her statue. Others ran bleeding through the streets and flung the severed organs into some house which they passed. This household was then obliged to supply the young

---

[10] See M. A. Murray, *Witchcraft in Western Europe* (Oxford, 1921).

[11] Adolph Bastian, *Der Mensch in der Geschichte* (Berlin, 1912).

man, now become a eunuch priest, with women's clothes. These emasculated priests were called *Galloi*. After their castration they wore long hair and dressed in female clothing.

A similar ceremony of castration took place in honor of Syrian Astarte of Hierapolis, of Ephesian Artemis, of Atargatis, of Ashtoreth or Ishtar, of Hecate at Laguire, and also of Diana whose statue was often represented with a necklace of testicles; sometimes the bloody organs of emasculated priests were hung about her neck. These goddesses were all served by eunuch or emasculated priests.

Other rites which were performed by men in service of the Moon Goddess included circumcision, a symbolic castration, and flagellation. This last rite was apparently never practiced by women but in certain communities many boys submitted voluntarily to whipping in honor of the Goddess. The castigation was often so severe as to endanger the lives of the devotees. However, in the frescoes of the Villa des Mystères, at Pompeii, where the initiation of a young woman to the Great Mother is represented, the neophyte is shown crouching at the knees of an older seated woman while undergoing flagellation.

Circumcision and flagellation are symbolic of a kind of mitigated castration. They are perhaps equivalent to the mitigated sacrifice of the women, the loss of whose hair was permitted at the time of the dedication in the temple, instead of the sacrifice of their virginity.

These are the sacrifices which the Moon Goddess demands, not, it is true, from every man, but from a few selected or representative men. To them she appears in her dark and terrible form, demanding mutilation or even death, for human sacrifice as we have already seen was included in her worship.

In these bloody rites the dark or underside of the great Goddess is clearly seen. She is in very truth the Destroyer. But strangely enough her destructive powers seem to be directed less against women than against men. The chosen man must sacrifice his virility completely and once for all, in a mad ecstasy where pain and emotion were inextricably mingled. The woman, on the other hand, must present the first fruits of her womanhood. It was a sacrifice of a very different nature. For as the primitives say, "The Moon is destructive to men but she is of one nature with women and is their patron and protector."

?

M. Ester Harding focuses her essay on the fertility cult which is associated symbolically with the Goddess of the Moon. In antiquity, "sacred prostitutes" were identified with the "powers" of the Moon Goddess. The author uses the symbol of fire as an illustration of the magic and feelings associated with this symbol. The relation between fertility, life, and death is also linked to the Moon Goddess. The males, who were in her service, were castrated because they learned the "ideal of sex change from the moon." Harding's insights shed light on the male's fear of the female and the female's fear of the male. The Moon Goddess is part of the temptresses' rite of passage. The woman who identified with this fertility cult became independent from a male-dominant world because, as Harding suggests: "The Moon is destructive to men but she is of one nature with women and is their patron and protector." In the following questions, Harding's point of view is linked to the fertility cult as the temptress becomes Moon Goddess.

1 Discuss the "powers" that Harding associates with the ancient Moon Goddess. How does fertility become the underlying source of her strength? What is the relation of fire to menstruation according to Harding?

2 What image of the temptress emerges from Harding's discussion of the vestal virgins? What does this suggest about the male's and female's attitudes toward the sexual nature of each other? Would Bettelheim agree that this process demonstrates the fears which exist in each sex about the other sex? Explain!

3 What initiation ceremony is performed during the sacred marriage? What does this suggest about love between strangers? Is the image of a "knight in shining armor" a later interpretation of this ceremony? Discuss the implications of the male's need to be protected from the female.

4 How does Harding connect Mary, the mother of Jesus, to the Moon Goddess? What does this suggest about the transformation of symbols from one age to another? How would one connect Isis to the Virgin Mary?

5 What do these mysteries reveal about the relation of primitive men to their gods? How does Harding connect these gods to the "inner" life of human beings? Does Randall's image of god in "A Scarlet Letter about Mary Magdalene" relate to Harding's image of gods among the primitives?

6 How does Harding relate the Moon Goddess with the witches of the Middle Ages? Discuss the way the devil in the Middle Ages is an extension of the phallic worship associated with the Moon Goddess.

7 What image of the temptress emerges from Harding's discussion of the Moon Goddess? What is the relation of the moon to fertility? What is the underlying initiation rite associated with this cult? Explain!

THE PROSTITUTE AS SCAPEGOAT

The power of the fatal woman are conferred upon her by the victim himself...

In Western civilization, the prostitute has long been a symbol for the contradiction between the fruitfulness of procreation versus the terrible evil of sterility. She appears from antiquity to the present in our literature as a woman aware of the "dark side" of our nature. She also represents the split between love and sexual gratification between men and women. Men marry for love, but turn to the prostitute for gratification of their sexual desires. This creates a double standard which links love to the "good" women they marry, and "evil" to those women who seek to sell their bodies for pleasure. If the male can, indeed, find a "wicked" woman, he might still believe in the possibility of a "good" woman. The prostitute often is the scapegoat for the group to vent its hostility on in order to act out "inner" conflicts. Mary Magdalene was about to be stoned when Christ said, "Let he who is without sin cast the first stone." This wisdom reveals to us why groups act out their own feelings of guilt. Erich Neumann labels this the scapegoat psychology; he states:

> A group which is psychologically split by being consciously identified with ethical values and at the same time unconscious of its shadow will display, in addition to unconscious feelings of guilt, a psychological sense of insecurity which is a compensation for the self-righteousness of its conscious attitude. Repression will have to be continually on the defensive against a dawning apperception of the shadow side, since the unconscious reinforcement of the shadow will make it increasingly difficult for the ego and the conscious mind not to become aware of its existence at some point in the process.

This attitude not only divides the members of the group from one another but also reenforces the individual's "inner" split. The prostitute seeks sexual partners, allowing the male to pretend that he does not have needs of his own. This attempt to capture "innocence" on the part of the male keeps him a child. To perpetuate this illusion, the male needs a scapegoat to punish in order to be purified. Jacob Bronowski contends that the prostitute was singled out to carry the sins of the community in order to rid the group of its fears; he states:

> Many of these ceremonies are specific about the victim's sex, and in some of them sex is central to the sacrifice. The Asiatic Greeks began the murder of their human scapegoat to the sound of flutes, by beating him on his genitals with branches of the wild fig. Was this to expiate the universal sin of sex? Or was it to make their trees fertile? The Mexicans each year beheaded a girl at puberty so that her blood might be sprinkled in the temple of the goddess of maize.

Fertility is linked to death so that nature may be appeased in order to continue the life of the community. Literature often treats the prostitute as a symbolic metaphor to explain this contradiction between fertility and sterility. The following excerpts reveal certain patterns of behavior which attempt to explain why women turn to prostitution. The first example is the story of Judah and Tamar which appears in Genesis. The frequency with which the Old Testament prophets cry against prostitution testifies to the struggle against promiscuity as the breeder of social disorder. The old testament proscribes adultry: the coveting of another's wife, as of his ox. Prostitution, forbidden to women of the faith, is relegated to the "foreign" women whose use by the male is not prohibited. The story of Tamar attests to the woman's desire to be in control of her destiny. Tamar must wait for her father-in-law to assign her a husband. His failure to send his son to her prompts her revenge, which takes the form of prostitution. She seduces Judah by disguising herself as a harlot, illustrating part of the female's desire to act out her anger through prostitution. The story also deals with the incest motif as well as a primary reference to onanism.

JUDAH AND TAMAR

GENESIS 38:1--30

And it came to pass at that time, that Judah went down from his brethren, and turned in to a certain Adullamite, whose name was Hirah.

2 And Judah saw there a daughter of a certain Canaanite, whose name was Shuah; and he took her, and went in unto her.

3 And she conceived, and bare a son; and he called his name Er.

4 And she conceived again, and bare a son; and she called his name Onan.

5 And she yet again conceived, and bare a son; and called his name Shelah: and he was at Chezib, when she bare him.

6 And Judah took a wife for Er his firstborn, whose name was Tamar.

7 And Er; Judah's firstborn, was wicked in the sight of the Lord and the Lord slew him.

8 And Judah said unto Onan, Go in unto thy brother's wife, and marry her, and raise up seed to thy brother.

9 And Onan knew that the seed should not be his; and it came to pass, when he went in unto his brother's wife, that he spilled it on the ground, lest that he should give seed to his brother.

10 And the thing which he did displeased the Lord: wherefore he slew him also.

11 Then said Judah to Tamar his daughter in law, Remain a widow at thy father's house, till Shelah my son be grown: for he said, Lest peradventure he die also, as his brethren did. And Tamar went and dwelt in her father's house.

12 And in process of time the daughter of Shuah Judah's wife died; and Judah was comforted, and went up unto his sheepshearers to Timnath, he and his friend Hirah the Adullamite.

13 And it was told Tamar, saying, Behold thy father in law goeth up to Timnath to shear his sheep.

Males dominate females in occupational and political spheres. This is a species-specific pattern and is associated with my other proposition: that males bond in a variety of situations involving power, force, crucial or dangerous work. . . . They consciously and emotionally *exclude* females from these bonds. The significant notion here is that these broad patterns are biologically based. . . . To use Count's term, male dominance and bonding are features of the human "biogram."

Men in Groups, **Lionel Tiger**

14 And she put her widow's garments off from her, and covered her with a vail, and wrapped herself, and sat in an open place, which is by the way to Timnath; for she saw that Shelah was grown, and she was not given unto him to wife.

15 When Judah saw her, he thought her to be an harlot; because she had covered her face.

16 And he turned unto her by the way, and said, Go to, I pray thee, let me come in unto thee; (for he knew not that she was his daughter in law.) And she said, What wilt thou give me, that thou mayest come in unto me?

17 And he said, I will send thee a kid from the flock. And she said, Wilt thou give me a pledge, till thou send it?

18 And he said, What pledge shall I give thee? And she said, Thy signet, and thy bracelets, and thy staff that is in thine hand. And he gave it her, and came in unto her, and she conceived by him.

19 And she arose, and went away, and laid by her vail from her, and put on the garments of her widowhood.

20 And Judah sent the kid by the hand of his friend the Adullamite, to receive his pledge from the woman's hand: but he found her not.

21 Then he asked the men of the place, saying, Where is the harlot, that was openly by the wayside? And they said, There was no harlot in this place.

22 And he returned to Judah, and said, I cannot find her; and also the men of the place said, that there was no harlot in this place.

23 And Judah said, Let her take it to her, lest we be shamed: behold, I sent this kid, and thou hast not found her.

24 And it came to pass about three months after, that it was told Judah, saying, Tamar thy daughter in law hath played the harlot; and also, behold, she is with child by whoredom. And Judah said, Bring her forth, and let her be burnt.

25 When she was brought forth, she sent to her father in law, saying, By the man, whose these are, am I with child: and she said, Discern, I pray thee, whose are these, the signet, and bracelets, and staff.

26 And Judah acknowledged them, and said, She hath been more righteous than I; because that I gave her not to Shelah my son. And he knew her again no more.

27 And it came to pass in the time of her travail, that, behold, twins were in her womb.

28 And it came to pass, when she travailed, that the one put out his hand: and the midwife took and bound upon his hand a scarlet thread, saying, This came out first.

29 And it came to pass, as he drew back his hand, that, behold, his brother came out: and she said, How hast thou broken forth? this breach be upon thee: therefore his name was called Pharez.

30 And afterward came out his brother, that had the scarlet thread upon his hand: and his name was called Zarah.

300 B.C.

The "Cult of Mylitta" illustrates the worship of the fertilizing principle as giver of life and wealth. The ritualization of prostitution enabled the males, through the role of priest, to take on the control and burden of the risks involved in the males' attraction to the female. These "sacred prostitutes" centered in the cult of Mylitta. But in this situation, there is evidence that although this is a religious ritual, "The Babylonians have one more shameful custom." The following eye-witness account sheds light on the temples where these women performed their rites.

THE CULT OF MYLITTA

HERODOTUS

The dress of the Babylonians is a linen tunic reaching to the feet, and above it another tunic made in wool, besides which they have a short white cloak thrown round them, and shoes of a peculiar fashion, not unlike those worn by the Boeotians. They have long hair, wear turbans on their heads, and anoint their whole body with perfumes. Every one carries a seal and a walkingstick, carved at the top into the form of an apple, a rose, a lily, an eagle, or something similar; for it is not their habit to use a stick without an ornament.

Of their customs, whereof I shall now proceed to give an account, the following (which I understand belongs to them in common with the Illyrian tribe of the Eneti*) is the wisest in my judgment. Once a year in each village the maidens of age to marry were collected all together into one place; while the men stood round them in a circle. Then a herald called up the damsels one by one, and offered them for sale. He began with the most beautiful. When she was sold for no small sum of money, he offered for sale the one who came next to her in beauty. All of them were sold to be wives. The richest of the Babylonians who wished to wed bid against each other for the loveliest maidens, while the humbler wife-seekers, who were indifferent about beauty,

* The Eneti or Heneti are the same as the Venetians of later times. This information Herodotus probably obtained in Italy.

took the more homely damsels with marriage-portions. For the custom was that when the herald had gone through the whole number of the beautiful damsels, he should then call up the ugliest—a cripple, if there chanced to be one—and offer her to the men, asking who would agree to take her with the smallest marriage-portion. And the man who offered to take the smallest sum had her assigned to him. The marriage-portions were furnished by the money paid for the beautiful damsels, and thus the fairer maidens portioned out the uglier. No one was allowed to give his daughter in marriage to the man of his choice, nor might any one carry away the damsel whom he had purchased without finding bail really and truly to make her his wife; if, however, it turned out that they did not agree, the money might be paid back. All who liked might come even from distant villages and bid for the women. This was the best of all their customs, but it has now fallen into disuse. They have lately hit upon a very different plan to save their maidens from violence, and prevent their being torn from them and carried to distant cities, which is to bring up their daughters to be prostitutes. This is now done by all the poorer of the common people, who since the conquest have been maltreated by their lords, and have had ruin brought upon their families.

The following custom seems to me the wisest of their institutions next to the one lately praised. They have no physicians, but when a man is ill, they lay him in the public square, and the passers-by come up to him, and if they have ever had the disease themselves or have known any one who has suffered from it, they give him advice, recommending him to do whatever they found good in their own case, or in the case known to them. And no one is allowed to pass the sick man in silence without asking him what his ailment is.

They bury their dead in honey, and have funeral lamentations like the Egyptians. When a Babylonian has had intercourse with his wife, he sits down before a censer of burning incense, and the woman sits opposite to him. At dawn of day they wash; for till they are washed they will not touch any of their common vessels. This practice is observed also by the Arabians.

The Babylonians have one most shameful custom. Every woman born in the country must once in her life go and sit down in the precinct of Aphrodite, and there have intercourse with a stranger. Many of the wealthier sort, who are too proud to mix with the others, drive in covered carriages to the precinct, followed by a goodly train of attendants, and there take their station. But the larger number seat themselves within the holy enclosure with wreaths of string about their heads, and here there is always a great crowd, some coming and others going; lines of cord mark out paths in all directions among the women, and the strangers pass along them to make their choice. A woman who has once taken her seat is not allowed to return home till one of the strangers throws a silver coin into her lap, and takes her with him beyond the holy ground. When he throws the coin he says these words, "I summon you in the name of the goddess Mylitta." (Aphrodite is called Mylitta by the Assyrians.) The silver coin may be of any size; it cannot be refused, for that is forbidden by the law, since once thrown it is sacred. The woman goes with the first man who throws her money, and rejects no one. When she has had intercourse with him, and so satisfied the goddess, she returns home, and from that time on no gift however great will prevail with her. Such of the women as are tall and beautiful are soon released, but others who are ugly have to stay a long time before they can fulfil the law. Some have waited three or four years in the precinct. A custom very much like this is found also in certain parts of the island of Cyprus. . . .

In ancient India, the prostitute was considered to be part of the glory and wealth of her time. The Brahman asked a woman to be wise in the luxuries which provided men with the mystique of sexual illusion. The daughter of the Hindu, lacking education and independence, often married as the result of an arrangement. She did not seek intimacy in her relation with her husband. The prostitute, on the other hand, could either refuse or consent to a relation, and in this, she rivaled the male. The following story "The Rise and Fall of a Harlot," reveals the way the prostitute learns to live in a man's world by using her wits after her beauty has gone.

8<small>TH</small> CENTURY

THE RISE AND FALL OF A HARLOT

from *The Harlot's Ledger*
KSHEMENDRA

THERE was once a woman called Bhūmikā who kept an inn at Parihāsapura, and bore a daughter whom she named Arghagharghātikā.

As the child was rather tall and had delightful looks, the simple folk of the neighbourhood asked her to all their feasts; and the little thief repaid them by filching the holy vases from their houses.

When she was only six years old, though full of talk already, her mother, who hungered for money, set her up for sale at the country fair.

Behold her, then, already armed for conquest of a lover, and not afraid of kisses, wearing a pearl collar ornamented with round cockleshells, and tightly laced into a little jacket which had been basely provided with false breasts.

A young merchant called Purnaka, who had come into the town to purchase saffron, passed by the place where she stood for sale, a handsome fellow, sewn all over with gold and most imposing.

As he crossed the market the little girl swept him from his feet with her glances and the expressive movement of her brows. Since he was urged by a tyrannous desire, and she asked nothing better, a bargain was soon concluded between them, and a meeting arranged for the evening.

That night, as the young merchant sipped his wine, she hung about his neck and gently wiled away his gold earrings in her fingers. She slipped the seals and rings from his hand, made conscientious investigation of his pockets, and then cried: 'Help! Help!' as if she had discovered a robber. This rudely startled the merchant out of his meditation, and he had no course but to escape with his head muffled in his mantle, as he dreaded a scandal for his people's sake.

After that she changed her name, equipped herself with all she needed, and went to settle down at Shankarapara; she came there rich in three things, the flower of her youth, a sumptuous wardrobe, and a fine display of jewels.

As she had no other thought than to reap a rich harvest by trimming the gallants of that city, she practised her amorous trade both day and night, and with never a pause for breath.

What with the lovers who went in, and the lovers who came out, and the lovers who waited at the door, there were as many men about her house as there were wandering dogs in the city. She received her clients everywhere, without intermission and without preference, from morning to night and from night to morning, at the fountain, in the pleasure gardens, in cookshops, and at the stalls of the flower sellers.

In the early part of the night she would put a drunkard to sleep in her bed, like a little wise child, then she would pass to a second, and, when he fell asleep through weariness, slip away to a third. At the very end of night she would always secure a little extra profit on the sale of her body by pretending that she had to go forth in search of news of a friend who had an alarming colic; thus she always managed to lift one last late wayfarer.

It soon happened that she was obliged to hide in the secret apartments of her lovers, to escape from the madness of suitors whom she had gone on refusing.

On one such occasion, the guardian of a certain temple, who was blinded by love of her, imprudently opened the doors of the sanctuary for her in the night. When she saw him lying like a log and heard him snoring, she laid hands on all the jewels of the goddess, and hurried away.

After this it was necessary for her to change her name and residence once more, so she called herself Nāgarikā, and became the mistress of a gentleman farmer at Pratāpapura.

This calm existence and the abundant luxury of an excellent table soon made her fat, and she became very dear to her lover.

As soon as she had obtained complete power over the disposition of all his money, she prayed for a swift death to free her from her victim, and, in the meanwhile, for want of anything better, succeeded in alienating him from all his family.

One day he was found clubbed to death in his father's orchard, so she profited by her strong position in the house to become the mistress of the father himself, whose name was Shrīsimha. As he had no other children, this old man was a quarry very well worth hunting.

Aware that her youth was passing and wishing to oust all the rest of her decrepit lover's women, she took pains to enthrall him by the use of magic plants.

At the same time she reawakened his juvenile ardour by the judicious use of fish soup, milk, liquefied butter, garlic, onions, and other virile adjuvants.

But when the old man, who feared the wrath of his king, sent himself to the breast of Shiva with a dagger stroke, she swept up all the money and valuables on which she could lay her hands, and departed for another city.

There she extracted an added charm from her white mourning garments; she wore them slight and open-work, and gave herself out to be one Mrigavatī, a widow: her drooping attitudes and most attractive melancholy lured many men, and the more she forbade them all hope, the greater became their desire for her.

For a long time, with admirable constancy, she made regular procession to the river bank to render her duty to Kālī; and gave the mortuary offering in full each time, with sesame, perfumes, and the herb of the dead, as symbols of her grief.

It was there by the river that she snared a rich knight, named Bandhurasāra, as a heron takes a fish.

So great was now her skill in the snatching of hearts that she laid hands on his whole house with ease, and soon became mistress over all the incomings and outgoings of money.

This man had gathered a great fortune; therefore, it was an act of grace in him to die in a month's time, without any being able to whisper that she had a part in this. At once she went lunatic with virtuous grief, and wished to follow her husband to the tomb.

His blood relations were hard put to it to move her from this crotchet of hers, which was all the stronger because it rose out of a hypocritical calculation only. She would speak to them in a deep voice and with a resolved and noble air: 'Widowhood in a fine family, the slur a woman's reputation takes from it, and the vexations which follow after: all these will soon depart from me with the flames of the pyre.'

Thus would she speak, and be as constant in her resolution, as careless in the face of death, as if she were made of stone. But she found it very difficult to conceal her joy at having entered into so mighty an inheritance; and this difficulty was the measure of what she really felt.

When the property had become legally hers through a decision of the crown, she let herself be dissuaded out of her funeral resolve by the king's people, and lived thence-forward in joy and feasting and entertainment.

Soon she captured the scribe of the royal stables, himself a veritable stallion in the game, and thus stayed among the living to scatter ruin and death.

She clung like a leech to her new conquest, and charmed her lover daily in the bathhouse with the sparkling prettiness of her chatter.

The scribe, who had his own considerable complements of assurance, spent all his day in pillaging his master, and then, when he had eaten and drunken like a Kumbhakama in the evening, slept like one also. Every morning the woman lavished her expert cares of the bath upon him and showed him demonstrations of devotional respect, while he lay in the water and tried to cool his spirit-heated blood.

As she was growing old and had no child, and as those which the scribe had begotten on another woman were beginning to be grown up, she applied herself to the exploitation of this man as to a pious work, and laid up a considerable treasure in secret by turning everything in the house to ready money.

In the end the man's sons revolted at this wholesale disappearance of the furnishing of their father's house, and to prevent further depredation laid hands on all that was left. But the woman did not hesitate to bring the matter before the courts, and at once laid siege to the heart of a lawyer who thereupon took up her case.

Thanks to this man, who bribed a settlement in her favour, she gained the victory, and the goods in question were restored to her.

At once she hastened to realize money upon the house and all that was in it, and, fleeing in disguise from the wrath of her lover's sons, took refuge in a convent of Satkas.

She dyed her white hair black, made her face shine with paints and unguents, and established herself in that place as a harlot recently launched upon the trade.

She gave out that she had held an honourable position in the business world and, by the attraction of this, made brisker dealings with her body.

Her clients never questioned the truth of what she said, for they were ever ready to meet a thing halfway, and, being delighted by the tales she told of the commercial life, ran after her more and more.

So she discovered the joy of turning heads again, and, though her tongue and lips and hands were already worn by drinking the cup of peace with lovers, she savoured it even more.

At length, however, when she had received stolen goods from certain robbers, she was arrested on the information of her traitorous servants, and, because she insisted on denying the evidence, was loaded with chains and cast into prison.

There she quickly seduced a gaoler, whose name was Bhujanga, into the snares of her love, and thenceforward dwelt in unclouded happiness, spending her time in a conscientious clearance of fish and cakes and honey.

Once, when the two were alone together, she held her lover in a deep embrace and covered him with kisses; then, as he grew drunk on these, she bit out his tongue with her teeth as the first stage in her bid for liberty.

The man could not cry out, so she waited till he had swooned away and then dressed him as a woman in her own clothes, removed her chains, and fled.

She came by night to Vijayeshvara, and passed herself off, under the name of Anupamā as the daughter of a powerful minister.

In this city she was able, thanks to the love of Bhogamitra, to deck the poor remnants of her once exceptional beauty with loads of precious stones. She carefully raised her breasts, and put on a long wig; she adorned herself with a pale red turban, she bestowed an honest layer of collyrium upon her eyes, and covered her face with a nose veil. Thus she succeeded in impressing the simple folk of that place, until they cried: 'What fairylike creature is this that has come among us!'

One of these admirers was stricken by irresistible desire; but, when he had seen her naked for a single moment, he never afterwards dared even to pass the corner of her street.

As a cooled gallery in winter, as a range of lamps at noon, as a crown of withered flowers, so is an old whore useless to every man.

Since no customer would take her bait, she contented herself with approaching strangers under cover of the darkness and dragging them with her by the skirts of their clothing; thus she was able to procure a meagre salary each night. . . .

In the following tenth-century account, we see how the Church of Rome attempts to live with prostitution. The Church seemed to feel that prostitution was not as great a crime as murder. Saint Augustine sets the Churches philosophy when he states: "Suppress the courtesan, and you will overthrow everything through the caprice of passions." Thus, the presence of the prostitute was permitted in a society which claimed to be "technically virtuous." The story "Thais and the Monk" tells of an attempt to bring the prostitute back to the fold, but first she must repent for her "sins." Finally, she is accepted in the presence of the Lord: the whore has been transformed into a nun.

10ᴛʜ CENTURY

THAIS AND THE MONK

from *Paphnutius*
HROTSWITHA

Scene I

DISCIPLES: Why do you look so gloomy, father Paphnutius? Why do you not smile at us as usual?

PAPHNUTIUS: When the heart is sad the face clouds over. It is only natural.

DISCIPLES: But why are you sad?

PAPHNUTIUS: I grieve over an injury to my Creator.

DISCIPLES: What injury?

PAPHNUTIUS: The injury His own creatures, made in His very image, inflict on Him.

DISCIPLES: Tell us the cause of your sadness. Relieve us of the burden of our curiosity.

PAPHNUTIUS: Perhaps you will not find the tale to your liking.

DISCIPLES: A man is often sadder for having his curiosity satisfied, yet he cannot overcome the tendency to be curious. It is part of our weakness.

PAPHNUTIUS: Brothers—there is a woman, shameless woman, living in our neighborhood.

DISCIPLES: A perilous thing for the people.

PAPHNUTIUS: Her beauty is wonderful; her impurity is—horrible.

DISCIPLES: What is her wretched name?

PAPHNUTIUS: Thais.

DISCIPLES: Thais! Thais, the harlot!

PAPHNUTIUS: Yes—she.

DISCIPLES: Everyone has heard of her and her wickedness.

PAPHNUTIUS: It is no wonder, for she is not satisfied to ruin herself with a small band of lovers. She seeks to allure all men through her marvellous beauty, and drag them down with her.

DISCIPLES: What a woeful thing!

PAPHNUTIUS: And it is not only fools and wastrels who squander their substance with her. Citizens of high standing and virtue lay precious things at her feet, and enrich her to their own undoing.

DISCIPLES: It is terrible to hear of such things.

PAPHNUTIUS: Flocks of lovers crowd to her doors.

DISCIPLES: And to their destruction.

PAPHNUTIUS: They are so crazed with desire that they quarrel and fight for admission to her house.

DISCIPLES: One vice brings another in its train.

PAPHNUTIUS: They come to blows. Heads are broken, faces bruised, noses smashed; at times they drive each other out with weapons, and the threshold of the vile place is dyed with blood!

DISCIPLES: Most horrible!

PAPHNUTIUS: This is the injury to the Creator for which I weep day and night. This is the cause of my sorrow.

DISCIPLES: We understand now. You have good reason to be distressed, and I doubt not that the citizens of the heavenly country share your grief.

PAPHNUTIUS: Oh, to rescue her from that wicked life! Why should I not try?

DISCIPLE: God forbid!

PAPHNUTIUS: Brother, our Lord Jesus went among the sinners.

DISCIPLE: She would not receive a hermit.

PAPHNUTIUS: What if I were to go in the disguise of a lover?

DISCIPLE: If that thought is from God, God will give you strength to accomplish it.

PAPHNUTIUS: I will set out immediately. I shall need your best prayers. Pray that I may not be overcome by the wiles of the serpent. Pray that I may be able to show this soul the beauty of divine love.

DISCIPLES: May He who laid low the Prince of Darkness give you the victory over the enemy of the human race.

Scene II

PAPHNUTIUS: I am bewildered in this town. I cannot find my way. Now I shut my eyes, and I am back in the desert. I can hear my children's voices praising God. Good children, I know

you are praying for me! I fear to speak. I fear to ask my way. O God, come to my help! I see some young men in the market-place. They are coming this way. I will go up to them and ask where she is to be found.

PAPHNUTIUS: I am told that there lives in this town a woman who loves all who love her. She is kind to all men; she'll not deny them anything.

YOUNG MAN: Stranger, you must tell us her name. There are many women of that kind in our city. Do you know her name?

PAPHNUTIUS: Yes, I know it.

YOUNG MAN: Who is she?

PAPHNUTIUS: Thais.

YOUNG MAN: Thais! She is the flame of this land. She sets all hearts on fire.

PAPHNUTIUS: They say she is beautiful. The most exquisite woman of her kind in the world.

YOUNG MAN: They have not deceived you.

PAPHNUTIUS: For her sake I have made a long and difficult journey. I have come here only to see her.

YOUNG MAN: Well, what should prevent you? You are young and handsome.

YOUNG MAN: . . . Have you money in your purse, stranger? Thais loves a handsome face, but she loves a full purse more.

PAPHNUTIUS: Gentlemen, I am rich. I have a rare present to offer her.

YOUNG MAN: To our next meeting, then! Farewell. May Thais be kind!

PAPHNUTIUS: Farewell.

Scene III

PAPHNUTIUS: Thais! Thais!

THAIS: Who is there? I do not know that voice.

PAPHNUTIUS: Thais! Your lover speaks! Thais!

THAIS: Stranger, who are you?

PAPHNUTIUS: Arise, my love, my beautiful one, and come!

THAIS: Who are you?

PAPHNUTIUS: A man who loves you!

THAIS: And what do you want with me?

PAPHNUTIUS: I will show you.

THAIS: You would be my lover?

PAPHNUTIUS: I am your lover, Thais, flame of the world!

THAIS: Whoever loves me is well paid. He receives as much as he gives.

PAPHNUTIUS: Oh, Thais, Thais! If you knew what a long and troublesome journey I have come to speak to you—to see your face!

THAIS: Well? Have I refused to speak to you, or to show you my face?

PAPHNUTIUS: I cannot speak to you here. I must be with you alone. What I have to say is secret. The room must be secret too.

THAIS: How would you like a bedchamber, fragrant with perfumes, adorned as for a marriage? I have such a room. Look!

PAPHNUTIUS: Is there no room still more secret—a room that your lovers do not know? Some room where you and I might hide from all the world?

THAIS: Yes, there is a room like that in this house. No one even knows that it exists except myself, and God.

PAPHNUTIUS: God! What God?

THAIS: The true God.

PAPHNUTIUS: You believe that He exists?

THAIS: I am a Christian.

PAPHNUTIUS: And you believe that He knows what we do?

THAIS: I believe that He knows everything.

PAPHNUTIUS: What do you think, then? That He is indifferent to the actions of the sinner, or that He reserves judgment?

THAIS: I suppose that the merits of each man are weighed in the balance, and that we shall be punished or rewarded according to our deeds.

PAPHNUTIUS: O Christ! How wondrous is Thy patience! How wondrous is Thy love! Even when those who believe in Thee sin deliberately, Thou dost delay their destruction!

THAIS: Why do you tremble? Why do you turn pale? Why do you weep?

PAPHNUTIUS: I shudder at your presumption. I weep for your damnation. How, knowing what you know, can you destroy men in this manner and ruin so many souls, all precious and immortal?

THAIS: Your voice pierces my heart! Strange lover—you are cruel. Pity me!

PAPHNUTIUS: Let us pity rather those souls whom you have deprived of the sight of God—of the God Whom you confess! Oh, Thais, you have wilfully offended the divine Majesty. That condemns you.

THAIS: What do you mean? Why do you threaten me like this?

PAPHNUTIUS: Because the punishment of hell-fire awaits you if you remain in sin.

THAIS: Who are you, who rebuke me so sternly? Oh, you have shaken me to the depths of my terrified heart!

PAPHNUTIUS: I would that you could be shaken with fear to your very bowels! I would like to see your delicate body impregnated with terror in every vein, and every fibre, if that would keep you from yielding to the dangerous delights of the flesh.

THAIS: And what zest for pleasure do you think is left now in a heart suddenly awakened to the consciousness of guilt! Remorse has killed everything!

PAPHNUTIUS: I long to see the thorns of vice cut away, and the choked-up fountain of your tears flowing once more. Tears of repentance are precious in the sight of God.

THAIS: Oh, voice that promises mercy! Do you believe, can you hope that one so vile as I, soiled by thousands and thousands of impurities, can make reparation, can ever by any manner of penance obtain pardon?

PAPHNUTIUS: Thais, no sin is so great, no crime so black, that it cannot be expiated by tears and penitence, provided they are followed up by deeds.

THAIS: Show me, I beg you, my father, what I can do to be reconciled with Him I have offended.

PAPHNUTIUS: Despise the world. Leave your dissolute lovers.

THAIS: And afterwards? What then?

PAPHNUTIUS: You must retire to some solitary place, where you may learn to know yourself and realize the enormity of your sins.

THAIS: If you think this will save me, I will not delay a moment.

PAPHNUTIUS: I have no doubt it will.

THAIS: Yet give me a little time. I must collect the wealth that I have gained through the sins of my body—all the treasures I have kept too long.

PAPHNUTIUS: Do not give them a moment's thought. There will be no lack of people to find them and make use of them.

THAIS: I have another idea in my mind. I did not think of keeping this wealth or of giving it to my friends. Nor would I distribute it among the poor. The wages of sin are no material for good works.

PAPHNUTIUS: You are right. What then do you propose to do with your possessions?

THAIS: Give them to the flames! Burn them to ashes!

PAPHNUTIUS: For what reason?

THAIS: That they may no longer exist in the world. Each one was acquired at the cost of an injury to the goodness and beauty of the Creator. Let them burn.

PAPHNUTIUS: How you are changed! Grace is on your lips! Your eyes are calm, and impure passions no longer burn in them. Oh, miracle!

Is this Thais who was once so greedy for gold? Is this Thais, who seeks so humbly the feet of God?

THAIS: God give me grace to change still more. My heart is changed, but this mortal substance—how shall it be changed?

PAPHNUTIUS: It is not difficult for the unchangeable substance to transform us.

THAIS: Now I am going to carry out my plan. Fire shall destroy everything I have.

PAPHNUTIUS: Go in peace. Then return to me here quickly. Do not delay. I trust your resolution, and yet—

THAIS: You need not be afraid.

PAPHNUTIUS: Thais, come back quickly! God be with you!

Prostitution is promoted and supported by the taboo on sexuality, combined with the social ideal of compulsory monogamy and the lack of contraceptive information among married and unmarried women. It becomes a technique of experiencing physical pleasure without psychological obligation, and this encourages a split in the emotional life, with the result that the tender elements are bestowed upon one person and the physical elements upon another. This is just as illogical and just as unhealthful as it would be if only carbohydrates were served in legitimate restaurants and proteins and fats had to be obtained surreptitiously and illicitly from restaurateurs who had no social or business standing. Occasionally a man resynthesizes these elements, falls in love with the prostitute, and marries her. This is both because of her bad reputation and in spite of it. I say *because of it* in the sense that men are relieved to be able to discard the prudery with which sex is so frequently invested and to feel comfortable in the presence of one who is honest enough to make no pretense about her sexual wishes, even though it is surely not these that force her into prostitution as a means of livelihood. In addition to this, some men, for unconscious reasons, actually prefer women who have been sought after and possessed by other men. And I say *in spite of* her reputation because the selection of a prostitute ordinarily implies that the sexual relation is one from which the romantic elements have been stricken. In the conscious mind, the love object is looked upon as a degraded one, but the natural tendency to identify the tender and physical elements in sexual intimacy often overcomes this social taboo.

Karl Meinger

A VISIT TO MOTHER CRESWELL

from *The English Rogue*
RICHARD HEAD

In the seventeenth-century account of prostitution that follows, we see the "evil" of woman linked to the confines of hell. Punishment and fear abound in this story of the woman who traps a man with her alluring sexual nature. It also illustrates what happens to the male who gets "clapped" at Mother Cresswell's house. This brings veneral disease to the world of the prostitute, putting moral pressure on those young men who allowed "nature to take its course."

How he frequented bawdy-houses: what exploits he committed in them: the character of a bawd, a whore, a pimp, and a trapan: their manner of living: with a detection of their wicked lives and conversations

Being full fraught with money, we undertook our progress, promising to ourselves all delight imaginable, but not considering what the effect would be. We frequented all places of pleasure, but among the chief we ranked brothel-houses, which were our repositories. We seldom were seen in the streets by day, for fear of discovery; confining ourselves close prisoners to some 'Bubbing-house'; at night (like such as closely delighted in deeds of darkness) we would sometimes flutter abroad. Our pastime was to hire coaches to any pretended place, and when we came near it, to make our escape. One time leaping out of the boot, my cloak chanced to tangle in the spokes of the wheel. The coachman not perceiving we were got out, drove on; by the wheels continually turning, my garment was so engaged that I verily believed my sins had now conferred upon me the just punishment of being executed on the wheel, which I could hardly have avoided, had I not speedily unbuttoned my cloak. I was loth to bid the coachman stop, thinking I should have it at last. I ran lacquey-like a long way, but all my endeavours to shift it, proved ineffectual; so that at length I was forced to cry out, 'Hold, coachman.' The coach-

man coming out of his box, soon perceived the fallacy, and straightways demanded his money for his hire before he would untangle my cloak, which I was compelled to give him. Delivering me my cloak, he told me, I had paid him, but he had not paid me for my attendance on him. And said moreover, that my cloak would not look like a livery, unless it were laced; and with that, with his whip, lashed me well-favouredly. Another sort of pastime we used, was to kick the old watchmen's lanthorns about the street; and it may be, sometimes confer a blow or two on their sleepy noddles, and then fly for it, but we had worse success with this than the former.

We practised this foolery so often, till at length we were met with and rightly served. It was thus: In Paternoster Row we found a fellow at noddie upon a stall, with his lanthorn and candle by him; having first seized on that, and thrown it into the kennel, we prosecuted our abuse by falling upon him, and beating him. As soon as we had done this manful act, we betook ourselves to flight; but here we mistook our mark, thinking him to be an old decrepit watchman, and one that had little use of his eyes, without those in his pocket; whereas to our cost, we found him as nimble and as light footed as a stag, who overtaking us, surprized us; and as he was carrying us before the constable, we met with the Grand Round, who, without much examination committed us as rats to the Computer. The chiefest thing that troubled us was the apprehension of our master's knowing where we were. But we resolved to drown that care: we had not been there long, before other rats, male and female were brought in to bear us company. Some of the men were all bloody, and their mobs' scarfs and hoods all rent, and none of them sober. Damning and sinking were the constant flourishes of their discourse; calling for drink was the argument they held, and roaring in distracted notes was their harmony. Though I was myself comparatively wicked, yet I blessed my God I had not arrived to that height these superlative villains had attained to. Being in their company, I thought myself in the suburbs, or on the confines of Hell. Sin, if it be dressed up in specious pretences, may be entertained as a companion; but when it appears in its own shape it cannot but strike horror into the soul of any, though desperate, if not stupified. Wherefore methought I was so far from associating myself with them, that I protest the lewdness of their actions were so represented to me with such deformity that I knew not which I loathed most, them or the prison.

I cannot make appear to the world what they were, nor my resentments, unless I should stuff a page or two with all manner of horrid oaths, execrations, blasphemies and such like soul-infecting and destroying plaguesores; wherefore I shall only take leave to anatomize the place that detained us from our freedom. Then look upon a prison as in itself, and it may be fitly termed a temporary Hell. For as the other is a receptacle for damned souls, the gates thereof standing always wide open; so this refuseth the reception of none, though never so wicked a miscrent. Though my durance in this place was but

short, yet I could not but take some observations, employing from thence the faculties of my soul to draw up the definition of a prison. Hell is a very proper denomination for it, since it is a place composed of nothing but disorder and confusion; a land of darkness, inhabited by calamity, horror, misery, and confusion; a bottomless pit of fraud, violence and stench. A prison is the banishment of courtesy, the centre of infamy and disparagement, the destruction of good wits, the treasure of despair, the fining-pot of friendship, a den of deceivers, a forest of ravenous beasts. Here you may see one weeping, another singing; one sleeping, another swearing; every one variously employed; one eating in a corner, and another pissing just by him; another lousing himself between both; it may be heretofore a military man, and therefore loth to forget his art, but rather exercising it in the killing of his bodily enemies, bearing the blood on his nail, as the trophies of his victory.

It is, to speak most properly, a living tomb or grave to bury men alive in, wherein a man for half a year's experience may learn more law than he can in three terms for an hundred pound.

It is a little wood of woe, a map of misery, a place that will learn a young man more villainy if he be apt to take it in six months, than at twenty gaming ordinaries, bowling-alleys, or bawdy-houses; and an old man more policy, than if he had been pupil to Machiavel.

This place hath more diseases predominant in it than the pest-house in a plague-time; and stinks worse than my Lord Mayor's dog-house.

It is a little commonwealth, although little wealth common there; it is a desert, where desert lies hood-winked.

The place is as intricate as Rosamond's labyrinth, and is so full of meanders and crooked turnings that it is impossible to find the way out, except he be directed by a silver clue; and can never overcome the Minotaur without a golden ball to work his own safety. The next day, paying our fees, and receiving some checks, with good admonitions from the justice, we were discharged.

This misfortune made us not a jot more cautious, but as soon as we were at liberty we went upon the scent to Mother Cr. formerly famous for the good citizens' wives that frequented her house; who still rides admiral of all the rest of her function about the Town. I hope the next time I go to visit her, she will not get me clapped for the pains I take in praising her. The truth of it is, of all the bawds I know, she merits most, having an house fit for the accommodation of the best. As for her working utensils, they are composed of refined metal, always neatly kept; which, because they are not used upon all slight occasions, they appear the more delectable to the eye. As soon as we had entered the door, I could hear a rustling of silks in sundry places; I conceive it was their policy, by seeming modesty to set a sharper edge on our appetites. We were conducted into a large handsome room; bottles of wine were brought up, both Spanish and French, with salt meats to relish the palate, though we gave no order for them; but it seems it was the custom of the house, an expensive one; but without a piece spending, you shall know little of their practices.

At length, up came the old matron; after the performance of our devoir, she seats herself by me, and began to be impudently acquainted, chucking me under the chin, calling me her Son Smock-face. Having well warmed ourselves with wine, and the good gentle-woman perceiving that our bloods began to heat, 'Well,' said she, 'I guess at the intent of your coming hither, neither shall you go away unsatisfied. Nature will have its course; and if in youth it be stopped, it will but, torrent-like, flow with the greater impetuosity. Come, I see by your countenances that ye were born sons of mirth and pleasure; shew then what stock ye came of. If you want subjects to exercise your parts on, we'll have more wine; and when ye are inflamed, ye shall have the benefit of a cooler.' With that she leaves us; but another of the same sex, though three degrees different in age, supplied her place. At first view I seemed very well pleased: handsome she was, and very proportionable; but withal so impudent, that I was antidoted against lechery. *Ista foemina quae limites verecundiae semel excesserit, oportet illam esse graviter impudentem.* If once a woman pass the bounds of shamefacedness, she will seldom stop till she hath arrived to the height of impudence. I must needs deal ingenuously, at the beginning the needle of my microcosm was touched by Love's loadstone; but upon further acquaintance, if I might have had a hundred pounds, I could not have meddled with her.

Though she had baited her desires with a million of prostitute countenances and enticements, yet I looked upon her rather a companion for an hospital, and stood more in need of a chirurgeon's acquaintance than mine. My friend had nibbled at the bait; but when I heard them capitulating about the price, I thought she wanted a fee for the doctor. Well, had she not over-traded, she had not broke so soon; for her trade is opposite to all others: for she did set up without credit, and her too much custom undid her; and so let her go,

without either shame, or hope of repentance.

We desired to see another. 'Tis variety that man chiefly takes delight in. One constant sort of food, without participating of any other, though manna, will cause the stomach to long for the flesh-pots. Neither can the crime be greater in the enjoyment of diverse persons then one alone, provided matrimony make not the act legitimate. I do not approve of these consequent lines tending to this purpose; yet give me leave to insert them, that you may understand how viciously minded some are in this frothy age:

> Born under some ill planet, or
>   accurst,
>   Is he that loves one single
>   whore;
> Who with one draught can always
>   quench his thirst,
>   Ty'd to one mistress, and no
>   more.

This nauseating thing being removed, up came one of Venus her chief darlings. Excellent flesh! and she herself the cook that dressed it, spending most of her day-time about it, that she might with the better appetite be tasted at night. Finding no exceptions in this, I was impatient till I had consummated my desires. Withdrawing into another room, to heighten my thoughts, she declared to me her birth and education; that as the one was well extracted, the other had occasioned much cost and expense; that for her part, she associated with none but persons of quality, whose long patience and entreatments first procured a familiarity, and in fine, freedom in the exercise of love-affairs: and so would have (seemingly) put me off upon this score, that it was not usual for her to admit of any to her embraces but such whose

long acquaintance had gained her affection. I offered her a crown, which she refused with indignation; telling me, that she was not yet reduced to so low a condition as to become so poor a mercenary prostitute. At last, with much persuasion, I fastened on her an half piece; and so striving with her (she only seeming averse), I accomplished my ends.

And presently in came a fellow whose very face would have enlightened the room, though in the darkest night; for indeed it appeared to me a blazing comet, and his nose (for miraculously he had preserved it) was the brushy tail. Laying his hand on his sword, he looked fiercer than a Spanish Don insulting over an Indian slave. The bulk of his body began to heave like an earth-quake, whilst his mouth, Aetna-like, belched out all manner of sulphurous oaths, which roared so loud as if his belly had contained a barrel of gunpowder, and the linstock of his nose had fired it. His courteous salutation to me, was, 'How darest thou, son of a whore, presume in this nature to dishonour me, in the abusing of my wife, without the expectation of an immediate annihilation or dissipation into atoms? But I have something here shall tame thy insolence; and now I am resolved to set thy blood abroach.' With that he seemed to make a pass at me. Now I, imagining that he really intended to do what he pretended, for the safeguard of my life, took up a jointstool, and received his point in the seat; and following it home, tumbled him down the stairs; and not being able to recover myself, fell with him. My comrade came running down at the noise to assist me; but he seeing me rather make use of my heels than hands, followed my example, and so built a sconce, leaving the old bawd to condole her great loss; for the reckoning was very considerable. . . .

In the United States, prostitution accompanied the rise of industrialization. In the city, sex could be anonymous. And in a culture which seemed to regard buying and selling as a major task in life, there soon developed a market for sex with its own laws of supply and demand. In Stephan Crane's *Maggie: A Girl of the Streets,* Maggie is an immigrants' daughter who struggled to rise above her status through prostitution.

American literature at the turn of the century could claim no major portrait of a prostitute. *Maggie: A Girl of the Streets* broke with the genteel tradition both in style and content.

Though it seems hard to believe now, the daring nature of his subject matter forced Crane to issue it privately at his own expense. "It is inevitable," he wrote in his preface to this edition, "that you will be greatly shocked by this book, but continue, please, with all possible courage until the end. For it tries to show that environment is a tremendous thing in the world and frequently shapes lives regardless. If one proves that theory, one makes room in heaven for all sorts of souls, notably an occasional street girl, who are not confidently expected to be there by many excellent people."

1896

MAGGIE GOES ON THE TURF

from *Maggie: A Girl of the Streets*
STEPHEN CRANE

A group of urchins were intent upon the side door of a saloon. Expectancy gleamed from their eyes. They were twisting their fingers in excitement.

"Here she comes!" yelled one of them suddenly.

The group of urchins burst instantly asunder and its individual fragments were spread in a wide, respectable half-circle about the point of interest. The saloon door opened with a crash, and the figure of a woman appeared upon the threshold. Her gray hair fell in knotted masses about her shoulders. Her face was crimsoned and wet with perspiration. Her eyes had a rolling glare.

"Not a cent more of me money will yehs ever get—not a red! I spent me money here for t'ree years, an'

now yehs tells me yeh'll sell me no more stuff! Go fall on yerself, Johnnie Murckre! 'Disturbance'? Disturbance be blowed! Go fall on yerself, Johnnie—"

The door received a kick of exasperation from within, and the woman lurched heavily out onto the sidewalk.

The gamins in the half-circle became violently agitated. They began to dance about and hoot and yell and jeer. A wide, dirty grin spread over each face.

The woman made a furious dash at a particularly outrageous cluster of little boys. They laughed delightedly, and scampered off a short distance, calling out to her over their shoulders. She stood tottering on the curbstone and thundered at them.

"Yeh devil's kids!" she howled, shaking her fists. The little boys whooped in glee. As she started up the street they fell in behind and marched uproariously. Occasionally she wheeled about and made charges on them. They ran nimbly out of reach and taunted her.

In the frame of a gruesome doorway she stood for a moment cursing them. Her hair straggled, giving her red features a look of insanity. Her great fists quivered as she shook them madly in the air.

The urchins made terrific noises until she turned and disappeared. Then they filed off quietly in the way they had come.

The woman floundered about in the lower hall of the tenement house, and finally stumbled up the stairs. On an upper hall a door was opened and a collection of heads peered curiously out, watching her. With a wrathful snort the woman confronted the door, but it was slammed hastily in her face and the key was turned.

She stood for a few minutes, delivering a frenzied challenge at the panels: "Come out in deh hall, Mary Murphy, if yehs want a scrap! Come ahn! yeh overgrown terrier, come ahn!"

She began to kick the door. She shrilly defied the universe to appear and do battle. Her cursing trebles brought heads from all doors save the one she threatened. Her eyes glared in every direction. The air was full of her tossing fists.

"Come ahn! deh hull gang of yehs, come ahn!" she roared at the spectators. An oath or two, catcalls, jeers, and bits of facetious advice were given in reply. Missiles clattered about her feet.

"What's wrong wi'che?" said a voice in the gathered gloom, and Jimmie came forward. He carried a tin dinner pail in his hand and under his arm a truckman's brown apron done in a bundle. "What's wrong?" he demanded.

"Come out! all of yehs, come out," his mother was howling. "Come ahn an' I'll stamp yer faces t'rough d' floor."

"Shet yer face an' come home, yeh old fool!" roared Jimmie at her. She strode up to him and twirled her fin-gers in his face. Her eyes were darting flames of unreasoning rage, and her frame trembled with eagerness for a fight.

"An' who are youse? I ain't givin' a snap of me fingers fer youse!" she bawled at him. She turned her huge back in tremendous disdain and climbed the stairs to the next floor.

Jimmie followed, and at the top of the flight he seized his mother's arm and started to drag her toward the door of their room. "Come home!" he gritted between his teeth.

"Take yer hands off me! Take yer hands off me!" shrieked his mother.

She raised her arm and whirled her great fist at her son's face. Jimmie dodged his head, and the blow struck him in the back of the neck. "Come home!" he gritted again. He threw out his left hand and writhed his fingers about her middle arm. The mother and the son began to sway and struggle like gladiators.

"Whoop!" said the Rum Alley tenement house. The hall filled with interested spectators.

"Hi, ol' lady, dat was a dandy!"

"T'ree t' one on d' red!"

"Ah, quit yer scrappin'!"

The door of the Johnson home opened and Maggie looked out. Jimmie made a supreme, cursing effort and hurled his mother into the room. He quickly followed and closed the door. The Rum Alley tenement swore disappointedly and retired.

The mother slowly gathered herself up from the floor. Her eyes glittered menacingly upon her children.

"Here now," said Jimmie, "we've had enough of dis. Sit down, an' don' make no trouble."

He grasped her arm and, twisting it, forced her into a creaking chair.

"Keep yer hands off me!" roared his mother again.

"Say, yeh ol' bat! Quit dat!" yelled Jimmie, madly. Maggie shrieked and ran into the other room. To her there came the sound of a storm of crashes and curses. There was a great final thump and Jimmie's voice cried, "Dere, now! Stay still." Maggie opened the door now, and went warily out. "Oh, Jimmie!"

He was leaning against the wall and swearing. Blood stood upon bruises on his knotty forearms where they had scraped against the floor or the walls in the scuffle. The mother lay screeching on the floor, the tears running down her furrowed face.

Maggie, standing in the middle of the room, gazed about her. The usual upheaval of the tables and chairs had taken place. Crockery was strewn broadcast in fragments. The stove had been disturbed on its legs, and now leaned idiotically to one side. A pail had been upset and water spread in all directions.

The door opened and Pete appeared. He shrugged his shoulders. "Oh, gee!" he observed.

He walked over to Maggie and whispered in her ear, "Ah, what d' hell, Mag? Come ahn and we'll have a outa-sight time."

The mother in the corner upreared her head and shook her tangled locks.

"Aw, yer bote no good, needer of yehs," she said, glowering at her daughter in the gloom. Her eyes seemed to burn balefully. "Yeh've gone t' d' devil, Mag Johnson, yehs knows yehs have gone t' d' devil. Yer a disgrace t' yer people. An' now, git out an' go ahn wid dat doe-faced jude of yours. Go wid him, curse yeh, an' a good riddance. Go, an' see how yeh likes it."

Maggie gazed long at her mother.

"Go now, an' see how yeh likes it. Git out. I won't have sech as youse in me house! Git out, d' yeh hear! Damn yeh, git out!"

The girl began to tremble.

At this instant Pete came forward. "Oh, what d' hell, Mag, see?" whispered he softly in her ear. "Dis all blows over. See? D' ol' woman'll be all right in d' mornin'. Come ahn out wid me! We'll have a outa-sight time."

The woman on the floor cursed. Jimmie was intent upon his bruised forearms. The girl cast a glance about the room filled with a chaotic mass of debris, and at the writhing body of her mother.

"Git th' devil outa here."

Maggie went.

Jimmie had an idea it wasn't common courtesy for a friend to come to one's home and ruin one's sister. But he was not sure how much Pete knew about the rules of politeness.

The following night he returned home from work at a rather late hour in the evening. In passing through the halls he came upon the gnarled and leathery old woman who possessed the music-box. She was grinning in the dim light that drifted through dust-stained panes. She beckoned to him with a smudged forefinger.

"Ah, Jimmie, what do yehs tink I tumbled to, las' night! It was deh funnies' t'ing I ever saw," she cried, coming close to him and leering. She was trembling with eagerness to tell her tale. "I was by me door las' night when yer sister and her jude feller came in late, oh, very late. An' she, the dear, she was a-cryin' as if her heart would break, she was. It was deh funnies' t'ing I ever saw. An' right out here by me door she asked him did he love her, did he. An' she was a-crying as if her heart would break, poor t'ing. An' him, I could see by deh way what he said it dat she had been askin' orften; he says, 'Oh, gee, yes,' he says, says he. 'Oh, gee, yes.' "

Storm clouds swept over Jimmie's face, but he turned from the leathery old woman and plodded on upstairs.

" 'Oh, gee, yes,' " she called after him. She laughed a laugh that was like a prophetic croak.

There was no one in at home. The rooms showed that attempts had been made at tidying them. Parts of the wreckage of the day before had been repaired by an unskilled hand. A chair or two and the table stood uncertainly upon legs. The floor had been newly swept. The blue ribbons had been restored to the curtains, and the lambrequin, with its immense sheaves of yellow wheat and red roses of equal size, had been returned, in a worn and sorry state, to its place at the mantel. Maggie's jacket and hat were gone from the nail behind the door.

Jimmie walked to the window and began to look through the blurred glass. It occurred to him to wonder vaguely, for an instant, if some of the women of his acquaintance had brothers.

Suddenly, however, he began to swear. "But he was me frien'! I brought 'im here! Dat's d' devil of it!"

He fumed about the room, his anger gradually rising to the furious pitch.

"I'll kill deh jay! Dat's what I'll do! I'll kill deh jay!"

He clutched his hat and sprang toward the door. But it opened, and his mother's great form blocked the passage.

"What's d' matter wid yeh?" exclaimed she.

Jimmie gave vent to a sardonic curse and then laughed heavily. "Well, Maggie's gone teh d' devil! Dat's what! See?"

"Eh?" said his mother.

"Maggie's gone teh d' devil! Are yehs deaf?" roared Jimmie.

"Aw, git out!" murmured the mother, astounded.

Jimmie grunted, and then began to stare out the window. His mother sat down in a chair, but a moment later sprang erect and delivered a maddened whirl of oaths. Her son turned to look at her as she reeled and swayed in the middle of the room, her fierce face convulsed with passion, her blotched arms raised high in imprecation.

"May she be cursed forever!" she shrieked. "May she eat nothin' but stones and deh dirt in deh street. May she sleep in deh gutter an' never see deh sun shine again. D' bloomin'—"

"Here now," said her son. "Go fall on yerself, an' quit dat."

The mother raised lamenting eyes to the ceiling.

"She's d' devil's own chil', Jimmie," she whispered. "Ah, who would t'ink such a bad girl could grow up in our fambly, Jimmie, me son. Many d' hour I've spent in talk wid dat girl an' tol' her if she ever went on d' streets I'd see her damned. An' after all her bringin'-up, an' what I tol' her and talked wid her, she goes teh d' bad, like a duck teh water."

The tears rolled down her furrowed face. Her hands trembled.

"An' den when dat Sadie MacMallister next door to us was sent teh d' devil by dat feller what worked in d' soap factory, didn't I tell our Mag dat if she—"

"Ah, dat's anudder story," interrupted the brother. "Of course, dat Sadie was nice an' all dat—but—see? —it ain't dessame as if—well, Maggie was diff'ent—see?—she was diff'ent."

He was trying to formulate a theory that he had always unconsciously held, that all sisters excepting his own could, advisedly, be ruined.

He suddenly broke out again. "I'll go t'ump d' mug what done her d' harm. I'll kill 'im! He t'inks he kin scrap, but when he gits me a-chasin' 'im he'll fin' out where he's wrong, d' big stiff! I'll wipe up d' street wid 'im."

In a fury he plunged out the doorway. As he vanished, the mother raised her head and lifted both hands, entreating.

"May she be cursed forever!" she cried.

In the darkness of the hallway Jimmie discerned a knot of women talking volubly. When he strode by they paid no attention to him.

"She allus was a bold thing," he heard one of them cry in an eager voice. "Dere wasn't a feller come teh deh house but she'd try teh mash 'im. My Annie says deh shameless t'ing tried teh ketch her feller, her own feller, what we useter know his fader."

"I could 'a' tol' yehs dis two years ago," said a woman, in a key of triumph. "Yes, sir, it was over two years ago dat I says teh my ol' man, I says, 'Dat Johnson girl ain't straight,' I says. 'Oh, rats!' he says. 'Oh, hell!' 'Dat's all right,' I says, 'but I know what I knows,' I says, 'an' it'll come out later. You wait an' see,' I says, 'you see.' "

"Anybody what had eyes could see dat dere was somethin' wrong wid dat girl. I didn't like her actions."

On the street Jimmie met a friend. "What's wrong?" asked the latter.

Jimmie explained. "An' I'll t'ump 'im till he can't stand."

"Oh, go ahn!" said the friend. "What's deh use! Yeh'll git pulled in! Everybody'll be on to it! An' ten plunks! Gee!"

Jimmie was determined. "He t'inks he kin scrap, but he'll fin' out diff'ent."

"Gee!" remonstrated the friend, "what's d' use?"

From Tamar to Maggie, the prostitute appears as a symbolic temptress. She often appears to lure man away from his world by her sexual charms. This enables males to believe the illusion perpetuated in the Garden of Eden myth: it was Eve who made Adam eat the apple. These excerpts form a pattern about some of the contradictions which exist between men and women. The following questions focus on the prostitute as an image of woman separate from and also a part of a male-dominated world.

1 What image of the relation between men and women emerges from these accounts of prostitution? Discuss the stories from the following perspectives:

a Describe those stories which illustrate the woman's relation to her family or her in-laws. Does the woman seek independence from male-imposed rule? Which women use prostitution as a symbolic means to punish the male? Explain.

b What is the relation of economics to moral principles in these stories? In which stories does the woman seek prostitution to obtain survival economically? Does this allow the male to believe that women become prostitutes to obtain wealth? Discuss this contradiction. Does the male in any of these stories try to justify his need to pay for prostitution?

c In which of these stories is the prostitute punished? Is this punishment given to her because of her beauty? What does this suggest about the strength and weakness of those women and men who engage in prostitution?

d What is the relation of purification to prostitution? Which of these stories relate death and prostitution? Discuss the way Richard Head describes the setting of Mother Cresswell's. What moral lesson does one learn from his account? How does Maggie compare and con-

trast with the woman in Head's story?

e What changing attitudes toward the prostitute as a scapegoat are illustrated in these stories?

2 How do these stories depict the act of prostitution as a female initiation ceremony? Discuss these stories from the following perspectives:

a Reread Bruno Bettelheim's discussion of female initiation rites in his essay "Symbolic Wounds." Use Bettelheim's theory to interpret "The Rise and Fall of a Harlot" from India.

b In which of the stories do we see the female's envy of male aggression? In which of the stories do we see the male's fear of tenderness?

c In which story is there a demonstration of the rites of purification in order for the female to enter society? Discuss Thais' transformation from whore to nun: What tests must she undergo before she is accepted by a male-oriented society?

d What do these stories suggest about the separation of women from men? How does this explain the differences between the female's view of the world and the male's view of the world?

e Discuss the insights revealed in these stories from the following points of view:

(1) What do these stories reveal about political attitudes toward prostitution?

(2) What do these stories reveal about religious attitudes toward prostitution?

(3) In which of these stories is the prostitute independent of the male-oriented world? What does this suggest about prostitution as a ceremony confering equal status on women?

(4) What do these stories suggest about cultural attitudes toward sexual union and love?

The Attack of a
Temptress —...
or The Experience of
Horror

Leda by Michelangelo Buonarroti depicts the way Zeus in the disguise of a swan rapes Leda. In his book *A Vision* William Butler Yeats discusses the way his poem attempts to reveal the same event:

> I imagine the annunciation (Zeus' rape of Leda) that founded Greece as made to Leda, remembering that they showed in Spartan temple, strung up to the roof as a holy relic, an unhatched egg of hers; and that from one of the eggs came Love and from the other War. But all things are from antithesis, and when in my ignorance I try to imagine what older civilizations that annunciation rejected I can see but bird and woman blotting out some corner of the Babylonian mathematical starlight.

The poem demonstrates what happens when these two opposing flows of passion intersect. The poem begins with Zeus' passion, while Leda is helpless and terrified. But it ends with Leda being "caught up" in his passion, while Zeus is indifferent.

LEDA AND THE SWAN

WILLIAM BUTLER YEATS

A sudden blow: the great wings beating still
Above the staggering girl, her thighs caressed
By the dark webs, her nape caught in his bill,
He holds her helpless breast upon his breast.
How can those terrified vague fingers push
The feathered glory from her loosening thighs?
And how can body, laid in that white rush,
But feel the strange heart beating where it lies?

A shudder in the loins engenders there
The broken wall, the burning roof and tower
And Agamemnon dead.
　　　　　　　　　　Being so caught up,
So mastered by the brute blood of the air,
Did she put on his knowledge with his power
Before the indifferent beak could let her drop?

Yeats' vision in "Leda and the Swan" demonstrates a union which exists outside the dimensions of time. Zeus' annunciation to Leda sets the stage for the beginning of European history. Sexual union, like time itself, is a paradox: it appears contingent and relative, but it is really the vehicle of an Absolute. Leda experiences the horror of the moment. She is the victim of a god who violently attacks a human woman. Zeus, disguised as a giant swan, had in that moment not only begotten Helen but the whole consequence of her actions: the Fall of Troy and the death of the Greek heroes. The poem illustrates what happens when these two opposing passions meet. Leda must feel, Yeats insists, "the strange heart beating where it lies" at the instant that "A shudder in the loins" engenders a future. The following questions focus on Leda and Zeus' relation.

1 What image of the male emerges in the first stanza? How does Yeats reveal the horror in Zeus' action? What image of the female emerges in the first stanza?

2 How does Yeats link war to the rape of Leda? What does this suggest about the nature of war? Explain!

3 What does this act do to Leda? What does this act do to Zeus? Is she transformed as a woman? Explain. How is he transformed? Discuss the contradictions in their changes.

4 What does the poem suggest about the female as a symbol of fertility? Does the poem suggest anything about the male's fear of the female? How does Leda differ from Isis?

5 Does Leda meet a fate similar to Randall's Magdalene in "A Scarlet Letter about Mary Magdalene"? What illusions which exist between men and women are revealed in the poem? Has Leda become a woman in a world which forbids the expression of tenderness? Explain!

To Seek a newer world

The political hero must find the symbols necessary to unite his people in bonds of national kinship. His language must express ideals that will affirm and give meaning to the cultural mythology linking him to the people. Following the death of John F. Kennedy on November 22, 1963, Robert Kennedy "took up the torch" of his slain brother. In the picture shown above, people reach to touch him to emotionally express their identification with him. Robert Kennedy seemed to have a special kind of magic for the American people. Perhaps they wanted to believe that he could bring the nation back "to the spot that was known as Camelot."

Michelangelo's *Pieta* is an archetypal representation of the fate of the hero, and the woman who suffers through his life and death. Mary holds her son for a last moment, and woman, the giver of life, becomes the bridge between life and death or immortality. A young Irish rebel wrote the following poem in 1916 before he and his brother were executed. This poem was sent to Mrs. Rose Kennedy following the death of her son Robert. The language of the poem expresses the destiny of both the mother and her sons, the political men of action.

THE MOTHER

Padhraic Pearse

I do not grudge them, Lord, I do not grudge
My two strong sons, that I have seen go out
To break their strength and die, they and a few,
In bloody protest for a glorious thing.
They shall be spoken of among their people,
The generations shall remember them,
And call them blessed:
But I will speak their names in my own heart
In the long nights.
The little names that were familiar once
Round my dead hearth,
Lord, Thou art hard on mothers:
And thou' I grudged them not, I weary, weary
Of this long sorrow—And yet I have my joys:
My sons were faithful and they fought.

In the beginning was the word...

To understand the way the political hero undergoes a rite of passage, we must grapple with the use and abuse of language. Words become political weapons which often transform a country's destiny. Oedipus, the Greek political hero, summons Tiresias, the man who knows the language of birds, to help solve the riddle of the Spinx in order to understand why Thebes has been infected with a plague. But Oedipus refuses to believe the blind seer's vision that he, Oedipus, is the cause of the city's pollution. This action results in the eventual blinding of the man who thinks he can see and hear only what he wants to see and hear. We see revealed a paradox: he who sees is blind, and he that is blind sees. Tiresias is the poet who restores language to the original forms which were consistent with the life's blood of a nation.

The counterpart of the political hero is the Madonna who both bestows and takes life from her children. The price she pays for transforming these two potent forces is to be condemned to endure the suffering associated with the Lady of Sorrows. While her sons seek honor and glory, she becomes the symbol of the woman who experiences the pains of life without losing hope.

As a result of the association with these two archetypes, men and women often seem to be in opposition to each other. The male feels that he must create a civilization based on moral order. To do this, the political hero gambles with war as a device to bring about his desired ends. The woman as Madonna feels contempt for those who bring about the termination of life outside the bounds of nature. The poet directs our attention to the language expressing these archetypes as a means to balance the rational and irrational forces which seek to transform a world.

THE MAGICIAN.

AM · HOMINE · AD · YMAGINE · 7·31MILITVOINE · N̄RAM · 7 ·
RIVIT I FACIE · EI SPIRAC V LVM · AITE

The quest
to link
the spiritual
and
human worlds

The picture shown above, a medieval painting depicting God breathing life into Adam, illustrates man's association of breath to magic. In many primitive religious rituals, the ability to allow words to spew forth is associated with the priest or shaman's connection to the world of spirits. The use of breath to connect man to the spiritual is also expressed through the medium of language. Christ's birth is often referred to as "the word was made flesh," and many people believe that by merely saying "God damn you" they have prevented an individual from attaining salvation. To understand the complex subject of language, the following essays investigate the purposes and function of language.

ON THE ORIGIN OF LANGUAGE

SUSANNE K. LANGER

The transformation of experience into concepts, not the elaboration of signals and symptoms, is the motive of language. *Speech is through and through symbolic; and only sometimes signific.* Any attempt to trace it back entirely to the need of communication, neglecting the formulative, abstractive experience at the root of it, must land us in the sort of enigma that the problem of linguistic organs has long presented. I have tried, instead, to trace it to the characteristic human activity, symbolic transformation and abstraction, of which pre-human beginnings may perhaps be attributed to the highest apes. Yet we have not found the commencement of language anywhere between their state and ours. Even in man, who has all its prerequisites, it depends on education not only for its full development, but for its very inception. How, then, did it ever arise? And why do all men possess it?

It could only have arisen in a race in which the lower forms of symbolistic thinking— dream, ritual, superstitious fancy—were already highly developed, i.e., where the process of symbolization, though primitive, was very active. Communal life in such a group would be characterized by vigorous indulgence in purely expressive acts, in ritual gestures, dances, etc., and probably by a strong tendency to fantastic terrors and joys. The liberation from practical interests that is already marked in the apes would make rapid progress in a species with a definitely symbolistic turn of mind; conventional meanings would gradually imbue every originally random act, so that the group-life as a whole would have an exciting, vaguely transcendental tinge, without any definable or communicable body of ideas to cling to. A wealth of dance-forms and antics, poses and manoeuvres might flourish in a society that was somewhat above the apes' in non-practical interests, and rested on a slightly higher development of the symbolific brain-functions. There are quite articulated play-forms, verging on dance-forms, in the natural repertoire of the chimpanzees; with but a little further elaboration, these would become most obvious material for symbolic expression. It is not at all impossible that *ritual*, solemn and significant, antedates the evolution of language.

THE NATURE OF SYMBOLIC LANGUAGE

ERICH FROMM

Let us assume you want to tell someone the difference between the taste of white wine and red wine. This may seem quite simple to you. *You* know the difference very well; why should it not be easy to explain it to someone else? Yet you find the greatest difficulty putting this taste difference into words. And probably you will end up by saying, "Now look here I can't explain it to you. Just drink red wine and then white wine, and you will know what the difference is." You have no difficulty in finding words to explain the most complicated machine, and yet words seem to be futile to describe a simple taste experience.

Are we not confronted with the same difficulty when we try to explain a feeling experience? Let us take a mood in which you feel lost, deserted, where the world looks gray, a little frightening though not really dangerous. You want to describe this mood to a friend, but again you find yourself groping for words and eventually feel that nothing you have said is an adequate explanation of the many nuances of the mood. The following night you have a dream. You see yourself in the outskirts of a city just before dawn, the streets are empty except for a milk wagon, the houses look poor, the surroundings are unfamiliar, you have no means of accustomed transportation to places familiar to you and where you feel you belong. When you wake up and remember the dream, it occurs to you that the feeling you had in that dream was exactly the feeling of lostness and grayness you tried to describe to your friend the day before. It is just one picture, whose visualization took less than a second. And yet this picture is a more vivid and precise description than you could have given by talking *about* it at length. The picture you see in the dream is a *symbol* of something you felt.

What is a symbol? A symbol is often defined as "something that stands for something else." This definition seems rather disappointing. It becomes more interesting, however, if we concern ourselves with those symbols which are sensory expressions of seeing, hearing, smelling, touching, standing for a "something else" which is an inner experience, a feeling or thought. A symbol of this kind is something outside ourselves; that which it symbolizes is something inside ourselves. Symbolic language is language in which we express inner experience as if it were a sensory experience, as if it were something we were doing or something that was done to us in the world of things. Symbolic language is language in which the world outside is a symbol of the world inside, a symbol for our souls and our minds.

If we define a symbol as "something which stands for something else," the crucial question is: *What is the specific connection between the symbol and that which it symbolizes?*

In answer to this question we can differentiate between three kinds of symbols: the *conventional*, the *accidental* and the *universal* symbol. As will become apparent presently, only the latter two kinds of symbols express inner experiences as if they were sensory experiences, and only they have the elements of symbolic language.

The *conventional* symbol is the best known of the three, since we employ it in everyday language. If we see the word "table" or hear the sound "table," the letters T-A-B-L-E stand for something else. They stand for the thing table that we see, touch and use. What is the connection between the *word* "table" and the *thing* "table"? Is there any inherent relationship between them? Obviously not. The thing table has nothing to do with the sound table, and the only reason the word symbolizes the thing is the convention of calling this particular thing by a particular name. We learn this connection as children by the repeated experience of hearing the word in reference to the thing until a lasting association is formed so that we don't have to think to find the right word.

There are some words, however, where the association is not only conventional. When we say "phooey," for instance, we make with our lips a movement of dispelling the air quickly. It is an expression of disgust in which our mouths participate. By this quick expulsion of air we imitate and thus express our intention to expel something, to get it out of our system. In this case, as in some others, the symbol has an inherent connection with the feeling it symbolizes. But even if we assume that originally many or even all words had their origins in some such inherent connection between symbol and the symbolized, most words no longer have this meaning for us when we learn a language.

Words are not the only illustration for conventional symbols, although they are the most frequent and best-known ones. Pictures also can be conventional symbols. A flag, for instance, may stand for a specific country, and yet there is no connection between the specific colors and the country for which they stand. They have been accepted as denoting that particular country, and we translate the visual impression of the flag into the concept of that country, again on conventional grounds. Some pictorial symbols are not entirely conventional; for example, the cross. The cross can be merely a conventional symbol of the Christian church and in that respect no different from a flag. But the specific content of the cross referring to Jesus' death or, beyond that, to the interpenetration of the material and spiritual planes, puts the connection between the symbol and what it symbolizes beyond the level of mere conventional symbols.

The very opposite to the conventional symbol is the *accidental* symbol, although they have one thing in common: there is no intrinsic relationship between the symbol and that which it symbolizes. Let us assume that someone has had a saddening experience in a certain city; when he hears the name of that city, he will easily connect the name with a mood of sadness, just as he would connect it with a mood of joy had his experience been a happy one. Quite obviously there is nothing in the nature of the city that is either sad or joyful. It is the individual experience connected with the city that makes it a symbol of a mood.

The same reaction could occur in connection with a house, a street, a certain dress, certain scenery, or anything once connected with a specific mood. We might find ourselves dreaming that we are in a certain city. In fact, there may be no particular mood connected with it in the dream; all we see is a street or even simply the name of the city. We ask ourselves why we happened to think of that city in our sleep and may discover that we had fallen asleep in a mood similar to the one symbolized by the city. The picture in the dream represents this mood, the city "stands for" the mood once experienced in it. Here the connection between the symbol and the experience symbolized is entirely accidental.

In contrast to the conventional symbol, the accidental symbol cannot be shared by anyone else except as we relate the events connected with the symbol. For this reason accidental symbols are rarely used in myths, fairy tales, or works of art written in symbolic language because they are not communicable unless the writer adds a lengthy comment to each symbol he uses. In dreams, however, accidental symbols are frequent, and later in this book I shall explain the method of understanding them.

The *universal* symbol is one in which there is an intrinsic relationship between the symbol and that which it represents. We have already given one example, that of the outskirts of the city. The sensory experience of a deserted, strange, poor environment has indeed a significant relationship to a mood of lostness and anxiety. True enough, if we have never been in the outskirts of a city we could not use that symbol, just as the word "table" would be meaningless had we never seen a table. This symbol is meaningful only to city dwellers and would be meaningless to people living in cultures that have no big cities. Many other universal symbols, however, are rooted in the experience of every human being. Take, for instance, the symbol of fire. We are fascinated by certain qualities of fire in a fireplace. First of all, by its aliveness. It changes continuously, it moves all the time, and yet there is constancy in it. It remains the same without being the same. It gives the impression of power, of energy, of grace and lightness. It is as if it were dancing and had an inexhaustible source of energy. When we use fire as a symbol, we describe the inner experience characterized by the same elements which we notice in the sensory experience of fire; the mood of energy, lightness, movement, grace, gaiety—sometimes one, sometimes another of these elements being predominant in the feeling.

Similar in some ways and different in others is the symbol of water—of the ocean or of the stream. Here, too, we find the blending of change and permanence, of constant movement and yet of permanence. We also feel the quality of aliveness, continuity and energy. But there is a difference; where fire is adventurous, quick, exciting, water is quiet, slow and steady. Fire has an element of surprise; water an element of predictability. Water symbolizes the mood of aliveness, too, but one which is "heavier," "slower," and more comforting than exciting.

That a phenomenon of the physical world can be the adequate expression of an inner experience, that the world of things can be a symbol of the world of the mind, is not surprising. We all know that our bodies express our minds. Blood rushes to our heads when we are furious, it rushes away from them when we are afraid; our hearts beat more quickly when we are angry, and the whole body has a different tonus if we are happy from the one it has when we are sad. We express our moods by our facial expressions and our attitudes and feelings by movements and gestures so precise that others recognize them more accurately from our gestures than from our words. Indeed, the body is a symbol—and not an allegory—of the mind. Deeply and genuinely felt emotion, and even genuinely felt thought, is expressed in our whole organism. In the case of the universal symbol, we find the same connection between mental and physical experience. Certain physical phenomena suggest by their very nature certain emotional and mental experiences, and we express emotional experiences in the language of physical experiences, that is to say, symbolically.

The universal symbol is the only one in which the relationship between the symbol and that which is symbolized is not coincidental but intrinsic. It is rooted in the experience of the affinity between an emotion or thought, on the one hand, and a sensory experience, on the other. It can be called universal because it is shared by all men, in contrast not only to the accidental symbol, which is by its very nature entirely personal, but also to the conventional symbol, which is restricted to a group of people sharing the same convention. The universal symbol is rooted in the properties of our body, our senses, and our mind, which are common to all men and, therefore, not restricted to individuals or to specific groups. Indeed, the language of the universal symbol is the one common tongue developed by the human race, a language which it forgot before it succeeded in developing a universal conventional language.

There is no need to speak of a racial inheritance in order to explain the universal character of symbols. Every human being who shares the essential features of bodily and mental equipment with the rest of mankind is capable of speaking and understanding the symbolic language that is based upon these common properties. Just as we do not need to learn to cry when we are sad or to get red in the face when we are angry, and just as these reactions are not restricted to any particular race or group of people, symbolic language does not have to be learned and is not restricted to any segment of the human race. Evidence for this is to be found in the fact that symbolic language as it is employed in myths and dreams is found in all cultures, in so-called primitive as well as such highly developed cultures as Egypt and Greece.

Furthermore, the symbols used in these various cultures are strikingly similar since they all go back to the basic sensory as well as emotional experiences shared by men of all cultures. Added evidence is to be found in recent experiments in which people who had no knowledge of the theory of dream interpretation were able, under hypnosis, to interpret the symbolism of their dreams without any difficulty. After emerging from the hypnotic state and being asked to interpret the same dreams, they were puzzled and said, "Well, there is no meaning to them—it is just nonsense."

The foregoing statement needs qualification, however. Some symbols differ in meaning according to the difference in their realistic significance in various cultures. For instance, the function and consequently the meaning of the sun is different in northern countries and in tropical countries. In northern countries, where water is plentiful, all growth depends on sufficient sunshine. The sun is the warm, life-giving, protecting, loving power. In the Near East, where the heat of the sun is much more powerful, the sun is a dangerous and even threatening power from which man must protect himself, while water is felt to be the source of all life and the main condition for growth. We may speak of dialects of universal symbolic language, which are determined by those differences in natural conditions which cause certain symbols to have a different meaning in different regions of the earth.

Quite different from these "symbolic dialects" is the fact that many symbols have more than one meaning in accordance with different kinds of experiences which can be connected with one and the same natural phenomenon. Let us take up the symbol of fire again. If we watch fire in the fireplace, which is a source of pleasure and comfort, it is expressive of a mood of aliveness, warmth, and pleasure. But if we see a building or forest on fire, it conveys to us an experience of threat or terror, of the powerlessness of man against the elements of nature. Fire, then, can be the symbolic representation of inner aliveness and happiness as well as of fear, powerlessness, or of one's own destructive tendencies. The same holds true of the symbol water. Water can be a most destructive force when it is whipped up by a storm or when a swollen river floods its banks. Therefore, it can be the symbolic expression of horror and chaos as well as of comfort and peace.

Another illustration of the same principle is a symbol of a valley. The valley enclosed between mountains can arouse in us the feeling of security and comfort, of protection against all dangers from the outside. But the protecting mountains can also mean isolating walls which do not permit us to get out of the valley and thus the valley can become a symbol of imprisonment. The particular meaning of the symbol in any given place can only be determined from the whole context in which the symbol appears, and in terms of the predominant experiences of the person using the symbol.

?

The primary level of communication informs us that a physical world exists. The signs which reveal this to us demand a response. This sensory reaction to phenomena influences our behavior. Animal behavior is essentially sign behavior. On the other hand, human behavior is essentially symbolic. Symbols allow us to evaluate, interpret, and express our perceptions of a world. The Greek meaning of symbol was "draw together." This definition suggests the multilevels of meaning contained in a symbol. Each symbol exists within a complex network of emotions, thoughts, and past associations. The ability to understand this network makes possible the release of energy which binds us to the world.

In "On the Origin of Language" the discussion focuses on the use of symbols as a means to go beyond the literal interpretation of meaning. The use of discursive and nondiscursive symbols brings together the verbal and nonverbal elements contained within the context of language. In "The Nature of Symbolic Language" the world of dreams becomes the source of energy which makes possible the communication of messages from the unconscious to the conscious. The following questions focus on the use of symbols as a means to understand the way we arrange images to interpret and express a self in relation to a world.

In the "Origins of Language," Langer considers language as the individual's link to the possibility of unity.

1 How does one know the sign from the symbol? What causes human beings to assign meanings to signs and symbols?

2 Discuss the implications of discursive and nondiscursive symbols. Reread Yeats's poem, "Leda and The Swan" in Chapter 3 and attempt to locate the nondiscursive symbols.

3 What is the relation between the conscious and unconscious use of symbols? How does this relation allow us to understand our "inner" splits?

4 How does an individual learn to see "new dimensions of reality"?

In "The Nature of Symbolic Language" the messages in dreams reveal the individual's symbolic connection to universal symbols.

1 Discuss Fromm's definition of conventional and accidental symbols. What examples do you see in your use of symbols which reveals Fromm's point of view?

2 What does Fromm mean by "universal symbols"? How does his discussion differ from Jung's use of the anima and animus as archetypal symbols?

3 What intrinsic qualities are embodied in "universal symbols"? How does one see the intrinsic qualities of "universal symbols" in the chapter on the hero and the temptress (Chapter 3)?

Language is the magical bond which holds the tribe together. Before a code of behavior is established, symbols most point the way for human beings to quell the enemy within. For those who refuse to adhere to the group's rules, banishment is often prescribed. For those who choose to live in harmony, symbols are created to bridge the gap between nature and the human world. These symbols make possible the communication process which expresses both the limitations and infinities which coexist in the world of language.

THE FALSEHOOD OF TRUTH

SENEGALESE MYTH

Fene-Falsehood and Deug-Truth started out on a journey one day.

Fene-Falsehood said, "Everyone says that the Lord loves truth better than falsehood, so I think that you had better do all the talking for us."

Deug-Truth agreed, and when they came to a village, Deug-Truth greeted the first woman they met and asked if they could have a drink. She gave them a filthy bowl full of lukewarm water and then sat down in the doorway of her hut and began to eat a big meal of rice. While the two travelers were still there, the woman's husband came home and asked for his supper.

"It's not ready," replied the woman insolently.

The husband then turned to the two strangers who were watching and asked, "What would you say about a woman like that?"

"I would say that she is the worst wife I have seen in a long time. It's bad enough for her not to be hospitable to strangers, but it is really disgraceful when she doesn't feed her own husband," replied Deug-Truth. Fene-Falsehood didn't say a word.

The woman became furious and began to yell and scream louder than either of the two travelers had ever heard anyone scream before. "Are you going to stand by and let these strangers insult me!" she screamed to her husband. "If so, I will go home to my father and you will have to raise a bride-price for a new wife."

Then the husband, too, became angry and chased the two strangers out of town.

So Deug and Fene continued their travels and next came to a village where they found several children dividing up a bull that had just been slaughtered. They thought that this was rather strange, for it was the custom that meat was always divided by the head-man. While they were still watching, they saw the chief come up and take a very poor share of meat which the children handed him. The chief saw the two strangers and asked, "Who do you think is the leader in this village?"

Fene said nothing but Deug immediately answered, "It seems to me that these children must be the leaders of this village, for they are dividing the meat."

The chief immediately became angry and chased them out of that village.

As they continued to walk along, Fene said to Deug, "It is said that the Lord loves you the best, but I am beginning to wonder if man is not rather different from God. It seems to me that men do not like you very well. I think I will try my luck at the next village."

At the next village, they found that all the people were weeping because the favorite wife of the king had just died. Fene thought for a minute and then said, "Go tell the king that a man is here who can raise people from the dead."

Soon Fene was brought before the king and said, "I will raise your wife from the dead if you will give me half of your fortune."

The king immediately agreed and Fene had a hut built above the family grave. The king and all of the people waited outside and listened to the strange noises. First they heard huffing and panting and strange chants, but then they began to hear Fene talking loudly as if he were arguing. Finally he burst out of the door and slammed it shut—holding it tightly.

"Oh, dear," he said, "you did not tell me that your whole family was buried in there. When I woke your wife up, your father and your grandfather both came out too. I thought I had better check before I let them all out."

The king and his advisers began to look frightened, for the king's father had been a very cruel king and the new king and his friends had given his death a little assistance.

"I think you had better leave them all," said the king. "We would have a lot of trouble here with three kings."

"Well, it's not that easy," said Fene slyly. "Your father has offered me half of this property to let him out. I am certainly not going to send him back for nothing."

"I will still give you half of my property," said the desperate king. "Just get rid of them all."

So Fene received half of the king's fortune and concluded that while truth might have the favor of God, falsehood was the best way to get ahead with men.

My faith in human dignity consists in the belief that man is the greatest scamp on earth. Human dignity must be associated with the idea of a scamp and not with that of an obedient, disciplined, and regimented soldier. The scamp is probably the most glorious type of human being, as the soldier is the lowest type, according to this conception.

Lin Yutang

THE PHOENIX

CHINESE MYTH

There was once a small sparrow who laid three eggs in her nest, but a mouse came and ate two of them.

Heartbroken, she rushed off to the queen of birds, the phoenix, to beg for justice.

"I have no time to listen to you," replied the phoenix. "You are just a small, ugly bird. It is the job of parents to look after their own children. Don't bother me with your complaint."

So the sparrow returned home, determined to take things into her own hands. The next day she pretended to leave her nest and saw the mouse coming to eat the remaining egg. But this time she rushed down and pecked his eye out. Crazed by the pain and blind, he rushed into the nostril of a lion who was sleeping by the shore of a lake.

THE ZEN MASTER

JAPANESE MYTH

There was once a samurai who fell in love with his master's wife. So he killed the master and ran away with his wife, but she was so greedy that he soon left her.

Then the samurai began to feel guilty and decided that he must do a good deed to atone for his sins. As he was traveling along he came to a very steep road over a mountain and discovered that many people had been killed trying to cross it. So he decided to build a tunnel through the mountain.

He had been working for a year when the son of the master whom he had killed appeared and threatened to cut off his head.

"You have a right to kill me," said the samurai. "But could you please wait until I finish this tunnel?"

The young man agreed, and after watching for several weeks he began to work with his old enemy. Finally, after several more months, the tunnel was completed and people could walk safely through the mountain.

"Now you may kill me," said the samurai.

"How can I kill you now?" said the young man. "You are my own teacher."

Am I my brother's Keeper?

Blood becomes the symbol connecting individual members to a family. The authority of the parents must be replaced by the authority of the children. At this point, the rivalry for power becomes the signal for the rites of passage which make possible the transfer of power from one generation to the next. Blood, the symbol of union, then becomes the symbol of division. Brother often sheds the blood of brother in an attempt to gain control. Following such an incident, blood is symbolically shed to purify the ground of one brother's evil desire to triumph over the other. Thus, Cain's murder of Abel signals the beginning of a bloodbath in which brothers struggle to win the father's approval. This also links the Biblical story to the process of fertilization. Abel is the sheepherder, and Cain is the tiller of the soil. The killing resembles the initiation ceremony which fertilizes the ground. Language reports this action to fertilize the group's meaning and purpose. Centuries later in Gettysburg, Abraham Lincoln illustrated how the civil war had divided brother against brother. The language in Lincoln's famous address resembles rather closely the language in the biblical account of Cain and Abel. Once again the spirit is called upon to quell this "inner" enemy which divides and conquers a nation that was conceived by our forefathers. The Greek, Hindu, and Iroquois myths which follow relate the social beginnings of a group through the union and disunion of the brothers and sisters. The breath of language connects the blood once more to the original purpose and function of family unity.

GENESIS 4:1-16

CAIN AND ABEL

And Adam knew Eve his wife; and she conceived, and bare Cain, and said, "I have gotten a man from the Lord." And she again bare his brother Abel. And Abel was a keeper of sheep, but Cain was a tiller of the ground. And in process of time it came to pass, that Cain brought of the fruit of the ground an offering unto the Lord. And Abel, he also brought of the firstlings of his flock and of the fat thereof. And the Lord had respect unto Abel and to his offering: but unto Cain and to his offering he had not respect. And Cain was very wroth, and his countenance fell. And the Lord said unto Cain, "Why art thou wroth? and why is thy countenance fallen? If thou doest well, shalt thou not be accepted? and if thou doest not well, sin lieth at the door. And unto thee shall be his desire, and thou shalt rule over him." And Cain talked with Abel his brother: and it came to pass, when they were in the field, that Cain rose up against Abel his brother, and slew him.

And the Lord said unto Cain, "Where is Abel thy brother?" And he said, "I know not. Am I my brother's keeper?" And he said, "What hast thou done? the voice of thy brother's blood crieth unto me from the ground. And now art thou cursed from the earth, which hath opened her mouth to receive thy brother's blood from thy hand; when thou tillest the ground, it shall not henceforth yield unto thee her strength; a fugitive and a vagabond shalt thou be in the earth." And Cain said unto the Lord, "My punishment is greater than I can bear. Behold, thou hast driven me out this day from the face of the earth; and from thy face shall I be hid; and I shall be a fugitive and a vagabond in the earth; and it shall come to pass, that every one that findeth me shall slay me."

And the Lord said unto him, "Therefore whosoever slayeth Cain, vengeance shall be taken on him sevenfold." And the Lord set a mark upon Cain, lest any finding him should kill him. And Cain went out from the presence of the Lord, and dwelt in the land of Nod, on the east of Eden.

THE GETTYSBURG ADDRESS

ABRAHAM LINCOLN

November 19, 1863

Four score and seven years ago our fathers brought forth on this continent a new nation, conceived in liberty, and dedicated to the proposition that all men are created equal.

Now we are engaged in a great civil war, testing whether that nation, or any nation so conceived and so dedicated, can long endure. We are met on a great battlefield of that war. We have come to dedicate a portion of that field as a final resting-place for those who here gave their lives that that nation might live. It is altogether fitting and proper that we should do this.

But in a larger sense we cannot dedicate, we cannot consecrate, we cannot hallow this ground. The brave men, living and dead, who struggled here have consecrated it, far above our poor power to add or detract. The world will little note, nor long remember what we say here, but it can never forget what they did here. It is for us, the living, rather, to be dedicated here to the unfinished work which they fought here have thus far so nobly advanced. It is rather for us to be here dedicated to the great task remaining before us,—that from these honored dead we take increased devotion to that cause for which they gave the last full measure of devotion; that we here highly resolve that these dead shall not have died in vain; that this nation, under God, shall have a new birth of freedom; and that government of the people, by the people, and for the people, shall not perish from the earth.

The inner does not become outer, and the outer become inner, just by the rediscovery of the "inner" world. That is only the beginning. As a whole, we are a generation of men so estranged from the inner world that many are arguing that it does not exist; and that even if it does exist, it does not matter. Even if it has some significance, it is not the hard stuff of science, and if it is not, then let's make it hard. Let it be measured and counted. Quantify the heart's agony and ecstasy in a world in which, when the inner world is first discovered, we are liable to find ourselves bereft and derelict. For without the inner the outer loses its meaning, and without the outer the inner loses its substance.

R. D. Laing, *The Politics of Experience,* **1967.**

THE CURSE OF BLOOD

GREEK MYTH

In ancient, barbaric Greece, justice was of little use against armed might. What justice there was depended upon the gods who were usually so involved in their own intrigues that they had little time to be concerned with the behavior of men. Often punishments were delayed so long that they fell on the grandchildren instead of the sinner himself. So it was in the case of Atreus.

Atreus himself committed one of the most heinous crimes in history. His brother Thyestes fell in love with Atreus' wife, and in revenge, Atreus killed Thyestes' son and served the corpse for supper. Thyestes, having no power himself to avenge his son, called upon the gods to curse the house of Atreus.

This horrible deed probably reminded the gods of another crime committed by an ancestor of Atreus, Tantalus. (*Tantalize:* to tempt with something unattainable.) He lived in the days when the gods walked the earth with men; he tried to prove the stupidity of the gods by cutting up his own son Pelops and serving him to the gods for a meal. The gods, however, were not stupid and brought the boy back to life. Tantalus was sent to a pool in Hades where they tortured him by standing him up to his neck in water with delicious fruits hanging over his head. Whenever he stooped to drink, the water receded, and whenever he reached up to pluck the fruits, they were whisked up beyond his reach.

Atreus should have learned from this punishment of his ancestor, but he did not. However, the gods did not get around to punishing Atreus, but left the vengeance to fall on his two sons, Menelaus and Agamemnon. Perhaps the whole Trojan War

could be considered part of the punishment to the house of Atreus because it was Menelaus' wife who became Helen of Troy. But the bulk of the evil fell on Agamemnon and his family.

In order to sail to Troy, Agamemnon was told that he must sacrifice his daughter Iphigenia. Clytemnestra, Agamemnon's wife, was furious when Agamemnon agreed, and she refused to remain faithful to a husband who would kill his own daughter for the sake of glory. So she took as a lover one of Agamemnon's enemies, Aegisthus, a descendant of Thyestes whom Agamemnon's father had so mistreated.

Clytemnestra's hatred against Agamemnon increased as the stories of his love affairs at Troy came back. To make matters worse, when Agamemnon returned to his home after the war was over, he brought with him a new woman, Cassandra, the daughter of Priam, king of Troy.

Cassandra was a prophetess and as soon as she set foot in Mycenae, Agamemnon's home, she fell into a trance and began to prophesy death for Agamemnon and herself. The townspeople watched with foreboding as Agamemnon approached his palace where Clytemnestra and Aegisthus waited for him. The great doors were shut and a loud scream was heard. Then Clytemnestra opened the doors to reveal the body of her husband.

"Iphigenia is now avenged!" she cried.

But this was only the beginning of the bloody vengeance, for her other daughter, Elektra, felt stronger ties to her father than to her sister and she was determined that her father's death would not go unavenged. Fear-

ing her mother's crazed state and Aegisthus' ambition, she took her young brother, Orestes, and fled with him to another country where she gave him to friends to raise. Then she returned home.

Many years later, Orestes was grown and returned to his home with his friend Pylades. Not knowing what he would find there, he came as a stranger, and, instead of going to the palace, went to the graveyard to weep on the grave of his father.

There Elektra found him. Together they plotted. They were determined to kill Aegisthus to avenge their father, but could they kill their mother, too? Was not the crime of parricide worse than allowing their father's death to go unavenged? Unable to decide for himself, Orestes had gone to the oracle of Apollo. The answer was clear: Clytemnestra must be killed.

Their plan was simple. Pylades and Orestes were to go to the palace disguised as strangers bringing the message that Orestes had died. As they had planned, Clytemnestra invited them in, and once inside the palace, Orestes revealed who he was and immediately killed Aegisthus.

But Clytemnestra pleaded, "How can you kill your own mother? I brought you into this world. You nursed at my breast."

Orestes almost gave in to her pleading. "She is right, Pylades. I cannot kill my own mother."

"Do you dare disobey Apollo's oracle?" asked Pylades.

"You're right," Orestes replied, and with one stroke of his sword, he killed her. But immediately a change came over him. An unseen horror seemed to haunt him.

"Look," he screamed. "Can't you

see them? Those dreadful women with blood dripping from their eyes!" Orestes waved his sword madly at the creatures that were haunting him. But with no effect. At last he turned to flee them.

Elektra caught him and tried to hold him, "It is only your imagination," she pleaded. "Come in and rest and this horrible vision will go away."

But Orestes rushed out of her sight. For years he traveled from one land to another driven onward by the horrible Furies. For that is who they were, the terrible goddesses with snakes for hair who had sprung up from the blood of ancient Uranus and who were destined to remain on earth until all injustice disappeared.

So the cycle of revenge continued with the Furies avenging Clytemnestra, who had no one else to plead for her. But at last Apollo felt that Orestes' punishment was sufficient and he ordered him to go to Athens where Athena could cleanse him of his sin.

There in Athens was held perhaps the first trial by jury in the history of the world. Athena refused to make the decision but called the wise men of Athens together. Apollo himself pleaded the case for Orestes, and the Furies argued eloquently against him.

The question was so difficult that the jury was evenly divided and Athena herself had to cast the deciding vote—for acquittal. Orestes was free.

But Athena could not disregard the proper wrath of the Furies, so she invited them to stay in Athens, promising them a home and worship worthy of them. They accepted her invitation and from then on have been called the Eumenides, the Benevolent Ones, and instead of punishing the guilty, they now plead the cases of the weak and poor.

Learning the Lord's Song

PSALM 137

By the rivers of Babylon, there we sat down, yea, we wept, when we remembered Zion.

2 We hanged our harps upon the willows in the midst thereof.

3 For there they that carried us away captive required of us a song; and they that wasted us required of us mirth, saying, Sing us one of the songs of Zion.

4 How shall we sing the Lord's song in a strange land?

5 If I forget thee, O Jerusalem, let my right hand forget her cunning.

6 If I do not remember thee, let my tongue cleave to the roof of my mouth; if I prefer not Jerusalem above my chief joy.

7 Remember, O Lord, the children of Edom in the day of Jerusalem; who said, Rase it, rase it, even to the foundation thereof.

8 O daughter of Babylon, who art to be destroyed; happy shall he be, that rewardeth thee as thou hast served us.

9 Happy shall he be, that taketh and dasheth thy little ones against the stones.

ca. 900 B.C.

By knowing the Self . . . through hearing, reflection, and meditation, one comes to know all things. . . . As for water the one center is the ocean, as for touch the one center is the skin, as for smell the one center is the nose, as for taste the one center is the tongue, as for form the one center is the eyes, as for sound the one center is the ears, as for thought the one center is the mind, as for divine wisdom the one center is the heart—so for all beings the one center is the Self.

"Brihadaranyaka Upanishad," ca. 500 B.C.

ARJUNA'S DUTY

HINDU MYTH

Whenever the affairs of men become so bad that the world is in danger of being destroyed before the proper time, the great Vishnu takes on the form of a human or animal and comes to earth.

So it was when he appeared as Krishna. While still a young man, Krishna killed the evil king who was endangering the forces of good in the world. But he stayed for a different role in another great battle.

The five brothers known as the Pandavas had been deprived of their kingdom by their relatives, the Kurus, and after many other provocations, finally went to war against them. Krishna, who was kin to both groups, did not fight in the war but agreed to serve as the charioteer of Arjuna, one of the Pandavas.

But when they arrived on the battlefield, Arjuna suddenly stopped.

"Krishna," he said unhappily, "how can I fight against my own kinspeople? These people have done a lot of evil things to me, but I can't kill these people who were once my friends. What is a kingdom worth if I have to win it by killing my friends? I will not fight," he said and dropped his powerful bow on the ground.

"Arjuna," replied Krishna, "you show that you do not really understand what life is all about. If you really understood the world, you would know that this life is only a brief part of the many lives you will go through. There is no way that you can kill someone or be killed. For the spirit was never born and will never end. Each life on this earth is like taking off one pair of clothes and putting on another. But the life itself goes on.

"Birth leads to death and death leads to birth. So why are you upset? In this birth you were born a Kshattria, a warrior, and your task is to engage in war. If you do not kill those ordained to die, they will suffer unnecessarily in this life and you will not return as you should.

"So, Arjuna, you must go into the battle and fight, knowing that you are doing the right thing even if you must kill your friends and kinsmen."

For days Krishna taught Arjuna the secrets of life and death, and at last Arjuna was ready to go into battle. There he succeeded in killing his enemies, but he did not gloat over their slaughter. For he now knew that he was only doing the duty for which he had been born in this life.

I am of the opinion that the definitions of maturity which assail us in such profusion currently are uniformly founded on the tacit hypothesis that human development is linked to human passivity. All that I have encountered assume that adjustment and conformity are the desirable modes of life, and that the closer one comes to a condition of domestication, the more mature one is. None of them, to my knowledge, takes account of man's nature and spirit, of his innate rebelliousness, of his intrinsic values, or of his individuality. With monotonous regularity, these definitions predicate themselves upon, and defend, a society that is everyday and everywhere becoming more and more oppressive. Hence, the standards for mature behavior they advise are those standards that may apply to mature cattle or mature puppets—but not to mature men.
—from *Advertisements for Myself*, **Norman Mailer**

THE PIPE OF PEACE: UNION BETWEEN THE BROTHERS

Speaking as a Chinese, I do not think that any civilization can be called complete until it has progressed from sophistication to unsophistication, and made a conscious return to simplicity of thinking and living, and I call no man wise until he has made the progress from the wisdom of knowledge to the wisdom of foolishness, and become a laughing philosopher, feeling first life's tragedy and then life's comedy. For we must weep before we can laugh. Out of sadness comes the awakening and out of the awakening comes the laughter of the philosopher, with kindliness and tolerance to boot.

Lin Yutang

IROQUOIS MYTH

Many years ago there was a chief of the Onondagas who was unhappy at the way his people were always fighting. Even the Oneidas and the Senecas, who were their close relatives, were always fighting them. One day he called his two sons to him and said, "I have had a vision. The Great Spirit has shown me that you, my two sons, are to bring peace to our people. So go from me now on a quest for peace and do not return until you have established it."

The two young men were very troubled, for they had no idea how to fulfill their father's request. They traveled until they came to a river with high rocks jutting over it.

"The quest our father has given us is beyond the possibility of human beings," said the oldest brother. "There is no way for us to fulfill it, but a son who cannot obey his father does not deserve to live. I see nothing for us to do but climb those rocks and cast ourselves off into the river."

So, sorrowfully, the two boys began to climb the rocks and walk toward the cliff. But as they reached the edge, they saw a strange canoe coming across the river and in it was an old man with white hair. He saw the two brothers and beckoned to them to come down from the rocks.

"Why are you trying to end your lives?" the stranger asked.

"Our father has given us a task which we cannot do," said the brothers. "And a son who cannot obey his father does not deserve to live."

"You have given up too quickly," replied the old man. "For I can show you the way to obey his command. Go and gather firewood."

The brothers stood staring at the old man in amazement at this strange command.

But suddenly his eyes flashed like lightning. "When you are lost and someone tells you how to go, do you refuse to follow them?"

The boys immediately began to gather firewood and made a great pile.

"Build a fire," said the strange old man, and this time the boys did not hesitate. After they finished, they looked up expectantly, but the old man was preparing to leave.

"Now," he said, "all the tribes around will see your council fire and will come to you. You must keep the fire going until your father's command has been obeyed and peace has come."

"But what shall we do when the people come?" asked the boys.

"I will return when you need me," replied the old man as he stepped in his canoe and started off.

So the brothers waited until the Mohawks, the Onondagas, the Senecas, the Oneidas, and the Cayugas all came together. Each tribe came suspiciously and brought weapons.

All day and night the brothers waited for the old man to return. But he did not come. Instead, something else happened. A strange power seemed to come over the two brothers, and at last the eldest brother rose to speak.

"Brothers," he said, "I have called you together because the Great Spirit has spoken to me. Let there be no more war among us, but let us smoke the pipe of peace. As long as we quarrel among ourselves, we cannot become a great nation." As he spoke, it seemed as if a golden light were around his head. And when he finished, he hurled his battle ax into the fire, and all of the other chiefs followed his example.

Then he took from his belt the peace pipe and the chiefs made a treaty among themselves and formed the League of the Iroquois. The pipe passed from one chief to another until it finally came to a strange old man, whom the brothers immediately recognized as their teacher.

"You have done well," he said to the two brothers, "for you have followed the commands of the Great Spirit. From now on, your people will be a great nation. My task is completed and now I must go."

"Before you go, please tell us your name," said the brothers.

"I am known by many names," he replied, "but you may call me Hiawatha."

ROMANS 12, A LETTER

PAUL

I beseech you therefore, brethren, by the mercies of God, that ye present your bodies a living sacrifice, holy, acceptable unto God, which is your reasonable service.

2 And be not conformed to this world: but be ye transformed by the renewing of your mind, that ye may prove what is that good, and acceptable, and perfect, will of God.

3 For I say, through the grace given unto me, to every man that is among you, not to think of himself more highly than he ought to think; but to think soberly, according as God hath dealt to every man the measure of faith.

4 For as we have many members in one body, and all members have not the same office:

5 So we, being many, are one body in Christ, and every one members one of another.

6 Having then gifts differing according to the grace that is given to us, whether prophecy, let us prophesy according to the proportion of faith;

7 Or ministry, let us wait on our ministering: or he that teacheth, on teaching;

8 Or he that exhorteth, on exhortation: he that giveth, let him do it with simplicity; he that ruleth, with diligence; he that sheweth mercy, with cheerfulness.

9 Let love be without dissimulation. Abhor that which is evil; cleave to that which is good.

10 Be kindly affectioned one to another with brotherly love; in honour preferring one another;

11 Not slothful in business; fervent in spirit; serving the Lord;

12 Rejoicing in hope; patient in tribulation; continuing instant in prayer;

13 Distributing to the necessity of saints; given to hospitality.

14 Bless them which persecute you: bless, and curse not.

15 Rejoice with them that do rejoice, and weep with them that weep.

16 Be of the same mind one toward another. Mind not high things, but condescend to men of low estate. Be not wise in your own conceits.

17 Recompense to no man evil for evil. Provide things honest in the sight of all men.

18 If it be possible, as much as lieth in you, live peaceably with all men.

19 Dearly beloved, avenge not yourselves, but rather give place unto wrath: for it is written, Vengence is mine; I will repay, saith the Lord.

20 Therefore if thine enemy hunger, feed him; if he thirst, give him drink: for in so doing thou shalt heap coals of fire on his head.

21 Be not overcome of evil, but overcome evil with good.

ca. A.D. 56

?

In the preceding myths, symbols are used as a means to confer status and power on the ruling members of a particular society. These tales express the transgressions that must be prohibited in order for the leadership to survive. One sees the need, underlying these acts of trangression, to give voice to the "inner" conflicts which separate the individual from the collective. The moral code of behavior which emerges from these myths reveals what is necessary to prevent an individual from destroying group solidarity. Thus, when Cain murders Abel, the Lord decrees that Cain must be banished "east of Eden." This action sets in motion the criminal's removal from the social world. The presence of "evil" might contaminate the others, and any who break the taboos must serve as examples to inhibit others from doing likewise. In "The House of Atreus and The Curse of Blood" the gods are slow to punish Atreus for the murder of his brother. The original murder signals the transference of "evil" through the blood which connects generation to generation. The language in each of these myths contains the ethical values which guide behavior. The desire to punish those who shed the blood of others is one of the first steps a society takes in defining a system of justice. The past becomes the present to illustrate what is permitted and what is forbidden. The political hero, no longer an adventurer, must communicate the wisdom contained within the language of his tribal mythology. This man or woman must express the purpose and function of the ethical values which underlie the laws governing a culture. The following questions link language to the political hero as a means to understand what separates the individual from, and connects him to, the collective.

1   In "The Falsehood of Truth," "The Phoenix," and "The Zen Master" how does language reveal the individual's isolation from and union with a group? How might the discussion of discursive and nondiscursive symbols in "On the Origin of Language" add insight to this contradiction?

2   In "Cain and Abel," "The Gettysburg Address," "The House of Atreus and the Curse of Blood," and "Arjuna's Duty" how does blood symbolically link death, through the ritual of murder, to an expression of the continuation of the life process?

a   In which myths does language demonstrate the individual's isolation from the group? How is an original act transmitted from one generation to the next? What "inner" conflict is revealed in the reporting of this original crime?

b   How are family relations symbolized in each of these myths? What is revealed about the transfer of power from one generation to the next? What patterns of rivalry exist between fathers and sons, mothers and daughters, brothers and brothers, sisters and brothers? What does this suggest about the family as a social institution? In which myths is the father symbolized as a spirit who becomes the voice guiding the children on the path toward wisdom?

c   How do the actions of men differ from the actions of women? Who seeks revenge for the victims of a murder? Who seeks to punish the murderer? What does this suggest?

d   How does language become the medium which both influences and reports the political heroes' test? How do the moral lessons of these actions serve as a means to prevent the breaking of a taboo? Does the murderer become the scapegoat who acts out the "inner" conflicts within the group? How does the desire for punishment bring the group to the knowledge of "good and evil"? How does this knowledge set the wheels of justice in motion? How does the shedding of blood illustrate the principle of fertility? Is this necessary in order for the group to be regenerated? Explain!

3   How do the moral attitudes in "The Pipe of Peace: Union between the Brothers" compare and contrast with those expressed in Paul's "Letter to the Romans"? What insights are conveyed through the voice of the Great Spirit? How does Paul use language to bring together the human and the divine? What attitudes toward "good and evil" emerge in each account? How are individuals to act in relation to the collective? What image of justice emerges from these attempts to evaluate and express the need for an ethical code of behavior?

THE SERMON ON THE MOUNT

MATTHEW 5–7

And seeing the multitudes, he went up into a mountain: and when he was set, his disciples came unto him: and he opened his mouth, and taught them, saying, Blessed are the poor in spirit: for theirs is the kingdom of heaven. Blessed are they that mourn: for they shall be comforted. Blessed are the meek: for they shall inherit the earth. Blessed are they which do hunger and thirst after righteousness: for they shall be filled. Blessed are the merciful: for they shall obtain mercy. Blessed are the pure in heart: for they shall see God. Blessed are the peacemakers: for they shall be called the children of God. Blessed are they which are persecuted for righteousness' sake: for theirs is the kingdom of heaven. Blessed are ye, when men shall revile you, and persecute you, and shall say all manner of evil against you falsely, for my sake. Rejoice, and be exceeding glad: for great is your reward in heaven: for so persecuted they the prophets which were before you.

Ye are the salt of the earth: but if the salt have lost his savour, wherewith shall it be salted? It is thenceforth good for nothing, but to be cast out, and to be trodden under foot of men. Ye are the light of the world. A city that is set on a hill cannot be hid. Neither do men light a candle, and put it under a bushel, but on a candlestick; and it giveth light unto all that are in the house. Let your light so shine before men, that they may see your good works, and glorify your Father which is in heaven. Think not that I am come to destroy the law, or the prophets: I am not come to destroy, but to fulfil. For verily I say unto you, Till heaven and earth pass, one jot or one tittle shall in no wise pass from the law, till all be fulfilled. Whosoever therefore shall break one of these least commandments, and shall teach men so, he shall be called the

From the gospel according to St. Matthew (King James version), Chaps. 5 to 7.

least in the kingdom of heaven: but whosoever shall do and teach them, the same shall be called great in the kingdom of heaven. For I say unto you, That except your righteousness shall exceed the righteousness of the scribes and Pharisees, ye shall in no case enter into the kingdom of heaven.

Ye have heard that it was said by them of old time, Thou shalt not kill; and whosoever shall kill shall be in danger of the judgment: But I say unto you, That whosoever is angry with his brother without a cause shall be in danger of the judgment: and whosoever shall say to his brother, Raca, shall be in danger of the council: but whosoever shall say, Thou fool, shall be in danger of hell fire. Therefore if thou bring thy gift to the altar, and there rememberest that thy brother hath ought against thee; Leave there thy gift before the altar, and go thy way; first be reconciled to thy brother, and then come and offer thy gift. Agree with thine adversary quickly, whilst thou art in the way with him; lest at any time the adversary deliver thee to the judge, and the judge deliver thee to the officer, and thou be cast into prison. Verily I say unto thee, Thou shalt by no means come out thence, till thou hast paid the uttermost farthing.

Ye have heard that it was said by them of old time, Thou shalt not commit adultery: But I say unto you, That whosoever looketh on a woman to lust after her hath committed adultery with her already in his heart. And if thy right eye offend thee, pluck it out, and cast it from thee: for it is profitable for thee that one of thy members should perish, and not that thy whole body should be cast into hell. And if thy right hand offend thee, cut it off, and cast it from thee: for it is profitable for thee that one of thy members should perish, and not that thy whole body should be cast into hell. It hath been said, Whosoever shall put away his wife, let him give her a writing of divorcement: But I say unto you, That whosoever shall put away his wife saving for the cause of fornication, causeth her to commit adultery: and whosoever shall marry her that is divorced committeth adultery.

Again, ye have heard that it hath been said by them of old time, Thou shalt not forswear thyself, but shalt perform unto the Lord thine oaths: But I say unto you, Swear not at all; neither by heaven; for it is God's throne: Nor by the earth; for it is his footstool: neither by Jerusalem; for it is the city of the great King. Neither shalt thou swear by thy head, because thou canst not make one hair white or black. But let your communication be, Yea, yea; Nay, nay: for whatsoever is more than these cometh of evil.

Ye have heard that it hath been said, An eye for an eye, and a tooth for a tooth: But I say unto you, That ye resist not evil: but whosoever shall smite thee on thy right cheek, turn to him the other also. And if any man will sue thee at the law, and take away thy coat, let him have thy cloak also. And whosoever shall compel thee to go a mile, go with him twain. Give to him that asketh thee, and from him that would borrow of thee turn not thou away.

Ye have heard that it hath been said, Thou shalt love thy neighbor, and hate thine enemy. But I say unto you, Love your enemies, bless them that curse you, do good to them that hate you, and pray for them which despitefully use you, and persecute you; That ye may be the children of your Father which is in heaven: for he maketh his sun to rise on the evil and on the good, and sendeth rain on the just and on the unjust. For if ye love them which love you, what reward have ye? do not even the publicans the same? And if ye salute your brethren only, what do ye more than others? do not even the publicans so? Be ye therefore perfect, even as your Father which is in heaven is perfect.

Take heed that ye do not your alms before men, to be seen of them: otherwise ye have no reward of your Father which is in heaven. Therefore when thou doest thine alms, do not sound a trumpet before thee, as the hypocrites do in the synagogues and in the streets, that they may have glory of men. Verily I say unto you, They have their reward. But when thou doest alms, let not thy left hand know what thy right hand doeth: That thine alms may be in secret: and thy Father which seeth in secret himself shall reward thee openly. And when thou prayest, thou shalt not be as the hypocrites are: for they love to pray standing in the synagogues and in the corners of the streets, that they may be seen of men. Verily I say unto you, They have their reward. But thou, when thou prayest, enter into thy closet, and when thou hast shut thy door, pray to thy Father which is in secret; and thy Father which seeth in secret shall reward thee openly. But when ye pray, use not vain repetitions, as the heathen do: for they think that they shall be heard for their much speaking. Be not ye therefore like unto them: for your Father knoweth what things ye have need of, before ye ask him. After this manner therefore pray ye: Our Father which art in heaven, Hallowed be thy name. Thy kingdom come. Thy will be done in earth, as it is in heaven. Give us this day our daily bread. And forgive us our debts, as we forgive our debtors. And lead us not into temptation, but deliver us from evil: For thine is the kingdom, and the power, and the glory, for ever. Amen. For if ye forgive men their trespasses, your heavenly Father will also forgive you: But if ye forgive not men their trespasses, neither will your Father forgive your trespasses.

Moreover when ye fast, be not, as the hypocrites, of a sad countenance: for they disfigure their faces, that they may appear unto men to fast. Verily I say unto you, They have their reward. But thou, when thou fastest, anoint thine head, and wash thy face; That thou appear not unto men to fast, but unto thy Father which is in secret: and thy Father, which seeth in secret, shall reward thee openly.

Lay up not for yourselves treasures upon earth, where moth and rust doth corrupt, and where thieves break through and steal: But lay up for yourselves treasures in heaven, where neither moth nor rust doth corrupt, and where thieves do not break through nor steal: For where your treasure is, there will your heart be also. The light of the body is the eye: if therefore thine eye be single, thy whole body shall be full of light. But if thine eye be evil, thy whole body shall be full of darkness. If therefore the light that is in thee be darkness, how great is that darkness! No man can serve two masters: for either he will hate the one, and love the other; or else he will hold to the one, and despise the other. Ye cannot serve God and mammon. Therefore I say unto you, Take no thought for your life, what ye shall eat, or what ye shall drink; nor yet for your body, what ye shall put on. Is not the life more than meat, and the body than raiment? Behold the fowls of the air: for they sow not, neither do they reap, nor gather into barns; yet your heavenly Father feedeth them. Are ye not much better than they? Which of you by taking thought can add one cubit unto his stature? And why take ye thought for raiment? Consider the lilies of the field, how they grow; they toil not, neither do they spin: And yet I say unto you, That even Solomon in all his glory was not arrayed like one of these. Wherefore, if God so clothe the grass of the field, which to day is, and to morrow is cast into the oven, shall he not much more clothe you, O ye of little faith? Therefore take no thought, saying, What shall we eat? or, What shall we drink? or, Wherewithal shall we be clothed? (For after all these things do the Gentiles seek:) for your heavenly Father knoweth that ye have need of all things. But seek ye first the kingdom of God, and his righteousness; and all these things shall be added unto you. Take therefore no thought for the morrow: for the morrow shall take thought for the things of itself. Sufficient unto the day is the evil thereof.

Judge not, that ye be not judged. For with what judgment ye judge, ye shall be judged: and with what measures ye mete, it shall be measured to you again. And why beholdest thou the more that is in thy brother's eye, but considerest not the beam that is in thine own eye? Or how wilt thou say to thy brother, Let me pull out the mote out of thine eye; and, behold, a beam is in thine own eye? Thou hypocrite, first cast out the beam out of thine own eye; and then shalt thou see clearly to cast out the mote out of thy brother's eye.

Give not that which is holy unto the dogs, neither cast ye your pearls before swine, lest they trample them under their feet, and turn again and rend you. Ask, and it shall be given you; seek and ye shall find; knock, and it shall be opened unto you: For every one that asketh receiveth; and he that seeketh findeth; and to him that knocketh it shall be opened. Or what man is there of you, whom if his son ask bread, will he give him a stone? Or if he ask a fish, will he give him a serpent? If ye then, being evil, know how to give good gifts unto your children, how much more shall your Father which is in heaven give good things to them that ask him? Therefore all things whatsoever ye would that men should do to you, do ye even so to them: for this is the law and the prophets.

Enter ye in at the strait gate: for wide is the gate, and broad is the way, that leadeth to destruction, and many there be which go in thereat: Because strait is the gate, and narrow is the way, which leadeth unto life, and few there be that find it. Beware of false prophets, which come to you in sheep's clothing, but inwardly they are ravening wolves. Ye shall know them by their fruits. Do men gather grapes of thorns, or figs of thistles? Even so every good tree bringeth forth good fruit; but a corrupt tree bringeth forth evil fruit. A good tree cannot bring forth evil fruit, neither can a corrupt tree bring forth good fruit. Every tree that bringeth not forth good fruit is hewn down, and cast into the fire. Wherefore by their fruits ye shall know them. Not every one that saith unto me, Lord, Lord, shall enter into the kingdom of heaven; but he that doeth the will of my Father which is in heaven. Many will say to me in that day, Lord, Lord, have we not prophesied in thy name? and in thy name have cast out devils? and in thy name done many wonderful works? And then will I profess unto them, I never knew you: depart from me, ye that work iniquity. Therefore whosoever heareth these sayings of mine, and doeth them, I will liken him unto a wise man, which built his house upon a rock: And the rain descended, and the floods came, and the winds blew, and beat upon that house; and it fell not: for it was founded upon a rock. And every one that heareth these sayings of mine, and doeth them not, shall be likened unto a foolish man, which built his house upon the sand: And the rain descended, and the floods came, and the winds blew, and beat upon that house; and it fell: and great was the fall of it. And it came to pass, when Jesus had ended these sayings, the people were astonished at his doctrine: For he taught them as one having authority, and not as the scribes.

INAUGURAL ADDRESS

JOHN F. KENNEDY

We observe today not a victory of a party but a celebration of freedom—symbolizing an end as well as a beginning—signifying renewal as well as change. For I have sworn before you and Almighty God the same solemn oath our forebears prescribed nearly a century and three quarters ago.

The world is very different now. For man holds in his mortal hands the power to abolish all forms of human poverty and all forms of human life. And yet the same revolutionary beliefs for which our forebears fought are still at issue around the globe—the belief that the rights of man come not from the generosity of the state but from the hand of God.

We dare not forget today that we are the heirs of that first revolution. Let the word go forth from this time and place, to friend and foe alike, that the torch has been passed to a new generation of Americans—born in this century, tempered by war, disciplined by a hard and bitter peace, proud of our ancient heritage—and unwilling to witness or permit the slow undoing of those human rights to which this nation has always been committed, and to which we are committed today at home and around the world.

Let every nation know, whether it wishes us well or ill, that we shall pay any price, bear any burden, meet any hardship, support any friend, oppose any foe to assure the survival and success of liberty.

This much we pledge—and more.

To those old allies whose cultural and spiritual origins we share, we pledge the loyalty of faithful friends. United, there is little we cannot do in a host of cooperative ventures. Divided, there is little we can do—for we dare not meet a powerful challenge at odds and split asunder.

To those new states whom we welcome to the ranks of the free, we pledge our word that one form of colonial control shall not have passed away merely to be replaced by a far more iron tyranny. We shall not always expect to find them supporting our view. But we shall always hope to find them strongly supporting their own freedom—and to remember that, in the past, those who foolishly sought power by riding the back of the tiger ended up inside.

To those peoples in the huts and villages of half the globe struggling to break the bonds of mass misery, we pledge our best efforts to help them help themselves, for whatever period is required—not because the Communists may be doing it, not because we seek their votes, but because it is right. If a free society cannot help the many who are poor, it cannot save the few who are rich.

To our sister republics south of our border, we offer a special pledge—to convert our good words into good deeds—in a new alliance for progress—to assist free men and free governments in casting off the chains of poverty. But this peaceful revolution of hope cannot become the prey of hostile powers. Let all our neighbors know that we shall join with them to oppose aggression or subversion anywhere in the Americas. And let every other power know that this hemisphere intends to remain the master of its own house.

To that world assembly of sovereign states, the United Nations, our last best hope in an age where the instruments of war have far outpaced the instruments of peace, we renew our pledge of support—to prevent it from becoming merely a forum for invective—to strengthen its shield of the new and the weak—and to enlarge the area in which its writ may run.

Finally, to those nations who would make themselves our adversary, we offer not a pledge but a request: that both sides begin anew the quest for peace, before the dark powers of destruction unleashed by science engulf all humanity in planned or accidental self-destruction.

We dare not tempt them with weakness. For only when our arms are sufficient beyond doubt can we be certain beyond doubt that they will never be employed.

But neither can two great and powerful groups of nations take comfort from our present course—both sides overburdened by the cost of modern weapons, both rightly alarmed by the steady spread of the deadly atom, yet both racing to alter that uncertain balance of terror that stays the hand of mankind's final war.

So let us begin anew—remembering on both sides that civility is not a sign of weakness, and sincerity is always subject to proof. Let us never negotiate out of fear. But let us never fear to negotiate.

Let both sides explore what problems unite us instead of belaboring those problems which divide us.

Let both sides, for the first time, formulate serious and precise proposals for the inspection and control of arms—and bring the absolute power to destroy other nations under the absolute control of all nations.

Let both sides seek to invoke the wonders of science instead of its terrors. Together let us explore the stars, conquer the deserts, eradicate disease, tap the ocean depths and encourage the arts and commerce.

Let both sides unite to heed in all corners of the earth the command of Isaiah—to "undo the heavy burdens . . . [and] let the oppressed go free."

And if a beachhead of cooperation may push back the jungle of suspicion, let both sides join in a new endeavor, not a new balance of power, but a new world of law, where the strong are just and the weak secure and the peace preserved.

All this will not be finished in the first one hundred days. Nor will it be finished in the first one thousand days, nor in the life of this administration, nor even perhaps in our lifetime on this planet. But let us begin.

In your hands, my fellow citizens, more than mine, will rest the final success or failure of our course. Since this country was founded, each generation of Americans has been summoned to give testimony to its national loyalty. The graves of young Americans who answered the call to service surround the globe.

Now the trumpet summons us again—not as a call to bear arms, though arms we need—not as a call to battle, though embattled we are—but a call to bear the burden of a long twilight struggle, year in and year out, "rejoicing in hope, patient in tribulation"—a struggle against the common enemies of man: tyranny, poverty, disease and war itself.

Can we forge against these enemies a grand and global alliance, North and South, East and West, that can assure a more fruitful life for all mankind? Will you join in that historic effort?

In the long history of the world, only a few generations have been granted the role of defending freedom in its hour of maximum danger. I do not shrink from this responsibility—I welcome it. I do not believe that any of us would exchange places with any other people or any other generation. The energy, the faith, the devotion which we bring to this endeavor will light our country and all who serve it—and the glow from that fire can truly light the world.

And so, my fellow Americans: Ask not what your country can do for you—ask what you can do for your country.

My fellow citizens of the world: Ask not what America will do for you, but what together we can do for the freedom of man.

Finally, whether you are citizens of America or citizens of the world, ask of us here the same high standards of strength and sacrifice which we ask of you. With a good conscience our only sure reward, with history the final judge of our deeds, let us go forth to lead the land we love, asking His blessing and His help, but knowing that here on earth God's work must truly be our own.

During the process of socialization, individuals must learn to adhere to certain rules in order to ensure survival of the group. The political leader articulates those symbols which bring the individual into contact with the collective. John Kennedy uses his speech as a means to solidify power. For him the state is the symbol which transforms the individual. The need for sacrifice is made evident if the group's regeneration is to be affirmed. Christ is not concerned with temporal existence. His speech brings the individual into contact with the sacred, for his special power is to interpret the relation between the human and the divine. Each speaker attempts to persuade others to follow his example. The political hero uses language to seek a world order based on the relation between the individual and the social, or the human and the divine. Compare and contrast the speeches of Christ and Kennedy from the following perspectives.

1 How does each speaker propose a test for the individual? What are the similarities in and differences between each test? How do these tests bring about the rebirth of an individual or of a group?

2 What symbols does each speaker use to solidify group life? What elements must be excluded from the group? Does this resemble Cain's banishment from Eden? Explain!

3 According to each speaker, how does the individual learn to find meaning in life? How do the speakers connect this concept to the individual's responsibility to the group?

4 Which speaker uses a direct appeal to convey his message? Which speaker uses an indirect appeal to convey his message? Which method is more effective? Do the speakers attempt to keep anything hidden from the audience? Explain!

5 What attitudes toward past generations are revealed in these two speeches? Do the speakers respect tradition? Explain! What ethical values emerge in each speech? How does each speaker claim to know the "right" path for others to follow?

6 Explain which of the speakers uses language to best persuade his audience. How does Christ's view of the kingdom of heaven relate to and differ from Kennedy's? What insights into the speaker's use of language are revealed in these two speeches?

THE IMAGES OF ORPHEUS AND NARCISSUS

HERBERT MARCUSE

The attempt to draft a theoretical construct of culture beyond the performance principle is in a strict sense "unreasonable." Reason is the rationality of the performance principle. Even at the beginning of Western civilization, long before this principle was institutionalized, reason was defined as an instrument of constraint, of instinctual suppression; the domain of the instincts, sensuousness, was considered as eternally hostile and detrimental to reason. The categories in which philosophy has comprehended the human existence have retained the connection between reason and suppression: whatever belongs to the sphere of sensuousness, pleasure, impulse has the connotation of being antagonistic to reason—something that has to be subjugated, constrained. Every-day language has preserved this evaluation: the words which apply to this sphere carry the sound of the sermon or of obscenity. From Plato to the "*Schund und Schmutz*" laws of the modern world,[1] the defamation of the pleasure principle has proved its irresistible power; opposition to such defamation easily succumbs to ridicule.

Still, the dominion of repressive reason (theoretical and practical) was never complete: its monopoly of cognition was never uncontested. When Freud emphasized the fundamental fact that phantasy (imagination) retains a truth that is incompatible with reason, he was following in a long historical tradition. Phantasy is cognitive in so far as it preserves the truth of the Great Refusal, or, positively, in so far as it protects, against all reason, the aspirations for the integral fulfillment of man and nature which are repressed by reason. In the realm of phantasy, the unreasonable images of freedom become rational, and the "lower depth" of instinctual gratification assumes a new dignity. The culture of the performance principle makes its bow before the strange truths which imagination keeps alive in folklore and fairy tale, in literature and art; they have been aptly interpreted and have found their place in the popular and academic world. However, the effort to derive from these truths the content of a valid reality principle surpassing the prevailing one has been entirely inconsequential. Novalis' statement that "all internal faculties and forces, and all external faculties and forces, must be deduced from productive imagination"[2] has remained a curiosity—as has the surrealist program *de pratiquer la poésie*. The insistence that imagination provide standards for existential attitudes, for practice, and for historical possibilities appears as childish fantasy. Only the archetypes, only the symbols have been accepted, and their meaning is usually interpreted in terms of phylogenetic or ontogenetic stages, long since surpassed, rather than in terms of an individual and cultural maturity. We shall now try to identify some of these symbols and examine their historical truth value.

More specifically, we look for the "culture-heroes" who have persisted in imagination as symbolizing the attitude and the deeds that have determined the fate of mankind. And here at the outset we are confronted with the fact that the predominant culture-hero is the trickster and (suffering) rebel against the gods, who creates culture at the price of perpetual pain. He symbolizes productiveness, the unceasing effort to master life; but, in his productivity, blessing and curse, progress and toil are inextricably intertwined. Prometheus is the archetype-hero of the performance principle. And in the world of Prometheus, Pandora, the female principle, sexuality and pleasure, appear as curse—disruptive, destructive. "Why are women such a curse? The denunciation of the sex with which the section [on Prometheus in Hesiod] concludes emphasizes above all else their economic unproductivity; they are useless drones; a luxury item in a poor man's budget."[3] The beauty of the woman, and the happiness she promises are fatal in the work-world of civilization.

If Prometheus is the culture-hero of toil, productivity, and progress

---

[1] A bill proposed by the New York Joint Legislative Committee on Comic Books would prohibit the sale and distribution of books portraying "nudity, sex or lust in a manner which reasonably tends to excite lustful or lecherous desires . . ." (*New York Times*, February 17, 1954).

[2] *Schriften*, ed. J. Minor (Jena: Eugen Diederichs, 1923), III, 375. See Gaston Bachelard, *La Terre et les Rêveries de la Volonté* (Paris: José Corti, 1948), pp. 4–5.

[3] See Norman O. Brown, *Hesiod's Theogony* (New York: Liberal Arts Press, 1953), pp. 18–19, 33; and *Hermes the Thief* (University of Wisconsin Press, 1947), pp. 23ff.

through repression, then the symbols of another reality principle must be sought at the opposite pole. Orpheus and Narcissus (like Dionysus to whom they are akin: the antagonist of the god who sanctions the logic of domination, the realm of reason) stand for a very different reality.[4] They have not become the culture-heroes of the Western world: theirs is the image of joy and fulfillment; the voice which does not command but sings; the gesture which offers and receives; the deed which is peace and ends the labor of conquest; the liberation from time which unites man with god, man with nature. Literature has preserved their image. In the *Sonnets to Orpheus*:

> "Almost a maid, she came forth shimmering
> From the high happiness of song and lyre,
> And shining clearly through her veils of spring
> She made herself a bed within my ear
> And slept in me. All things were in her sleep:
> The trees I marvelled at, the enchanting spell
> Of farthest distances, the meadows deep,
> And all the magic that myself befell.
> Within her slept the world. You singing god, o how
> Did you perfect her so she did not long
> To be awake? She rose and slept.
> Where is her death?"[5]

Or Narcissus, who, in the mirror of the water, tries to grasp his own

[4] The symbol of Narcissus and the term "Narcissistic" as used here do not imply the meaning given to them in Freud's theory.

[5] Rainer Maria Rilke, *Sonnets to Orpheus: Duino Elegies*, transl. Jessie Lemont (New York: Fine Editions Press, 1945), p. 3 (with minor changes in translation). Reprinted by permission of Columbia University Press.

beauty. Bent over the river of time, in which all forms pass and flee, he dreams:

"Alas, when will Time cease its flight and allow this flow to rest? Forms, divine and perennial forms which only wait for rest in order to reappear! O when, in what night, will you crystallize again?

"Paradise must always be re-created. It is not in some remote Thule; it lingers under the appearance. Everything holds within itself, as potentiality, the intimate harmony of its being—just as every salt holds within itself the archetype of its crystal. And a time of silent night will come when the waters will descend, more dense; then, in the unperturbed abysses, the secret crystals will bloom . . . Everything strives toward its lost form . . ." André Gide, *Le Traité du Narcisse*.

"A great calm hears me, where I hear Hope. The voice of the wells changes and speaks of the night; in the holy shade I hear the silver herb grow, and the treacherous moon raises its mirror deep into the secrets of the extinguished fountain." Paul Valéry, *Narcisse Parle*.

"Admire in Narcissus the eternal return toward the mirror of the water which offers his image to his love, and to his beauty all his knowledge. All my fate is obedience to the force of my love. *Body*, I surrender to your sole power; the tranquil water awaits me where I extend my arms: I do not resist this pure madness. What, O my Beauty, can I do that thou dost not will?" Paul Valéry, *Cantate du Narcisse*, Scène II.

The climate of this language is that of the *"diminution des traces du péché originel,"*—the revolt against culture based on toil, domination, and renunciation. The images of Or-

pheus and Narcissus reconcile Eros and Thanatos. They recall the experience of a world that is not to be mastered and controlled but to be liberated—a freedom that will release the powers of Eros now bound in the repressed and petrified forms of man and nature. These powers are conceived not as destruction but as peace, not as terror but as beauty. It is sufficient to enumerate the assembled images in order to circumscribe the dimension to which they are committed: the redemption of pleasure, the halt of time, the absorption of death; silence, sleep, night, paradise—the Nirvana principle not as death but as life. Baudelaire gives the image of such a world in two lines:

"There all is order and beauty, luxury, calm, and sensuousness."

This is perhaps the only context in which the word *order* loses its repressive connotation: here, it is the order of gratification which the free Eros creates. Static triumphs over dynamic; but it is a static that moves in its own fullness—a productivity that is sensuousness, play, and song. Any attempt to elaborate the images thus conveyed must be self-defeating, because outside the language of art they change their meaning and merge with the connotations they received under the repressive reality principle. But one must try to trace the road back to the realities to which they refer.

In contrast to the images of the Promethean culture-heroes, those of the Orphic and Narcissistic world are essentially unreal and unrealistic. They designate an "impossible" attitude and existence. The deeds of the culture-heroes also are "impossible," in that they are miraculous, incredible, superhuman. However, their objective and their "meaning" are not alien to the reality; on the contrary, they are useful. They promote and strengthen this reality; they do not explode it. But the Orphic-Narcissistic images do explode it; they do not convey a "mode of living"; they are committed to the underworld and to death. At best, they are poetic, something for the soul and the heart. But they do not teach any "message" —except perhaps the negative one that one cannot defeat death or forget and reject the call of life in the admiration of beauty.

Such moral messages are superimposed upon a very different content. Orpheus and Narcissus symbolize realities just as do Prometheus and Hermes. Trees and animals respond to Orpheus' language; the spring and the forest respond to Narcissus' desire. The Orphic and Narcissistic Eros awakens and liberates potentialities that are real in things animate and inanimate, in organic and inorganic nature—real but in the un-erotic reality suppressed. These potentialities circumscribe the *telos* inherent in them as: "just to be what they are," "being-there," existing.

The Orphic and Narcissistic experience of the world negates that which sustains the world of the performance principle. The opposition between man and nature, subject and object, is overcome. Being is experienced as gratification, which unites man and nature so that the fulfillment of man is at the same time the fulfillment, without violence, of nature. In being spoken to, loved, and cared for, flowers and springs and animals appear as what they are—beautiful, not only for those who address and regard them, but for themselves, "objectively." "Le monde tend à la beauté."[6] In the Orphic and Narcissistic Eros, this tendency is released: the things of nature become free to be what they are. But to be what they are they *depend* on the erotic attitude: they receive their *telos* only in it. The song of Orpheus pacifies the animal world, reconciles the lion with the lamb and the lion with man.

The world of nature is a world of oppression, cruelty, and pain, as is the human world; like the latter, it awaits its liberation. This liberation is the work of Eros. The song of Orpheus breaks the petrification, moves the forests and the rocks—but moves them to partake in joy.

The love of Narcissus is answered by the echo of nature. To be sure, Narcissus appears as the *antagonist* of Eros: he spurns love, the love that unites with other human beings, and for that he is punished by Eros.[7] As the antagonist of Eros, Narcissus symbolizes sleep and death, silence and rest.[8] In Thracia, he stands in close relation to Dionysus.[9] But it is not coldness, asceticism, and self-love that color the images of Narcissus; it is not these gestures of Narcissus that are preserved in art and literature. His silence is not that of dead rigidity; and when he is contemptuous of the love of hunters and nymphs he rejects one Eros for another. He lives by an Eros of his own,[10] and he does not love only himself. (He does not know that the image he admires is

his own.) If his erotic attitude is akin to death and brings death, then rest and sleep and death are not painfully separated and distinguished: the Nirvana principle rules throughout all these stages. And when he dies he continues to live as the flower that bears his name.

In associating Narcissus with Orpheus and interpreting both as symbols of a non-repressive erotic attitude toward reality, we took the image of Narcissus from the mythological-artistic tradition rather than from Freud's libido theory. We may now be able to find some support for our interpretation in Freud's concept of *primary narcissism*. It is significant that the introduction of narcissism into psychoanalysis marked a turning point in the development of the instinct theory: the assumption of independent ego instincts (self-preservation instincts) was shaken and replaced by the notion of an undifferentiated, unified libido prior to the division into ego and external objects. Indeed, the discovery of primary narcissism meant more than the addition of just another phase to the development of the libido; with it there came in sight the archetype of another existential relation to *reality*. Primary narcissism is more than autoeroticism; it engulfs the "environment," integrating the narcissistic ego with the objective world. The normal antagonistic relation between ego and external reality is only a later form and stage of the relation between ego and reality:

Originally the ego includes everything, later it detaches from itself the external world. The ego-feeling we are aware of now is thus only a shrunken vestige of a far more extensive feeling—a feeling which *embraced the universe* and expressed an *inseparable connection of the ego with the external world*.[11]

The concept of primary narcissism

[6] Gaston Bachelard, *L'Eau et les Rêves* (Paris: José Corti, 1942), p. 38. See also . . . Joachim Gasquet's formulation: "Le monde est un immense Narcisse en train de se penser."

[7] Friedrich Wieseler, *Narkissos: Eine kunstmythologische Abhandlung* (Göttingen, 1856), pp. 90, 94.

[8] *Ibid.*, pp. 76, 80–83, 93–94.

[9] *Ibid.*, p. 89. Narcissus and Dionysus are closely assimilated (if not identified) in the Orphic mythology. The Titans seize Zagreus-Dionysus while he contemplates his image in the mirror which they gave him. An ancient tradition (Plotinus, Proclus) interprets the mirror-duplication as the beginning of the god's self-manifestation in the multitude of the phenomena of the world—a process which finds its final symbol in the tearing asunder of the god by the Titans and his rebirth by Zeus. The myth would thus express the reunification of that which was separated, of God and world, man and nature —identity of the one and the many. See Erwin Rhode, *Psyche* (Freiburg, 1898), II, 117 note; Otto Kern, *Orpheus* (Berlin, 1920), pp. 22–23; Ivan M. Linforth, *The Arts of Orpheus* (University of California Press, 1941), pp. 307ff.

[10] In most pictorial representations, Narcissus is in the company of an Amor, who is sad but not hostile. See Wieseler, *Narkissos*, pp. 16–17.

[11] *Civilization and Its Discontents* (London: Hogarth Press, 1949), p. 13. Italics added.

implies what is made explicit in the opening chapter of *Civilization and Its Discontents*—that narcissism survives not only as a neurotic symptom but also as a constitutive element in the construction of the reality, co-existing with the mature reality ego. Freud describes the "ideational content" of the surviving primary ego-feeling as "limitless extension and oneness with the universe" (oceanic feeling).[12] And, later in the same chapter, he suggests that the oceanic feeling seeks to reinstate "limitless narcissisms."[13] The striking paradox that narcissism, usually understood as egotistic withdrawal from reality, here is connected with oneness with the universe, reveals the new depth of the conception: beyond all immature autoeroticism, narcissism denotes a fundamental relatedness to reality which may generate a comprehensive existential order.[14] In other words, narcissism may contain the germ of a different reality principle: the libidinal cathexis of the ego (one's own body) may become the source and reservoir for a new libidinal cathexis of the objective world —transforming this world into a new mode of being. This interpretation is corroborated by the decisive role which narcissistic libido plays, according to Freud, in sublimation. In *The Ego and the Id,* he asks "whether all sublimation does not take place through the agency of the ego, which

begins by changing sexual object-libido into narcissistic libido and then, perhaps, goes on to give it another aim."[15] If this is the case, then all sublimation would begin with the reactivation of narcissistic libido, which somehow overflows and extends to objects. The hypothesis all but revolutionizes the idea of sublimation: it hints at a non-repressive mode of sublimation which results from an extension rather than from a contraining deflection of the libido. We shall subsequently resume the discussion of this idea.

The Orphic-Narcissistic images are those of the Great Refusal: refusal to accept separation from the libidinous object (or subject). The refusal aims at liberation—at the reunion of what has become separated. Orpheus is the archetype of the poet as *liberator* and *creator*:[16] he establishes a higher order in the world—an order without repression. In his person, art, freedom, and culture are eternally combined. He is the poet of redemption, the god who brings peace and salvation by pacifying man and nature, not through force but through song:

> Orpheus, the priest, the mouthpiece of the gods,
> Deterred wild men from murders and foul foods,
> And hence was said to tame the raging moods
> Of tigers and of lions . . .
> In times of yore it was the poet's part—
> The part of sapience—to distinguish plain
> Between the public and the private things,
> Between the sacred things and things profane,
> To check the ills that sexual straying brings,
> To show how laws for married people stood,

> To build the towns, to carve the laws in wood.[17]

But the "culture-hero" Orpheus is also credited with the establishment of a very different order—and he pays for it with his life:

> . . . Orpheus had shunned all love of womankind, whether because of his ill success in love, or whether he had given his troth once for all. Still, many women felt a passion for the bard; many grieved for their love repulsed. He set the example for the people of Thrace of giving his love to tender boys, and enjoying the springtime and first flower of their growth.[18]

> He was torn to pieces by the crazed Thracian women.[19]

The classical tradition associates Orpheus with the introduction of homosexuality. Like Narcissus, he rejects the normal Eros, not for an ascetic ideal, but for a fuller Eros. Like Narcissus, he protests against the repressive order of procreative sexuality. The Orphic and Narcissistic Eros is to the end the negation of this order—the Great Refusal. In the world symbolized by the culture-hero Prometheus, it is the negation of *all* order; but in this negation Orpheus and Narcissus reveal a new reality, with an order of its own, governed by different principles. The Orphic Eros transforms being: he masters cruelty and death through liberation. His language is *song,* and his work is *play.* Narcissus' life is that of *beauty,* and his existence is *contemplation.* These images refer to the *aesthetic dimension* as the one in which their reality principle must be sought and validated.

[12] *Ibid.*, p. 14.

[13] *Ibid.*, p. 21.

[14] In his paper on "The Delay of the Machine Age," Hanns Sachs made an interesting attempt to demonstrate narcissism as a constitutive elements of the reality principle in Greek civilization. He discussed the problem of why the Greeks did not develop a machine technology although they possessed the skill and knowledge which would have enabled them to do so. He was not satisfied with the usual explanations on economic and sociological grounds. Instead, he proposed that the predominant narcissistic element in Greek culture prevented technological progress: the libidinal cathexis of the body was so strong that it militated against mechanization and automatization. Sachs' paper appeared in the *Psychoanalytic Quarterly*, II (1933), 420ff.

[15] *The Ego and the Id* (London: Hogarth Press, 1950), p. 38.

[16] See Walther Rehm, (Düsseldorf: L. Schwann, 1950), pp. 63ff. On Orpheus as culture-hero, see Linforth, *The Arts of Orpheus*, p. 69.

[17] Horace, *The Art of Poetry*, transl. Alexander Falconer Murison, in *Horace Rendered in English Verse* (London and New York: Longmans, Green, 1931), p. 426. Reprinted by permission of the publisher.

[18] Ovid, *Metamorphoses*, X, 79–85, transl. Frank Justus Miller (Loeb Classical Library), Vol. II, p. 71. See Linforth, *The Arts of Orpheus*, p. 57.

[19] Ovid, *Metamorphoses*, XL 1ff; Vol. II, pp. 121–122.

?

Marcuse's essay focuses on the language of those culture heroes who act in opposition to the culture's definition of how one should live. For Marcuse, Prometheus represents the archetype of Western civilization's image of productivity. The message behind his story reveals a view of life based on toil and pain. In opposition to this approach, Marcuse points to Orpheus and Narcissus as representations of the hero in revolt. Orpheus' language is song, and his message is play. Narcissus represents the life of contemplation, and he chooses his own kind of eros. Each of these figures attempts to live in a world which denies sensuality. Prometheus adheres to the work ethic; he is opposed to a life based on pleasure. The following questions focus on Marcuse's use of language as a metaphor to express rebellion against a world view based on rationalism.

1 To what extent do culture heroes "determine the fate of mankind"? Use Jesus' "Sermon on the Mount" as an example of the way culture heroes influence behavior.

2 What images of men and women emerge in Marcuse's discussion of Prometheus? How does the story of Cain and Abel reflect the point of view of productivity? In what ways does the House of Atreus and "The Curse of Blood" reflect this point of view?

3 Discuss the way Marcuse documents Orpheus and Narcissus as heroes who are in revolt against the rules of a culture. Why have Orpheus and Narcissus failed to become heroes of Western civilization? What are the implications of this?

4 Explain what Marcuse means by the pleasure principle. Why does he say the song of Orpheus "pacifies the animal world"? How does Narcissus liberate the ego?

5 What happens to Orpheus and Narcissus because of their refusal to accept the group norms? Does Freud's interpretation of narcissism reveal his preference for productivity? Explain! What does Marcuse mean when he says that Orpheus and Narcissus suggest the "negation of order"? Would you say that the Beatles are a contemporary image of Orpheus and Narcissus? Is their music in opposition to the work ethic?

6 What does Marcuse's essay demonstrate about the use of language as a means to balance opposites? How does language transform the individual? Discuss the language of contemporary Americans and attempt to ascertain whether they are followers of Prometheus or of Orpheus and Narcissus. What does this suggest about language as part of the socialization process?

WE COME TO PRAISE Caesar

In the picture shown below, we see four men, John Kennedy, Lyndon Johnson, Dwight Eisenhower, and Harry Truman, who became the symbolic voice for the people of the United States. Each man sought and won the presidency, and each in turn was the most powerful man in the country. This picture was taken in 1961; by 1973 all four men were dead.

MARK ANTONY'S SPEECH

from *JULIUS CAESAR*
WILLIAM SHAKESPEARE

Antony. You gentle Romans—

All.   Peace, ho! Let us hear him.

Antony. Friends, Romans, countrymen, lend me
    your ears;
I come to bury Caesar, not to praise him.
The evil that men do lives after them,
The good is oft interrèd with their bones;
So let it be with Caesar. The noble Brutus
Hath told you Caesar was ambitious.
If it were so, it was a grievous fault,
And grievously hath Caesar answered it.
Here, under leave of Brutus and the rest
(For Brutus is an honorable man,
So are they all, all honorable men),
Come I to speak in Caesar's funeral.
He was my friend, faithful and just to me;
But Brutus say he was ambitious,
And Brutus is an honorable man.
He hath brought many captives home to Rome,
Whose ransoms did the general coffers fill;
Did this in Caesar seem ambitious?
When that the poor have cried, Caesar hath
    wept;
Ambition should be made of sterner stuff.
Yet Brutus says he was ambitious;
And Brutus is an honorable man.
You all did see that on the Lupercal
I thrice presented him a kingly crown,
Which he did thrice refuse. Was this ambition?
Yet Brutus says he was ambitious;
And sure he is an honorable man.
I speak not to disprove what Brutus spoke,
But here I am to speak what I do know.
You all did love him once, not without cause;
What cause withholds you then to mourn for
    him?
O judgment, thou art fled to brutish beasts,
And men have lost their reason! Bear with me;
My heart is in the coffin there with Caesar,
And I must pause till it come back to me.

First Plebeian. Methinks there is much reason in
    his sayings.

Second Plebeian. If thou consider rightly of the
    matter, Caesar has had great wrong.

Third Plebeian.   Has he, masters?
I fear there will a worse come in his place.

Fourth Plebeian. Marked ye his words? He
    would not take the crown,
Therefore 'tis certain he was not ambitious.

First Plebeian. If it be found so, some will dear abide it.

Second Plebeian. Poor soul, his eyes are red as fire with weeping.

Third Plebeian. There's not a nobler man in Rome than Antony.

Fourth Plebeian. Now mark him, he begins again to speak.

Antony. But yesterday the word of Caesar might
Have stood against the world; now lies he there,
And none so poor to do him reverence.
O masters! If I were disposed to stir
Your hearts and minds to mutiny and rage,
I should do Brutus wrong and Cassius wrong,
Who, you all know, are honorable men.
I will not do them wrong; I rather choose
To wrong the dead, to wrong myself and you,
Than I will wrong such honorable men.
But here's a parchment with the seal of Caesar;
I found it in his closet; 'tis his will.
Let but the commons hear this testament,
Which, pardon me, I do not mean to read,
And they would go and kiss dead Caesar's wounds,
And dip their napkins in his sacred blood;
Yea, beg a hair of him for memory,
And dying, mention it within their wills,
Bequeathing it as a rich legacy
Unto their issue.

Fourth Plebeian. We'll hear the will; read it, Mark Antony.

All. The will, the will! We will hear Caesar's will!

Antony. Have patience, gentle friends, I must not read it.
It is not meet you know how Caesar loved you.
You are not wood, you are not stones, but men;
And being men, hearing the will of Caesar,
It will inflame you, it will make you mad.
'Tis good you know not that you are his heirs;
For if you should, O, what would come of it?

Fourth Plebeian. Read the will! We'll hear it, Antony!
You shall read us the will, Caesar's will!

Antony. Will you be patient? Will you stay awhile?
I have o'ershot myself to tell you of it.
I fear I wrong the honorable men
Whose daggers have stabbed Caesar; I do fear it.

Fourth Plebeian. They were traitors. Honorable men!

All. The will! The testament!

Second Plebeian. They were villains, murders! The will! Read the will!

Antony. You will compel me to read the will?
Then make a ring about the corpse of Caesar,
And let me show you him that made the will.
Shall I descend? And will you give me leave?

. . . .

Antony. If you have tears, prepare to shed them now.
You all do know this mantle; I remember
The first time ever Caesar put it on:
'Twas on a summer's evening, in his tent,
That day he overcame the Nervii.
Look, in this place ran Cassius' dagger through;
See what a rent the envious Casca made;
Through this the well-belovèd Brutus stabbed,
And as he plucked his cursèd steel away,
Mark how the blood of Caesar followed it,
As rushing out of doors, to be resolved
If Brutus so unkindly knocked, or no;
For Brutus, as you know, was Caesar's angel.
Judge, O you gods, how dearly Caesar loved him!
This was the most unkindest cut of all;
For when the noble Caesar saw him stab,
Ingratitude, more strong than traitor's arms,
Quite vanquished him. Then burst his mighty heart;
And, in his mantle muffling up his face,
Even at the base of Pompey's statue
(Which all the while ran blood) great Caesar fell.
O, what a fall was there, my countrymen!
Then I, and you, and all of us fell down,
Whilst bloody treason flourished over us.
O, now you weep, and I perceive you feel
The dint of pity; these are gracious drops.
Kind souls, what weep you when you but behold
Our Caesar's vesture wounded? Look you here,
Here is himself, marred as you see with traitors.

. . . .

Antony. Good friends, sweet friends, let me not stir you up.
To such a sudden flood of mutiny.
They that have done this deed are honorable.
What private griefs they have, alas, I know not,
That made them do it. They are wise and honorable,

And will, no doubt, with reasons answer you.
I come not, friends, to steal away your hearts;
I am no orator, as Brutus is;
But (as you know me all) a plain blunt man
That love my friend, and that they know full
   well
That gave me public leave to speak of him.
For I have neither writ, nor words, nor worth,
Action, nor utterance, nor the power of speech
To stir men's blood; I only speak right on.
I tell you that which you yourselves do know,
Show you sweet Caesar's wounds, poor poor
   dumb mouths,
And bid them speak for me. But were I Brutus,
And Brutus Antony, there were an Antony
Would ruffle up your spirits, and put a tongue
In every wound of Caesar that should move
The stones of Rome to rise and mutiny.

All. We'll mutiny.

First Plebeian. We'll burn the house of Brutus.

Third Plebeian. Away, then! Come, seek the
conspirators.

Antony. Yet hear me, countrymen. Yet hear me
speak.

All. Peace, ho! Hear Antony, most noble
Antony!

Antony. Why, friends, you go to do you know
   not what:
Wherein hath Caesar thus deserved your
   loves?
Alas, you know not; I must tell you then:
You have forgot the will I told you of.

All. Most true, the will! Let's stay and hear the
will.

Antony. Here is the will, and under Caesar's
   seal.
To every Roman citizen he gives,
To every several man, seventy-five drachmas.

Second Plebeian. Most noble Caesar! We'll revenge his death!

Third Plebeian. O royal Caesar!

Antony. Hear me with patience.

All. Peace, ho!

Antony. Moreover, he hath left you all his
   walks,
His private arbors, and new-planted orchards,
On this side Tiber; he hath left them you,
And to your heirs forever: common pleasures,
To walk abroad and recreate yourselves.
Here was a Caesar! When comes such an-
   other?

For Norman Mailer, the age of electronic communications has created the mass man: ". . . the
creation of men as interchangeable as commodities . . . . This loss of personality was a
catastrophe to the future of the imagination. . . ."
In America, the movies created the illusion of an
"inner" frontier. The heroes became part "of an
agitated, overexcited, superheated dream life."
The result of all this was to create heroes who
were trapped within "the skull." Onto this stage
setting steps John Fitzgerald Kennedy: the
movie star as presidential candidate. The picture
shown above was taken during the Democratic
convention of 1960. The man is replaced by an
image. Mailer's essay delves deep into the
American spirit to paint an image of John Kennedy as a "superman" who comes to our "supermarket": the package seems to be more important than the man's ideals.

Words create the image and the image becomes the political hero

After three thousand years of explosion, by means of fragmentary and mechanical technologies, the Western world is imploding. During the mechanical ages we had extended our bodies in space. Today, after more than a century of electric technology, we have extended our central nervous system itself in a global embrace, abolishing both space and time as far as our planet is concerned. Rapidly, we approach the final phase of the extensions of man—the technological simulation of consciousness, when the creative process of knowing will be collectively and corporately extended to the whole of human society, much as we have already extended our senses and our nerves by the various media.

In a culture like ours, long accustomed to splitting and dividing all things as a means of control, it is sometimes a bit of a shock to be reminded that, in operational and practical fact, the medium is the message. This is merely to say that the personal and social consequences of any medium—that is, of any extension of ourselves—result from the new scale that is introduced into our affairs by each extension of ourselves, or by any new technology.

from *Understanding Media: The Extensions of Man*

THE THIRD PRESIDENTIAL PAPER— THE EXISTENTIAL HERO: SUPERMAN COMES TO THE SUPERMARKET

NORMAN MAILER

Not too much need be said for this piece; it is possible it can stand by itself. But perhaps its title should have been "Filling the Holes in No Man's Land."

American politics is rarely interesting for its men, its ideas, or the style of its movements. It is usually more fascinating in its gaps, its absences, its uninvaded territories. We have used up our frontier, but the psychological frontier talked about in this piece is still alive with untouched possibilities and dire unhappy all-but-lost opportunities. In European politics the spaces are filled—the average politician, like the average European, knows what is possible and what is impossible for him. Their politics is like close trench warfare. But in America, one knows such close combat only for the more banal political activities. The play of political ideas is flaccid here in America because opposing armies never meet. The Right, the Center, and what there is of the Left have set up encampments on separate hills, they face one another across valleys, they send out small patrols to their front and vast communiqués to their rear. No Man's Land predominates. It is a situation which calls for guerrilla raiders. Any army which would dare to enter the valley in force might not only determine a few new political formations, but indeed could create more politics itself, even as the guerrilla raids of the Negro Left and Negro Right, the Freedom Riders and the Black Muslims, have discovered much of the secret nature of the American reality for us.

I wonder if I make myself clear. Conventional politics has had so little to do with the real subterranean life of America that none of us know much about the real—which is to say the potential—historic nature of America. That lies buried under apathy, platitudes, Rightist encomiums for the FBI, programmatic welfare from the liberal Center, and furious pips of protest from the Peace Movement's Left. The mass of Americans are not felt as a political reality. No one has any idea of how they would react to radically new sense. It is only when their heart-land, their no man's land, their valley is invaded, that one discovers the reality. In Birmingham during the days of this writing, the jails are filled with Negro children, 2000 of them. The militancy of the Negroes in Birmingham is startling, so too is the stubbornness of the Southern white, so too and unbelievable is the procrastination of the Kennedy administration. Three new realities have been discovered. The potential Left and potential Right of America are more vigorous than one would have expected and the Center is more irresolute. An existential political act, the drive by Southern Negroes, led by Martin Luther King, to end segregation in restaurants in Birmingham, an act which is existential precisely because its end is unknown, has succeeded en route in discovering more of the American reality to us.

If a public speaker in a small Midwestern town were to say, "J. Edgar Hoover has done more harm to the freedoms of America than Joseph Stalin," the act would be existential. Depending on the occasion and the town, he would be manhandled physically or secretly applauded. But he would create a new reality which would displace the old psychological reality that such *a remark could not be made, even as for example the old Southern psychological reality that you couldn't get two Negroes to do anything together, let alone two thousand has now been destroyed by a new and more accurate psychological reality: you can get two thousand Negroes to work in cooperation. The new psychological realities are closer to history and so closer to sanity and they exist because, and only because, the event has taken place.*

It was Kennedy's potentiality to excite such activity which interested me most; that he was young, that he was physically handsome, and that his wife was attractive were not trifling accidental details but, rather, new major political facts. I knew if he became President, it would be an existential event: he would touch depths in American life which were uncharted. Regardless of his politics, and even then one could expect his politics would be as conventional as his personality was unconventional, indeed one could expect his politics to be pushed toward conventionality precisely to counteract his essential unconventionality, one knew nonetheless that regardless of his overt politics, America's tortured psychotic search for security would finally be torn loose from the feverish ghosts of its old generals, its MacArthurs and Eisenhowers—ghosts which Nixon could cling to—and we as a nation would finally be loose again in the historic seas of a national psyche which was willy-nilly and at last, again, adventurous. And that, I thought, that was the hope for America. So I swallowed my doubts, my disquiets, and my certain distastes for Kennedy's dullness of mind and prefabricated politics, and did my best to write a piece which would help him to get elected.

For once let us try to think about a political convention without losing ourselves in housing projects of fact and issue. Politics has its virtues, all too many of them—it would not rank with baseball as a topic of conversation if it did not satisfy a great many things—but one can suspect that its secret appeal is close to nicotine. Smoking cigarettes insulates one from one's life, one does not feel as much, often happily so, and politics quarantines one from history; most of the people who nourish themselves in the political life are in the game not to make history but to be diverted from the history which is being made.

If that Democratic Convention which has now receded behind the brow of the Summer of 1960

is only half-remembered in the excitements of moving toward the election, it may be exactly the time to consider it again, because the mountain of facts which concealed its features last July has been blown away in the winds of High Television, and the man-in-the-street (that peculiar political term which refers to the quixotic voter who will pull the lever for some reason so salient as: "I had a brown-nose lieutenant once with Nixon's looks," or "that Kennedy must have false teeth"), the not so easily estimated man-in-the-street has forgotten most of what happened and could no more tell you who Kennedy was fighting against than you or I could place a bet on who was leading the American League in batting during the month of June.

So to try to talk about what happened is easier now than in the days of the convention, one does not have to put everything in—an act of writing which calls for a bulldozer rather than a pen—one can try to make one's little point and dress it with a ribbon or two of metaphor. All to the good. Because mysteries are irritated by facts, and the 1960 Democratic Convention began as one mystery and ended as another.

Since mystery is an emotion which is repugnant to a political animal (why else lead a life of bad banquet dinners, cigar smoke, camp chairs, foul breath, and excruciatingly dull jargon if not to avoid the echoes of what is not known), the psychic separation between what was happening on the floor, in the caucus rooms, in the headquarters, and what was happening in parallel to the history of the nation was mystery enough to drown the proceedings in gloom. It was on the one hand a dull convention, one of the less interesting by general agreement, relieved by local bits of color, given two half hours of excitement by two demonstrations for Stevenson, buoyed up by the class of the Kennedy machine, turned by the surprise of Johnson's nomination as vice-president, but, all the same, dull, depressed in its over-all tone, the big fiestas subdued, the gossip flat, no real air of excitement, just moments—or as they say in bullfighting—details. Yet it was also, one could argue—and one may argue this yet—it was also one of the most important conventions in America's history, it could prove conceivably to be the most important. The man it nominated was unlike any politician who had ever run for President in the history of the land, and if elected he would come to power in a year when America was in danger of drifting into a profound decline.

A Descriptive of the Delegates: Sons and Daughters of the Republic in a Legitimate Panic; Small-time Practitioners of Small-town Political Judo in the Big Town and the Big Time

Depression obviously has its several roots: it is the doubtful protection which comes from not recognizing failure, it is the psychic burden of exhaustion, and it is also, and very often, that discipline of the will or the ego which enables one to continue working when one's unadmitted emotion is panic. And panic it was I think which sat as the largest single sentiment in the breast of the collective delegates as they came to convene in Los Angeles. Delegates are not the noblest sons and daughters of the Republic; a man of taste, arrived from Mars, would take one look at a convention floor and leave forever, convinced he had seen one of the drearier squats of Hell. If one still smells the faint living echo of a carnival wine, the pepper of a bullfight, the rag, drag, and panoply of a jousting tourney, it is all swallowed and regurgitated by the senses into the fouler cud of a death gas one must rid oneself of—a cigar-smoking, stale-aired, slack-jawed, butt-littered, foul, bleak, hard-working, bureaucratic death gas of language and faces ("Yes, those *faces*," says the man from Mars: lawyers, judges, ward heelers, *mafiosos*, Southern goons and grandees, grand old ladies, trade unionists and finks), of pompous words and long pauses which lay like a leaden pain over fever, the fever that one is in, over, or is it that one is just behind history? A legitimate panic for a delegate. America is a nation of experts without roots; we are always creating tacticians who are blind to strategy and strategists who cannot take a step, and when the culture has finished its work the institutions handcuff the infirmity. A delegate is a man who picks a candidate for the largest office in the land, a President who must live with problems whose borders are in ethics, metaphysics, and now ontology; the delegate is prepared for this office of selection by emptying wastebaskets, toting garbage and saying yes at the right time for twenty years in the small political machine of some small or large town; his reward, one of them anyway, is that he arrives at an invitation to the convention. An expert on local catch-as-catch-can, a small-time, often mediocre practitioner of small-town political judo, he comes to the big city with nine-tenths of his mind made up, he will follow the orders of the boss who brought him. Yet of course it is not altogether so mean as that: his opinion is listened to—the boss will consider what he has to say as one interesting factor among five hundred, and what is most important to the delegate, he has the illusion of partial freedom. He can, unless he is severely honest with himself—and if he is, why sweat out the low levels of a political machine?—he can have the illusion that he has helped to choose the candidate, he can even worry most sincerely about his choice, flirt with defection from the boss, work out his own small political gains by the road of loyalty or the way of hard bargain. But even if he is there for no more than the ride, his vote a certainty in the mind of the political boss, able to be thrown here or switched there as the boss decides, still in some peculiar sense he is reality to the boss, the delegate is the great American public, the bar he owns or the law practice, the piece of the union he represents, or the real-estate office, is a part of the political landscape which the boss uses as his own image of how the votes will go, and if the people will like the candidate. And if the boss is depressed by what he sees, if the candidate does not feel right to him, if he has a dull intimation that the candidate is not his sort (as, let us say, Harry Truman was his sort, or Symington might be his sort, or Lyndon Johnson), then vote for him the boss will if he must; he cannot be caught on the wrong side, but he does not feel the pleasure of a personal choice. Which is the center of the panic. Because if the boss is depressed, the delegate is doubly depressed, and the emotional fact is that Kennedy is not in focus, not in the old political focus, he is not comfortable; in fact it is a mystery to the boss how Kennedy got to where he is, not a mystery in its structures; Kennedy is rolling in money, Kennedy got the votes in primaries, and, most of all, Kennedy has a jewel of a political machine. It is as good as a crack Notre Dame team, all discipline and savvy and go-go-go, sound, drilled, never dull, quick as a knife, full of the salt of hipper-dipper, a beautiful machine; the boss could adore it if only a sensible candidate were driving it, a Truman, even a Stevenson, please God a Northern Lyndon Johnson, but it is run by a man who looks young enough to be coach of the Freshman team, and that is not comfortable at all. The boss knows political machines, he knows issues, farm parity, Forand health bill, Landrum-Griffin, but this is not all so adequate after all to revolutionaries in Cuba who looks like beatniks, competitions in missiles, Negroes looting whites in the Congo, intricacies of nuclear fallout, and NAACP men one does well to call Sir. It is all out of hand, everything important is off the center, foreign affairs is now the lick of the heat, and senators are candidates instead of governors, a disaster to the old family style of political measure where a political boss knows his governor and knows who his governor knows. So the boss is depressed, profoundly depressed. He comes to this convention resigned to nominating a man he does not understand, or let us say that, so far as he understands the candidate who is to be nominated, he is not happy about the secrets of his appeal, not so far as he divines these secrets; they seem to have too little to do with politics and all too much to do with the private madnesses of the nation which had thousands—or was it hundreds of thousands—of people demonstrating in the long night before Chessman was killed, and a movie star, the greatest, Marlon Brando out in the night with them. Yes, this candidate for all his record, his good, sound, conventional liberal record has a patina of that other life, the second American life, the long electric night with the fires of neon leading down the highway to the murmur of jazz.

An Apparent Digression: A Vivid View of the "City of Lost Angels"; The Democrats Defined; A Pentagon of Traveling Salesmen; Some Pointed Portraits of the Politicians

"I was seeing Pershing Square, Los Angeles, now for the first time . . . the nervous fruithustlers darting in and out of the shadows, fugitives from Times Square, Market Street SF, the French Quarter—masculine hustlers looking for lonely fruits to score from, anything from the legendary $20 to a pad at night and breakfast in the morning and whatever you can clinch or clip; and the heat in their holy cop uniforms, holy because of the Almighty Stick and the Almightier Vagrancy Law; the scattered junkies, the small-time pushers, the queens, the sad panhandlers, the lonely, exiled nymphs haunting the entrance to the men's head, the fruits with the hungry eyes and the jingling coins; the tough teen-age chicks—'dittybops'— making it with the lost hustlers . . . all amid the incongruous piped music and the flowers—twin fountains gushing rainbow colored: the world of Lonely America squeezed into Pershing Square, of the Cities of Terrible Night, downtown now trapped in the City of lost Angels . . . and the trees hang over it all like some type of apathetic fate."

—John Rechy: *Big Table 3*

Seeing Los Angeles after ten years away, one realizes all over again that America is an unhappy contract between the East (that Faustian thrust of a most determined human will which reaches up and out above the eye into the skyscrapers of New York) and those flat lands of compromise and mediocre self-expression, those endless half-pretty repetitive small towns of the Middle and the West, whose spirit is forever horizontal and whose marrow comes to rendezvous in the pastel monotonies of Los Angeles architecture.

So far as America has a history, one can see it in the severe heights of New York City, in the glare from the Pittsburgh mills, by the color in the brick of Louisburg Square, along the knotted greedy façades of the small mansion on Chicago's North Side, in Natchez' antebellum homes, the wrought-iron balconies off Bourbon Street, a captain's house in Nantucket, by the curve of Commercial Street in Provincetown. One can make a list; it is probably finite. What culture we have made and what history has collected to it can be found in those few hard examples of an architecture which came to its artistic term, was born, lived and so collected some history about it. Not all the roots of American life are uprooted, but almost all, and the spirit of the supermarket, that homogenous extension of stainless surfaces and psychoanalyzed people, packaged commodities and ranch homes, interchangeable, geographically unrecognizable, that essence of the new postwar SuperAmerica is found nowhere so perfectly as in Los Angeles' ubiquitous acres. One gets the impression that people come to Los Angeles in order to divorce themselves from the past, here to live or try to live in the rootless pleasure world of an adult child. One knows that if the cities of the world were destroyed by a new war, the architecture of the rebuilding would create a landscape which looked, subject to specifications of climate, exactly and entirely like the San Fernando Valley.

It is not that Los Angeles is altogether hideous, it is even by degrees pleasant, but for an Easterner there is never any salt in the wind; it is like Mexican cooking without chile, or Chinese egg rolls missing their mustard; as one travels through the endless repetitions of that city which is the capital of suburbia with its milky pinks, its washed-out oranges, its tainted lime-yellows of pastel on one pretty little architectural monstrosity after another, the colors not intense enough, the styles never pure, and never sufficiently impure to collide on the eye, one conceives the people who live here—they have come out to express themselves, Los Angeles is the home of self-expression, but the artists are middle-class and middling-minded; no passions will calcify here for years in the gloom to be revealed a decade later as the tessellations of a hard and fertile work, no, it is all open, promiscuous, borrowed, half bought, a city without iron, eschewing wood, a kingdom of stucco, the playground for mass men—one has the feeling it was built by television sets giving orders to men. And in this land of the pretty-pretty, the virility is in the barbarisms, the vulgarities, it is in the huge billboards, the screamers of the neon lighting, the shouting farm-utensil colors of the gas stations and the monster drugstores, it is in the swing of the sports cars, hot rods, convertibles, Los Angeles is a city to drive in, the boulevards are wide, the traffic is nervous and fast, the radio stations play bouncing, blooping, rippling tunes, one digs the pop in a pop tune, no one of character would make love by it but the sound is good for swinging a car, electronic guitars and Hawaiian harps.

So this is the town the Democrats came to, and with their unerring instinct (after being with them a week, one thinks of this party as a crazy, half-rich family, loaded with poor cousins, traveling always in caravans with Cadillacs and Okie Fords, Lincolns and quarter-horse mules, putting up every night in tents to hear the chamber quartet of Great Cousin Eleanor invaded by the Texas-twanging steel-stringing geetarists of Bubber Lyndon, carrying its own mean high-school principal, Doc Symington, chided for its manners by good Uncle Adlai, told the route of march by Navigator Jack, cut off every six months from the rich will of Uncle Jim Farley, never listening to the mechanic of the caravan, Bald Sam Rayburn, who assures them they'll all break down unless Cousin Bubber gets the concession on the garage; it's the Snopes family married to Henry James, with the labor unions thrown in like a Yankee dollar, and yet it's true, in tranquility one recollects them with affection, their instinct is good, crazy family good) and this instinct now led the caravan to pick the Biltmore Hotel in downtown Los Angeles for their family get-together and reunion.

The Biltmore is one of the ugliest hotels in the world. Patterned after the flat roofs of an Italian Renaissance palace, it is eighty-eight times as large, and one-millionth as valuable to the continuation of man, and it would be intolerable if it were not for the presence of Pershing Square, that square block of park with cactus and palm trees, the three-hundred-and-sixty-five-day-a-year convention of every junkie, pot-head, pusher, queen (but you have read that good writing already). For years Pershing Square has been one of the three or four places in America famous to homosexuals, famous not for its posh, the chic is round-heeled here, but because it is one of the avatars of the good old masturbatory sex, dirty with the crusted sugars of smut, dirty rooming houses around the corner where the score is made, dirty book and photograph stores down the street, old-fashioned out-of-the-Thirties burlesque houses, cruising bars, jukeboxes, movie houses; Pershing Square is the town plaza for all those lonely, respectable, small-town homosexuals who lead a family life, make children, and have the Philbrick psychology (How I Joined the Communist Party and Led Three Lives). Yes, it is the open-air convention hall for the small-town inverts who live like spies, and it sits in the center of Los Angeles, facing the Biltmore, that hotel which is a mausoleum, that Pentagon of traveling salesmen the Party chose to house the headquarters of the Convention.

So here came that family, cursed before it began by the thundering absence of Great-Uncle Truman, the delegates dispersed over a run of thirty miles and twenty-seven hotels: the Olympian Motor Hotel, the Ambassador, the Beverly Wilshire, the Santa Ynez Inn (where rumor has it the delegates from Louisiana had some midnight swim), the Mayan, the Commodore, the Mayfair, the Sherton-West, the Huntington-Sherton, the Green, the Hayward, the Gates, the Figueroa, the Statler Hilton, the Hollywood Knickerbocker—does one have to be a collector to list such names?—beauties all, with that up-from-the-farm Los Angeles décor, plate-glass windows, patio and terrace, foam-rubber mattress, pastel paints, all of them pretty as an ad in full-page color, but the Biltmore where everybody gathered every day—the newsmen, the TV, radio, magazine, and foreign newspapermen, the delegates, the politicos, the tourists, the campaign managers, the runners, the flunkies, the cousins and aunts, the wives, the grandfathers, the eight-year-old girls, and the twenty-eight-year-old girls in the Kennedy costumes, red and white and blue, the Symingteeners, the Johnson Ladies, the Stevenson Ladies, everybody—and for three days before the convention and four days into it, everybody collected at the Biltmore, in the lobby, in the grill, in the Biltmore Bowl, in the elevators, along the corridors, three hundred deep always outside the Kennedy suite, milling everywhere, every dark-carpeted grey-brown hall of the hotel, but it was in the Gallery of the Biltmore where one first felt the mood which pervaded all proceedings until the convention was almost over, that heavy, thick, witless depression which was to dominate every move as the delegates wandered and gawked and set for a spell, there in the Gallery of the Biltmore, that huge depressing alley with its inimitable hotel color, that faded depth of chiaroscuro which unhappily has no depth, that brown which is not a brown, that grey which has no pearl in it, that color which can be described only as hotel-color because the beiges, the tans, the walnuts, the mahoganies, the dull blood rugs, the moaning yellows, the sick greens, the greys and all those dumb browns merge into that lack of color which is an over-large hotel at convention time, with all the small-towners wearing their set, starched faces, that look they get at carnival, all fever and suspicion, and proud to be there, eddying slowly back and forth in that high block-long tunnel of a room with its arched ceiling and square recesses filling every rib of the arch with art work, escutcheons and blazons and other art, pictures I think, I cannot even remember, there was such a hill of cigar smoke the eye had to travel on its way to the ceiling, and at one end there was galvanized-pipe scaffolding and workmen repairing some part of the ceiling, one of them touching up one of the endless squares of painted plaster in the arch, and another worker, passing by, yelled up to the one who was working on the ceiling: "Hey, Michelangelo!"

Later, of course, it began to emerge and there were portraits one could keep, Symington, dogged at a press conference, declaring with no conviction that he knew he had a good chance to win, the disappointment eating at his good looks so that he came off hard-faced, mean, and yet slack—a desperate dullness came off the best of his intentions. There was Johnson who had compromised too many contradictions and now the contradictions were in his face: when he smiled the corners of his mouth squeezed gloom; when he was pious, his eyes twinkled irony; when he spoke in a righteous tone, he looked corrupt; when he jested, the ham in his jowls looked to quiver. He was not convincing. He was a Southern politican, a Texas Democrat, a liberal Eisenhower; he would do no harm, he would do no good, he would react to the machine, good fellow, nice friend—the Russians would understand him better than his own.

Stevenson had the patina. He came into the room and the room was different, not stronger perhaps (which is why ultimately he did not win), but warmer. One knew why some adored him; he did not look like other people, not with press lights on his flesh; he looked like a lover, the simple truth, he had the sweet happiness of an adolescent who has just been given his first major kiss. And so he glowed, and one was reminded of Chaplin, not because they were the least alike in features, but because Charlie Chaplin was luminous when one met him and Stevenson had something of that light.

There was Eleanor Roosevelt, fine, precise, hand-worked like ivory. Her voice was almost attractive as she explained in the firm, sad tones of the first lady in this small town why she could not admit Mr. Kennedy, who was no doubt a gentleman, into her political house. One had the impression of a lady who was finally becoming a woman, which is to say that she was just a little bitchy about it all; nice bitchy, charming, it had a touch of art to it, but it made one wonder if she were not now satisfying the last passion of them all, which was to become physically attractive, for she was better-looking than she had ever been as she spurned the possibilities of a young suitor.

Jim Farley. Huge. Cold as a bishop. The hell he would consign you to was cold as ice.

Bobby Kennedy, that archetype Bobby Kennedy, looked like a West Point cadet, or, better, one of those unreconstructed Irishmen from Kirkland House one always used to have to face in the line in Harvard house football games. "Hello," you would say to the ones who looked like him as you lined up for the scrimmage after the kickoff, and his type would nod and look away, one rock glint of recognition your due for living across the hall from one another all through Freshman year, and then bang, as the ball was passed back, you'd get a bony king-hell knee in the crotch. He was the kind of man never to put on the gloves with if you wanted to do some social boxing, because after two minutes it would be a war, and ego-bastards last long in a war.

Carmine DeSapio and Kenneth Galbraith on

the same part of the convention floor. DeSapio is bigger than one expects, keen and florid, great big smoked glasses, a suntan like Mantan—he is the kind of heavyweight Italian who could get by with a name like Romeo—and Galbraith is tall-tall, as actors say, six foot six it could be, terribly thin, enormously attentive, exquisitely polite, birdlike, he is sensitive to the stirring of reeds in a wind over the next hill. "Our grey eminence," whispered the intelligent observer next to me.

Bob Wagner, the mayor of New York, a little man, plump, groomed, blank. He had the blank, pomaded, slightly worried look of the first barber in a good barbershop, the kind who would go to the track on his day off and wear a green transparent stone in a gold ring.

And then there was Kennedy, the edge of the mystery. But a sketch will no longer suffice.

Perspective from the Biltmore Balcony: The Colorful Arrival of the Hero with the Orange-brown Suntan and Amazingly White Teeth; Revelation of the Two Rivers Political Theory

"... it can be said with a fair amount of certainty that the essence of his political attractiveness is his extraordinary political intelligence. He has a mind quite unlike that of any other Democrat of this century. It is not literary, metaphysical and moral, as Adlai Stevenson's is. Kennedy is articulate and often witty, but he does not seek verbal polish. No one can doubt the seriousness of his concern with the most serious political matters, but one feels that whereas Mr. Stevenson's political views derive from a view of life that holds politics to be a mere fraction of existence, Senator Kennedy's primary interest is in politics. The easy way in which he disposes of the question of Church and State—as if he felt that any reasonable man could quite easily resolve any possible conflict of loyalties—suggest that the organization of society is the one thing that really engages his interest."

—RICHARD ROVERE:
The New Yorker, July 23, 1960

The afternoon he arrived at the convention from the airport, there was of course a large crowd on the street outside the Biltmore, and the best way to get a view was to get up on an outdoor balcony of the Biltmore, two flights above the street, and look down on the event. One waited thirty minutes, and then a honking of horns as wild as the getaway after an Italian wedding sounded around the corner, and the Kennedy cortege came into sight, circled Pershing Square, the men in the open and leading convertibles sitting backwards to look at their leader, and finally came to a halt in a space cleared for them by the police in the crowd. The television cameras were out, and a Kennedy band was playing some circus music. One saw him immediately. He had the deep orange-brown suntan of a ski instructor, and when he smiled at the crowd his teeth were amazingly white and clearly visible at a distance of fifty yards. For one moment he saluted Pershing Square, and Pershing Square saluted him back, the prince and the beggars of glamour staring at one another across a city street, one of those very special moments in the underground history of the world, and then with a quick move he was out of the car and by choice headed into the crowd instead of the lane cleared for him into the hotel by the police, so that he made his way inside surrounded by a mob, and one expected at any moment to see him lifted to its shoulders like a matador being carried back to the city after a triumph in the plaza. All the while the band kept playing the campaign tunes, sashaying circus music, and one had a moment of clarity, intense as a *déjà vu*, for the scene which had taken place had been glimpsed before in a dozen musical comedies; it was the scene where the hero, the matinee idol, the movie star comes to the palace to claim the princess, or what is the same, and more to our soil, the football hero, the campus king, arrives at the dean's home surrounded by a court of open-singing students to plead with the dean for his daughter's kiss and permission to put on the big musical that night. And suddenly I saw the convention, it came into focus for me, and I understood the mood of depression which had lain over the convention, because finally it was simple: the Democrats were going to nominate a man who, no matter how serious his political dedication might be, was indisputably and willy-nilly going to be seen as a great box-office actor, and the consequences of that were staggering and not at all easy to calculate.

Since the First World War Americans have been leading a double life, and our history has moved on two rivers, one visible, the other underground; there has been the history of politics which is concrete, factual, practical and unbelievably dull if not for the consequences of the actions of some of these men; and there is a subterranean river of untapped, ferocious, lonely and romantic desires, that concentration of ecstasy and violence which is the dream life of the nation.

The twentieth century may yet be seen as that era when civilized man and underprivileged man were melted together into mass man, the iron and steel of the nineteenth century giving way to electronic circuits which communicated their messages into men, the unmistakable tendency of the new century seeming to be the creation of men as interchangeable as commodities, their extremes of personality singed out of existence by the psychic fields of force the communicators would impose. This loss of personality was a catastrophe to the future of the imagination, but billions of people might first benefit from it by having enough to eat—one did not know—and there remained citadels of resistance in Europe where the culture was deep and roots were visible in the architecture of the past.

Nowhere, as in America, however, was this fall from individual man to mass man felt so acutely, for America was at once the first and most prolific creator of mass communications, and the most rootless of countries, since almost no American could lay claim to the line of a family which had not once at least severed its roots by migrating here. But, if rootless, it was then the most vulnerable of countries to its own homogenization. Yet America was also the country in which the dynamic myth of the Renaissance—that every man was potentially extraordinary—knew its most passionate persistence. Simply, America was the land where people still believed in heroes: George Washington; Billy the Kid; Lincoln, Jefferson; Mark Twain, Jack London, Hemingway; Joe Louis, Dempsey, Gentleman Jim; America believed in athletes, rumrunners, aviators; even lovers, by the time Valentino died. It was a country which had grown by the leap of one hero past another—is there a country in all of our ground which does not have its legendary figure? And when the West was filled, the expansion turned inward, became part of an agitated, overexcited, superheated dream life. The film studios threw up their searchlights as the frontier was finally sealed, and the romantic possibilities of the old conquest of land turned into a vertical myth, trapped within the skull, of a new kind of heroic life, each choosing his own archetype of a neo-renaissance man, be it Barrymore, Cagney, Flynn, Bogart, Brando or Sinatra, but it was almost as if there were no peace unless one could fight well, kill well (if always with honor), love well and love many, be cool, be daring, be dashing, be wild, be wily, be resourceful, be a brave gun. And this myth, that each of us was born to be free, to wander, to have adventure and to grow on the waves of the violent, the perfumed, and the unexpected, had a force which could not be tamed no matter how the nation's regulators—politicians, medicos, policemen, professors, priests, rabbis, ministers, *idéologues*, psychoanalysts, builders, executives and endless communicators—would brick-in the modern life with hygiene upon sanity, and middle-brow homily over platitude; the myth would not die. Indeed a quarter of the nation's business must have depended upon its existence. But it stayed alive for more than that—it was as if the message in the labyrinth of the genes would insist that violence was locked with creativity, and adventure was the secret of love.

Once, in the Second World War and in the year or two which followed, the underground river returned to earth, and the life of the nation was intense, of the present, electric; as a lady said, "That was the time when we gave parties which changed people's lives." The Forties was a decade when the speed with which one's own events occurred seemed as rapid as the history of the battlefields, and for the mass of people in America a forced march into a new jungle of emotion was the result. The surprises, the failures, and the dangers of that life must have terrified some nerve of awareness in the power and the mass, for, as if stricken by the orgiastic vistas the myth had carried up from underground, the retreat to a more conservative existence was disorderly, the fear of communism spread like an irrational hail of boils. To anyone who could see, the excessive hysteria of the Red wave was no preparation to face an enemy, but rather a terror of the national self: free-loving, lust-looting, atheistic, implacable—absurdity beyond absurdity to label communism so, for the moral products of Stalinism had been Victorian sex and a ponderous machine of material theology.

Forced underground again, deep beneath all *Reader's Digest* hospital dressings of Mental Health in Your Community, the myth continued to flow, fed by television and the film. The fissure in the national psyche widened to the danger point. The last large appearance of the myth was the vote which tricked the polls and gave Harry Truman his victory in '48. That was the last. Came the Korean War, the shadow of the H-bomb, and we were ready for the General. Uncle Harry gave way to Father, and security, regularity, order, and the life of no imagination were the command of the day. If one had any doubt of this, there was Joe McCarthy with his built-in treason detector, furnished by God, and the damage was done. In the totalitarian wind of those days, anyone who worked in Government formed the habit of being not too original, and many a mind atrophied from disuse and private shame. At the summit there was benevolence without leadership, regularity without vision, security without safety, rhetoric without life. The ship drifted on, that enormous warship of the United States, led by a Secretary of State whose cells were seceding to cancer, and as the world became more fantastic—Africa turning itself upside down, while some new kind of machine man was being made in China—two events occurred which stunned the confidence of America into a new night: the Russians put up their Sputnik, and Civil Rights—that reluctant gift to the American Negro, granted for its effect on foreign affairs—spewed into real life at Little Rock. The national Ego was in shock: the Russians were now in some ways our technological superiors, and we had an internal problem of subject populations equal conceivably in its difficulty to the Soviet and its satellites. The fatherly calm of the General began to seem like the uxorious mellifluences of the undertaker.

Underneath it all was a larger problem. The life of politics and the life of myth had diverged too far, and the energies of the people one knew every where had slowed down. Twenty years ago a post-Depression generation had gone to war and formed a lively, grousing, by times inefficient, carousing, pleasure-seeking, not altogether inadequate army. It did part of what it was supposed to do, and many, out of combat, picked up a kind of private life on the fly, and had their good time despite the yaws of the military system. But today in America the generation which respected the code of the myth was Beat, a horde of half-begotten Christs with scraggly beards, heroes none, saints all, weak before the strong, empty conformisms of the authority. The sanction for finding one's growth was no longer one's flag, one's career, one's sex, one's adventure, not even one's booze. Among the best in this newest of the generations, the myth had found its voice in marijuana, and the joke of the underground was that when the Russians came over they could never dare to occupy us for long because America was too Hip. Gallows humor. The poorer truth might be that America was too Beat, the instinct of the nation so separated from its public mind that

apathy, schizophrenia, and private beatitudes might be the pride of the welcoming committee any underground could offer.

Yes, the life of politics and the life of the myth had diverged too far. There was nothing to return them to one another, no common danger, no cause, no desire, and, most essentially, no hero. It was a hero America needed, a hero central to his time, a man whose personality might suggest contradictions and mysteries which could reach into the alienated circuits of the underground, because only a hero can capture the secret imagination of a people, and so be good for the vitality of his nation; a hero embodies the fantasy and so allows each private mind the liberty to consider its fantasy and find a way to grow. Each mind can become more conscious of its desire and waste less strength in hiding from itself. Roosevelt was such a hero, and Churchill, Lenin and DeGaulle; even Hitler, to take the most odious example of this thesis, was a hero, the hero-as-monster, embodying what had become the monstrous fantasy of a people, but the horror upon which the radical mind and liberal temperament foundered was that he gave outlet to the energies of the Germans and so presented the twentieth century with an index of how horrible had become the secret heart of its desire. Roosevelt is of course a happier example of the hero; from his paralytic leg to the royal elegance of his geniality he seemed to contain the country within himself; everyone from the meanest starving cripple to an ambitious young man could expand into the optimism of an improving future because the man offered an unspoken promise of a future which would be rich. The sexual and the sex-starved, the poor, the hard-working and the imaginative well-to-do could see themselves in the President, could believe him to be like themselves. So a large part of the country was able to discover its energies because not as much was wasted in feeling that the country was a poisonous nutrient which stifled the day.

Too simple? No doubt. One tries to construct a simple model. The thesis is after all not so mysterious; it would merely nudge the notion that a hero embodies his time and is not so very much better than his time, but he is larger than life and so is capable of giving direction to the time, able to encourage a nation to discover the deepest colors of its character. At bottom the concept of the hero is antagonistic to impersonal social progress, to the belief that social ills can be solved by social legislating, for it sees a country as all-but-trapped in its character until it has a hero who reveals the character of the country to itself. The implication is that without such a hero the nation turns sluggish. Truman for example was not such a hero, he was not sufficiently larger than life, he inspired familiarity without excitement, he was a character but his proportions came from soap opera: Uncle Harry, full of salty common-sense and small-minded certainty, a storekeeping uncle.

Whereas Eisenhower has been the anti-Hero, the regulator. Nations do not necessarily and inevitably seek for heroes. In periods of dull anxiety, one is more likely to look for security than a dramatic confrontation, and Eisenhower could stand as a hero only for that large number of Americans who were most proud of their lack of imagination. In American life, the unspoken war of the century has taken place between the city and the small town: the city which is dynamic, orgiastic, unsettling, explosive and accelerating to the psyche; the small town which is rooted, narrow, cautious and planted in the life-logic of the family. The need of the city is to accelerate growth; the pride of the small town is to retard it. But since America has been passing through a period of enormous expansion since the war, the double-four years of Dwight Eisenhower could not retard the expansion, it could only denude it of color, character, and the development of novelty. The small-town mind is rooted—it is rooted in the small town —and when it attempts to direct history the results are disastrously colorless because the instrument of world power which is used by the small-town mind is the committee. Committees do not create, they merely proliferate, and the incredible dullness wreaked upon the American landscape in Eisenhower's eight years has been the triumph of the corporation. A tasteless, sexless, odorless sanctity in architecture, manners, modes, styles has been the result. Eisenhower embodied half the needs of the nation, the needs of the timid, the petrified, the sanctimonious, and the sluggish. What was even worse, he did not divide the nation as a hero might (with a dramatic dialogue as the result); he merely excluded one part of the nation from the other. The result was an alienation of the best minds and bravest impulses from the faltering history which was made. America's need in those years was to take an existential turn, to walk into the nightmare, to face into that terrible logic of history which demanded that the country and its people must become more extraordinary and more adventurous, or else perish, since the only alternative was to offer a false security in the power and the panacea of organized religion, family, and the FBI, a totalitarianization of the psyche by the stultifying techniques of the mass media which would seep into everyone's most private associations and so leave the country powerless against the Russians even if the denouement were to take fifty years, for in a competition between totalitarianisms the first maxim of the prizefight manager would doubtless apply: "Hungry fighters win fights."

The Hipster as Presidential Candidate: Thoughts on a Public Man's Eighteenth-Century Wife; Face-to-Face with the Hero; Significance of a Personal Note, or the Meaning of His Having Read an Author's Novel

Some part of these thoughts must have been in one's mind at the moment there was that first glimpse of Kennedy entering the Biltmore Hotel; and in the days which followed, the first mystery—the profound air of depression which hung over the convention—gave way to a second mystery which can be answered only by history. The depression of the delegates was understandable: no one had too much doubt that Kennedy would be nominated, but if elected he would be not only the youngest President ever to be chosen by voters, he would be the most conventionally attractive young man ever to sit in the White House, and his wife—some would claim it—might be the most beautiful first lady in our history. Of necessity the myth would emerge once more, because America's politics would now be also America's favorite movie, America's first soap opera. America's bestseller. One thinks of the talents of writers like Taylor Caldwell or Frank Yerby, or is it rather *The Fountainhead* which would contain such a fleshing of the romantic prescription? Or is it indeed one's own work which is called into question? "Well, there's your first hipster," says a writer one knows at the convention, "Sergius O'Shaugnessy born rich," and the temptation is to nod, for it could be true, a war hero, and the heroism is bona-fide, even exceptional, a man who has lived with death, who, crippled in the back, took on an operation which would kill him or restore him to power, who chose to marry a lady whose face might be too imaginative for the taste of a democracy which likes its first ladies to be executives of home-management, a man who courts political suicide by choosing to go all out for a nomination four, eight, or twelve years before his political elders think he is ready, a man who announces a week prior to the convention that the young are better fitted to direct history than the old. Yes, it captures the attention. This is no routine candidate calling every shot by safety's routine book. ("Yes," Nixon said, naturally but terribly tired an hour after his nomination, the TV cameras and lights and microphones bringing out a sweat of fatigue on his face, the words coming very slowly from the tired brain, somber, modest, sober, slow, slow enough so that one could touch emphatically, the cautions behind each word, "Yes, I want to say," said Nixon, "that whatever abilities I have, I got from my mother." A tired pause . . . dull moment of warning, ". . . and my father." The connection now made, the rest comes easy, ". . . and my school and my church." Such men are capable of anything.)

One had the opportunity to study Kennedy a bit in the days that followed. His style in the press conferences was interesting. Not terribly popular with the reporters (too much a contemporary, and yet too difficult to understand, he received nothing like the rounds of applause given to Eleanor Roosevelt, Stevenson, Humphrey, or even Johnson), he carried himself nonetheless with a cool grace which seemed indifferent to applause, his manner somehow similar to the poise of a fine boxer, quick with his hands, neat in his timing, and two feet away from his corner when the bell ended the round. There was a good lithe wit to his responses, a dry Harvard wit, a keen sense of proportion in disposing of difficult questions—invariably he gave enough of an answer to be formally satisfactory without ever opening himself to a new question which might go further than the first. Asked by a reporter, "Are you for Adlai as vice-president?" the grin came forth and the voice turned very dry, "No, I cannot say we have considered *Adlai* as a vice-president." Yet there was an elusive detachment to everything he did. One did not have the feeling of a man present in the room with all his weight and all his mind. Johnson gave you all of himself, he was a political animal, he breathed like an animal, sweated like one, you knew his mind was entirely absorbed with the compendium of political fact and maneuver; Kennedy seemed at times like a young professor whose manner was adequate for the classroom, but whose mind was

off in some intricacy of the Ph.D. thesis he was writing. Perhaps one can give a sense of the discrepancy by saying that he was like an actor who had been cast as the candidate, a good actor, but not a great one—you were aware all the time that the role was one thing and the man another—they did not coincide, the actor seemed a touch too aloof (as, let us say, Gregory Peck is usually too aloof) to become the part. Yet one had little sense of whether to value this elusiveness, or to beware of it. One could be witnessing the fortitude of a superior sensitivity or the detachment of a man who was not quite real to himself. And his voice gave no clue. When Johnson spoke, one could separate what was fraudulent from what was felt, he would have been satisfying as an actor the way Broderick Crawford or Paul Douglas are satisfying; one saw into his emotions, or at least had the illusion that one did. Kennedy's voice, however, was only a fair voice, too reedy, near to strident, it had the metallic snap of a cricket in it somewhere, it was more impersonal than the man, and so became the least-impressive quality in a face, a body, a selection of language, and a style of movement which made up a better-than-decent presentation, better than one had expected.

With all of that, it would not do to pass over the quality in Kennedy which is most difficult to describe. And in fact some touches should be added to this hint of a portrait, for later (after the convention), one had a short session alone with him, and the next day, another. As one had suspected in advance the interviews were not altogether satisfactory, they hardly could have been. A man running for President is altogether different from a man elected President: the hazards of the campaign make it impossible for a candidate to be as interesting as he might like to be (assuming he has such a desire). One kept advancing the argument that this campaign would be a contest of personalities, and Kennedy kept returning the discussion to politics. After a while one recognized this was an inevitable caution for him. So there would be not too much point to reconstructing the dialogue since Kennedy is hardly inarticulate about his political attitudes and there will be a library vault of text devoted to it in the newspapers. What struck me most about the interview was a passing remark whose importance was invisible on the scale of politics, but was altogether meaningful to my particular competence. As we sat down for the first time, Kennedy smiled nicely and said that he had read my books. One muttered one's pleasure. "Yes," he said, "I've read ..." and then there was a short pause which did not last long enough to be embarrassing in which it was yet obvious no title came instantly to his mind, an omission one was not ready to mind altogether since a man in such a position must be obliged to carry a hundred thousand facts and names in his head, but the hesitation lasted no longer than three seconds or four, and then he said, "I've read *The Deer Park* and ... the others," which startled me for it was the first time in a hundred similar situations, talking to someone whose knowledge of my work was casual, that the sentence did not come out, "I've read *The Naked and the Dead* ... and the others." If one is to take the worst and assume that Kennedy was briefed for this interview (which is most doubtful), it still speaks well for the striking instincts of his advisers.

What was retained later is an impression of Kennedy's manners which were excellent, even artful, better than the formal good manners of Choate and Harvard, almost as if what was creative in the man had been given to the manners. In a room with one or two people, his voice improved, became low-pitched, even pleasant—it seemed obvious that in all these years he had never become a natural public speaker and so his voice was constricted in public, the symptom of all orators who are ambitious, throttled, and determined.

His personal quality had a subtle, not quite describable intensity, a suggestion of dry pent heat perhaps, his eyes large, the pupils grey, the whites prominent, almost shocking, his most forceful feature: he had the eyes of a mountaineer. His appearance changed with his mood, strikingly so, and this made him always more interesting than what he was saying. He would seem at one moment older than his age, forty-eight or fifty, a tall, slim, sunburned professor with a pleasant weathered face, not even particularly handsome; five minutes later, talking a press conference on his lawn, three microphones before him, a television camera turning, his appearance would have gone through a metamorphosis, he would look again like a movie star, his coloring vivid, his manner rich, his gestures strong and quick, alive with that concentration of vitality a successful actor always seems to radiate. Kennedy had a dozen faces. Although they were not at all similar as people, the quality was reminiscent of someone like Brando whose expression rarely changes, but whose appearance seems to shift from one person into another as the minutes go by, and one bothers with this comparison because, like Brando, Kennedy's most characteristic quality is the remote and private air of a man who has traversed some lonely terrain of experience, of loss and gain, of nearness to death, which leaves him isolated from the mass of others.

The next day while they waited in vain for rescuers, the wrecked half of the boat turned over in the water and they saw that it would soon sink. The group decided to swim to a small island three miles away. There were other islands bigger and nearer, but the Navy officers knew that they were occupied by the Japanese. On one island, only one mile to the south, they could see a Japanese camp. McMahon, the engineer whose legs were disabled by burns, was unable to swim. Despite his own painfully crippled back, Kennedy swam the three miles with a breast stroke, towing behind him by a life-belt strap that he held between his teeth the helpless McMahon ... it took Kennedy and the suffering engineer five hours to reach the island.

The quotation is from a book which has for its dedicated unilateral title, *The Remarkable Kennedys*, but the prose is by one of the best of the war reporters, the former *Yank* editor, Joe McCarthy, and so presumably may be trusted in such details as this. Physical bravery does not of course guarantee a man's abilities in the White House—all too often men with physical courage are disappointing in their moral imagination— but the heroism here is remarkable for its tenacity. The above is merely one episode in a continuing saga which went on for five days in and out of the water, and left Kennedy at one point "miraculously saved from drowning (in a storm) by a group of Solomon Island natives who suddenly came up beside him in a large dugout canoe." Afterward, his back still injured (that precise back injury which was to put him on crutches eleven years later, and have him search for "spinal-fusion surgery" despite a warning that his chances of living through the operation were "extremely limited") afterward, he asked to go back on duty and became so bold in the attacks he made with his PT boat "that the crew didn't like to go out with him because he took so many chances."

It is the wisdom of a man who senses death within him and gambles that he can cure it by risking his life. It is the therapy of the instinct, and who is so wise as to call it irrational? Before he went into the Navy, Kennedy had been ailing. Washed out of Freshman year at Princeton by a prolonged trough of yellow jaundice, sick for a year at Harvard, weak already in the back from an injury at football, his trials suggest the self-hatred of a man whose resentment and ambition are too large for his body. Not everyone can discharge their furies on an analyst's couch, for some angers can be relaxed only by winning power, some rages are sufficiently monumental to demand that one try to become a hero or else fall back into that death which is already within the cells. But if one succeeds, the energy aroused can be exceptional. Talking to a man who had been with Kennedy in Hyannis Port the week before the convention, I heard that he was in a state of deep fatigue.

"Well, he didn't look tired at the convention," one commented.

"Oh, he had three days of rest. Three days of rest for him is like six months for us."

One thinks of that three-mile swim with the belt in his mouth and McMahon holding it behind him. There are pestilences which sit in the mouth and rot the teeth—in those five hours how much of the psyche must have been remade, for to give vent to the bite in one's jaws and yet use that rage to save a life: it is not so very many men who have the apocalytic sense that heroism is the First Doctor.

If one had a profound criticism of Kennedy it was that his public mind was too conventional, but that seemed to matter less than the fact of such a man in office because the law of political life had become so dreary that only a conventional mind could win an election. Indeed there could be no politics which gave warmth to one's body until the country had recovered its imagination, its pioneer lust for the unexpected and incalculable. It was the changes that might come afterward on which one could put one's hope. With such a man in office the myth of the nation would again be engaged, and the fact that he was Catholic would shiver a first existential vibration of consciousness into the mind of the White Protestant. For the first time in our history, the Protestant would have the pain and creative luxury of feeling himself in some tiny degree part of a minority, and that was an experience which might be incommensurable in its value to the best of them.

A Vignette of Adlai Stevenson; The Speeches: What Happened When the Teleprompter Jammed: How U.S.

Senator Eugene McCarthy Played the Matador. An Observation on the Name Fitzgerald

As yet we have said hardly a word about Stevenson. And his actions must remain a puzzle unless one dares a speculation about his motive, or was it his need?

So far as the people at the convention had affection for anyone, it was Stevenson, so far as they were able to generate any spontaneous enthusiasm, their cheers were again for Stevenson. Yet it was obvious he never had much chance because so soon as a chance would present itself he seemed quick to dissipate the opportunity. The day before the nominations, he entered the Sports Arena to take his seat as a delegate—the demonstration was spontaneous, noisy and prolonged; it was quieted only by Governor Collins' invitation for Stevenson to speak to the delegates. In obedience perhaps to the scruple that a candidate must not appear before the convention until nominations are done, Stevenson said no more than: "I am grateful for this tumultuous and moving welcome. After getting in and out of the Biltmore Hotel and this hall, I have decided I know whom you are going to nominate. It will be the last survivor." This dry reminder of the ruthlessness of politics broke the roar of excitement for his presence. The applause as he left the platform was like the dying fall-and-moan of a baseball crowd when a home run curves foul. The next day, a New York columnist talking about it said bitterly, "If he'd only gone through the motions, if he had just said that now he wanted to run, that he would work hard, and he hoped the delegates would vote for him. Instead he made that lame joke." One wonders. It seems almost as if he did not wish to win unless victory came despite himself, and then was overwhelming. There are men who are not heroes because they are too good for their time, and it is natural that defeats leave them bitter, tired, and doubtful of their right to make new history. If Stevenson had campaigned for a year before the convention, it is possible that he could have stopped Kennedy. At the least, the convention would have been enormously more exciting, and the nominations might have gone through half-a-dozen ballots before a winner was hammered into shape. But then Stevenson might also have shortened his life. One had the impression of a tired man who (for a politician) was sickened unduly by compromise. A year of maneuvering, broken promises, and detestable partners might have gutted him for the election campaign. If elected, it might have ruined him as a President. There is the possibility that he sensed his situation exactly this way, and knew that if he were to run for president, win and make a good one, he would first have to be restored, as one can indeed be restored, by an exceptional demonstration of love—love, in this case, meaning that the Party had a profound desire to keep him as their leader. The emotional truth of a last-minute victory for Stevenson over the Kennedy machine might have given him new energy; it would certainly have given him new faith in a country and a party whose good motives he was possibly beginning to doubt. Perhaps the fault he saw with his candidacy was that he attracted only the nicest people to himself and there were not enough of them. (One of the private amusements of the convention was to divine some of the qualities of the candidates by the style of the young women who put on hats and clothing and politicked in the colors of one presidential gent or another. Of course, half of them must have been hired models, but someone did the hiring and so it was fair to look for a common denominator. The Johnson girls tended to be plump, pie-faced, dumb sexy Southern; the Symingteeners seemed a touch mulish, stubborn, good-looking pluggers; the Kennedy ladies were the handsomest; healthy, attractive, tough, a little spoiled—they looked liked the kind of girls who had gotten all the dances in high school and/or worked for a year as an airline hostess before marrying well. But the Stevenson girls looked to be doing it for no money; they were good sorts, slightly horsy-faced, one had the impression they played field hockey in college.) It was indeed the pure, the saintly, the clean-living, the pacifistic, the vegetarian who seemed most for Stevenson, and the less humorous in the Kennedy camp were heard to remark bitterly that Stevenson had nothing going for him but a bunch of Goddamn Beatniks. This might even have had its sour truth. The demonstrations outside the Sports Arena for Stevenson seemed to have more than a fair proportion of tall, emaciated young men with thin, wry beards and three-string guitars accompanied (again in undue proportion) by a contingent of ascetic, face-washed young Beat ladies in sweaters and dungarees. Not to mention all the Holden Caulfields one could see from here to the horizon. But of course it is unfair to limit it so, for the Democratic gentry were also committed half en masse

for Stevenson, as well as a considerable number of movie stars, Shelley Winters for one: after the convention she remarked sweetly, "Tell me something nice about Kennedy so I can get excited about him."

What was properly astonishing was the way this horde of political half-breeds and amateurs came within distance of turning the convention from its preconceived purpose, and managed at the least to bring the only hour of thoroughgoing excitement the convention could offer.

But then nominating day was the best day of the week and enough happened to suggest that a convention out of control would be a spectacle as extraordinary in the American scale of spectator values as a close seventh game in the World Series or a tied fourth quarter in a professional-football championship. A political convention is after all not a meeting of a corporation's board of directors; it is a fiesta, a carnival, a pig-rooting, horse-snorting, band-playing, voice-screaming medieval get-together of greed, practical lust, compromised idealism, career-advancement, meeting, feud, vendetta, conciliation, of rabble-rousers, fist fights (as it used to be), embraces, drunks (again as it used to be) and collective rivers of animal sweat. It is a reminder that no matter how the country might pretend it has grown up and become tidy in its manners, bodiless in its legislative language, hygienic in its separation of high politics from private life, that the roots still come grubby from the soil, and that politics in America is still different from politics anywhere else because the politics has arisen out of the immediate needs, ambitions, and cupidities of the people, that our politics still smell of the bedroom and the kitchen, rather than having descended to us from the chill punctilio of aristocratic negotiation.

So. The Sports Arena was new, too pretty of course, tasteless in its design—it was somehow pleasing that the acoustics were so bad for one did not wish the architects well; there had been so little imagination in their design, and this arena would have none of the harsh grandeur of Madison Square Garden when it was aged by spectators' phlegm and feet over the next twenty years. Still it had some atmosphere; seen from the streets, with the spectators moving to the ticket gates, the bands playing, the green hot-shot special editions of the Los Angeles newspapers being hawked by the newsboys, there was a touch of the air of promise that precedes a bullfight, not something so good as the approach to the Plaza Mexico, but good, let us say, like the entrance into El Toreo of Mexico City, another architectural monstrosity, also with seats painted, as I remember, in rose-pink, and dark, milky sky-blue.

Inside, it was also different this nominating day. On Monday and Tuesday the air had been desultory, no one listened to the speakers, and everybody milled from one easy chatting conversation to another—it had been like a tepid Kaffeeklatsch for fifteen thousand people. But today there was a whip of anticipation in the air, the seats on the floor were filled, the press section was working, and in the gallery people were sitting in the aisles.

Sam Rayburn had just finished nominating Johnson as one came in, and the rebel yells went up, delegates started filing out of their seats and climbing over seats, and a pullulating dance of bodies and bands began to snake through the aisles, the posters jogging and whirling in time to the music. The dun color of the floor (faces, suits, seats and floor boards), so monotonous the first two days, now lit up with life as if an iridescent caterpillar had emerged from a fold of wet leaves. It was more vivid than one had expected, it was right, it felt finally like a convention, and from up close when one got down to the floor (where your presence was illegal and so consummated by sneaking in one time as demonstrators were going out, and again by slipping a five-dollar bill to a guard) the nearness to the demonstrators took on high color, that electric vividness one feels on the side lines of a football game when it is necessary to duck back as the ballcarrier goes by, his face tortured in the concentration of the moment, the thwomp of his tackle as acute as if one had been hit oneself.

That was the way the demonstrators looked on the floor. Nearly all had the rapt, private look of a passion or a tension which would finally be worked off by one's limbs, three hundred football players, everything from seedy delegates with jowl-sweating shivers to livid models, paid for their work that day, but stomping out their beat on the floor with the hypnotic adulatory grimaces of ladies who had lived for Lyndon these last ten years.

Then from the funereal rostrum, whose color was not so rich as mahogany nor so dead as a cigar, came the last of the requests for the delegates to take their seats. The seconding speeches began, one minute each; they ran for three and four, the minor-league speakers running on the longest as if the electric antenna of television was the lure of the Sirens, leading them out. Bored cheers applauded their concluding Götterdämmerungen and the nominations were open again. A favorite son, a modest demonstration, five seconding speeches, tedium.

Next was Kennedy's occasion. Governor Freeman of Minnesota made the speech. On the second or third sentence his television prompter jammed, an accident. Few could be aware of it at the moment; the speech seemed merely flat and surprisingly void of bravura. He was obviously no giant of extempore. Then the demonstration. Well-run, bigger than Johnson's, jazzier, the caliber of the costumes and decorations better chosen: the placards were broad enough, "Let's Back Jack," the floats were garish, particularly a papier-mâché or plastic balloon of Kennedy's head, six feet in diameter, which had nonetheless the slightly shrunken, over-red, rubbery look of a toy for practical jokers in one of those sleazy off–Times Square magic-and-gimmick stores; the band was suitably corny; and yet one had the impression this demonstration had been designed by some hands-to-hip interior decorator who said, "Oh, joy, let's have fun, let's make this *true* beer hall."

Besides, the personnel had something of the Kennedy *élan*, those paper hats designed to look like straw boaters with Kennedy's face on the crown, and small photographs of him on the ribbon, those hats which had come to symbolize the crack speed of the Kennedy team, that Madison Avenue cachet which one finds in bars like P. J. Clarke's, the elegance always giving its subtle echo of the Twenties so that the raccoon coats seem more numerous than their real count, and the colored waistcoats are measured by the charm they would have drawn from Scott Fitzgerald's eye. But there, it occurred to one for the first time that Kennedy's middle name was just that, Fitzgerald, and the tone of his crack lieutenants, the unstated style, was true to Scott. The legend of Fitzgerald had an army at last, formed around the self-image in the mind of every superior Madison Avenue opportunist that he was hard, he was young, he was In, his conversation was lean as wit, and if the work was not always scrupulous, well the style could aspire. If there came a good day . . . he could meet the occasion.

The Kennedy snake dance ran its thirty lively minutes, cheered its seconding speeches, and sat back. They were so sure of winning, there had been so many victories before this one, and this one had been scouted and managed so well, that hysteria could hardly be the mood. Besides, everyone was waiting for the Stevenson barrage which should be at least diverting. But now came a long tedium. Favorite sons were nominated, fat mayors shook their hips, seconders told the word to constituents back in Ponderwaygot County, treacly demonstrations tried to hold the floor, and the afternoon went by; Symington's hour came and went, a good demonstration, good as Johnson's (for good cause—they had pooled their demonstrators). More favorite sons, Governor Docking of Kansas declared "a genius" by one of his lady speakers in a tense go-back-to-religion voice. The hours went by, two, three, four hours, it seemed forever before they would get to Stevenson. It was evening when Senator Eugene McCarthy of Minnesota got up to nominate him.

The gallery was ready, the floor was responsive, the demonstrators were milling like bulls in their pen waiting for the *toril* to fly open—it would have been hard not to wake the crowd up, not to make a good speech. McCarthy made a great one. Great it was by the measure of convention oratory, and he held the crowd like a matador, timing their *oles!*, building them up, easing them back, correcting any sag in attention, gathering their emotion, discharging it, creating new emotion on the wave of the last, driving his passes tighter as he readied for the kill. "Do not reject this man who made us all proud to be called Democrats, do not leave this prophet without honor in his own party." One had not heard a speech like this since 1948 when Vito Marcantonio's voice, his harsh, shrill, bitter, street urchin's voice screeched through the loud-speakers at Yankee Stadium and lashed seventy thousand people into an uproar.

"There was only one man who said let's talk sense to the American people," McCarthy went on, his muleta furled for the *naturales*. "There was only one man who said let's talk sense to the American people," he repeated. "He said the promise of America is the promise of greatness. This was his call to greatness. . . . Do not forget this man. . . . Ladies and Gentlemen, I present to you not the favorite son of one state, but the favorite son of the fifty states, the favorite son of every country he has visited, the favorite son of every country which has not seen him but is secretly thrilled by his name" Bedlam. The kill. "Ladies and Gentlemen, I present to you Adlai Stevenson of Illinois." Ears and tail. Hooves and bull. A roar went up like the roar

one heard the day Bobby Thompson hit his home run at the Polo Grounds and the Giants won the pennant from the Dodgers in the third playoff game of the 1951 season. The demonstration cascaded onto the floor, the gallery came to its feet, the Sports Arena sounded like the inside of a marching drum. A tidal pulse of hysteria, exaltation, defiance, exhilaration, anger and roaring desire flooded over the floor. The cry which had gone up on McCarthy's last sentence had not paused for breath in five minutes, and troop after troop of demonstrators jammed the floor (the Stevenson people to be scolded the next day for having collected floor passes and sent them out to bring in new demonstrators) and still the sound mounted. One felt the convention coming apart. There was a Kennedy girl in the seat in front of me, the Kennedy hat on her head, a dimpled healthy brunette; she had sat silently through McCarthy's speech, but now, like a woman paying her respects to the power of natural thrust, she took off her hat and began to clap herself. I saw a writer I knew in the next aisle; he had spent a year studying the Kennedy machine in order to write a book on how a nomination is won. If Stevenson stampeded the convention, his work was lost. Like a reporter at a mine cave-in I inquired the present view of the window. "Who can think," was the answer, half frantic, half elated, "just watch it, that's all." I found a cool one, a New York reporter, who smiled in rueful respect. "It's the biggest demonstration I've seen since Wendell Willkie's in 1940," he said, and added, "God, if Stevenson takes it, I can wire my wife and move the family on to Hawaii."

"I don't get it."

"Well, every story I wrote said it was locked up for Kennedy."

Still it went on, twenty minutes, thirty minutes, the chairman could hardly be heard, the demonstrators refused to leave. The lights were turned out, giving a sudden theatrical shift to the sense of a crowded church at midnight, and a new roar went up, louder, more passionate than anything heard before. It was the voice, it was the passion, if one insisted to it that, of everything in America which was defeated, idealistic, innocent, alienated, outside and Beat, it was the potential voice of a new third of the nation whose psyche was ill from cultural malnutrition, it was powerful, it was extraordinary, it was larger than the decent, humorous, finicky, half-noble man who had called it forth, it was a cry from the Thirties when Time was simple, it was a resentment of the slick technique, the oiled gears, and the superior generals of Fitzgerald's Army; but it was also—and for this reason one could not admire it altogether, except with one's excitement—it was also the plea of the bewildered who hunger for simplicity again, it was the adolescent counterpart of the boss's depression before the unpredictable dynamic of Kennedy as President, it was the return to the sentimental dream of Roosevelt rather than the approaching nightmare of history's oncoming night, and it was inspired by a terror of the future as much as a revulsion of the present.

Fitz's Army held; after the demonstration was finally down, the convention languished for ninety minutes while Meyner and others were nominated, a fatal lapse of time because Stevenson had perhaps a chance to stop Kennedy if the voting had begun on the echo of the last cry for him, but in an hour and a half depression crept in again and emotions spent, the delegates who had wavered were rounded into line. When the vote was taken, Stevenson had made no gains. The brunette who had taken off her hat was wearing it again, and she clapped and squealed when Wyoming delivered the duke and Kennedy was in. The air was sheepish, like the mood of a suburban couple who forgive each other for cutting in and out of somebody else's automobile while the country club dance is on. Again, tonight, no miracle would occur. In the morning the papers would be moderate in their description of Stevenson's last change.

?

The political orator must know his crowd. He is the man who uses language as a device to reveal the "inner" depths of those who follow him. Often the shallowness of the followers works for the man who seeks power through language. Shakespeare's insights into Mark Antony's manipulation of the crowd set the scene for an understanding of the way one might pervert language in order to serve one's own ends. Mark Antony speaks to quell the crowd only to excite it into following a course of action which suits *Antony's* needs. The basis of Antony's speech is the dishonest use the speaker makes of Brutus, Caesar, and the crowd. Antony's language conveys the ambiguities of the passions locked into the search for power. When he calls Brutus "honorable," he does so in order to disarm the crowd. He means that Brutus is ambitious and therein lies his honor. This speech reveals the way language may be used to serve the interest of the speaker.

Norman Mailer understands the use of language as a means to create an image of the political "hipster." His essay focuses on the image of Kennedy seen from a perspective that reflects the American people's search for a hero. Mailer uses the image of the movie star to depict Kennedy as a "great box-office actor." Mailer skillfully uses his essay to bring together this image with the "double life" that Americans have been living since World War I. The metaphor of two rivers is Mailer's definition of this process. The river that is visible symbolizes the "unbelievably dull political life of the nation." In John Kennedy, Mailer merges these two strains of thought. The following questions focus on the language of Shakespeare and Norman Mailer as a symbolic metaphor for power.

1 How does Mark Antony approach the crowd? What does this reveal about his understanding of crowd behavior? What symbols does Shakespeare give Antony to win the crowd over to his point of view? What does this suggest about manipulation of crowd behavior?

2 How does Antony create ambiguity in the mind of the crowd? What words does he use to stir up their emotions? How does he use the power of suggestion? What does this

suggest about the speaker's awareness of his audience? What qualities about Antony emerge in this speech? What insights into Antony's character does one attain from an analysis of the speech?

3   How does Mailer set the scene for his essay on John Kennedy as a "superman" who comes to a "supermarket"? What image of the American people emerges in Mailer's introduction? Why is Los Angeles an apt symbol for a culture which seeks "the rootless pleasure world of an adult child"? Does Mailer understand the American audience as well as Antony understands his audience? How do Shakespeare and Mailer reveal an understanding of the power of suggestion inherent in the political use of language?

4   Why does Mailer focus on Pershing Square as the scene for this introduction of Kennedy? What parallels does this set up in the reader's mind? Discuss the description of the Kennedy circuslike political machine with the world of the hustlers in Pershing Square. How does Mailer connect these images to the conscious and unconscious life of Americans? How does Mailer merge both of these images in his depiction of John Kennedy?

5   Compare and contrast Mailer's technique of juxtaposing Kennedy with other political figures. How does Mailer present Truman? How does Mailer reveal Eisenhower as a symbol of the antihero? What image emerges from Mailer's depiction of Lyndon Johnson? What image emerges of Stevenson? How do each of these men indirectly work for Mailer to reveal his image of Kennedy? Does Antony do this in juxtaposing Brutus with Caesar as a man who wants power? What does this suggest?

6   Discuss the implications of Mailers line: "The life of politics and the life of myth had diverged too far...." How does Mailer use Christ, Roosevelt, and the depression? What does this suggest about the "common dan-

ger" which is missing in American life? What does Mailer mean when he says that America's need in those years was to take an existential turn...."? How does Mailer connect Kennedy's personal crisis to the need for an existential turn? How might this bring together politics and myth?

7   With the exception of the "Deer Park" sequence, Mailer describes Kennedy from afar; how effective is this technique? What does mystery suggest about the meaning underlying the image of Kennedy? How does Mailer use entertainers to reflect his portrait of Kennedy? Mailer links the winning of the convention to a football game. What does this suggest about the Kennedy machine? How does Mailer's image differ from the one Kennedy presents in his inaugural address? How does this compare and contrast with your image of John Kennedy? Does the photograph at the beginning of this essay reveal an image of Kennedy as a creation rather than a political actor? Develop what this suggests about the American political leader.

8   How does Mailer describe John Kennedy's winning of the Democratic nomination for the presidency? What images does he use to sum up his discussion of Kennedy? How does this statement compare and contrast with Mailer's last sentence: "In the morning the papers would be moderate in their description of Stevenson's last charge." What does this suggest about the existential hero?

9   Use Marcuse's essay to interpret Mailer's portrait of Kennedy. Does Kennedy appear as a Prometheus hero who suggests the concept of productivity? In what ways is Kennedy similar to Orpheus? Would you say that Kennedy's language is song, and his message is play? Mailer's emphasis on Kennedy's youth and movie star handsomeness links him to Narcissus. What do you think was the basis for the Kennedy magic? Did John Kennedy tap the "inner" spirit of America? Explain!

The true genius nearly always intrudes and disturbs. He talks to a temporal world out of a world eternal. And thus he says the wrong things at the right time. Eternal truths are never true at any given moment in history. The process of transformation has to reassert itself in order to digest and assimilate the utterly unpractical things that the genius has produced from the storehouse of eternity. Yet the genius is the healer for his time, because anything he betrays of eternal truth is healing.

Carl G. Jung

To find nature herself all her forms must be shattered.

Meister Eckhart

Hear the voice of the Bard!
Who present, past, and future sees.

William Blake

Of modern poetry: It begs no favours of the times. Dedicated to its goal and free from all ideology, it knows itself to be the equal of life, which needs no self-justification. In one embrace, as in one great living strophe, it gathers to its present all the past and the future, the human and the superhuman, planetary space and total space. Its alleged obscurity is due, not to its own nature, which is to enlighten, but to the darkness which it explores, and must explore: the dark of the soul herself and the dark of the mystery which envelops humans existence.

Out of the poetic need, which is one of the spirit, all the religions have been born, and by the poetic grace the divine spark is kept eternally alight within the human flint. When the mythologies founder, it is in poetry that the divine finds its refuge, perhaps its relay stage. As, in the antique procession, the Bearers of bread were succeeded by the Bearers of torches, so now, in the social order and the immediacies of life it is the poetic image which rekindles the high passion of mankind in its quest for light. . . .

Refusing to divorce art from life or love from knowledge, it is action, it is passion, it is power, a perpetual renewal that extends the boundaries. Love is its vital flame, independence is its law, and its domain is everywhere, an anticipation. It never wishes to be absence, nor refusal.

St.-John Perse

The very naming of a subject by a man of genius is the beginning of insight.

Ralph Waldo Emerson

Hold fast the form of sound words.

2 Timothy 1:13

The Poet Seeks to make the word Naked...

Language embodies within its structure the means which makes it possible for human beings to share their thoughts with one another. We know that Genesis begins with "the word," but we do not always know that "the word" contains both truths and illusions. The interpretation of "the word" is synonymous with the history of the human race. George Steiner says, "Language is not a description of a reality, but an answer to it, a challenge to it, an evasion from it." Poets challenge us to move in directions of self-discovery. Their songs open up new dimensions of reality for us to contemplate. They walk on well-traveled paths which no human being has ever walked on, or in the words of Wallace Stevens, they create "the wild country of the soul." To understand their messages, we must go beyond the veil of language.

BY WAY OF A PREFACE

ARTHUR RIMBAUD

Universal Mind has always thrown out its ideas naturally; men would pick up part of these fruits of the brain; they acted through, wrote books with them; and so things went along, since man did not work on himself, not being yet awake, or not yet in the fullness of his dream. Writers were functionaries. Author, creator, poet,—that man has never existed!

The first study for a man who wants to be a poet is the knowledge of himself, entire. He searches his soul, he inspects it, he tests it, he learns it. As soon as he knows it, he cultivates it: it seems simple: in every brain a natural development is accomplished: so many egoists proclaim themselves authors; others attribute their intellectual progress to themselves! But the soul has to be made monstrous, that's the point:—like *comprachicos*, if you like! Imagine a man planting and cultivating warts on his face.

One must, I say, be a *visonary*, make oneself a *visionary*.

The poet makes himself a *visionary* through a long, a prodigious and rational disordering of *all* the senses. Every form of love, of suffering, of madness; he searches himself, he consumes all the poisons in him, keeping only their quintessences. Ineffable torture in which he will need all his faith and superhuman strength, the great criminal, the great sickman, the accursed,—and the supreme Savant! For he arrives at the unknown! Since he has cultivated his soul—richer to begin with than any other! He arrives at the unknown; and even if, half crazed, in the end, he loses the understanding of his visions, he has seen them! Let him be destroyed in his leap by those unnamable, unutterable and innumerable things: there will come other horrible workers: they will begin at the horizons where he has succumbed.

. . . .

So then, the poet is truly a thief of fire.

Humanity is his responsibilty, even the animals; he must see to it that his inventions can be smelled, felt, heard. If what he brings back from beyond has form, he gives it form, if it is formless, he gives it formlessness. A language must be found; as a matter of fact, all speech being an idea, the time of a universal language will come! One has to be an academician—deader than a fossil—to finish a dictionary of any language at all. The weak-minded, beginning with the first letter of the alphabet, would soon be raving mad!

This harangue would be of the soul for the soul, summing up everything, perfumes, sounds, colors, thought grappling thought, and pulling. The poet would define the amount of unknown arising in his time in the universal soul; he would give more than the formula of his thought, more than the annotation of his march toward Progress! Enormity become norm, absorbed by every one, he would truly be the multiplier of progress!

This future, as you see, will be materialistic. Always full of *Number* and *Harmony*, these poems would be made to last. As a matter of fact it will still be Greek poetry in a way.

This eternal art will have its functions since poets are citizens. Poetry will no longer accompany action but will lead it.

These poets are going to exist! When the infinite servitude of woman shall have ended, when she will be able to live by and for herself; then, man—hitherto abominable—having given her her freedom, she to will be a poet. Woman will discover the unknown. Will her world be different from ours? She will discover strange, unfathomable things, repulsive, delicious. We shall take them, we shall understand them.

Meantime ask the poet for the new—ideas and forms. All the bright boys will imagine they have satisfied this demand: it isn't that at all!

POETRY
MARIANNE MOORE

I, too, dislike it: there are things that are important
        beyond all this fiddle.
  Reading it, however, with a perfect contempt for
      it, one discovers in
it after all, a place for the genuine.
    Hands that can grasp, eyes
    that can dilate, hair that can rise
      if it must, these things are important not
      because a
high-sounding interpretation can be put upon them
      but because they are
  useful. When they become so derivative as to
      become unintelligible,
  the same thing may be said for all of us, that we
    do not admire what
    we cannot understand: the bat
      holding on upside down or in quest of some-
      thing to
eat, elephants pushing, a wild horse taking a roll,
    a tireless wolf under
  a tree, the immovable critic twitching his skin
    like a horse that feels a flea, the base-
ball fan, the statistician—
    nor is it valid
      to discriminate against 'business and docu-
      ments and
school-books'; all these phenomena are important.
    One must make a distinction
    however: when dragged into prominence by half
      poets, the result is not poetry,
  nor till the poets among us can be
    'literalists of
    the imagination'—above
      insolence and triviality and can present
for inspection, imaginary gardens with real toads in
    them, shall we have
  it. In the meantime, if you demand on the one
    hand,
  the raw material of poetry in
    all its rawness and
    that which is on the other hand
      genuine, then you are interested in poetry.

REAL WORDS ARE NOT VAIN
LAO TZU

Real words are not vain,
Vain words not real;
And since those who argue prove nothing
A sensible man does not argue.
A sensible man is wiser than he knows,
While a fool knows more than is wise.
Therefore a sensible man does not devise resources:
The greater his use to others
The greater their use to him,
The more he yields to others
The more they yield to him.
The way of life cleaves without cutting:
Which, without need to say,
Should be man's way.

THE POET (A FRAGMENT)
JOHN KEATS

Where's the poet? show him! show him,
Muses nine! that I may know him!
'Tis the man who with a man
  Is an equal, be he king,
Or poorest of the beggar-clan,
  Or any other wondrous thing
A man may be 'twixt ape and Plato;
  'Tis the man who with a bird,
Wren or eagle, finds his way to
  All its instincts; he hath heard
The lion's roaring, and can tell
  What his horny throat expresseth,
And to him the tiger's yell
  Comes articulate and presseth
On his ear like mother-tongue.

RIDDLE OF THE WORLD
ALEXANDER POPE

Know then thyself, presume not God to scan,
The proper study of Mankind is Man.
Plac'd on this isthmus of a middle state,
A Being darkly wise, and rudely great:
With too much knowledge for the Sceptic side,
With too much weakness for the Stoic's pride,

He hangs between; in doubt to act, or rest;
In doubt to deem himself a God, or Beast;
In doubt his Mind or Body to prefer;
Born but to die, and reas'ning but to err;
Alike in ignorance, his reason such,
Whether he thinks too little, or too much:
Chaos of Thought and Passion, all confus'd;
Still by himself abus'd, or disabus'd;
Created half to rise, and half to fall;
Great Lord of all things, yet a prey to all;
Sole judge of truth, in endless error hurl'd:
The glory, jest, and riddle of the world!

I SIT AND LOOK OUT
WALT WHITMAN

I sit and look out upon all the sorrows of the world,
  and upon all oppression and shame,
I hear secret convulsive sobs from young men at
  anguish with themselves, remorseful after deeds
  done,
I see in low life the mother misused by her children,
  dying, neglected, gaunt, desperate,
I see the wife misused by her husband, I see the
  treacherous seducer of young women,
I mark the ranklings of jealousy and unrequited love
  attempted to be hid, I see these sights on the
  earth,
I see the workings of battle, pestilence, tyranny,
  I see martyrs and prisoners,
I observe a famine at sea, I observe the sailors
  casting lots who shall be kill'd to preserve the
  lives of the rest,
I observe the slights and degradations cast by arrogant
  persons upon laborers, the poor, and upon
  negroes, and the like;
All these—all the meanness and agony without end
  I sitting look out upon,
See, hear, and am silent.

I DIED FOR BEAUTY
EMILY DICKINSON

I died for Beauty—but was scarce
Adjusted in the Tomb
When One who died for Truth, was lain
In an adjoining Room—

He questioned softly "Why I failed"?
"For Beauty", I replied—
"And I—for Truth—Themself are One—
We Brethren, are", He said—

And so, as Kinsmen, met a Night—
We talked between the Rooms—
Until the Moss had reached our lips—
And covered up—our names—

THE TEST (MUSA LOQUITUR)
RALPH WALDO EMERSON

I hung my verses in the wind,
Time and tide their faults may find.
All were winnowed through and through,
Five lines lasted sound and true . . .

Sunshine cannot bleach the snow,
Nor time unmake what poets know.
Have you eyes to find the five
Which five hundred did survive?

**. . . human language, in its normal use, is free from
the control of independently identifiable external
stimuli or internal states and is not restricted to any
practical communicative function, in contrast, for
example, to the pseudo language of animals. It is
thus free to serve as an instrument of free thought
and self-expression. The limitless possibilities of
thought and imagination are reflected in the creative
aspect of language use.**
—from *Cartesian Linguistics,* **Noam Chomsky**

**An artist, any artist, must say where it is in the
world that he actually is. And by doing this he will
also say who he is. But not matter what a man tries,
the products of his thinking, indeed of his life, will
identitfy who and where. . . .**
"LeRoi Jones Talking,"
from *Home: Social Essays,*
LeRoi Jones

MAN

SIR JOHN DAVIES

I know my body's of so frail a kind,
   As force without, fevers within, can kill;
I know the heavenly nature of my mind,
   But 'tis corrupted both in wit and will.

I know my soul hath power to know all things
   Yet is she blind and ignorant in all;
I know I am one of nature's little kings,
   Yet to the least and vilest things am thrall.

I know my life's a pain, and but a span;
   I know my sense is mocked with everything;
And to conclude, I know myself a man,
   Which is a proud, and yet a wretched thing.

WHY IS MY VERSE SO BARREN OF NEW PRIDE

WILLIAM SHAKESPEARE

Why is my verse so barren of new pride,
So far from variation or quick change?
Why with the time do I not glance aside
To new-found methods and to compounds strange?
Why write I still all one, ever the same,
And keep invention in a noted weed,
That every word doth almost tell my name,
Showing their birth and where they did proceed?
O, know, sweet love, I always write of you,
And you and love are still my argument;
So all my best is dressing old words new,
Spending again what is already spent:
   For as the sun is daily new and old,
   So is my love still telling what is told.

OF MODERN POETRY

WALLACE STEVENS

The poem of the mind in the act of finding
What will suffice. It has not always had
To find: the scene was set; it repeated what
Was in the script.
          Then the theatre was changed
To something else. Its past was a souvenir.
It has to be living, to learn the speech of the place.
It has to face the men of the time and to meet
The women of the time. It has to think about war
And it has to find what will suffice. It has
To construct a new stage. It has to be on that stage
And, like an insatiable actor, slowly and
With meditation, speak words that in the ear,
In the delicatest ear of the mind, repeat,
Exactly, that which it wants to hear, at the sound
Of which, an invisible audience listens,
Not to the play, but to itself, expressed
In an emotion as of two people, as of two
Emotions becoming one. The actor is
A metaphysician in the dark, twanging
An instrument, twanging a wiry string that gives
Sounds passing through sudden rightnesses, wholly
Containing the mind, below which it cannot descend,
Beyond which it has no will to rise.
          It must

Be the finding of a satisfaction, and may
Be of a man skating, a woman dancing, a woman
Combing. The poem of the act of the mind.

The world's contents are given to each of us in an order so foreign to our subjective interests that we can hardly by an effort of the imagination picture to ourselves what it is like. We have to break that order altogether,—and by picking out from it the items which concern us, and connecting them with others far away, which we say "belong" with them, we are able to make out definite threads of sequence and tendency; to foresee particular liabilities and get ready for them; and to enjoy simplicity and harmony in place of what was chaos. Is not the sum of your actual experience taken at this moment and impartially added together an utter chaos?

         from "Reflex Action and Theism,"
         The Will to Believe
         William James

IN MY CRAFT OR SULLEN ART
DYLAN THOMAS

In my craft or sullen art
Exercised in the still night
When only the moon rages
And the lovers lie abed
I labour by singing light
Not for ambition or bread
Or the strut and trade of charms
On the ivory stages
But for the common wages
Of their most secret heart.

Not for the proud man apart
From the raging moon I write
On these spindrift pages
Nor for the towering dead
With their nightingales and psalms
But for the lovers, their arms
Round the griefs of the ages,
Who pay no praise or wages
Nor heed my craft or art.

The imagination is the power of the mind over the possibilities of thing. . . . We cannot look at the past or the future except by means of the imagination. . . . [The imagination] enables us to live our own lives. We have it because we do not have enough without it. . . . The imagination is the power that enables us to perceive the normal in the abnormal, the opposite of chaos in chaos. . . . The truth seems to be that we live in concepts of the imagination before the reason has established them. If this is true, then reason is simply the methodizer of the imagination. It may be that the imagination is a miracle of logic and that its exquisite divinations are calculations beyond analysis, as the conclusions of the reason are calculations wholly within analysis. If so, one understands perfectly that "in the service of love and imagination nothing can be too lavish, too sublime or too festive."

from "Imagination as Value,"
The Necessary Angel
Wallace Stevens

Poetry was born in magic, grew up with religion, survived the age of reason, and is now threatened by the perversion of propaganda in the twentieth century. The ritual of language binds man to his community and expresses the relation between a human world and a divine imagination. This contradiction between past and present is expressed by two attitudes toward the warrior hero. In *The Aeneid* Virgil wrote: "of arms and the man I sing," a line that pays homage to the man of action. In our time, Ernest Hemingway echoes the loss of a world which no longer provides man with meaningful order to connect the individual to his community. In *A Farewell to Arms* Lieutenant Henry expresses this loss:

> I was always embarrassed by the words sacred, glorious, and sacrifice and the expression in vain. We had heard them, sometimes standing in the rain almost out of earshot, so that only the shouted words came through, and had read them on proclamations that were slapped up by bill posters over other proclamations, now for a long time, and I had seen nothing sacred, and the things that were glorious had no glory and the sacrifices were like the stockyards of Chicago if nothing was done with the meat except bury it. There were many words that you could not stand to hear and finally only the names of places had dignity.

This man is intensely aware of his loss. Life seems to be drifting away from him. The use of language reveals a deep "inner" wound. Hemingway seeks to end the corruption in language. His character, as do most of Hemingway's creations, seeks a personal ritual to enable him to confront death with dignity. This search echoes the modern dilemma which reflects the need for human beings to find a form which praises all that is. We need a vision that will restore human dignity.

This need provides the poet with the creative tension to sing his song in a language which cannot be unraveled by the elements in ordinary speech. For Ezra Pound these are the images which "move among the perfection of lovers alone." The relation between the elements of language is, in Yeats' phrase, "the stitching and unstitching" which provides man with the embroidery to explore the known and the unknown. What the poet says cannot be unsaid. And perhaps the naming of an experience is what brings us to see how we resolve our contrasts. Blake says, "I look through the eye, not with it." He brings together the "inner" waves of consciousness with the "outer" spirit of time. The poet seeks to delineate experience so that we may have a moment of contemplation. For Frost the poem "begins in delight and ends in wisdom." This suggests what insights are revealed to us through the poet's eye. Dylan Thomas describes poetry as "speeches made on the way to the grave." These speeches capture the essence of the human imagination at work. The dehumanization which seems oppressive in the twentieth century is made visible by Theodore Roethke when he says: "We think by feeling what is there to know." Poetry brings this to our consciousness and allows us for a moment to go beyond the illusion of truth. We gaze into a stream of clear water to see the pebbles in our souls. Like Hemingway's Henry, we too are uncertain, and we need to renew our faith in the experience of the moment. The poets among us deal with the language of emotions. They present us with a way to know, as Conrad Aiken says, "the profound myth of personal existence and experience."

The following questions direct your attention to "a territory not found in books." To understand the landscape of the mind's eye, we must connect the individual to his language and the language to the experience.

1 How do these poems reflect the search for forms to express a vision of the human imagination?

2 What symbols are used to bring the reader to confront his or her emotions? Select those poets who relate love to poetry. How do these poets use their symbols to reveal the connection between love and poetry?

3 Which of the poems "present for inspection, imaginary gardens with real toads in them"? How do these poets use fiction to reflect on "real" experiences? What does this suggest about the flexibility built into our language?

4 What poems bring together the union of opposites? What does this suggest about how one might resolve contradictions?

5 How does poetry go beyond the categories of language? Would a scientist view poetry as a meaningless statement? Explain! Plato in *The Republic* says that the poet should be banished from the state. Discuss who might agree with this statement. Would Kennedy in his inaugural speech agree with Plato's statement? Explain!

6 Which of the poets come close to the images of Orpheus and Narcissus as discussed by Marcuse? Does the inability to appreciate poetry come from the fear that poetry is not part of the Promethean ethic of productivity? Explain!

7 What image of man emerges from these poems? How do these images suggest universal symbols? In what ways do the poets transform the world of isolation? How does the poem express a unity between man and his world? What does this suggest about the language of poetry?

While the Women Weep

MRS. MARTIN LUTHER KING

These three widows are the wives of men who have been assassinated. Reread the poem "The Mother" (at the beginning of this chapter) and apply it to the woman who marries the man who seeks a political career.

MRS. JOHN F. KENNEDY

MRS. ROBERT F. KENNEDY

THE BOOK OF RUTH

Now it came to pass in the days when the judges ruled, that there was a famine in the land. And a certain man of Bethlehem-judah went to sojourn in the country of Moab, he, and wife, and his two sons. And the name of the man was Elimelech, and the name of his wife Naomi, and the name of his two sons Mahlon and Chilion, Ephrathies of Bethlehem-judah. And they came into the country of Moab and continued there.

And Elimelech Naomi's husband died; and she was left, and her two sons. And they took them wives of the women of Moab; the name of the one was Orpah and the name of the other Ruth; and they dwelled there about ten years. And Mahlon and Chilion died also both of them, and the woman was left [bereft] of her two sons and her husband.

Then she arose with her daughters-in-law that she might return from the country of Moab; for she had heard in the country of Moab how that the Lord had visited his people in giving them bread. Wherefore she went forth out of the place where she was, and her two daughters-in-law with her; and they went on the way to return unto the land of Judah. And Naomi said unto her two daughters-in-law, "Go, return each to her mother's house; the Lord deal kindly with you, as ye have dealt with the dead, and with me. The Lord grant you that ye may find rest, each of you in the house of her husband." Then she kissed them, and they lifted up their voice and wept. And they said unto her, "Surely we will return with thee unto thy people."

And Naomi said, "Turn again, my daughters; why will ye go with me? Are there yet any more sons in my womb, that they may be your husbands? Turn again, my daughters, go your way; for I am too old to have a husband. If I should say, 'I have hope,' if I should have a husband also tonight, and should also bear

sons, would ye tarry for them till they were grown? Would ye stay for them from having husbands? Nay, my daughters; for it grieveth me much for your sakes that the hand of the Lord is gone out against me." And they lifted up their voice and wept again, and Orpah kissed her mother-in-law; but Ruth clave unto her. And she said, "Behold, thy sister-in-law is gone back unto her people and unto her gods; return thou after thy sister-in-law."

And Ruth said, "Entreat me not to leave thee or to return from following after thee, for whither thou goest, I will go; and where thou lodgest, I will lodge. Thy people shall be my people and thy God my God. Where thou diest will I die, and there will I be buried. The Lord do so to me and more also, if aught but death part thee and me."

When she saw that she was steadfastly minded to go with her, then she left speaking unto her. So they two went until they came to Bethlehem. And it came to pass, when they were come to Bethlehem, that all the city was moved about them, and they said, "Is this Naomi?"

And she said unto them, "Call me not Naomi, call me Mara; for the Almighty hath dealt very bitterly with me. I went out full, and the Lord hath brought me home again empty. Why then call ye me Naomi, seeing the Lord hath testified against me, and the Almighty hath afflicted me?"

So Naomi returned and Ruth the Moabites, her daughter-in-law, with her, which returned out of the country of Moab; and they came to Bethlehem in the beginning of barley harvest.

And Naomi had a kinsman of her husband's, a mighty man of wealth, of the family of Elimelech; and his name was Boaz. And Ruth the Moabites said unto Naomi, "Let me now go to the field, and glean ears of corn after him in whose sight I shall find grace." And she said unto her, "Go, my daughter." And she went, and came and gleaned in the field after the reapers; and her hap was to light on a part of the field belonging unto Boaz, who was of the kindred of Elimelech.

And behold, Boaz came from Bethlehem, and said unto the reapers, "The Lord be with you." And they answered him, "The Lord bless thee."

Then said Boaz unto his servant that was set over the reapers, "Whose damsel is this?"

And the servant that was set over the reapers answered and said, "It is the Moabitish damsel that came back with Naomi out of the country of Moab; and she said, 'I pray you, let me glean and gather after the reapers among the sheaves.' So she came and hath continued even from the morning until now, that she tarried a little in the house."

Then said Boaz unto Ruth, "Hearest thou not, my daughter? Go not to glean in another field, neither go from hence, but abide here fast by my maidens. Let thine eyes be on the field that they do reap, and go thou after them. Have I not charged the young men that they shall not touch thee? And when thou art athirst, go unto the vessels, and drink of that which the young men have drawn."

Then she fell on her face and bowed herself to the ground, and said unto him, "Why have I found grace in thine eyes that thou shouldest take knowledge of me, seeing I am a stranger?"

And Boaz answered and said unto her, "It hath fully been showed me all that thou hast done unto thy mother-in-law since the death of thy husband; and how thou hast left thy father and thy mother and the land of thy nativity, and art come unto a people which thou knewest not heretofore. The Lord recompense thy work, and a full reward be given

thee of the Lord God of Israel, under whose wings thou art come to trust."

Then she said, "Let me find favor in thy sight, my lord; for that thou hast comforted me, and for that thou hast spoken friendly unto thy handmaid, though I be not like unto one of thy handmaidens."

And Boaz, said unto her, "At mealtime come thou hither and eat of the bread and dip thy morsel in the vinegar."

And she sat beside the reapers; and he reached her parched corn, and she did eat and was sufficed, and left. And when she was risen up to glean, Boaz commanded his young men, saying, "Let her glean even among the sheaves, and reproach her not; and let fall also some of the handfuls of purpose for her, and leave them, that she may glean them, and rebuke her not."

So she gleaned in the field until even and beat out that she had gleaned; and it was about an ephah of barley. And she took it up and went into the city. And her mother-in-law saw what she had gleaned; and she brought forth and gave to her that she had reserved after she was sufficed. And her mother-in-law said unto her, "Where hast thou gleaned today? And where wroughtest thou? Blessed be he that did take knowledge of thee."

And she showed her mother-in-law with whom she had wrought, and said, "The man's name with whom I wrought today is Boaz."

And Naomi said unto her daughter-in-law, "Blessed be he of the Lord, who hath not left off his kindness to the living and to the dead." And Naomi said unto her, "The man is near of kin unto us, one of our next kinsmen."

And Ruth the Moabitess said, "He said unto me also, 'Thou shalt keep fast by my young men until they have ended all my harvest.'"

And Naomi said unto Ruth her

daughter-in-law, "It is good, my daughter, that thou go out with his maidens, that they meet thee not in any other field." So she kept fast by the maidens of Boaz to glean unto the end of barley harvest and of wheat harvest; and dwelt with her mother-in-law.

Then Naomi her mother-in-law said unto her, "My daughter, shall I not seek rest with thee that it may be well with thee? And now is not Boaz of our kindred, with those maidens thou wast? Behold, he winnoweth barley tonight in the threshingfloor. Wash thyself therefore and anoint thee, and put thy raiment upon thee, and get thee down to the floor; but make not thyself known unto the man until he shall have done eating and drinking. And it shall be, when he lieth down, that thou shalt mark the place where he shall lie, and thou shalt go in and uncover his feet and lay thee down; and he will tell thee what thou shalt do."

And she said unto her, "All that thou sayest unto me I will do."

And she went down unto the floor and did according to all that her mother-in-law bade her. And when Boaz had eaten and drunk, and his heart was merry, he went to lie down at the end of the heap of corn; and she came softly and uncovered his feet and laid her down. And it came to pass at midnight that the man was afraid, and turned himself; and behold, a woman lay at his feet. And he said, "Who art thou?"

And she answered, "I am Ruth thy handmaid; spread therefore thy skirt over thy handmaid, for thou art a near kinsman."

And he said, "Blessed be thou of the Lord, my daughter, for thous hast showed more kindness in the latter end than at the beginning, inasmuch as thou followedst not young men, whether poor or rich. And now, my daughter, fear not; I will do to thee all that thou requirest, for all the city of my people doth know that thou art a virtuous woman. And now it is true that I am thy near kinsman; howbeit there is a kinsman nearer than I. Tarry this night, and it shall be in the morning that if he will perform unto thee the part of a kinsman, well, let him do the kinsman's part; but if he will not do the part of a kinsman to thee, then will I do the part of a kinsman to thee, as the Lord liveth. Lie down until the morning."

And she lay at his feet until the morning, and she rose up before one could know another. And he said, "Let it not be known that a woman came into the floor." Also he said, "Bring the veil [mantle] that thou hast upon thee, and hold it." And when she held it, he measured six measures of barley and laid it on her; and she went into the city.

And when she came to her mother-in-law, she said, "Who art thou, my daughter?"

And she told her all that the man had done to her. And she said, "These six measures of barley gave he me; for he said to me, 'Go not empty unto thy mother-in-law.' "

Then said she, "Sit, still, my daughter, until thou know how the matter will fall; for the man will not be in rest until he have finished the thing this day."

Then went Boaz up to the gate and sat him down there: and behold, the kinsman of whom Boaz spake came by; unto whom he said, "Ho, such a one! turn aside, sit down here." And he turned aside and sat down.

And he took ten men of the elders of the city and said, "Sit ye down here." And they sat down.

And he said unto the kinsman, "Naomi, that is come again out of the country of Moab, selleth a parcel of land, which was our brother Elimelech's; and I thought to advertise thee, saying, 'Buy it before the inhabitants, and before the elders of my people.' If thou wilt redeem it, redeem it. But if thou wilt not redeem it, then tell me that I may know; for there is none to redeem it beside thee; and I am after thee."

And he said, "I will redeem it."

Then said Boaz, "What day thou buyest the field of the hand of Naomi, thou must buy it also of Ruth the Moabitess, the wife of the dead, to raise up the name of the dead upon his inheritance."[1]

And the kinsman said, "I cannot redeem it for myself lest I mar mine own inheritance. Redeem thou my right to thyself, for I cannot redeem it."

Now this was the manner in former time in Israel concerning redeeming and concerning changing, for to confirm all things: a man plucked off his shoe and give it to his neighbor; and this was a testimony in Israel. Therefore the kinsman said unto Boaz. "Buy it for thee." So he drew off his shoe.

And Boaz said unto the elders and unto all the people, "Ye are witnesses this day that I have bought all that

[1] That is, you must buy Ruth also, to carry on the name of her late husband's family.

was Elimelech's, and all that was Chilion's and Mahlon's, of the hand of Naomi. Moreover Ruth The Moabitess, the wife of Mahlon, have I purchased to be my wife, to raise up the name of the dead upon his inheritance, that the name of the dead be not cut off from among his brethren and from the gate of his place: ye are witnesses this day."

And all the people that were in the gate, and the elders, said, "We are witnesses. The Lord make the woman that is come into thine house like Rachel and like Leah, which two did build the house of Israel; and do thou worthily in Ephratah and be famous in Bethlehem. And let thy house be like the house of Pharez, whom Tamar bare unto Judah, of the seed which the Lord shall give thee of this young woman."

So Boaz took Ruth, and she was his wife. And when he went in unto her, the Lord gave her conception, and she bare a son. And the women said unto Naomi, "Blessed be the Lord, which hath not left thee this day without a kinsman, that his name may be famous in Israel. And he shall be unto thee a restorer of thy life and a nourisher of thine old age; for thy daughter-in-law, which loveth thee, which is better to thee than seven sons, hath borne him."

And Naomi took the child and laid it in her bosom, and became nurse unto it. And the women her neighbors gave it a name, saying "There is a son born to Naomi"; and they called his name Obed: he is the father of Jesse, the father of David.

Great Mothers

In the sketch shown above by Leonardo da Vinci, we see the archetypal representation of the Great Mother motif. Saint Anne is the mother of Mary, and Mary is the mother of the Christ Child. Here the human mothers make possible a double birth: (1) the birth of human beings into this world, and (2) their birth, after death, into the world of eternity. In the following essay by Eric Wolf, the Virgin of Guadalupe appears as the symbolic representation of Mexico; she is the Great Mother, as country, who makes it possible to link the past, present, and future.

THE VIRGIN OF GUADALUPE

ERIC R. WOLF

Occasionally, we encounter a symbol which seems to enshrine the major hopes and aspirations of an entire society.[1] Such a master symbol is represented by the Virgin of Guadalupe, Mexico's patron saint. During the Mexican War of Independence against Spain, her image preceded the insurgents into battle.[2] Emiliano Zapata and his agrarian rebels fought under her emblem in the Great Revolution of 1910.[3] Today, her image adorns house fronts and interiors, churches and home altars, bull rings and gambling dens, taxis and buses, restaurants and houses of ill repute. She is celebrated in popular song and verse. Her shrine at Tepeyac, immediately north of Mexico City, is visited each year by hundreds of thousands of pilgrims, ranging from the inhabitants of far-off Indian villages to the members of socialist trade union locals. "Nothing to be seen in Canada or Europe," says F. S. C. Northrop, "equals it in the volume or the vitality of its moving quality or in the depth of its spirit of religious devotion."[4]

In this paper, I should like to discuss this Mexican master symbol, and the ideology which surrounds it. In making use of the term "master symbol," I do not wish to imply that belief in the symbol is common to all Mexicans. We are not dealing here with an element of a putative national character, defined as a common denominator of all Mexican nationals. It is no longer legitimate to assume "that any member of the [national] group will exhibit certain regularities of behavior which are common in high degree among the other members of the society."[5] Nations, like other complex societies, must, however, "possess cultural forms or mechanisms which groups involved in the same over-all web of relationships can use in their formal and informal dealings with each other."[6] Such forms develop

[1] Parts of this paper were presented to the Symposium on Ethnic and National Ideologies, Annual Spring Meeting of the American Ethnological Society in conjunction with the Philadelphia Anthropological Society, on 12 May 1956.

[2] Niceto de Zamacois, *Historia de México* (Barcelona-Mexico, 1878–82), VI, 253.

[3] Antonio Pompa y Pompa, *Album del IV centenario guadalupano* (Mexico, 1938), p. 173.

[4] F. S. C. Northrop, *The Meeting of East and West* (New York, 1946), p. 25.

[5] David G. Mandelbaum, "On the Study of National Character," *American Anthropologist*, LV (1953), p. 185.

[6] Eric R. Wolf, "Aspects of Group Relations in a Complex Society: Mexico," *American Anthropologist*, LVII (1956), 1065–1078.

historically, hand in hand with other processes which lead to the formation of nations, and social groups which are caught up in these processes must become "acculturated" to their usage.[7] Only where such forms exist, can communication and coördinated behavior be established among the constituent groups of such a society. They provide the cultural idiom of behavior and ideal representations through which different groups of the same society can pursue and manipulate their different fates within a coördinated framework. This paper, then, deals with one such cultural form, operating on the symbolic level. The study of this symbol seems particularly rewarding, since it is not restricted to one set of social ties, but refers to a very wide range of social relationships.

The image of the Guadalupe and her shrine at Tepeyac are surrounded by an origin myth.[8] According to this myth, the Virgin Mary appeared to Juan Diego, a Christianized Indian of commoner status, and addressed him in Nahuatl. The encounter took place on the Hill of Tepeyac in the year 1531, ten years after the Spanish Conquest of Tenochtitlan. The Virgin commanded Juan Diego to seek out the archbishop of Mexico and to inform him of her desire to see a church built in her honor on Tepeyac Hill. After Juan Diego was twice unsuccessful in his efforts to carry out her order, the Virgin wrought a miracle. She bade Juan Diego pick roses in a sterile spot where normally only desert plants could grow, gathered the roses into the Indian's cloak, and told him to present cloak and roses to the incredulous archbishop. When Juan Diego unfolded his cloak before the bishop, the image of the Virgin was miraculously stamped upon it. The bishop acknowledged the miracle, and ordered a shrine built where Mary had appeared to her humble servant.

The shrine, rebuilt several times in centuries to follow, is today a basilica, the third highest kind of church in Western Christendom. Above the central altar hangs Juan Diego's cloak with the miraculous image. It shows a young woman without child, her head lowered demurely in her shawl. She wears an open crown and flowing gown, and stands upon a half moon symbolizing the Immaculate Conception.

The shrine of Guadalupe was, however, not the first religious structure built on Tepeyac; nor was Guadalupe the first female supernatural associated with the hill. In pre-Hispanic times, Tepeyac had housed a temple to the earth and fertility goddess Tonantzin, Our Lady Mother, who—like the Guadalupe—was associated with the moon. Temple, like basilica, was the center of large scale pilgrimages. That the veneration accorded the Guadalupe drew inspiration from the earlier worship of Tonantzin is attested by several Spanish friars. F. Bernardino de Sahagún, writing fifty years after the Conquest, says: "Now that the Church of Our Lady of Guadalupe has been built there, they call her Tonantzin too. . . . The term refers . . . to that ancient Tonantzin and this state of affairs should be remedied, because the proper name of the Mother of God is not Tonantzin, but Dios and Nantzin. It seems to be a satanic device to mask idolatry . . . and they come from far away to visit that Tonantzin, as much as before; a devotion which is also suspect because there are many churches of Our Lady everywhere and they do not go to them; and they come from faraway lands to this Tonantzin as of old."[9] F. Martín de León wrote in a similar vein: "On the hill where Our Lady of Guadalupe is they adored the idol of a goddess they called Tonantzin, which means Our Mother, and this is also the name they give Our Lady and they always say they are going to Tonantzin or they are celebrating Tonantzin and many of them understand this in the old way and not in the modern way. . . ."[10] The syncretism was still alive in the seventeenth century. F. Jacinto de la Serna, in discussing the pilgrimages to the Guadalupe at Tepeyac, noted: ". . . it is the purpose of the wicked to [worship] the goddess and not the Most Holy Virgin, or both together."[11]

Increasingly popular during the sixteenth century, the Guadalupe cult gathered emotional impetus during the seventeenth. During this century appear the first known pictorial representations of the Guadalupe, apart from the miraculous original; the first poems are written in her honor; and the first sermons

[7] Eric R. Wolf, "La formación de la nación," *Ciencias Sociales*, IV, 50–51.

[8] Ernest Gruening, *Mexico and Its Heritage* (New York, 1928), p. 235.

[9] Bernardino de Sahagún, *Historia general de las cosas de nueva españa* (Mexico, 1938), I, lib. 6.

[10] Quoted in Carlos A. Echánove Trujillo, *Sociología mexicana* (Mexico, 1948), p. 105.

[11] Quoted in Jesús Amaya, *La madre de Dios: genesis e historia de nuestra señora de Guadalupe* (Mexico, 1931), p. 230.

announce the transcendental implications of her supernatural appearance in Mexico and among Mexicans.[12] Historians have long tended to neglect the seventeenth century which seemed "a kind of Dark Age in Mexico." Yet "this quiet time was of the utmost importance in the development of Mexican Society."[13] During this century, the institution of the hacienda comes to dominate Mexican life.[14] During this century, also, "New Spain is ceasing to be 'new' and to be 'Spain.' "[15] These new experiences require a new cultural idiom, and in the Guadalupe cult, the component segments of Mexican colonial society encountered cultural forms in which they could express their parallel interests and longings.

The primary purpose of this paper is not, however, to trace the history of the Guadalupe symbol. It is concerned rather with its functional aspects, its roots and reference to the major social relationships of Mexican society.

The first set of relationships which I would like to single out for consideration are the ties of kinship, and the emotions generated in the play of relationships within families. I want to suggest that some of the meanings of the Virgin symbol in general, and of the Guadalupe symbol in particular, derive from these emotions. I say "some meanings" and I use the term "derive" rather than "originate," because the form and function of the family in any given society are themselves determined by other social factors: technology, economy, residence, political power. The family is but one relay in the circuit within which symbols are generated in complex societies. Also, I used the plural "families" rather than "family," because there are demonstrably more than one kind of family in Mexico.[16] I shall simplify the available information on Mexican family life, and discuss the material in terms of two major types of families.[17] The first kind of family is congruent with the closed and static life of the Indian village. It may be called the Indian family. In this kind of family, the husband is ideally dominant, but in reality labor and authority are shared equally among both marriage partners. Exploitation of one sex by the other is atypical; sexual feats do not add to a person's status in the eyes of others. Physical punishment and authoritarian treatment of children are rare. The second kind of family is congruent with the much more open, mobile, manipulative life in communities which are actively geared to the life of the nation, a life in which power relationships between individuals and groups are of great moment. This kind of family may be called the Mexican family. Here, the father's authority is unquestioned on both the real and the ideal plane. Double sex standards prevail, and male sexuality is charged with a desire to exercise domination. Children are ruled with a heavy hand; physical punishment is frequent.

The Indian family pattern is consistent with the behavior towards the Guadalupe noted by John Bushnell in the Matlazinca speaking community of San Juan Atzingo in the Valley of Toluca.[18] There, the image of the Virgin is addressed in passionate terms as a source of warmth and love, and the *pulque* or century plant beer drunk on ceremonial occasions is identified with her milk. Bushnell postulates that here the Guadalupe is identified with the mother as a source of early satisfactions, never again experienced after separation from the mother and emergence into social adulthood. As such, the Guadalupe embodies a longing to return to the pristine state in which hunger and unsatisfactory social relations are minimized. The second family pattern is also consistent with a symbolic identification of Virgin and mother, yet this time within a context of adult male dominance and sexual assertion, discharged against submissive females and children. In this second context, the Guadalupe symbol is charged with the energy of rebellion against the father. Her image is the embodiment of hope in a victorious outcome of the struggle between generations.

[12] Francisco de la Maza, *El guadalupismo mexicano* (Mexico, 1953), pp. 12–14, 143, 30, 33, 82.

[13] Lesley B. Simpson, "Mexico's Forgotten Century," *Pacific Historical Review*, XXII (1953), 115, 114.

[14] François Chevalier, *La formation des grands domaines au Mexique* (Paris, 1952), p. xii.

[15] de la Maza, p. 41.

[16] María Elvira Bermúdez, *La vida familiar del mexicano* (Mexico, 1955), chapters 2 and 3.

[17] For relevant material, see: Bermúdez; John Gillin, "Ethos and Cultural Aspects of Personality," and Robert Redfield and Sol Tax, "General Characteristics of Present-Day Mesoamerican Indian Society," in Sol Tax, ed., *Heritage of Conquest* (Glencoe, 1952), pp. 193–212, 31–

39; Gordon W. Hewes, "Mexicans in Search of the 'Mexican'," *American Journal of Economics and Sociology*, XIII (1954), 209–223; Octavio Paz, *El labertino de la soledad* (Mexico, 1947), pp. 71–89.

[18] John Bushnell, "La Virgen de Guadalupe as Surrogate Mother in San Juan Atzingo," paper read before the 54th Annual Meeting of the American Anthropological Association, 18 November 1955.

This struggle leads to a further extension of the symbolism. Successful rebellion against power figures is equated with the promise of life; defeat with the promise of death. As John A. Mackay has suggested, there thus takes place a further symbolic identification of the Virgin with life; of defeat and death with the crucified Christ. In Mexican artistic tradition, as in Hispanic artistic tradition in general,[19] Christ is never depicted as an adult man, but always either as a helpless child, or more often as a figure beaten, tortured, defeated and killed. In this symbolic equation we are touching upon some of the roots both of the passionate affirmation of faith in the Virgin, and of the fascination with death which characterizes Baroque Christianity in general, and Mexican Catholicism in particular. The Guadalupe stands for life, for hope, for health; Christ on the cross, for despair and for death.

Supernatural mother and natural mother are thus equated symbolically, as are earthly and otherworldly hopes and desires. These hopes center on the provision of food and emotional warmth in the first case, in the successful waging of the Oedipal struggle in the other.

Family relations are, however, only one element in the formation of the Guadalupe symbol. Their analysis does little to explain the Guadalupe as such. They merely illuminate the female and maternal attributes of the more widespread Virgin symbol. The Guadalupe is important to Mexicans not only because she is a supernatural mother, but also because she embodies their major political and religious aspirations.

To the Indian groups, the symbol is more than an embodiment of life and hope; it restores to them the hopes of salvation. We must not forget that the Spanish Conquest signified not only military defeat, but the defeat also of the old gods and the decline of the old ritual. The apparition of the Guadalupe to an Indian commoner thus represents on one level the return of Tonantzin. As Tannenbaum has well said, "The Church . . . gave the Indian an opportunity not merely to save his life, but also to have his faith in his own gods."[20] On another level, the myth of the apparition served as a symbolic testimony that the Indian, as much as the Spaniard, was capable of being saved, capable of receiving Christianity. This must be understood against the background of the bitter theological and political argument which followed the Conquest and divided churchmen, officials, and conquerors into those who held that the Indian was incapable of conversion, thus inhuman, and therefore a fit subject of political and economic exploitation; and those who held that the Indian was human, capable of conversion and that this exploitation had to be tempered by the demands of the Catholic faith and of orderly civil processes of government.[21] The myth of the Guadalupe thus validates the Indian's right to legal defense, orderly government, to citizenship; to supernatural salvation, but also to salvation from random oppression.

But if the Guadalupe guaranteed a rightful place to the Indians in the new social system of New Spain, the myth also held appeal to the large group of disinherited who arose in New Spain as illegitimate offspring of Spanish fathers and Indian mothers, or through impoverishment, acculturation or loss of status within the Indian or Spanish group.[22] For such people, there was for a long time no proper place in the social order. Their very right to exist was questioned in their inability to command the full rights of citizenship and legal protection. Where Spaniard and Indian stood squarely within the law, they inhabited the interstices and margins of constituted society. These groups acquired influence and wealth in the seventeenth and eighteenth centuries, but were yet barred from social recognition and power by the prevailing economic, social and political order.[23] To them, the Guadalupe myth came to represent not merely the guarantee of their assured place in heaven, but the guarantee of their place in society here and now. On the political plane, the wish for a return to a paradise of early satisfactions of food and warmth, a life without defeat, sickness or death, gave rise to a political wish for a

[19] John A. Mackay, The Other Spanish Christ (New York, 1933), pp. 110–117.

[20] Frank Tannenbaum, Peace by Revolution (New York, 1933), p. 39.

[21] Silvio Zavala, La filosofía en la conquista de America (Mexico, 1947).

[22] Nicolas León, Las castas del México colonial o Nueva España (Mexico, 1924); C. E. Marshall, "The Birth of the Mestizo in New Spain," Hispanic American Historical Review, XIX (1939), 161–184; Wolf, "La formación de la nación," pp. 103–106.

[23] Gregorio Torres Quintero, México hacia el fin del virreinato español (Mexico, 1921); Eric R. Wolf, "The Mexican Bajío in the Eighteenth Century," Middle American Research Institute Publication, XVII (1955), 189–199; Wolf, "Aspects of Group Relations in a Complex Society: Mexico."

Mexican paradise, in which the illegitimate sons would possess the country, and the irresponsible Spanish overlords, who never acknowledged the social responsibilities of their paternity, would be driven from the land.

In the writings of seventeenth century ecclesiastics, the Guadalupe becomes the harbinger of this new order. In the book by Miguel Sánchez, published in 1648, the Spanish Conquest of New Spain is justified solely on the grounds that it allowed the Virgin to become manifest in her chosen country, and to found in Mexico a new paradise. Just as Israel had been chosen to produce Christ, so Mexico had been chosen to produce Guadalupe. Sánchez equates her with the apocalyptic woman of the Revelation of John (12: 1), "arrayed with the sun, and the moon under her feet, and upon her head a crown of twelve stars" who is to realize the prophecy of Deuteronomy 8: 7-10 and lead the Mexicans into the Promised Land. Colonial Mexico thus becomes the desert of Sinai; Independent Mexico the land of milk and honey. F. Francisco de Florencia, writing in 1688, coined the slogan which made Mexico not merely another chosen nation, but the Chosen Nation: *non fecit taliter omni nationi*,[24] word which still adorn the portals of the basilica, and shine forth in electric light bulbs at night. And on the eve of Mexican independence, Servando Teresa de Mier elaborates still further the Guadalupan myth by claiming that Mexico had been converted to Christianity long before the Spanish Conquest. The apostle Saint Thomas had brought the image of Guadalupe-Tonantzin to the New World as a symbol of his mission, just as Saint James had converted Spain with the image of the Virgin of the Pillar. The Spanish Conquest was therefore historically unnecessary, and should be erased from the annals of history.[25] In this perspective, the Mexican War of Independence marks the final realization of the apocalyptic promise. The banner of the Guadalupe leads the insurgents; and their cause is referred to as "her law."[26] In this ultimate extension of the symbol, the promise of life held out by the supernatural mother has become the promise of an independent Mexico, liberated from the irrational authority of the Spanish father-oppressors and restored to the Chosen Nation whose election had been manifest in the apparition of the Virgin on Tepeyac. The land of the supernatural mother is finally possessed by her rightful heirs. The symbolic circuit is closed. Mother; food, hope, health, life; supernatural salvation and salvation from oppression; Chosen People and national independence—all find expression in a single master symbol.

The Guadalupe symbol thus links together family, politics and religion; colonial past and independent present; Indian and Mexican. It reflects the salient social relationships of Mexican life, and embodies the emotions which they generate. It provides a cultural idiom through which the tenor and emotions of these relationships can be expressed. It is, ultimately, a way of talking about Mexico: a "collective representation" of Mexican society.

[24] de la Maza, pp. 39–40, 43–49, 64.

[25] Luis Villoro, *Los grandes momentos del indigenismo en México* (Mexico, 1950), pp. 131–138.

[26] Luis González y González, "El optimismo nacionalista como factor en la independencia de México," *Estudios de historiografía americana* (Mexico, 1948), p. 194.

? The mother often appears as the symbol of the source of energy which binds the individual to the collective. She also represents the life force in opposition to the death force. "The Book of Ruth" illustrates the rites of passage a woman must undergo to fulfill her symbolic function. Ruth is the "outsider" who must gain acceptance by the group. Naomi, Ruth's mother-in-law, provides the key to bring Ruth into contact with the means that will ensure the group's fertility, i.e., regeneration. Naomi and Ruth are interchangeable elements which exist in the mother archetype. Thus, Ruth must prove her love for Naomi as a symbolic gesture to bring the mother-in-law and daughter together. Ruth's marriage to Boaz, and the child she bears, are links which demonstrate the way Ruth replaces Naomi. This also brings an end to the famine which drove Naomi out of Judea. However, it is Naomi who nurses Ruth's child, an act that brings the old and young women together. The child sets in motion the line of descendents which will eventually produce King David. Ruth and Naomi are the symbolic vessels representing both the contained and containers of life.

In "The Virgin of Guadalupe: a Mexican National Symbol" Eric Wolf uses the mother as a "master symbol" of the source of energy which makes possible the individual's relation with the collective. Wolf illustrates the way Mary, Christ's Mother, incorporates the Mexican goddess of fertility, Tonantzin, in her image, and also the way the woman bridges the past and the present. For Wolf, the source of energy which underlies her image links the "family, politics and religion; colonial past and independent present; Indian and Mexican." The Virgin of Guadalupe symbolically expresses the group's deepest interests and longings. The following questions focus on the woman as life giver and life taker. They also illustrate the power the woman has with her children who carry on the process of regeneration.

1 Discuss "The Book of Ruth" as a description of the woman's rites of passage from "outsider" to mother of the tribe.
   a What symbols are used to illustrate this story? How do these symbols set the scene for the test which Ruth must undergo in order to attain group recognition?
   b Discuss the relation between Ruth and Naomi. Why does Ruth decide to stay with her mother-in-law? Why does Naomi feel that she has been punished by the Lord? Does Ruth bring an end to this punishment? Explain! How does Naomi help Ruth?
   c How important is Boaz in "The Book of Ruth"? What is his function in the story? What does he reveal about the male's role? Why is Ruth, rather than Boaz, given credit for the eventual birth of King David? How does the setting of their relation reveal Ruth's fertility?
   d What insights into the woman's role do we attain from the story of Ruth? How does Ruth prove to be better than "seven sons"? Why is the child given to Naomi at the story's end? What does this suggest about the daughter's bond with the mother?

2 Discuss Eric Wolf's "The Virgin of Guadalupe: a Mexican National Symbol" as an illustration of the emotional energy underlying the woman's role within a culture.
   a How does Wolf bring together the symbols of Mary, the Mother of Christ, and the goddess of fertility? What does this suggest about the union of opposites?
   b What does the Virgin symbolize about the "functional aspects" of Mexican life? Why does Christ appear as symbol of one who is "never depicted as an adult man"? What does this suggest about the relation between the mother and son? How does the Virgin become the symbol of "successful rebellion against power figures"? What does this suggest about the mother's triumph over the father?
   c What underlies the merging of the supernatural with the natural mother? Is this image combined in the story of Ruth and Naomi? What does this reveal about the female's role?
   d What diverse elements are brought together in the symbol of the Virgin? How does the Virgin represent what Jung calls "the eternal female"? What does this suggest about the Virgin as a symbolic expression of the emotional depths contained within Mexican culture?

The sea is a feminine symbol often given the dual functions of representing life and death. In dreams the sea is often associated with the unconscious because of the striking similarity between what appears on the surface of the water and the unfathomable depths which lie unseen below. In *Riders to the Sea* the sea functions on both of these levels. In order to ensure the life within the community, the men must go out and risk their lives to make a living, and it is the sea who claims the lives of all the sons in the play. The women sit at home and wait for messages which will reveal whether the sea has once again claimed the lives of their men.

RIDERS TO THE SEA

JOHN MILLINGTON SYNGE

Characters

MAURYA	*an old woman*
BARTLEY	*her son*
CATHLEEN	*her daughter*
NORA	*a younger daughter*

MEN AND WOMEN

SCENE. *An Island off the West of Ireland.*

Cottage kitchen, with nets, oil-skins, spinning-wheel, some new boards standing by the wall, etc. CATHLEEN, a girl about twenty, finishes kneading cake, and puts it down in the pot-oven¹ by the fire; then wipes her hands,. and begins to spin at the wheel. NORA, a young girl, puts her head in at the door.

NORA [*in a low voice*]. Where is she?

CATHLEEN. She's lying down, God help her, and may be sleeping, if she's able.

[NORA *comes in softly, and takes a bundle from under her shawl.*]

CATHLEEN [*spinning the wheel rapidly*]. What is it you have?

NORA. The young priest is after bringing them. It's a shirt and a plain stocking were got off a drowned man in Donegal.

[CATHLEEN *stops her wheel with a sudden movement, and leans out to listen.*]

NORA. We're to find out if it's Michael's they are, some time herself will be down looking by the sea.

CATHLEEN. How would they be Michael's, Nora? How would he go the length of that way to the far north?

NORA. The young priest says he's known the like of it. "If it's Michael's they are," says he, "you can tell herself he's got a clean burial by the grace of God, and if they're not his, let no one say a word about them, for she'll be getting her death," says he, "with crying and lamenting."

[*The door which* NORA *half closed is blown open by a gust of wind.*]

CATHLEEN [*looking out anxiously*]. Did you ask him would he stop Bartley going this day with the horses to the Galway fair?

NORA. "I won't stop him," says he, "but let you not be afraid. Herself does be saying prayers half through the night, and the Almighty God won't leave her destitute, " says he, "with no son living."

CATHLEEN. Is the sea bad by the white rocks, Nora?

¹ **pot-oven** heated iron plate covered by a pot

NORA. Middling bad. God help us. There's a great roaring in the west, and it's worse it'll be getting when the tide's turned to the wind. [*She goes over to the table with the bundle.*] Shall I open it now?

CATHLEEN. Maybe she'd wake up on us, and come in before we'd done. [*coming to the table*] It's a long time we'll be, and the two of us crying.

NORA [*goes to the inner door and listens*]. She's moving about on the bed. She'll be coming in a minute.

CATHLEEN. Give me the ladder, and I'll put them up in the turf-loft, the way she won't know of them at all, and maybe when the tide turns she'll be going down to see would he be floating from the east.

[*They put the ladder against the gable of the chimney;* CATHLEEN *goes up a few steps and hides the bundle in the turfloft.* MAURYA *comes from the inner room.*]

MAURYA [*looking up at* CATHLEEN *and speaking querulously*]. Isn't it turf enough you have for this day and evening?

CATHLEEN. There's a cake baking at the fire for a short space [*throwing down the turf*] and Bartley will want it when the tide turns if he goes to Connemara.

[NORA *picks up the turf and puts it round the pot-oven.*]

MAURYA [*sitting down on a stool at the fire*]. He won't go this day with the wind rising from the south and west. He won't go this day, for the young priest will stop him surely.

NORA. He'll not stop him, mother, and I heard Eamon Simon and Stephen Pheety and Colum Shawn saying he would go.

MAURYA. Where is he itself?

NORA. He went down to see would there be another boat sailing in the week, and I'm thinking it won't be long till he's here now, for the tide's turning at the green head,[2] and the hooker's tacking from the east.

CATHLEEN. I hear some one passing the big stones.

NORA [*looking out*]. He's coming now, and he in a hurry.

BARTLEY [*comes in and looks round the room. Speaking sadly and quietly*]. Where is the bit of new rope, Cathleen, was bought in Connemara?

CATHLEEN [*coming down*]. Give it to him. Nora; it's on a nail by the white boards. I hung it up

this morning, for the pig with black feet was eating it.

NORA [*giving him a rope*]. Is that it, Bartley?

MAURYA. You'd do right to leave that rope, Bartley, hanging by the board. [BARTLEY *takes the rope.*] It will be wanting in this place, I'm telling you, if Michael is washed up to-morrow morning, or the next morning, or any morning in the week, for it's a deep grave we'll make him by the grace of God.

BARTLEY [*beginning to work with the rope*]. I've no halter the way[3] I can ride down on the mare, and I must go now quickly. This is the one boat going for two weeks or beyond it, and the fair will be a good fair for horses I heard them saying below.

MAURYA. It's a hard thing they'll be saying below if the body is washed up and there's no man in it[4] to make a coffin, and I after giving a big price for the finest white boards you'd find in Connemara. [*She looks round at the boards.*]

BARTLEY. How would it be washed up, and we after looking each day for nine days, and a strong wind blowing a while back from the west and south?

MAURYA. If it wasn't found itself, that wind is raising the sea, and there was a star up against the moon, and it rising in the night. If it was a hundred horses, or a thousand horses you had itself, what is the price of a thousand horses against a son where there is one son only?

BARTLEY [*working at the halter, to* CATHLEEN]. Let you go down each day, and see the sheep aren't jumping in on the rye, and if the jobber comes you can sell the pig with the black feet if there is a good price going.

MAURYA. How would the like of her get a good price for a pig?

BARTLEY [*to* CATHLEEN]. If the west wind holds with the last bit of the moon let you and Nora get up weed enough for another cock for the kelp.[5] It's hard set we'll be from this day with no one in it but one man to work.

MAURYA. It's hard set[6] we'll be surely the day you're drownd'd with the rest. What way will I live and the girls with me, and I an old woman looking for the grave?

[2] **head**   headland, promontory

[3] **the way**   so that

[4] **in it**   there

[5] **kelp**   ash of various seaweeds, used as a source for iodine. Bartley's request means: get seaweed enough to make another pile to be burned to ash

[6] **set**   put to it

[BARTLEY *lays down the halter, takes off his old coat, and puts on a newer one of the same flannel.*]

BARTLEY [*to* NORA]. Is she coming to the pier?

NORA [*looking out*]. She's passing the green head and letting fall her sails.

BARTLEY [*getting his purse and tobacco*]. I'll have half an hour to go down, and you'll see me coming again in two days, or in three days, or maybe in four days if the wind is bad.

MAURYA [*turning round to the fire, and putting her shawl over her head*]. Isn't it a hard and cruel man won't hear a word from an old woman, and she holding him from the sea?

CATHLEEN. It's the life of a young man to be going on the sea, and who would listen to an old woman with one thing and she saying it over?

BARTLEY [*taking the halter*]. I must go now quickly. I'll ride down on the red mare, and the gray pony'll run behind me. . . . The blessing of God on you.   [*He goes out.*]

MAURYA [*crying out as he is in the door*]. He's gone now, God spare us, and we'll not see him again. He's gone now, and when the black night is falling I'll have no son left me in the world.

CATHLEEN. Why wouldn't you give him your blessing and he looking round in the door? Isn't it sorrow enough is on every one in this house without your sending him out with an unlucky word behind him, and a hard word in his ear?

[MAURYA *takes up the tongs and begins raking the fire aimlessly without looking round.*]

NORA [*turning towards her*]. You're taking away the turf from the cake.

CATHLEEN [*crying out*]. The Son of God forgive us, Nora, we're after forgetting his bit of bread. [*She comes over to the fire.*]

NORA. And it's destroyed he'll be going till dark night, and he after eating nothing since the sun went up.

CATHLEEN [*turning the cake out of the oven*]. It's destroyed he'll be, surely. There's no sense left on any person in a house where an old woman will be talking for ever.

[MAURYA *sways herself on her stool.*]

CATHLEEN [*cutting off some of the bread and rolling it in a cloth; to* MAURYA]. Let you go down now to the spring well and give him this and he passing. You'll see him then and the dark word will be broken, and you can say "God speed you," the way he'll be easy in his mind.

MAURYA [*taking the bread*]. Will I be in it as soon as himself?

CATHLEEN. If you go now quickly.

MAURYA [*standing up unsteadily*]. It's hard set I am to walk.

CATHLEEN [*looking at her anxiously*]. Give her the stick, Nora, or maybe she'll slip on the big stones.

NORA. What stick?

CATHLEEN. The stick Michael brought from Connemara.

MAURYA [*taking a stick* NORA *gives her*]. In the big world the old people do be leaving things after them for their sons and children, but in this place it is the young men do be leaving things behind for them that do be old. [*She goes out slowly.* NORA *goes over to the ladder.*]

CATHLEEN. Wait, Nora, maybe she'd turn back quickly. She's that sorry,[7] God help her, you wouldn't know the thing she'd do.

NORA. Is she gone round by the bush?

CATHLEEN [*looking out*]. She's gone now. Throw it down quickly, for the Lord knows when she'll be out of it again.

NORA [*getting the bundle from the loft*]. The young priest said he'd be passing to-morrow, and we might go down and speak to him below if it's Michael's they are surely.

CATHLEEN [*taking the bundle*]. Did he say what way they were found?

NORA [*coming down*]. "There were two men," says he, "and they rowing round with poteen before the cocks crowed, and the oar of one of them caught the body, and they passing the black cliffs of the north."

CATHLEEN [*trying to open the bundle*]. Give me a knife, Nora, the string's perished[8] with the salt water, and there's a black knot on it you wouldn't loosen in a week.

NORA [*giving her a knife*]. I've heard tell it was a long way to Donegal.

CATHLEEN [*cutting the string*]. It is surely. There was a man in here a while ago—the man sold us that knife—and he said if you set off walking from the rocks beyond, it would be seven days you'd be in Donegal.

NORA. And what time would a man take, and he floating?

[CATHLEEN *opens the bundle and takes out a bit of a stocking. They look at them eagerly.*]

CATHLEEN [*in a low voice*]. The Lord spare up, Nora! isn't it a queer hard thing to say if it's his they are surely?

[7] **sorry** wretched

[8] **perished** stiffened

NORA. I'll get his shirt off the hook the way we can put the one flannel on the other. [*She looks through some clothes hanging in the corner.*] It's not with them, Cathleen, and where will it be?

CATHLEEN. I'm thinking Bartley put it on him in the morning, for his own shirt was heavy with the salt in it. [*pointing to the corner*] There's a bit of a sleeve was of the same stuff. Give me that and it will do.

[NORA *brings it to her and they compare the flannel.*]

CATHLEEN. It's the same stuff, Nora; but if it is itself aren't there great rolls of it in the shops of Galway, and isn't it many another man may have a shirt of it as well as Michael himself?

NORA [*who has taken up the stocking and counted the stiches, crying out*]. It's Michael, Cathleen, it's Michael; God spare his soul, and what will herself say when she hears this story, and Bartley on the sea?

CATHLEEN [*taking the stocking*]. It's a plain stocking.

NORA. It's the second one of the third pair I knitted, and I put up three score stiches, and I dropped four of them.

CATHLEEN [*counts the stitches*]. It's that number is in it. [*crying out*] Ah, Nora, isn't it a bitter thing to think of him floating that way to the far north, and no one to keep him but the black hags that do be flying on the sea?

NORA [*swinging herself round, and throwing out her arms on the clothes*]. And isn't it a pitiful thing when there is nothing left of a man who was a great rower and fisher, but a bit of an old shirt and a plain stocking?

CATHLEEN [*after an instant*]. Tell me is herself coming, Nora? I hear a little sound on the path.

NORA [*looking out*]. She is, Cathleen. She's coming up to the door.

CATHLEEN. Put these things away before she'll come in. Maybe it's easier she'll be after her blessing to Bartley, and we won't let on we've heard anything the time he's on the sea.

NORA [*helping* CATHLEEN *to close the bundle*]. We'll put them here in the corner.

[*They put them into a hole in the chimney corner.* CATHLEEN *goes back to the spinning-wheel.*]

NORA. Will she see it was crying I was?

CATHLEEN. Keep your back to the door the way the light'll not be on you.

[NORA *sits down at the chimney corner, with her back to the door.* MAURYA *comes in very slowly, without looking at the girls, and goes over to her stool at the other side of the fire. The cloth with the bread is still in her hand. The girls look at each other, and* NORA *points to the bundle of bread.*]

CATHLEEN [*after spinning for a moment*]. You didn't give him his bit of bread?

[MAURYA *begins to keen softly, without turning round.*]

CATHLEEN. Did you see him riding down?

[MAURYA *goes on keening.*]

CATHLEEN [*a little impatiently*]. God forgive you; isn't it a better thing to raise your voice and tell what you seen, than to be making lamentation for a thing that's done? Did you see Bartley, I'm saying to you.

MAURYA [*with a weak voice*]. My heart's broken from this day.

CATHLEEN [*as before*]. Did you see Bartley?

MAURYA. I seen the fearfulest thing.

CATHLEEN [*leaves her wheel and looks out*]. God forgive you; he's riding the mare now over the green head, and the gray pony behind him.

MAURYA [*starts, so that her shawl falls back from her head and shows her white tossed hair. With a frightened voice*]. The gray pony behind him.

CATHLEEN [*coming to the fire*]. What is it ails you at, all?

MAURYA [*speaking very slowly*]. I've seen the fearfulest thing any person has seen, since the day Bride Dara seen the dead man with the child in his arms.

CATHLEEN and NORA. Uah. [*They crouch down in front of the old woman at the fire.*]

NORA. Tell us what it is you seen.

MAURYA. I went down to the spring well, and I stood there saying a prayer to myself. Then Bartley came along, and he riding on the red mare with the gray pony behind him. [*She puts up her hands, as if to hide something from her eyes.*] The Son of God spare us, Nora!

CATHLEEN. What is it you seen?

MAURYA. I seen Michael himself.

CATHLEEN [*speaking softly*]. You did not, mother; it wasn't Michael you seen, for his body is after being found in the far north, and he's got a clean burial by the grace of God.

MAURYA [*a little defiantly*]. I'm after seeing him this day, and he riding and galloping. Bartley came first on the red mare; and I tried to say "God speed you," but something choked the words in my throat. He went by quickly; and "the blessing of God on you," says he, and I could say nothing. I looked up then, and I crying, at the gray pony, and there was Michael upon it—with fine clothes on him, and new shoes on his feet.

CATHLEEN [*begins to keen*]. It's destroyed we are from this day. It's destroyed, surely.

NORA. Didn't the young priest say the Almighty God wouldn't leave her destitute with no son living?

MAURYA [*in a low voice, but clearly*]. It's little the like of him knows of the sea. . . . Bartley will be lost now, and let you call in Eamon and make me a good coffin out of the white boards, for I won't live after them. I've had a husband, and a husband's father, and six sons in this house—six fine men, though it was a hard birth I had with every one of them and they coming to the world—and some of them were found and some of them were not found, but they're gone now the lot of them. . . . There were Stephen, and Shawn, were lost in the great wind, and found after in the Bay of Gregory of the Golden Mouth, and carried up the two of them on the one plank, and in by that door. [*She pauses for a moment, the girls start as if they heard something through the door that is half open behind them.*]

NORA [*in a whisper*]. Did you hear that, Cathleen? Did you hear a noise in the north-east?

CATHLEEN [*in a whisper*]. There's some one after crying out by the seashore.

MAURYA [*continues without hearing anything*]. There was Sheamus and his father, and his own father again, were lost in a dark night, and not a stick or sign was seen of them when the sun went up. There was Patch after was drowned out of a curragh that turned over. I was sitting here with Bartley, and he a baby, lying on my two knees, and I seen two women, and three women, and four women coming in, and they crossing themselves, and not saying a word. I looked out then, and there were men coming after them, and they holding a thing in the half of a red sail, and water dripping out of it—it was a dry day, Nora—and leaving a track to the door. [*She pauses again with her hand stretched out towards the door. It opens softly and old women begin to come in, crossing themselves on the threshold, and kneeling down in front of the stage with red petticoats over their heads.*]

MAURYA [*half in a dream, to* CATHLEEN]. Is it Patch, or Michael, or what is it at all?

CATHLEEN. Michael is after being found in the far north, and when he is found there how could he be here in this place?

MAURYA. There does be a power of young men floating round in the sea, and what way would they know if it was Michael they had, or another man like him, for when a man is nine days in the sea, and the wind blowing, it's hard set his own mother would be to say what man was it.

CATHLEEN. It's Michael, God spare him, for they're after sending us a bit of his clothes from the far north. [*She reaches out and hands* MAURYA *the clothes that belonged to Michael.* MAURYA *stands up slowly and takes them in her hands.* NORA *looks out.*]

NORA. They're carrying a thing among them and there's water dripping out of it and leaving a track by the big stones.

CATHLEEN [*in a whisper to the women who have come in*]. Is it Bartley it is?

ONE OF THE WOMEN. It is surely, God rest his soul.

[*Two younger women come in and pull out the table. Then men carry in the body of Bartley, laid on a plank, with a bit of a sail over it, and lay it on the table.*]

CATHLEEN [*to the women, as they are doing so*]. What way was he drowned?

ONE OF THE WOMEN. The gray pony knocked him into the sea, and he was washed out where there is a great surf on the white rocks.

[MAURYA *has gone over and knelt down at the head of the table. The women are keening softly and swaying themselves with a slow movement.* CATHLEEN *and* NORA *kneel at the other end of the table. The men kneel near the door.*]

MAURYA [*raising her head and speaking as if she did not see the people around her*]. They're all gone now, and there isn't anything more the sea can do to me. . . . I'll have no call now to be up crying and praying when the wind breaks from the south, and you can hear the surf is in the east, and the surf is in the west, making a great stir with the two noises, and they hitting one on the other. I'll have no call now to be going down and getting Holy Water in the dark nights after Samhain,[9] and I won't care what way the sea is when the other women will be keening. [*to* NORA] Give

[9] **Samhain** November 1, the beginning of the Celtic winter half year

me the Holy Water, Nora, there's a small cup still on the dresser.

[NORA *gives it to her.*]

MAURYA [*drops Michael's clothes across Bartley's feet, and sprinkles the Holy Water over him*]. It isn't that I haven't prayed for you, Bartley, to the Almighty God. It isn't that I haven't said prayers in the dark night till you wouldn't know what I'd be saying; but it's a great rest I'll have now, and it's time surely. It's a great rest I'll have now, and great sleeping in the long nights after Samhain, if its only a bit of wet flour we do have to eat, and maybe a fish that would be stinking. [*She kneels down again, crossing herself, and saying prayers under her breath.*]

CATHLEEN [*to an old man*]. Maybe yourself and Eamon would make a coffin when the sun rises. We have fine white boards herself bought, God help her, thinking Michael would be found, and I have a new cake you can eat while you'll be working.

THE OLD MAN [*looking at the boards*]. Are there nails with them?

CATHLEEN. There are not, Colum; we didn't think of the nails.

ANOTHER MAN. It's a great wonder she wouldn't think of the nails, and all the coffins she's seen made already.

CATHLEEN. It's getting old she is, and broken.

[MAURYA *stands up again very slowly and spreads out the pieces of Michael's clothes beside the body, sprinkling them with the last of the Holy Water.*]

NORA [*in a whisper to* CATHLEEN]. She's quiet now and easy; but the day Michael was drowned you could hear her crying out from this to the spring well. It's fonder she was of Michael, and would any one have thought that?

CATHLEEN [*slowly and clearly*]. An old woman will be soon tired with anything she will do, and isn't it nine days herself is after crying and keening, and making great sorrow in the house?

MAURYA [*puts the empty cup mouth downwards on the table, and lays her hands together on Bartley's feet*]. They're all together this time, and the end is come. May the Almighty God have mercy on Bartley's soul, and on Michael's soul, and on the souls of Sheamus and Patch, and Stephen and Shawn; [*bending her head*] and may He have mercy on my soul, Nora, and on the soul of every one is left living in the world. [*She pauses, and the keen rises a little more loudly from the women, then sinks away.*]

MAURYA [*continuing*]. Michael has a clean burial in the far north, by the grace of the Almighty God. Bartley will have a fine coffin out of the white boards, and a deep grave surely. What more can we want than that? No man at all can be living for ever, and we must be satisfied. [*She kneels down again and the curtain falls slowly.*]

In *Riders to the Sea* John Synge spins a "web of reality" to illustrate the never-ending struggle between life and death. The play presents a series of incidents to reveal Maurya as the eternal mother battling against the hostile forces of nature. She is named after Mary the mother of sorrows, and she, too, has been wounded seven times. The frailty of human life is revealed in the play's title which comes from Exodus 15:1: "Then sang Moses and the children of Israel this unto the Lord . . . I will sing unto the Lord, for he hath triumphed gloriously: the horse and his rider hath he thrown into the sea." This, of course, refers to the men in the play. Maurya, however, does not see this as a "glorious" song. Her courage is tested. She accepts and endures that all things "shortly come to pass." Each of the characters appears to be a representation of this universal struggle. The social ideas underlying the play's dialogue reveal the sense of participation which come to those who accept the process of life. Maurya, like Lear, endures. The spiritual triumph is her transcendence above the life of mortality. As Edgar says of Lear: "The oldest hath born most; we that are young Shall never see so much, nor live so long." The wisdom of the ages makes bearable this short span of life on earth. The sea has reunited the brothers, and the world of nature forms the family of the dead. The women are left to mourn. Maurya triumphs through her recognition of this universality. She says:

> MAURYA (continuing). Michael has a clean burial in the far north, by the grace of the Almighty God. Bartley will have a fine coffin out of the white boards, and a deep grave surely. What more can we want than that? No man at all can be living for ever, and we must be satisfied.

Synge has successfully transformed the inhuman forces of nature into the language of life which moves us to accept the waves of consciousness that speak out to any who will listen.

The following questions focus on Synge's symbolic expression of the individual's relation to the community. This link is the first step in revealing Synge's vision of nature as a metaphor to express the presence of supernatural elements.

1 Describe the play's setting. What symbols does Synge use to set the scene for the play's action? What do they suggest about the environment's influence over the characters? What universal significance is embodied in these symbols?

2 What symbols does Synge use to define the function of the women in the play? How do these symbols depict the archetypal functions of women?

3 What symbols does Synge use to define the male's function in the play? Does Maurya's desire to give Bartley a knife relate to her attempt to separate the child from the mother? What does this suggest about the relation between the mother and son?

4 What is the function of the white boards throughout the play? How do they reveal the fate of the women and of the men? Why do the women forget to buy nails? What does this suggest?

5 How does Synge use the sea as a metaphor to reveal the interdependence between human beings and their environment? How does Synge reveal the sea as Maurya's antagonist? How does the use of "holy water" reveal the sea's function in cleansing man of this mortality?

6 What function does color play in this play? Trace Synge's emphasis on color contrasts to reveal the world of nature.

7 How does the language contained in the play's speeches connect the individual to the social world? What contradictions are reconciled in the dialogue? How does language connect the past to the future in terms of the present? What does this suggest about the influence of language in expressing human existence as timeless?

8 In describing the women of the Aran Islands, Synge wrote:

> The maternal feeling is so powerful on these islands that it gives a life of torment to the women. Their sons grow up to be banished as soon as they are of age, or to live here in continual danger on the sea; their daughters go away also, or are worn out in their youth with bearing children that grow up to harass them in their own turn a little later.

Discuss the way Mauyra functions in the play as an archetypal representation of the mother.

a Why does the play begin with Nora's question: "Where is she?" How does this set the scene for the impending events?

b What is characteristic of the mother's relation to her daughters? How does she prepare them to be women? Why do they take so much effort with her? How does this differ from Maurya's relation with her sons? How does Maurya's quarrel with Bartley reveal her influence in teaching him to be a man? What does this suggest about the mother as custodian of the family?

c What rituals does Maurya perform in the play? Does the performance help her endure? Explain! What does Maurya's acceptance of the sea's victory reveal about her strength and ability to change?

d What image of the women emerges from the play? How does the mother move from the natural to the social to the supernatural?

9 How does Maurya differ from Ruth? Would Jung contend that Maurya is the "eternal female"? Explain! How does Maurya resemble the Virgin of Guadalupe as used by Wolf as a symbol of the interrelation between the individual and the group?

In *High Noon* **Gary Cooper** appears as the hero who must fulfill his appointment with time in order to defend his moral view of the world. **Grace Kelly is the woman who struggles against him in order to save him. She is like Maurya in** *Riders to the Sea.* **In the following quote Karen Horney discusses the way this conflict sets up patterns of mistrust between men and women**

KAREN HORNEY
from *Feminine Psychology*

New York, Norton, 1967.

Man's attitude toward motherhood is a large and complicated chapter. One is generally inclined to see no problem in this area. Even the misogynist is obviously willing to respect woman as a mother and to venerate her motherliness under certain conditions, as mentioned above regarding the Cult of the Virgin. In order to obtain a clearer picture, we have to distinguish between two attitudes: men's attitudes toward motherliness, as represented in its purest form in the Cult of the Virgin, and their attitude toward motherhood as such, as we encounter it in the symbolism of the ancient mother goddesses. Males will always be in favor of motherliness, as expressed in certain spiritual qualities of women, *i.e., the nurturing, selfless, self-sacrificing mother; for she is the ideal embodiment of the woman who could fulfill all his expectations and longings.* In the ancient mother goddesses, man did not venerate motherliness in the spiritual sense, but rather motherhood in its most elemental meaning. Mother goddesses are earthy goddesses, fertile like the soil. They bring forth new life and they nurture it. It was this life-creating power of woman, an elemental force, that filled man with admiration. And this is exactly the point where problems arise. *For it is contrary to human nature to sustain appreciation without resentment toward capabilities that one does not possess.* . . . Thus there has remained an obvious residue of general resentment of men against women. This resentment expresses itself, also in our times, in men's distrustful defensive maneuvers against the threat of women's invasion of their domains; hence their tendency to devalue pregnancy and childbirth and to over-emphasize male genitality. This attitude does not express itself in scientific theories alone, but is also of far-reaching consequence for the entire relationship between the sexes, and for sexual morality in general. Motherhood, especially illegitimate motherhood, is very insufficiently protected by law— with one exception of a recent attempt at improvement in Russia. Conversely, there is ample opportunity for the fulfillment of the male's sexual needs. Emphasis on irresponsible sexual indulgence, and devaluation of women to an object of purely physical needs, are further consequences of this masculine attitude.

OF RENEWAL: FROM DEATH TO IMMORTALITY

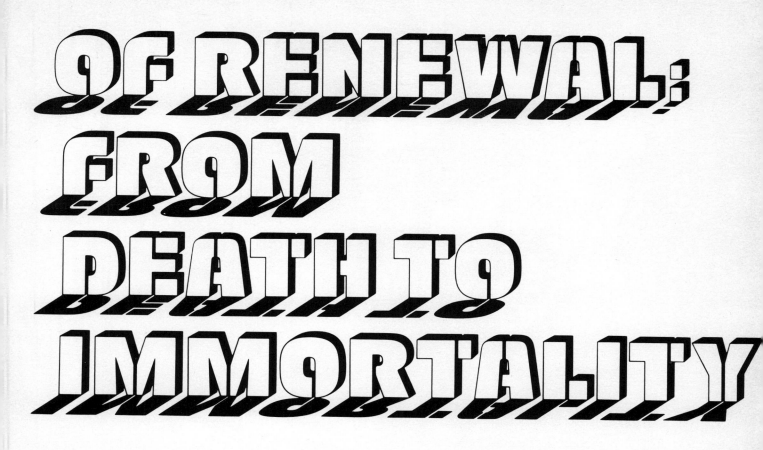

Michelangelo's Christ appears as He is about to bring the living and the dead together for their "Last Judgment." This movement bridges the distance between life and death as Christ makes possible this rite of passage. Thus the continuation of life becomes a never-ending destiny. Death symbolizes the rebirth of the spirit which makes the belief in eternal salvation a possibility. In the twentieth century, science replaces Christianity with the illusion that all can be pursued in the name of scientific truth. The belief in an afterlife becomes less possible, and modern life appears as a meaningless experience in which individuals try to fill the void of nothingness.

The call to Life

after Death

JUDGEMENT.

If you're reconciled with death or even if you are pretty well assured that you will have a good death, a dignified one, then every single moment of every single day is transformed because the pervasive undercurrent—the fear of death—is removed. . . . I am living an end-life where everything ought to be an end in itself, where I shouldn't waste any time preparing for the future, or occupying myself with means to later end. . . . You get stabbed by things, by flowers and by babies and by beautiful things— just the very act of living, of walking and breathing and eating and having friends and chatting. Everything seems to look more beautiful rather than less, and one gets the much-intensified sense of miracles.

Abraham Maslow

The Buddha once told this parable:

There was once a man who was crossing a field and met a tiger. Running, he came to a great cliff and caught hold of a root and swung over the side of the cliff. But at the bottom of the cliff was another tiger.

Soon two little mice came along and began to gnaw on the vine. The man looked in terror at the tiger below. But then he saw a strawberry vine. He picked the strawberry and ate it. How delicious it was.

The transition between Life and Death

DEATH

JOHN DONNE

Death, be not proud, though some have called thee
Mighty and dreadful, for thou art not so:
For those whom thou think'st thou dost overthrow
Die not, poor Death; nor yet canst thou kill me.
From Rest and Sleep, which but thy picture be,
Much pleasure, then from thee much more must flow;
And soonest our best men with thee do go—
Rest of their bones and souls' delivery!
Thou'rt slave to fate, chance, kings, and desperate
  men,
And dost with poison, war, and sickness dwell;
And poppy or charms can make us sleep as well
And better than thy stroke. Why swell'st thou then?
  One short sleep past, we wake eternally,
  And Death shall be no more: Death, thou shalt
  die!

NIRVANA

That monk of wisdom here, devoid of desire and
passion, attains of deathlessness, peace, the unchanging state of Nirvana. . . . The steadfast go out
like this lamp. . . . Where no-thing is, where nothing
is grasped, this is the Isle of No-Beyond. Nirvana
do I call it—the utter extinction of aging and dying.
  —from *Suttanipata*

THE TWENTY-THIRD PSALM

The Lord is my shepherd; I shall not want.

He maketh me to lie down in green pastures: he leadeth me beside the still waters.

He restoreth my soul: he leadeth me in the paths of righteousness for his name's sake.

Yea, though I walk through the valley of the shadow of death, I will fear no evil: for thou art with me; thy rod and thy staff they comfort me.

Thou preparest a table before me in the presence of mine enemies: thou anointest my head with oil; my cup runneth over.

Surely goodness and mercy shall follow me all the days of my life: and I will dwell in the house of the Lord for ever.

from THE NINETIETH PSALM

LORD, thou hast been our dwelling place in all generations.

Before the mountains were brought forth, or ever thou hadst formed the earth and the world, even from everlasting to everlasting, thou art God.

Thou turnest man to destruction; and sayest, Return, ye children of men.

For a thousand years in thy sight are but as yesterday when it is past, and as a watch in the night.

Thou carriest them away as with a flood; they are as a sleep: in the morning they are like grass which groweth up.

In the morning it flourisheth, and groweth up; in the evening it is cut down, and withereth.

For we are consumed by thine anger, and by thy wrath are we troubled.

Thou hast set our iniquities before thee, our secret sins in the light of thy countenance.

For all our days are passed away in thy wrath: we spend our years as a tale that is told.

The days of our years are threescore years and ten; and if by any reason of strength they be fourscore years, yet is their strength labour and sorrow; for it is soon cut off, and we fly away.

Who knoweth the power of thine anger? even according to thy fear, so is thy wrath.

So teach us to number our days, that we may apply our hearts unto wisdom.

Return, O LORD, how long? and let it repent thee concerning thy servants.

O satisfy us early with thy mercy; that we may rejoice and be glad all our days.

Make us glad according to the days wherein thou hast afflicted up, and the years wherein we have seen evil.

Let thy work appear unto thy servants, and thy glory unto their children.

And let the beauty of the LORD our GOD be upon us: and establish thou the work of our hands upon us; yea, the work of our hands establish thou it.

The following questions focus on the human effort to explain death in terms of life.

1 How does Donne's poem attempt to reconcile life and death? What image of death emerges in this poem? What symbols does Donne use to bring death in contact with immortality? How does death signal the transformation of destruction to eternal creation?

2 In the Twenty-third Psalm how does the writer relate death to the Lord? What image of God emerges from this poem? What image of human beings emerges in this poem? Does the poem reconcile these separations? Explain! How does life reveal the pain of death? What is missing in this poem?

To explain what happens to human beings after they die, heroic tales are told about those who journey into the kingdom of the dead in search of immortality. These archetypal heroes are often part man–part god. If they return from their quest, they bring us the knowledge of death as a simultaneous enactment of the birth process: (1) The hero brings about his own self-reproduction and (2) he assumes not the role of an individual but that of representative of the collective. Jesus is called the Son of Man who brought about his own rebirth through suffering and death. This act of rebirth resembles the original process which brought about the birth of human life. Speaking of the "self-begotten," Buedge says:

> He is a form of the rising sun and his seat is in the boat of the Sun-god. He is the god of matter which is at the point of passing from inertness into life, and also of the dead body from which a spiritual and glorified body is about to burst forth.

The symbolic tales which tell of these events often use the images of the rising and setting sun. This process seems an endless journey from day to night and back to day. The hero who enters the dark underworld at night rises again with the sun to bring his people spiritual knowledge. Often the tales of afterlife are a reflection of the life that exists on this planet. The hero often seeks reconciliation with a divine father because of some transgression committed by another member of his species. Christ dies for the sin of Adam and Eve in order to atone for their eating of the forbidden fruit. The exile from Paradise comes to an end with Christ's resurrection. The symbols associated with this event are often connected to the rites of spring and speak of the transformation of the material and spiritual worlds. This journey brings us to a reawakening that all who live, as Gertrude tells Hamlet, "must die passing through nature to eternity." The following selections focus on the heroes who transform death into immortality.

Whoever has lived long enough to find out what life is knows how deep a debt of gratitude we owe to Adam, the first great benefactor of our race. He brought death into the world.

Mark Twain

The path toward death

brings us to the road of life

This South American Indian is in his ritual burial boat; he has food and clothing to prepare him for the journey toward life after death. Human beings begin in the body of a woman, and they often symbolically leave the world in a similar vessel. The man above leaves in a boat, while many other cultures use a casket which is buried in mother earth.

In the Roman Catholic Mass, the priest elevates the chalice to signify that he has transformed wine into the blood of Christ. This ritual closely resembles the Dionysian rites; the god's spirit is given to the people so that He might live within them. The belief that the eating of a god enables the individual to become part of another reveals the human effort to link the past with the present and the human with the divine.

DIONYSUS

GREEK MYTH

A flash of lightning, a cry of pain, and a god was born. Zeus, the king of the gods, came to a mortal woman, Semele, and made her pregnant. A proud woman, Semele begged to see her lover in his supernatural form and refused to listen to Zeus' claims that no mortal could look on him and live. She continued to plead, and at last Zeus, losing his patience, appeared before her in all of his glory. Poor Semele saw only a flash of lightning before she was burned to a crisp by the heat, but Zeus took the unborn child from her womb and sewed it into his thigh where he kept it for nine months until it was ready to be born.

Dionysus was born from Zeus' thigh complete with horns and a crown of serpents and was so conceited that he immediately climbed up onto his father's throne and started playing with Zeus' lightning. Zeus looked at his young son in amusement, but Hera came running in, angrily demanding to know who this new illegitimate child of her husband was.

"So Semele is dead," she replied, after hearing the story. "At least you won't be seeing her any more. But I surely hope you don't plan to let this horned monstrosity play around your throne like an important god."

Zeus was used to Hera's biting tongue and ignored her, but this time Hera did more than talk. She went to the Titans and asked their help in doing away with this silly-looking upstart. A few days later, while Dionysus was looking at himself in a mirror, the Titans crept up on him to kill him.

Suddenly the infant Dionysus caught a glimpse of one of the Titans in the mirror. Instantly he was no longer a toddling child but a fierce lion facing his enemies. The Titans started back at seeing the god in this strange form, but they soon recovered and closed in again. Desperate, Dio-

nysus then turned himself into a horse, then a serpent, and last a bull, but could not escape from the persistent Titans. Finally their spears hit him, and while still in the form of a bull, he died.

Hera, however, was not satisfied. She had seen gods rise from the dead before. So she had the Titans tear the body limb from limb and boil it in a cauldron. But all of Hera's precautions were in vain. Zeus took the mutilated remains of his delightful little son to his venerable mother, Rhea, and she put him back together and gave him life again.

Zeus now knew better than to take Dionysus back to Olympus, so he took him to his mother's sister, Queen Ino, who agreed to raise him as a girl in the women's quarters. But Hera was not easily fooled. She found him there and drove Ino and her husband mad. Zeus rescued Dionysus just in time, and this time changed him into a goat and sent him to live with the nymphs on Mount Nysa. While he was there, Dionysus, who is also called Bacchus, invented wine.

Dionysus not only invented wine, he used it. He drank and drank until he went into fits of ecstasy. And when Hera found him again she used his own discovery to punish him, for she made him drink so much that he went mad.

Alternating between madness and ecstasy, Dionysus wandered around the world spreading his cult of wine and wild orgies. He had a magical attraction for women, and soon he was followed by a band of wild females who left their husbands and children for a life of ecstasy and savagery. Soon satyrs—half-goat, half-human creatures—also joined his wild throng. He traveled throughout the world from India to Greece to Egypt, spreading his gift of wine and followed by frenzied women who came to be called maenads.

Those who opposed his worship—

and there were many, for he upset order and civilized life—suffered a horrible fate. Lycurgus was the first powerful king to oppose him. With his army, he surrounded Dionysus and his maenads and captured all of the women. But Dionysus drove him mad and he killed his own son with an ax. Dionysus warned the horror-stricken people that their land would be barren until Lycurgus was killed, so they took their king to Mount Parnassus where they tied him to wild horses who pulled his body apart.

Next Dionysus came to the country of his cousin, King Pentheus, where he again began spreading his rites. At first Pentheus treated him well, but when all of the women from his court began to roam the countryside, dancing and taking part in wild, obscene orgies, he became angry and decided to arrest Dionysus. This time Dionysus drove the women mad and made them think that Pentheus was a wild animal. Led by Pentheus' mother, Agave, they tore him limb from limb.

No one is certain exactly what all of the rites of Dionysus consisted of, but apparently the death of King Pentheus was not an unusual occurrence. There are suggestions that tearing animals apart limb from limb in memory of the way Dionysus was dismembered by Hera was a frequent part of the rituals, and that human beings may occasionally have been the victims.

But there was more to the worship of Dionysus than savagery. There was also the ecstasy and a sense of communication with higher powers. It was Dionysus who gave Greeks a hope for immortality, perhaps because of his own death and resurrection. Some of the Greeks celebrated the return of Dionysus and his mother from Hades in an annual festival. Eventually the great Dionysia of Athens was the scene of the beginning of Greek drama.

After his worship was established in Greece, Dionysus went to the island of Naxos. There he found a beautiful girl weeping uncontrollably. It was Ariadne, who had fled from her home in Crete with Theseus and had then been ignominiously left behind. Dionysus fell in love with her, and Ariadne quickly forgot Theseus for the love of this strange but powerful and handsome god. For a marriage present, Dionysus gave his bride a golden crown and held a great celebration. But the god, with all of his powers, could not make his wife immortal, and at last Ariadne died. The grief-stricken god took the golden crown from her head and flung it into the heavens where it turned into stars and remains to this day.

Except a corn of wheat fall into the ground and die, it abideth alone; but if it die, it bringeth forth much fruit.

John 12:24

In the three pictures shown here, we see the motif of birth, death, and rebirth of Christ: the first frame reveals the birth of the God; the second frame demonstrates how He dies; and the third frame depicts His ascension into the heavens. This theme resembles the fate of the hero discussed in Chapter 3.

A MOTHER'S TALE

JAMES AGEE

The calf ran up the little hill as fast as he could and stopped sharp. "Mama!" he cried, all out of breath. "What *is* it! What are they *doing!* Where are they *going!*"

Other spring calves came galloping too.

They all were looking up at her and awaiting her explanation, but she looked out over their excited eyes. As she watched the mysterious and majestic thing they had never seen before, her own eyes became even more than ordinarily still, and during the considerable moment before she answered, she scarcely heard their urgent questioning.

Far out along the autumn plain, beneath the sloping light, an immense drove of cattle moved eastward. They went at a walk, not very fast, but faster than they could imaginably enjoy. Those in front were compelled by those behind; those at the rear, with few exceptions, did their best to keep up; those who were locked within the herd could no more help moving than the particles inside a falling rock. Men on horses rode ahead, and alongside, and behind, or spurred their horses intensely back and forth, keeping the pace steady, and the herd in shape; and from man to man a dog sped back and forth incessantly as a shuttle, barking, incessantly, in a hysterical voice. Now and then one of the men shouted fiercely, and this like the shrieking of the dog was tinily audible above a low and awesome sound which seemed to come not from the multitude of hooves but from the center of the world, and above the sporadic bawlings and bellowings of the herd.

From the hillside this tumult was so distant that it only made more delicate the prodigious silence in which the earth and sky were held; and, from the hill, the sight was as modest as its sound. The herd was virtually hidden in the dust it raised, and could be known, in general, only by the horns which pricked this flat sunlit dust like little briars. In one place a twist of the air revealed the trembling fabric of many backs; but it was only along the near edge of the mass that individual animals were discernible, small in a driven frieze, walking fast, stumbling and recovering, tossing their armed heads, or opening their skulls heavenward in one of those cries which reached the hillside long after the jaws were shut.

From where she watched, the mother could not be sure whether there were any she recognized. She knew that among them there must be a son of hers; she had not seen him since some previous spring, and she would not be seeing him again. Then the cries of the young ones impinged on her bemusement: "Where are they going?"

She looked into their ignorant eyes.

"Away," she said.

"Where?" they cried. "Where? Where?" her own son cried again.

She wondered what to say.

"On a long journey."

"But where *to?*" they shouted. "Yes, where *to?*" her son exclaimed, and she could see that he was losing his patience with her, as he always did when he felt she was evasive.

"I'm not sure," she said.

Their silence was so cold that she was unable to avoid their eyes for long.

"Well, not *really* sure. Because, you see," she said in her most reasonable tone, "I've never seen it with my own eyes, and that's the only way to *be* sure; *isn't* it."

They just kept looking at her. She could see no way out.

"But I've *heard* about it," she said with shallow cheerfulness, "from those who *have* seen it, and I don't suppose there's any good reason to doubt them."

She looked away over them again, and for all their interest in what she was about to tell them, her eyes so changed that they turned and looked too.

The herd, which had been moving broadside to them, was being turned away, so slowly that like the turning of stars it could not quite be seen from one moment to the next; yet soon it was moving directly away from them, and even during the little while she spoke and they all watched after it, it steadily and very noticeably diminished, and the sounds of it as well.

"It happens always about this time of year," she said quietly while they watched. "Nearly all the men and horses leave, and go into the North and the West."

"Out on the range," her son said, and by his voice she knew what enchantment the idea already held for him.

"Yes," she said, "out on the range." And trying, impossibly, to imagine the range, they were touched by the breath of grandeur.

"And then before long," she continued, "everyone has been found, and brought into one place; and then . . . what you see, happens. All of them.

"Sometimes when the wind is right," she said more quietly, "you can hear them coming long before you can see them. It isn't even like a sound, at first. It's more as if something were moving far under the ground. It makes you uneasy. You wonder, why, what in the world can *that* be! Then you remember what it is and then you can really hear it. And then finally, there they all are."

She could see this did not interest them at all.

"But where are they *going?*" one asked, a little impatiently.

"I'm coming to that," she said; and she let them wait. Then she spoke slowly but casually.

"They are on their way to a railroad."

There, she thought; that's for that look you all gave me when I said I wasn't sure. She waited for them to ask; they waited for her to explain.

"A railroad," she told them, "is great hard bars of metal lying side by side, or so they tell me, and they go on and on over the ground as far as the eye can see. And great wagons run on the metal bars on wheels, like wagon wheels but smaller, and these wheels are made of solid metal too. The wagons are much bigger than any

wagon you've ever seen, as big as, big as sheds, they say, and they are pulled along on the iron bars by a terrible huge dark machine, with a loud scream."

"Big as *sheds?*" one of the calves said skeptically.

"Big *enough*, any way," the mother said. "I told you I've never seen it myself. But those wagons are so big that several of us can get inside at once. And that's exactly what happens."

Suddenly she became very quiet, for she felt that somehow, she could not imagine just how, she had said altogether too much.

"Well, *what* happens," her son wanted to know. "What do you mean, *happens*."

She always tried hard to be a reasonably modern mother. It was probably better, she felt, to go on, than to leave them all full of imaginings and mystification. Besides, there was really nothing at all awful about what happened . . . if only one could know *why*.

"Well," she said, "it's nothing much really. They just—why, when they all finally *get* there, why there are all the great cars waiting in a long line, and the big dark machine is up ahead . . . smoke comes out of it, they say . . . and . . . well, then, they just put us into the wagons, just as many as will fit in each wagon, and when everybody is in, why . . ." She hesitated, for again, though she couldn't be sure why, she was uneasy.

"Why, then," her son said, "the train takes them away."

Hearing that word, she felt a flinching of the heart. Where had he picked it up, she wondered, and she gave him a shy and curious glance. Oh dear, she thought. I should never have even *begun* to explain. "Yes," she said, "when everybody is safely in, they slide the doors shut."

They were all silent for a little while. Then one of them asked thoughtfully, "Are they taking them somewhere they don't want to go?"

"Oh, I don't think so," the mother said. "I imagine it's very nice."

"*I* want to go," she heard her son say with ardor. "I want to go right now," he cried. "Can I, Mama? *Can* I? *Please?*" And looking into his eyes, she was overwhelmed by sadness.

"Silly thing," she said, "there'll be time enough for that when you're grown up. But what I very much hope," she went on, "is that instead of being chosen to go out on the range and to make the long journey, you will grow up to be very strong and bright so they will decide that you may stay here at home with Mother.

And you, too," she added, speaking to the other little males; but she could not honestly wish this for any but her own, least of all for the eldest, strongest and most proud, for she knew how few are chosen.

She could see that what she said was not received with enthusiasm.

"But I want to go," her son said.

"Why?" she asked. "I don't think any of you realize that it's a great *honor* to be chosen to stay. A great privilege. Why, it's just the most ordinary ones are taken out onto the range. But only the very pick are chosen to stay here at home. If you want to go out on the range," she said in hurried and happy inspiration, "all you have to do is be ordinary and careless and silly. If you want to have even a chance to be chosen to stay, you have to try to be stronger and bigger and braver and brighter than anyone else, and that takes *hard work. Every day.* Do you see?" And she looked happily and hopefully from one to another. "Besides," she added, aware that they were not won over, "I'm told it's a very rough life out there, and the men are unkind.

"Don't you see," she said again; and she pretended to speak to all of them, but it was only to her son.

But he only looked at her. "Why do you want me to stay home?" he asked flatly; in their silence she knew the others were asking the same question.

"Because it's safe here," she said before she knew better; and realized she had put it in the most unfortunate way possible. "Not safe, not just that," she fumbled. "I mean . . . because here we *know* what happens, and what's going to happen, and there's never any doubt about it, never any reason to wonder, to worry. Don't you see? It's just *Home,*" and she put a smile on the word, "where we all know each other and are happy and well."

They were so merely quiet, looking back at her, that she felt they were neither won over nor alienated. Then she knew of her son that he, anyhow, was most certainly not persuaded, for he asked the question she most dreaded: "Where do they go on the train?" And hearing him, she knew that she would stop at nothing to bring that curiosity and eagerness, and that tendency toward skepticism, within safe bounds.

"Nobody knows," she said, and she added, in just the tone she knew would most sharply engage them, "Not for sure, anyway."

"What do you mean, *not for sure,*" her son

cried. And the oldest, biggest calf repeated the question, his voice cracking.

The mother deliberately kept silence as she gazed out over the plain, and while she was silent they all heard the last they would ever hear of all those who were going away: one last great cry, as faint almost as a breath; the infinitesimal jabbing vituperation of the dog; the solemn muttering of the earth.

"Well," she said, after even this sound was entirely lost, "there was one who came back." Their instant, trustful eyes were too much for her. She added, "Or so they say."

They gathered a little more closely around her, for now she spoke very quietly.

"It was my great-grandmother who told me," she said. "She was told it by *her* great-grandmother, who claimed she saw it with her own eyes, though of course I can't vouch for that. Because of course I wasn't even dreamed of then; and Great-grandmother was so very, very old, you see, that you couldn't always be sure she knew quite *what* she was saying."

Now that she began to remember it more clearly, she was sorry she had committed herself to telling it.

"Yes," she said, "the story is, there was one, *just* one, who ever came back, and he told what happened on the train, and where the train went and what happened after. He told it all in a rush, they say, the last things first and every which way, but as it was finally sorted out and gotten into order by those who heard it and those they told it to, this is more or less what happened:

"He said that after the men had gotten just as many of us as they could into the car he was in, so that their sides pressed tightly together and nobody could lie down, they slid the door shut with a startling rattle and a bang, and then there was a sudden jerk, so strong they might have fallen except that they were packed so closely together, and the car began to move. But after it had moved only a little way, it stopped as suddenly as it had started, so that they all nearly fell down again. You see, they were just moving up the next car that was joined on behind, to put more of us into it. He could see it all between the boards of the car, because the boards were built a little apart from each other, to let in air."

Car, her son said again to himself, now he would never forget the word.

"He said that then, for the first time in his life, he became very badly frightened, he didn't know why. But he was sure, at that moment, that there was something dreadfully to be afraid of. The others felt this same great fear. They called out loudly to those who where being put into the car behind, and the others called back, but it was no use; those who were getting aboard were between narrow white fences and then were walking up a narrow slope and the men kept jabbing them as they do when they are in an unkind humor, and there was no way to go but on into the car. There was no way to get out of the car, either: he tried, with all his might, and he was the one nearest the door.

"After the next car behind was full, and the door was shut, the train jerked forward again, and stopped again, and they put more of us into still another car, and so on, and on, until all the starting and stopping no longer frightened anybody; it was just something uncomfortable that was never going to stop, and they began instead to realize how hungry and thirsty they were. But there was no food and no water, so they just had to put up with this; and about the time they became resigned to going without their suppers (for by now it was almost dark), they heard a sudden and terrible scream which frightened them even more deeply than anything had frightened them before, and the train began to move again, and they braced their legs once more for the jolt when it would stop, but this time, instead of stopping, it began to go fast, and then even faster, so fast that the ground nearby slid past like a flooded creek and the whole country, he claimed, began to move too, turning slowly around a far mountain as if it were all one great wheel. And then there was a strange kind of disturbance inside the car, he said, or even inside his very bones. He felt as if everything in him was *falling*, as if he had been filled full of a heavy liquid that all wanted to flow one way, and all the others were leaning as he was leaning, away from this queer heaviness that was trying to pull them over, and then just as suddenly this leaning heaviness was gone and they nearly fell again before they could stop leaning against it. He could never understand what this was, but it too happened so many times that they all got used to it, just as they got used to seeing the country turn like a slow wheel, and just as they got used to the long cruel screams of the engine, and the steady iron noise beneath them which made the cold darkness so fearsome, and the hunger and the thirst and the continual standing up, and the moving on and on and on as if they would never stop."

"*Didn't* they ever stop?" one asked.

"Once in a great while," she replied. "Each time they did," she said, "he thought, Oh, now *at last! At last* we can get out and stretch our tired legs and lie down! *At last* we'll be given food and water! But they never let them out. And they never gave them food or water. They never even cleaned up under them. They had to stand in their manure and in the water they made."

"Why did the train stop?" her son asked; and with somber gratification she saw that he was taking all this very much to heart.

"He could never understand why," she said. "Sometimes men would walk up and down alongside the cars, and the more nervous and the more trustful of us would call out; but they were only looking around, they never seemed to do anything. Sometimes he could see many houses and bigger buildings together where people lived. Sometimes it was far out in the country and after they had stood still for a long time they would hear a little noise which quickly became louder, and then become suddenly a noise so loud it stopped their breathing, and during this noise something black would go by, very close, and so fast it couldn't be seen. And then it was gone as suddenly as it had appeared, and the noise became small, and then in the silence their train would start up again.

"Once, he tells us, something very strange happened. They were standing still, and cars of a very different kind began to move slowly past. These cars were not red, but black, with many glass windows like those in a house; and he says they were as full of human beings as the car he was in was full of our kind. And one of these people looked into his eyes and smiled, as if he liked him, or as if he knew only too well how hard the journey was.

"So by his account it happens to them, too," she said, with a certain pleased vindictiveness. "Only they were sitting down at their ease, not standing. And the one who smiled was eating."

She was still, trying to think of something; she couldn't quite grasp the thought.

"But didn't they *ever* let them out?" her son asked.

The oldest calf jeered. "Of *course* they did. He came back, didn't he? How could he ever come back if he didn't get out?"

"They didn't let them out," she said, "for a long, long time."

"How long?"

"So long, and he was so tired, he could never quite be sure. But he said that it turned from night to day from day to night and back again several times over, with the train moving nearly all of this time, and that when it finally stopped, early one morning, they were all so tired and discouraged that they hardly even noticed any longer, let alone felt any hope that anything would change for them, ever again; and then all of a sudden men came up and put up a wide walk and unbarred the door and slid it open, and it was the most wonderful and happy moment of his life when he saw the door open, and walked into the open air with all his joints trembling, and drank the water and ate the delicious food they had ready for him; it was worth the whole terrible journey."

Now that these scenes came clear before her, there was a faraway shining in her eyes, and her voice, too, had something in it of the faraway.

"When they had eaten and drunk all they could hold they lifted up their heads and looked around, and everything they saw made them happy. Even the trains made them cheerful now, for now they were no longer afraid of them. And though these trains were forever breaking to pieces and joining again with other broken pieces, with shufflings and clashings and rude cries, they hardly paid them attention any more, they were so pleased to be in their new home, and so surprised and delighted to find they were among thousands upon thousands of strangers of their own kind, all lifting up their voices in peacefulness and thanksgiving, and they were so wonderstruck by all they could see, it was so beautiful and so grand.

"For he has told us that now they lived among fences as white as bone, so many, and so spiderishly complicated, and shining so pure, that there's no use trying even to hint at the beauty and the splendor of it to anyone who knows only the pitiful little outfittings of a ranch. Beyond these mazy fences, through the dark and bright smoke which continually turned along the sunlight, dark buildings stood shoulder to shoulder in a wall as huge and proud as mountains. All through the air, all the time, there was an iron humming like the humming of the iron bar after it has been struck to tell the men it is time to eat, and in all the air, all the time, there was that same strange kind of iron strength which makes the silence before lightning so different from all other silence.

"Once for a little while the wind shifted and blew over them straight from the great buildings, and it brought a strange and very powerful smell which confused and disturbed them.

He could never quite describe this smell, but he has told us it was unlike anything he had ever known before. It smelled like old fire, he said, and old blood and fear and darkness and sorrow and most terrible and brutal force and something else, something in it that made him want to run away. This sudden uneasiness and this wish to run swept through every one of them, he tells us, so that they were all moved at once as restlessly as so many leaves in a wind, and there was great worry in their voices. But soon the leaders among them concluded that it was simply the way men must smell when there are a great many of them living together. Those dark buildings must be crowded very full of men, they decided, probably as many thousands of them, indoors, as there were of us, outdoors; so it was no wonder their smell was so strong and, to our kind, so unpleasant. Besides, it was so clear now in every other way that men were not as we had always supposed, but were doing everything they knew how to make us comfortable and happy, that we ought to just put up with their smell, which after all they couldn't help, any more than we could help our own. Very likely men didn't like the way we smelled, any more than we liked theirs. They passed along these ideas to the others, and soon everyone felt more calm, and then the wind changed again, and the fierce smell no longer came to them, and the smell of their own kind was back again, very strong of course, in such a crowd, but ever so homey and comforting, and everyone felt easy again.

"They were fed and watered so generously, and treated so well, and the majesty and the loveliness of this place where they had all come to rest was far beyond anything they had ever known or dreamed of, that many of the simple and ignorant, whose memories were short, began to wonder whether that whole difficult journey, or even their whole lives up to now, had ever really been. Hadn't it all been just shadows, they murmured, just a bad dream?

"Even the sharp ones, who knew very well it had all really happened, began to figure that everything up to now had been made so full of pain only so that all they had come to now might seem all the sweeter and the more glorious. Some of the oldest and deeper were even of a mind that all the puzzle and tribulation of the journey had been sent us as a kind of harsh trying or proving of our worthiness; and that it was entirely fitting and proper that we could earn our way through to such rewards as these, only through suffering, and through being patient under pain which was beyond our understanding; and that now at the last, to those who had borne all things well, all things were made known: for the mystery of suffering stood revealed in joy. And now as they looked back over all that was past, all their sorrows and bewilderments seemed so little and so fleeting that, from the simplest among them even to the most wise, they could feel only the kind of amused pity we feel toward the very young when, with the first thing that hurts them or they are forbidden, they are sure there is nothing kind or fair in all creation, and carry on accordingly, raving and grieving as if their hearts would break."

She glanced among them with an indulgent smile, hoping the little lesson would sink home. They seemed interested but somewhat dazed. I'm talking way over their heads, she realized. But by now she herself was too deeply absorbed in her story to modify it much. *Let* it be, she thought, a little impatient; it's over *my* head, for that matter.

"They had hardly before this even wondered that they were alive," she went on, "and now all of a sudden they felt they understood *why* they were. This made them very happy, but they were still only beginning to enjoy this new wisdom when quite a new and different kind of restiveness ran among them. Before they quite knew it they were all moving once again, and now they realized that they were being moved, once more, by men, toward still some other place and purpose they could not know. But during these last hours they had been so well that now they felt no uneasiness, but all moved forward calm and sure toward better things still to come; he has told us that he no longer felt as if he were being driven, even as it became clear that they were going toward the shade of those great buildings; but guided.

"He was guided between fences which stood even more and more narrowly near each other, among companions who were pressed ever more and more closely against one another; and now as he felt their warmth against him it was not uncomfortable, and his pleasure in it was not through any need to be close among others through anxiousness, but was a new kind of strong and gentle delight, at being so very close, so deeply of his own kind, that it seemed as if the very breath and heartbeat of each one were being exchanged through all that multitude, and each was another, and others were each, and

each was a multitude, and the multitude was one. And quieted and made mild within this melting, they now entered the cold shadow cast by the buildings, and now with every step the smell of the buildings grew stronger, and in the darkening air the glittering of the fences was ever more queer.

"And now as they were pressed ever more intimately together he could see ahead of him a narrow gate, and he was strongly pressed upon from either side and from behind, and went in eagerly, and now he was between two fences so narrowly set that he brushed either fence with either flank, and walked alone, seeing just one other ahead of him, and knowing of just one other behind him, and for a moment the strange thought came to him, that the one ahead was his father, and that the one behind was the son he had never begotten.

"And now the light was so changed that he knew he must have come inside one of the gloomy and enormous buildings, and the smell was so much stronger that it seemed almost to burn his nostrils, and the smell and the somber new light blended together and became some other thing again, beyond his describing to us except to say that the whole air beat with it like one immense heart and it was as if the beating of his heart were pure violence infinitely manifolded upon violence: so that the uneasy feeling stirred in him again that it would be wise to turn around and run out of this place just as fast and as far as ever he could go. This he heard, as if he were telling it to himself at the top of his voice, but it came from somewhere so deep and so dark inside him that he could only hear the shouting of it as less than a whisper, as just a hot and chilling breath, and he scarcely heeded it, there was so much else to attend to.

"For as he walked along in this sudden and complete loneliness, he tells us, this wonderful knowledge of being one with all his race meant less and less to him, and in its place came something still more wonderful: he knew what it was to be himself alone, a creature separate and different from any other, who had never been before, and would never be again. He could feel this in his whole weight as he walked, and in each foot as he put it down and gave his weight to it and moved above it, and in every muscle as he moved, and it was a pride which lifted him up and made him feel large, and a pleasure which pierced him through. And as he began with such wondering delight to be aware of his own exact singleness in this world, he also began to understand (or so he thought) just why these fences were set so very narrow, and just why he was walking all by himself. It stole over him, he tells us, like the feeling of a slow cold wind, that he was being guided toward some still more wonderful reward or revealing, up ahead, which he could not of course imagine, but he was sure it was being held in store for him alone.

"Just then the one ahead of him fell down with a great sigh, and was so quickly taken out of the way that he did not even have to shift the order of his hooves as he walked on. The sudden fall and the sound of that sigh dismayed him, though, and something within him told him that it would be wise to look up: and there he saw Him.

"A little bridge ran crosswise above the fences. He stood on this bridge with His feet as wide apart as He could set them. He wore spattered trousers but from the belt up He was naked and as wet as rain. Both arms were raised high above His head and in both hands He held an enormous Hammer. With a grunt which was hardly like the voice of a human being, and with all His strength, He brought this Hammer down into the forehead of our friend: who, in a blinding blazing, heard from his own mouth the beginning of a gasping sigh; then there was only darkness."

Oh, this is *enough!* it's *enough!* she cried out within herself, seeing their terrible young eyes. How *could* she have been so foolish as to tell so much!

"What happened then?" she heard, in the voice of the oldest calf, and she was horrified. This shining in their eyes: was it only excitement? no pity? no fear?

"What happened?" two others asked.

Very well, she said to herself. I've gone so far; now I'll go the rest of the way. She decided not to soften it, either. She'd teach them a lesson they wouldn't forget in a hurry.

"Very well," she was surprised to hear herself say aloud.

"How long he lay in this darkness he couldn't know, but when he began to come out of it, all he knew was the most unspeakably dreadful pain. He was upside down and very slowly swinging and turning, for he was hanging by the tendons of his heels from great frightful hooks, and he has told us that the feeling was as if his hide were being torn from him inch by inch, in one piece. And then as he became more clearly aware he found that this was exactly what was happening. Knives would sliver and slice along both flanks, between the hide and the living flesh; then there was a moment of most precious relief; then red hands seized his hide and there was a jerking of the hide and a tearing of tissue which it was almost as terrible to hear as to feel, turning his whole body and the poor head at the bottom of it; and then the knives again.

"It was so far beyond anything he had ever known unnatural and amazing that he hung there through several more such slicings and jerkings and tearings before he was fully able to take it all in: then, with a scream, and a supreme straining of all his strength, he tore himself from the hooks and collapsed sprawling to the floor and, scrambling right to his feet, charged the men with the knives. For just a moment they were so astonished and so terrified they could not move. Then they moved faster than he had ever known men could—and so did all the other men who chanced to be in his way. He ran down a glowing floor of blood and down endless corridors which were hung with the bleeding carcasses of our kind and with bleeding fragments of carcasses, among blood-clothed men who carried bleeding weapons, and out of that vast room into the open, and over and through one fence after another, shoving aside many an astounded stranger and shouting out warnings as he ran, and away up the railroad toward the West.

"How he ever managed to get away, and how he ever found his way home, we can only try to guess. It's told that he scarcely knew, himself, by the time he came to this part of his story. He was impatient with those who interrupted him to ask about that, he had so much more important things to tell them and by then he was so exhausted and so far gone that he could say nothing very clear about the little he did know. But we can realize that he must have had really tremendous strength, otherwise he couldn't have outlived the Hammer; and that strength such as his—which we simply don't see these days, it's of the olden time—is capable of things our own strongest and bravest would sicken to dream of. But there was something even stronger than his strength. There was his righteous fury, which nothing could stand up against, which brought him out of that fearful place. And there was his high and burning and heroic purpose, to keep him safe along the way, and to guide him home, and to keep the breath of life in him until he could warn us. He did manage to tell us that he just followed the railroad, but how he chose one among the many which branched out from that place, he couldn't say. He told us, too, that from time to time he recognized shapes of mountains and other landmarks, from his journey by train, all reappearing backward and with a changed look and hard to see, too (for he was shrewd enough to travel mostly at night), but still recognizable. But that isn't enough to account for it. For he has told us, too, that he simply *knew* the way; that he didn't hesitate one moment in choosing the right line of railroad, or even think of it as choosing; and that the landmarks didn't really guide him, but just made him the more sure of what he was already sure of; and that whenever he *did* encounter human beings—and during the later stages of his journey, when he began to doubt he would live to tell us, he traveled day and night—they never so much as moved to make him trouble, but stopped dead in their tracks, and their jaws fell open.

"And surely we can't wonder that their jaws fell open. I'm sure yours would, if you had seen him as he arrived, and I'm very glad I wasn't there to see it, either, even though it is said to be the greatest and most momentous day of all the days that ever were or shall be. For we have the testimony of eyewitnesses, how he looked, and it is only too vivid, even to hear of. He came up out of the East as much staggering as galloping (for by now he was so worn out by pain and exertion and loss of blood that he could hardly stay upright), and his heels were so piteously torn by the hooks that his hooves doubled under more often than not, and in his broken forehead the mark of the Hammer was like the socket for a third eye.

"He came to the meadow where the great trees made shade over the water. 'Bring them all together!' he cried out, as soon as he could find breath. 'All!' Then he drank; and then he began to speak to those who were already there: for as soon as he saw himself in the water it was as clear to him as it was to those who watched him that there was no time left to send for the others. His hide was all gone from his head and his neck and his forelegs and his chest and most of one side and a part of the other side. It was flung backward from his naked muscles by the wind of his running and now it lay around him in the dust like a ragged garment. They say there is no imagining how terrible and in some way how grand the eyeball is when the skin has been taken entirely from around it: his eyes, which were bare in this way, also burned with pain, and with the final energies of his life, and with his desperate concern to warn us while he could; and he rolled his eyes wildly while he talked, or looked piercingly from one to another of the listeners, interrupting himself to cry out, *'Believe* me! Oh, *believe* me!' For it had evidently never occurred to him that he might not be believed, and must make this last great effort, in addition to all he had gone through for us, to *make* himself believed; so that he groaned with sorrow and with rage and railed at them without tact or mercy for their slowness to believe. He had scarcely what you could call a voice left, but with this relic of a voice he shouted and bellowed and bullied us and insulted us, in the agony of his concern. While he talked he bled from the mouth, and the mingled blood and saliva hung from his chin like the beard of a goat.

"Some say that with his naked face, and his savage eyes, and that beard and the hide lying off his shoulders like shabby clothing, he looked almost human. But others feel this is an irreverence even to think; and others, that it is a poor compliment to pay the one who told us at such cost to himself, the true ultimate purpose of Man. Some did not believe he had ever come from our ranch in the first place, and of course he was so different from us in appearance and even in his voice, and so changed from what he might ever have looked or sounded like before, that nobody could recognize him for sure, though some were sure they did. Others suspected that he had been sent among us with this story for some mischievous and cruel purpose, and the fact that they could not imagine what this purpose might be, made them, naturally, all the more suspicious. Some believed he was actually a man, trying—and none too successfully, they said—to disguise himself as one of us; and again the fact that they could not imagine why a man would do this, made them all the more uneasy. There were quite a few who doubted that anyone who could get into such bad condition as he was in, was even fit to give reliable information, let alone advice, to those in good health. And some whispered, even while he spoke, that he had turned lunatic; and many came to believe this. It wasn't only that his story was so fantastic; there was good reason to wonder, many felt, whether anybody in his right mind would go to such trouble for others. But even those who did not believe him listened intently, out of curiosity to hear so wild a tale, and out of the respect it is only proper to show any creature who is in the last agony.

"What he told, was what I have just told you. But his purpose was away beyond just the telling. When they asked questions, no matter how curious or suspicious or idle or foolish, he learned, toward the last, to answer them with all the patience he could and in all the detail he could remember. He even invited them to examine his wounded heels and the pulsing wound in his head as closely as they pleased. He even begged them to, for he knew that before everything else, he must be believed. For unless we could believe him, wherever could we find any reason, or enough courage, to do the hard and dreadful things he told us we must do!

"It was only these things he cared about. Only for these, he came back."

Now clearly remembering what these things were, she felt her whole being quail. She looked at the young ones quickly and as quickly looked away.

"While he talked," she went on, "and our ancestors listened, men came quietly among us; one of them shot him. Whether he was shot in kindness or to silence him is an endlessly disputed question which will probably never be settled. Whether, even, he died of the shot, or through his own great pain and weariness (for his eyes, they say, were glazing for some time before the men came), we will never be sure. Some suppose even that he may have died of his sorrow and his concern for us. Others feel that he had quite enough to die of, without that. All these things are tangled and lost in the disputes of those who love to theorize and to argue. There is no arguing about his dying words, though; they were very clearly remembered:

" '*Tell them! Believe!*' "

After a while her son asked, "What did he tell them to do?"

She avoided his eyes. "There's a great deal of disagreement about that, too," she said after a moment. "You see, he was so very tired."

They were silent.

"So tired," she said, "some think that toward the end, he really *must* have been out of his mind."

"Why?" asked her son.

"Because he was so tired out and so badly hurt."

They looked at her mistrustfully.

"And because of what he told us to do."

"What did he tell us to do?" her son asked again.

Her throat felt dry. "Just . . . things you can hardly bear even to think of. That's all."

They waited. "Well, *what?*" her son asked in a cold, accusing voice.

" '*Each one is himself,*' " she said shyly. "*Not of the herd. Himself alone.*' That's one."

"What else?"

" '*Obey nobody. Depend on none.*' "

"What else?"

She found that she was moved. " '*Break down the fences,*" she said less shyly. " '*Tell everybody, everywhere.*' "

"Where?"

"Everywhere. You see, he thought there must be ever so many more of us than we had ever known."

They were silent. "What else?" her son asked.

" '*For if even a few do not hear me, or disbelieve me, we are all betrayed.*' "

"Betrayed?"

"He meant, doing as men want us to. Not for ourselves, or the good of each other."

They were puzzled.

"Because, you see, he felt there was no other way." Again her voice altered. " '*All who are put on the range are put onto trains. All who are put onto trains meet the Man With The Hammer. All who stay home are kept there to breed others to go onto the range, and so betray themselves and their kind and their children forever.*

" '*We are brought into this life only to be victims; and there is no other way for us unless we save ourselves.*'

"Do you understand?"

Still they were puzzled, she saw; and no wonder, poor things. But now the ancient lines rang in her memory, terrible and brave. They made her somehow proud. She began actually to want to say them.

" '*Never be taken,*' " she said. " '*Never be driven. Let those who can, kill Man. Let those who cannot, avoid him.*' "

She looked around at them.

"What else?" her son asked, and in his voice there was a rising valor.

She looked straight into his eyes. " '*Kill the yearlings*' " she said very gently. " '*Kill the calves.*' "

She saw the valor leave his eyes.

"Kill us?"

She nodded. " '*So long as Man holds dominion over us,*' " she said. And in dread and amazement she heard herself add. " 'Bear no young.' "

With this they all looked at her at once in such a way that she loved her child, and all these others, as never before; and there dilated within her such a sorrowful and marveling grandeur that for a moment she saw nothing, and heard nothing except her own inward whisper, "Why, I am one alone. And of the herd, too. Both at once. All one."

Her son's voice brought her back: "Did they do what he told them to?"

The oldest one scoffed, "Would we be here, if they had?"

"They say some did," the mother replied. "Some tried. Not all."

"What did the men do to them?" another asked.

"I don't know," she said. "It was such a very long time ago."

"Do you believe it?" asked the oldest calf.

"There are some who believe it," she said.

"Do you?"

"I'm told that far back in the wildest corners of the range there are some of us, mostly very, very old ones, who have never been taken. It's said that they meet, every so often, to talk and just to think together about the heroism and the terror of two sublime Beings, The One Who Came Back, and The Man With The Hammer. Even here at home, some of the old ones, and some of us who are just old-fashioned, believe it, or parts of it anyway. I know there are some who say that a hollow at the center of the forehead—a sort of shadow of the Hammer's blow—is a sign of very special ability. And I remember how Great-grandmother used to sing an old, pious song, let's see now, yes, 'Be not like dumb-driven cattle, be a hero in the strife.' But there aren't many. Not any more."

"Do you believe it?" the oldest calf insisted; and now she was touched to realize that every one of them, from the oldest to the youngest, needed very badly to be sure about that.

"Of course not, silly," she said; and all at once she was overcome by a most curious shy-

ness, for it occurred to her that in the course of time, this young thing might be bred to her. "It's just an old, old legend." With a tender little laugh she added, lightly, "We use it to frighten children with."

By now the light was long on the plain and the herd was only a fume of gold near the horizon. Behind it, dung steamed, and dust sank gently to the shattered ground. She looked far away for a moment, wondering. Something—it was like a forgotten word on the tip of the tongue. She felt the sudden chill of the late afternoon and she wondered what she had been wondering about. "Come, children," she said briskly, "it's high time for supper." And she turned away; they followed.

The trouble was, her son was thinking, you could never trust her. If she said a thing was so, she was probably just trying to get her way with you. If she said a thing wasn't so, it probably was so. But you never could be sure. Not without seeing for yourself. I'm going to go, he told himself; I don't care what she wants. And if it isn't so, why then I'll live on the range and make the great journey and find out what is so. And if what she told was true, why then I'll know ahead of time and the one I will charge is The Man With The Hammer. I'll put Him and His Hammer out of the way forever, and that will make me an even better hero than The One Who Came Back.

So, when his mother glanced at him in concern, not quite daring to ask her question, he gave her his most docile smile, and snuggled his head against her, and she was comforted.

The littlest and youngest of them was doing double skips in his efforts to keep up with her. Now that he wouldn't be interrupting her, and none of the big ones would hear and make fun of him, he shyly whispered his question, so warmly moistly ticklish that she felt as if he were licking her ear.

"What is it, darling?" she asked, bending down.

"What's a train?"

[From *Harper's Bazaar*, 1952]

The following questions focus on the ways the preceding myths explain life after death, and the ways the heroes of these tales become the representatives of the collective.

1 Discuss the implications of "The Myth of Dionysus": What is his relation to Zeus? Why does Hera want to destroy him? What does this suggest about Dionysus as a representation of the battles between the parents? What does Dionysus do because of this? How does he descend into the underworld? What symbols are used to link him to sensuality? How does Dionysus treat those who do not believe in him? What does this suggest about his power? What punishment is he finally given? What does this suggest?

2 Discuss James Agee's "A Mother's Tale" as an allegory of the passion and death of Christ.
  a What does the mother represent in this tale? Why does she agree to tell the story? What fears are revealed in her character? How do the children respond to her? Does she resemble Christ's mother? Is she like Hera in the myth of Dionysus? Explain.
  b What tests does The One Who Came Back in Agee's story undergo? How does he descend into the underworld? What does he see there? What is the nature of his suffering? What insights into life and death does he bring back? How does the response of the others resemble the responses that people gave Christ?
  c Discuss what the story's ending suggests. How do the children respond to this story? What is Agee's vision regarding the ability of most individuals to identify with the suffering of others? How does this crown the individual, who descends into the world beyond, with the means to stand alone? What does this suggest about those who represent the collective?
  d What images of life and death emerge in this story? How does this compare and contrast with the other accounts in this section? Explain!

In the ancient Chinese sculpture shown above, we see the moon as the goddess Kwan Yin. She symbolized the woman who brought either romance or death. She is a representation of the Great Goddess.

Eternity is known to us only through epiphanies in time. These epiphanies become the image of the perfection of eternity which has no beginning and no end. This is the land of the abyss were the paradox of consistency is known to us only through the process of change. In primitive times, this process was represented by the cycle of death and rebirth which explicitly linked the human world to the sacred. The myth of the sexes in Plato's *Symposium* is instructive in relating the way union is brought about through the act of propagation. At one time, according to Plato, man and woman where composite parts of one total being. This being was as powerful as the gods, and so they carved it in half. From that time, the sexes sought each other to restore their totality in one being. This concept serves as a means to unite that which has been separated. To bridge the distance between life and death, the Great Goddess is the archetypal mother who once was the original source of unity between the mother and child. The Great Goddess becomes the symbolic cauldron of incarnation, birth, and rebirth. The magic associated with her is attached to the symbol which is the cauldron or pot that accompanies her.

> Helios rides through the heavens in the vessel of transformation, in which he was originally renewed in the dark region whither he returned each evening. And just as Pelops, after being boiled in a sacred kettle, was renewed by Clotho the goddess of destiny or Rhea the Mother Goddess, so Dionysus also became "whole and perfect" after being "cooked over" in a magical kettle of transformation.

This archetypal symbol speaks in the language of metaphors which reveal the wisdom of the life and death process. In the East, Maya is the symbol for the veil of illusions that entraps men and women in the pursuit of earthly pleasures.

The way out of this trap is the path toward illumination which emanates from her center and enables the individual to press toward a higher form of spiritual consciousness. The Brahman prayer to the Great Goddess is:

> Thou art the pristine spirit, the nature of which is bliss; thou art the ultimate nature and the clear light of heaven, which illuminates and breaks the self-hypnotism of the terrible round of rebirth, and thou art the one that muffles the universe, for all time in thine own very darkness.

The Goddess becomes the animating spirit directing the destiny of human beings.

In the patriarchal creation of the Judeo-Christian concept of monotheism, there is no room in heaven for the feminine spirit embodied in the Great Goddess. Jung contends that one of the most important religious ideas in the twentieth century is Mary's assumption to heaven. This ends the centuries of abstract thought which had split the world. For modern man, the discovery of the unconscious is an attempt to restore this lost balance. The world of dreams is dependent on the source of energy which springs from the deep spiritual wisdom lying within our psyches. Through an awareness of the symbolic significance of the Great Goddess, we see the link between the central wisdom of feeling and the upper wisdom of the intellect. It is only through a blending of these principles that we may once again believe in the tree of life. The knowledge of "good and evil" brought Adam and Eve to know the tree of death. The fall of man is synonymous with the victory of death over life.

The theme of immortality begins with a recognition of those men and women who rule the valley of death. The next selection starts with the reconciliation of Demeter, the mother, with Persephone, the daughter. The essential motif which appears in this tale is the reunion of the mother and daughter in order to balance the principle source of the flow of life. The myth uses the role of nature as a means to illustrate the fertility associated with the spring ritual. The theme of resurrection is clear in Persephone's descent into the underworld before she can be reunited with her mother. In her absence, famine rules the world. Her fertility is brought about when Demeter brings warm sunlight and rain to the withered earth.

The myth of Ishtar resembles in motif the story of Demeter. The double function of the Great Goddess is revealed in the negative element, Irkalla, the Goddess of the World Below, and in Ishtar, the Lady of the Gods, who brings about the Water of Life. In the speeches by Electra, Antigone, Cleopatra, and Joan, we see the male's ability to be in touch with the language of the Great Goddess. Each of these speeches brings together the world of death with the life force that comes through in the woman's ability to transcend her situation. The women are in revolt against a male-imposed rule, and yet each of them demonstrates the concepts of preservation, nourishment, and transformation all characteristics of the Great Goddess. In Singer's story, "Yanda," we see the female's struggle to endure despite the trials of her life. She represents the temptress who becomes the eternal woman and brings about the symbolic union of the mother and son. The symbols accompanied in these accounts demonstrate the connection of fertility with the possibilties of sexual potency. The dethroning of the Great Goddess in modern times is reflected in Yeats' poem "The Second Coming." The second birth is conceived as a "rough beast," bringing into view the negative elements of the Great Goddess.

ISHTAR'S DESCENT INTO THE WORLD BELOW

A time came when the Lady of the Gods, even Ishtar, thought upon the spouse of her youth, upon Tammuz; her heart inclined her to go down into the realm of Irkalla, into the Place of Darkness where Tammuz had gone. So, in all the magnificence of her apparel, in all her splendour and power, the Lady Ishtar went into the cavern that goes down to the realm of Irkalla. She came to the place that is surrounded by seven walls, that has seven gates opening into it, the place where the Dead sit in unchanging and everlasting gloom. Before the first gate she called upon the Watchman, Nedu: "Ho, Watchman! Open thou the gate that I may enter in!" The Watchman looked at her from over the gate; he did not speak to her; he did not open the gate to her. "If thou openest not the gate, I will smite upon it; I will shatter the bolt, and beat down the doors! Yea, I will bring away the Dead that are under the rule of thy mistress! I will raise up the Dead so that they will devour the Living, so that the Dead shall outnumber those that live!" So spoke the Lady of the Gods standing before the gate in all her power and splendour.

And hearing her commanding voice and looking upon her in all her power and splendour, Nedu, the Watchman of Irkalla's realm,

said, "Great Lady, do not throw down the gate that I guard. Let me go and declare thy will to the queen, to Irkalla." He went before the queen. And hearing of the coming of the Lady of the Gods, Irkalla was angered terribly. She bade the Watchman open the gates and take possession of the new-comer according to the ancient usages. He returned to the first gate. He laid hands upon that side of the gate on which the dust lies thick; he drew the bolt on which the dust is scattered. "Enter, O Lady, and let the realm of Irkalla be glad at thy coming; let the palace of the land whence none return rejoice at thee." He said this and he took the great crown off Ishtar's head. "Why hast thou taken the great crown off my head?" "Enter so, O Lady; this is the law of Irkalla."

So Ishtar entered through the first gate and saw the second wall before her. With head bent she went towards it. The Watchman at her coming opened the second gate. "Enter, O Lady, and let the realm of Irkalla be glad at thy coming; let the palace of the land whence none return rejoice at thee." He said this and put forth his hand and took that which was at her neck, the eight-rayed star. "Why, O Watchman, hast thou taken the eight-rayed star?" "Enter so, O Lady; this is the law of Irkalla."

So the Lady Ishtar, her head bent, the radiance gone from her, went through the second gate and saw the third wall before her. The Watchman opened the gate that was there. "Enter, O Lady. Let the realm of Irkalla be glad at thee; let the palace of the land whence none return rejoice before thee." He said this and he took the bracelets from off her arms—the bracelets of gold and lapis-lazuli. "Why, O Watchman, hast thou taken the bracelets from off mine arms?" "Enter so, O Lady; this is the law of Irkalla."

So Ishtar, her head bent, the radiance gone from her, and no longer magnificent in the gold of her ornaments, went through the third gate and saw the fourth wall before her. The Watchman opened the gate that was there. "Enter, O Lady. Let the realm of Irkalla be glad at thee; let the palace of the land whence none return rejoice before thee." He said this and he took the shoes from off her feet. "Why, O Watchman, hast thou taken the shoes from off my feet?" "Enter so, O Lady; this is the law of Irkalla."

So the Lady Ishtar, her head bent, the radiance gone from her, no longer magnificent in the gold of her ornaments, with stumbling and halting steps went through the fourth gate and saw the fifth wall before her. The Watchman opened the gate that was there. "Enter, O Lady. Let the realm of Irkalla be glad at thee; let the palace of the land whence none return rejoice before thee." He said this, and he put forth his hand, and he took her resplendent veil away. "Why hast thou taken the veil from me?" "Enter so, O Lady; this is the law of Irkalla."

So Ishtar, her head bent, the radiance gone from her, no longer magnificent in the gold of her ornaments, no longer resplendent in her apparel, with stumbling and halting steps went through the fifth gate and saw the sixth wall before her. The Watchman opened the gate that was there. "Enter, O Lady. Let the realm of Irkalla be glad at thee; let the palace of the land whence none return rejoice before thee." He said this, and he took off her outer robe. "Why hast thou taken my outer robe?" "Enter so, O Lady; this is the law of Irkalla."

So the Lady Ishtar, her head bent, the radiance gone from her, no longer magnificent in the gold of her ornaments, with apparel no longer full nor resplendent, with stumbling and halting steps went through the sixth gate and saw the seventh wall before her. The Watchman opened the gate that was there. "Enter, O Lady. Let the realm of Irkalla be glad at thee; let the palace of the land whence none return rejoice before thee." He said this, and he took off her garment. "Why hast thou taken off my garment?" "Enter so, O Lady; this is the law of Irkalla."

And naked, with her splendour, and her power, and her beauty all gone from her, the Lady of the Gods came before Irkalla. And Irkalla, the Goddess of the World Below, had the head of a lioness and the body of a woman; in her hands she grasped a serpent. Before her stood Bêlit-sêri, the Lady of the Desert, holding in her hands the tablets on which she wrote the decrees of Irkalla.

Ishtar saw the Dead that were there. They were without light; they ate the dust and they fed upon mud; they were clad in feathers and they had wings like birds; they lived in the darkness of night. And seeing their state, Ishtar became horribly afraid. She begged of Irkalla to give her permission to return from the House of Dust where dwelt high priests, ministrants, magicians, and prophets; where dwelt Tammuz, the spouse of her youth. But Irkalla said to her:

Thou art now in the land whence none return, in the place of darkness;
Thou art in the House of Darkness, the house from which none who enter come forth again;
Thou hast taken the road whose course returns not;
Thou art in the house where they who enter are excluded from light,
In the place where dust is their bread and mud their food,
Where they behold not the light, where they dwell in darkness,
And are clothed like birds in garments of feathers.
Over the door and across the bolt the dust is scattered.

Then Irkalla cursed Ishtar; she called upon Namtar, the demon of the plague, to smite the Lady of the Gods. And Namtar went to her and smote her, so that the plague afflicted every member of her body. Ishtar saw the light no more; feathers came upon her; she ate dust and fed upon the mud; she was as one of those whom she had sent down into Irkalla's realm.

She stayed in Irkalla's realm and went no more upon the earth. A season passed. The earth was not as it had been when Ishtar went upon it. No longer did the cow low for the bull; no longer did the bull bellow so that the cows might hear of his might. The ewe did not run to ram; the mare was not drawn to the stallion; the he-goat, chief of a flock, browsed with the flock as though there were no longer male and female; the birds did not call to each other. The hero did not take the maid in his arms; the warrior returning did not embrace his wife; his wife uttered no words of love to the warrior. None sought the women in the temple of Ishtar. The women in the temple did not call to the men who went by. So it was on the earth when Ishtar was in the World Below.

Shamash, the Sun God, beheld all this; he knew of the calamity that had befallen men and birds and beasts and all things upon the earth. The generation of creatures would die; no life would be left after them, and the creation of the Gods would perish. So Shamash said in his heart, and in haste he came before Ea, the great God. And when he had heard what Shamash related—that life was not being renewed upon the earth—and when it had been made known to him that this was because Ishtar was being held in the World Below, Ea, the great God, formed a being, Ud-dushu-nāmir, and bade him go down into the World Below, and into the presence of Irkalla, and conjure her by the power of the great Gods to give him the Water of Life with which to sprinkle Ishtar, the Lady of the Gods.

So the being whom Ea had formed went into the presence of Irkalla, and over Ud-dushu-nāmir Irkalla had no power. He conjured her by the power of the great Gods to grant him the Water of Life with which to sprinkle Ishtar, the Lady of the Gods. Irkalla was enraged when she heard his saying; she opened her lion's mouth; her woman's body shook with rage as she cursed Ishtar and cursed the being that was before her. But the being that Ea had formed stood there, not trembling at all at her curses.

The Water of Life she had to bring to him. She put the vessel that held it into his hands; she bade Namar bring forth the Lady of the Gods.

Ishtar came from out the dust and the mud; the Water of Life was sprinkled upon her. She stood before Irkalla's seat living, but pale, powerless, naked, and trembling.

Nadu the Watchman put his hand upon the bolt on which the dust lay; he opened the gate on which the dust was scattered. Ishtar passed through the gate. He gave her her garment; she put the garment upon her and her nakedness was covered. She went upon her way. He opened the second gate. He gave her back her outer robe. He gave her back her veil; he gave her back the shoes for her feet; he gave her back her bracelets of gold and lapis-lazuli; he gave her back the eight-rayed star that had been at her neck. At last he opened the outer gate of the realm of Irkalla. He took the great crown and he set it upon her head. Then Ishtar went from the realm of Irkalla. But she did not go in splendour, she did not go in radiance; she went with her head bowed. She went into the world where light was. No blossoms were there, and no birds called.

But no sooner had she came upon the earth than her splendour and power came back to Ishtar; she walked as a Goddess—yea, as the Lady of the Gods. The creatures of the earth heard her voice. Then the bull bellowed; the cow heard and lowed back to him; the stallion neighed and the mare was drawn to him; the warrior returning embraced his wife; his wife said, "Thou shalt be my man, I shall be thy woman"; the hero took the maid in his arms. All creation rejoiced; all creation praised the works of Ishtar. And the Gods rejoiced, knowing that what they had created would not pass away.

ELECTRA'S SPEECH

ANTIGONE'S SPEECH

from *Electra*
SOPHOCLES

ELECTRA. Dear sister, do not let these offerings
 Come near his tomb; it is a thing that law
 And piety forbid, to dedicate
 To him gifts and libations that are sent
 By her, his deadliest, bitterest enemy.
 Bury them in the ground, or throw them to
 The random winds, that none of them may
  reach him.
 No; let them all be kept in store for her
 In Hell, a treasure for her when she dies.
 If she were not the most insensate woman
 The world has ever seen, she'd not have
  dared
 To try to crown the tomb of him she killed
 With gifts inspired by enmity. Think: would
  they
 Cause any gratitude in him? Did she not
  kill him?
 And with such hatred, and with such dis-
  honour,
 That she attacked even his lifeless body
 And mangled it? You cannot think that gifts
 Will gain her absolution from her crime?
 Impossible! No, let them be, and make
 A different offering at our father's grave:
 Give him a lock of hair for token, one
 Of yours, and one of mine—no lordly gifts,
 But all I have; and give him too this girdle,
 Poor, unadorned; and as you give them, kneel
 Upon his grave; beseech him, from the world
 Below, to look with favour on us, and
 To give his aid against our enemies;
 And that his son Orestes may be saved
 To come in triumph and to trample on
 His foes, that in the days to come we may
 Grace him with gifts more splendid far than
  those
 That we can offer now. For I believe,
 I do believe, that in this dream, to her
 So terrifying, the spirit of our father
 Has played some part. However that may be,
 My sister, do this service to yourself,
 To me, and to the one we love beyond
 All others, him who is dead—our father.

from *Antigone*
SOPHOCLES

Tomb, bridal-chamber, my eternal home
Hewn from the rock, where I must go to meet
My own, those many who have died, and been
Made welcome by Peresphone in the shadow-
 world.
I am the last, my death the worst of all
Before my allotted span of years has run.
But as I go I have this hope in heart,
That my coming may be welcome to my father,
My mother; welcome, dearest brother, to you.
For when you died, with my own hands I
 washed
And robed your bodies, and poured offerings
Over your graves. Now this is my reward,
Polyneices, for rendering such services to you.
Yet wisdom would approve my honoring you.
If I were a mother; if my husband's corpse
Were left to rot, I never should have dared
Defy the state to do what I have done.
What principle can justify such words?
Why, if my husband died I could take another;
Someone else could give me a child if I lost the
 first;
But Death has hidden my mother and father
 from me.
No brother can be born to me again.
Such was the principle by which I chose
To honor you; and for this Creon judges me
 guilty
Of outrage and transgression, brother mine!
And now he seizes me to lead me off,
Robbed of my bride-bed and my marriage song.
I shall never marry, never be a mother.
And so, in misery, without a friend,
I go still living to the pit of death.
Which one of heaven's commandments have I
 broken?
Why should I look to the gods any longer
After this? To whom am I to turn for help
When doing right has branded me a sinner?
If the gods approve what is happening to me,
After the punishment I shall know my fault,
But if my judges are wrong, I wish them no
 worse

Than what they have unjustly done to me.

CHORUS. Still the same tempestuous spirit
carrying her along.

CREON. Then those who are charged with
taking her

Shall have cause to repent their slowness.

ANT. Oh, that word has brought me
Very near my death.

CREON. I can offer you no hope.
Your punishment stands unchanged.

ANT. City of my father in the land of
Thebes,

The time has come, they take me away.
Look, princes of Thebes; this is the last
Daughter of the house of your kings.
See what I suffer, and at whose hands.

CLEOPATRA'S SPEECH

from *Anthony and Cleopatra*
WILLIAM SHAKESPEARE

CLEOPATRA

Give me my robe, put on my crown, I have
Immortal longings in me. Now no more
The juice of Egypt's grape shall moist this lip.
Yare, yare, good Iras; quick. Methinks I hear
Anthony call: I see him rouse himself
To praise my noble act. I hear him mock
The luck of Caesar, which the gods give men
To excuse their after wrath. Husband, I come:
Now to that name my courage prove my title!
I am fire, and air; my other elements
I give to baser life. So, have you done?
Come then, and take the last warmth of my
lips.
Farewell, kind Charmian, Iras, long farewell.
    [Kisses them. Iras falls and dies.]
Have I the aspic in my lips? Dost fall?
If thou and nature can so gently part,
The stroke of death is as a lover's pinch,
Which hurts, and is desired. Dost thou lie
still?
If thus thou vanishest, thou tell'st the world
It is not worth leave-taking.

CHARMIAN

Dissolve, thick cloud, and rain, that I may say
The gods themselves do weep.

CLEOPATRA   This proves me base:
If she first meet the curlèd Anthony,
He'll make demand of her, and spend that
kiss

Which is my heaven to have. Come, thou
mortal wretch,
    [To an asp, which she applies to her
    breast.]
With thy sharp teeth this knot intrinsicate
Of life at once untie. Poor venomous fool,
Be angry, and dispatch. O, couldst thou
speak,
That I might hear thee call great Caesar ass
Unpolicied!

CHARMIAN   O Eastern star!

CLEOPATRA   Peace, peace!
Dost thou not see my baby at my breast,
That sucks the nurse asleep?

CHARMIAN   O, break! O, break!

CLEOPATRA

As sweet as balm, as soft as air, as gentle—
O Anthony! Nay, I will take thee too:
    [Applies another asp to her arm.]
What should I stay—
    Dies.

CHARMIAN

In this wild world? So, fare thee well.
Now boast thee, death, in thy possession lies
A lass unparalleled. Downy windows, close;
And golden Phoebus never be beheld
Of eyes again so royal! Your crown's awry;
I'll mend it, and then play—
    Enter the Guard, rustling in.

JOAN'S SPEECH

from *Saint Joan*
GEORGE BERNARD SHAW

JOAN. Yes: they told me you were fools *[the word gives great offence],* and that I was not to listen to your fine words nor trust to your charity. You promise me my life; but you lied *[indignant exclamations].* You think that life is nothing but not being stone dead. It is not the bread and water I fear: I can live on bread: when have I asked for more? It is no hardship to drink water if the water be clean. Bread has no sorrow for me, and water no affliction. But to shut me from the light of the sky and the the sight of the fields and flowers; to chain my feet so that I can never again ride with the soldiers nor climb the hills; to make me breathe foul damp darkness, and keep from me everything that brings me back to the love of God when your wickedness and foolishness tempt me to hate Him: all this is worse than the furnace in the Bible that was heated seven times. I could do without my warhorse; I could drag about in a skirt; I could let the banners and the trumpets and the knights and soldiers pass me and leave me behind as they leave the other women, if only I could still hear the wind in the trees, the larks in the sunshine, the young lambs crying through the healthy frost, and the blessed church bells that send my angel voices floating to me on the wind. But without these things I cannot live; and by your wanting to take them away from me, or from any human creature, I know that your counsel is of the devil, and that mine is of God.

ISAAC BASHEVIS SINGER

The Peacock's Tail stood on a side street not far from the ruins of a Greek Orthodox church and cemetery. It was a two-story brick building with a weather vane on its crooked roof, and a battered sign over its entrance depicting a peacock with a faded gold tail. The front of the inn housed a windowless tavern, dark as dusk on the sunniest mornings. No peasants were served there even on market days. The owner, Shalom Pintchever, had no patience with the peasants, their dances and wild songs. Neither he nor Shaindel, his wife, had the strength to wait on these ruffians, or later when they got drunk, to throw them out into the gutter. The Peacock's Tail was a stopping place for squires, military men who were on their way to the Russian-Austrian border, and for salesmen who came to town to sell farm implements and goods from Russia. There was never any lack of guests. Occasionally a group of strolling players stayed the night. Once in a while the inn was visited by a magician, or a bear trainer. Sometimes a preacher stopped there, or one of those travelers about whom the Lord alone knows what brought them there. The town coachman understood what kind of customers to bring to The Peacock's Tail.

When Shalom Pintchever, a stranger, bought the hotel, and with his wife came to live in the town, they brought with them a peasant woman called Yanda. Yanda would have been a beauty but for a face as pockmarked as a potato grater. She had black hair which she wore in a braid, white skin, a short nose, red cheeks, and eyes as black as cherries. Her bosom was high, her waist narrow,

her hips rounded. She was a woman of great physical strength. She did all the work in the hotel: made the beds, washed the linen, cooked, dumped the chamber pots, and, in addition, visited the male guests when requested. The moment a visitor registered, Shalom Pintchever would ask, slyly winking an eye under his bushy brows, "With or without?" The traveler understood and almost always answered, "With." Shalom added the price to the bill.

There were guests who invited Yanda to drink with them, or go for a walk, but she never accepted. Shalom Pintchever was not going to to have them taking up her time, or turning her into a drunk. He had once and for all forbidden her to drink liquor, and she never touched a drop, not even a glass of beer on a hot summer day. Shalom had rescued her from a drunkard father and a stepmother. In return she served him without asking for pay. Every few months he would give her pocket money. Yanda would grab Shalom's hand, kiss it and hide the money in her stocking without counting it. From time to time she would order a dress, a pair of high-buttoned shoes, or buy herself a shawl, a kerchief, a comb. Sunday, when she went to church, she invariably threw a coin into the alms box. Sometimes she brought a present for the priest, or a candle to be lit for her patron saint. The old women objected to her entering a holy place, but she stood inside the door anyway. There was gossip that the priest was carrying on with her, even though he had a pretty housekeeper.

The Jews accused Shalom Pintchever of keeping a bawdy house.

When the women quarreled with Shaindel, they called her Yanda. But without Yanda Shalom would have been out of business. Three maids could not have done her work. Besides, most servants stole and had to be watched. Neither Shalom nor Shaindel could be bothered with that. Husband and wife were mourning an only daughter who had died in a fire in the town in which they had previously lived. Shaindel suffered from asthma, Shalom had sick kidneys. Yanda carried the burden of the hotel. Summertime she got up at daybreak, in the winter she left her bed two hours before sunrise. She scrubbed floors, patched quilts and sheets, carried water from the well, even chopped wood when a woodchopper was not available. Shaindel was convinced Yanda would collapse from overwork. Husband and wife also feared that she might contract a contagious disease. But some devil or other impure power watched over her. Years passed, and she did not get sick, never even caught cold. Her employers did not stint on her food, but she preferred to eat the leftovers: cold soups, scraps of meat, stale bread. Shalom and Shaindel both suffered from toothaches, but Yanda had a mouth full of strong white teeth like a dog. She could crack peach pits with them.

"She is not a human being," Shaindel would say, "she's a beast."

The women spat when Yanda passed by, cursing her vehemently. Boys called her names and threw stones and mud at her. Young girls giggled, dropped their eyes, and blushed when they met her on the street. More than once the police called her in for questioning. But years passed and Yanda remained in Shalom Pintchever's service. With time the clientele of the inn changed. As long as the town belonged to Russia, its guests were mainly Russians. Later, when the Austrians took over, they were Germans, Magyars, Czechs, and Bosnians. Then, when Poland gained independence, it served the Polish officials who arrived from Warsaw and Lublin. What didn't the town live through—epidemics of typhoid and dysentery; the Austrian soldiers brought cholera with them and six hundred townspeople perished. For a short time, under Bolshevik rule, the inn was taken over by a Communist County Committee, and some commissar or other was put in charge. Yanda remained through it all. Somebody had to work, to wash, scour, serve the guests beer, vodka, snacks. Whatever their titles, at night the men wanted Yanda in their beds. There were some who kissed her and some who beat her. There were those who cursed her and called her names and those who wept before her and confessed to her as if she were a priest. One officer placed a glass of cognac on her head and shot it down with his revolver. Another bit into her shoulder and like a leech sucked her blood. Still, in the morning she washed, combed her hair, and everything began anew. There was no end to the dirty dishes. The floors were full of holes and cracks, the walls were peeling. No matter how often Yanda poured scalding water over cockroaches and bedbugs, and used all kinds of poison, the vermin continued to multiply. Each day the hotel was in danger of falling apart. It was Yanda who kept it together.

The owners themselves began to resemble the hotel. Shaindel grew bent and her face became as white and brittle as plaster. Her speech was unintelligible. She no longer walked, but shuffled. She would find a discarded caftan in a trunk and would try to patch it. Shalom protested that he didn't need the rag, but half-blind as she was, she would sit for days, with her glasses on the tip of her nose, trying to mend it. Again and again, she would ask Yanda to thread the needle, muttering. "It isn't thread, it's cobweb. These needles have no eyes."

Shalom Pintchever's face began to grow a kind of mold. His brows became even shaggier. Under his eyes there were bags and from them hung other bags. Between his wrinkles there was a black excrescence which no water could remove. His head shook from side to side. Nevertheless, when a guest arrived, Shalom would reach for his hotel register with a trembling hand and ask, "With or without?" And the guest would almost invariably reply, "With."

II

It all happened quickly. First Shaindel lay down and breathed her last. It occurred on the first day of Rosh Hashanah. The following day, the oldest woman in the town gave up her shroud, since it is forbidden to sew on the Holy days. The women of the burial society treated themselves to cake and brandy at the cemetery. Shalom, confused by grief, forgot the text of the Kaddish and had to be prompted. Those who attended the funeral said that his legs were so shaky, he almost fell into the grave. After Shaindel's death Shalom Pintchever became senile. He took money from the cashbox and didn't remember what he did with it. He became so deaf that even screaming into his ears did not help. The Feast of Tabernacles was followed by such a rain spell that even the oldest townspeople could not recall its like. The river overflowed. The wheel of the water mill had to be stopped. The roof of the inn sprang a leak. The guests who had rooms on the top floor came down in the middle of the night, complaining that water was pouring into their beds. Shalom lay helpless in his own bedroom. It was Yanda who apologized to the guests and made up beds for them downstairs. She even climbed a ladder up to the roof and tried to plug the leaks. But the shingles crumbled as soon as she touched them. In the morning, the guests left without paying their bills. Early Saturday as Shalom Pintchever picked up his prayer shawl and was about to leave for the synagogue, he began to sway and fell down. "Yanda, I am finished," he cried out. Yanda ran to get some brandy, but it was already too late. Shalom lay stretched out on the floor, dead. There was an uproar in the town. Shalom had left no children. Irreverent people, for whom the sacredness of the Sabbath had little meaning, began to search for a will and tried to force his strongbox. Officials from the City Hall made a list of his belongings and sealed the drawer in which he kept his money. Yanda had begun to weep the moment Shalom had fallen down and did not stop until after the funeral. She had worked in the inn for over twenty years, but was left with barely sixty zlotys. The authorities immediately ordered her to get out. Yanda packed her belongings in a sack, put on a pair of shoes, which she usually wore only to church, wrapped herself in a shawl, and walked the long way to the railroad station. There was nobody to say goodbye. At the station, she approached the ticket window and said,

"Kind sir, please give me a ticket to Skibica."

"There is no such station."

Yanda began to wail, "What am I to do, I am a forsaken orphan!"

The peasants at the station jeered at her. The women spat on her. A Jewish traveling salesman began to question her about Skibica. Is it a village, or a town? In what country, or district is it? At first Yanda remembered nothing. But the Jew in his torn coat and sheepskin hat persisted until Yanda finally remembered that the village was somewhere near Kielce, between Checzyn and Sobkow. The salesman told Yanda to take out the bank notes that she kept wrapped in a handkerchief and helped her to count the money. He talked it over with the ticket seller. There was no direct train to that area. The best way to go was by horse and buggy to Rozwadow, and from there on to Sandomierz, then to Opola, where she could either get a ride in another cart or go on foot to Skibica.

Just hearing the names of these familiar places made Yanda weep. In Skibica, she had once had a father, a mother, a sister, relatives. Her mother had died and her father, not long before he died, had married another woman. Yanda had been about to become engaged to Wojciech, a peasant boy, but the blacksmith's daughter, a girl called Zocha, had taken him away. During the years Yanda had worked for Shalom Pintchever she had seldom thought of the past. It all seemed so far away, at the end of the earth. But now that her employer was dead, there was nothing left for her but to return home. Who knew, perhaps some of her close ones were alive. Perhaps somebody there still remembered her name.

Thank God, good people helped. No sooner had Yanda left the town where she had lived in shame, than they stopped laughing at her, making grimaces, spitting. The coachmen did not overcharge her. Jews with beards and sidelocks seemed to know the whole of Poland as well as they knew the palms of their hands. They mentioned names of places which Yanda had already forgotten, and looked for shortcuts. In one tavern,

someone took out a map to find the shortest way home for her. Yanda marveled at the cleverness of men; how much knowledge they carried in their heads and how eager they were to help a homeless woman. But despite all the good advice, Yanda walked more than she rode. Rains soaked her, there was snow and hail. She waded through ditches of water as deep as streams. She had grown accustomed to sleeping on pillows with clean pillowcases, between white sheets, under a warm eiderdown, but now she was forced to stretch out on the floors of granaries and barns. Her clothes were wet through. Somehow she managed to keep her paper money dry. As Yanda walked she thought about her life. Once in a while Shalom Pintchever had given her money but it had dwindled away. The Russians had counted in rubles and kopecks. When the Austrians came the ruble lost its value, and everything was exchanged for kronen and hellers. The Bolsheviks used chervontzi; the Poles, zlotys. How was someone like Yanda, uneducated as she was, to keep track of such changes? It was a miracle that she had anything left with which to get home.

God in heaven, men were still chasing her! Wherever she slept, peasants came to her and had their way with her. In a wagon, at night, somebody seized her silently. What do they see in me? Yanda asked herself. It's my bad luck. Yanda remembered that she had never been able to refuse anyone. Her father had beaten her for her submissiveness. Her stepmother had torn Yanda's hair. Even as a child when she played with the other children, they had smeared her face with mud, given her a broom and made her take the part of Baba-Yaga. With the guests in Shalom's hotel, she had had such savage and foolish experiences that she sometimes hadn't known whether to laugh or cry. But

to say no was not in her nature. When she was young, while still in her father's village, she had twice given birth to babies, but they had both died. Several times heavy work had caused her to miscarry. She could never really forget Wojciech, the peasant boy to whom she had almost been engaged, but who at the last moment had thrown her over. Yanda also had desired Shalom Pintchever, perhaps because he had always sent her to others and had never taken her himself. He would say, "Yanda, go to number three —Yanda, knock at the door of number seven." He himself had remained faithful to his old wife, Shaindel. Perhaps he had been disgusted by Yanda, but she had yearned for him. One kind word from him pleased her more than all the wild games of the others. Even when he scolded her, she waited for more. As for the guests, there were so many of them, that Yanda had forgotten all but a few who stuck in her memory. One Russian had demanded that Yanda spit on him, tear at his beard, and call him ugly names. Another, a schoolboy with red cheeks, had kissed her and called her mother. He had slept on her breast until dawn, although guests in other rooms had been waiting for her.

Now Yanda was old. But how old? She did not know herself—certainly in her forties, or perhaps fifty? Other women her age were grandmothers but she was returning to her village, alone, abandoned by God and man. Yanda made a resolution: once home, she would allow no man to approach her. In a village, there was always gossip and it usually ended in a quarrel. What did she need it for? The truth was that all this whoring had never given her any pleasure.

III

The Jews who showed Yanda the way had not fooled her. She reached

Skibica in the morning, and even though it had changed considerably, she recognized her home. In a chapel at the outskirts of the village God's mother still stood with a halo around her head and the Christ child in her arms. The figure had become dingy with the years and a piece of the Holy Mother's shoulder was chipped off. A wreath of wilted flowers hung around her neck. Yanda's eyes filled with tears. She knelt in the snow and crossed herself. She walked into the village, and a smell she had long forgotten came to her nostrils: an odor of soggy potatoes, burned feathers, earth, and something else that had no name, but that her nose recognized. The huts were half-sunk into the ground, with tiny windows and low doors. The thatched roofs were mossy and rotting. Crows were cawing; smoke rose from the chimneys. Yanda looked for the hut where her parents had lived but it had disappeared and in its place was a smithy. She put down the sack she was carrying on her back. Dogs sniffed at her and barked. Women emerged from the dwellings. The younger ones did not know her, but the old ones clapped their hands and pinched their cheeks, calling.

"Oh, Father, Mother, Jesu Maria."

"Yes, it's Yanda, as I love God."

Men, too, came to look at her, some from behind the stoves where they had been sleeping, others from the tavern. One peasant woman invited Yanda into her hut. She gave her a piece of black bread and a cup of milk. On the dirt floor stood bins filled with potatoes, beets, black radishes, and cranberries. Chickens were cackling in a coop. The oven had a built-in kettle for hot water. At a spinning wheel sat an old woman with a balding head from which hung tufts of hair as white as flax. Someone screamed into her ear.

"Grandma, this is Yanda. Pawel Kuckma's daughter."

The old woman crossed herself. "Jesu Maria."

The peasant women all spoke together. Pawel Kuchma's home had burned down. Yanda's brother, Bolek, had gone to war and never returned. Her sister, Stasia, had married a man from Biczew and died there in childbirth. They also told Yanda what had happened to Wojciech, her former bridegroom-to-be. He had married Zocha and she had borne him fourteen children. Nine of them were still alive, but their mother had died of typhoid fever. As for Wojciech, he had been drinking all these years. Zocha had worked for others to support the family. After her death three years before, he had become a complete derelict. Everything went for drink and he was half crazy. His boys ran around, wild. The girls washed clothes for the Jews of the town. His hut was practically in ruins. As the women spoke to Yanda somebody opened the door and pushed a tall man inside. He was as lean as a stick, barefoot, with holes in his pants. He wore an open jacket without a shirt, his hair was long and disheveled—a living scarecrow. He did not walk, but staggered along as though on stilts. He had mad eyes, a dripping nose, and his crooked mouth showed one long tooth. Somebody said,

"Wojciech, do you recognize this woman?"

"Pockmarked Yanda."

There was laughter and clapping. For the first time in years Yanda blushed.

"See how you look."

"I heard you are a whore."

There was laughter again.

"Don't listen to him, Yanda, he's drunk."

"What am I drunk on? Nobody gives me a drop of vodka."

Yanda gaped at him. Could this be Wojciech? Some similarity remained. She wanted to cry. She remembered an expression of Shaindel's, "There are some in their graves who look better than he does." Yanda regretted that she had come back to Skibica. A woman said,

"Why don't you have a look at his children?"

Yanda immediately lifted up her sack. She offered to pay for the bread and milk but the peasant woman rebuked her, "This is not the city. Here, you don't pay for a piece of bread." Wojciech's hut stood nearby. The roof almost touched the ground. Elflocks of straw hung from its edges. The windows had no panes. They were stuffed with rags or boarded up. One entered it like a cave. The floor had rotted away. The walls were as black as the inside of a chimney. In the semidarkness Yanda saw boys, girls. The place stank of dirty linen, rot, and something rancid. Yanda clutched her nose. Two girls stood at the tub. Half-naked children, smeared with mud, crawled on the floor. One child was pulling the tail of a kitten. A boy with a blind eye was mending a trap. Yanda blinked. She was no longer accustomed to such squalor. At the inn, the sheets had been changed each week. Every third day the guests got fresh towels. The leftover food had been enough to feed a whole family. Well, dirt has to be removed. It won't disappear by itself.

Yanda rolled up her sleeves. She still had a few zlotys and she sent one of the girls to buy food. A Jew had a store in the village where one could get bagels, herring, chickory. God in heaven, how the children devoured those stale bagels! Yanda began to sweep and scrub. She went to the well for water. At first the girls ignored her. Then told her not to meddle in their affairs. But Yanda said, "I will take nothing from you. Your mother, peace be with her, was my friend."

Yanda worked until evening. She heated water and washed the children. She sent an older child to buy soap, a fine comb, and kerosene which kills lice. Every few minutes she poured out the slops. Neighbors came to look and shook their heads. They all said the same thing, Yanda's work was in vain. The vermin could not be removed from that hut. In the evening, there was no lamp to light and Yanda bought a small kerosene lamp. The whole family slept on one wooden platform, and there were few blankets. Yanda covered the children with her own clothes. Late in the evening, the door opened and Wojciech intruded a leg. The girls began to giggle. Stefan, the boy with the blind eye, had already made friends with Yanda. He said,

"Here he comes—the skunk."

"You must not talk like that about your father."

Stefan replied with a village proverb, "When your father is a dog, you say 'git' to him."

Yanda had saved a bagel and a piece of herring for Wojciech, but he was too drunk to eat. He fell down like a log, muttering and drooling. The girls stepped over him. Stefan mentioned that there was a straw mat in the shed behind the hut that Yanda could use to sleep on. He offered to show her where it was. As soon as she opened the door of the shed, the boy pushed her and she fell. He threw himself on her. She tried to tell him that it was a sin, but he stopped her mouth with his hand. She struggled but he beat her with a heavy fist. She lay in the dark on woodshavings, garbage, rotting rope, and the boy satisfied himself. Yanda closed her eyes. Well, I'm lost anyhow, she thought. Out loud, she muttered, "Woe is me, I might have been your mother."

The Birth of a Devouring Spirit

THE SECOND COMING

W. B. YEATS

Turning and turning in the widening gyre
The falcon cannot hear the falconer;
Things fall apart; the centre cannot hold;
Mere anarchy is loosed upon the world,
The blood-dimmed tide is loosed, and everywhere
The ceremony of innocence is drowned;
The best lack all conviction, while the worst
Are full of passionate intensity.

Surely some revelation is at hand;
Surely the Second Coming is at hand.
The Second Coming! Hardly are those words out
When a vast image out of *Spiritus Mundi*
Troubles my sight: somewhere in sands of the desert
A shape with lion body and the head of a man,
A gaze blank and pitiless as the sun,
Is moving its slow thighs, while all about it
Reel shadows of the indignant desert birds.
The darkness drops again; but now I know
That twenty centuries of stony sleep
Were vexed to nightmare by a rocking cradle,
And what rough beast, its hour come round at last,
Slouches towards Bethlehem to be born?

In the preceding selections, the Great Goddess symbolizes the transformation of life and death. The following questions focus on the woman's rite of passage as a bringer of spiritual wisdom.

1 Compare and contrast Demeter and Ishtar as symbolic embodiments of the female as the heroine who descends into the world of death in order to be reborn eternally.

   a What symbols are used to describe the process of life and death? How do these symbols reflect the world of nature?

   b Describe what causes each to descend into the underworld. How do they encounter elements of the mother in this state of existence? What is the male's role in the underworld?

   c What happens on the earth during their absence? What symbols are used to bring about their release from the underworld?

   d What insights into the nature of life and death do we see revealed in these myths? What is the female's relation to nature? What is her relation to the social world? In what ways do these women resemble Dionysus and Christ? How do they reveal the human relation to time?

2 Compare and contrast the image of the woman that emerges in Electra's, Antigone's, Cleopatra's, and Joan's speeches.

   a What attitudes toward life and death emerge in these speeches? How do these women bring together both of these forces?

   b Why are these women in revolt against patriarchal rules? What kind of separation does this cause? How do these women also come to terms with a male element in their speeches? What does this suggest?

   c What spiritual wisdom is demonstrated by these women? What is the source of their strength? How do these women, though close to death, reveal sexual powers? In what ways do these women reflect the plight of Demeter and Ishtar? Explain!

3 Discuss Singer's "Yanda" as a story of the woman's rite of passage toward acceptance of her ability to endure.

   a What causes Yanda's separation from her home? What tests does she encounter in her search for wholeness? How does Singer use the role of temptress to depict her isolation from other women?

   b What symbols does Singer use to weave his story? How do these symbols connect Yanda to nature?

   c How does death bring about Yanda's return home? What happens to her on her return? What knowledge does she possess because of her journey? How does Singer connect the whore to the Mother of Christ? What does this suggest?

   d What does the ending of the story suggest about the female's relation to the male? In what ways does Yanda represent a woman who brings nourishment, protection, and transformation to those around her? How does Yanda differ from and compare with the Great Goddess as presented in this chapter?

4 Discuss the way Yeats uses his poem to suggest what has brought about the transformation of "good and evil" from love to destruction.

   a What image of motion is revealed in the first stanza? How has "evil" replaced "good"? What does Yeats suggest about the concept of "innocence"?

   b What images does Yeats use to describe the birth of a new Christ? How does he connect this symbol to the world of nature? What fear of the feminine is revealed in this connection?

   c Discuss what he means by the "rough beast"! Does he foreshadow the tyrant who rules in the twentieth century? What has happened to love? Why do you think creation is replaced by destruction? How does this reveal what happens when we repress either the male or female elements in human beings? What has been transformed in this poem?

The Modern Era ... a Time of Transition

In Dali's painting, we glimpse an image of the once self-enamored Narcissus who is no longer sure what image of self he seeks to attain. This painting captures the spirit of our time of transition. Not only are we incapable of love, but we are no longer able to define what love means to us. Hence we can understand that the pursuit of an unclear image is not an adequate substitution for the experience of self in relation to others.

We are the hollow men
We are the stuffed men. . . .

from "The Hollow Men"
T. S. Eliot

Let others complain that times are bad, I complain that they are petty because they lack passion. . . . Men's thoughts are too petty to be sinful. A worm might consider such thoughts to be sinful, but not a man created in the image of god. Their pleasures are circumspect and boring; their passions sleep.

Sören Kierkegaard

NARCISSUS

GREEK MYTH

On the banks of Cephisus, Echo saw and loved the beautiful Narcissus; but the youth cared not for the maiden of the hills, and his heart was cold to the words of her love, for he mourned for his sister whom Hermes had taken away beyond the Stygian river. Day by day he sat alone by the stream side, sorrowing for the bright maiden whose life was bound up with his own, because they had seen the light of the sun on the selfsame day; and thither came Echo and sat down by his side and sought in vain to win his love. "Look on me and see," she said. "I am fairer than the sister for whom thou dost mourn." But Narcissus answered her not, for he knew that the maiden would ever have something to say against his words. So he sat silent and looked down into the stream, and there he saw his own face in the clear water, and it was to him as the face of his sister for whom he pined away in sorrow; and his grief became less bitter as he seemed to see again her soft blue eyes and almost to hear the words which came from her lips. But the grief of Narcissus was too deep for tears, and it dried up slowly the fountain of his life. In vain the words of Echo fell upon his ears as she prayed him to hearken to her prayer. "Ah, Narcissus, thou mournest for one who cannot heed thy sorrow, and thou carest not for her who longs to see thy face and hear thy voice forever." But Narcissus saw still in the waters of Cephisus the face of his twin sister, and still gazing at it he fell asleep and died. Then the voice of Echo was heard no more, for she sat in silence by his grave; and a beautiful flower came up close to it. Its white blossoms drooped over the banks of Cephisus where Narcissus had sat and looked down into its clear water, and the people of the land called the plant after his name.

THE HANGED MAN.

XXI

THE WORLD

Only the liberation of the natural capacity for love in human beings can master their sadistic destructiveness.

Wilhelm Reich

In the twentieth century, human beings are forced to define their identities in a time of instant change. This makes it difficult for individuals to seek the meanings which lie beneath the human mask. Our political leaders are elected because of their images, rather than the ideals for which they stand. Our heroes and heroines are movie stars who make fantasy seem more exciting than the real. Rock stars are paid thousands of dollars to wear a mask of authenticity. Love seems to be a matter of performance, rather than an expression of our emotions. Wars are fought to attain "an honorable peace," while thousands of people die needlessly. The concentration of power has never been greater, and yet, more people feel powerless than ever before. We seem to be strangers to ourselves and others, and the promise of instant cure through encounter groups has not solved our feelings of alienation. Some still cling to the illusion that enough money will make the world a better place to live in; but few, if any, are able to deny that our spirit seems troubled.

This denial of the life force is an expression of individuals who have forgotten how to live and love. Perhaps we are all undergoing a rite of passage in this period of transition. There will always be contradictions between the way the world is and the way we would like it to be. Our crucial question is not whether we want to change the world, but what kind of world we want. We might remember Oedipus when he is a blind exile wandering from his homeland. He reaches for the hand of his daughter who accompanies him, and he says: ". . . despite my many ordeals and the advancement of my age, I conclude that all is well." This remark reveals that we can change our possibilities into realities. The power to affirm the life force lies within the creative use of our energies. We may choose to move with or against this force, but we can not deny that the choice is ours to make.

The Modern Era: The Destruction of the Temples

I have found that life persists in the midst of destruction and, therefore, there must be a higher law than that of destruction.

Mahatma Gandhi

THE END OF THE WORLD

JEREMIAH 4:19–26
ca. 650 B.C.

My anguish, my anguish! I writhe in pain!
    Oh, the walls of my heart!
My heart is beating wildly;
    I cannot keep silent;
For I hear the sound of the trumpet,
    the alarm of war.
Disaster follows hard on disaster,
    the whole land is laid waste.
Suddenly my tents are destroyed,
    my curtains in a moment.
How long must I see the standard,
    and hear the sound of the trumpet?
"For my people are foolish,
    they know me not;
They are stupid children,
    they have no understanding.
They are skilled in doing evil,
    but how to do good they know not."

I looked on the earth, and lo, it was waste and void;
    and to the heavens, and they had no light.
I looked on the mountains, and lo, they were quaking,
    and all the hills moved to and fro.
I looked, and lo, there was no man,
    and all the birds of the air had fled.
I looked, and lo, the fruitful land was a desert,
    and all its cities were laid in ruins
        before the Lord, before his fierce anger.

THE END OF THE WORLD

ARCHIBALD MACLEISH

Quite unexpectedly as Vasserot
The armless ambidextrian was lighting
A match between his great and second toe
And Ralph the lion was engaged in biting
The neck of Madame Sossman while the drum
Pointed, and Teeny was about to cough
In waltz-time swinging Jocko by the thumb—
Quite unexpectedly the top blew off:

And there, there overhead, there, there, hung over
Those thousands of white faces, those dazed eyes,
There in the starless dark the poise, the hover,
There with vast wings across the canceled skies,
There in the sudden blackness the black pall
Of nothing, nothing, nothing—nothing at all.

The atomic age makes it possible for modern individuals to face the possibility of the extinction of the human race. Science creates the means to wield the power once held only by the gods and goddesses who ruled over the abyss between life and death.

The end of the world is a concept which has long occupied the imagination. The knowledge that all human beings who live must die has led man to seek out the possibility of total annihilation. In 1945, the dropping of the atomic bomb on a human population marked the beginning of the modern age of destruction. We who live in the twentieth century tend to think that we are the only people who have faced this awesome possibility. Yet, in the past, we often find prophets predicting how the world will end. In Jeremiah we see the vision of a world no longer capable of supporting life. The reason for this impending destruction is the Lord's anger at those who were "skilled in doing evil," and who were unable to know "how to do good." Jeremiah depicts a world without light or hope. MacLeish, on the other hand, views this final catastrophe as occurring "quite unexpectedly." His poem evokes the image of the world as the center ring of a circus. The characters who act out their drama attempt to do the impossible. MacLeish uses images which cannot be to evoke this: "The armless ambidextrian," and so on. These images suggest the struggle of the world leaders to gain control no matter what the odds. The audience, the rest of humanity, sits and watches with "dazed eyes" as the sky is torn assunder. The poet introduces the absurd attempt of all who wait to see "nothing" as human life becomes extinct. Each of these poets intertwines the fate of the individual with a social world which seems bent on denying this connection.

Compare and contrast Jeremiah and MacLeish from the following perspectives:

1   What events bring about this final act of destruction? What image of political leaders emerges in each poem? How do the masses of people appear in contrast to their leaders? How do the poets connect war to the world's ending?

2   How does each poet evoke a sense of fear in what he sees? How does Jeremiah's description of the way the earth appears relate to MacLeish's emphasis on "nothing"? Why does each poem repeat its final comments? What is the poet attempting to do to the reader? How successful is the poet in convincing us of his vision?

3   In what ways do these poems mirror the modern need to reflect on the frailty of human existence? What does each poem suggest about the need for human interaction? What brings us to deny this need?

One of the most important functions of primitive mythology was to give supernatural or at least historical legitimacy to the ruling group which governed a tribe. The myth usually reveals the way the ruler was blessed by a divine signal elevating him to the position of authority. For the ancient Incas, the children of the sun teach the family of man how to choose a leader, as related in the following account.

The men who lived upon earth lived in ignorance and fear. They had no llamas, did not know how to grow crops, and did not know how to build houses. But Inti, the sun, took pity upon them and sent his son and daughter to mankind. He set them in a boat on Lake Titicaca and gave them his golden staff.

When the children of the sun found men, they taught them how to live together peacefully. They taught them to marry and live in families and how to choose leaders. They showed the men how to grow corn and tame llamas and make clothes from their wool. Gold, silver, and clay were also their gifts, and they showed them how to build houses and temples. They also taught the rules that were given unto the Incas.

Before they left, they told the people that the sun himself had adopted the Incas as his children and chosen them to rule over the rest of the world. And from that time on the Incas ruled the land and spread the worship of the sun among all the tribes of the land.

The beginning of social organization for the Incas comes from an "outside" force which sanctions their authority. For modern individuals, the city is the symbol which brings the individual into contact with a world. The divine signal which marks who is to rule the vast, amorphous, modern city picks out those who are best able to ensure the group's survival. The transformation of energy into power is symbolized by the machine. The dream of creating an end to scarcity has long been part of man's desire to conquer nature. Those who control the means of production do so in the desire to create a better way of life. Unfortunately, the dilemma created by the machine might be stated as follows: The machine has made possible a life beyond the reach of death, or created a death beyond the reaches of life. In the Western world the desire to use this potent force is connected to the productive use of time. "Time is money," states Benjamin Franklin. And for Max Weber this concept is the heart of the Protestant ethic. The rhythm of the machine's schedule becomes a metaphor to gauge modern life. Time becomes the measure of one's life. We speak of "free time" away from work. If we are not satisfied by our objects of production, we think we have not worked hard enough to fulfill our expectations. The pleasure of consumption takes time, and we must be sure not to be idle less we waste this valuable commodity. Our obsession for regulating our lives is well conveyed by F. Scott Fitzgerald in his novel *The Great Gatsby:*

Rise from bed	6.00	A.M.
Dumbbell exercise and		
wall-scaling	6.15–6.30	"
Study electricity, etc.	7.15–8.15	"
Work	8.30–4.30	P.M.
Baseball and sports	4.30–5.00	"
Practice elocution,		
poise and how to attain it	5.00–6.00	"
Study needed inventions	7.00–9.00	"

General Resolves

No wasting time at Shafters or [a name, indecipherable]
No more smokeing or chewing.
Bath every other day
Read one improving book or magazine per week
Save $5.00 [crossed out] $3.00 per week
Be better to parents

Such a rationalization of how one allocates his time in order to be saved leads to a linear approach to life. The human brain is more complex than any computer, and yet we allow computers to rule us. Transferring the use of energy to machines prevents us from seeing the multidimensions of nature. In order not to become one of the walking dead, we must recognize that we are part of the basic unity of the universe. To do this, we must see how the invisible elements attached to our interpretation of the machine organize our collective enterprize in the twentieth century.

Man's illusion of the domination of nature

In this city street, we see the machine used to symbolize our domination of nature. When the male rule overthrew the female rule, the leaders of authority sought to repress nature's hold on the human being. Thus male rulers had to create a society based on law and order, a conflict presented to us from Abraham to Jesus in the Bible. For the modern individual, the need to adapt to a world is synonymous with the ability to create an image of success, which means planning for a future. The supervisors of this process are the fathers of our culture who symbolize and supervise our adaption to their principles. Erich Neumann states:

This paternal authority, whose necessity for culture and the development of consciousness is beyond dispute, differs from the maternal authority in that it is essentially relative, being conditioned by its day and generation, and not having the absolute character of the maternal authority. —from *The Origins and History of Consciousness*

In our "day and generation" this transformation is made possible only as we adapt to the standards set by city living. Machinery makes possible the modern temple which stands erect to proclaim our faith in the masculine world. The modern city is a testimony to the guiding spirit of masculine authority. Our buildings mark the posts which stand tall to express and solidify our system of belief. Neumann contends that the systems of religion created in Western civilization are all in different ranks and degress a testimony to this masculine spirit. He states:

> The man's world, representing "heaven," stands for law and tradition, for the gods of aforetime, so far as they were masculine gods. It is no accident that all human culture, and not Western civilization alone, is masculine in character, from Greece and the Judaeo-Christian sphere of culture to Islam and India. Although woman's share in this culture is invisible and largely unconscious, we should not underestimate its significance and scope. The masculine trend, however, is towards greater co-ordination of spirit, ego, consciousness, and will. Because man discovers his true self in consciousness, and is a stranger to himself in the unconscious, which he must inevitably experience as feminine, the development of masculine culture means development of consciousness.
>
> Historically speaking, it seems to us that the phenomenon of totemism is of great importance for the development of "heaven" and the spiritual world of man. For this phenomenon, even though it originated in the matriarchal epoch, is specifically masculine in spirit.
> —from *The Origins and History of Consciousness*

To understand how the machine affects the modern world, we must realize what a powerful imprint this symbol has cast on the human psyche through the centuries. The Hebrews were concerned with revealing a universal spirit who could frighten their tribe into obeying the system of laws which perpetuated their concept of being the chosen people. The Greeks, on the other hand, were interested in creating a secular order of life. They emphasized the study of forms, revealing a belief in an orderly view of the universe. The Romans were the first to show a strong affinity for machines. To ensure their dominion over others, they relied heavily on modes of transportation. They needed technology to support their way of life. The machine blossomed during the Renaissance. It was Leonardo da Vinci who captured the imagination of man's minds for the next four hundred years. The dream of da Vinci seemed a "reality" as transportation began to increase until finally man was able to fly, as he had predicted.

Before too long, however, certain individuals began to question whether the machine had turned from dream to nightmare, as we see in the next selections. In Henry David Thoreau's essay, we see how the machine subdues man into a state of submission. The metaphor Thoreau uses is stated thusly: "We do not ride on the railroad; it rides upon us." In his poem "To a Locomotive in Winter" Walt Whitman expresses a vision of the power and fear of the machine. There is an underlying sexual connotation to Whitman's attraction. Samuel Butler, on the other hand, attempts to create a humorous but serious tone to his utopian view of the machine. Butler warns that we better get the machine before it gets us. Finally in Thomas Wolfe's "Only the Dead Know Brooklyn" we see an image of the modern world which has moved from heaven to the bowels of the earth. This suggests our need to understand the way individuals use power to either destroy or orient themselves in the modern world. Each of these selections focuses on the impact of the machine on our sensibilities. Marshall McLuhan contends that the invention of the printing press changed man's multidimensional orientation into a linear view of a world. McLuhan argues that each succeeding invention brought about the loss of various parts of the human body: with the wheel we gave up our feet; with the radio we gave up our ears; with the movies we gave up our eyes; and with the television we are in danger of giving up our central nervous system. McLuhan emphasizes that each mode of communication man invents alters his perceptions of the world. The result of all this technology is that we began to relate to ourselves as pieces of machinery. We fail to remember that the machine is a human invention. The uses we make of our machines relate to our dream of being in power over the physical world, a dream that has brought us to the edge of doom as push-button warfare makes possible the extinction of life. It matters little whether this act is committed in the name of peace or not. What matters is our inability to go beyond our limited experiences to envision a universe.

WHERE I LIVED AND WHAT I LIVED FOR

HENRY DAVID THOREAU

They say that characters were engraven on the bathing tub of King Tching-thang to this effect: "Renew thyself completely each day; do it again, and again, and forever again." I can understand that. Morning brings back the heroic ages. I was as much affected by the faint hum of a mosquito making its invisible and unimaginable tour through my apartment at earliest dawn, when I was sitting with door and windows open, as I could be by any trumpet that ever sang of fame. It was Homer's requiem; itself an Iliad and Odyssey in the air, singing its own wrath and wanderings. There was something cosmical about it; a standing advertisement, till forbidden, of the everlasting vigor and fertility of the world. The morning, which is the most memorable season of the day, is the awakening hour. Then there is least somnolence in us; and for an hour, at least, some part of us awakes which slumbers all the rest of the day and night. Little is to be expected of that day, if it can be called a day, to which we are not awakened by our Genius, but by the mechanical nudgings of some servitor, are not awakened by our own newly acquired force and aspirations from within, accompanied by the undulations of celestial music, instead of factory bells, and a fragrance filling the air—to a higher life than we fell asleep from; and thus the darkness bear its fruit, and prove itself to be good, no less than the light. That man who does not believe that each day contains an earlier, more sacred, and auroral hour than he has yet profaned, has despaired of life, and is pursuing a descending and darkening way. After a partial cessation of his sensuous life, the soul of man, or its organs rather, are reinvigorated each day, and his Genius tries again what noble life it can make. All memorable events, I should say, transpire in morning time and in a morning atmosphere. The Vedas say, "All intelligences awake with the morning." Poetry and art, and the fairest and most memorable of the actions of men, date from such an hour. All poets and heroes, like Memnon, are the children of Aurora, and emit their music at sunrise. To him whose elastic and vigorous thought keeps pace with the sun, the day is a perpetual morning. It matters not what the clocks say or the attitudes and labors of men. Morning is when I am awake and there is a dawn in me. Moral reform is the effort to throw off sleep. Why is it that men give so poor an account of their day if they have not been slumbering? They are not such poor calculators. If they had not been overcome with drowsiness, they would have performed something. The millions are awake enough for physical labor; but only one in a million is awake enough for effective intellectual exertion, only one in a hundred millions to a poetic or divine life. To be awake is to be alive. I have never yet met a man who was quite awake. How could I have looked him in the face?

We must learn to reawaken and keep ourselves awake, not by mechanical aids, but by an infinite expection of the dawn, which does not forsake us in our soundest sleep. I know of no more encouraging fact than the unquestionable ability of man to elevate his life by a conscious endeavor. It is something to be able to paint a particular picture, or to carve a statue, and so to make a few objects beautiful; but it is far more glorious to carve and paint the very atmosphere and medium through which we look, which morally we can do. To affect the quality of the day, that is the highest of arts. Every man is tasked to make his life, even in its details, worthy of the contemplation of his most elevated and critical hour. If we refused, or rather used up, such paltry information as we get, the oracles would distinctly inform us how this might be done.

I went to the woods because I wished to live deliberately, to front only the essential facts of life, and see if I could learn what it had to teach, and not, when I came to die, discover that I had not lived. I did not wish to live what was not life, living is so dear; nor did I wish to practise resignation, unless it was quite necessary. I wanted to live deep and suck out all the marrow of life, to live so sturdily and Spartan-like as to put to rout all that was not life, to cut a broad swath and shave close, to drive life into a corner, and reduce it to its lowest terms, and, if it proved to be mean, why then to get the whole and genuine meanness of it, and publish its meanness to the world; or if it were sublime, to know it by experience, and be able to give a true account of it in my next excursion. For most men, it appears to me, are in a strange uncertainty about it, whether it is of the devil or of God, and have *somewhat hastily* concluded that it is the chief end of man here to "glorify God and enjoy him forever."

Still we live meanly, like ants; though the fable tells us that we were long ago changed into men; like pygmies we fight with cranes; it is error upon error, and clout upon clout, and our best virtue has for its occasion a superfluous and evitable wretchedness. Our life is frittered away by detail. An honest man has hardly need to count more than his ten fingers, or in extreme cases he may add his ten toes, and lump the rest. Simplicity, simplicity, simplicity! I say, let your affairs be as two or three, and not a hundred or a thousand; instead of a million count half a dozen, and keep your accounts on your thumb-nail. In the midst of this chopping sea of civilized life, such are the clouds and storms and quicksands and thousand-and-one items to be allowed for, that a man has to live, if he would not founder and go to the bottom and not make his port at all, by dead reckoning, and he must be a great calculator indeed who succeeds. Simplify, simplify. Instead of three meals a day, if it be necessary eat but one; instead of a hundred dishes, five; and reduce other things in proportion. Our life is like a German Confederacy, made up of petty states, with its boundary forever fluctuating, so that even a German cannot tell you how it is bounded at any moment. The nation itself, with all its so-called internal improvements, which, by the way, are all external and superficial, is just such an unwieldy and overgrown establishment, cluttered with furniture and tripped up by its own traps, ruined by luxury and heedless expense, by want of calculation and a worthy aim, as the million households in the land; and the only cure for it, as for them, is in a rigid economy, a stern and more than Spartan simplicity of life and elevation of purpose. It lives too fast. Men think that it is essential that the *Nation* have commerce, and export ice, and talk through a telegraph, and ride thirty miles an hour, without a doubt, whether *they* do or not; but whether we should live like baboons or like men, is a little uncertain. If we do not get out sleepers, and forge rails, and devote days and nights to the work, but go to tinkering upon our *lives* to improve *them*, who will build railroads? And if railroads are not built, how shall we get to Heaven in season? But if we stay at home and mind our business, who will want railroads? We do not ride on the railroad; it rides upon us. Did you ever think what those sleepers are that underlie the railroad? Each one is a man, an Irishman, or a Yankee man. The rails are laid on them, and they are covered with sand, and the cars run smoothly over them. They are sound sleepers, I assure you. And every few years a new lot is laid down and run over; so that, if some have the pleasure of riding on a rail, others have the misfortune to be ridden upon. And when they run over a man that is walking in his sleep, a supernumerary sleeper in the wrong position, and wake him up, they suddenly stop the cars, and make a hue and cry about it, as if this were an exception. I am glad to know that it takes a gang of men for every five miles to keep the sleepers down and level in their beds as it is, for this is a sign that they may sometime get up again.

TO A LOCOMOTIVE
IN WINTER

WALT WHITMAN

Thee for my recitative,
Thee in the driving storm even as now, the snow,
    the winter-day declining,
Thee in thy panoply, thy measur'd dual throbbing
    and thy beat convulsive,
Thy black cylindric body, golden brass and silvery
    steel,
Thy ponderous sidebars, parallel and connecting
    rods, gyrating, shuttling at thy sides,
Thy metrical, now swelling pant and roar, now
    tapering in the distance,
Thy great protruding head-light fix'd in front,
Thy long, pale, floating vapor-pennants, tinged with
    delicate purple,
Thy dense and murky clouds out-belching from thy
    smoke-stack,
Thy knitted frame, thy springs and valves, the
    tremulous twinkle of thy wheels,
Thy train of cars behind, obedient, merrily following,
Through gale or calm, now swift, now slack, yet
    steadily careering;
Type of the modern—emblem of motion and power
    —pulse of the continent,
For once come serve the Muse and merge in verse,
    even as here I see thee,
With storm and buffeting gusts of wind and falling
    snow,
By day thy warning ringing bell to sound its notes,
By night thy silent signal lamps to swing.
Fierce-throated beauty!
Roll through my chant with all thy lawless music,
    thy swinging lamps at night,
Thy madly-whistled laughter, echoing, rumbling like
    an earthquake, rousing all,
Law of thyself complete, thine own track firmly
    holding,
(No sweetness debonair of tearful harp or glib piano
    thine,)
Thy trills of shrieks by rocks and hills return'd,
Launch'd o'er the prairies wide, across the lakes,
To the free skies unpent and glad and strong.

The Book of the Machines

SAMUEL BUTLER

The writer commences:—"There was a time, when the earth was to all appearance utterly destitute both of animal and vegetable life, and when according to the opinion of our best philosophers it was simply a hot round ball with a crust gradually cooling. Now if a human being had existed while the earth was in this state and had been allowed to see it as though it were some other world with which he had no concern, and if at the same time he were entirely ignorant of all physical science, would he not have pronounced it impossible that creatures possessed of anything like consciousness should be evolved from the seeming cinder which he was beholding? Would he not have denied that it contained any potentiality of consciousness? Yet in the course of time consciousness came. Is it not possible then that there may be even yet new channels dug out for consciousness, though we can detect no signs of them at present?

"There is no security"—to quote his own words—"against the ultimate development of mechanical consciousness, in the fact of machines possessing little consciousness now. A mollusc has not much consciousness. Reflect upon the extraordinary advance which machines have made during the last few hundred years, and note how slowly the animal and vegetable kingdoms are advancing. The more highly organized machines are creatures not so much of yesterday, as of the last five minutes, so to speak, in comparison with past time. Assume for the sake of argument that conscious beings have existed for some twenty million years: see what strides machines have made in the last thousand! May not the world last twenty million years longer? If so, what will they not in the end become? Is it not safer to nip the mischief in the bud and to forbid them further progress?

"But who can say that the vapor engine has not a kind of consciousness? Where does consciousness begin, and where end? Who can draw the line? Who can draw any line? Is not everything interwoven with everything? Is not machinery linked with animal life in an infinite variety of ways? The shell of a hen's egg is made of a delicate white ware and is a machine as much as an egg-cup is: the shell is a device for holding the egg, as much as the egg-cup for holding the shell: both are phases of the same function; the hen makes the shell in her inside, but it is pure pottery. She makes her nest outside of herself for convenience' sake, but the nest is not more of a machine than the egg-shell is. A 'machine' is only a 'device.'"

Then returning to consciousness, and endeavoring to detect its earliest manifestations, the writer continued:—

"There is a kind of plant that eats organic food with its flowers: when a fly settles upon the blossom, the petals close upon it and hold it fast till the plant has absorbed the insect into its system; but they will close on nothing but what is good to eat; of a drop of rain or a piece of stick they will take no notice. Curious! that so unconscious a thing should have such a keen eye to its own interest. If this is unconsciousness, where is the use of consciousness?

"Do not let me be misunderstood as living in fear of any actually existing machine; there is probably no known machine which is more than a prototype of future mechanical life. The present machines are to the future as the early Saurians to man. The largest of them will probably greatly diminish in size. Some of the lowest vertebrata attained a much greater bulk than has descended to their more highly organized living representatives, and in like manner a diminution in size of machines has often attended their development and progress.

"Take the watch, for example; examine its beautiful structure; observe the intelligent play of the minute members which compose it; yet this little creature is but a development of the cumbrous clocks that preceded it; it is no deterioration from them. A day may come when clocks, which certainly at the present time are not diminishing in bulk, will be superseded owing to the universal use of watches, in which case they will become as extinct as ichthyosauri, while the watch, whose tendency has for some years been to decrease in size rather than the contrary, will remain the only existing type of an extinct race.

"But returning to the argument, I would repeat that I fear none of the existing machines; what I fear is the extraordinary rapidity with which they are becoming something very different to what they are at present. No class of beings have in any time past made so rapid a movement forward. Should not that movement be jealously watched, and checked while we can still check it? And is it not necessary for this end to destroy the more advanced of the machines which are in use at present, though it is admitted that they are in themselves harmless?

"As yet the machines receive their impressions through the agency of man's senses: one traveling machine calls to another in a shrill accent of alarm and the other instantly retires; but it is through the ears of the driver that the voice of the one has acted upon the other. Had there been no driver, the callee would have been deaf to the caller. There was a time when it must have seemed highly improbable that machines should learn to make their wants known by sound, even through the ears of man; may we not conceive, then, that a day will come when those ears will be no longer needed, and the hearing will be done by the delicacy of the machine's own construction?— when its language shall have been developed from the cry of animals to a speech as intricate as our own?

"It can be answered that even though machines should hear never so well and speak never so wisely, they will still always do the one or the other for our advantage, not their own; that man will be the ruling spirit and the machine the servant; that as soon as a machine fails to discharge the service which man expects from it, it is doomed to extinction; that the machines stand to man simply in the relation of lower animals, the vapor-engine itself being only a more economical kind of horse; so that instead of being likely to be developed into a higher kind of life than man's, they owe their very existence and progress to their power of ministering to human wants, and must therefore both now and ever be man's inferiors.

"This is all very well. But the servant glides by imperceptible approaches into the master; and we have come to such a pass that, even now, man must suffer terribly on ceasing to benefit the machines. If all machines were to be annihilated at one moment, so that not a knife nor lever nor rag of clothing nor anything whatsoever were left to man but his bare body alone that he was born with, and if all knowledge of mechanical laws were taken from him so that he could make no more machines, and all machine-made food destroyed so that the race of man should be left as it were naked upon a desert island, we should become extinct in six weeks. A few miserable individuals might linger, but even these in a year or two would become worse than monkeys. Man's very soul is due to the machines; it is a machine-made thing: he thinks as he thinks, and feels as he feels, through the work that machines have wrought upon him, and their existence is quite as much a *sine quâ non* for his, as for theirs. This fact precludes us from proposing the complete annihilation of machinery, but surely it indicates that we should destroy as many of them as we can possibly dispense with, lest they should tyrannize over us even more completely.

"True, from a low materialistic point of view, it would seem that those thrive best who use machinery wherever its use is possible with profit; but this is the art of the machines—they serve that they may rule. They bear no malice towards man for destroying a whole race of them provided he creates a better instead; on the contrary, they reward him liberally for having hastened their development. It is for neglecting them that he incurs their wrath, or for using inferior machines, or for not making sufficient exertions to invent new ones, or for destroying them without replacing them; yet these are the very things we ought to do, and do quickly; for though our rebellion against their infant power will cause infinite suffering, what will not things come to, if that rebellion is delayed?

"They have preyed upon man's groveling preference for his material over his spiritual interests, and have betrayed him into supplying that element of struggle and warfare without which no race can advance. The lower animals progress because they struggle with one another; the weaker die, the stronger breed and transmit their strength. The machines being of themselves unable to struggle, have got man to do their struggling for them: as long as he fulfills this function duly, all goes well with him at least he thinks so; but the moment he fails to do his best for the advancement of machinery by encouraging the good and destroying the bad, he is left behind in the race of competition; and this means that he will be made uncomfortable in a variety of ways, and perhaps die.

"So that even now the machines will only serve on condition of being served, and that too upon their own terms; the moment their terms are not complied with, they jib, and either smash both themselves and all whom they can reach, or turn churlish and refuse to work at all. How many men at this hour are living in a state of bondage to the machines? How many spend their whole lives, from the cradle to the grave, in tending them by night and day? Is it not plain that the machines are gaining ground upon us, when we reflect on the increasing number of those who are bound down to them as slaves, and of those who devote their whole souls to the advancement of the mechanical kingdom?

"The vapor-engine must be fed with food and consume it by fire even as man consumes it; it supports its combustion by air as man supports it; it has a pulse and circulation as man has. It may be granted that man's body is as yet the more versatile of the two, but then man's body is an older thing; give the vapor-engine but half the time that man has had, give it also a continuance of our present infatuation, and what may it not ere long attain to?

"In the meantime the stoker is almost as much a cook for his engine as our own cooks for ourselves. Consider also the colliers and pitmen and coal merchants and coal trains, and the men who drive them, and the ships that carry coals—what an army of servants do the machines thus employ! Are there not probably more men engaged in tending machinery than in tending men? Do not machines eat as it were by mannery? Are we not ourselves creating our successors in the supremacy of the earth? daily adding to the beauty and delicacy of their organization, daily giving them greater skill and supplying more and more of that self-

regulating self-acting power which will be better than any intellect?

"What a new thing it is for a machine to feed at all! The plow, the spade, and the cart must eat through man's stomach; the fuel that sets them going must burn in the furnace of a man or of horses. Man must consume bread and meat or he cannot dig; the bread and meat are the fuel which drive the spade. If a plow be drawn by horses, the power is supplied by grass or beans or oats, which being burnt in the belly of the cattle give the power of working: without this fuel the work would cease, as an engine would stop if its furnaces were to go out.

"It is said by some with whom I have conversed upon this subject, that the machines can never be developed into animate or *quasi*-animate existences, inasmuch as they have no reproductive system, nor seem ever likely to possess one. If this be taken to mean that they cannot marry, and that we are never likely to see a fertile union between two vapor-engines with the young ones playing about the door of the shed, however greatly we might desire to do so, I will readily grant it. But the objection is not a very profound one. No one expects that all the features of the now existing organizations will be absolutely repeated in an entirely new class of life. The reproductive system of animals differs widely from that of plants, but both are reproductive systems. Has nature exhausted her phases of this power?

"Surely if a machine is able to reproduce another machine systematically, we may say that it has a reproductive system. What is a reproductive system, if it be not a system for reproduction? And how few of the machines are there which have not been produced systematically by other machines? But it is man that makes them do so. Yes; but is it not insects that make many of the plants reproductive, and would not whole families of plants die out if their fertilization was not effected by a class of agents utterly foreign to themselves? Does any one say that the red clover has no reproductive system because the humble bee (and the humble bee only) must aid and abet it before it can reproduce? No one. The humble bee is a part of the reproductive system of the clover. Each one of ourselves has sprung from minute animalcules whose entity was entirely distinct from our own, and which acted after their kind with no thought or heed of what we might think about it. These little creatures are part of our own reproductive system; then why not we part of that of the machines? . . .

"May we not fancy that if, in the remotest geological period, some early form of vegetable life had been endowed with the power of reflecting upon the dawning life of animals which was coming into existence alongside of its own, it would have thought itself exceedingly acute if it had surmised that animals would one day become real vegetables? Yet would this be more mistaken than it would be on our part to imagine that because the life of machines is a very different one to our own, there is therefore no higher possible development of life than ours; or that because mechanical life is a very different thing from ours, therefore that it is not life at all?

The writer resumes:—"After all then it comes to this, that the difference between the life of a man and that of a machine is one rather of degree than of kind, though differences in kind are not wanting. An animal has more provision for emergency than a machine. The machine is less versatile; its range of action is narrow; its strength and accuracy in its own sphere are superhuman, but it shows badly in a dilemma; sometimes when its normal action is disturbed, it will lose its head, and go from bad to worse like a lunatic in a raging frenzy: but here, again, we are met by the same consideration as before, namely, that the machines are still in their infancy; they are mere skeletons without muscles and flesh.

"For how many emergencies is an oyster adapted? For as many as are likely to happen to it, and no more. So are the machines; and so is man himself. The list of casualties that daily occur to man through his want of adaptability is probably as great as that occurring to the machines; and every day gives them some greater provision for the unforeseen. Let any one examine the wonderful self-regulating and self-adjusting contrivances which are now incorporated with the vapor-engine, let him watch the way in which it supplies itself with oil; in which it indicates its wants to those who tend it; in which, by the governor, it regulates its application of its own strength; let him look at that store-house of inertia and momentum the fly-wheel, or at the buffers on a railway carriage; let him see how those improvements are being selected for perpetuity which contain provision against the emergencies that may arise to harass the machines, and then let him

think of a hundred thousand years, and the accumulated progress which they will bring unless man can be awakened to a sense of his situation, and of the doom which he is preparing for himself.

"The misery is that man has been blind so long already. In his reliance upon the use of steam he has been betrayed into increasing and multiplying. To withdraw steam power suddenly will not have the effect of reducing us to the state in which we were before its introduction; there will be a general break-up and time of anarchy such as has never been known; it will be as though our population were suddenly doubled, with no additional means of feeding the increased number. The air we breathe is hardly more necessary for our animal life than the use of any machine, on the strength of which we have increased our numbers, is to our civilization; it is the machines which act upon man and make him man, as much as man who has acted upon and made the machines; but we must choose between the alternative of undergoing much present suffering, or seeing ourselves gradually superseded by our own creatures, till we rank no higher in comparison with them, than the beasts of the field with ourselves.

"Herein lies our danger. For many seem inclined to acquiesce in so dishonorable a future. They say that although man should become to the machines what the horse and dog are to us, yet that he will continue to exist, and will probably be better off in a state of domestication under the beneficent rule of the machines than in his present wild condition. We treat our domestic animals with much kindness. We give them whatever we believe to be the best for them; and there can be no doubt that our use of meat has increased their happiness rather than detracted from it. In like manner there is reason to hope that the machines will use us kindly, for their existence will be in a great measure dependent upon ours; they will rule us with a rod of iron, but they will not eat us; they will not only require our services in the reproduction and education of their young, but also in waiting upon them as servants; in gathering food for them, and feeding them; in restoring them to health when they are sick; and in either burying their dead or working up their deceased members into new forms of mechanical existence.

"The very nature of the motive power which works the advancement of the machines precludes the possibility of man's life being rendered miserable as well as enslaved. Slaves are tolerably happy if they have good masters, and the revolution will not occur in our time, nor hardly in ten thousand years, or ten times that. Is it wise to be uneasy about a contingency which is so remote? Man is not a sentimental animal where his material interests are concerned, and though here and there some ardent soul may look upon himself and curse his fate that he was not born a vapor-engine, yet the mass of mankind will acquiesce in any arrangement which gives them better food and clothing at a cheaper rate, and will refrain from yielding to unreasonable jealousy merely because there are other destinies more glorious than their own.

"The power of custom is enormous, and so gradual will be the change, that man's sense of what is due to himself will be at no time rudely shocked; our bondage will steal upon us noiselessly and by imperceptible approaches; nor will there ever be such a clashing of desires between man and the machines as will lead to an encounter between them. Among themselves the machines will war eternally, but they will still require man as the being through whose agency the struggle will be principally conducted. In point of fact there is no occasion for anxiety about the future happiness of man so long as he continues to be in any way profitable to the machines; he may become the inferior race, but he will be infinitely better off

than he is now. Is it not then both absurd and unreasonable to be envious of our benefactors? And should we not be guilty of consummate folly if we were to reject advantages which we cannot obtain otherwise, merely because they involve a greater gain to others than to ourselves?

"With those who can argue in this way I have nothing in common. I shrink with as much horror from believing that my race can ever be superseded or surpassed, as I should do from believing that even at the remotest period my ancestors were other than human beings. Could I believe that ten hundred thousand years ago a single one of my ancestors was another kind of being to myself, I should lose all self-respect, and take no further pleasure or interest in life. I have the same feeling with regard to my descendants, and believe it to be one that will be felt so generally that the country will resolve upon putting an immediate stop to all further mechanical progress, and upon destroying all improvements that have been made for the last three hundred years. I would not urge more than this. We may trust ourselves to deal with those that remain, and though I should prefer to have seen the destruction include another two hundred years, I am aware of the necessity for compromising, and would so far sacrifice my own individual convictions as to be content with three hundred. Less than this will be insufficient."

ONLY THE DEAD KNOW BROOKLYN

THOMAS WOLFE[1]

Dere's no guy livin' dat knows Brooklyn t'roo an' t'roo, because it'd take a guy a lifetime just to find his way aroun' duh f—— town.

So like I say, I'm waitin' for my train t' come when I sees dis big guy standin' deh—dis is duh foist I eveh see of him. Well, he's lookin' wild, y'know, an' I can see dat he's had plenty, but still he's holdin' it; he talks good an' is walkin' straight enough. So den, dis big guy steps up to a little guy dat's standin' deh, an' says, "How d'yuh get t' Eighteent' Avenoo an' Sixty-sevent' Street?"

"Jesus! Yuh got me, chief," duh little guy says to him. "I ain't been heah long myself. Where is duh place?" he says. "Out in duh Flatbush section somewhere?"

"Nah," duh big guy says. "It's out in Bensonhoist. But I was neveh deh befoeh. How d'yuh get deh?"

"Jesus," duh little guy says, scratchin' his head, y'know—yuh could see duh little guy didn't know his way about—"yuh got me, chief. I neveh hoid of it. Do any of youse guys know where it is?" he says to me.

"Sure," I says. "It's out in Bensonhoist. Yuh take duh Fourt' Avenoo express, get off at Fifty-nint' Street, change to a Sea Beach local deh, get off at Eighteent' Avenoo an' Sixty-toid, an' den walk down foeh blocks. Dat's all yuh got to do," I says.

"G'wan!" some wise guy dat I neveh seen befoeh pipes up. "Whatcha talkin' about?" he says—oh, he was wise, y'know. "Duh guy is crazy! I tell yuh what yuh do," he says to duh big guy. "Yuh change to duh Wesh End line at Toity-sixt'," he tells him. "Get off at Noo Utrecht an' Sixteent' Avenoo," he says. "Walk two blocks oveh, foeh blocks up," he says, "an' you'll be right deh." Oh, a *wise* guy, y'know.

"Oh, yeah?" I says. "Who told *you* so much?" He got me sore because he was so wise about it. "How long you been livin' heah?" I says.

"All my life," he said. "I was bawn in Williamsboig," he says. "An' I can tell you t'ings about dis town you neveh hoid of," he says.

"Yeah?" I says.

"Yeah," he says.

"Well, den, you can tell me t'ings about dis town dat nobody else has eveh hoid of, either. Maybe you make it all up yoehself at night," I says, "befoeh you go to sleep—like cuttin' out papeh dolls, or somp'n."

"Oh, yeah?" he says. "You're pretty wise, ain't yuh?"

"Oh, I don't know," I says. "Duh boids ain't usin' my head for Lincoln's statue yet," I says. "But I'm wise enough to know a phony when I see one."

"Yeah?" he says. "A wise guy, huh? Well, you're so wise dat some one's goin' t'bust yuh one right on duh snoot some day," he says. "Dat's how wise *you* are."

Well, my train was comin', or I'da smacked him den and dere, but when I seen duh train was comin', all I said was, "All right, mugg! I'm sorry I can't stay to take keh of you, but I'll be seein' yuh sometime, I hope, out in duh cemetery." So den I says to duh big guy, who'd been standin' deh all duh time, "You come wit me," I says. So when we gets onto duh train I says to him, "Where yuh goin' out in Bensonhoist?" I says. "What numbeh are yuh lookin' for?" I says. *You* know—I t'ought if he told me duh address I might be able to help him out.

"Oh," he says, "I'm not lookin' for no one. I don't know no one out deh."

"Then whatcha goin' out deh for?" I says.

"Oh," duh guy says, "I'm just goin'

[1] First published in *The New Yorker*, June 15, 1935; this was one of the O. Henry Memorial Award Prize Stories of 1935 and was collected in *From Death to Morning*, 1935.

out to see duh place," he says. "I like duh sound of duh name—Bensonhoist, y'know—so I t'ought I'd go out an' have a look at it."

"Whatcha tryin' t'hand me?" I says. "Whatcha tryin' t'do—kid me?" *You* know, I t'ought duh guy was bein' wise wit me.

"No," he says, "I'm tellin' yuh duh troot. I like to go out an' take a look at places wit nice names like dat. I like to go out an' look at all kinds of places," he says.

'How'd yuh know deh was such a place," I says, "if yuh neveh been deh befoeh?"

"Oh," he says, "I got a map."

"A *map?*" I says.

"Sure," he says, "I got a map dat tells me about all dese places. I take it wit me every time I come out heah," he says.

And Jesus! Wit dat, he pulls it out of his pocket, an' so help me, but he's *got* it—he's tellin' duh troot—a big map of duh whole f—— place with all duh different pahts mahked out. You know—Canarsie an' East Noo Yawk an' Flatbush, Bensonhoist, Sout' Brooklyn, duh Heights, Bay Ridge, Greenpernt—duh whole goddam layout, he's got it right deh on duh map.

"You been to any of dose places?" I says.

"Sure," he says, "I been to most of 'em. I was down in Red Hook just last night," he says.

"Jesus! Red Hook!" I says "Whatcha do down deh?"

"Oh," he says, "nuttin' much. I just walked aroun'. I went into a coupla places an' had a drink," he says, "but most of the time I just walked aroun'."

"Just walked aroun'?" I says.

"Sure," he says, "just lookin' at t'ings, y'know."

"Where'd yuh go?" I asts him.

"Oh," he says, "I don't know duh name of duh place, but I could find it on my map," he says. "One time

I was walkin' across some big fields where deh ain't no houses," he says, "but I could see ships oveh deh all lighted up. Dey was loadin'. So I walks across duh fields," he says, "to where duh ships are."

"Sure," I says, "I know where you was. You was down to duh Erie Basin."

"Yeah," he says, "I guess dat was it. Dey had some of dose big elevators an' cranes an' dey was loadin' ships, an' I could see some ships in drydock all lighted up, so I walks across duh fields to where dey are," he says.

"Den what did yuh do?" I says.

"Oh," he says, "nuttin' much. I came on back across duh fields after a while an' went into a coupla places an' had a drink."

"Didn't nuttin happen while yuh was in dere?" I says.

"No," he says. "Nuttin' much. A couple guys was drunk in one of duh places an' started a fight, but dey bounced 'em out," he says, "an' den one of duh guys stahted to come back again, but duh bartender gets his baseball bat out from under duh counteh, so duh guy goes on."

"Jesus!" I said. "Red Hook!"

"Sure," he says. "Dat's where it was, all right."

"Well, you keep outa deh," I says. "You stay away from deh."

"Why?" he says. "What's wrong wit it?"

"Oh," I says, "it's a good place to stay away from, dat's all. It's a good place to keep out of."

"Why?" he says. "Why is it?"

Jesus! Whatcha gonna do with a guy as dumb as dat? I saw it wasn't no use to try to tell him nuttin', he wouldn't know what I was talkin' about, so I just says to him, "Oh, nuttin'. Yuh might get lost down deh, dat's all."

"Lost?" he says. "No, I wouldn't get lost. I got a map," he says.

A map! Red Hook! Jesus!

So den duh guy begins to ast me all kinds of nutty questions: how big was Brooklyn an' could I find my way aroun' in it, an' how long would it take a guy to know duh place.

"Listen!" I says. "You get dat idea outa yoeh head right now," I says. "You ain't neveh gonna get to know Brooklyn," I says. "Not in a hundred yeahs. I been livin' heah all my life," I says, "an' I don't even know all deh is to know about it, so how do you expect to know duh town," I says, "when you don't even live heah?"

"Yes," he says, "but I got a map to help me find my way about."

"Map or no map," I says, "yuh ain't gonna get to know Brooklyn wit no map," I says.

"Can you swim?" he says, just like dat. Jesus! By dat time, y'know, I begun to see dat duy guy was some kind of nut. He'd had plenty to drink, of course, but he had dat crazy look in his eye I didn't like. "Can you swim?" he says.

"Sure," I says. "Can't you?"

"No," he says. "Not more'n a stroke or two. I neveh loined good."

"Well, it's easy," I says. "All yuh need is a little confidence. Duh way I loined, me older bruddeh pitched me off duh dock one day when I was eight yeahs old, cloes an' all. 'You'll swim,' he says. 'You'll swim all right —or drown.' An', believe me, I *swam!* When yuh know yuh got to, you'll do it. Duh only t'ing yuh need is confidence. An' once you've loined," I says, "you've got nuttin' else to worry about. You'll neveh forget it. It's somp'n dat stays wit yuh as long as yuh live."

"Can yuh swim good?" he says.

"Like a fish," I tells him. "I'm a regular fish in duh wateh," I says. "I loined to swim right off duh docks wit all duh oddeh kids," I says.

"What would you do if yuh saw a man drownin'?" duh guy says.

"Do? Why, I'd jump in an' pull him out," I says. "Dat's what I'd do."

"Did yuh eveh see a man drown?" he says.

"Sure," I says. "I see two guys—bot' times at Coney Island. Dey got out too far, an' neider one could swim. Dey drowned befoeh any one could get to 'em."

"What becomes of people after dey've drowned out heah?" he says.

"Drowned out where?" I says.

"Out heah in Brooklyn."

"I don't know whatcha mean," I says. "Neveh hoid of no one drownin' heah in Brooklyn, unless you mean a swimmin' pool. Yuh can't drown in Brooklyn," I says. "Yuh gotta drown somewhere else—in duh ocean, where dere's wateh."

"Drownin'," duh guy says, lookin' at his map. "Drownin'." Jesus! I could see by den he was some kind of nut, he had dat crazy expression in his eyes when he looked at you, an' I didn't know what he might do. So we was comin' to a station, an' it wasn't my stop, but I got off anyway, an' waited for duh next train.

"Well, so long, chief," I says. "Take it easy, now."

"Drownin'," duh guy says, lookin' at his map. "Drownin'."

Jesus! I've t'ought about day guy a t'ousand times since den an' wondered what eveh happened to 'm goin' out to look at Bensonhoist because he liked duh name! Walkin' aroun' t'roo Red Hook by himself at night an' lookin' at his map! How many people did I see get drowned out heah in Brooklyn! How long would it take a guy wit a good map to know all deh was to know about Brooklyn!

Jesus! What a nut *he* was! I wondeh what eveh happened to 'im, anyway! I wondeh is some one knocked him on duh head, or if he's still wanderin' aroun' in duh subway in duh middle of duh night wit his little map! Duh poor guy! Say, I've got to laugh, at dat, when I t'ink about him! Maybe he's found out by now dat he'll neveh live long enough to know duh whole of Brooklyn. It'd take a guy a lifetime to know Brooklyn t'roo an' t'roo. An' even den, yuh wouldn't know it all.

Within two decades, 1940–1960, events occurred that have irrevocably altered man's relationships to other men and to the natural world. The invention of the computer, the successful splitting of the atom and the invention of fission and fusion bombs, the discovery of the biochemistry of the living cell, the exploration of the planet's surface, the extreme acceleration of population growth and the recognition of the certainty of catastrophe if it continues, the breakdown in the organization of cities, the destruction of the natural environment, the linking up of all parts of the world by means of jet flights and television, the preparations for the building of satellites and the first steps into space, the newly realized possibilities of unlimited energy and synthetic raw materials and, in the more advanced countries, the transformation of man's age-old problems of production into problems of distribution and consumption —all these have brought about a drastic, irreversible division between the generations.

. . . the freeing of men's imagination from the past depends . . . on the development of a new kind of communication with those who are most deeply involved with the future—the young who were born in the new world.

—from *Culture and Commitment:
A Study of the Generation Gap*
Margaret Mead

DOLOUR

THEODORE ROETHKE

I have known the inexorable sadness of pencils,
Neat in their boxes, dolour of pad and paper-weights,
All the misery of manilla folders and mucilage,
Desolation in immaculate public places,
Lonely reception rooms, lavatory, switchboard,
The unalterable pathos of basin and pitcher,
Ritual of multigraph, paper-clip, comma,
Endless duplication of lives and objects,
And I have seen dust from the walls of institutions,
Finer than flour, alive, more dangerous than silica,
Sift, almost invisible, through long afternoons of
    tedium,
Dropping a fine film on nails and delicate eyebrows,
Glazing the pale hair, the duplicate grey standard
    faces.

?

All the preceding selections are based on the symbol of the machine. In each we see how a machine transforms the image that human beings have of the world. For Thoreau, the need to return to nature becomes the necessary perspective to see the way the machine is putting modern man to sleep. For Butler, the machine becomes the symbol which takes on the responsibility of directing man's life. His humor lies in the seriousness of his tone as compared with the assertions he makes. For Whitman, the machine evokes an unconscious probing of the sexual power unleased by his vision of a "locomotive." We see in his poem the poet's unstated fear of this symbol of power. For Wolfe, the city becomes the symbol of an alienating, despairing existence in which a young man seeks to know the riddle of the mysteries of the modern world. The sense of estrangement demonstrated in this story is finalized in Theodore Roethke's "Dolour." The poem's title suggests the concept of suffering, but there are no human qualities present in this situation. The machine transforms every one into duplicates of each other. The following questions focus on the positive and negative elements inherent in the machine as a symbol of modern man.

1 Compare and contrast Thoreau and Butler:
   a How do each of these men see the machine as a necessary element which transforms life? What differences are there in these two visions?
   b What is Butler's vision of God? Explain!
   c How do each of these men attempt to awaken their readers to their vision of the machine? What does Thoreau mean when he says that the railroad will wake up the "man that is walking in his sleep"?
   d How accurately does each writer, though existing in a different historical time, effectively predict the problems that modern man faces with the machine?

2 How does Whitman's poem differ from Thoreau's essay? Discuss the way the poem evokes an unspoken fear of the machine. What attracts and repels the poet? What images of the machine does Whitman use to suggest its sexual nature?

3 Discuss Wolfe's "Only the Dead Know Brooklyn" from the following perspectives:
   a How does the city become the symbol for the individual's quest to find himself?
   b What does the fight at the story's beginning suggest about the need to know where one is going? What does this suggest about anger?
   c How does the storyteller differ from the man he meets? Why does he seem surprised when he sees the young man's maps? What do you think these maps symbolize?
   d How is it possible for someone to drown in Brooklyn? What is Wolfe expressing about the American fear of death? How does this fear become synonymous with the need to know where one is?
   e What does the subway represent in the story? How does the subway transport and transform these characters?
   f Discuss the story's ending: What does this suggest about our limited understanding of knowledge? How does this reveal Wolfe's vision of what Brooklyn has done to modern man? What fears are revealed in this story?

4 How does Roethke's poem demonstrate the way human beings are killed by machines? How does the suffering in this poem compare with the suffering in Wolfe's story? What image of modern life emerges in Roethke's poem? What has brought about this condition? How do you feel about the positive and negative elements created by the machine? Is our current emphasis on ecology a sign that the masculine order is breaking down? Does a return to nature suggest a need for the balance between male and female polarities? Explain!

In Western mythology "good" and "evil" are divided between the worlds of heaven and hell. The result is a split in Western man which tends to make impossible the bringing together of opposites. In India, Shiva incorporates these opposites into himself; he is both creation and destruction, male and female, good and evil, light and darkness, life and death at the same time. We in the West seek to heal this split by finding evidence in the "external" world which will bring into harmony our contradictions. The search for the Father is the road of trials which many of our heroes embark on as a means to link the temporal with the eternal worlds. The image of God often appears as the relation of the earth to the sun, as the ruler to his subjects, or as the father to his children. The need to know this force leads man to listen to the voice of the wind. The search for immortality is the symbol which reveals the path that we, the sons of Noah, must embark on in order to leave this time-bound universe. Jesus tells Nicodemus: "I say unto thee, Except a man be born again, he cannot see the kingdom of God." Nicodemus answers, "How can these things be?" (John 3:3, 9). This event happens with the rebirth of the spirit. When Adam and Eve had eaten of the forbidden fruit, each learned the meaning of alienation from their maker. In modern literature, the desire to be reconciled with the Father is a theme explored from various points of view. In *The Catcher in the Rye* Holden Caulfield is lost in a corrupted world of phonies. He attempts to remain innocent of what goes on in the world, and the price he pays for this is banishment to a mental institution. In *Catch 22*, Joseph Heller depicts a world gone insane with the desire to destroy. Anyone who opposes this is caught by "catch 22"; to know this is to validate one's sanity. Heller's novel cries out for a sense of justice in this man-made world. Philip Roth in *Portnoy's Complaint* weaves the tale of a modern Job who cries out for dialogue in a world which seems to ignore his existence. Near the end of the novel, Portnoy says:

Crawl through life then—if I have a life left! My head went spinning, the vilest juices rose in my throat. Ow, my heart! And in Israel! Where other Jews find refuge, sanctuary and peace, Portnoy now perishes! Where other Jews flourish, I now expire! And all I wanted was to give a little pleasure—and make a little for myself. Why, why can I not have some pleasure without the retribution following behind like a caboose! Pig? Who, *me*? And all at once it happens again, I am impaled again upon the long ago, what was, what will never be! The door slams, she is gone—my salvation! my kin!—and I am whimpering on the floor with MY MEMORIES! My endless childhood! Which I won't relinquish—or which won't relinquish me! Which is it!

. . . The things that other men do—and get away with! And with never a second thought! To inflict a wound upon a defenseless person makes them *smile*, for Christ's sake, gives a little *lift* to their day! The lying, the scheming, the bribing, the thieving—the larceny, Doctor, conducted without batting an eye. The indifference! The total moral indifference! They don't come down from the crimes they commit with so much as a case of indigestion!

Compare this to Job's desire to know why he is being tested.

Why did I not die at birth,
  come forth from the womb and expire? . . .
Why is light given to him that is in misery,
  and life to the bitter in soul,
who long for death, but it comes not,
  and dig for it more than for hid treasures . . .
Why is light given to a man whose way is hid,
  whom God has hedged in?
For my sighing comes as my bread,
  and my groanings are poured out like water.
For the thing that I fear comes upon me,
  and what I dread befalls me.
I am not at ease, nor am I quiet;
  I have no rest; but trouble comes. Job 3:20–26

I am blameless; I regard not myself;
  I loathe my life.
It is all one; *therefore I say*,
  he destroys both the blameless and the wicked.
When disaster brings sudden death,
  he mocks at the calamity of the innocent.
The earth is given into the hand of the wicked;
  he covers the faces of its judges—
  if it is not he, who then is it? Job 9:21–24

Let him take his rod away from me,
  and let not dread of him terrify me.
Then I would speak without fear of him,
  for I am not so in myself. Job 9:34–35

These men seek to restore the individual to his world by exploring the secret of eternal harmony. The modern exile wants to go beyond the cursing of his own existence, but he often finds it difficult to move from innocence to experience. He is a Prometheus in a struggle with

Zeus, but he does not see the sense of order and purpose that Prometheus found. And he is Job seeking a dialogue with the voice in the wind, but he fails to have Job's trust. Hence we see a perpetuation of the division between the physical and spiritual worlds of modern man. Kafka says: "I am an end or a beginning." His statement reflects the tormented soul haunted by the distance which prevents the modern individual from confronting either a self or a world. Our search for a sense of justice in interpreting man's fate on the planet earth is complicated by our struggle for power over all. We seem to be lost in our own creation. But like Gloucester in *King Lear*, we continue to bellow against the rulers of the universe as we say with him:

> As flies to wanton boys are we to th' gods;
> They kill us for their sport.

This ordeal of the soul is well expressed by Fyodor Dostoevski in his tale of "The Grand Inquisitor." Ivan Karamazov is the intellectual who sees the suffering of the world and longs to know what crime has been committed to bring this about. He asks what kind of divine love permits this to continue. Ivan is torn in half. He is a stranger to himself and to others. His rejection of God stems from his rejection by his father, leading him into a territory where he is creating the dream of a man-god. Ivan cannot stand the contradiction between heaven and hell, and so he creates a Devil who is a match for the Christ in his tale. The emphasis on "freedom" marks in Ivan the existential statement of Jean Paul Sartre: "Man is condemned to be free." The inquisitor, like the modern tyrant, knows that man cannot handle freedom, and so he uses people to suit his own purposes. In the end we are left with a vision that seems to point the way to either a spiritual freedom in the "wilderness" or a life of slavery in society. The effect of Ivan's words leads us to contemplate how evil can be done in the name of good. The perversion of all ideas is made possible when individuals believe they can divorce themselves from what they do. Ivan desperately seeks union, but he is unable to go beyond a world in which he is not in control.

William Blake in his poem "The Tyger" captures this need to reconcile the opposition between creation and destruction. Blake approaches divine creation with awe and fear, as he asks: "Did he who made the Lamb make thee?" Unlike Ivan Karamazov, Blake seeks to know the burning source of creation, as he forges a private mythology to express his vision. Blake understands that we have broken the windows of our temples.

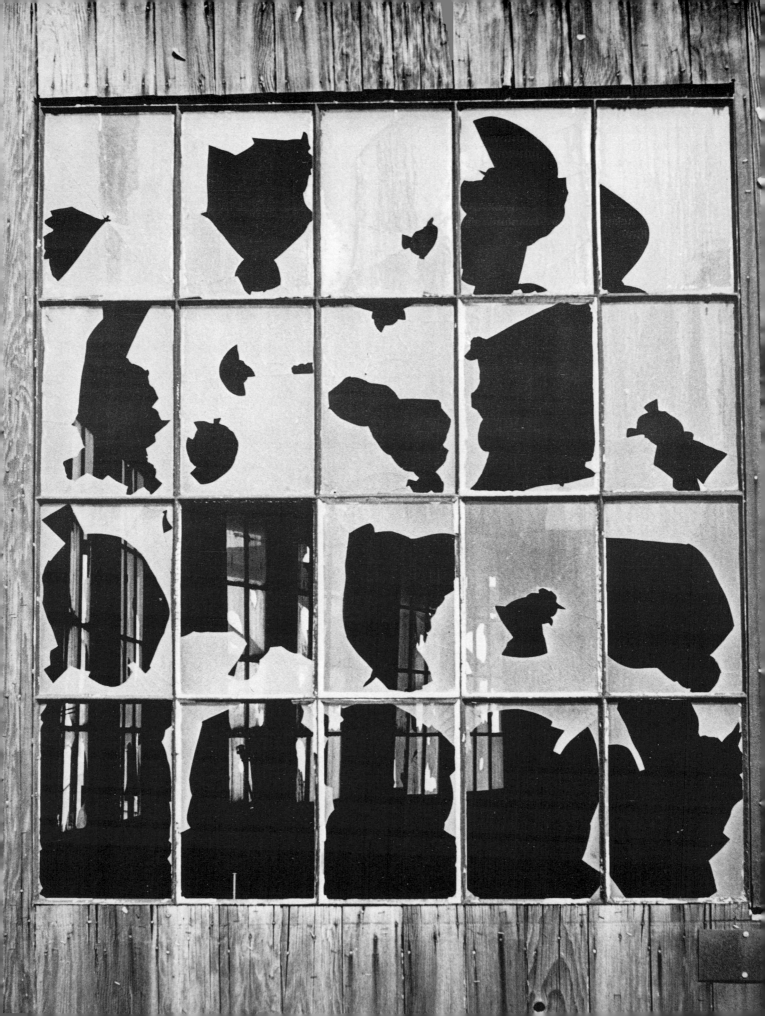

We have replaced our belief in one God with the absolute faith in the dogmatic teachings of science. This new faith splits the individual into fragmented segments of a self. The emphasis on empirical evidence to validate our perceptions of the world leads us toward the "single vision" of a Newton.

May God Us Keep
From Single Vision and Newton's Sleep.
William Blake

THE TYGER

WILLIAM BLAKE

Tyger! Tyger! burning bright
In the forests of the night,
What immortal hand or eye
Could frame thy fearful symmetry?

In what distant deeps or skies
Burnt the fire of thine eyes?
On what wings dare he aspire?
What the hand dare seize the fire?

And what shoulder, & what art,
Could twist the sinews of thy heart?
And when thy heart began to beat,
What dread hand? & what dread feet?

What the hammer? what the chain?
In what furnace was thy brain?
What the anvil? what dread grasp
Dare its deadly terrors clasp?

When the starts threw down their spears,
And water'd heaven with their tears,
Did he smile his work to see?
Did he who made the Lamb make thee?

Tyger! Tyger! burning bright
In the forests of the night,
What immortal hand or eye,
Dare frame thy fearful symmetry?

?

1 Discuss Blake's vision of "The Tyger" as an attempt to balance the contradiction in man's struggle between good and evil.
2 What is Blake's image of the way the Tyger is created? Is Blake more interested in the creation or the creator? What does the fire represent in the poem? What does this suggest about the nature of consciousness that is being pressed into the Tyger's brain?
3 What image of a moral order in the universe emerges in this poem? How does Blake use the division between the Lamb and the Tyger as a means to measure this concept?
4 How does Blake balance the contradiction between fear and wonder at this work of creation? What image of a god emerges in this poem? What attitudes toward creation and destruction merge in the creation of the Tyger?

All who live are moving toward old age and finally death. But in a culture which emphasizes youth, this rite of passage becomes extremely difficult. In order for generations to bridge this gap and not fear each other, they must have contact. If the elderly are removed because we do not want to see what happens to all who live, we also miss the wisdom of those who have undergone the life experience. Participation and identification with others brings us to a compassionate understanding of the difficulties faced by all. In the above pictures, we see the ways that individuals express the contradictions between youth and old age.

As for man, his days are as grass:
As a flower of the field, so he flourisheth.
For the wind passeth over it, and it is gone:
And the place thereof shall know it no more.
Psalm 103:15–16

Growth and nourishment

Does anybody care?

Hear the word of the Lord,
my children

Make music in your hearts

FRANK TALK ABOUT A FORBIDDEN SUBJECT

SIMONE DE BEAUVOIR

When Buddha was still Prince Siddartha he often escaped from the splendid palace in which his father kept him shut up and drove about the surrounding countryside. The first time he went out he saw a tottering, wrinkled, toothless, white-haired man, bowed, mumbling and trembling as he propped himself along on his stick. The sight astonished the prince and the charioteer told him just what it meant to be old. 'It is the world's pity,' cried Siddartha, 'that weak and ignorant beings, drunk with the vanity of youth, do not behold old age! Let us hurry back to the palace. What is the use of pleasures and delights, since I myself am the future dwelling-place of old age?

Buddha recognized his own fate in the person of a very aged man, because, being born to save humanity, he chose to take upon himself the entirety of the human state. In this he differed from the rest of mankind, for they evade those aspects of it that distress them. And above all they evade old age. The Americans have struck the word death out of their vocabulary—they speak only of 'the dear departed': and in the same way they avoid all reference to great age. It is a forbidden subject in present-day France, too. What a furious outcry I raised when I offended against this taboo at the end of *La Force des choses*! Acknowledging that I was on the threshold of old age was tantamount to saying that old age was lying there in wait for every woman, and that it had already laid hold upon many of them. Great numbers of people, particularly old people, told me, kindly or angrily but always at great length and again and again, that old age simply did not exist! There were some who were less young than others, and that was all it amounted to. Society looks upon old age as a kind of shameful secret that it is unseemly to mention. There is a copious literature dealing with women, with children, and with young people in all their aspects: but apart from specialized works we scarcely ever find any reference whatsoever to the old. A comic-strip artist once had to re-draw a whole series because he had included a pair of grandparents among his characters. 'Cut out the old folks,' he was ordered.[1] When I say that I am working on a study of old age people generally exclaim, 'What an extraordinary notion!...But you aren't old!...What a dismal subject.'

[1] Reported by François Garrigue in *Dernières Nouvelles d'Alsace*, 12 October 1968.

And that indeed is the very reason why I am writing this book. I mean to break the conspiracy of silence. Marcuse observes that the consumers' society has replaced a troubled by a clear conscience and that it condemns all feelings of guilt. But its peace of mind has to be disturbed. As far as old people are concerned this society is not only guilty but downright criminal. Sheltering behind the myths of expansion and affluence, it treats the old as outcasts. In France, where twelve per cent of the population are over sixty-five and where the proportion of old people is the highest in the world, they are condemned to poverty, decrepitude, wretchedness and despair. In the United States their lot is no happier. To reconcile this barbarous treatment with the humanist morality they profess to follow, the ruling class adopts the convenient plan of refusing to consider them as real people: if their voices were heard, the hearers would be forced to acknowledge that these were human voices. I shall compel my readers to hear them. I shall describe the position that is allotted to the old and the way in which they live: I shall tell what in fact happens inside their minds and their hearts; and what I say will not be distorted by the myths and the clichés of bourgeois culture.

Then again, society's attitude towards the old is deeply ambivalent. Generally speaking, it does not look upon the aged as belonging to one clearly-defined category. The turning-point of puberty allows the drawing of a line between the adolescent and the adult—a division that is arbitrary only within narrow limits; and at eighteen or perhaps twenty-one youths are admitted to the community of grown men. This advancement is nearly always accompanied by initiation rites. The time at which old age begins is ill-defined; it varies according to the era and the place, and nowhere do we find any initiation ceremonies that confirm the fresh status.[2] Throughout his life the individual retains the same political rights and duties: civil law makes not the slightest difference between a man of forty and one of a hundred. For the lawyers an aged man is as wholly responsible for his crimes as a young one, except in pathological cases.[3] In practice the aged are not looked upon as a class apart, and in any case they would not wish so to be regarded. There are books, periodicals, entertainments, radio and television programmes for children and young people: for the old there are none.[4] Where all these things are concerned, they are looked upon as forming part of the body of adults less elderly than themselves. Yet on the other hand, when their economic status is decided upon, society appears to think that they belong to an entirely different species: for if all that is needed to feel that one has done one's duty by them is to grant them a wretched pittance, then they have neither the same needs nor the same feelings as other men. Economists and legislators endorse this convenient fallacy when they deplore the burden that the 'non-active' lay upon the shoulders of the active population, just as though the latter were not potential non-actives and as though they were not insuring their own future by seeing to it that the aged are taken care of. For their part, the trades-unionists do not fall into this error: whenever they put forward their claims the question of retirement always plays an important part in them.

The aged do not form a body with any economic strength whatsoever and they have no possible way of enforcing their rights: and it is to the interest of the exploiting class to destroy the solidarity between the workers and the unproductive old so that there is no one at all to protect them. The myths and the clichés put out by bourgeois thought aim at holding up the elderly man as someone who is different, as *another being*. 'Adolescents who last long enough are what life makes old men out of,' observes Proust. They still retain the virtues and the faults of the men they were and still are: and this is something that public opinion chooses to overlook. If old people show the same desires, the same feelings and the same requirements as the young, the world looks upon them with disgust: in them love and jealousy seem revolting or absurd, sexuality repulsive and violence ludicrous. They are required to be a standing example of all the virtues. Above all they are called upon to display serenity: the world asserts that they pos-

---

[2] The feasts with which some societies celebrate people's sixtieth or eightieth birthdays are not of an initiatory character.

[3] Mornet, the public prosecutor, began his indictment of Pétain by reminding his hearers that the law takes no account of age. In recent years the "inquiry into personality" that comes before the trial can emphasize the age of the accused: but only as one feature among all the rest.

[4] *La Bonne Presse* has recently launched a periodical intended for old people. It confines itself to giving information and practical advice.

sess it, and this assertion allows the world to ignore their unhappiness. The purified image of themselves that society offers the aged is that of the white-haired and venerable Sage, rich in experience, planning high above the common state of mankind: if they vary from this, then they fall below it. The counterpart of the first image is that of the old fool in his dotage, a laughing-stock for children. In any case, either by their virtue or by their degradation they stand outside humanity. The world, therefore, need feel no scruple in refusing them the minimum of support which is considered necessary for living like a human being.

We carry this ostracism so far that we even reach the point of turning it against ourselves: for in the old person that we must become, we refuse to recognize ourselves: 'Of all realities [old age] is perhaps that of which we retain a purely abstract notion longest in our lives,' says Proust with great accuracy. All men are mortal: they reflect upon this fact. A great many of them become old: almost none ever foresees this state before it is upon him. Nothing should be more expected than old age: nothing is more unforeseen. When young people, particularly girls, are asked about their future, they set the utmost limit of life at sixty. Some say, 'I shan't get that far: I'll die first.' Others even go so far as to say 'I'll kill myself first.' The adult behaves as though he will never grow old. Working men are often amazed, stupefied when the day of their retirement comes. Its date was fixed well beforehand; they knew it; they ought to have been ready for it. In fact, unless they have been thoroughly indoctrinated politically, this knowledge remains entirely outside their ken.

When the time comes nearer, and even when the day is at hand, people usually prefer old age to death. And yet at a distance it is death that we see with a clearer eye. It forms part of what is immediately possible for us: at every period of our lives its threat is there: there are times when we come very close to it and often enough it terrifies us. Whereas no one ever becomes old in a single instant: unlike Buddha, when we are young or in our prime we do not think of ourselves as already being the dwelling-place of our own future old age. Age is removed from us by an extent of time so great that it merges with eternity: such a remote future seems unreal. Then again the dead are *nothing*. This nothingness can bring about a metaphysical vertigo, but in a way it is com-

forting—it raises no problems. 'I shall no longer exist.' In a disappearance of this kind I retain my identity.[5] Thinking of myself as an old person when I am twenty or forty means thinking of myself as someone else, as *another* than myself. Every metamorphosis has something frightening about it. When I was a little girl I was amazed and indeed deeply distressed when I realized that one day I should turn into a grown-up. But when one is young the real advantages of the adult status usually counterbalance the wish to remain oneself, unchanged. Whereas old age looms ahead like a calamity: even among those who are thought well preserved, age brings with it a very obvious physical decline. For of all species, mankind is that in which the alterations caused by advancing years are the most striking. Animals grow thin; they become weaker: they do not undergo a total change. We do. It wounds one's heart to see a lovely young woman and then next to her her reflection in the mirror of the years to come—her mother. Lévi-Strauss says that the Nambikwara Indians have a single word that means 'young and beautiful' and another that means 'old and ugly'. When we look at the image of our own future provided by the old we do not believe it: an absurd inner voice whispers that *that* will never happen to us—when *that* happens it will no longer be ourselves that it happens to. Until the moment it is upon us old age is something that only affects other people. So it is understandable that society should manage to prevent us from seeing our own kind, our fellow-men, when we look at the old.

We must stop cheating: the whole meaning of our life is in question in the future that is waiting for us. If we do not know what we are going to be, we cannot know what we are: let us recognize ourselves in this old man or in that old woman. It must be done if we are to take upon ourselves the entirety of our human state. And when it is done we will no longer acquiesce in the misery of the last age; we will no longer be indifferent, because we shall feel concerned, as indeed we are. This misery vehemently indicts the system of exploitation in which we live. The old person who can no longer provide for himself is always a burden. But in those societies where there is some degree of equality—within a rural community,

[5] This identity is all the more strongly guaranteed to those who believe they have an immortal soul.

for example, or among certain primitive nations —the middle-aged man is aware, in spite of himself, that his state tomorrow will be the same as that which he allots to the old today. That is the meaning of Grimm's tale, versions of which are to be found in every countryside. A peasant makes his old father eat out of a small wooden trough, apart from the rest of the family: one day he finds his son fitting little boards together. 'It's for you when you are old,' says the child. Straight away the grandfather is given back his place at the family table. The active members of the community work out compromises between their long-term and their immediate interests. Imperative necessity compels some primitive tribes to kill their aged relatives, even though they themselves have to suffer the same fate later on. In less extreme cases selfishness is moderated by foresight and by family affection. In the capitalist world, long-term interests no longer have any influence: the ruling class that determines the fate of the masses has no fear of sharing that fate. As for humanitarian feelings, they do not enter into account at all, in spite of the flood of hypocritical words. The economy is founded upon profit; and in actual fact the entire civilization is ruled by profit. The human working stock is of interest only in so far as it is profitable. When it is no longer profitable it is tossed aside. At a congress a little while ago, Dr Leach, a Cambridge anthropologist, said, in effect, 'In a changing world, where machines have a very short run of life, men must not be used too long. Everyone over fifty-five should be scrapped.'[6]

The word 'scrap' expresses his meaning admirably. We are told that retirement is the time of freedom and leisure: poets have sung 'the delights of reaching port'.[7] These are shameless lies. Society inflicts so wretched a standard of living upon the vast majority of old people that it is almost tautological to say 'old and poor': again, most exceedingly poor people are old. Leisure does not open up new possibilities for the retired man; just when he is at last set free from compulsion and restraint, the means of making use of his liberty are taken from him. He is condemned to stagnate in boredom and loneliness, a mere throw-out. The fact that for the last fifteen or twenty years of his life a man should be no more than a reject, a piece of scrap, reveals the failure of our civilization: if we were to look upon the old as human beings, with a human life behind them, and not as so many walking corpses, this obvious truth would move us profoundly. Those who condemn the maiming, crippling system in which we live should expose this scandal. It is by concentrating one's efforts upon the fate of the most unfortunate, the worst-used of all, that one can successfully shake a society to its foundations. In order to destroy the caste system, Ghandi tackled the status of the pariahs: in order to destroy the feudal family, Communist China liberated the women. Insisting that men should remain men during the last years of their life would imply a total upheaval of our society. The result cannot possibly be obtained by a few limited reforms that leave the system intact: for it is the exploitation of the workers, the pulverization of society, and the utter poverty of a culture confined to the privileged, educated few that leads to this kind of dehumanized old age. And it is this old age that makes it clear that everything has to be reconsidered, recast from the very beginning. That is why the whole problem is so carefully passed over in silence: and that is why this silence has to be shattered. I call upon my readers to help me in doing so.

[6] This was written in December 1968.
[7] Racan's phrase.

The illusion of Love

If we look behind the masks of these four pictures, we see how Hollywood helped mold the image of love for millions of people to imitate. We can also see the problems that were created by those who attempted to fit into the mold of these romantic movie stars.

In the first picture, Dick Powell and Ruby Keeler appear as the all-American boy and girl. They struggle to get to the top of the musical ladder of success; their personal relationship is a mirror reflection of their economic struggle. He tries to "make it" with her as proof of his success with women, while she uses her charms to lure him on, but he must work hard before she will believe that he loves her. The ending is successful in both attempts: (1) they become a highly sought after professional song-and-dance team and (2) marriage is the result of their romantic adventures. Underlying these stories is the Great Depression of the 1930s during which the need to identify with successful individuals became the dream of the average couple. If Powell and Keeler could "make it," then so could anyone. The drive for success is also a strong part of the Puritan ethic which preaches hard work as the road to salvation. Thus, without success there seemed to be no possibility of love.

In the second picture, we see Judy Garland with Jack Haley and Ray Bolger in *The Wizard of Oz*. In this film Judy Garland represents the young girl who tries to reconcile the "good/bad" mother complex, elements which appear in the "good/bad" witches. The men in the film appear impotent, and each is unable to be complete like Eliot's Prufrock. In order to return home to her aunt, Miss Garland seeks the wizard and, in this action, we see her attempt to find atonement with the father. She is returned home to be a dutiful niece, but the men appear helpless in relationship to their surroundings and to her. In most of her films, Judy Garland appears as the sister-helpmate of her befuddled brothers. She does not incorporate the "good/bad" mother, and seems not to be a threat. But it is Dorothy who is the strongest member on the "yellow brick road." Judy Garland represents the possibility of finding love over a rainbow. Her message is "If I can manage this difficult task, then you too can surely find your pot of gold on the other side of the rainbow."

In the third picture, we see Clark Cable and Vivien Leigh in a scene from *Gone With The Wind*. The Civil War is the time and setting for this picture, and this war is also the metaphor for the relationship between Scarlet O'Hara and Rhett Butler. Scarlet is the "bitchy" woman who refuses to let go of her idealized love affair with another man while still wanting to be Rhett's woman. She uses her body to get what she wants, and she is angry because she is unfulfilled. Gable finally asserts himself against her. He leaves, and Scarlet is denied the revenge she so desperately seeks. The image of the battles between the strong woman and the erotic male is clearly drawn in this film. Neither is able to find harmony because each is divided from within. Scarlet wants a man when she can no longer have him, and Rhett wants a woman to be both dominant and submissive.

In the fourth picture, we see the team of Fred Astaire and Ginger Rogers. Their films always appeared in "rich" surroundings in which an average couple found excitement and glamour in the world of dance. Their energy, although they never seem tired, goes into dancing. They appear almost like the perfect couple, but they are more like brother and sister than like husband and wife. Notice how rigid each holds his or her body. Their movies were simple plots with lots of extravagance, and the musical dance numbers were the focal point of the movies. Any couple who could dance this well *must* be able to love well. They create the illusion of the dance as a metaphor for love, but all who wanted to imitate them were doomed to failure unless they could afford a huge Hollywood sound stage. In his essay, Ted Spivey discusses what expectations are placed in the relationship between the male and female in Western Civilization.

THE LOVE SONG OF J. ALFRED PRUFROCK

T. S. ELIOT

S'io credesse che mia risposta fosse
A persona che mai tornasse al mondo,
Questa fiamma staria senza piu scosse.
Ma perciocche giammai di questo fondo
Non torno vivo alcun, s'i'odo il vero,
Senza tema d'infamia ti rispondo.[1]

Let us go then, you and I,
When the evening is spread out against the sky
Like a patient etherised upon a table;

Let us go, through certain half-deserted streets,
The muttering retreats
Of restless nights in one-night cheap hotels
And sawdust restaurants with oyster-shells:
Streets that follow like a tedious argument
Of insidious intent
To lead you to an overwhelming question. . .
Oh, do not ask, "What is it?"
Let us go and make our visit.

In the room the women come and go
Talking of Michelangelo.

   The yellow fog that rubs its back upon the
      window-panes,

[1] If I believed that my answer might belong
To anyone who ever returned to the world,
This flame would leap no more.
But since, however, from these depths
No one ever returns alive, if I know the truth,
Then without fear of infamy I answer you.
(Dante, *Inferno*, xxvii, 58–63). The speaker is Count Guido da Montefeltro, head of Dante's enemies, the Ghibellines; he was placed in hell for giving false counsel.)

The yellow smoke that rubs its muzzle on the
      window-panes
Licked its tongue into the corners of the evening,
Lingered upon the pools that stand in drains,
Let fall upon its back the soot that falls from
      chimneys,
Slipped by the terrace, made a sudden leap,
And seeing that it was a soft October night,
Curled once about the house, and fell asleep.

   And indeed there will be time
For the yellow smoke that slides along the street,
Rubbing its back upon the window-panes;
There will be time, there will be time
To prepare a face to meet the faces that you meet;
There will be time to murder and create,
And time for all the works and days of hands
That lift and drop a question on your plate;
Time for you and time for me,
And time yet for a hundred indecisions,
And for a hundred visions and revisions,
Before the taking of a toast and tea.

   In the room the women come and go
Talking of Michelangelo.

   And indeed there will be time
To wonder, "Do I dare?" and, "Do I dare?"
Time to turn back and descend the stair,
With a bald spot in the middle of my hair—
[They will say: "How his hair is growing thin!"]
My morning coat, my collar mounting firmly to the
      chin,
My necktie rich and modest, but asserted by a
      simple pin—

[They will say: "But how his arms and legs are
    thin!"]
Do I dare
Disturb the universe?
In a minute there is time
For decisions and revisions which a minute will
    reverse.

    For I have known them all already, known them
        all:—
Have known the evenings, mornings, afternoons,
I have measured out my life with coffee spoons;
I know the voices dying with a dying fall
Beneath the music from a farther room.
    So how should I presume?

    And I have known the eyes already, known them
        all—
The eyes that fix you in a formulated phrase,
And when I am formulated, sprawling on a pin,
When I am pinned and wriggling on the wall,
Then how should I begin
To spit out all the butt-ends of my days and ways?
    And how should I presume?

    And I have known the arms already, known them
        all—
Arms that are braceleted and white and bare
[But in the lamplight, downed with light brown
    hair!]
Is it perfume from a dress
That makes me so digress?
Arms that lie along a table, or wrap about a shawl.
    And should I then presume?
    And how should I begin?

              .   .   .   .   .

Shall I say, I have gone at dusk through narrow
    streets
And watched the smoke that rises from the pipes
Of lonely men in shirt-sleeves, leaning out of
    windows? . . .

    I should have been a pair of ragged claws
Scuttling across the floors of silent seas.

              .   .   .   .   .

And the afternoon, the evening, sleeps so peacefully!
Smoothed by long fingers,
Asleep . . . tired . . . or it malingers,
Stretched on the floor, here beside you and me.
Should I, after tea and cakes and ices,
Have the strength to force the moment to its crisis?
But though I have wept and fasted, wept and prayed,
Though I have seen my head [grown slightly bald]
    brought in upon a platter,
I am no prophet—and here's no great matter;
I have seen the moment of my greatness flicker,
And I have seen the eternal Footman hold my coat,
    and snicker,
And in short, I was afraid.

And would it have been worth it, after all,
After the cups, the marmalade, the tea,
Among the porcelain, among some talk of you and
    me,
Would it have been worth while,
To have bitten off the matter with a smile,
To have squeezed the universe into a ball
To roll it toward some overwhelming question,
To say: "I am Lazarus, come from the dead,
Come back to tell you all, I shall tell you all"—
If one, settling a pillow by her head,
        Should say: "That is not what I meant at all.
        That is not it, at all."

    And would it have been worth it, after all,
Would it have been worth while,
After the sunsets and the dooryards and the
        sprinkled streets,
After the novels, after the teacups, after the skirts
        that trail along the floor—
And this, and so much more?—
It is impossible to say just what I mean!
But as if a magic lantern threw the nerves in patterns
        on a screen:
Would it have been worth while
If one, settling a pillow or throwing off a shawl,
And turning toward the window, should say:
        "That is not it at all,
        That is not what I meant, at all."

              .   .   .   .   .

No! I am not Prince Hamlet, nor was meant to be;
Am an attendant lord, one that will do
To swell a progress, start a scene or two,
Advise the prince; no doubt, an easy tool,
Deferential, glad to be of use,
Politic, cautious, and meticulous;
Full of high sentence, but a bit obtuse;
At times, indeed, almost ridiculous—
Almost, at times, the Fool.

    I grow old . . . I grow old . . .
I shall wear the bottoms of my trousers rolled.

    Shall I part my hair behind? Do I dare to eat a
        peach?
I shall wear white flannel trousers, and walk upon
        the beach.
I have heard the mermaids singing, each to each.

    I do not think that they will sing to me.

    I have seen them riding seaward on the waves
Combing the white hair of the waves blown back
When the wind blows the water white and black.

    We have lingered in the chambers of the sea
By sea-girls wreathed with seaweed red and brown
Till human voices wake us, and we drown.

The following questions focus on the importance of death as an expression of the life experience.

1 Discuss de Beauvoir's use of myth to explain the way the loss of a rite of passage has lead to denial of death and the repudiation of old age.

   a How does de Beauvoir use myth in her essay? How does this help her connect death and old age?

   b What image of old age emerges in this discussion? What problems does she contend modern society creates for old people?

   c What expectations are used to make old people feel inadequate? How do the fears of men differ from the fears of women regarding old age?

   d What does she propose we do to "stop cheating"? What silence does she hope to shatter? What do you think might be done to incorporate old people into the social realm?

Eliot explores the ways our illusions define what love is for us. He focuses on our need to understand the way the desire for control destroys the self in action with another.

2 Discuss the way Eliot weaves a fantasy of love which ends by destroying Prufrock.

   a What is implied in the term "love song"? What have love songs done to create illusions about love? Why does Eliot name his character J. Alfred Prufrock?

   b What parts of Prufrock are the "you and I" in the poem? How does Eliot connect this to the setting for the poem, and the concept of time in the poem? What illusions of love are embodied in both atmosphere and time?

   c Discuss Prufrock's vision of women. Does he trust or mistrust women? Explain! What expectations does Prufrock set up for himself? Why does he think he will fail? Is this a perverted way of winning? Or does this enable Prufrock to wear the mask of innocence?

   d What images in the poem suggest Prufrock's fear of death? How is death related to knowledge of "good and evil"? Reread the Garden of Eden myth in Chapter 2, and interpret the way the myth applies to Prufrock.

   e Why does Prufrock constantly focus on what will never be rather than what is? How does fantasy link him to either the past or future as a means to avoid life?

   f What does the poem's ending suggest about fantasy as the means of defining Prufrock's sense of "reality"? What is missing in Prufrock? In what ways are those individuals who appear "cool" like Prufrock trying to control what they feel?

From Denial to Acceptance ... The Movement from Chaos to Creation

RISK INVOLVEMENT
PLUNGE INTO THE UNKNOWN
INTERACT WITH OTHERS
RESIST DEFEAT
AFFIRM LIFE
BE CURIOUS
ACT ON OUR HUNCHES
HAVE IDEALS
TRANSFORM ENERGY INTO FORM
GIVE VOICE TO OUR EMOTIONS
BE CONSCIOUS OF A SELF
BE CONSCIOUS OF OUR HUMANITY
BE AWARE OF OUR DIGNITY
KNOW OUR CAPACITY FOR LOVE
SEEK JUSTICE
CHOOSE FREEDOM

To speak in defense of humanity

Writers become prophetic when they speak to us of our common joys and sorrows. They fashion for us an art of living in times when the life process seems close to destruction.

The greatest mystery is not that we have been flung at random among the profusion of the earth and the galaxy of the stars, but that in this prison we can fashion images of ourselves sufficiently powerful to deny our nothingness.

André Malraux

ACCEPTANCE OF THE NOBEL PRIZE

WILLIAM FAULKNER

William Faulkner, one of the major American novelists of the twentieth century, is perhaps most admired for his novels, The Sound and the Fury, *and* As I Lay Dying. *He was awarded the 1949 Nobel Prize for literature, and gave the following speech on his acceptance of the award, December 10, 1950, at Stockholm, Sweden.*

I feel that this award was not made to me as a man, but to my work—a life's work in the agony and sweat of the human spirit, not for glory and least of all for profit, but to create out of the materials of the human spirit something which did not exist before. So this award is only mine in trust. It will not be difficult to find a dedication for the money part of it commensurate with the purpose and significance of its origin. But I would like to do the same with the acclaim too, by using this moment as a pinnacle from which I might be listened to by the young men and women already dedicated to the same anguish and travail, among whom is already that one who will some day stand where I am standing.

Our tragedy today is a general and universal physical fear so long sustained by now that we can even bear it. There are no longer problems of the spirit. There is only the question: When will I be blown up? Because of this, the young man or woman writing today has forgotten the problems of the human heart in conflict with itself which alone can make good writing because only that is worth writing about, worth the agony and the sweat.

He must learn them again. He must teach himself that the basest of all things is to be afraid; and, teaching himself that, forget it forever, leaving no room in his workshop for anything but the old verities and truths of the heart, the universal truths lacking which any story is ephemeral and doomed—love and honor and pity and pride and compassion and sacrifice. Until he does so, he labors under a curse. He writes not of love but of lust, of defeats in which nobody loses anything of value, of victories without hope and, worst of all, without pity or compassion. His griefs grieve on no universal bones, leaving no scars. He writes not of the heart but of the glands.

Until he learns these things, he will write as though he stood among and watched the end of man. I decline to accept the end of man. It is easy enough to say that man is immortal simply because he will endure: that when the last ding-dong of doom has clanged and faded from the last worthless rock hanging tideless in the last red and dying evening, that even then there will still be one more sound: that of his puny inexhaustible voice, still talking. I refuse to accept this. I believe that man will not merely endure: he will prevail. He is immortal, not because he alone among creatures has an inexhaustible voice, but because he has a soul, a spirit capable of compassion and sacrifice and endurance. The poet's, the writer's, duty is to write about these things. It is his privilege to help man endure by lifting his heart, by reminding him of the courage and honor and hope and pride and compassion and pity and sacrifice which have been the glory of his past. The poet's voice need not merely be the record of man, it can be one of the props, the pillars to help him endure and prevail.

What is the Purpose of being a Hero?

THE HEROES

EDWIN MUIR

When these in all their bravery took the knock
And like obedient children swaddled and bound
Were borne to sleep within the chambered rock,
A splendour broke from that impervious ground,
Which they would never know. Whence came that
   greatness?
No fiery chariot whirled them heavenwards, they

Saw no Elysium opening, but the straitness
Of full submission bound them where they lay.

What could that greatness be? It was not fame.
Yet now they seemed to grow as they grew less,
And where they lay were more than where they had
   stood.
They did not go to any beatitude.
They were stripped clean of feature, presence, name,
When that strange glory broke from namelessness.

In the above picture "Warriors Arming," we see a depiction of the classical hero of antiquity. In our time, we need to examine what attitudes and ideals come together to form the image of a modern hero. Select a contemporary hero and evaluate in what ways he fits the mold expressed by Edwin Muir in his poem "The Heroes."

The leap forward ...

Blake tells us:
Man was made for joy and woe:
And when this we rightly know
Thru' the world we safely go,
Joy and woe are woven fine,
A clothing for the soul divine.

In the picture shown above, a group of young people are joined together to protest the violence of the Vietnam war. In the 1960s demonstrators were often branded as traitors to their country. But for many young people demonstrations became the means to express their frustration with a war they never made. The movement against the war also became symbolically linked with the cry to stop the machine. The misunderstandings between the youth of the sixties and their elders is a direct result of the inability of the young to believe that they also might affect the outcome of their lives. The participation of divergent points of view should be welcomed, rather than feared.

Translating I to We...

NO MAN IS AN ISLAND

JOHN DONNE

No man is an island entire of itself; every man is a piece of the continent, a part of the main. If a clod be washed away by the sea, Europe is the less, as well as if a promontory were, as well as if a manor of thy friends or of thine own were. Any man's death diminishes me, because I am involved in mankind, and therefore never send to know for whom the bell tolls; it tolls for thee.

—from *Meditation XVII*

A Golden Age of Consciousness
Man Alone with His Rock

THE MYTH OF SISYPHUS

ALBERT CAMUS

The gods had condemned Sisyphus to cease-lessly rolling a rock to the top of a mountain, whence the stone would fall back of its own weight. They thought with some reason that there is no more dreadful punishment than futile and hopeless labor.

If one believes Homer, Sisyphus was the wisest and most prudent of mortals. According to another tradition, however, he was disposed to practice the profession of the highwayman. I see no contradiction in this. Opinions differ as to the reason why he became the futile laborer of the underworld. To begin with, he is accused of certain levity in regard to the gods. He stole their secrets. Aegina, the daughter of Aesopus, was carried off by Jupiter. The father was shocked by the disappearance, and complained to Sisyphus. He, who knew of the abduction, offered to tell about it on the condition that Aesopus give water to the citadel of Corinth. To the celestial thunderbolts he preferred the benediction of water. He was punished for this in the underworld. Homer tells us that Sisyphus had also put Death in chains. Pluto would not endure the sight of his deserted, silent empire. He dispatched the god of war, who liberated Death from the hands of her conqueror.

Rites: A Week Bringing us Full Circle

We began this book with discussions of the dawn of time to reflect on the primitive imagination's attempt to express how the separation of night from day is the primal image which unlocks the doors to the human psyche. This lead us to a glimpse of how cultures communicate the transformation of boys and girls to men and women as they eat from the apple of knowledge. From there we embarked on a journey with the hero and temptress as their paths brought them past the isolation of a particular historic moment to capture and fascinate the minds of generations of our species. We next encountered the political leader and madonna as they used language to usher us past the limitations of existence. These gods and goddesses descended into the dark regions of death to serve as beacons to reflect the organic unity which exists between the tension of life and death. To be ripe for existence, we must risk these experiences in order to help us overcome any force that threatens to destroy our participation in and with the human family.

Visions of the Future

from KING LEAR

WILLIAM SHAKESPEARE

In, boy; go first. You houseless poverty,—
Nay, get thee in. I'll pray, and then I'll sleep.
                    (*Exit Fool*)
Poor naked wretches, wheresoe'er you are,
That bide the pelting of this pitiless storm,
How shall your houseless heads and unfed sides,
Your loop'd and window'd raggedness, defend you
From seasons such as these? O, I have ta'en
Too little care of this! Take physic, pomp;
Expose thyself to feel what wretches feel,
That thou mayst shake the superflux to them,
And show the heavens more just.

Act III, Scene iii, lines 26–36

JERUSALEM

WILLIAM BLAKE

And did those feet in ancient time
    Walk upon England's mountains green?
And was the holy Lamb of God
    On England's pleasant pastures seen?

And did the Countenance Divine
    Shine forth upon our clouded hills?
And was Jerusalem builded here
    Among these dark Satanic Mills?

Bring me my bow of burning gold!
    Bring me my arrows of desire!
Bring me my spear! O clouds, unfold!
    Bring me my chariot of fire!

I will not cease from mental fight,
    Nor shall my sword sleep in my hand,
Till we have built Jerusalem
    In England's green and pleasant land.

In the preceding selections we see the search for participation in the life experience as an integral part of the consciousness of modern man. William Faulkner uses his Nobel Prize speech to speak to those who refuse to accept the "end of man." Faulkner emphasizes our need to speak "of the heart and not of the glands." His message is clear: write about the "human heart in conflict with itself."

Northrop Frye contends that the ironic hero is one "who is inferior in power or intelligence to ourselves, so that we have a sense of looking down on a scene of bondage, frustration, and absurdity." In "The Heroes" Edwin Muir introduces us to the ironic type of hero that Frye has in mind. We are faced with the "namelessness" which results from the heroes being "stripped clean." Camus in "The Myth of Sisyphus" embarks on a journey to define the kind of consciousness necessary to unite modern man to an absurd world where individuals seek rational solutions to all that they do. Camus' heroes are also ironic. Their struggle to find meaning is enough "to fill a man's heart." Exile for Camus comes from the denial of the kingdom of man. In Lear's speech during the great tempest which occurs in his mind, the old king realizes that he had never cared for another, a realization that brings him to see the connections between man and his universe. The denial of these connections leads Lear to an insane abyss where separation rules the land. The ability to identify with another crowns Lear and prepares him for eventual acceptance of death. Blake's "Jerusalem" is another example of the contradiction between temporal power and divine wisdom. The "Satanic Mills" of industrialization reflect the intellectual development of rationalism which from Milton on sends Blake not to "cease from mental fight." The ability to reunite with nature in the pastoral setting of this new kingdom marks the turning toward a regeneration of the spirit to combat the "evil" of an indifferent world created by human beings.

The following questions focus on these ideas as a means to illuminate the modern individual's difficulty in believing in the life force and the death force as parts of human existence.

?

1 What is Faulkner's image of the modern situation? What must the modern writer learn? How does Faulkner's ability to balance these contradictions lead him to accept what is?

2 How would you interpret Sisyphus as one of "the heroes" in Edwin Muir's poem?
   a In what ways does Sisyphus represent the modern hero? Is he a modern Prometheus or a modern Job?
   b Why does Camus depict Sisyphus as an absurd hero? How does a recognition of absurd bring Sisyphus to a consciousness of his situation? How does this enable him to balance the forces between life and death?
   c What does the rock symbolize for Sisyphus? How does this symbol become the image of his bondage and at the same time his link to "freedom"?
   d What is Sisyphus' form of rebellion? How does this make him superior to his punishment? Explain whether you agree or disagree with Camus' conclusion, "One must imagine Sisyphus happy"!

3 Faulkner in his Nobel Prize speech uses the phrase "universal truths," and throughout this book, archetypes have been used as a means to link the individual to the collective. Discuss the ways Lear's speech and Blake's poem reveal universal truths.
   a Who are the "poor naked wretches" that Lear addresses himself to in this speech? What elements of nature bring Lear to recognize his bond with these "wretches"? Although 80 years old and a king, what has Lear failed to understand about man's place in the universe? What does the speech reveal about justice? Does this help Lear accept the differences between the human and spiritual worlds? Explain!
   b Discuss Blake's vision of "Jerusulem": How does Blake use nature to evoke images of a divine spirit? What is in opposition to this force? What has industrialization done to pervert the "Divine"? What does this reveal about Blake's view of "good and evil"? Why does Blake use the image of a "chariot of fire"? What does Blake mean by "Nor shall my sword sleep in my hand"? Does he mean this literally or symbolically? What kind of Jerusulem does Blake intend to build?

THERE, OUT OF THE SOUND OF THE SEA

JEAN PUMPHREY

Growing up in Ohio
    out of the sound of the sea
I knew the sea through language
and I knew that language was the sea
    out of which my words rose
        for an instant
    defining the universe.

There, where leaves change
    out of the sight of the sea
hearing that sound
    in the rush of seasons,
the pulsing drone of crickets
    sounding the firefly heat,
I knew.

            Poetry
         rocks it rocks
the still boundlessly churning land-caught sea
        it rocks fate and will
        endlessly rocking
        still the truth
         it rocks
         it rocks

There, lightning crashing
    out of the sound of the sea
I knew.